BRITISH BATTLESHIPS 1889-1904

Below: *Commonwealth* bow-on. Note the relatively low freeboard at the bows.

Below: *Africa* at Weymouth, 1909–10. She was the first British battleship to be fitted with forced lubrication for the machinery.

BRITISH BATTLESHIPS 1889-1904

R. A. BURT

Arms and
Armour

To the late W. P. Trotter, MC★

ACKNOWLEDGEMENTS

During the preparation of this book I have received assistance from several quarters. In particular, I acknowledge with appreciation the help given freely by Dr Morris and Michael Webb of the Manuscript Department, and G. Slatter of the Draught Room, at the National Maritime Museum. Many thanks are extended also to A. J. Francis of the Naval Historical Library (MOD); T. H. King of the Naval Ordnance Museum; and D. W. Robinson of Vickers Shipbuilding Group. Good friends must be mentioned: John Roberts and Alan Norris who helped with significant material and comments. I should like to express my indebtedness to my publishers and their production team; to David Gibbons, Beryl Gibbons and Anthony Evans, who have been tireless in their efforts to comply with my wishes. A special thank you is given to my editor, Michael Boxall. Finally, I must express my sincere gratitude to my wife Janice, who has been a peerless tower of strength throughout, and who encouraged me greatly if I showed signs of flagging. The photographs are all from the author's collection. The drawings are based on the shipbuilders' draughts, now held at the National Maritime Museum, Greenwich. R.A.B.

First published in Great Britain in 1988 by Arms and Armour Press, Artillery House, Artillery Row, London SW1P 1RT.

Distributed in Australia by Capricorn Link (Australia) Pty. Ltd., P.O. Box 665, Lane Cove, New South Wales 2066, Australia.

British Library Cataloguing in Publication Data:

Burt, R. A.
British battleships, 1889-1904.
1. Great Britain. Royal Navy. Battleships
I. Title
623.8′252′0941
ISBN 0-85368-914-8

Jacket illustration: *Majestic* leaving Portsmouth in 1889, as Flagship (1895-1904) of the Channel Fleet. Note her splendid Victorian paintwork, which she wore until 1902. The white canvas covers on the mainmast were fitted to prevent the dense smoke from spoiling the paint. The coloured stripes running through the bridgework and boat deck were often painted-up according to the whim of the Captain or acting Admiral to indicate that this was 'his ship' during the period of his commission. The considerable latitude allowed meant that the colour scheme was liable to change when a new Captain was appointed. Shields are still in evidence on the 3pdrs in the fighting tops (removed from 1899). Note semaphore on main masthead; upper deck torpedo net defence; fixed topmasts. As completed (1895), *Majestic* was the finest example of British battleship construction to date, and was indeed the *magnum opus* of her designer, Sir William White, DNC.

Designed and edited by DAG Publications Ltd. Designed by David Gibbons; edited by Michael Boxall; layout by Anthony A. Evans; typeset by Typesetters (Birmingham) Ltd and Ronset Typesetters Ltd; camerawork by M&E Reproductions, North Fambridge, Essex; printed and bound in Great Britain by The Bath Press, Avon.

CONTENTS

PREFACE

After the Battle of Trafalgar in 1805, Great Britain enjoyed a naval supremacy that was virtually unchallenged until the turn of the 19th century. During this period, which was more or less free from major sea wars, the battlefleet quickly became a political force as well as a practical one—and never more so than during the reign of Queen Victoria. By 1890 the combined British fleets enjoyed a numerical superiority hitherto unknown; the pride of the British people focused on the Royal Navy, which seemed to embody all that was quintessentially English to the man in the street. No matter what qualities or defects the ships possessed, he saw the battlefleet as the true backbone of the country and the empire.

For an island nation, it was paramount that command of the seas by a superior force be kept in a state of readiness and generally this was accomplished, even if there were periods when it seemed that the lion was asleep.

From about 1900, matters relating to naval affairs, strategy, design of warships and general administration changed somewhat, and the decline of Great Britain as a two-power naval force began. Other nations were beginning to flex their muscles and, looking at the Royal Navy, and what it had achieved over the past fifty years, began to build warships and invest heavily in the development of their own nautical interests. Not to be outdone, however, the Royal Navy showed that the experience gained during the Victorian era had not been wasted, and began a new battleship building programme second to none, but that is another story.

This book deals with the vessels which formulated the battlefleet from 1876 through to the innovatory *Dreadnought* of 1905, and ultimately, the shock of the First World War. Most of the information has been drawn from official sources, although it was found that many of the older documents had either perished, been mislaid or simply destroyed over a period of time; so there is less data available for the Victorian period than for 1920–45. This is a great pity because that era was one of transition and very rapid technological advance.

Four of the most important personalities in British naval history during the late Victorian period.

1

2

3

4

1 Sir William Henry White

Born in Devonport 2 February 1845 and educated at the Royal School of Naval Architecture. In 1883 he joined Sir William Armstrong and developed many new techniques within the firm.

He became Director of Naval Construction (DNC) in 1885 and held that post until 1902. While DNC he virtually revolutionized battleship design and created a fleet which was the envy of the civilized world. Made KCB in 1895. He wrote the classic *Manual of Naval Architecture* and many papers on naval affairs. He left office in 1902, but sustained his naval interest until his death in 1913, never to see how the fleet he created would fare in world war.

2 John Arbuthnot Fisher (First Baron Fisher of Kilverstone)

Born at Rambodde 25 January 1841 and entered the navy on 12 June 1854, on board the *Victory* at Portsmouth, 'penniless, friendless, and forlorn', as he once wrote of himself. Active service in *Calcutta* with the Baltic Fleet during the Crimean War and later in China. Promoted to Captain in 1874, he commanded the battleship *Inflexible* at the bombardment of Alexandria in 1882, landing there with the Naval Brigade, and using an armoured train which he commanded in several engagements, receiving the CB for his services. In February 1892 he was appointed to the Board of Admiralty as Controller (Third Sea Lord) and held that post until 1897. From 1899 to 1902 he was Commander-in-Chief, Mediterranean Fleet where he worked on designs for the 'all big gunned' battleship. Responsible for many changes within the system of the

Royal Navy and introduced a scheme of entry and training for naval officers which abolished the *Britannia* (training school) and substituted colleges at Osborne and Dartmouth which trained executive officers, engineers and marines up to the rank of lieutenant. Commander-in-Chief, Portsmouth from 1903 to 1904. Made First Sea Lord 21 October 1904 and held office until 1910. Knighted in 1894.

He pushed home his ideas for a new 'all big gunned' battlefleet, introduced oil fuel into large warships, and improved the system of shooting. He was strongly opposed to the Dardanelles campaign and with difficulty was prevented from resigning over the matter. He died 10 July 1920, having retained his vigour of mind and speech to the end.

3 Charles Willam De La Poer Beresford, Baron

Born 10 November 1846. A naval cadet in 1859, he came to notice when he commanded *Condor* at the bombardment of Alexandria in 1882. In 1884 he commanded the Naval Brigade in the Nile expedition, fought at Abu Klea and in *Sofia* he effected the rescue of Sir Charles Wilson. Commanded *Undaunted* 1893–95 and became Rear-Admiral in 1897. Second in Command, Mediterranean 1900–02; Commander Channel Fleet 1903–05 and Commander, Mediterranean Fleet 1905–07; again Commander, Channel Fleet 1907–09. Made full Admiral in 1906. Entered Parliament in 1874 when he gained Waterford as Conservative and held that post until 1880. MP for East Marylebone 1885 to 1889. Also a Lord of the Admiralty from 1886 to 1888. MP for York 1897–1900. Worked very hard for the

benefit of the navy and always expressed his opinions very strongly when in Parliament (*see* his memoranda in Naval Defence Act, 1889). Often criticized the administration of the navy and called for a special Board to be set up to deal with war staff and national Intelligence.

Wrote many important papers and books including, *The Break-up of China*, *Facts concerning Naval Policy*, *Administration*, *Memories*. Died suddenly in Caithness 6 September 1919.

4 Sir Percy Moreton Scott

Born 10 July 1853 and educated at University College, London. Entered the Navy in 1886 and became Captain by 1893. His name can be intimately linked with the development of scientific methods in naval gunnery; he was a member of the Ordnance Committee from 1894 to 1896. Came to notice with his excellent shooting record when serving in *Scylla* and *Terrible* (*see* gunnery).

Served in the Ashanti and Egyptian wars and landed with a Naval Brigade in South Africa in 1899, improvising mountings for heavy guns at Ladysmith. Captain of '*Excellent*' the RN gunnery school, from 1903 to 1905, and Inspector for target practice 1905–7; commanded cruiser squadrons, 1907–09. Created KCB 1910, Rear-Admiral in 1905, and Baronet 1913. Specially recognized by government for his numerous inventions towards improving naval gunnery and general shooting at sea. Retired as Admiral in 1913, but rejoined the service on outbreak of war.

Perhaps the most well-known incident in his career was his clash with Lord Charles Beresford, which received heavy coverage in the tabloids of the time.

In 1903 Scott was flying his flag in the cruiser *Good Hope*, which was anchored just inside the breakwater at Portland. *Roxburgh* was just outside, some 300 yards away. Both ships received orders from Lord Charles Beresford to paint ship in readiness for the reception of the German Emperor. No order was sent, however, to suspend gunnery practice in which the two cruisers were engaged. Scott sent a message by semaphore to *Roxburgh*, 'Paintwork appears to be more in demand than gunnery, so you had better come in, in time to make yourself look pretty by the 8th.' The reply came, 'As the weather is suitable, we can red lead the rust marks off our funnels and get ready for painting out here.'

Roxburgh remained outside, and two hours later Beresford arrived, and after anchoring made a signal to *Roxburgh*, to 'be out of routine', and that she was to suspend gunnery and devote her energy to painting. *Roxburgh* then came inside the breakwater, and to use a very common service phrase, started to make herself 'look pretty' which was exactly what Scott had told her to do two hours before Beresford's arrival. Someone overheard Scott's remarks and passed them on to Beresford. Without asking for an explanation, Beresford severely reprimanded Scott and requested the Admiralty that he be superseded. Scott offerered an explanation, but Beresford would not listen. Scott was later to say that the signal had been, 'a misrepresentation of fact due to Lord Charles Beresford not having inquired into the facts before he took action'. The affair made good reading for some time after the incident, and was not quickly forgotten.

INTRODUCTION

DEVELOPMENT OF THE BATTLESHIP

The late 19th-century battleship—now termed 'pre-dreadnought'—had its conception as far back as 1869, when all vessels, whether cruiser, sloop, frigate or battleship were fitted with masts, yards and sail. In late 1868, the First Sea Lord, Hugh Childers, asked the Chief Constructor (Edward Reed) to prepare a design to ascertain if a seagoing turret ship smaller than *Monarch* and *Captain* (then under construction) was practicable. Reed was asked to limit displacement to about 6,100 tons, and to provide sail rig but only on a limited scale. On 3 February 1869 Reed reported that such a design would be impracticable but quickly submitted a paper with his own proposals showing certain features:

'The object of the Admiralty in the preparation of this design has been to produce a warship of great offensive and defensive qualities, adapted for naval warfare in Europe. The capabilities of the ship to cross the Atlantic has also been considered; but the primary object, and that in which view of the qualities of the ship have been regulated, is that of fitness for engaging the enemies' ships and squadrons in the British Channel, Mediterranean and other European seas. The offensive power has been regulated by the desire to furnish her with guns which would penetrate the armour of the 1st class of Europe, with few or no exceptions, to give these guns an uninterrupted command in all directions, and to so place and work them, that they may be efficient and secure in a sea-way under all but extreme conditions.

1. Displacement 9,035 tons. Low freeboard, semi-monitor type hull with raised breastwork amidships enclosing the turrets, but not carried out to the sides. Freeboard 9ft along forecastle, by 4½ft to upper deck abaft this. Short high superstructure on breastwork through which funnel uptakes and hatches would lead; a flying deck for boat stowage and navigating position, etc. Prominent ram fitted, and sides strengthened against such an attack.
2. Four 12in (25 ton) guns in two twin turrets, both on centre-line on breastwork, one forward and one aft.
3. Side armour 12in maximum, decks 2in, turrets 12in.
4. Twin screws fitted in the event of a shaft breakage.

5. No sail rig, only light poles at end of each breastwork.

The latter item has its advantages in the following: A low freeboard type is possible, carrying with it a reduced amount of armour; a clear range for guns all round; half the complement owing to absence of rigging.'

The design was actually nothing more than an enlarged edition of the breastwork monitors of the earlier *Cerebus* class, developed to seagoing proportions within acceptable displacement limits, and resulted in the most controversial warship design ever submitted by the Constructor's Department to that date.

The adoption of the low-freeboard hull is said to have been influenced to some extent by the visit to Britain of the US monitor *Miantonomoh* during 1866-7 although Reed's design was considerably less extreme in this respect. From the point of view of seagoing qualities and habitability it was also the most unsatisfactory, and was subjected to severe criticisim as being unsafe.

The design, nevertheless, featured some outstanding innovations, for a seagoing type: low-freeboard, semi-monitor type hull and absence of sail rig. By discarding sail rig, a number of structural and tactical advantages had been secured for the first time in a seagoing ship of such size.

In the 1869–70 programme provision was made for two such ships, *Devastation* and *Thunderer*, with a third to be called *Fury* and laid down in the following year. Following the loss of the rigged turret ship *Captain*, however, the *Devastation* type became very suspect, it being held (erroneously) in the service that such ships would probably be similarly overwhelmed and capsize in heavy seas despite the absence of masts and sail.

The severe criticism from both service and public sectors necessitated action to restore confidence in the design and in the technical authorities, and to vindicate the new principles governing naval layouts. A Committee was convened to examine all designs recently laid down, and in particular that of *Devastation*. At its first meeting, in January 1871, Nathaniel Barnaby (new Chief Constructor, succeeding Reed) proposed modifications to the original *Devastation* design with a view to improving stability offensive power, protection and habitability:

1. Extension of breastwork right out to sides in the form of a light, enclosed superstructure with wings

carried about 30 feet abaft breastwork on each side.
2. Substitution of 12in (35 ton) for the original 12in (25 ton).
3. Increased protection to the horizontal and internal parts of the ship (total of 874 tons added with all improvements).

These modifications, which increased the nominal displacement to 9,900 tons, were approved by the Committee. The additional freeboard provided by the new superstructure resulted in a far more seaworthy and satisfactory design which attained a reputable standard for ships of the semi-monitor type.

Apart from certain general recommendations, which in no way affected the basic principles of the design, the Committee, in a report on *Devastation* issued in March 1871, expressed great satisfaction with the type in general and approved it as a basis for further development.

A majority report recommended also, that no more first class battleships should be built with full sail rig, irrespective of whether the main armament was mounted in turrets or on the broadside. In support of this the report pointed out that it was impossible to combine any real efficiency under sail with a high degree of offensive and defensive qualities, and advanced the following basic objections to sail rig:

1. With a turret armament, full rig restricted arcs of fire, and prevented full benefit being derived from the advantages of turrets in respect of all-round fire, thereby placing rigged turret ships at a distinct disadvantage in engaging even smaller and cheaper mastless types.
2. It represented a hazard in action owing to its inflammable nature, and the risks of falling masts, spars and gear which might obstruct guns and propellers.
3. It absorbed weight which could be expended to advantage in increasing fuel capacity, especially in the case of twin-screwed ships, where the risk of breakdown requiring the use of sail was minimized.
4. It reduced speeds when steaming head to wind and encumbered deck space when topgallant masts and upper yards were struck for going into action.

These objections met with considerable adverse service opinion at the time of their release, however, and the report was completely ignored by the Admiralty in the following designs for *Alexandra*, *Temeraire* and *Inflexible*, which were laid down in 1873–4.

Despite the early criticism, which was stronger than had been directed at any other British warship, *Devastation* entirely fulfilled the intentions of the design, and turned out to be a safe, seaworthy ship, although, as in all ships of this type, the low freeboard at the extremities imposed definite limitations on fighting and steaming abilities in a sea-way.

As time went by, service opinion became progressively more favourable and, ten years after commissioning, her all-round fighting qualities were considered higher than those of later ships such as *Alexandria*, *Temeraire*, *Colossus* and even the *Admiral* classes.

Those two vessels, *Devastation* and *Thunderer*, with their aggressive names and grim, invincible appearance, were just what appealed to the man in the street; when Messrs. Bryant & May required a warship to typify Britannia's sea power on their matchboxes, *Devastation* and *Thunderer* were the obvious choices. Although now discontinued, if you come across one of these boxes, look with a fresh eye, and imagine how these illustrations were seen by the public in those bygone days of the late 19th and early 20th centuries.

The original design for *Fury*, as prepared by Reed in 1870, was merely an enlarged and faster edition of his *Devastation* which had been governed by displacement restrictions no longer in force. Compared with *Devastation* the new design was 35 feet longer and 1,130 tons heavier with the same armament and similar protection except that the belt armour was carried right through to the bows above as well as below the waterline.

The ship was laid down to this design in September 1870, but because of the disturbance caused by the *Devastation* design, construction was suspended pending the report from the newly appointed Committee.

Barnaby proposed that the draught be increased by at least six inches, and freeboard forward and aft be reduced so as to increase basic stability. Further

DEVASTATION
Outboard profile and cutaway, as refitted and rearmed 1894

Devastation and *Thunderer* were completely reconstructed during 1890 to 1894 to conform with modern technology. The 12in guns were replaced by 29ton 10in guns. They were re-engined and reboilered with inverted triple-expansion machinery and cylindrical boilers; the IHP was thereby raised to 7,000 for 14 knots maximum speed. A navigating bridge was added over the chart house at the forward end of the hurricane deck and a signal bridge at the after end. The funnels were remodelled, and other minor alterations gave them a fresh appearance when the refits were completed in 1894.
1 Boiler rooms
2 Engine room
3 Magazines and shell rooms

proposals included:

1. Extension to breastwork at sides giving freeboard of 11ft 6in amidships.
2. Provision of open flying deck, 9 feet above the waterline.
3. Placing the main gun turrets 10—12 feet off centre on opposite sides to enable three guns to fire directly ahead or astern.
4. Extension of belt armour down over the ram forward, and increasing the maximum thickness of the main belt from 12in to 14in.

   A further proposal was put forward by Admirals Elliot and Ryder who called for extensions of the breastwork level to bow and stern by light plating,

---

Devastation: Steam trials, 31 October 1872

Stokes Bay run
Wind: 2
Sea: smooth, conditions good
Draught: 26ft 4in forward, 26ft 6in aft
Pressure in boilers: 27psi
Revolutions: 76.756
IHP: 6,633
Speed: 13.8 knots.

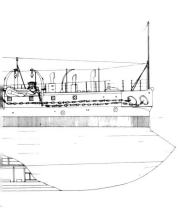

Devastation and *Thunderer*: Particulars, as completed

Construction
Devastation: Portsmouth DY; laid down 1̇2 Nov 1869; floated out 12 July 1871; completed Jan 1873
Thunderer: Pembroke DY; laid down 26 June 1869; launched 25 March 1872; completed and began trials 1877.
Both ships extensively rebuilt 1890–1 and 1893–4 respectively to conform with modern warship technology (guns renewed, re-engined and noticeable appearance changes).

Displacement (tons)
Devastation: 9,190 (load), 9,827 (deep)
Thunderer: 9,380 (load), 9,641 (deep).

Dimensions
Length: 285ft pp, 307ft oa
Beam: 62ft 3in
Draught: 25ft 9in forward, 26ft 6in aft.

Armament
Devastation:
Four 12in 35ton MLR
One 9pdr
Thunderer:
Two 12.5in 38ton MLR
Two 12in 35ton MLR
One 9pdr
Two 16in torpedo carriages (in breastwork ports).

Armour (iron)
Main belt: 12in–10in–9in–8½in
Breastwork: 12in–10in
Bulkheads: 12in–6in–5in
Turrets: 14in–12in
Breastwork deck: 2in
Upper deck: 3in midships, 2in aft
Main deck: 3in
Conning tower: 9in–6in.

Machinery
Two sets horizontal single-cylinder (*Thunderer* double-cylinder) direct-acting trunk engines, two Griffiths propellers
Cylinder diameter: 88in (*Thunderer* 77in)
Stroke: 3ft 3in (*Thunderer* 3ft 6in)
Propellers: 4-bladed
Propeller diameter: 17ft 6in
Propeller pitch: 19ft 6in
Boilers: eight rectangular in two compartments, working pressure 27–30psi
Total heating surface: 17,806sq ft
Total length of engine + boiler rooms: 127ft 11½in
Designed SHP: 5,600 for 12.5 knots
Fuel: 1,350 tons coal normal, 1,800 tons max.
Coal consumption: 3lb per hour per HP
Radius of action: 4,700nm at 10 knots.
Devastation was last RN battleship to have single-cylinder trunk engines.

Ship's boats
Pinnaces (steam): one 37ft, one 28ft
Whale gigs: one 25ft
Gigs: one 30ft, two 28ft, one 26ft
Punts: one 11ft
Dinghies: one 14ft.

Searchlights
None as completed
Two 24in 1880, four more 1893.

Complement
As designed: 250
As completed: 358.

Cost
£361,438 (plus guns £43,780, *Thunderer* £88,431).

Sold
Devastation: 12 May 1908
Thunderer: 13 July 1909.

thus providing a flush deck, and removing the vessel from the monitor category.

Barnaby's plan for the open deck and echelon turrets were rejected by the Committee, but that suggested by the two Admirals was fitted to some extent after *Devastation* had run her preliminary trials. Later on, the guns were revised, and the 12in 35ton were changed for 12.5in 38ton pieces. Most of the revisions took place during 1872, and the ship was renamed *Dreadnought*. As completed, she turned out as the only battleship built during Barnaby's reign as DNC that never came in for severe criticism. When the design for *Trafalgar* was under consideration (1886) the initial layout was almost identical with that of *Dreadnought*, which had become known as the 'officers' ideal'.

The 1873 estimates produced *Alexandra*, the last central battery type battleship built for the Royal Navy. She was the most powerfully armed (two 11in and ten 10in), most heavily armoured, fastest and most successful of the thirteen ships of this group, built during the period of transition from broadside to turret type. The design, which was quite unique, had nothing even approaching a sister vessel, and represented the apotheosis of broadside central battery theory coupled with the best ideas ever put into practice for combining good all-round fire with full sail rig. Her overall fighting qualities were never equalled by any other British or foreign broadside armed ship. The decision to adhere to the fully rigged ship was taken despite the recommendations of the 1871 Committee on designs, which urged that full rig be abandoned. *Alexandra*'s rig, although close to perfection in so far as mastless broadside ships were concerned, made her virtually obsolete by the time she was completed in 1877.

Laid down in the same year as *Alexandra*, was *Temeraire*, also a central battery type—but with a difference; she was also given barbettes! The design, which embodied several unique features, was a direct outcome of proposals by Admirals Elliot and Ryder of the 1871 Design Committee, and represented a distinctly hybrid type, combining the central battery system with a separate, and at that time novel, barbette arrangement for securing increased fire end on. A wide frigate-type stern sloping strongly outwards from the waterline was reverted to for the last time in any British battleship. This reversion was probably influenced by current ideas regarding

appearance, despite the additional weight involved, and other disadvantages as compared with the more modern pattern. Topgallant, forecastle and poop were fitted, but these were kept as low as possible so as to reduce freeboard in view of the weight of the barbettes.

This was certainly a 'one-off' vessel, but she was exceptionally steady and well armed. The novel barbette mountings, sited one forward and one aft (two 11in in each), were fitted with the Moncrieff

system for raising and lowering the guns; the system had, in fact, been designed for coast-defence guns, and afforded complete protection to gun crews while loading. The principle defects for shipboard use were the excessive weight and the absence of overhead protection to the barbettes.

Admiral Ballard said of *Temeraire*: 'In the *Temaraire*, we could not fire the after barbette guns on any bearing whatever without damage to the fittings and bulkheads under the poop, so quarterly

Below: *Devastation*, June 1897. A magnificent view showing the extremely low freeboard. Rather striking in appearance with the long raised breastwork and short high superstructure with hurricane deck above. Replaced *Swiftsure* (old) at Devonport as Port Guard Ship from 5 December 1893 until January 1898. Present at Diamond Jubilee Fleet Review on 26 June 1897 at Portsmouth, when this photograph was taken.

Above: *Dreadnought* cleared for action during a practice run, c.1887–9. Like *Devastation*, she was designed by Reed and modified by Barnaby and W. White, after Reed had left office. She was in fact an enlarged and improved *Devastation*, and on completion was the most powerfully armed and completely armoured battleship in service. Her fighting value, however, was rather less than appeared on paper because the volume of fire was limited to one broadside (four rounds) every two minutes.

Left: *Dreadnought*, 1904–5. Seen here towards the end of her active career when she was employed as Depot Ship for destroyers during annual manoeuvres in the Irish Sea.

practices with that gun's crew were carried out in the fore barbette in three out of the annual four. The damage caused by the fourth was not beyond repair, but nevertheless it cost some money to put

---

Dreadnought: Particulars, as completed

Construction
Pembroke DY; laid down 10 Sept 1870; launched 8 March 1875; completed 15 Feb 1879.

Displacement (tons)
10,893 (load), 11,486 (deep).

Dimensions
Length: 320ft pp, 343ft oa
Beam: 63ft 10in
Draught: 26ft 3in forward, 26ft 9in aft
Freeboard: 10ft 9in forward, 11ft 6in amidships, 10ft aft.

Armament
Four 12.5in 38ton MLR
Ten Nordenfelt QF guns added 1884
Two 16in torpedo carriages.

Armour (iron)
Main belt: 14in–8in
Citadel: 11in–14in
Bulkheads: 13in
Turrets: 14in
Conning tower: 14in–8in–6in
Main deck: 2½in
Citadel deck: 3in.

Machinery
Two sets 3-cylinder vertical inverted compound engines, two Griffiths propellers
Cylinder diameter: HP 66in, LP 90in
Stroke: 4ft 6in
Propeller diameter: 20ft
Boilers: twelve cylindrical, back to back in four compartments, working pressure 60psi
Designed SHP: 8,000 for 14 knots (made 14.5 knots with 8,216shp on trials)
Fuel: 1,200 tons coal normal, 1,800 tons max.
Estimated radius of action: 5,650nm at 10 knots.

Searchlights
Two 24in added later: one over charthouse, one on after end of hurricane deck.

Complement
369 (1879)
374 (1882).

Cost
£619,739.

Sold
14 July 1908.

---

right again.'

The barbette central battery arrangement adopted in this ship was never repeated, and she was the last battleship laid down for the British Navy to carry any part of her main armament below the upper deck.

Another vessel to join the ranks of the Royal Navy was *Superb* which was designed by Reed as the Turkish *Hamidieh* in 1873. She was completed in 1877, but detained in the United Kingdom because of neutrality obligations during the Russo-Turkish war. She was purchased for the Royal Navy in February 1878 and renamed *Superb*.

In general design, *Superb* was merely an enlarged edition of *Hercules* (1865) with heavier armament, thicker armour and about a knot less speed. She was the last broadside armed battleship ever to enter service with the Royal Navy. She had thicker battery armour than any of the others, and a heavier weight of broadside than any previous British warship.

Although slightly modified for use in the Royal Navy, and proving herself a steady ship in a sea-way, she was quite unmanageable under sail. This was not surprising, because she was very much undercanvassed and the weight of her spars and rigging materially reduced her reserve of buoyancy and affected speed against head winds.

Seventy-five per cent of her armament was arranged in a single battery on the main deck, where guns were difficult to fight in a sea-way. This was immediately criticised as a major weak point in the design, and made the ship inferior in fighting qualities compared with the *Alexandra* despite her heavier broadside.

Her purchase from the Turkish Government was mainly due to political tension with Russia, and also to a belated realization that British building programmes had fallen far behind those of France and Italy, then the second and third naval powers. The modifications to her hull, armament, accommodation, etc., before joining the Royal Navy, took some time, and she did not enter service until 1880, by which time she was bordering on obsolescence.

Leaving aside the coastal-defence ships, the next design prepared in 1873 was more or less a direct reply to the Italian *Duilio* and *Dandalo*, and embodied the maximum gun calibre and heaviest armour principle. It marked a milestone in British naval architecture, being a completely radical

departure from all previous standards of design in the British Navy.

On a displacement of 10,400 tons, the *Duilio*s, laid down in 1872, were designed to carry four 15in (60ton) guns in two twin turrets, echeloned amidships to secure nominal all-round fire. They would have a 21½in armour belt and 17in citadel armour, and a designed speed of 15 knots. In 1875, however, the 15in guns were replaced by 17.7in (100ton) which increased displacement to 11,140 tons. Not only were these Italian ships, as designed, the largest, most powerfully armed, heavily armoured and among the fastest warships projected to that date, but they also represented a distinctly novel type. The principle innovation was the abandonment of the complete waterline belt in favour of a short thick belt and heavily armoured citadel amidships enclosing turret bases, machinery and boilers, with armour protection to the extremities confined to an underwater deck.

The actual fighting value of the Italian ships, however, was rather less than appeared on paper. With the heaviest armament, they were heavily overgunned for their displacement, and the hulls could not have withstood the strain of continuous firing from guns of this calibre. In practice only one gun could be fired at a time, on any bearing, without causing considerable damage to the ship's structure. The novel character and high paper qualities of the design created a considerable impression, and as the most powerful British battleship in hand was *Fury* (later *Dreadnought*), carrying four 12.5in (38ton) guns with 14in armour, it was considered essential to produce a reply to the Italian threat. This materialized in *Inflexible*—the only battleship of the 1873–4 programme. Admiralty requirements for such a design, officially known at first as the 'New *Fury*' called for:

1. Dimensions not to exceed those of *Fury*, with ability to enter docks at Portsmouth, Chatham, Malta and the dry dock at Bombay. Ship must be able to pass through Panama Canal in the light condition.

2. Heaviest available guns, thick armour and maximum possible speed.

3. Greatest possible fuel capacity, and have seaworthiness adequate for operations in the Channel, Mediterranean and Baltic with minimum sail rig consistent with peacetime duties.

4. Cost not to exceed that of *Fury*.

Below: *Temeraire*, Malta, 1886. She was a good ship, but pitched heavily in head seas. She was a direct outcome of proposals put forward by Admirals Elliot and Ryder of the 1871 Design Committee.

Below: *Alexandra*, 1880. A unique design which had no equal in the Royal Navy. She took part in the bombardment of Alexandria, firing the first shot on 11 July 1882. During the day she was hit about 60 times, 24 in the hull, yet sustained only minimal damage and four casualties. In January 1885 she contributed a contingent to the Naval Brigade which fought under Lord Charles Beresford at the Battle of Abu Klea and Metemneh.

Bottom: *Superb*, Malta 1884. Built at Blackwall as *Hamidieh* for the Turkish Government. In February 1878 towards the close of the Russo-Turkish war, when a conflict between England and Russia seemed probable, she was purchased for the Royal Navy for £443,000 and renamed *Superb*. A great deal more was spent on her to bring her into line with Royal Navy requirements, and she did not enter service until 1880.

Temeraire: Particulars, as completed

Construction
Chatham DY; laid down 18 Aug 1873; floated out 9 May 1876; completed Aug 1877.

Displacement (tons)
8,550 (load), 8,766 (deep).

Dimensions
Length: 285ft wl
Beam: 62ft
Draught: 26ft 8in forward, 27ft 2in aft.

Armament
Four 11in 25ton MLR
Four 10in 18ton MLR
Four 20pdr Armstrong BL
One 9pdr MLR
One 3pdr QF plus MG (boat)
Two 14in torpedo carriages.

Armour (iron)
Main belt: 11in–9in–6in–5½in and 3in
Battery: 8in

Forward bulkhead: 10in
After bulkhead: 5in (between upper and lower edges of belt armour)
Bulkhead: 8in (closing each end of battery)
Forward barbette: 10in
After barbette: 8in
Ammunition trunks: 8in
Upper deck: 1in
Main deck: 1½in.

Machinery
Two sets 2-cylinder vertical inverted compound engines, two Griffiths propellers
Propellers: 2-bladed
Cylinder diameter: HP 70in, LP 114in
Stroke: 34ft 10in
Boilers: twelve cylindrical back to back in four compartments, working pressure 60psi
Designed SHP: 7,000 for 14 knots (made 14.65 knots on measured mile, six runs)
Fuel: 400 tons coal normal, 620 tons max.

Radius of action: 2,680nm at 8–9 knots (economical speed).

Sail and rig
Two masts, heavy brig rig
Sail area: 25,000sq ft, main truck 169ft above deck
Iron lower mast, all other masts wood
Poor sailer, but owing to short hull, one of the handiest ships in the fleet. Fast in tacking and wore well in eight minutes in a moderate sea.

Searchlights
Two 24in 1884, two more 1895.

Complement
531–581.

Cost
£489,822.

Sold
26 May 1921.

Superb: Particulars, as completed

Construction
Thames Ironworks; laid down late 1873; launched 16 Nov 1875; completed late 1877; purchased for Navy 20 Feb 1878 and renamed *Superb*.

Displacement (tons)
9,173 (load), 9,557 (deep).

Dimensions
Length: 332ft 3in pp
Beam: 59ft
Draught: 24ft 4in forward, 26ft 5in aft.

Armament
Sixteen 10in 18ton MLR
Six 20pdrs Armstrong BL (saluting)
Ten boat guns
Four 14in torpedo carriages.

Armour (iron)
Main belt: 12in–10in–7in–6in–4in
Battery: 12in sides, 10in–7in–6in–5in bulkheads
Upper deck: 1½in
Main deck: 1½in
Conning tower: 8in.

Machinery
One set 2-cylinder horizontal single pressure engines, single propeller
Propeller: 2-bladed, left-hand
Cylinder diameter: 116in
Stroke: 4ft
Boilers: nine box-type, working pressure 30psi
Designed SHP: 7,000 for 13–14 knots (on trials made 13.78 knots with 7,431shp)
Fuel: 600 tons coal normal, 970 tons max.
Radius of action: 1,770nm at 9–10 knots.

Sail and rig
Three masts, barque rig on modified second scale
Sail area: 26,000sq ft approx., main truck 142ft above deck. Very much under-canvassed, sail power being quite inadequate for reliable movement. Very stiff and almost impossible to handle under sail only.

Searchlights
Two 24in 1885.

Complement
623 as completed
655 1880.

Costs
£443,000 (plus guns and machinery £88,846).

Sold
15 May 1906.

On 3 June 1873, the Chief Constructor (Barnaby) submitted a preliminary draft plan, together with several alternative sketch plans showing improvements on the *Fury* layout. It was generally appreciated, however, that with the introduction of guns larger than 12in calibre, it was no longer practicable to provide the complete armouring of the *Devastation-Fury* types, and that adequate protection to turret bases and machinery could only be secured by adopting the *Duilio* arrangement of concentrating this in a short, heavily armoured enclosure amidships, with only deck protection and internal sub-division at the extremities.

Features of the proposed *Inflexible* design which were accepted by the Admiralty were:
1. Dimensions: 320ft x 75ft x 24ft. Displacement: 11,000tons.
2. Low freeboard along upper deck with narrow superstructure forward and aft giving a hatch freeboard of about 17 feet.
3. Four 15in guns in twin turrets, echeloned amidships, with limited end-on and cross-deck arcs of fire.
4. Short central citadel, with 24in maximum armour, enclosing turret bases, machinery and boilers, with 16in turrets.
5. Underwater armoured deck outside citadel, with cellular layer above this.
6. Speed 14 knots with steaming radius of 3,000 miles at 10 knots.

Right: *Inflexible* as completed, 1881–2. One of the most experimental ships ever built. Throughout her construction new developments were being incorporated and she was subjected to such a large number of changes that she was not completed until seven years after being laid down (1874). Her first commanding officer was Captain J. A. Fisher (later Admiral 'Jackie' Fisher).

Below right: *Inflexible*, as refitted with military rig, 1887. Her monster 16in (80ton) guns proved most useful when she bombarded Alexandria in 1882, but their blast caused much structural damage and smashed many of her own boats. She carried the thickest armoured belt (24in) ever fitted to a warship (a record that still stands).

Alexandra: Particulars, as completed

Construction
Chatham DY; laid down 5 March 1873; launched 7 April 1875; completed 2 Jan 1877.

Displacement (tons)
9,454 (load), 9,712 (deep).

Dimensions
Length: 325ft pp
Beam: 63ft 8in
Draught: 26ft forward, 26ft 6in aft.

Armament
Two 11in 25ton MLR
Ten 10in 18ton MLR
Six 20pdr (Armstrong BL)
Three 9pdr (boat)
Two Gatling .303in (boat)
Four 16in torpedo carriages.

Armour (iron)
Main belt: 12in–10in–6in
Battery belt: 12in
Upper battery: 8in
After bulkheads: 5in
Main deck: 1in–1½in.

Machinery
Two sets 3-cylinder vertical inverted compound engines, twin Mangin propellers
Cylinder diameter: HP 69in, LP 90in
Stroke: 4ft
Boilers: twelve cylindrical, back to back in four compartments along centre-line, working pressure 60psi
(First battleship completed with compound engines)
Designed SHP: 8,000 for 14 knots (trials: 8,610shp for 15.1 knots on Maplin measured mile)
Fuel: 500 tons coal normal, 685 tons max.
Radius: 3,800nm at 8–9 knots.

Sail and rig
Three masts, heavy barque rig on second scale
Iron lower masts, all other masts wood
Sail area: 27,000sq ft (excluding stunsails)
Ship never exceeded 6 knots under sail alone.

Searchlights
Two 24in 1883.

Wireless
Experimental W/T fitted in 1899 manoeuvres, the first big ship to have this. W/T gaff fitted on mizzenmast.

Complement
665 as private ship
674 as flagship (1878)
685 as flagship (1880).

Costs
£538,293.

Sold
8 October 1908.

7. Two funnels placed amidships between turrets, close together and slightly echeloned.
8. Two pole masts for signalling purposes with provision for steadying or emergency sail only.

The armament provided corresponded to that of the *Duilio*s but later, it became possible to mount a heavier calibre (16in 80ton) while the ship was under construction. The Italians responded of course, and adapted their ships to carry the 17.7in Armstrong guns which had just been developed.

The final design was generally similar to the Italian pair, but about 740 tons heavier, with 16in guns against 17in. *Inflexible* was well received in the service at first, but her stability in a damaged condition was questioned in 1876, and as a result construction was suspended pending an investigation by a special Committee. This delay coupled with government economies meant that the ship was seven and a half years under construction. On completion in 1881, the heavy guns and thick armour (thickest ever carried) exerted considerable popular appeal, but the rate of fire from the muzzle-loading 80ton guns was too slow to provide adequate volume of fire, and although the many novel features placed it among the noteworthy designs of the Barnaby era, the ship had only a limited success and quickly became obsolete after the appearance of the much faster firing 12in BLR guns in 1886.

Inflexible: Particulars, as completed

Construction
Portsmouth DY; laid down 24 Feb 1874; launched 27 April 1876; completed Dec 1880.

Displacement (tons)
10,822 (load), 11,760 (deep).

Dimensions
Length: 320ft pp, 344ft oa
Beam: 75ft
Draught: 24ft 5in forward and 25ft 0¾in aft at above displacements.

Armament
Four 16in 80ton MLR
Six 20pdrs
Four torpedo tubes: two submerged, two on carriages.

Armour (iron and compound and iron)
Main strake of citadel: 24in (two 12in plates), 20in above 16in below
Bulkheads: 22in–18in–14in (Teak backing: 24in–20in–16in)
Deck: 3in
Turrets: 16in (outer 3½in compound plates on 5½in iron, then 8in teak backed by 7in iron)
Main armoured citadel: 110ft long
Armour: 9ft 7in above waterline at normal load.

Machinery
Two sets 3-cylinder inverted compound engines, Griffiths twin propellers
Cylinder diameter: HP 70in, LP 90in
Stroke: 4ft
Propellers: 2-bladed
Propeller diameter: 20ft 2½in
Propeller pitch: 23ft 0½in
Boilers: twelve cylindrical: eight single-ended 9ft × 13ft 7in; four double-ended 17ft × 9ft 3in, working pressure 61psi
Weight of machinery: 1,366 tons
Designed SHP: 8,000 for 14 knots
Fuel: 1,200 tons coal normal, 1,300 tons max.
Coal consumption: 16½ tons per day at 5¼ knots
Radius of action: 4,140nm at 10 knots.

Ship's boats (estimated in final legend)
Pinnaces (steam): two 36ft, one 30ft
Pinnaces (sail): two 28ft
Galleys: one 30ft
Cutters: two 28ft
Whale gigs: one 27ft, one 26ft
Dinghies: one 14ft
Life rafts: one 25ft.

Searchlights
Two 24in in sponsons echeloned on flying deck.

Complement
443 in 1881.

Costs
Hull and materials: £589,481
Machinery: £125,981
Hydraulic gun machinery: £48,396
Masts: £1,823
Total as completed: £809,594.

Sold
15 September 1903.

Another vessel joined the Royal Navy after being appropriated in February 1878 while completing for the Brazilian Navy. Taken over because of the ever-mounting tension with Russia, and after some modification, *Neptune* (ex-*Independencia*) completed in 1881.

She was designed by Reed in 1872 to meet the requirements of the Brazilian Navy who wanted a fully rigged ship of the largest size and carrying the heaviest guns possible. The order for the ship stemmed largely from the impression made by *Devastation*; the Brazilians wanted something along the same lines but were not prepared to sacrifice the full sail rig. She was the last rigged battleship to enter service with the Royal Navy, but proved generally unsatisfactory, suffering from the inherent disadvantages of combining turrets with full rig. Moreover, she was a poor sea-boat, a heavy roller and difficult to handle, and because of this she was relegated to Port Guardship after only three years' active service.

The 1876–77 programme provided the Royal Navy with two more battleships, *Ajax* and *Agamemnon*, which, in all essentials, were reduced editions of *Inflexible*, exaggerating the defects in that design, but without any of her virtues. They represented one of the worst examples of restricting displacement and fighting efficiency in order to cut costs.

They were the last British battleships to have

muzzle-loading armament, and their design also marked the end of sail rig in the Royal Navy.

As a result of Government economies, and indecision regarding the main armament, they were seven years under construction. The hull design, which was similar to that of *Inflexible* but on a reduced scale, embodied great proportionate beam, moderate draught, a very flat bottom with full lines and unusually flat run. They proved poor sea-boats on completion, suffering from excessive beam and a tendency to lurch and plunge heavily in a sea-way. They were extremely unhandy, a large degree of port or starboard helm being required to maintain an even course. This pair, as completed, must go down on record as the most unsatisfactory battleships ever built for the Royal Navy.

Government economies were still in force when the allowance for the 1878–9 programme came up and only two battleships were provided for the Royal Navy. Designed in the spring of 1878, *Colossus* and *Edinburgh* were enlarged and improved editions of the *Agamemnon* class, with a larger secondary armament, a knot more speed, better seakeeping capacity due to increased displacement, and some improvements in detail. Originally they were to have had the same armament as *Agamemnon* (12.5in MLR), but this was changed to 12in BLR at a later date. On a displacement of 9,620 tons and dimensions of 325ft x 68ft x 27ft, the design proved a success compared to the previous pair. They were the last of the group of five central citadel battleships laid down for the Royal Navy from 1874 to 1879.

Completion of the *Colossus* class ended a 20-year experimental period that was notable for the variety of types produced, but for little else.

The genesis of the homogeneous, pre-dreadnought type had its conception in the Admirals dating from 1879–80, a class produced solely for the purpose of countering French ships of the *Formidable*, *Requin* and *Admiral Baudin* classes.

The six Admirals fell naturally into three distinct groups by virtue of armament, dimensions, armouring and other various differing details; they were the first British battleships to have more than two ships to a class since the *Audacious* group, laid down in 1867. Various sketch designs were submitted by the Chief Constructor (Barnaby) to their Lordships which included the following features:

1. A much improved edition of the Italian

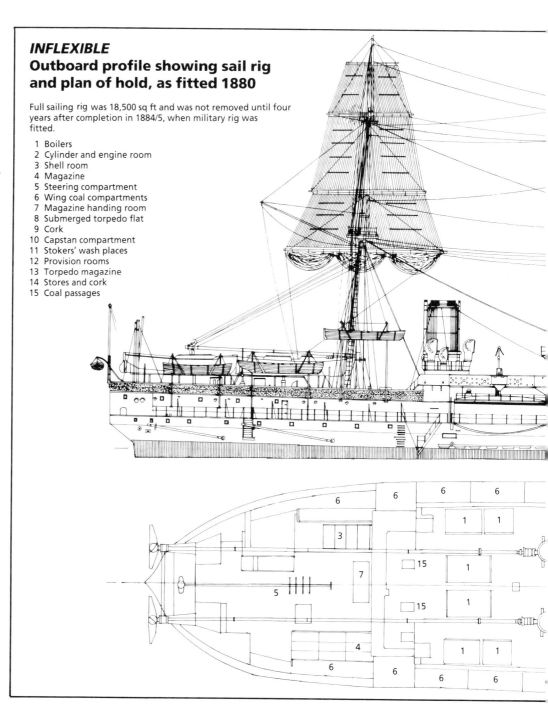

INFLEXIBLE
Outboard profile showing sail rig and plan of hold, as fitted 1880

Full sailing rig was 18,500 sq ft and was not removed until four years after completion in 1884/5, when military rig was fitted.

1 Boilers
2 Cylinder and engine room
3 Shell room
4 Magazine
5 Steering compartment
6 Wing coal compartments
7 Magazine handing room
8 Submerged torpedo flat
9 Cork
10 Capstan compartment
11 Stokers' wash places
12 Provision rooms
13 Torpedo magazine
14 Stores and cork
15 Coal passages

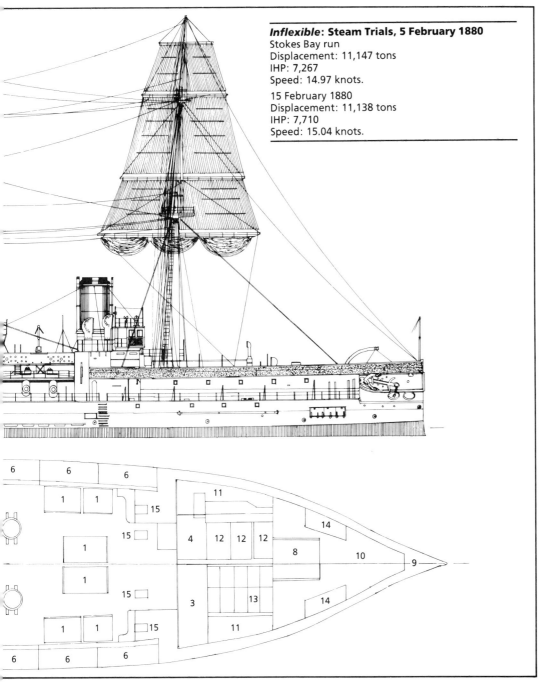

Inflexible: Steam Trials, 5 February 1880
Stokes Bay run
Displacement: 11,147 tons
IHP: 7,267
Speed: 14.97 knots.

15 February 1880
Displacement: 11,138 tons
IHP: 7,710
Speed: 15.04 knots.

battleship *Italia*, laid down in 1878 and which carried four 17in BL guns. The design had no armoured belt, but deck protection only, and a speed of 18 knots.

2. An improved edition of *Inflexible*, but still carrying sail.

3. An *Inflexible* type built along the lines suggested by former DNC Reed, which theoretically could remain afloat even with extremities flooded.

4. A *Dreadnought* type (1870), but with central citadel and unarmoured ends.

Unfortunately for Barnaby, the Board regarded none of the proposals as particularly innovatory and rejected them all. The DNC submitted other layouts within a few weeks, but this time showed all turret ships with gun commands only 10–14 feet abve waterline, a feature which was certainly frowned upon by the Board.

Barnaby found it increasingly difficult to satisfy their Lordships, especially when he had to work within the limits of 10,000 tons which was influenced to some extent by the increased risk of a vessel's loss by torpedo attack. In the opinion of the Constructor's Department this restriction certainly precluded the production of any satisfactory vessel capable of dealing with foreign battleships, be they French or Italian.

During the preparation of this design, their Lordships showed signs of unrest, but the professionalism of Barnaby came up with a synopsis which he quickly presented to the Controller. It showed that the average efficiency per ship in the French fleet was, in 1872, nearly the same as in the British fleet, but the British had a total of 45 ships as against their 26. In 1879, however, the number of French ships had increased to 38, but figures showed that average efficiency per ship had not increased; on the other hand, the Royal Navy's ships had become more efficient and could claim an increase of at least 40 per cent over 1872 figures.

Barnaby's original sketch proposal provided a displacement of only 7,200 tons on a speed of 14 knots, and had been given stimulus from the concept of the French *Caimen* type, a low freeboard vessel which carried two 16.5in guns in separate barbettes. Armament for the British vessels was provisionally fixed for either two 80ton or 100ton guns in separate mountings; the secondary battery to be four 6in guns on the main deck level.

Barnaby and his brilliant assistant, William White, prepared another set of layouts, drawings,

Neptune: Particulars, as completed

Construction
J. & W. Dudgeon, Milwall; laid down 1874 for Brazilean Navy as *Independencia*; launched 1 Sept 1874; purchased by Royal Navy Feb 1878; commenced trials May 1880; completed 3 Sept 1881.

Displacement (tons)
8,964 (load), 9,311 (deep).

Dimensions
Length: 300ft pp
Beam: 63ft
Draught: 25ft (mean)
Freeboard: 11ft to upper deck amidships.

Armament
Four 12.5in 38ton MLR
Two 9in 12ton MLR
Ten 20pdrs BL
Two 16in torpedo carriages.

Armour (iron)
Main belt: 12in–10in–9in
Citadel: 10in sides, 8in bulkheads

Forecastle side: 8in
Turrets: 13in faces, 11in sides
Upper deck: 1½–1in
Main deck: 3in–2in
Conning tower: 8in–6in
Teak backing: 15in–12in–10in.

Machinery
One set 2-cylinder trunk engines, single Griffiths propeller
Cylinder diameter: 127ft
Stroke: 4ft 6in
Propeller: 4-bladed
Propeller diameter: 26ft
Boilers: eight rectangular in two compartments with furnaces facing inboard, working pressure 32psi
Designed SHP: 8,000 for 14 knots (reached 14.66 knots with 8,832ihp in Feb 1878)
Fuel: 670 tons coal
Radius of action: 1,480nm at 10 knots.
The machinery installation comprised the largest set of trunk engines and biggest cylinders ever

built by Penn for a warship, the contract horsepower of 8,000ihp being the highest ever obtained from just two cylinders.

Sail and rig
Three masts, barque rig
Mainmast uncomfortably close to funnels and caused sails and rigging to become rotted by smoke and heat.
Last rigged battleship to enter service in the Royal Navy.

Searchlights
Four 24in 1887.

Complement
540 reduced to 468 when rig reduced in 1887.

Costs
Purchase price: £600,000
Alterations: £89,172.

Sold
15 September 1903.

Left: *Neptune,* c.1883. Designed by E. J. Reed for the Brazilian Government and built at Millwall as the *Independencia.* Purchased for the Royal Navy for £614,000 when an Anglo-Russian war seemed likely, and completed as *Neptune* in May 1880. Her all-round fire from the four 12.5in guns mounted in turrets was rather restricted because of her full rig and forecastle and poop arrangements.

Ajax and *Agamemnon*: Particulars, as completed

Construction
Ajax: Pembroke DY; laid down 21 March 1876; launched 10 March 1880; commissioned 30 March 1883
Agamemnon: Chatham DY; laid down 9 May 1876; launched 17 Sept 1879; completed 29 March 1883.

Displacement (tons)
8,510 (load), 8,812 (deep).

Dimensions
Length: 280ft pp
Beam: 66ft
Draught: 23ft forward, 24ft aft
Freeboard: 17ft 3in along superstructure forward and aft; 9ft 6in to upper deck.

Armament
Four 12.5in 38ton MLR
Two 6in 81cwt BLR
Six Nordenfelt QF
Thirteen MG
Two 14in torpedo carriages.

Armour
(Citadel and decks iron, turrets compound)
Citadel: 18in–15in sides
Bulkheads: 16½in–13½in
Upper deck: 3in
Lower deck: 3in–2½in
Turrets: 16in faces, 14in sides
Conning tower: 12in.

Machinery
Two sets 3-cylinder vertical inverted compound engines, twin propellers
Cylinder diameter: 54in
Stroke: 3ft 3in
Boilers: ten cylindrical return tube, working pressure 60psi
Designed SHP: 6,000 for 13 knots (Made 13.27 knots with 5,440ihp on trials, light condition)
Fuel: 700 tons coal normal, 970 tons max.
Radius of action: 2,100nm at 9 knots.

Searchlights
Three 24in on high platforms on superstructure.

Complement
344–359.

Cost
£548,393 *Ajax*
£530,015 *Agamemnon*.

Sold
1 March 1904 *Ajax*
13 January 1903 *Agamemnon*.

Colossus and *Edinburgh*: Particulars, as completed

Construction
Colossus: Portsmouth DY; laid down 6 June 1879; launched 21 May 1882; trials Jan 1884; commissioned 13 April 1886
Edinburgh: Pembroke DY; laid down 20 March 1879; launched 18 March 1882; trials Sept 1883; commissioned 8 July 1887.

Displacement (tons)
9,522 (load), 9,732 (deep).

Dimensions
Length: 325ft pp
Beam: 68ft
Draught: 26ft forward, 27ft aft
Freeboard: 8ft 9in amidships (load).

Armament
Four 12in 45ton BLR
Five 6in 89cwt BLR
Eight Nordenfelt QF
Fifteen MG
Two 14in torpedo carriages.

Armour (citadel, bulkheads and turrets compound, decks iron)
Citadel: 18in–14in
Bulkheads: 16in–13in
Turrets: 16in faces, 14in sides
Upper deck: 3in
Lower deck: 3in–2½in
Conning tower: 14in
Teak backing on armour: 22in–10in.

Machinery
Two sets 3-cylinder direct-acting inverted compound engines, two propellers, one HP two LP cylinders in each set
Cylinder diameter: HP 58in, LP 74in
Stroke: 3ft 3in
Propeller: 4-bladed
Boilers: ten cylindrical, working pressure 64psi
Designed SHP: 6,000 for 14 knots (Trials: *Colossus* 16.4 knots with 7,488ihp; *Edinburgh* 15.991 knots with 6,754ihp)
Fuel: 850 tons coal normal, 950 tons max.
Radius of action: 2,740nm at 9–10 knots.

Searchlights
Three 24in.

Wireless
Fitted in *Edinburgh* 1901.

Complement
397–409.

Costs
Colossus: £661,716
Edinburgh: £662,773.

Sold
Colossus: 6 October 1908
Edinburgh: 11 October 1910.

legend figures and model results, and submitted them to the Board. He assured against any lingering doubts about torpedo attack by referring to his speech of 1876, given before the Institute of Naval Architects, in which he had said:

'The assailants ought to be brought to bay before they get within striking distance of the ironclads by consorts armed like the attacking vessel, with ram and torpedo. Each costly ironclad ought to be in divisions defended against torpedo and ram by numerous smaller but less important parts of the general force.'

The Admiralty knew only too well that the closest defence against torpedo attack was by means of nets, but these could not be used under all circumstances. The best method would be to meet torpedo-boat with torpedo-boat, or better still a torpedo-boat catcher, as recently suggested by Edward Reed. A fleet action would almost certainly start with a boat attack, and all the powers were presently engaged in building small boats to accompany the fleets to sea.

This idea was warmly welcomed by authorities including Admiral Sir Spencer Robinson, Sir Edward Reed, John Scott Russell and many others in naval construction circles. Their Lordships decided that the new layouts were worthy of consideration even though the size and cost had exceeded their original desires. On acceptance the design was sent to Pembroke Dockyard for further confirmation and guidance.

The approved layout showed a rise in displacement to 9,200 tons on a draught of 25–26 feet, but even with this increase over Barnaby's original design, it made her a distinctly cramped vessel which curtailed high freeboard at the extremities and vertical armoured side; protection being subordinated to the requirements of armament and speed when allocating weights within the design.

The final legend was approved in January 1880 and was named *Collingwood*; she was to be the

Above: *Agamemnon* during a Mediterranean commission 1886–7. *Ajax* and *Agamemnon* were probably the most unsatisfactory battleships ever constructed for the Royal Navy. Reduced versions of *Inflexible* and armed with 12.5in muzzle-loaders – the last British battleships ever to have MLR guns.

Left: *Ajax* whilst in Fleet Reserve, 1887. On leaving Sheerness, she demonstrated while completely unmanageable she was by nearly running down an Indiaman crowded with troops. Next, she parted her cable in a dead calm in Dover Roads by going about with the tide and bringing the cable across her ram. Next day, going down the Channel at full speed, she carried her helm three turns astarboard for three hours, and then without warning 'broke her sheer' and came around on a pivot scattering merchant vessels in all directions.

Right, top and bottom: *Colossus*, both photographs taken on Mediterranean service, 1890–3. *Colossus* and *Edinburgh* turned out passable sea-boats but had a heavy roll. To counteract this, they were fitted with experimental anti-rolling water tanks (*Inflexible* was first to have these). They were placed at each side of the hull with a connecting cross-pipe. They were only partially successful, however, as large quantities of water washing from side to side caused violent shocks, and made it difficult to stand on the deck above; their retention was not recommended.

As a result of Government economy and changes in armament, she was six years under construction. She was the first British battleship to carry BL guns in barbettes. She was a limited success, but suffered greatly from her low freeboard even though she was a passable sea-boat with a moderate roll in good conditions. Note no net booms.

prototype of the *Admiral* class. This design marked the abandonment of the principle of end-on action as embodied in the older *Alexandra*, *Inflexible* and *Colossus* types, in favour of the line-ahead battle formation with emphasis on broadside fire. Moreover, it showed the increasing recognition of the value of a good secondary armament of medium-calibre guns, together with the need for protection against close-range attack from this type of gun.

The ship was provided with low freeboard at the extremities and had full-width superstructure amidships in place of the narrow superstructure forward and aft as in the *Inflexible* and *Colossus* types. Hull lines were hollowed forward and aft, and were finer than in preceding classes in order to reduce unarmoured areas liable to flooding in the event of damage. Internal sub-division at the ends above the armoured deck contained coal, stores and provisions, but layers of cork were not fitted as in *Inflexible* and *Colossus*. Tests showed that with both extremities flooded seaworthiness and fighting efficiency was unimpaired, and the ship would still be able to manoeuvre safely with a loss of only a few knots in speed.

The original design had specified a main armament of four muzzle-loading guns mounted in pairs on low turntables on the centre-line forward and aft, but this was later modified to two breech-loaders mounted singly on each turntable. With the adoption of breech-loaders, however, barbette mountings became practicable, and turntables were subsequently replaced by a new type of barbette designed especially for this class by George Rendel of Elswick. This gave a considerably higher gun command than could have been obtained with turrets, and had the benefit that no increase in protection weight was needed, the redoubt armour to protect the turret training gear now being available for the barbettes.

Collingwood was officially rated as a central citadel type, although the absence of side armour above main deck level excluded her from this category. Because the protection had been subordinated to armament and speed, the scale of armouring as applied was the best that could be provided on the displacement limit, but it resulted in a vessel not widely different from contemporary battleships, and only slightly better than in the *Colossus* type.

Protection layout was influenced to some extent by the appearance of the medium-calibre gun

Collingwood: Particulars, as completed

Construction
Pembroke DY; laid down 12 July 1880; launched 22 Nov 1882, completed 1884; gunnery trials 3 May 1886.

Displacement (tons)
8,750 (load), 9,700 (deep).

Dimensions
Length: 325ft pp
Beam: 68ft
Draught: 25ft 5¾in forward, 26ft 4in aft.

Armament
Four 12in 44ton BL Mk II; 85rpg
Six 6in Mk III; 85rpg
Two 9pdr; 500rpg
Ten 1in Nordenfelt
Four 0.45in Gardiner MG
Five 14in torpedo tubes (above water; one bow, four beam) twelve torpedoes.

Armour (compound iron main belt, bulkheads and ammunition tubes, rest mild steel)
Main belt: 18in–8in, 140ft long; 18in for depth of 4ft and 8in below this
Bulkheads: 16in–7in
Barbettes: 11½in faces, 10in rears, 1in roof plates, 3in floor
Ammunition tubes: 12in–10in
Battery bulkheads: 6in
Conning tower: 12in sides, 2in roof

Main deck: 3in
Lower deck: 2½in–2in at ends.

Machinery
Two sets 3-cylinder vertical inverted compound engines, two propellers, one HP, two LP cylinders each set
Cylinder diameter: HP 52in, LP 74in
Stroke: 3ft 6in
Boilers: twelve cylindrical single-ended return tube in four compartments, back to back against centre-line bulkhead; thirty-six furnaces, working pressure 90psi
IHP: 7,000 normal, 9,500 forced
Fuel: 900 tons coal normal, 1,200 tons max.
Radius of action: 6,400nm (approx.) at 10 knots.

Ship's boats
See Admiral class.

Searchlights
Six 24in: four in sponsons, one over bridge, one high on platform at after end of superstructure.

Anchors
See Admiral class.

Complement
1887: 459
1904: 455.

Cost
£636,996.

Collingwood: Steam trials, May 1884

Runs:	1	2	3	4
Mean Draught:	23ft 6in	23ft 9in	23ft 10in	23ft 11in
Displacement (tons):	8,000	8,200	8,240	8,280
IHP:	9,573	8,369	7,071	3,040
Revs. (mean):	95.57	89.05	85.47	65.67
Speed (knots):	16.88	16.60	16.051	12.621

Average steam pressure in boilers: 93.45psi.

Below: *Collingwood.* A splendid view taken during the Diamond Jubilee Fleet Review for Queen Victoria, 12 June 1897. She continued to take part in annual manoeuvres, and acted as Guardship until 1904 when she was laid up and finally sold in 1909.

Left: *Collingwood*, Chatham c.1889–90. Officially rated as a central citadel type, but the absence of side armour above the main deck excluded the vessel from this category. Protection was subordinated to armament and speed, and the scale of armouring was the best that could be applied within the limits of displacement. She was the first British battleship fitted with forced draught.

Collingwood: GM and stability

January 1884

	Displacement (tons)	GM	Maximum stability
Load condition (fully equipped plus 900 tons coal)	9,505	6ft	39°
Light condition	8,310	5.75ft	
Experimental condition	7,525	6.09ft	

which was quite capable of delivering a significant volume of fire against unarmoured areas at close range, and represented a modification of the central citadel system with armour extended along the waterline and removed from the upper side; *Collingwood* being the first British battleship whose side armour was confined to the waterline only. The short, thin, narrow waterline belt ran for just 140 feet by 7½ feet wide amidships, and was closed by heavy transverse bulkheads, covered by a flat deck. The belt, although 18 inches thick, was liable to be completely submerged at sea in the deep load condition, which meant that there was practically no defence against shells of any calibre. The barbettes formed separate armoured redoubts with armoured floors, standing on the upper deck, and connected to the main belt by armoured ammunition trunks. The barbette roof plates were not armoured, being intended to protect the gun crews from machine-gun fire.

A very weak point in the system was the provision in all watertight bulkheads of drainage apertures connecting to the main drain and then into the engine room. The closing valves were apt to become clogged with dirt, and as many were almost inaccessible shutting them properly in an emergency proved extremely difficult.

The system of protection adopted was severely criticized by Edward Reed on the grounds of the extremely low armoured side. In defence Barnaby submitted the following points:

1. The main armament, ammunition trunks and ventilating trunks to engine and boiler rooms are very well protected for the size of the ship.

2. Protection to the machinery and boilers is much stronger than would have been the case if the same weight of belt had been applied over the whole length of the hull.

3. Owing to the fact that the total weight available to protection would not premit a full-length belt without a considerable reduction in thickness at the ends, other areas have been better treated and in particular, the magazines, shell rooms and steering gear have received more efficient protection in the way of a better underwater deck.

On completion, *Collingwood* was the fastest battleship in the Royal Navy, and reached 16.884 knots on trials. Achievement of this high figure, however, was a result of the compromise within the design, including certain sacrifices in the protective qualities. The high speed looked excellent on paper, but in practice could only be maintained in good weather; it fell off very rapidly in a seaway because of the low freeboard.

The following four ships, *Rodney, Howe, Camperdown* and *Anson* were all laid down in 1882–3 and differed from *Collingwood* in having 13.5in guns instead of 12in armament, plus a longer main belt and thicker barbette armour in *Anson* and *Camperdown* whose length and beam were increased 5 feet and 6in respectively to carry the additional weight of armour without further increase in draught.

The 1882–3 programme allowed for an extra vessel, but because of a shortage of building slips within the Royal dockyards, the vessel was allocated to a private yard (Thames Ironworks). Originally she was to have belonged to the *Camperdown* group, but owing to the anticipated delay in deliverance of the new 13.5in guns selected for these ships, and which was unacceptable in a contract-built ship, the design was modified to carry the Armstrong 16.25in gun which at that time was just becoming available. Great consideration was given to this move, but the only other proven heavy gun generally available was the 12in as fitted in *Collingwood*. In foreign constructions, it was noted that the Italian Navy were mounting 16.5in

CAMPERDOWN
Outboard profile, sections and plan of hold, as fitted 1890

Section 124
1 Barbette
2 Gun room
3 Wardroom pantry
4 Patent fuel
5 Coal
6 Magazine
7 Engineers' stores
8 Engineers' stores
9 Shaft passage
10 Machinery

Section 112
1 Barbette
2 Gun room
3 Passageway
4 Wardroom servants
5 Patent fuel
6 Coal
7 Shell room and magazine
8 Engineers' stores
9 Small gun magazine
10 Shaft passage

Section 124
looking aft

Section 112
looking aft

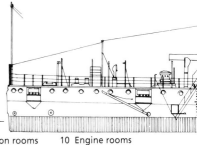

1 Wet provision rooms
2 Provision room
3 Spirit room
4 Shaft passage
5 Watertight compartments
6 Engineers' stores
7 Wings
8 Condensers
9 Coal hatches
10 Engine rooms
11 Coal bunkers
12 Boilers
13 After stoke-hold flat
14 Forward stoke-hold flat

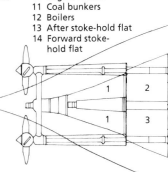

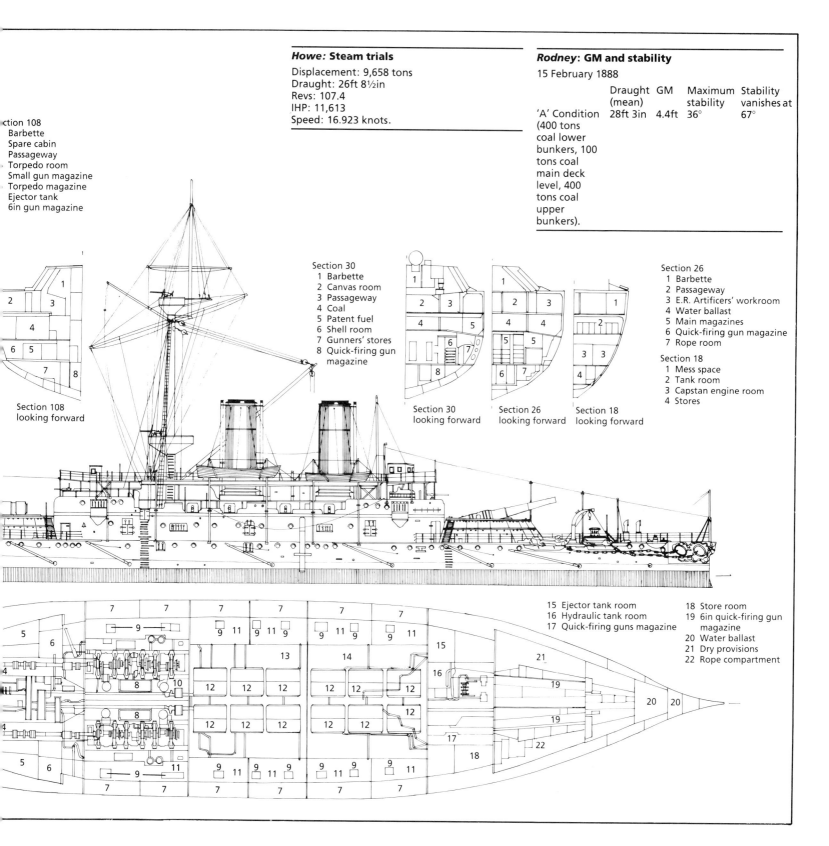

Howe: Steam trials

Displacement: 9,658 tons
Draught: 26ft 8½in
Revs: 107.4
IHP: 11,613
Speed: 16.923 knots.

Rodney: GM and stability

15 February 1888

	Draught (mean)	GM	Maximum stability	Stability vanishes at
'A' Condition (400 tons coal lower bunkers, 100 tons coal main deck level, 400 tons coal upper bunkers).	28ft 3in	4.4ft	36°	67°

...ction 108
Barbette
Spare cabin
Passageway
Torpedo room
Small gun magazine
Torpedo magazine
Ejector tank
6in gun magazine

Section 108
looking forward

Section 30
1 Barbette
2 Canvas room
3 Passageway
4 Coal
5 Patent fuel
6 Shell room
7 Gunners' stores
8 Quick-firing gun
magazine

Section 30
looking forward

Section 26
looking forward

Section 18
looking forward

Section 26
1 Barbette
2 Passageway
3 E.R. Artificers' workroom
4 Water ballast
5 Main magazines
6 Quick-firing gun magazine
7 Rope room

Section 18
1 Mess space
2 Tank room
3 Capstan engine room
4 Stores

15 Ejector tank room
16 Hydraulic tank room
17 Quick-firing guns magazine

18 Store room
19 6in quick-firing gun
magazine
20 Water ballast
21 Dry provisions
22 Rope compartment

Admiral class: Particulars, as completed

Construction

Anson: Pembroke DY; laid down 24 April 1883; launched 17 Feb 1886; transferred to Portsmouth DY for completion of armament March 1887

Howe: Pembroke DY; laid down 7 June 1882; launched 28 April 1885; transferred to Portsmouth DY for completion of armament 15 Nov 1885

Camperdown: Portsmouth DY; laid down 18 Dec 1882; launched 24 Nov 1885; completed trials 14 March 1887

Rodney: Chatham DY; laid down 6 Feb 1882; launched 24 Nov 1885; completed trials 14 March 1887.

Displacement (tons)
10,007 (as designed), 10,619 (load), 10,919 (deep) (*Camperdown*).

Dimensions
Length: 330ft pp
Beam: 68ft 6in
Draught: 28ft 6½in (deep).

Armament
Four 13.5in 67ton Mk I (*Rodney* three 67ton, one 69ton experimental)
Six 6in 26cal Mk IV
Twelve 6pdr
Two 3pdr
Seven–ten Nordenfelt
Five 14in torpedo tubes (*Rodney* not fitted with bow tube).

Armour (compound iron)
Belt: 18in–8in (150ft long, *Rodney* and *Howe* 140ft)
Bulkheads: 16in–7in
Barbettes: 11½in faces, 10in sides and rear
Ammunition tubes: 12in–10in

Conning tower: 12in sides, 2in roof
Battery: 6in bulkheads, 1in faceplates
Main deck: 3in
Lower deck: 2½in.

Machinery
Two sets 3-cylinder vertical inverted engines, two propellers
Cylinder diameter: HP 52in, LP 74in
Stroke: 3ft 9in
Boilers: twelve cylindrical single-ended return tube (*Anson* eight cylindrical single-ended), working pressure 100psi; all fitted for forced draught
IHP: 7,500 normal, 11,000 forced (*Howe* 16.923 knots on trials)
Fuel: 900 tons coal normal, 1,200 tons max.
Radius of action: 6,400nm at 10 knots.

Ship's boats
Torpedo boat 1st class: one 63ft
Pinnaces (steam): one 52ft, one 37ft
Launches (steam): one 42ft
Cutters: two 30ft, one 20ft
Whalers: two 27ft
Gigs: one 30ft
Dinghies: one 14ft
Skiff dinghies: one 10ft.

Searchlights
Six 24in (five *Rodney*).

Anchors
Rogers modified type
Three 115cwt, one 30cwt, one 25cwt, one 12cwt
Cable: 525 fathoms 2⅜in, 200 fathoms 1½in.

Complement
454–472.

Cost
Anson £662,582
Rodney £665,963.

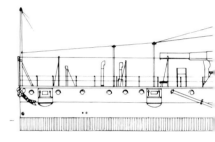

1 Boilers
2 Machinery and engine rooms
3 Shell rooms
4 Magazines
5 13.5in barbettes
6 Boiler room uptakes
7 Engine room vents
8 Steering compartment
9 Torpedo rooms
10 Conning tower
11 Stores and watertight compartments
12 Capstan room

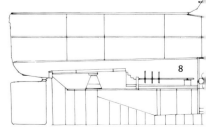

(75ton) guns in the *Andrea Doria* class, and the French *Formidable* had been given 14.5in (75ton). The 12in was considered by their Lordships to be inadequate and the 16.25in was chosen, although it was realized that its great weight made it impracticable to carry more than two guns. Named *Benbow*, she was the first of only three ships ever to mount the 16.25in gun.

In most respects, the class as a whole, were generally successful except for the low freeboard. The design does show that the Admiralty was seeking greatly to improve qualities of British battleships, and to bring some sort of homogeneity to the battlefleet

As a result of interim changes in the Board of Admiralty, the principles of attack and defence on which the design of the *Admiral* class had been based were no longer favoured when the design for the two battleships of the 1885–86 programme came up for discussion, and there was a demand for a reversion to turrets with full height of armoured side below these and complete waterline protection in place of the open barbettes, unprotected upper side and short, narrow waterline belt of the *Admiral*s.

In line with the current trend towards moderate dimensions and cost, the original Admiralty demand was for something along the lines of an

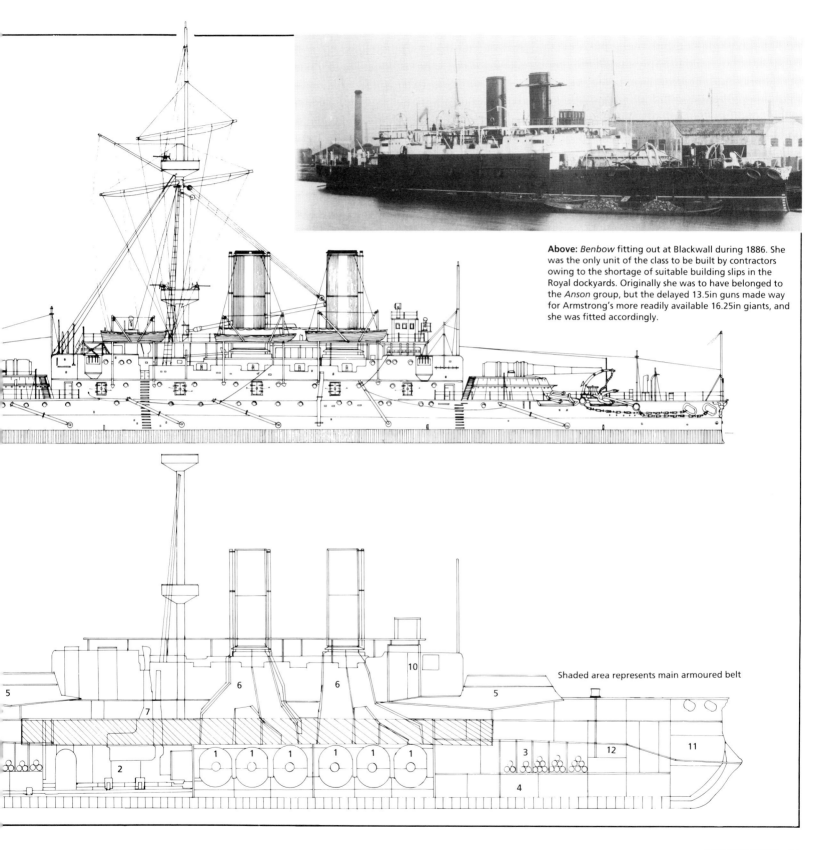

Above: *Benbow* fitting out at Blackwall during 1886. She was the only unit of the class to be built by contractors owing to the shortage of suitable building slips in the Royal dockyards. Originally she was to have belonged to the *Anson* group, but the delayed 13.5in guns made way for Armstrong's more readily available 16.25in giants, and she was fitted accordingly.

Shaded area represents main armoured belt

improved *Conqueror* (laid down 1879), a rather unsatisfactory type in which the main armament was concentrated forward in a twin turret with low command, embodying the subsequently discarded tactical principle of end-on attack. The vessel displaced 6,200 tons in the load condition and had been constructed as a coastal defence ship. It had been decided to provide maximum battleship standards of armament and protection in the new ships, and to raise the displacement to 10,500 tons while retaining the basic features of the *Conqueror* type. This decision accentuated the existing confusion of thought regarding battleship design and, in the minds of many, was thought to be a retrograde step on the grounds that the *Conqueror* concept was faulty as a coastal defence type, and even more disastrous in a seagoing battleship in which high gun command and effective all-round fire were paramount.

The Construction Department received verbal instructions from their Lordships to provide sketch designs for new battleships conforming with their ideas in respect of *Conqueror*, but if the DNC wished to include other designs he should feel free to do so. From September to October 1884, the DNC forwarded six basic sketch designs for

Benbow: Particulars, as completed

Construction
Thames Ironworks, Blackwall; laid down 1 Nov 1882; launched 15 June 1888; transferred to Chatham Aug 1886 to await main armament; completed 1888.

Displacement (tons)
10,040 (load), 10,750 (deep).

Dimensions
Length: 330ft pp
Beam: 68ft
Draught: 26ft 3in forward, 27ft 3in aft.

Armament
Two 16.25in 30cal 111ton Mk I; 92rpg
Ten 6in Mk IV
Eight 6pdr
Ten Nordenfelt
Six Gardner MG
Five 14in torpedo tubes above water (four beam, one bow).

Armour
Belt: 18in–8in, 150ft long
Bulkheads: 17in–16in
Barbettes: 14in–12in
Ammunition tubes: 12in
Decks: 3in main, 2½in lower
Battery: 6in
Conning tower: 12in–9in
Total weight of armour 3,999 tons.

Machinery
Two sets 3-cylinder inverted compound engines, two propellers
Cylinder diameter: as other ships of the Admiral group.
Stroke: 3ft 6in
Boilers: twelve cylindrical single-ended return tube, working pressure 90psi
IHP: 7,500 normal, 11,000 forced (17.5 knots with 10,860shp on trials)
Fuel: 900 tons coal normal, 1,200 tons max.
Radius of action: 6,300nm at 10 knots.

Searchlights
Four 24in.

Complement
523–538.

Cost
£764,022.

approval, on the basis of Admiralty requirements in respect of moderate displacement and turret mountings, the topweight of the turrets and redoubts implying acceptance of low freeboard and gun command if permitted limits of displacement were not exceeded. The sketch designs were marked 'A' to 'E'. In accordance with further instructions an alternative to sketch 'C' was prepared and submitted which showed dimensions of 340ft x 70ft x 26ft 6in on a displacement of 10,050 tons, and carrying four 43ton and sixteen 6in guns.

Costs varied from £867,500 for 'A'; £857,000 for 'B'; and £847,500 for 'C'.

Throughout the development of the design, it was found that weight considerations, in view of the restricted displacement, made it impracticable to provide more than one turret without either exceeding the displacement limit or sacrificing the required standards in gun calibre or armour thickness. As a result of this, it was decided to adopt the twin turret mounted in the forward part of the ship as shown in plan 'E'. This concentration of the entire main armament forward was influenced to some extent by the views of a small lobby that still favoured ramming tactics and end-on attack, and by Mediterranean considerations which, at that time, included the possibility of having to force the Dardanelles for which purpose maximum ahead fire would be an advantage.

A minority of the Board, however, was critical of the absence of all-round fire which was seen as essential for fleet actions, and some concession was made to their wishes by the inclusion of a single 9.2in or 10in gun astern. This move was initiated by modifying design 'E' to include the after mounting by reducing the number of 6in guns to twelve, and a reduction in the main belt thickness from 20in to 18in (*see* legend table).

Their Lordships had always required that the new vessels be armed with the heaviest guns possible on the given displacement; as completed they were the only British battleships (apart from coastal defence ships) to have their main armament in one turret. The decision to mount 16.25in (111ton) in the turret forward was due to the anticipated delay in delivery of the Woolwich-made 13.5in, as had been the case with *Benbow* (*Admiral* class). During the proving ground trials, however, one of the new guns was found to have bent after firing, and then had to undergo a lengthy series of

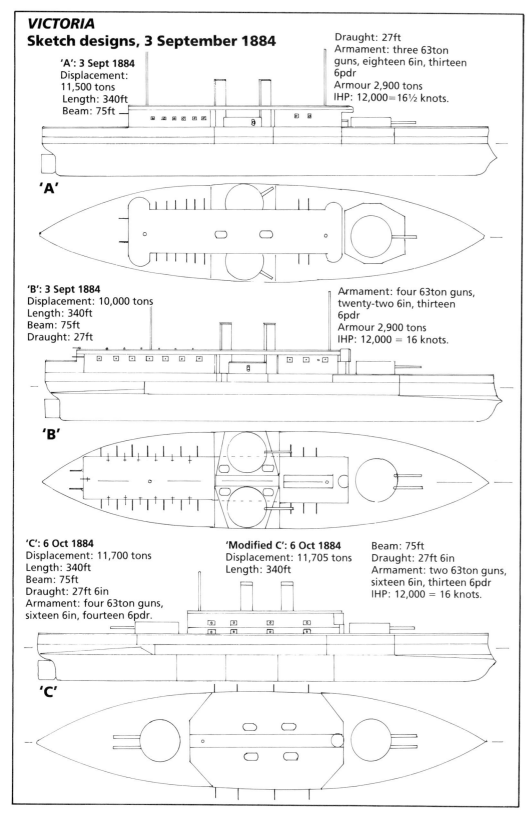

VICTORIA
Sketch designs, 3 September 1884

'A': 3 Sept 1884
Displacement:
11,500 tons
Length: 340ft
Beam: 75ft

Draught: 27ft
Armament: three 63ton
guns, eighteen 6in, thirteen
6pdr
Armour 2,900 tons
IHP: 12,000 = 16½ knots.

'A'

'B': 3 Sept 1884
Displacement: 10,000 tons
Length: 340ft
Beam: 75ft
Draught: 27ft

Armament: four 63ton guns,
twenty-two 6in, thirteen
6pdr
Armour 2,900 tons
IHP: 12,000 = 16 knots.

'B'

'C': 6 Oct 1884
Displacement: 11,700 tons
Length: 340ft
Beam: 75ft
Draught: 27ft 6in
Armament: four 63ton guns,
sixteen 6in, fourteen 6pdr.

'Modified C': 6 Oct 1884
Displacement: 11,705 tons
Length: 340ft

Beam: 75ft
Draught: 27ft 6in
Armament: two 63ton guns,
sixteen 6in, thirteen 6pdr
IHP: 12,000 = 16 knots.

'C'

trials before acceptance, which resulted in a good deal of modification to the structure of the gun.

Although the turret was mounted much farther aft in the new ships than had been the case in *Benbow*, the gun command was considerably lower (5ft) than in the latter and was considered to be insufficient for a good seagoing ship because of the impossiblity of fighting guns if the ships were being driven against head seas.

The after gun was provisionally fixed as being a 9.2in piece, but consideration was given to the *Esmeralda* (Chile) which had been built and armed with 10in guns by Elswick in 1883. It seemed natural to arm a British battleship with the best gun possible, and one which was greatly superior to anything mounted in foreign vessels, so the Elswick company was asked to supply the new ship (building in their own yard) with one of their 10in guns.

The percentage of armour weight in the new ships (named *Sans Pareil* and *Renown*, later renamed *Victoria* to honour the Queen) was higher than in any other British battleship since *Dreadnought* (1879) and the arrangement of the armouring differed somewhat from the almost complete waterline belt and central citadel of the *Conqueror* class on which the new design had been largely based. In general it was similar to the *Admiral*s but with an increased height of belt (as put forward by ex-DNC, Sir Edward Reed) and with main armament in a closed turret standing in an armoured redoubt instead of open barbettes with thin floors at upper deck level and armoured ammunition trunks below.

The redoubt was carried well abaft the turret, enclosing the turret base and the foot of the conning tower. Reversion to the closed turret mounting provided more complete protection than the open barbettes of the *Admiral* class, and was probably due to the fact that the quick-firing secondary gun could smother an open barbette and thus render the main armament of a battleship unworkable.

Maximum thickness of belt and deck armour was the same as in the *Admiral* group, but the turret armour was 3in to 5½in heavier than the barbettes in those ships. The belt, which extended slightly beyond the turret and enclosed the machinery, boiler and most magazine spaces, was 12ft to 22ft longer and 1ft wider than in the *Admiral*s and carried 2ft higher above the waterline with a slightly reduced depth below.

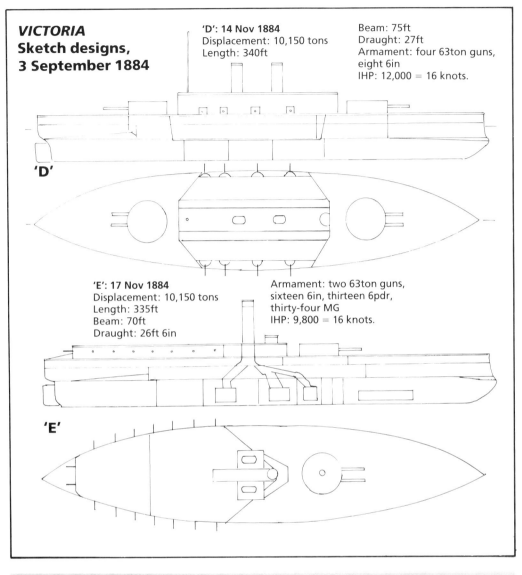

VICTORIA
Sketch designs,
3 September 1884

'D': 14 Nov 1884
Displacement: 10,150 tons
Length: 340ft

Beam: 75ft
Draught: 27ft
Armament: four 63ton guns,
eight 6in
IHP: 12,000 = 16 knots.

'D'

'E': 17 Nov 1884
Displacement: 10,150 tons
Length: 335ft
Beam: 70ft
Draught: 26ft 6in

Armament: two 63ton guns,
sixteen 6in, thirteen 6pdr,
thirty-four MG
IHP: 9,800 = 16 knots.

'E'

Bottom left: *Victoria* during trials in the summer of 1888. Compared with *Benbow*, *Victoria* and *Sans Pareil* were 10 feet longer, 420 tons heavier, had the same main armament, re-arranged for ahead instead of all-round fire, with a lower gun command, heavier secondary armament and about ½-knot faster. On completion, they were considered by many to be the last word in battleship design, an opinion, it may be added, that was by no means general.

Provision of a complete end to end belt was at first considered, but as this would have necessitated a reduction in maximum armour thickness to about 14in with 12in at the ends so as not to exceed the permissible displacement limit, the idea was abandoned and the underwater deck of the *Admirals* was repeated instead. Moreover, a complete belt was considered unnecessary in these ships, in any event, owing to the fine lines forward and aft with corresponding reduction in area, outside belt, liable to flooding by waterline damage. On 22 June 1893, during exercises in the Mediterranean, *Victoria* was rammed forward by *Camperdown* and sank in about ten minutes (23 officers, 336 ratings lost). Watertight doors and hatches had not been closed prior to the collision and extensive flooding outside the breached compartments caused the ship to capsize. The subsequent inquiry established the principle causes for the loss of the ship:

1. Open watertight doors and hatches which could not be shut after the collision.

2. Low freeboard forward with consequent reduction in safe angle of heel.

3. Longitudinal bulkheads in forward compartments tended to confine flooding to the damaged side, and increase capsizing effect (these bulkheads were removed in *Sans Pareil* in 1899).

Victoria's maximum stability, was considered by the Court to be adequate by existing standards, although the margin of safety and the point where maximum stability vanished was not great enough.

It was considered, that if all watertight doors and hatches could have been closed before the collision, the stem head could have been brought to waterline level, with a heel of about 9°, and that the ship would have remained safe and under control in prevailing good weather, although likely to have been critical in any seaway.

Prior to this accident, they were considered by some naval experts to have been the most successful battleships of the Barnaby era, although owing to the very low gun command, and absence of all-round fire, this view was by no means generally accepted.

The two vessels proposed for the 1886–7 programme were to be the last of the British single citadel turret battleships, and were enlarged and modified versions of *Dreadnought*, embodying the recommendations of the First Sea Lord, Sir Arthur Hood, in respect of low freeboard and a maximum

Below: *Victoria*, fitting out at Armstrong, 1888. She was the first British battleship to be built and armed by a private firm.

Victoria and *Sans Pareil*: Particulars, as completed

Construction
Victoria: Armstrong, Elswick; laid down 23 April 1885; launched 9 April 1887; completed June 1888
Sans Pareil: Thames Ironworks; laid down 21 April 1885; launched 9 May 1887; completed Sept 1888.

Displacement (tons)
11,096 (load), 11,346 (deep).

Dimensions
length: 340ft pp
Beam: 70ft 1in
Draught: 27ft 10in (mean) load, 28ft 4in deep.

Armament
Two 16.25in 130cal 111ton BL Mk I
One 10in 30cal 29ton
Twelve 6in Mk IV BL
Twelve 6pdr
Nine 3pdr
Two 1in Nordenfelt
Four 14in torpedo tubes (one bow, one stern above water, two submerged, broadside); 24 torpedoes.

Armour
Main belt: 18in–16in (162ft × 8ft 6in)
Bulkheads: 16in
Redoubts: 18in–16in
Turrets: 17in
Sheild to 10in gun: 6in
Battery: 3in sides, 5in bulkheads, 3in ammunition tubes
Decks: 3in main and lower
Conning tower: 14in sides, 2in roof
Teak backing 6in–7in behind vertical armour.

Machinery
Two sets triple expansion engines, twin propellers
Cylinder diameter: HP 43in, IP 62in, LP 96in
Stroke: 4ft 3in
Boilers: eight cylindrical in four compartments, two each side centre-line with fore and aft ammunition passage between them, working pressure 135psi
Designed SHP: 7,500 natural draught, 12,000 forced
Designed speed: 15.3 knots natural, 17.2 knots forced (trials: 14,250shp, no speeds recorded; second runs: 16–16¼ knots (forced) 15 June 1888)
Fuel: 750 tons coal normal, 1,200 tons max.
Radius of action: 7,000nm at 10 knots.

Ship's boats
Torpedo-boats 1st class: one 63ft
Pinnaces (steam): one 52ft, one 37ft
Launches (steam): one 42ft
Cutters: two 30ft
Whalers: two 27ft
Gigs: one 30ft
Dinghies: one 14ft.

Searchlights
Four 24in *Victoria*
Three 24in *Sans Pareil*.

Anchors
Three 115cwt (2 Martins, 1 Inglefield)
One 32cwt Admiralty pattern
One 25cwt Admiralty pattern
One 12cwt Admiralty pattern 525 fathoms cable (2⅜in).

Complement
430 as designed
530 *Sans Pareil* 1903
549 *Victoria* 1890.

Cost
£625,000 estimated (1885) (exclusive of guns)
£844,922 *Victoria*
£778,659 *Sans Pareil*.

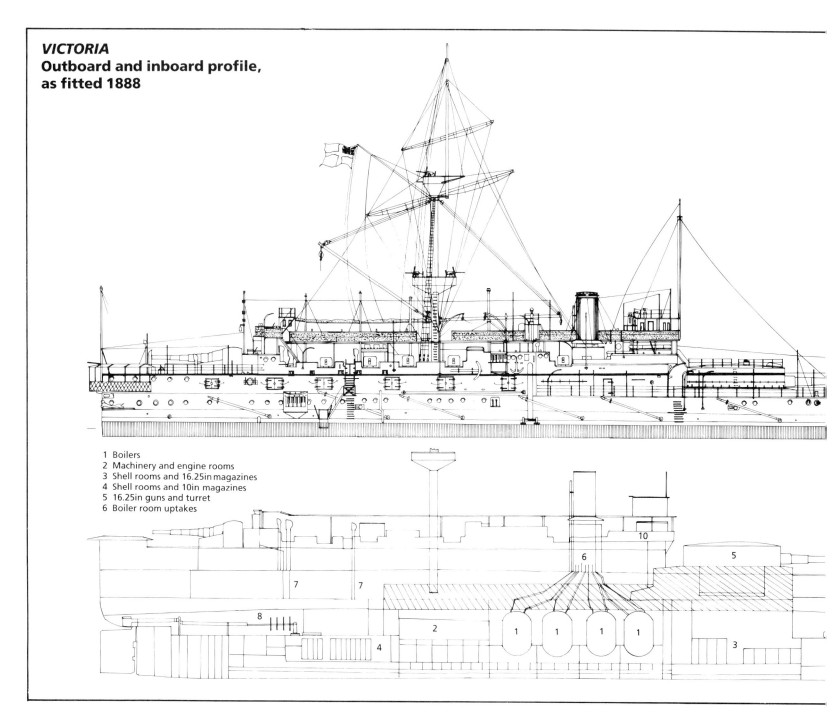

VICTORIA
**Outboard and inboard profile,
as fitted 1888**

1 Boilers
2 Machinery and engine rooms
3 Shell rooms and 16.25in magazines
4 Shell rooms and 10in magazines
5 16.25in guns and turret
6 Boiler room uptakes

Below: *Victoria*, as completed, 1890. During gunnery trials the 16.25in (110ton) guns proved rather a failure and her completion was greatly delayed. She was to have a short but eventful life. On 29 January 1892 she ran aground on rocks at Luipe Point off the coast of Greece and was badly damaged. Finally, on 22 June 1893, while on manoeuvres, she was accidently rammed and sunk by *Camperdown* (*Admiral* class) off the coast of Syria.

Bottom: *Sans Pareil*, 1904. All grey, W/T gaff, foremast and funnels raised. Both were completed with short funnels, but were considerably increased in height during August 1890 to improve natural draught. They were the first British battleships to have the twin funnel arrangement.

Victoria: GM and stability

Based on inclining experiments, January 1890

	Draught	GM	Maximum stability	Stability vanishes at
'A' Condition (= load)*	27ft 10in	5.05ft	35°	68°
'B' Condition (= deep load)**	28ft 4in	5.05ft		

Launch weight: 5,556 tons (*Sans Pareil*)

*Fully equipped plus 750 tons coal.
**Fully equipped plus 1,000 tons coal.

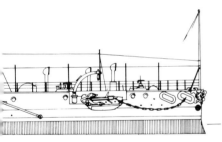

7 Engine room vents
8 Steering compartment
9 Torpedo rooms
10 Conning tower
11 Stores and watertight compartment
12 Capstan room

Shaded area represents main armour belt

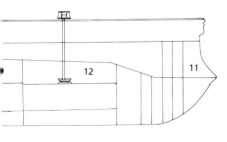

standard of protection. The design was first considered early in 1885, and the original proposals submitted by Barnaby are believed to have been similar to, or a revival of, an 11,700ton separate redoubt turret version of the *Admirals* which had been suggested by him in October 1884 for the *Sans Pareil* class. (Official records show very little on these early suggestions, but it appears to have been very like design 'C'; *see* sketches.)

No decision on any final design, however, had been reached by June 1885, when a new Board of Admiralty, with Sir Arthur Hood as First Sea Lord, took office, and the displacement restrictions which had exercised a cramping effect on the *Admirals* and *Sans Pareil* pair were no longer enforced. Hood strongly opposed the DNC's (Barnaby) ideas, especially regarding the separate redoubt system of protection, but instead favoured

low freeboard with a single citadel. A proposed design dated 8 July 1885, initiated by him, and representing a development of *Dreadnought*, was put forward as being regarded by many naval officers as the ideal battleship type.

Displacement was 11,800 tons, and armament, armour thickness and speed were all increased over *Dreadnought*, but the basic principles of the *Dreadnought* design were retained except that belt armour was not carried right to the extremities, but replaced by an underwater deck forward and aft as in the *Admiral* and *Sans Pareil* groups. As in *Dreadnought*, no secondary battery was provided and there was nothing between the main armament and five or six 6pdrs for anti-torpedo-boat work. On 28 July 1885, however, this plan was rejected by many of those on the Board, in favour of an alternative, separate redoubt turret design of the same

displacement, which may have been Barnaby's original proposal with extra side armour added. Hood replied by revising his *Dreadnought* plan to include an armoured secondary battery of eight 5in guns and increasing the displacement to 11,940 tons. As put forward, this was initially accepted on 12 August 1885 as the final basis for the *Trafalgar* class.

On a displacement of 11,940 tons, the design provided four 13.5in guns in two twin turrets on the upper deck forward and aft, with a command of about 15 feet, a secondary battery of eight 5in BL amidships, five 6pdr quick-firing and four 14in torpedo tubes.

The maximum armour on belt, citadel and turrets was 20in 18in and 18in respectively, with 3in on the citadel and underwater decks. The DNC (Barnaby) was on sick leave at the time (he

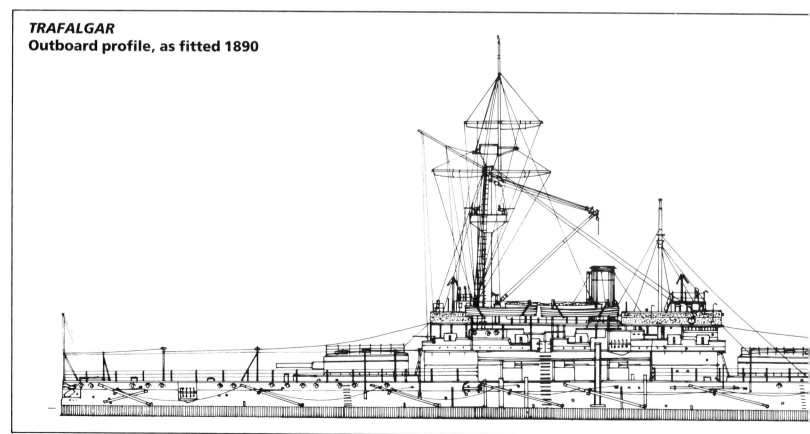

TRAFALGAR
Outboard profile, as fitted 1890

had actually tendered his resignation in July), and details of the design were worked out by a Council of Construction, consisting of Mr Morgan and Mr Crossland, assisted by Constructor Allington and Assistant Constructor J. H. Cardwell.

After the layout and general design had become known, neither Barnaby nor William White, who succeeded him as DNC on 1 October 1885, approved of the design, largely on the grounds that it placed exaggerated emphasis on protection to the detriment of other qualities, and each of them officially disclaimed any responsibility.

Barnaby claimed that displacement could not legitimately be increased without corresponding advance in offensive power, and although the proposed new ships were some 1,300 and 900 tons heavier than the *Admiral* and *Sans Pareil* classes respectively, there was no increase in armament,

and even a slight reduction in nominal speed; the additional displacement being wholly allocated, in each case, to protection.

Both Barnaby and White favoured barbette mountings, with separate redoubts instead of turrets, and a single citadel; moreover, White preferred a greater length and much higher freeboard for maintenance of speed in a seaway. At the same time, they suggested, in a joint memorandum, that in view of the existing uncertainty

regarding the whole question of battleship design, a special committee be appointed to investigate this, and that construction of any new ships be delayed pending the committee's report. This recommendation was rejected, however, on the grounds that in view of the unsatisfactory state of the British battlefleet, it was most desirable to complete new armoured tonnage as quickly as possible, while it was also of great importance to maintain continuity of employment in the Royal dockyards.

Trafalgar: GM and stability

Based on inclining experiments, 31 October 1889

	Displacement (tons)	Draught	GM
'A' Condition (= load)*		26ft 5in (mean)	4.9ft
'B' Condition (= deep load)**		28ft 8in (mean)	4.9ft
'C' Condition (= light)	11,270	26ft 2in	4.87ft

*Fully equipped plus 900 tons coal, boilers and feed tanks to working height.
**Fully equipped plus 1,100 tons coal.

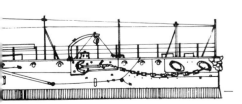

Trafalgar class: Particulars, as completed

Construction
Trafalgar: Portsmouth DY; laid down 1 Jan 1886; launched 20 Sept 1887; completed March 1890
Nile: Pembroke DY; laid down 8 April 1886; launched 27 March 1888; completed July 1891.

Displacement (tons)
12,016 (load), 12,660 (deep).

Dimensions
Length: 345ft pp
Beam: 73ft
Draught: 27ft 6in load, 28ft 8in deep.

Armament
Four 13.5in 67ton BL; 80rpg
Six 4.7in
Eight 6pdr
Four MG
Six 14in torpedo tubes (two port/starboard in ports on main deck, one bow and stern, two submerged port and starboard); 24 torpedoes.

Armour
Main belt: 20in–18in–16in
Bulkheads: 16in–14in
Citadel: 18in–16in
Protective deck: 3in
Conning tower: 14in
Turrets: 18in
Battery: 4in.

Machinery
Two sets vertical inverted triple expansion engines
Cylinder diameter: HP 43in, IP 62in, LP 96in
Stroke: 4ft 6in
Designed SHP: 7,500 natural, 12,000 forced
Boilers: six cylindrical single-ended in two compartments one each side of centre-line, with magazine space and ammunition passage between
Total heating surface: 19,380sq ft
Grate area: 604sq ft
Fuel: 900 tons coal normal, 1,100 tons max

Radius of action: 6,300nm at 10 knots.

Ship's boats
Pinnaces (steam): one 53ft picket boat
Launches (steam): one 40ft
Launches (sail): one 42ft
Cutters (steam): one 30ft
Cutters (sail): two 30ft, one 23ft
Whalers: two 27ft
Galleys: one 32ft
Skiff dinghies: one 16ft
Balsa raft: one 13ft.

Searchlights
Five 24in: Four on sponsons port and starboard at sides of superstructure amidships and main deck right aft; one over after charthouse.

Anchors
Two 115–120cwt Martins improved type
One 120cwt Inglefield (*Nile*)
525 fathoms 2⅜in cable.

Complement
540 *Trafalgar* 1897
537 *Nile* 1903
527 *Nile* 1905.

Cost
Trafalgar: £859,070
Nile: £885,718.

Weight breakdown (tons) (*Nile* as fitted)
Hull: 4,210
Armour: 4,352
Armament: 1,085
Machinery: 1,080
General equipment: 440
Engineer's stores: 45
Coal: 900
Total: 12,112.

Steam trials
Trafalgar: 12,900shp = 17.28 knots; 8,440shp = 16.22 knots
Nile: 12,102sho = 16.88 knots.

Below: *Nile* in 1896. With an armoured belt of 20in–18in–14in and turret thickness of 18in, they were extremely well protected ships. Steady gun platforms, but suffered, like the *Admiral*s, from low freeboard. Nicknamed the 'Jew' because of her funnel tops, she was still on the active list as late as 1910.

Below: *Trafalgar, c.*1897. She was completed with short funnels like *Victoria*, but was refitted during 1891 to give them greater height, as in *Nile*. They were good ships, but quickly became outdated with the arrival of the high freeboard battleship (*Royal Sovereigns*); nevertheless, they were extremely popular in service.

Although speed and fighting efficiency in a seaway were adversely affected by the low freeboard forward and aft, the fighting qualities of the new ships (*Trafalgar* and *Nile*) were always highly regarded in the service, and preferred by many to the succeeding *Royal Sovereign* group, owing to the smaller target offered, and heavier protection.

Because the original design provided for a normal displacement of 11,940 tons with a mean draught of 27ft 6in and a freeboard of 11ft 3in, and later modifications during construction increased draught and displacement by 1ft and 650 tons respectively, with a corresponding reduction in freeboard, the Admiralty directed that, in future, a Board Margin of 4 per cent was to be added to the nominal displacement in the final legend to allow for extra weights imposed while under construction.

As completed, they were about 1,570 tons heavier than *Sans Pareil* and *Victoria*, with an increase of 5ft in length (pp), 3ft more beam, 9in draught, and were the heaviest British battleships to date.

They had low freeboard forward and aft, with short, full-width superstructure amidships, angled obliquely in at each end forming an octagonal structure. As in the *Admirals* and *Sans Pareil*, hull lines were hollowed (much more than in previous classes) at the fore and aft parts of the ship, which reduced the area liable to flooding in the event of a waterline hit; estimated sinkage, with forward extremity above the armoured deck flooded, was only 3 inches.

Construction of the ships, especially behind the armour, was exceptionally strong. Two thicknesses of skin plating (30lb and 60lb) were used for the frames, which were 2ft deep and spaced 2ft apart. A second system of light-ended frames, 3ft deep and 4ft apart, were fitted behind the belt armour only and the outer coal bunker bulkhead was secured to the inner side of these.

The main gun command was insufficient for a seagoing ship, and very difficult to fight in a seaway. The gun muzzles themselves, were only 3ft 6in above the upper deck, but trials indicated that they could still be fired directly end-on at 3° elevation with only slight damage to the deck.

Improvements in handling and control of the hydraulic gear enabled four rounds to be fired singly in nine minutes on trials. An improved mounting for these guns greatly facilitated loading, and enabled a high rate of fire to be maintained.

As mentioned, the original design provided for eight 5in guns, but this was modified in January 1890, while still under construction, to six 4.7in, because of that gun's combination of long range with rapidity and accuracy of fire. The total weight of secondary armament was increased from 135 tons to 185 tons owing to the larger ammunition supply required for the quick-firing guns.

To meet the requirements of the First Sea Lord, Sir Arthur Hood, freeboard, armament and speed were subordinated to protection, and percentage of armour weight to displacement was greater than in any previous British battleship, respectively 7 per cent and 5.4 per cent higher than in the *Admiral* class or *Sans Pareil*.

The general scheme of armouring represented a combination of the ideas of Sir Edward Reed and the recommendations of the 1871 Committee on Designs, embodying more complete overall protection than had been provided in the *Admiral* and *Sans Pareil* classes and comprising a thick waterline belt over about two-thirds of the hull length, surmounted by a heavily armoured citadel enclosing both turret bases and carried right to the upper deck.

The extremities forward and aft, outside the belt, were protected by an underwater deck with watertight sub-division above this to the main deck, as in the previous classes. The belt was 68ft longer than in *Sans Pareil*, and enclosed all magazines, machinery and boiler room spaces. Both ships spent their entire active careers in the Mediterranean where conditions were more suited to the low freeboard than in home waters, and where the disadvantages of this were minimized.

GUNNERY

Since the days of sail there had been two methods of firing practised within the Royal Navy: 'independent firing', when the captain of each gun laid and fired it independently, and 'broadside or concentrated firing', in which all guns were laid on the same target, its bearing, heel of ship and range being given from the upper deck; the broadside was fired simultaneously by order.

In truck guns, elevation was given by degrees marked on the quoin, or by a wooden scale held vertically with one end on deck so that a mark on the rear of the gun could be brought into line with the required degree on the scale.

Training was by means of 'converging lines', the beam over each gun being marked to denote 'right abeam' one-and-a-half points before and abaft the beam, and three points (extreme training) before and abaft the beam. Each converging line had one end hooked over the centre of the port, and the other held by No. 1 at the rear of the gun exactly under the required mark on the beam overhead. The gun was then trained until its axis corresponded with the converging lines. Broadsides were fired by a 'directing gun' whose captain was considered the best marksman available, his No. 1 giving the elevation and the moment of firing to all the others, the bearing of the entire broadside having been decided from the upper deck.

During the early 1850s Captain Moorsom, RN had introduced a 'director' by which the bearing, heel, and distance were all determined, and the guns laid accordingly. It was generally fixed over the centre main deck gun, on the upper deck, or some other convenient position; and the order to fire was given by the officer attending it, as soon as the target came into its sights. This 'director' was greatly improved by Lieutenant R. H. Pairse in 1885, but in the absence of efficient communications it was found impracticable, and generally discarded in favour of broadside firing. The mounting of secondary guns in casemates, however, precluded broadside firing, and any former methods of control had to be abandoned in favour of independent firing.

During the 1880s the Royal Navy received some exceptionally fine warships, all featuring balanced design (as far as possible), good armament, adequate armour protection for the period in which they were built, reliable machinery, good seagoing qualities and trained crews to man them. The weakness was the inability to hit a target with any degree of accuracy or indeed consistency. If one studies official records, one might be forgiven for thinking that before 1900 gunnery practice and expertise was practically non-existent.

There were many gunnery officers within the service who would have liked to see many changes in the system but, during this period, the Admiralty turned a blind eye to any radical change.

One gunnery officer in particular, Captain Percy Scott, who was most meticulous in his approach, had revived methods of standard gunnery, and introduced a loading trough to teach rapid loading as well as a 'dotter' by which a hit or miss, showed up on a miniature target. He trained his crew in *Scylla* during 1899, to keep telescope sights on target so that hits or misses could be observed. During the ship's firing tests of that year, he took the matter in hand and scored 80 per cent hits on the given target – to the delight of his crew, but unfortunately, nobody else – least of all the Admiralty.

In the following year he commanded *Terrible* and repeated the performance. All doubts were dispelled, and the general bad shooting in the Royal Navy was exposed. Speaking of gunnery in general, he wrote:

'The gunnery of the Fleet is not what it should be. Most of the Commanders of our battleships and cruisers are gunnery men, and have probably reached that rank through having been so, but in how many cases has the ladder by which they have climbed been kicked away, and gunnery been made to take a back seat in favour of Paint and brass.'

When Sir William May became Controller and Third Sea Lord in 1902, although certainly not the first to notice and remark on the poor state of shooting in the service, he put into practice his own ideas, that this subject of gunnery at sea should be thoroughly investigated. At the same time, the Press, who were never slow in taking up a cause, set about attacking Admiralty standard policy: in fact, they had been gnawing away at the subject for some years prior to 1900.

Jottings from Lionel Yexley in 'Bluejacket' set the pace:

'Gunnery, Gunnery, Gunnery, that is the chant of the naval song and the refrain that has been taken up by the nation, which is at last beginning to realize the supreme importance of the men behind the gun. Even the First Lord has been kind enough to tell us he is more important than guns, armour, projectiles or powder, and that every effort was made to draw the attention to this fact. But Lord Selbourne must have had his tongue in his cheek.

To what extent naval gunnery was regarded in the past, may be gathered from the fact that 20 years ago, it was not at all uncommon to drop whole quarter firing allowance quietly over the side in the

first watch, to escape the hearty mess consequent on target practice, while those ships that did go to target practice carried it out in a perfunctory manner, the sole object being, to get through as quickly as possible. To hit the target was a crime, because it caused delay. I myself remember one ship I served in, the Captain of one of the guns was a remarkably good shot, and probably, if put to the test, would have proved the grounds of his day. Whilst on target practice outside Malta, he succeeded in hitting the target with his first three shots. This instead of eliciting applause, simply drew from the bridge the exclamation "What's the damn fool doing of; does he want to keep us out here all day?" '

The experiments of 1902 were carried out by a most fastidious staff and in the August of that year an interim report was submitted to their Lordships for perusal, throwing light on many interesting arguments. The report had been compiled from many discussions by gunnery officers as to whether the present system was best calculated to prepare men and ships for the supreme test of battle.

Most of the officers were vociferous in their opinion that the entire system lacked that cohesion which was necessary to form the links in the chain of command required for successful gun attacks against an enemy.

At the turn of the century, the only method encouraging in shooting practice was that of the 'prize firing' (introduced by Sir John Fisher while CinC, Mediterranean). The crux of the situation lay in the fact that conditions under which 'prize firing' was conducted, would almost certainly never be repeated in conditions of war. Large amounts of ammunition were expended during these tests, but as Lionel Yexley's letter shows, nothing good ever came of them; along with any other type of practice shooting, it had become standard practice to fire the guns and merely hope for a limited degree of success in hitting the target.

The longest battle ranges of the day were about 1,000 yards, but it was becoming increasingly obvious to many officers, that the need to open fire sooner, and at greater ranges, was paramount.

Criticism of the, 'If the target cannot be successfully hit at short range, it will not be hit at long range,' kind was voiced, and it was also argued that, 'perhaps it is best to walk before you run'.

To use the same method for both short and long range, however, would cause many problems. The report showed that short range should be defined as anything up to 3,000 yards, and long range up to as much as 8,000 yards—hitherto an unheard of figure. (During tests carried out in *Venerable* during 1903 in the Mediterranean, by Rear-Admiral Sir Reginald Custance, he remarked: 'It is practically useless to open fire at ranges beyond 4,000 yards, and 8,000 yards is a ridiculous and impossible range at which to fight.'

With guns becoming more powerful, and more experiments highlighting the possibility of increasing the ranges slowly from 4,000 to 8,000 yards, and even, as it was suggested, 10,000 yards, it became obvious that if this could be achieved, the ability to strike the first blow at such great distances would be a very great advantage.

The 1902 report mentioned practically everything that was important about gunnery at sea: 'Range Finding

The first question which arises is how the range is to be obtained. At long ranges it was the opinion of the majority of gunnery lieutenants of the Mediterranean Squadron in 1902 that the present Barr and Stroud rangefinder was most unsatisfactory. Suppose we had a perfect rangefinder our trouble would not then all be over, owing to the fact that the range we require is not the true range, but a purely artificial one which I shall call the gun range, and which will be found very different to the true one owing to the following causes, viz:

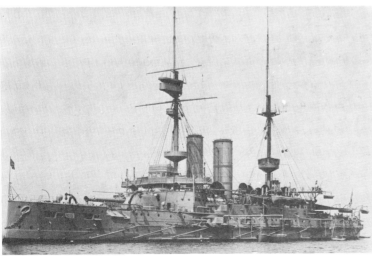

13.5in 30cal Mk III Gun
as mounted in *Royal Sovereign*, *Admiral* and *Trafalgar* classes

Weight (excluding breech): 67tons 1cwt
Weight of breech: 1 ton 3cwt
Length: 433in
Chamber length: 66.5in
Muzzle velocity: 2,061fps
Muzzle energy: 35,230ft tons
Elevation in turret: 13½°
Range: 11,950 yards (full elevation)
Rate of fire: 1 round per two minutes
Weight of shell: 1,250lb
Weight of charge: 630lb (slow-burning cocoa)
Cost: £10,859 (approx).

12in 35cal Mk VIII Gun
mounted in pairs in oval-shaped turrets (except *Caesar* and *Illustrious*).

Supplied with left- or right-hand breeches, according to position occupied

Construction: steel, wire wound
Weight (excluding breech): 44 tons 18cwt
Weight of breech: 1ton 2cwt
Length: 445.5in
Bore: 35cal (425.15in)
Chamber length: 70in
Chamber diameter: 16in largest; 12.8in smallest
Rifling system: polygroove modified plain section
Length of rifling: 349.285in
Twist: straight from breech to 278.95in from muzzle, then increasing from 0 to 1 turn in 30cals at muzzle

Number of grooves: 48
Depth of grooves: 1in straight; .08in (twist)
Width of grooves: .62in (straight); .607in (twist)
Muzzle velocity: 2,367fps (when 2,400ft was attempted, there were serious accidents)
Muzzle energy: 33,020ft tons
Elevation in turret: 13½°
Rate of fire: 1 round per 1 minute 50 seconds (*Caesar*)
Weight of shell: 850lb
Weight of full charge: 2,000lb MD cordite made up of ¼-charges in 'R' cases
Performance: 32in wrought iron pierced at 1,000 yards; 13in Krupp steel pierced at 3,000 yards.

12in 40cal Mk IX Gun
mountings BVI London, *Bulwark*, *Formidable*, etc.; BVII in *Irresistible*

Construction: steel, wire wound
Weight (with breech): 50 tons
Length: 496.5in
Bore: 40cal (480in)
Chamber diameter: 17.5in largest; 13in smallest
Rifling system: polygroove modified plain section; Mk I rifling
Length of rifling: 386.74in
Twist: straight for 48in from breech, them increasing from 0 to 30cal at muzzle
Muzzle velocity: 2,516fps
Muzzle energy: 37,564ft tons
Weight of shell: 850lb
Weight of charge: 211lb cordite (full charge); 158¼lb reduced
Performance: 31.3in steel pierced at 1,000 yards.

Wear of gun. Height of barometer. Temperature of cordite. Wind, etc., and, owing to the fact that unless the range is very accurately known at a long range, the target cannot be hit; we must fall back on finding the gun range by the gun because this false range varies from day to day.

While on this subject and in connection with the temperature of cordite, I am of the opinion that the cease-firing position for all guns should be "Cartridge out" for the following reasons: Suppose several rounds have been fired from a gun and it is placed in the cease-firing position. The chamber of the gun is very hot, and the charge of the cordite will get baked up in the gun, and perhaps after 20 minutes baking the gun opens fire again. The first charge is hot, the 2nd is cool. Different ballistics will therefore result and the most important first shot will give you a false range. The extra time taken to put the cartridge in the gun when required to open fire is infinitesimal. The note dealing with this subject in new Gunnery Drill Book does not appear to be drastic enough. As we must therefore find the range by the gun the best method in my opinion is by a ranging group of three 6in guns. Each gun should be given the same range on the sights and at order from Group Officer they should

---

12in 45cal Mk X Gun
as mounted in *Lord Nelson*

Construction: steel wire wound
Weight (excluding breech): 56 tons 16 cwt
Length: 557.55in
Bore: 45cal (540in)
Rifling system: polygroove plain section
Twist: uniform, one turn in 30cal
Muzzle velocity: 2,725–2,821fps
Muzzle energy: 47,800ft tons
Range: 16,400 yards full elevation (13½°)
Rate of fire: 2 rounds per minute (approx.)
Weight of shell: 850lb
Weight of charge: 258lb MD cordite.

10in 32cal Mk III Gun
as mounted in *Centurion, Barfleur, Renown*

Weight: 29 tons
Length: 342.4in
Bore: 32cal
Rifling system: plain section, modified
Twist: straight to 60in from breech, increasing from 0 to 1 turn in 30cal at muzzle
Number of grooves: 60.

10in 45cal Mk VI Gun
as mounted in *Swiftsure*

Weight (excluding breech): 39 tons 8 cwt
Length: 467.6in
Chamber length: 71.5175in
Chamber width: 14.5in
Chamber pressure: 17.5tons
Rifling system: polygroove plain section

Twist: uniform right-hand twist, 1 turn in 30cal
Number of grooves: 60
Depth of grooves: 0.07in at commencement, decreasing to 0.06in at 60in from commencement
Width of grooves: .3491in
Muzzle velocity: 2,840fps (normal shell); 2,787fps (capped shell)
Muzzle energy: 27,965ft tons (normal shell); 26,930ft tons (capped shell)
Elevation in turret: 13½°
Depression in turret: −5°
Barbette diameter: 21ft (internal)
Loading angle: 5°
Weight of shell: 500lb
Weight of charge: 210lb (nitrocellulose); 178.0½lb (cordite)
Performance: 11½in steel pierced at 3,000 yards.

9.2in 46cal Mk X Gun
as mounted in *King Edward VII Class*

Construction: steel wire wound
Weight (with breech): 28 tons
Length: 442.35in
Bore: 46.66cal (429.33in)
Chamber length: 71in
Chamber diameter: 13in largest; 10.2in smallest
Rifling system: polygroove modified plain section
Length of rifling: 353.8in
Twist: straight from breech to 303.585in from muzzle, then increasing from 0 to 1 turn in 30cal at muzzle
Number of grooves: 37
Depth of grooves: .08in (straight); .06in (twist)

Width of groove: .062in (straight); .062in (twist)
Muzzle velocity: 2,640fps
Muzzle energy: 18,400ft tons
Weight of shell: 380lb
Weight of charge: 511lb (MD cordite) (two for full charge 102lb)
Performance: 33in wrought iron pierced at muzzle; 22in at 1,000 yards.

7.5in 50cal Mk I Gun
as mounted in *Swiftsure* and *Triumph*

Weight (excluding breech): 15 tons 15 cwt
Length: 388.2in
Bore: 50cal (375in)
Chamber length: 46.9in
Chamber width: 10.5in
Chamber capacity: 3,750 cubic inches
Rifling system: polygroove modified plain system
Twist: 1 turn in 30cal
Number of grooves: 44
Depth of grooves: .357in
Muzzle velocity: 2,955fps with nitro; 2,769fps with MDC
Muzzle energy: 12,110ft tons with nitro; 10,633ft tons with MDC
Elevation in citadel mountings: 14°
Depression in citadel mountings: −5°
Weight of shell: 200lb
Weight of charge: 79½lb (nitro); 56lb (MDC)
Performance: 7in nickel steel pierced at 3,000 yards.

6in Mks VII and VIII Gun

Weight (excluding breech): 7 tons 7 cwt 2 qr

Weight of breech: 3 cwt 8 lb
Length: 279.228in
Bore: 44.9cal (269.5in)
Chamber length: 32.3in (standard); 32.658in (modified)
Rifling system: modified plain section
Length of rifling: 233.6in
Muzzle velocity: 2,536fps with Mk I rifling
Muzzle energy: 4,600ft tons with Mk I rifling
Range: 2,500 yards with Mk I rifling; 2,950 yards with Mk III rifling
Weight of shell: 100lb; burster 8lb 11oz
Weight of charge: 20lb Mk I; 23lb Mk I with modified chamber; 28lb 10oz Mk III with modified chamber.

14pdr 3in Gun
as mounted in *Triumph*

Weight: 16 cwt
Muzzle velocity: 2,690fps
Muzzle energy: 702.56ft tons
Weight of shell: 14lb
Weight of charge: 4.31lb cordite.

6pdr Gun
Triumph

Weight (including mechanism): 8 cwt 1 qr 18 lb
Weight of mounting: 8 cwt 3 qr 11 lb
Length: 97.63in
Bore: 40cal
Muzzle velocity: 1,818fps
Muzzle energy: 137.5ft tons
Weight of shell: 6lb
Weight of charge: 7¾oz cordite
Performance: 4in wrought iron pierced at muzzle.

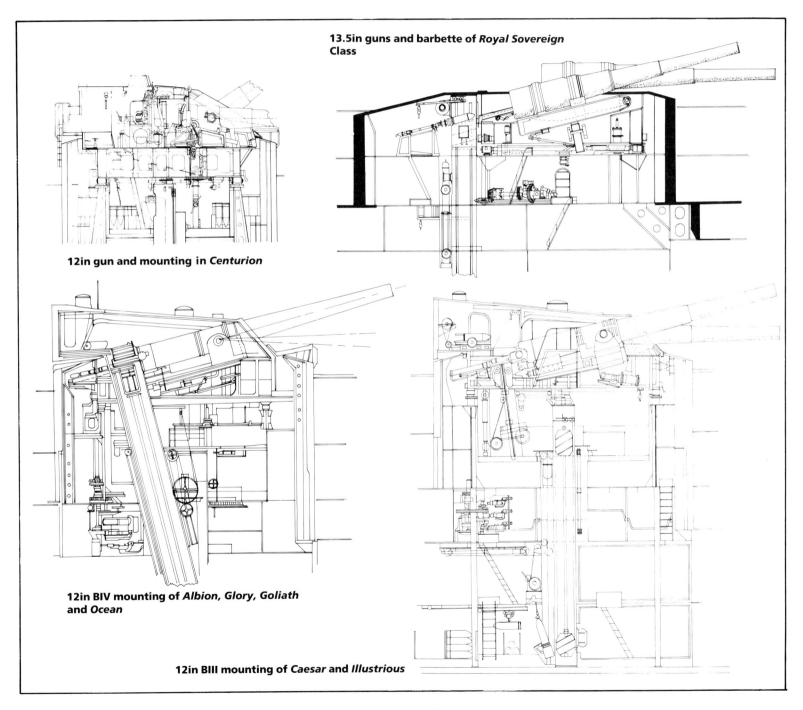

13.5in guns and barbette of *Royal Sovereign* Class

12in gun and mounting in *Centurion*

12in BIV mounting of *Albion, Glory, Goliath* and *Ocean*

12in BIII mounting of *Caesar* and *Illustrious*

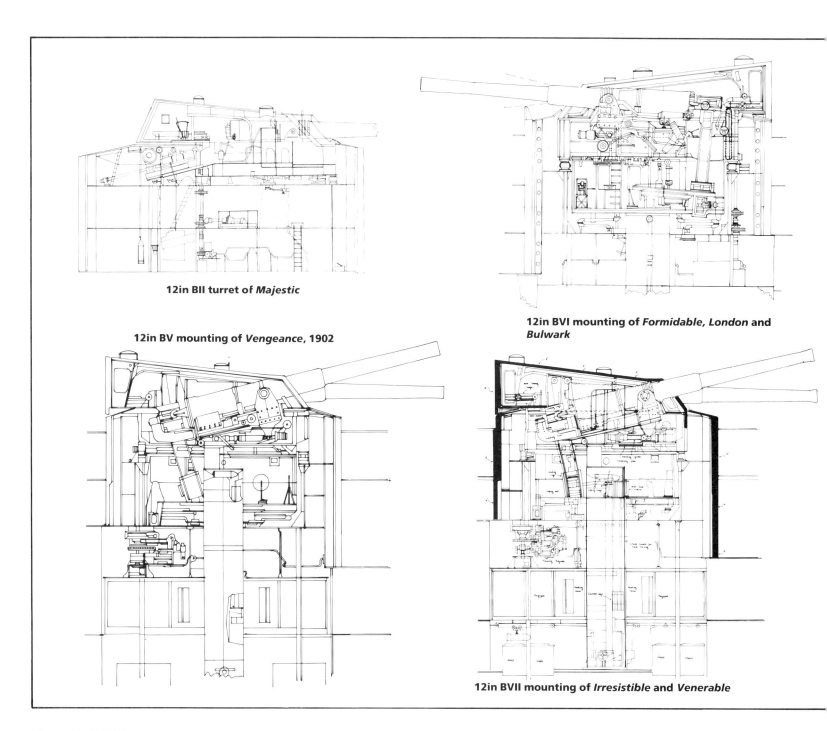

12in BII turret of *Majestic*

12in BV mounting of *Vengeance*, 1902

12in BVI mounting of *Formidable*, *London* and *Bulwark*

12in BVII mounting of *Irresistible* and *Venerable*

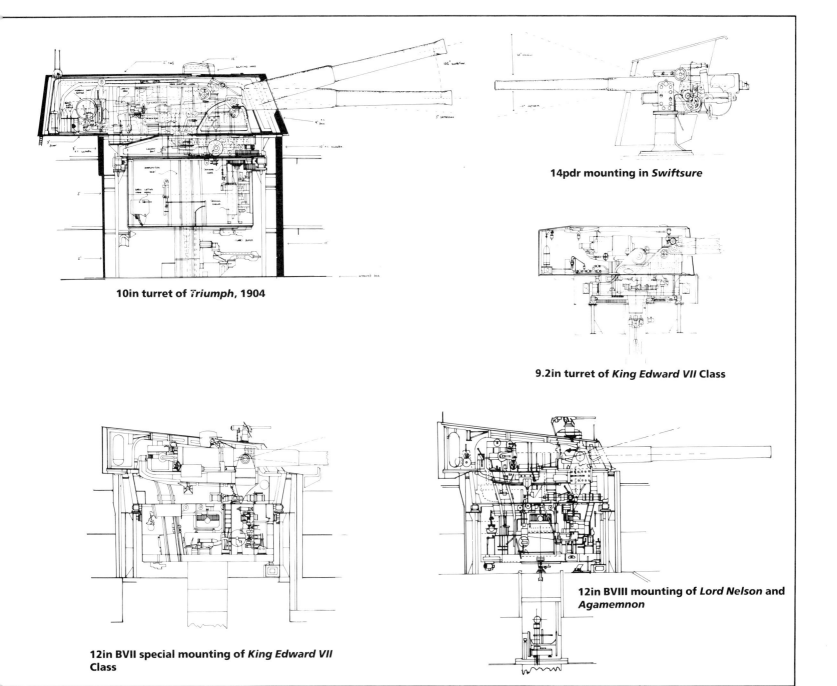

10in turret of *Triumph*, 1904

14pdr mounting in *Swiftsure*

9.2in turret of *King Edward VII* Class

12in BVII special mounting of *King Edward VII* Class

12in BVIII mounting of *Lord Nelson* and *Agamemnon*

fire as simultaneously as possible, this has the effect of eliminating the error of one man and one gun and gives a surer guide as to whether you have the range or not. The extra rounds are well worth expending if the range is obtained.

Spotting Shots

There is very great difficulty in noting the fall of the shot and this is almost impossible from the gun positions. It is advisable to go aloft for this purpose and the higher the better. This spotting of shots is an all-important factor and it will be necessary to train officers specially for this duty.

He should have the assistance of a very powerful telescope which has been suggested by Lt Wray and has been constructed.

It is on the following principles:

It consists of a high-power telescope with two movable hair lines in the objective focus which are capable of being closed or opened one from the other. The distance the lines are apart corresponds to the apparent vertical height of splash above water line of target, when a shot is 500 yards over or short of the target.

As the range increases these wires by means of scale at side become closer together, as ranges get less these wires become further apart, thus a very good approximate guide is given to the spotting officer as to what is 500 yards over or short of target.

Keeping the Range

When the range is found what is then the best method to pursue? The following in my opinion has the best chance of success. Direct each gun in the ship to have the same distance on their sights and all lower or raise together under the direction of Controlling Officer.

I do not think it should be permitted for a moment at a long range for the Captain of the guns and various officers of the quarter to alter their sights themselves for the following reason:

At long ranges it is almost impossible to judge with any useful degree of accuracy the fall of the shot from the gun positions, and owing to a large number of shots pitching together, and the length of the time of flight, it will be exceedingly difficult for the most experienced Captain of guns to even judge which is his individual shot. Consequently it will result in some shots being a long way short, others a long way over, etc., and no control will be effective, firing will become wild, and it will be

necessary constantly to check the firing by a "check fire" bugle and redetermine range.

On the other hand if every gun in the ship is given the same range, and using, as is now the custom, telescopic sights, only small errors in aim are made in long ranges, and therefore if six 6in guns are firing on the broadside, and provided the elevation is the same, their six shots will pitch very close together (errors in aim have very little effect at long ranges) and we shall create, which is all important a "zone of fire". This zone of fire can be placed nearer or further away by the Controlling Officer lowering or raising all sights in the ship simultaneously and if it is put about a ship by a skillful Controlling Officer she is sure to be hit fairly frequently and with a given number of rounds fired, I am sure more hits would be obtained by this method of fire zone than by allowing each Captain of guns or Officer of Quarters to alter his sights independently.

With this method it would be necessary from time to time, to determine in each ship that each gun, at the same elevation of sight, would, approximately, pitch its shot at the same distance from the ship, for if not each particular gun would require a table of its own corrections, as the amount of wear would almost certainly vary and it is absolutely essential that such a table should be supplied for turret guns. It is also of great importance that projectiles should be rammed home properly and every effort should be made to ensure this similarity of gun range so that at long ranges the ship can be treated as one big gun firing practically a big shrapnel shell.

Passing the range

Where should the control be from?

Fall of shot must be noted from aloft, and if controlling position is not there any other position which is selelcted has the following difficulties. Delay necessary in passing result of fall of shot to controlling officer who is to determine range, this delay is fatal to good shooting. Difficulty in passing range to guns. The proximity of controlling officer to the disturbing influence around any position of deck. If he is, as some advocate, in the conning tower the transmitting of ranges and orders to gun positions would have the effect of distracting the attention of the Captain or Navigating Officer from their all-important duty of conning ship. And it appears to me that Controlling Officer should be

aloft. Who should be the Controlling Officer? I am of the opinion that he should be the Gunnery Lieutenant as he is not required on the gun deck. This organization should be complete before going into action. If it is not, it will certainly not be remedied during an action, and I can conceive of no occasion on which his services will be required at the guns during the heat of an action if efficient training is given to Officers of Quarters and guns' crews beforehand. He should have to assist him a Marine Officer, a junior Accountant Officer and a Midshipman.

How is the range to be passed simultaneously?

In modern battleships all group casemates have a sighting hood in upper one, which is in full view of this position aloft, and the range can therefore be passed by range dial, i.e., by the quickest of all methods, sight. This has been tried in several ships with very good results and is important insomuch as rapidity in passing the range cannot be over-estimated. In addition, a reliable range and order dial should be fitted in each gun position connected to the top controlling position and not with the conning tower. A straight and large voice pipe and a telephone should be fitted from the top to the conning tower thus putting controlling officer in direct communication with the Captain.

Keeping the Range

Having obtained the range the next difficulty is to keep it. This can be done easily, rapidly, and correctly by means of the rate of change instrument and Lt Wray's rate of change clock. The former instrument is so well known that it is unnecessary to describe it here although great improvements have been made in it since it was originally designed. It shows the rate of change in range in yards per 10 seconds: provided that the enemy's course and speed can be approximately determined. 10 seconds is taken as the unit of time as it is roughly the interval between two rounds of a 6in gun when firing fairly rapidly, i.e., 6 rounds per minute, and also 10 is a convenient unit to work to. It therefore becomes necessary to have some guide as to the time taken between rounds and the rate of change clock has been devised for this purpose. The arrangements are as follows.

It consists of a clock which makes one revolution in 20 seconds: opposite every 2 seconds is a slot which shows automatically what the rate of change is every 2 seconds, starting from 0 to 20 seconds.

The numbers are worked by wheel X which is turned until desired rate of change per 10 seconds shows through slot and it in its turn works all the remaining wheels which shows required rate of change up to 20 seconds: for example:

If the rate of change of range is 150 yards per 10 seconds the following figures will show through the slot.

30, 60, 90, 120, 150, 180, 210, 240, 270, 300.

If the rate of change was 100 the figures would be:

20, 40, 60, 80, 100, 120, 140, 160, 180, and 200.

The clock is started by the gun or by the sight-setter at will.

Every time the gun fires the clock flies back to zero, or the sight setter can put it to zero, and by this means, the sight setter knows exactly the rate of change to put on and how much to raise or lower his sight independently of the rate of fire.

The importance of this instrument for long and even short range firing cannot be over-estimated, and the cost is very small. This rate of change clock does not in any way interfere with the ordinary sighting arrangements. Every time it is necessary to alter the range or rate of change of range through the zone of fire getting off the target due to a wrong estimate of enemy's speed and course, a short sharp blast on the syren would call the attention of the officers in the sighting hoods to the dial, or it could be so arranged that one short blast could be a signal to lower or raise 50 yards, two short blasts, 100 yards, one long blast, raise sight 50 yards, two long blasts, raise sights 100 yards, only this preconcerted signal by syren must be known by consort ships, so that their attention will not be distracted.

As the range gets closer it is most probable that the communication between the position aloft and the guns will fail, but the mast is a small object, and there is quite a good chance of this system lasting as long as any other which has so far been advocated, while if it does its duty at a long range it will have served its purpose, and as the range gets down to 3,000 yards, or even less, the Officers of the Quarters and Captain of the guns will less and less require this outside assistance to enable them to hit their target, and it is then that their careful training will tell.

Defects in present training

Is the training that the Officers of the Quarters and Captains of guns at present receive adapted for the requirements of war? I do not think it is, as in most cases far too much assistance is given them in noting the fail of the shot, and the Captains of the guns consequently get so much in the habit of having this done for them that they get to rely on always having such advice. The present system of prize firing has that great defect and its principal faults are as follows: Such rivalry exists between ships that to obtain high scores a very large number of dodges are resorted to, which are not legislated for in the regulations.

These are:

Firing with the same sight and shifting it from gun to gun.

Firing from guns highest up.

Using no rammer.

Spotting from aloft.

Gunnery Lieutenant as sight-setter.

Practising this particular form of firing.

Every assistance given to the firer by officers noting the fall of shot.

The effect of this, is to reduce the Captain of the guns duties to simply lay his gun on the object, which in action, when this external assistance is not forthcoming, will be one of his simplest duties of noting the fall of shot himself, and the speed at which the target is approaching with its consequent alteration of range and deflection not being called into play. Consequently this firing is not so much a test of the Captain of the guns, as it is of the immorality and cunning of the Gunnery Lieutenant and does not necessarily form a good criterion of the gunnery efficiency of the ship.

Training of Officers of Quarters

I do not propose here to go into the subject of the training of Officers of Quarters. Each Officer of Quarters should be given a rate of change instrument, and if possible be provided with a portable range finder, such an article is now being experimented with. It is essential that the Officers of Quarters should receive far more thorough and practical training in gunnery than they do at present.

In summing up, it will be seen that I advocate:
1. More long range practice.
2. An arbitary definition of long and short ranges.
3. Obtaining from practical experience some data as to the results at our longest ranges.
4. The obtaining of the range by a group of three 6in guns, thus eliminating error.
5. The provision of an officer aloft to note the fall of shot.
6. The provision of indicating instruments from that position to the guns.
7. The removal of such instruments from the conning tower.
8. The eliminating of judgement from Captains of guns when firing at long ranges, i.e., (8,000 yards to 3,000 yards).
9. The consequent reintroduction of director firing with this difference that it is carried out at long, instead of such short ranges.
10. The consequent provision of zones of fire.
11. The careful tabulation of results of individual guns at such long ranges.
12. The universal provision of the rate of change instrument and rate of change clock.
13. A change in the present system of prize firing designed so as to make this practice of real use for war.
14. General consideration of the above points.

In putting forward these remarks, I would submit that they are obtained from the combined experience of many gunnery Lieutenants and are written in the hope that exhaustive experiments may be carried out to test their value.

If this is done, I am convinced that a well-defined system of training laid down on broad lines may be introduced and that such a system is urgently required cannot, I submit, be doubted for a moment.

At present, the whole of our system centres around short range firing, while owing to our lack of prescience, such short ranges may never be arrived at.

It is certain that firing must be commenced at long ranges. It is at those ranges therefore that the first blow will be struck.

It would be melancholy indeed if we are unable from lack of practice to strike that all-important blow.

A.V. Vyoyan., Lt. RN.'

When this report was circulated privately to their Lordships it had great effect, and caused much alarm. There was great praise and severe criticism from differing lobbies, but there was no denying that the ground work had been laid for a considerable alteration within the system. In practice, however, improvements were extremely slow in being implemented: gun sights were improved in some ships, in others not at all. There still seemed to be no consistency of proceedure.

In 1903, while on a practice shoot, *Formidable* made such a hash of it that she was dubbed the 'Tame Mouse', an embarrassing sobriquet indeed for such a powerful man-of-war. Moreover, during firing tests in 1904 on the China Station, an observer in *Centurion* sent a message to A. White (journalist): 'You have so often referred in the Press to our bad gun sights, that you will be glad to hear that notwithstanding their defects, we in long range firing, are far from being the last in the Fleet. We hit the target once! Many ships did not hit it at all.'

As more and more experiments were carried out, and newer inventions were introduced, there were signs of improvement, but it was still not consistent, and left much to be desired. On 23 February 1905 one Able Seaman Hollinghurst scored seven hits out of ten on a target 8ft by 6ft at ranges of 1,500 to 1,600 yards, and Captain Percy Scott seized another opportunity to be heard: 'For the moment A. Hollinghurst is the "Only pebble on the Beach". He stands now in the proud position of having made the finest firing that has ever been made by anyone in H.M. Fleet—or any other Fleet.'

The Press had a field day with a headline, 'Only Pebble on the Beach', and it did not end there. Nevertheless, slowly but surely matters were taken in hand, and gradually put right as far as possible. Scott, who had been put in charge of '*Excellent*' (Gunnery School) on Whale Island was later awarded a knighthood for his relentless pursuance of an accurate, reliable and standard system of director control for the Royal Navy. Many others, too numerous to mention, played a part in the advancement of gunnery at sea, including the very progressive 'Jackie' Fisher, who made sure nothing was left to chance and put other officers' ideas into practice as well as his own. Captain Scott, and others like him, were extremely unpopular at the time of the metamorphosis in naval gunnery, but he was a hard man who demanded as much from himself, as he did from his staff; Lord Charles Beresford said of him: 'Like all reformists Captain Scott has had an uphill fight, he has been misunderstood, and has had the old ladies of both sexes against him.'

Fore-control tops made their appearance in ships from about 1905–6 and great improvements were made as far as rangefinders were concerned. The textbooks were revised as a result of the 1902 report and later experiments, but unfortunately for the older predreadnoughts, the latest equipment was given to the newer and more powerful revolutionary dreadnoughts, and many of the ships dealt with in this book never received very advanced fire control until the war broke out in 1914 when they received limited equipment to do the job in hand. Experience gained during the war resulted in director-controlled firing becoming, by the end of it, a highly elaborate system—certainly far superior to that in other navies.

MACHINERY

The *Inflexible* of 1873 was the first British capital ship designed with compound engines and cylindrical boilers, which replaced the single-pressure engines and low-pressure rectangular boilers of previous designs.

The installation in *Inflexible* was a considerable improvement and provided increased power for reduced fuel consumption.

The system was greatly developed in the succeeding *Agamemnon*, *Colossus* and *Admiral* classes, and triple expansion engines were introduced in *Victoria* and *Sans Pareil* in 1886. Single- and double-ended cylindrical boilers were used in all types of warships during this period, but they proved endlessly troublesome, and needed frequent overhauls. In 1892 as a consequence of these frequent defects, the Admiralty ordered a Committee to be set up under Admiral Buller, CB to consider existing types of single-combustion boilers, especially the double-ended pattern, and to suggest any improvements that could be made. The Admiralty knew that any steps they might take in haste would, as usual, be severely criticized from within and without the service. The navy atributed propulsion defects to the use of too-high a steam pressure and triple expansion engines; the Press and public were agitating about the general state of propulsion installations in existing warships. Indeed the Press referred to the subject so often that one member of the Institution of Naval Architects stated that if the same attention were directed towards the Mercantile Marine also, there would be no room for much other news.

Two main points were deliberated: the use of high-pressure steam up to 150psi was considered too high; the speed of shaft revolutions in triple expansion engines was considered too high. The Committee found, however, that most of the difficulties previously experienced were simply the result of attempting to get too much out of the boilers by the use of forced draught, and making the engines capable of producing too large a margin above the specified IHP which in turn led to uneconomical working at low power. They expressed a decided preference for single-ended rather than double-ended boilers, and wanted a separate combusion chamber to be fitted to each furnace where practicable; they also recommended limits on the heating surfaces, which would prevent any over-pressing of the cylindrical boilers. Their final conclusion was that trials for water tube boilers should be undertaken with a view to their being fitted in large ships as well as torpedo-boats, etc. (Experiments had been carried out since 1890 in the torpedo-boat *Speedy*, the first British warship with water tube boilers, and had proved an unqualified success.) Other tests were carried out in the torpedo-boats *Spanker*, *Daring*, *Decoy*, and the torpedo-gunboat *Sharpshooter* in 1892–4. The conclusion was that *Spanker*, with her French Du Temple small water tube boilers, was not at all successful, and this saw the demise of the type. *Daring* and *Decoy*, fitted with Yarrow water tube boilers, were matched against *Havock* and her locomotive boilers. The results showed that while the Yarrow were superior to the locomotive type, the former were not all that satisfactory, and needed some modification to make them suitable for marine purposes. This was accomplished later when Yarrow altered the design to conform with Admiralty demands. After this, however, it was recommended that no more locomotive boilers be installed in small ships. At the time (1890–2), it was pointed out by Captains Compton Domville and W.H.May that the French Navy had been having limited success with large tube boilers of the Belleville and D'Allert types.

The *Sharpshooter* trials were carried out in 1894 after she had been refitted with Belleville boilers; she made 19 knots with 3,238 at normal draught. Unwilling to wait for further, lengthy experiments with this type of boiler, the Admiralty decided, in the face of opposition, to fit Belleville large tube boilers to the massive cruisers *Powerful* and *Terrible* laid down in that year. This adoption, however, was approved only on the recommendation of the Engineer-in-Chief, Sir John Durston, and endorsed by the DNC (White). Both ships made over

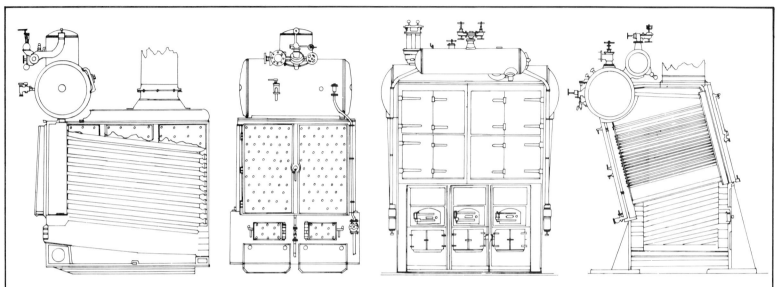

Niclausse Boiler This worked on the same principle as the Babcock and Wilcox and also had sloping water tubes with furnaces (2) below and an upper water drum. It was a good boiler, but required constant attention.

Babcock and Wilcox Boiler The straight, sloping water tubes connected a number of water boxes of square section and sinuous outline, which were connected to a cylindrical upper drum half-filled with water, half-filled with steam. The three furnaces were filled below the water tubes. It was considered the best boiler for large warships.

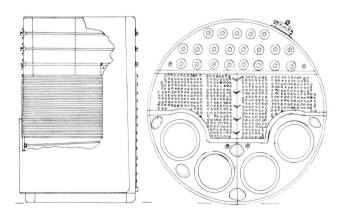

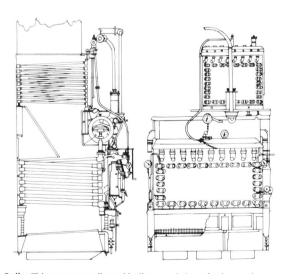

Cylindrical Boiler or 'Scotch boiler'. These varied in size up to 20ft in length and could be single- or double-ended, up to four furnaces for single, eight for double. It was a reliable boiler but extremely heavy.

Belleville Boiler This was a complicated boiler, consisting of tubes and a separator. It was not economical at high speeds and needed more attention than other boilers. It was lighter than the cylindrical type, but costly in terms of upkeep.

21 knots on preliminary trials and proved most successful; the result being that it was recommended that water tube boilers be used in all succeeding warships. Bellevilles were fitted in the *Canopus* class and all following classes up to the *King Edward*s in 1902. In these ships the whole question of boiler types came under examination as the previous years had shown a bad record for Belleville boilers, which were frequently breaking down. This problem came to the fore when the large cruiser *Europa* suffered machinery and boiler defects, and showed considerable increased coal consumption.

Their Lordships appointed another Committee to consider certain questions in respect to modern types of water tube boilers used in large warships. The Committee consisted of Vice-Admiral Compton Domville, KCB (Chairman); Mr J.A. Smith, (Inspector of machinery); Mr. J. List, RNR, Superintendent Engineer, Castle Line; Mr James Bain, RNR, Superintendent, Engineer, Cunard Line; Mr J.T. Milton, Chief Engineer-Surveyor of Lloyd's Register of Shipping; Professor A.B.W. Kennedy; Mr J. Inglis, LL.D, Head of A.J. Inglis, Engineers & Shipbuilders, Glasgow; Commander Montague E. Browning, RN; Chief Engineer H. Wood, RN.

The points requiring elucidation by the Admiralty were:

1. To ascertain practically and experimentally the relative advantages and disadvantages of the Belleville boiler, as compared with the cylindrical type.

2. To investigate the causes of defects which have occurred in these boilers, and in machinery that serves them.

3. To report generally on the suitability of the propelling and auxiliary machinery fitted in recent warships, and offer any suggestions for improvement, to the effect of weight and space.

4. To look generally into the merits of the Niclausse and Babcock & Wilcox boilers in comparison with the Belleville; and report whether any other type of boiler then available had sufficient advantages over the Belleville, or the other two types, as a boiler for HM large cruisers and battleships .

For the purpose of direct comparison, the ships *Hyacinth* (Belleville), *Adriadne* (Belleville), *Gladiator* (Belleville), *Perseus* and *Prometheus* (Thornycroft) would be made available for the Committee to carry out trials as they saw fit. Also, opportunities to inspect the cruisers *Furious*, *Niobe*, *Diadem*, *Arrogant* (Belleville) and *Pactolus* (Blechynden) could be carried out when in dock for refit. *Pelorus* (Normand) and *Powerful*, after heavy steaming at sea, would also be made available for inspection. It was particularly desired that any conclusions be backed up with experimental proof as far as possible, and that the Committee should propose any further tests they might think fit.

During the following years exacting tests were made in these, and other vessels, and highlighted many of the defects in machinery/boiler installations in Royal Navy service. In an interim report, the Committee listed many conclusions:

1. As regards ships which are to be ordered in the future: Belleville boilers not to be fitted in any case.

2. As regards ships ordered for which the work on the boilers is not too far advanced: Belleville boilers should not be fitted.

3. Regarding ships under construction for which work is so far advanced, that to alter boilers would halt the completion of the ship substantially, Belleville boilers should be retained.

4. Regarding completed ships, Belleville should be kept in those ships.

In addition to the Belleville type, which was found to be more expensive in upkeep than cylindrical boilers, the expense in the opinion of the Committee increasing substantially with the age of the boiler, consideration was given to four types of large straight type (tubes) boilers which had been tried out in warships with much success and were now being adopted in foreign navies. These were: Babcock & Wilcox; Niclausse; Durr; Yarrow large tube.

On 2 July 1904 the Babcock & Wilcox, and the Yarrow were recommended as being the most suitable, but without any combination of cylindrical boilers. This decision was arrived at after many combinations had been fitted in the *King Edward VII* class (eight ships) during their years of construction (1902–4). Also, during the design stages of the battleships *Queen* (1901) and *Prince of Wales*, it had been debated whether or not to fit *Queen* with all Babcock boilers and compare her with her sister (POW) fitted with Bellevilles. Harland & Wolff (*Queen*) looked into the question of altering the ship to take all Babcock boilers, and seeing that it would affect little, proceeded to install them (*see* relevant chapters on ships for details of trials). Far from dismissing the Belleville as a failure, the Chairman of the Committee, Sir Compton Domville, while serving in *Bulwark* at Rapallo in June 1904, sent a report to their Lordships giving a glowing recommendation for the type:

'I have the honour to submit, herewith to be laid before the Lords Commissioners of the Admiralty, the final report of the Boiler Committee of which I am President. Although I have not been present at the experiments carried out during the last two years, I have received from time to time all the reports, and they show the great care and pains taken by the Committee to obtain correct results. With reference to our previous report, I am compelled to say that my experience with the Belleville boilers on the Mediterranean Station has been very favourable to them as a steam generator, and it is clear to me that the earlier boilers of this description were badly constructed and badly used. We have had no serious boiler defects in any of the ships out here, and the fact that two ships are about to be recommissioned, with only the ordinary annual repairs being undertaken shows that their life is not so short as I originally supposed.

However, the second commission of these ships will be a very good test of the staying capabilities of their boilers.

In conclusion, I cannot express too highly my opinion of the work done by my colleagues on the Committee.'

The cylindrical boiler as fitted to ships of the *Majestic* class, *Formidable* classes, etc., was not discarded as totally useless either. It was stated that the steaming capabilities of *Hannibal* (*Majestic* class) left very little to be desired, but their inability to raise steam quickly from a cold start precluded the use of the type. But with these, and the Belleville, development had reached its limits, whereas the Babcock & Wilcox and Yarrow types were only just getting off the mark. The entire boiler investigation had lasted almost twelve years, and had accomplished a great deal towards uniform design within warship types. However, an independent report of the conclusions showed some distaste for the whole concern:

'Large sums of money were spent in making useless changes of boilers, and the Navy was deprived of the services of important ships for many months owing to the state of uncertainty and indecision which prevailed. The labours of the Boiler Committee, which were so costly, were most nugatory in their results, as they saddled the Navy with 18 ships of reduced efficiency, caused a serious delay in construction of new warships; caused an immense amount of work for the engineering staff of the Admiralty, by which other warships had suffered, and condemned a boiler (Belleville) which after two years definite experience in the largest fleet, the President could only praise.'

One fact which did emerge was that the Babcock & Wilcox were preferred to those of the Yarrow type. To replace one or more tubes in the Yarrow entailed the removal of several others. Moreover, the Babcock boiler showed approximately 12 per cent more efficiency than the Yarrow, and occupied less floor space and weight. It can also be added, that difficulties experienced with high speeds in reciprocating machinery were solved when forced lubrication was introduced, and proved most successful. In passing, it may be mentioned that most of the Boiler Committee's reports and recommendations were made public, and the maritime powers of the world benefited greatly from this.

PAINTWORK AND CAMOUFLAGE

'Spic and span', 'clean and shipshape', 'shining like a new pin', and 'buffed up so that you can see your face in it', were all terms used when describing the appearance of a man-of-war during the Victorian period. But just imagine having to clean and keep in pristine condition in all weathers, colours such as yellow ochre, gloss black and, worst of all, brilliant white. It was general practice for two dozen sheets of emery and two dozen tins of polishing paste to be used every week on one turret—and that was considered moderate. Moreover, there was a great deal of brass on board, which also had to be polished and which kept the crew in constant work.

At the turn of the century, the service allowance of paint was just one coat of zinc white per annum. A battleship was permanent home for about 600–700 men, so it was only natural that great pains were taken to keep everything clean and brightly painted. However, if the service allowance only were used, it would wear off before the end of the year; in fact, depending on the area in which the vessel was serving (Atlantic, Mediterranean, China Station), it would look disgraceful before the end of three months. Very often, real enamel paint was used, which lasted much longer (up to nine months) and being hard and glossy, did not show up the dirt so much and was a great saving in

labour. During the 1890s the Admiralty realized that the ships could not remain in this easily spotted bright paintwork if hostilities broke out, but it had not been decided what new colour schemes to adopt. The livery buff then in use had been kept so long, partly to comply with Queen Victoria's wishes, but also in accordance with the wishes of a strong lobby who simply thought the scheme most suitable.

Looking abroad, the Austrian Navy, after repeated trials, found that a greenish-tinted grey seemed to be the best for their ships; the French had decided on *toile mouillé* (like damp canvas), while the German Navy preferred a medium shade of all-over grey. It would seem then, that Austria, France, Germany and indeed Japan, kept their ships in simple colours which they considered would be suitable in the event of war. The Royal Navy, however, did not start experiments with 'invisible painting' until about 1902.

Most of these trials (all that official records seem to show) were carried out on three of the *Majestic* class battleships: *Hannibal*, *Magnificent* and *Majestic* herself, during 1902–3 while the ships were serving together in the Channel Fleet, to determine the most efficient colour to replace the existing Victorian buff. At first, *Hannibal* was painted in a dull greenish-brown and later, with light-green upper works and a return to the black hull (this time in matt finish). *Magnificent* sported all-grey then all-black, which in certain conditions proved the most successful. *Majestic* received grey upper works and a black hull. The light-green of *Hannibal* proved the most difficult to pick up at a distance, but at times, in certain dull conditions, she stood out rather boldly. The black hulls, it was found, were generally good for overcast weather; the grey, depending on its shade, blending in with most conditions—certainly far more than the green, brown or black.

Finally, late in 1902, it was decided to adopt an all-over grey, slightly darked than that used in the German Navy. There was for some time, however, a great deal of variation between ships which followed the old system under which considerable latitude was allowed in painting (captains' and officers' choice, within certain limits, etc.). A slightly lighter grey was adopted for ships serving on the Far East Stations and in the Mediterranean, and towards the beginning of the First World War a much darker grey on battleships was in evidence.

When war came in 1914, the old predreadnoughts, like the revolutionary dreadnoughts, received a variety of unofficial camouflage schemes; the most noticeable being at the Dardanelles early in 1915.

One of the first to show weird paintwork, however, was the oldest British battleship to serve in the war. When *Revenge* (later *Redoubtable*) was refitted for bombarding the Belgian coast in late 1914–15 she came out of dock wearing large, dark-grey (possibly blue) patches over a medium-grey background. A whole variety of wonderful paintwork featured in the Dardanelles at various times throughout the campaign, and each was different. False bow waves were very common, but apart from that, *Canopus*, *Irresistible*, *Vengeance*, *Implacable* and *Agamemnon* were all given the full treatment. The first four showed colours of medium-grey backgrounds, with dark-grey irregular patterns all over. Blue was used at times instead of the dark-grey, but lack of official records leaves the schemes unclear. *Agamemnon* was painted up not unlike the battle cruiser *Inflexible*; grey background, dark patterns on the upperworks, and a white second funnel.

All of these seem to have disppeared by early 1916—in the predreadnoughts at least—and did not re-appear until 1918 when *London* was used as a minelayer and as an experimental ship for dazzle painting.

Colours consisted of greys, blues, green and black. The only active predreadnought to receive official Norman Wilkinson dazzle was *Commonwealth* from the *King Edward VII* class, after she had been refitted with bulges and tripod, etc. (*see* that class); a one-off pattern, as all battleships were—shades of blue, grey and green (painted out before the end of the war).

THE NAVAL DEFENCE ACT

During the Russo-Turkish war of 1879, a Committee was formed to ensure that British defences were adequate to cope with any situation that might draw the country into conflict. The Committee concluded its deliberations by stating that the Royal Navy as a whole was far from adequate to fulfill its role as safeguard to the empire. Moreover, many of the vessels then on the Navy List were more than eight years old, and perhaps could not hope to match some of the latest French battleships then completing or on the stocks.

The Board felt that the report was somewhat alarmist, but further construction was sanctioned with *Collingwood* in 1880, *Rodney*, *Camperdown*, *Howe*, *Anson* and *Benbow* during 1882–4 and *Hero* in 1884. Content that the ranks had been greatly augmented, the Board sat back with some satisfaction, feeling that although fresh construction was under way, it was at a leisurely pace, and one that could be accommodated nicely as far as the Treasury was concerned.

This was a bad situation and a strong body of opinion opposed the Board for not forcing the issue and building more large seagoing battleships in which we were quite defficient, but with the Egyptian war going on, and the constant changes in government (and in the Board itself) these urgings were ignored.

During 1884, the matter of defence reared its head again. The government as a whole was opposed to further costly construction, but the matter was now being aired in public, and all parties within the government were seen to be squabbling over which path they should take.

With only the *Admiral*s under construction, and viewing the meagre handful of ships Britain had acquired during the Russo-Turkish war, there was grave doubt as to whether or not the Royal Navy could take the decisive role in a two-power standard situation.

The cat was thrown among the pigeons in September 1884 when in the *Pall Mall Gazette*, a series of questions were put forward by an anonymous writer which cast serious reflections on the strength and ability of the Royal Navy as the leading seapower.

THE TRUTH ABOUT THE NAVY

'1. Our war risks have enormously increased. Has our Navy, which is our national insurance, been correspondingly strengthened?
2. Can we or can we not demonstrate beyond all gainsaying our "irresistible superiority" in armour, guns, speed and coal-carrying capacity over any combination of fleets which it is reasonable to believe could be brought against us?
3. If at this moment we are in this position, how will it be in five years hence, when the ironclads now building are in commission?
4. Have repairs been sacrificed to building, or are our ships in commission really serviceable?
5. If our ironclads are superior in hull, is their armament up to the mark? Is it or is it not true that both the French and Italian navies are armed with heavier guns of greater precision, and more convenient for handling than are our own ships?
6. In case of a sudden outbreak of war with any naval power, have we at this moment a fighting ship on each of our foreign stations better than the best that the enemy could send against us?
7. Have we sufficient store of fast ocean cruisers to scour the seas in search of the innumerable vessels which in case of war would at once be let loose upon our commerce?
8. Are our coal and telegraph stations secured against the sudden descent of a hostile ship?
9. Are our own seaports in a state of defence, and our own harbours adequately protected?
10. If an ironclad were disabled in any part of the world, have we provided docks wherein it could be refitted within reasonable distance of the scene of action?
11. Have we sufficient trained sailors and gunners, first, to man our ships, and secondly to supply the wear and tear of service in time of war?
12. And lastly, if all these questions can be answered in the affirmative have we a sufficiently numerous mosquito fleet of torpedo-boats, steam launches and picket boats to fend off the attacks of an enemy's torpedoes and save our gigantic ironclads from sudden destruction?'

To these questions, it was said, the nation had a right to an accurate and unbiased answer. The public became agitated and scanned the *Pall Mall Gazette* a few days later:

'What is this England whose very existence is in peril, that we have a right to expose her thus to a risk of a fatal overthrow? England is not merely our country and the teeming mother of new Englands beyond the seas, she is the power which with all her faults yet leads the progress of the world in civilization—pacific, industrial and free. Among the great powers of the old world, England stands for liberty—liberty of conscience, liberty of trade, liberty of association, and for the free Government of free men by their own voice and vote.'

Just three days after the above synopsis had appeared, the most startling disclosure, in considerable length and detail, was sent in for publication. For obvious reasons, the writer's name was withheld to avoid personnel criticizm, but the full facts were answered against the 'Truth about the Navy' and headed as, 'By one who Knows'. (In fact it was written by Captain J.A. Fisher assisted by Lord Esher and Mr H.O. Arnold-Forster. The whole series had been put together by these three men.)

The answers were far too lengthy to reproduce here, but in short they were:
1. Increased risks: 'Naval expenditure has definitely not been increased to meet the ever-imposing threat of foreign invasion, which by 1884 was much greater than in 1869 when the question was asked'.
2. Our superiority in Ironclads afloat: 'The following table shows the facts:

	British	Tons
First class ironclads, 8 years old and under:	4	38,900
Ditto over 8 years old:	6	56,940
Second class, from 5 to 16 years old:	13	79,740
Third class, from 7 to 21 years old:	14	112,410
Coast defence, 10in armour, 13 years old:	5	18,830
Ditto second class, 18 to 21 years old:	6	13,120
Ditto in the Colonies, 14 to 16 years old:	3	9,580
	French	
First class, 8 years old and under:	3	28,990
Second class, from 4 to 16 years old:	11	79,338
Third class, iron, 7 to 21 years old:	12	55,981
Coast defence, 6 to 16 years old:	6	22,276
Ditto, 2nd class 18 to 21 years old:	5	7,190

Comparison of these tables shows that although inferior to the Royal Navy, in first class, they equal us in second class ships, which compose the chief fighting force, and the British preponderance, such as it was, is due to old ironclads of an antiquated type with extremely thin armour compared with modern day plates [1884].'
3. Our superiority in building ironclads:
The actual state of the navy being unsatisfactory, was the lost ground now being made up? On the contrary, ground was being lost. Construction was going ahead, but the French were ahead with the number of ships on the stocks. The writer said:
'To put this country into the same relative pace to that which she maintained ten years ago, without

making any allowance for the necessity for making up lost ground, there should be at least a million a year added to the shipbuilding vote.'

4. Repairs:

The Government was accused of not spending money on older ships to keep them fit for the line of battle, while giving money for limited new construction. On the other hand, it was asked whether or not, it was actually worth keeping many of the older ships which were obsolete—refit or not.

5. Our inferiority in guns:

The French are superior to the Royal Navy in guns, although not so decidedly as first sight would appear. With the exception of six vessels, however, there is not a breechloader in the ironclad navy, and the new ships, now under construction (*Admiral* class) are having to wait for the new 63ton and 110ton guns proposed for them.

6. Our danger on our Foreign Stations:

'In case of a sudden outbreak of war with France, the whole of our Chinese Squadron would be at her mercy. As a matter of fact, England is not in a position adequately to protect her mercantile marine in case of war against any considerable naval power.'

7. There were not enough fast cruisers to protect British merchant vessels.

8. Are our coaling and telegraph stations protected?

'This question is easily answered. More than half our telegraph and coaling stations are exposed to destruction by the sudden descent of a hostile ship.'

9. Protection of Home Harbours:

There were eight foreign station and four docks. There was no dock in the whole of India which could refit an ironclad. There was a dock then building in Hong Kong, but far from adequate.

10. Defence of Home Ports: There were not more than two harbours in the United Kingdom which were adequately protected.

11. Personnel of the Navy: There were not nearly enough trained crews (especially gunners) to man the Fleet if war had been declared.

12. The Mosquito Fleet: In the cheapest and deadliest mode of the Fleet, the naval supremacy, instead of being absolutely irresistible, was practically non-existent.

The startling revelation of the weakness of the Navy, and the utter unpreparedness for war, hit some hard and brought an overwhelming response from all quarters which indicated that the statements in 'The Truth about the Navy' no longer rested on the authority of an anonymous correspondent.

Admiral of the Fleet Sir Thomas Symonds said:

'I have not words in which to thank you for this most patriotic endeavour to save Great Britain and its dependencies. May God grant that John Bull may attend to it in time – soon or never. This article has the great advantage of understanding the case 50%. It does not follow the French estimates, which are Cuirasses d,Escadre, Cuirasses de Station, etc., etc. He leaves out six large French ironclads, and two small ones.'

Certainly nothing like this report had ever been published before and there had never been a stronger attack on the capabilities of the Royal Navy. The measure of response, however, was paradoxically mild and the building programme of 1884 consisted of only two battleships (*Victoria* and *Sans Pareil*) plus seven belted cruisers, which were to be spread over a period of five years. All the lobbying and general public agitation had done little to persuade the government to increase expenditure for further naval construction on a large scale, which caused much unrest within the media.

By 1886 the Royal Navy had under construction, or nearing completion the battleships *Colossus*, *Edinburgh*, *Conqueror*, *Hero*, *Collingwood*, *Anson*, *Rodney*, *Camperdown*, *Howe*, *Benbow*, *Sans Pareil* and *Victoria* although with much reluctance the government did sanction funds for a further two battleships in the 1885 estimates (*Trafalgar* and *Nile*). Changes in government, however, saw fresh faces on the Board and brought about a divergence of opinion over the many old ships still showing on the Navy List and in active service. In numbers the Royal Navy was not deficient in battleships, but many had been modernized, their hulls were old, and their guns out of date, and they could no longer be classed as first class ships of the line.

Moreover, the question of battleship design was under discussion with reference to the principles of attack and defence, even to the extent of using the old ironclad *Resistance* as a target to gain practical experience on how a ship would take considerable gunfire. (*Resistance* had a displacement of 6,150 tons with dimensions of 280ftpp x 54ft x 26ft, armed with eight 7in BLR and had been completed in 1861–2.) She was protected with 4½in iron plates 140ft long amidships from upper deck to 6ft below the waterline and covering all the main deck battery. This was backed by 18in teak. Fired on by medium-size shells only, it was seen that there was a great necessity for armour strakes above the main belt to keep out raking fire and stop the upper works of a ship being wrecked by medium-calibre guns. Later, special plates were placed on her sides to ascertain how thick the plates would have to be, and whether it were a feasible proposition.

The experiments continued for many years, but the early tests provided the Royal Navy test centre with much valuable data which was filtered into British warships for the next decade.

With the change of government Lord Charles Beresford was appointed to the Board. He understood the need to keep the fleet in a constant state of readiness, and shortly after taking office drew up an important document on 'War Organization' to be circulated among their Lordships. A copy of the report was obtained by another member of the staff, who passed it to the *Pall Mall Gazette*. Much of it was published on 16 October 1886.

'1. Our deficiencies:

The perilous absence of any complete plan of preparation for war, and the gravity and imminence of the dangers which may result to this country from such a state of affairs, have reduced me to submit this paper for the consideration of the present board of Admiralty.

2. No Scheme of War Preparation:

The scare of 1885 showed approximately what we should actually require in officers and men, shipping, armament, and ammunition, coal and medical stores, over what is now at our disposal. It is quite incredible that with the knowledge as to what will be required at the time of a declaration of war, no steps have been taken to organize or prepare any method for showing how or where these indispensible requirements are to be got.

3. No security for being first in the field:

In these days of electricity and great speed the first point scored may save millions to the country that secures it, and have the probable effect of winning the campaign. This remark applies with particular force to our foreign stations. Through want of organization and systematic instruction, as well as want of ordinary foresight, the Admiralty render it possible for an enterprising enemy, like France or Russia might be, easily to score this first advantage, because a delay of two days is allowed to elapse owing to the antiquated formalities of the present system before the Admiralty could communicate the proclamation of war to the Commanders-in-Chief of different stations.

4. Deficiency of personnel:
It would appear that there are sufficient numbers of Captains and Commanders for the vessels which could be got ready for commission in three months, but irrespective of war. In regard to the present number of lieutenant rank, I should think we are 300 deficient.

5. Store Department:
With respect to the stores in the Medical Department a similar want of forethought is discernible, taking far off stations like Hong Kong, the Cape of Good Hope and Esquimalt, where the stores are kept in certain proportions, which of course would have to be immensely increased. There are actually ready more reserve stores for the medical than for any other department in the navy, I find at Deptford, Plymouth & etc.; but there is no detailed plan for their quick distribution.

6. How we invite panic and Court disaster:
Knowing as we do, of the necessity for an increase in officers, men, merchant shipping, coal, ammunition, medical and commisariat stores, why, I would ask, in the name of common sense, do we not organize in time of peace for these requirements by having detailed lists arranged of officers and men that we can instruct by telegraph to proceed at once to their destinations, instead of adding to the panic and confusion certain to occur on any declaration of war, through not having worked out this otherwise simple question in advance?

7. Mobilization: France 48 hours ... England 5 days.
Now, why does this wicked state of affairs exist? Simply because there is no efficient staff of Admiralty employed in organizing our fleets for war, and no attempt is made at practising this most necessary evolution.

8. Short of coal, and short of ammunition:
It is needless to say that coal is the life and breath of the fleet, and to point out the danger of not having thought out how the 60,000 tons of fuel necessary for foreign stations on the outbreak of war is to be got there. The question of ammunition is still more grave. Nothing has been done to remedy this shocking state of affairs which was pointed out in a private and confidential paper.

9. No plan of campaign:
Other nations have a plan of campaign clearly defined at headquarters which is altered or adapted to the nation they may find themselves engaged with, which plan is also communicated to Admirals commanding fleets. The disadvantage England rests under through not possessing a plan of campaign at all is a matter for very grave uneasiness to anybody who studies the question.

10. The essentials for efficiency:
Having to the best of my ability pointed out the indispensible necessity for immediately recognizing the gravity of the present state of affairs, I will now submit a proposal for placing matters in that state of efficiency which everyone must acknowledge is positively essential. I am not egotistical enough to imagine that I have made some novel discovery, as I know full well from conversations that have sat on the Board of Admiralty of late years has felt the importance of the subjects embodied in this paper.

11. An Intelligence Department for the Navy:
To meet the difficulties of extra duties entailed, I would submit the following proposals. Extend the present Foreign Intelligence Committee and call it the Intelligence Department, dividing it into sections 1 and 2. The head of this department should be an Admiral with a staff of two junior Captains, two Commanders or lieutenants, two marine officers, three clerks and two writers.
Section 1 would gather all information relative to foreign navies, inventions, trials, and foreign maritime matters generally; while section 2 would organize war preparations, including naval mobilization and the making out of plans for naval campaigns for all contingencies, corrected frequently and periodically.'

An alarming situation was revealed, and great foresight on the part of Beresford. It had echoes from the past and told a tale much the same as that of 1884 (The Truth about the Navy'). The tabloids reacted strongly, none more so than the *York Herald*:
'The matter to which Lord Charles Bereseford directs attention must strike every reader as absolutely necessary in case of war, unless, indeed, we are content to go on the old system of bungling through a first campaign, and by degrees arriving at a condition in which we are able to beat our enemies.'

Although the message was well and truly hammered home from all quarters, no capital ships were laid down from 1886 until 1889! During 1888,

the DNC, William White, drew up a report detailing the ever-deteriorating condition of ships of war, and what was needed to rectify the situation regarding fresh construction. At the same time, Beresford resigned from the Board and prepared his own synopsis of mandatory requirements. With the backing of the majority of the Board and the DNC's approval, Beresford brought forward his proposals in detail on 13 December 1888 and asked for £20,000,000 to be spent on building 74 ships over a period of years.

The First Lord (Lord George Hamilton) jeered at him, saying that he (Lord Hamilton) obtained his information from authoritative sources and not from newspapers—he said that Britain was equal to any two powers, and that Lord Beresford was a seaman 'given to exaggeration'.

To add weight to the argument that fresh construction was necessary, the report of the 1888 fleet manoeuvres had just been made available, which showed that many of our ships were deficient in good seagoing qualities. It also stated that the fleet would find it difficult to confront even one of the major powers, let alone two.

The political ramifications were considerable, but the day was finally won, and just thirteen weeks after Lord Beresford's speech, Lord George Hamilton reluctantly brought in the Naval Defence Act in March 1889 which provided for the construction of 70 ships at a cost of £21,500,000. All were to be spread over a period of 5 years, and included the famous *Royal Sovereign*s, Hood, *Centurion* and *Barfleur* plus 41 cruisers of different types. The turn of the tide had arrived, and armed with adequate finance, fresh constructional advice, and generally a free hand, the DNC remarked before the members of the Naval Institute in a somewhat prognostic mood:

'If, with such a staff, with all our recorded data and experience, with our grand experimental establishment at Haslar, so ably conducted by my friend Mr Froude, and with all the valuable assistance and suggestions coming to us from the Naval Service, and our professional colleagues in the Dockyards, as well as the constant benefits we derive from a full knowledge of the work done by private shipbuilders and foreign competitors, we do not in the "Whitehall Office" succeed in producing "the best possible ships" consistent with the instructions of the Board of Admiralty, then there can be no excuse.'

ROYAL SOVEREIGN CLASS

1889 ESTIMATES

DESIGN

On 17 August 1888, a meeting of the Board of Admiralty took place at Devonport Dockyard during the Board's annual inspection of the yard, to decide on the specifications and dimensions of the battleships to be ordered under the estimates for 1889. The members of the Board had papers and plans detailing various battleship types and in the course of discussions reviewed the merits of the various features of these vessels. The main topics were:

1. Whether the new ships should have high freeboard or low freeboard (the former only possible with a barbette-mounted main armament).
2. The number, distribution and mounting arrangements of the main armament.
3. The disposition of the secondary armament.
4. The arrangements and thickness of armour protection.
5. Main machinery.

After a lengthy debate the following points were agreed by all present:
1. There should be four heavy guns in two separated, protected stations, each gun having arcs of at least 260° and both being capable of firing on each beam. After considerable discussion it was agreed that these guns should be 13.5in calibre which would bring them into line with the newest battleships then completing (*Trafalgar* and *Nile*).
2. The secondary armament was to consist of ten 6in guns, the main element of which should be placed in a long, broadside central battery between the main gun positions, with light protection if possible. The remaining secondary guns to be placed a deck higher to reduce mutual blast interference and limit the number of guns that could be put out of action by a single hit. This latter resulted from consideration of recent developments in high explosives and medium-calibre quick-firing guns.
3. The main armour belt was to be of the same ratio-to-length as in the *Trafalgar* class. The main belt was to be at least 18in thick with a 4in or 5in upper belt and a 3in protective deck.

There was also discussion on the citadel and redoubt systems of armouring, figures of 14in and 12in being given for citadel armour. No decision was made as to the type of ship to be adopted, but it was made clear that which ever was chosen would be subject to the same cost limitation, although ample funds had been allowed for the final design.

On returning to the office, the DNC, William White, informed his department that: 'The Board has directed that after considerable discussion, outline sketches be prepared on the following alternatives: **1.** A modified *Trafalgar*. **2.** A modified *Anson*.'

From these requirements, the DNC Department prepared several outline designs for both turret and barbette ships which were the subject of considerable discussions and some controversy. The DNC forcefully expounded on the advantages of the barbette ship, with redoubt protection and particularly high freeboard. The First Naval Lord, Admiral Hood, preferred the more extensive protection available in the turret type, which due to considerable topweight, required low freeboard. Details of the principal types of design prepared in accordance with requirements and placed before the Board can be seen in the table.

Investigations were called for also in to:
1. Displacement and cost of turret ships with a natural draught speed of 17 knots and 30 per cent larger fuel capacity.
2. The standard of main armament and protection that could be provided in a turret ship of 12,000 tons, having the same freeboard, gun command, speed and fuel capacity as in citadel turret and redoubt types (B and C).

This reduced design is reported to have been desired for close comparison with the French battleship *Brennus* (then under construction) of 11,200 tons, carrying three 13.4in guns in one twin and one single turret, a secondary battery of ten 6.5in with 15.8in of armour on the main belt, 17.7in on turrets, and a speed of 17 knots.

On 16 November 1888 the various alternative plans were considered by a special Committee comprising the members of the Board of Admiralty together with Admirals Dowell, Vesey Hamilton and Richards, Vice-Admiral Baird, Captain Lord Walter Kerr, Captain J. Fisher (DNO) and the DNC.

The special design that called for a natural speed of 17 knots and 30 per cent fuel capacity increase, together with the reduced versions were virtually rejected out of hand; the former because of its unacceptable size (found to be approximately 16,000 tons at a cost of £1,000,000 excluding armament) and the latter on the grounds that the displacement was insufficient to provide adequate standards of armament and protection. The basic point of issue, however, lay in the relative merits of the turret and barbette types. The former afforded

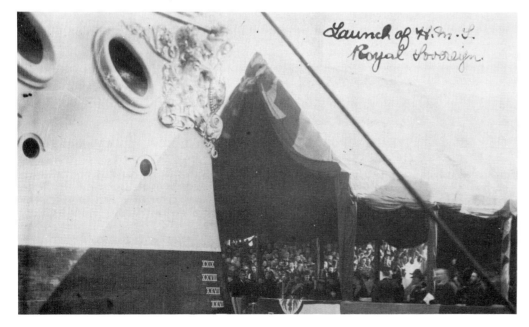

Left: *Repulse*, fitting out at Pembroke Dockyard during the early part of 1892. She was taken to Portsmouth on 5 December 1892 where she was completed for sea.

more complete protection to the main armament, plus increased height of heavily armoured side in the single citadel arrangement, but the considerable topweight of armour involved necessitated low freeboard with its concomitant disadvantages in respect of gun command and sea speed. The latter, with a low distribution of weight, allowed higher freeboard and gun command with increased fighting efficiency and maintenance of speed, at some sacrifice in protection to the gun positions.

ROYAL SOVEREIGN
Outboard profile, as fitted 1893

Royal Sovereign class: Launch figures

Launching weight:
Royal Sovereign: 6,300 tons approx.
Ramillies: 6,500 tons.
Although official launch records for the class have not survived, there is mention of the great length of the slipway on which *Ramillies* had to run (75 feet) and this ties in well with the resulting difficulties of her launch (*see* History). *Royal Sovereign* was launched with main belt in place, side 4in Harvey plates fitted, and all internal armoured bulkheads complete.

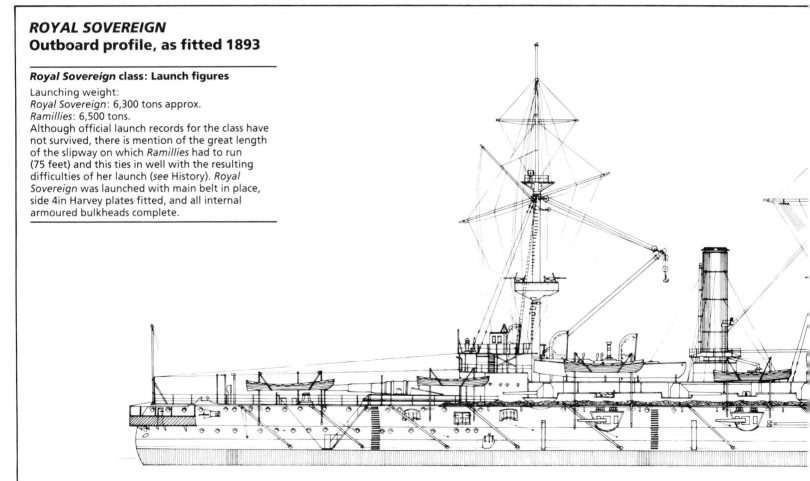

The turret plan was strongly favoured by the First Sea Lord, Admiral Sir Arthur Hood (who had been largely responsible for the *Trafalgar* design) while White preferred the barbette arrangement and, when submitting the alternative designs called for by the Board, included a memo strongly criticizing the *Trafalgar*s and the turret type in general, and urging the adoption of the barbette plan for the new ships.

The three designs for the 14,000-ton citadel turret ship, the 13,650-ton redoubt turret ship (C)

and 11,600-ton barbette ship (c) were accepted as the most satisfactory representatives of their respective types, and in further considering these the Committee initially rejected the single citadel design in favour of the separate redoubt system, the barbette version of this finally being selected in view of its higher freeboard. The final decision to adopt the high freeboard barbette ship was subsequently confirmed by the Report of the 1888 Manoeuvres Committee which revealed a number of defects in the design of the fleet's vessels, and in

particular emphasized a major problem with the battleships. The report stressed that the low freeboard turret ships, and the barbette ships of the *Admiral* class suffered badly in a sea-way, and in some cases rolled and pitched so violently that they would have been unable to fight their guns efficiently, if it all. In the turret vessels, the problem was worsened by the fact that the main armament was positioned so close to the waterline that it was not unusual for the muzzles of the forward guns to be dipping into the foam shipped over the forecastle.

The final deliberations of the Committee were published in a Parliamentary White Paper, and also in a statement from the First Lord which confirmed:

1. Speeds of 15 knots for continuous steaming, and about 17 knots as the maximum speed was regarded as sufficient for first class battleships.

2. After some discussion, and after further explanations had been given of the alternative arrangements for disposing armaments in use in other navies, it was unanimously agreed that the general features of the disposition of heavy guns, and the auxiliary armament, illustrated in the vessels of the *Admiral* class, as well as in the *Nile* and *Trafalgar*, were on the whole best possible.

3. It was generally agreed that when the armoured belt was carried over such a large portion of the length of the ship as in the designs under consideration, so that the spaces above the protective deck, before and after the belt were of small capacity, and the entry of water to them would produce only small sinkage and very moderate changes of trim, it was preferable to dispose the weight available for waterline protection in the form of thicker armour on the belt not carried to the ends.

4. After full discussion it was agreed to have two separate strongly protected stations for the four heavy guns, rather than a single citadel.

5. It was agreed that for maintenance of speed and fighting power at sea, the high freeboard and high placed guns in the design for the barbette ship were preferable to the lower freeboard of the turret ship.

6. The advantages and disadvantages of turrets versus barbettes has been fully reviewed and the barbette arrangement was preferred in a battleship intended for general sea-going purposes.

A week after the meeting, the DNC sent a letter to J. O. Hopkins, the Controller, stating:

'The two designs C and c are to be worked out in

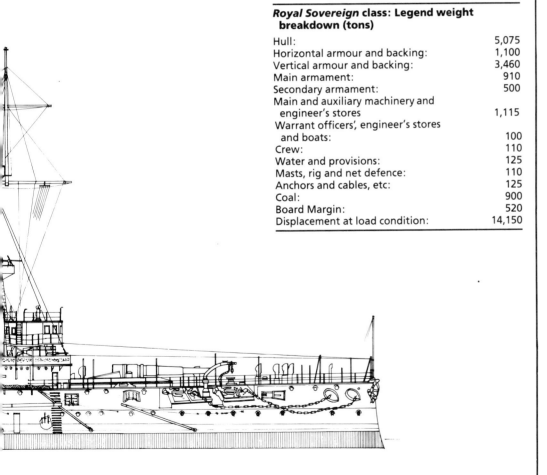

Royal Sovereign class: Legend weight breakdown (tons)	
Hull:	5,075
Horizontal armour and backing:	1,100
Vertical armour and backing:	3,460
Main armament:	910
Secondary armament:	500
Main and auxiliary machinery and engineer's stores	1,115
Warrant officers', engineer's stores and boats:	100
Crew:	110
Water and provisions:	125
Masts, rig and net defence:	110
Anchors and cables, etc:	125
Coal:	900
Board Margin:	520
Displacement at load condition:	14,150

Designs for *Royal Sovereign* class

	Barbette ship (Admirals)	Citadel turret ship	Redoubt turret ship	Barbette ship	*Trafalgar*	Design B (citadel turret)	Design C (redoubt turret)	Design C (barbette)	Redoubt turret ship	Barbette ship
Displacement (tons):	10,550	14,000	12,000	12,000	12,000	15,000	13,650	11,600	14,000	14,000
Length:	330ft	380ft	350ft	350ft	345ft	400ft	380ft	350ft	380ft	380ft
Beam:	68½ft	75ft	70ft	70ft	73ft	74ft	73ft	68ft	75ft	75ft
Draught:	27½ft	27½ft	27ft	27½ft	27½ft	27½ft	27½ft	27ft	27½ft	27½ft
Freeboard:	10¼ft	11¼ft	11¼ft	18ft	11¼ft	18ft	18ft	18ft	11¼ft	18ft
SHP (forced):	11,000	13,000	12,000	12,000	12,000	18,000	13,000	12,000	13,000	13,000
Speed (forced):	16¾kts	17kts	17kts	17kts	16½kts	18½kts	17kts	17kts	17kts	17kts
Speed (normal):	15kts	15kts	15kts	15kts	15kts	16½kts	15½kts	15½kts	15kts	15kts
Coal (tons):	900	900	900	900	900	900	900	900	900	900
Armament:	four 67ton BL / six 6in BL / twelve 6pdr / seven 3pdr	four 67ton BL / ten 6in QF / ten 6pdr / eight 3pdr	four 45ton BL / ten 6in QF / ten 6pdr / eight 3pdr	four 45ton BL / ten 6in QF / sixteen 6pdr / eight 3pdr	four 67ton BL / six 4.7in BL / eight 6pdr / ten 3pdr	four 67ton BL / ten 6in QF	four 67ton BL / ten 6in QF	four 43ton BL / six 6in QF	four 67ton BL / ten 6in QF	four 67ton BL / ten 6in
Length of belt:	150ft	250ft	230ft	230ft	230ft	230ft	250ft	230ft	250ft	250ft
Armour:	18in	18in–14in	14in	14in	20in–14in	20in	18in	14in	18in–14in	18in–14in

detail. I have directed Mr W. H. Whiting (Constructor) to be in charge of C, and Mr Beaton to be in charge of c. The calculations which are common to both designs are to be discussed between both men, as they may mutually arrange and thoroughly countercheck. Of the rig, the funnels will be brought together as in the *Victoria*, and a second light mast provided abaft the conning tower.'

On 23 February 1889 the final legend was produced (*see* table) which showed a vessel of 380ft x 75ft x 27ft 6in on a displacement of 14,150 tons in the load condition.

The question of docking accommodation materially influenced dimensions; particularly the beam. The restriction of draught to 27½ft corresponded to that of *Trafalgar*s as designed, but necessitated a marked increase in length over those ships to accommodate the extra weights carried, these including higher freeboard, heavier secondary armament, more powerful machinery plus the 4 per cent Board Margin. Owing to the nominal draught and displacement in the *Trafalgar* having been considerably exceeded by modifications during construction with consequent reduction in height of belt, the Admiralty required a Board Margin of unappropriated weight amounting to 4 per cent to be included in the design of the *Royal Sovereign*s, and the legend displacement was calculated to include a margin of 500 tons. Various additions amounting to 250 tons were deducted from this while building and the unexpended balance was utilized to increase coal stowage at the designed normal draught from 900 to 1,100 tons.

The high freeboard, which was the outstanding feature of the design, was obtained by the addition of one complete deck (middle), the above weights and centre of gravity being raised appreciably in consequence. This factor, together with the height of the barbettes, unprecedented weight of armour and wide range of displacement between normal and deep conditions, presented special and unusual problems to the Construction Department, which, it may be added, were overcome with much success. The design work being complete, seven battleships of the *Royal Sovereign* class were ordered under the Naval Defence Act of 1889, and another to be built as a low freeboard type (*Hood*). Three ships went to Royal Dockyards, and the remainder to private contractors.

As completed, they represented a great success for William White and his staff. They had seen clearly the faults of existing battleships and had had the ability to solve difficult problems and push through their ideas in the teeth of serious opposition. The *Royal Sovereign*s broke a long-lasting size limitation on British battleships and were the largest such vessels so far built for the Royal Navy. They were also the largest group of battleships built to a single design since the introduction of the ironclad and heralded a decade of uniformity for the British Fleet in which homogeneous battle squadrons once again became possible.

Royal Sovereign: Legend, 23 February 1889

Displacement: 14,000 tons
Length: 380ft
Beam: 75ft
Draught: 27ft forward, 28ft aft
Freeboard: 19ft 6in forward, 17ft 3in amidships, 18ft aft
Height of main guns above waterline: 23ft

SHP: 9,000 natural draught = 16 knots; 13,000 forced draught = 17½ knots
Fuel: 900 tons coal normal

Complement: 640

Armament
Four 13.5in
Ten 6in
Sixteen 6pdr
Eight 3pdr
Five torpedo tubes above water, two submerged, 24 torpedoes

Armour
Main belt: 18in–14in (8in–4in teak backing plus 1½in steel skin)
Bulkheads: 16in–14in
Battery side: 5in (later 4in)
Barbettes: 17in–13in
6in Ammunition tubes: 2in
Conning tower: 14in forward, 3in aft
Communications tube: 8in
Deck: 3in–2½in

Hull weight: 4,875 tons

Royal Sovereign class: Particulars, as completed

Construction
Royal Sovereign: Portsmouth DY; laid down 30 Sept 1889; launched 26 Feb 1891; completed May 1892

Empress of India: Pembroke DY; laid down 9 July 1889; launched 7 May 1891; completed August 1893

Ramillies: Thompson; laid down 11 Aug 1890; launched 1 March 1892; completed Oct 1893

Resolution: Palmer; laid down 14 June 1890; launched 28 May 1892; completed Nov 1893

Revenge: Palmer; laid down 12 Feb 1891; launched 3 Nov 1892; completed March 1894

Repulse: Pembroke DY; laid down 1 Jan 1890; launched 27 Feb 1892; completed April 1894

Royal Oak: Cammell Laird; laid down 29 May 1890; launched 5 Nov 1892; completed June 1894.

Displacement (tons)
Royal Sovereign: 14,150 (legend), 14,262 (load), 14,860 (deep).
Revenge: 14,635 (load), 15,535 (extra deep).

Dimensions
Length: 380ft pp, 410ft 6in oa
Beam: 75ft
Draught: 28–29ft 6in (mean)
Height of guns above lower waterline: 23ft.

Armament
Four 13.5in 30cal 67ton Mk I–IV; 80rpg
Ten 6in 40cal; 200rpg
Sixteen 6pdr QF
Twelve 3pdr QF
Eight Maxim MG

Seven 18in torpedo tubes, five above water, two submerged.

Armour (Compound and nickel steel)
Main belt: 18in–16in–14in (250ft long)
Upper belt: 4in (150ft long)
Bulkheads: 16in (forward), 14in (aft)
Screen bulkheads: 3in
Decks: 3in middle, 2½in lower
Barbettes: 17in–16in–11in
Casemates: (main deck 6in guns only) 6in
Conning tower: 14in–12in
Conning tower tube: 8in
After conning tower: 3in
After conning tower tube: 3in.

Machinery
Two sets 3-cylinder vertical triple expansion engines, twin propellers
Cylinder diameter: HP 40in, IP 59in, LP 88in
Boilers: eight cylindrical single-ended return tube in four compartments, working pressure 155psi
Heating surface: 19,560sq ft
Grate area: 700sq ft
Designed SHP: 9,000 = 16 knots natural draught, 11,000 = 17.5 knots forced draught
Fuel: 900 tons coal legend, 1,100 tons normal, 1,490 tons max.
Coal consumption: 230 tons per day full power; 35 tons per day at 7 knots
Radius of action: 2,780nm at 14 knots; 4,720nm at 10 knots
Engine room complement: 138.

Ship's boats (*Revenge* 1896)
Pinnaces (steam): two 56ft, one 40ft
Pinnaces (sail): one 36ft
Barges (steam): one 40ft
Launches (sail): one 42ft
Cutters (sail): two 30ft, one 26ft
Whalers (sail): one 30ft, one 25ft
Galleys (sail): one 32ft
Gigs (sail): one 28ft
Skiff dinghies: one 16ft.

Searchlights
Five 24in: two (P+S) forward and aft main deck, one pair close before foremast, one close abaft mainmast.

Anchors
Two Inglefield 118cwt (bower), one 117cwt (sheet)
Two Martins 55cwt, two 43cwt.

Wireless
Fitted 1900–02, removed later.

Complement
670 average
692 *Empress of India* as flagship, 1903
672 *Resolution*, 1903
695 *Revenge* as flagship, 1903
466 *Revenge* as training ship, 1906.

Costs
Royal Sovereign: £839,136 plus guns £74,850
Empress of India: £846,321 plus guns £65,841
Ramillies: £902,600 plus guns £78,295
Resolution: £875,522 plus guns £78,295
Revenge: £876,101 plus guns £78,724
Royal Oak: £899,272 plus guns £78,724
Repulse: £915,302 (including guns).

While under construction some minor modifications were made to the design and were incorporated in the ships. These included increasing the heights of the funnels, which added 13 tons, increasing the fighting tops, adding 4 tons, and increasing the thickness of the boiler tubes, adding 20 tons. The complement was enlarged, adding a further 10 tons, three more 3pdr QF guns were fitted and the carpenter's stores and number of boats increased. These, with other minor additions amounted to a total calculated weight of 137.5 tons which was taken from the Board margin.

The ships completed during 1892–4 and soon proved highly successful; at that time they were probably unequalled in all-round fighting efficiency. They were also of impressive and elegant appearance and could be easily identified by their twin athwartships funnels, high freeboard and open-topped barbettes. The class came as a welcome change to all concerned with their construction, and the public sector felt that the extra cost of such large vessels had been more than justified. Construction was exceptionally strong and heavy; on completion they were the most substantial warships ever built for the Royal Navy, and suffered, it must be said, to some extent, from excessive weight of fittings, etc. A provision for bilge keels was considered in the original design, but the final decision was deferred pending sea trials without them. The main reason for this was summed up by White who stated:

'No one has more strenuously urged the utility of bilge keels than myself. But while it is undoubted that they can never do harm, and in many cases may do great good in limiting rolling, their influence varies under different circumstances. In small ships of quick period, and in ships of moderate weight and moment of inertia, they are likely to prove most beneficial. In slow-moving ships of great inertia the influence of bilge keels must clearly be less felt, and may be very small. That influence depends upon the area of the keels, their radial distance from the axis of rotation, and their rate of motion through the water, which rate is governed

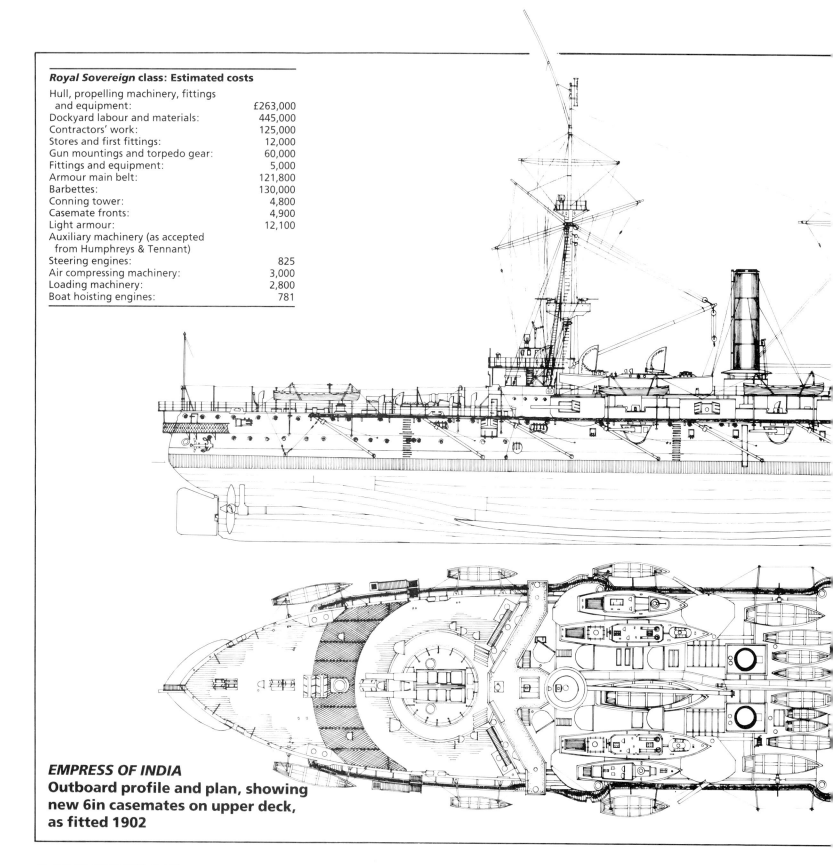

Royal Sovereign class: Estimated costs

Hull, propelling machinery, fittings and equipment:	£263,000
Dockyard labour and materials:	445,000
Contractors' work:	125,000
Stores and first fittings:	12,000
Gun mountings and torpedo gear:	60,000
Fittings and equipment:	5,000
Armour main belt:	121,800
Barbettes:	130,000
Conning tower:	4,800
Casemate fronts:	4,900
Light armour:	12,100
Auxiliary machinery (as accepted from Humphreys & Tennant)	
Steering engines:	825
Air compressing machinery:	3,000
Loading machinery:	2,800
Boat hoisting engines:	781

EMPRESS OF INDIA
Outboard profile and plan, showing new 6in casemates on upper deck, as fitted 1902

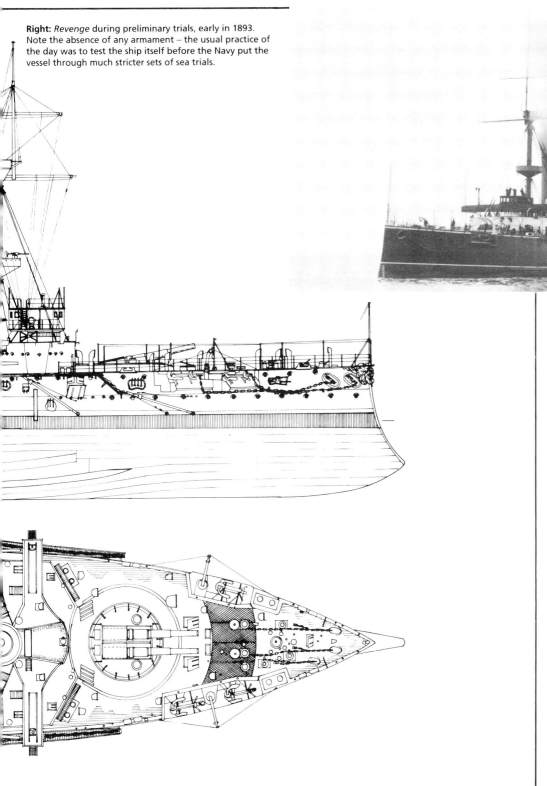

Royal Sovereign class: Armour weight breakdown (tons)

	As designed	As built
Main belt and bulkheads:	1,350	1,310
Upper belt and battery sides:	450	
Upper belt:		225
Casemates:		150
Barbettes:	1,385	1,345
Conning tower:	85	80
Wood backing to sides and bulkheads:	80	75
Wood backing on barbettes:	50	40
Deck plating and shellproof gratings:	1,010	1,060

by the arc of oscillation and the period of the oscillation. Since, within considerable limits of oscillation, ships are practically isochronous in their motions, the mean rate of motion of bilge keels through the water varies with the arc of oscillation. In other words, fluid resistance to the motion of the bilge keels has a small value and moment about the axis of rotation in a slow-moving ship until considerable angles of oscillation are reached.

Moreover, with a given moment about the axis of rotation of fluid resistance to the moment of bilge keels, the check put upon the rolling of a ship to which they are attached depends upon the weight, the stiffness, and the moment of inertia of the ship. It may happen, therefore, in large, slow-moving ships that the influence of the largest practicable bilge keels will be scarcely felt until considerable angles of rolling are reached. This appears to be the case in the *Royal Sovereign* class, and it was, therefore, decided not to fit bilge keels from the outset, until experience had been gained at sea with the ships.'

Below: *Empress of India*, 1894. Seen in the Clyde in her original rig and paintwork scheme.

Bottom: *Resolution* as completed, 1895. Dressed overall. The incident in December 1893 when she was forced to return to base because of severe rolling in a heavy sea earned the class the nickname of 'Rolling Ressies', but to be fair it was a one-off incident that was corrected by the fitting of long bilge keels.

This, however, did not prove to be the case. Although the ships turned out to be good, dry seaboats, they were found to develop a deep and disconcerting roll in certain conditions of sea, and they quickly became known as the 'Rolling Ressies' in the service. One particular, highlighted incident was when *Resolution* left Plymouth on 18 December 1893 to join the Channel Squadron at Gibraltar, and on the 19/20th met severe gales and tremendous squalls. Wave heights were reported as being 42 feet from hollow to crest, and lengths of up to 300 feet. The ship was brought head to sea, but was found to roll exceptionally heavily, and on at least two occasions the sea broke over the upper deck amidships and caused superficial damage.

After the incident, and after some considerable study of the situation, it was proved that the ship had not inclined to meet the water to the extent of the upper deck, but, in fact, it was the heavy swell which had reached that height. There was no doubt that the vessel had rolled a little too much for practicable purposes, which would certainly have been a hindrance had she been trying to fire her

guns. An alarmist in the Press claimed that *Resolution* had rolled up to 40 degrees on each beam! As a result of this experience, and to help alleviate the problem, bilge keels of 200 feet x 3 feet were fitted experimentally to *Repulse* while she was in the fitting-out stage. Later she underwent a series of tests with *Resolution* which showed that she rolled up to 11 degrees against 23 degrees in the latter. If further proof were needed, the report from Captain W. H. Hall in *Resolution* on 1 November 1894 showed conclusive results:

'On leaving Chatham bound for Gibraltar we did a series of trials which showed that the new bilge keels seem to have made a reduction in speed, but this may be due to the heavy swell in which the bows are frequently underwater. The swell was on the bow at first, and then on the beam, and had we not been fitted with bilge keels we should have rolled heavy – as it was, we hardly moved. As soon as we left Chatham, I made a series of circle turn trials to see if the bilge keels had affected the tactical diameter, and found that the diameter was

reduced from 680 yards to 500 yards, with both screws going full ahead, and from 450 to 300 yards reversing one screw.

This I attribute to the keels having a better grip of the water and stopping the crab like motion. The bilge keels, therefore, appear to be in every way a success, and have made the vessels efficient fighting ships which they certainly were not without them.'

This report was later backed up by Vice-Admiral Walter Kerr, aboard *Emperor of India* in November 1895, who said:

Below: *Repulse*, fully dressed 1895. In 1895–6 they were called 'The Flying Squadron of the Channel Fleet'.

Top right: *Revenge*. View from quarterdeck, showing battle honours along the breastwork.

'The *Emperor of India* caught it bad one night, and rode it out very well. I judge the ship as being A1 in heavy weather and I have never before found it possible to praise a ship in this manner.'

All ships of the class were fitted with bilge keels during 1894–5.

In general, the ships were well received in the service. While serving in *Ramillies* in 1895, Commander John Jellicoe (later Admiral of the Grand Fleet) stated that he had never seen a ship turned out so well from a builder's yard, especially a contractor. He went over the ship with a fine-tooth comb, and all he found to criticize were a few minor details of the design and nothing regarding the fighting capabilities of the vessel. The only major point he raised was that the ship was very stuffy in eastern and Mediterranean stations, particularly in the accommodation spaces, both for the officers and men; this was due to lack of suitable ventilation. There seemed to be plenty of cowl

vents in the areas concerned, but their arrangement did not ensure that air in sufficient quantities reached all compartments.

Their Lordships and the construction staff were well aware of this problem which beset practically every warship in the Royal Navy.

ARMAMENT

Throughout the meetings of the Design Committee, a considerable weight of opinion favoured for the main armament the adoption of a new, wire-wound 12in gun which at that time was still under construction. In March 1889, however, it became apparent that the new gun would not be ready in time, and as the Board required four of the heaviest guns available, it became Hobson's choice over the 13.5in 67ton piece which had proved so successful in the *Admiral*s. Although their Lordships gave preference to the heavy guns being mounted on barbettes, adverse criticism had been launched

against existing systems carried in the *Admiral* group, which in the main, was levelled at some of the interior workings, and lack of armour protection underneath. At that time barbettes were little more than shallow, armoured cylinders with plated bottoms, placed well above the armoured deck, the only means of connection being the ammunition trunks. The system obviously saved a good deal of armour weight, but it meant that the ammunition trunks, shell rooms and magazines were dangerously vulnerable to heavy shellfire, especially when there was no armour at all above the main belt.

White was quick to seize the opportunity of making some rectification and proposed several modifications. The thin 1in steel floor was omitted, the ammunition trunks were abolished, and an inside ring bulkhead was fitted. He also proposed full armour protection for the barbettes which would reach down to the armoured deck level. Experience in the *Admiral*s had shown that the height of the upper deck above the waterline needed to be raised as much as possible to increase the height of the barbette from the deck, but this could not be accomplished in these ships because of their low freeboard. During the controversy over barbettes versus turrets, White had written to Admiral A. K. Wilson, a most knowledgeable man who had a great understanding of what was required in Her Majesty's ships to make them more efficient. Wilson was a no-nonsense character, liked by all, even though he voiced many scathing remarks on the condition of the Royal Navy in general. At a party in his honour, Queen Alexandra presented him with a gold tie-pin; Wilson said calmly, 'Sorry, I don't wear tie-pins.' On 10 November 1888 Wilson wrote to White saying:

'The adoption of the two separate redoubts as in the *Admiral*s instead of the armoured single citadel as in designs E and C no doubt effect a saving in weight, if you only consider the protection of the machinery within the turret and barbette, but it leaves the whole broadside open to penetration by light guns, and greatly increases the exposure of the armoured deck, and correspondingly the boiler rooms and machinery when the ship is rolling. By plating the whole side of the level up to the main deck with comparatively thick armour, the penetration of these parts of the ship by anything other than AP shells will be prevented, and if the plan of plating the level up to the main deck battery is carried out in 4in thickness, which I would

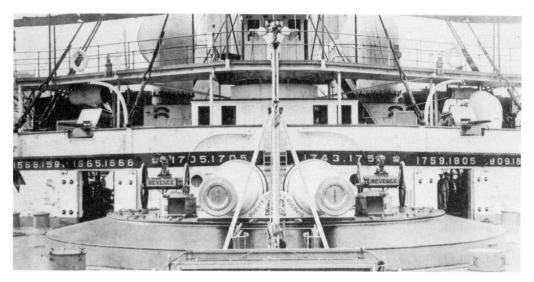

recommend, then the chance of shot penetration below the boiler/machinery, even when rolling would be small.

The matter could be determined over the course of a month with one of the *Admirals* and one of the turret ships in the Bay of Biscay. If the armoured citadel is adopted, I recommend that the un-armoured portion be reduced to a minimum and I submit that until actually tried, the effect of pene-tration of unarmoured parts at sea, we are not in a position to fairly consider the problem. My opinion is entirely in favour of the barbette; the saving in weight for the same height of guns is considerable.'

Armed with Wilson's reputable service opinion, White was able to sway the conclusions of the Board at the next meeting on 16 November 1888 in complete favour of the barbette system, especially as the lesser topweight in armour over the turret system, could enable the guns to be placed on a higher command, with consequently increased fighting efficiency of the guns in a sea-way.

The barbettes were pear-shaped to accommodate fixed loading positions at the rear. The bases were extended right down to the armoured deck, with the upper storey containing the turntable and the lower storey the hydraulic training gear, etc (*see* drawing). The arrangement finally selected was considerably superior to all other mountings of this type, and particularly in securing maximum broadside firing with minimum interference from the secondary battery.

During the meeting in August 1888, the secondary armament received extra-special atten-tion, and it was decided to adopt the 6in QF gun in place of the 6in BL of earlier ships, even though the new gun was still in the experimental stage. In the French cruiser *Dupuy de Lôme*, ordered in 1888, the armament of two 7.6in and six 6.4in were to be mounted in small single turrets, all on the upper deck, and White had originally proposed to carry the secondary armament of the *Royal Sovereign*s in the same way. This plan, however, was later rejected, on the grounds that training facilities would be provided by manual power with fixed armour protection and central pivot mountings.

The two deck system was adopted, and was so designed to secure minimum interference between main and secondary armaments, together with sufficiently wide spacing of guns to minimize mutual interference and simultaneous disablement of any number by a single hit. This arrangement

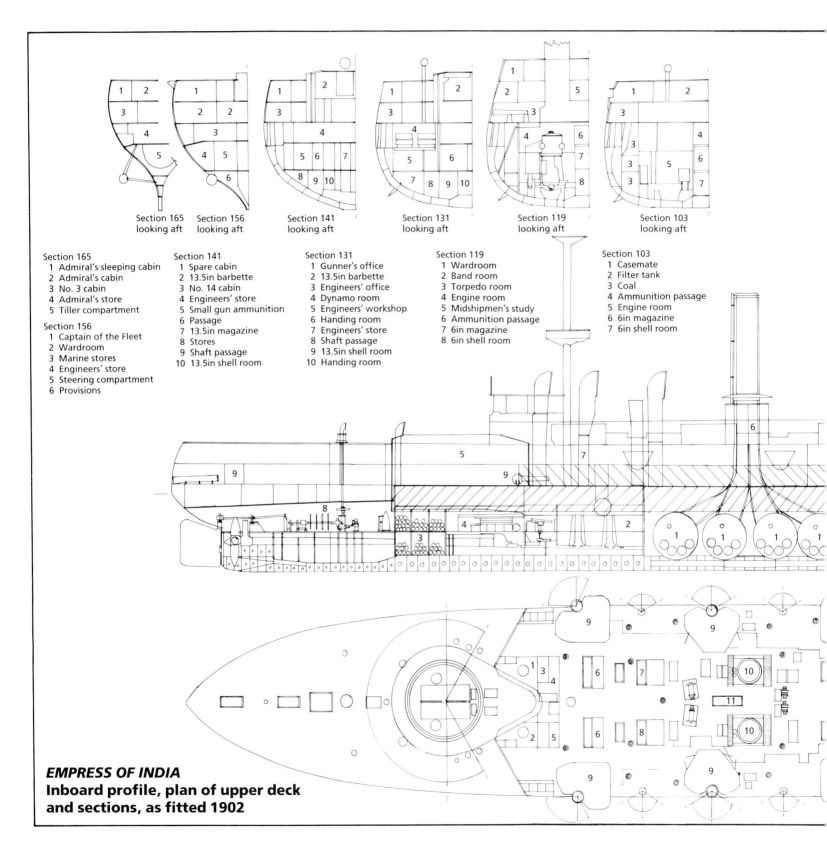

Section 165
looking aft

Section 156
looking aft

Section 141
looking aft

Section 131
looking aft

Section 119
looking aft

Section 103
looking aft

Section 165
1 Admiral's sleeping cabin
2 Admiral's cabin
3 No. 3 cabin
4 Admiral's store
5 Tiller compartment

Section 156
1 Captain of the Fleet
2 Wardroom
3 Marine stores
4 Engineers' store
5 Steering compartment
6 Provisions

Section 141
1 Spare cabin
2 13.5in barbette
3 No. 14 cabin
4 Engineers' store
5 Small gun ammunition
6 Passage
7 13.5in magazine
8 Stores
9 Shaft passage
10 13.5in shell room

Section 131
1 Gunner's office
2 13.5in barbette
3 Engineers' office
4 Dynamo room
5 Engineers' workshop
6 Handing room
7 Engineers' store
8 Shaft passage
9 13.5in shell room
10 Handing room

Section 119
1 Wardroom
2 Band room
3 Torpedo room
4 Engine room
5 Midshipmen's study
6 Ammunition passage
7 6in magazine
8 6in shell room

Section 103
1 Casemate
2 Filter tank
3 Coal
4 Ammunition passage
5 Engine room
6 6in magazine
7 6in shell room

EMPRESS OF INDIA
Inboard profile, plan of upper deck
and sections, as fitted 1902

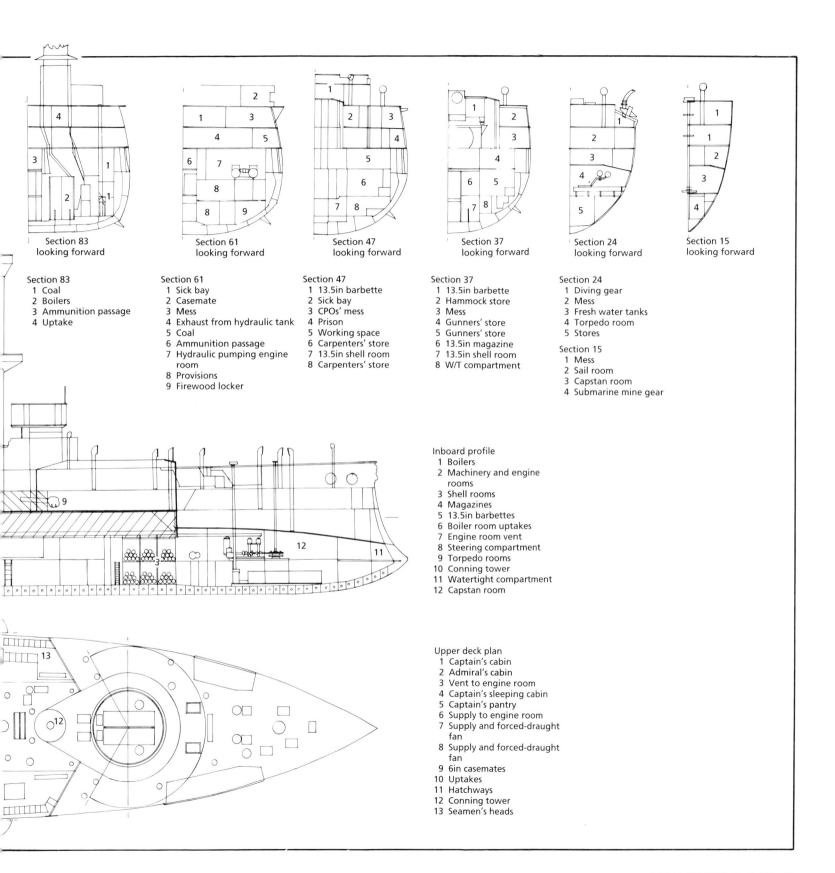

Section 83
looking forward

Section 61
looking forward

Section 47
looking forward

Section 37
looking forward

Section 24
looking forward

Section 15
looking forward

Section 83
1 Coal
2 Boilers
3 Ammunition passage
4 Uptake

Section 61
1 Sick bay
2 Casemate
3 Mess
4 Exhaust from hydraulic tank
5 Coal
6 Ammunition passage
7 Hydraulic pumping engine room
8 Provisions
9 Firewood locker

Section 47
1 13.5in barbette
2 Sick bay
3 CPOs' mess
4 Prison
5 Working space
6 Carpenters' store
7 13.5in shell room
8 Carpenters' store

Section 37
1 13.5in barbette
2 Hammock store
3 Mess
4 Gunners' store
5 Gunners' store
6 13.5in magazine
7 13.5in shell room
8 W/T compartment

Section 24
1 Diving gear
2 Mess
3 Fresh water tanks
4 Torpedo room
5 Stores

Section 15
1 Mess
2 Sail room
3 Capstan room
4 Submarine mine gear

Inboard profile
1 Boilers
2 Machinery and engine rooms
3 Shell rooms
4 Magazines
5 13.5in barbettes
6 Boiler room uptakes
7 Engine room vent
8 Steering compartment
9 Torpedo rooms
10 Conning tower
11 Watertight compartment
12 Capstan room

Upper deck plan
1 Captain's cabin
2 Admiral's cabin
3 Vent to engine room
4 Captain's sleeping cabin
5 Captain's pantry
6 Supply to engine room
7 Supply and forced-draught fan
8 Supply and forced-draught fan
9 6in casemates
10 Uptakes
11 Hatchways
12 Conning tower
13 Seamen's heads

was retained in the Royal Navy for the next decade or so. It afforded a wide distribution of guns, although the main deck location suffered from the disadvantages of low command and inability to fight the guns effectively in a sea-way; except in fine weather the gun ports in these positions had to be kept closed to avoid substantial flooding of the deck.

Following special firing experiments against the target ship *Resistance* during 1888–9, separate armoured casemates, designed by White, were provided for the main deck guns, and appeared in the *Royal Sovereign*s for the first time in the British Navy. The weight of the ten 6in quick-firing guns as mounted, together with the large ammunition supply provided, was approximately equivalent to that of twenty 6in BL guns, and exceeded by 500 tons the weight of the six 4.7in of the *Trafalgar* class.

The provision for this extra load, posed some problems within the design for White and his staff, but sacrifices were made elsewhere to allow for it.

ARMOUR

When the design first came under discussion in August 1888 it was generally agreed that the waterline belt should have the same relative length as in the *Trafalgar* class, but decisions on other details of protection were deferred pending consideration of designs embodying different arrangements of armouring which the DNC Department was preparing.

Three basic alternative systems of protection were subsequently considered by a special Committee appointed for the task in 1888, which would decide details, and evaluate on the basis of similar displacement, armament, speed and fuel capacity in each case. Each plan provided a waterline belt over approximately 65 per cent of the hull length with the same basic underwater protection. In other respects they differed as follows:

1. Single citadel turret types: Main armament in turrets standing at each end of a long armoured citadel extending the full width of the ship above the belt, and enclosing bases of both turrets. Citadel carried 11¼ft above the waterline with a flat armoured deck across the top. Maximum armour thickness on citadel and turrets, 14in and 15in respectively.

2. Separate redoubt plan: Each turret in a separate armoured redoubt with light armour above the belt

amidships, to 9½ft above the waterline. Armoured belt in this plan placed across top of belt. Maximum armour thickness on redoubts, sides and turrets, 17in, 5in and 18in respectively:

3. Separate redoubt barbette plan: Main armament in open barbettes with sides carried down to belt deck to form individual armoured redoubts. Light side armour amidships to 9½ft above waterline as in 2. Armoured deck across belt. Maximum armour thickness on barbette and sides, 17in and 4in respectively.

Compared with the single citadel, the separate redoubt arrangement provided increased protection to turrets and turret bases, and to the more isolated gun positions, and was preferred for this reason only. The barbette version was finally adopted on the grounds that it embodied the high freeboard considered essential for maintenance of speed and fighting efficiency—qualities which, in view of sea experience with preceding low freeboard types, were considered to outweigh the more complete protection to the guns afforded by closed,

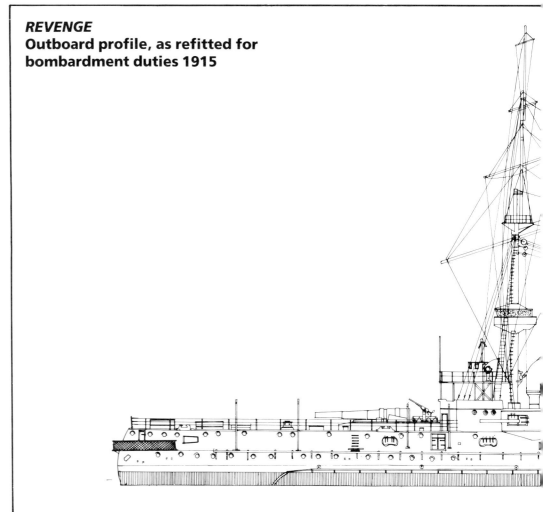

REVENGE
Outboard profile, as refitted for bombardment duties 1915

heavily armoured turrets. Because of the new method of application for the latest vessels it may be viewed as a subordination of armour protection to some extent, if compared to *Trafalgar*, but with special consideration given for the first time to protection of the secondary armament. In view of the development of medium-calibre shell performance, the new group of battleships as completed were actually better off than the *Trafalgar* class.

The thickness of the middle side armour above the main belt was determined from lengthy experimental firing tests carried out on the target ship *Resistance* during and after 1886, which indicated that at least 3in to 4in of the new improved quality armour then under preparation would provide adequate protection against modern medium-calibre shells. The Committee recommended, however, that if any weight became available in the design, it should be allotted to the belt to increase it to 5in. In the event, the extra weights that were available were taken up by the new secondary 6in guns, but the 4in Harvey as fitted (*Royal Sovereign* only, others were nickel steel) was given a steel skin of $^3/_8$in which brought it as near to 5in as possible—a solution which satisfied all concerned.

At an early stage White had it in mind that the thick armoured waterline belt, with light middle side armour above and flat armoured deck on top, might be abandoned in favour of a much wider medium thickness which would provide the same total armoured side, and could be topped off with a thicker sloping armoured deck. This early pro-

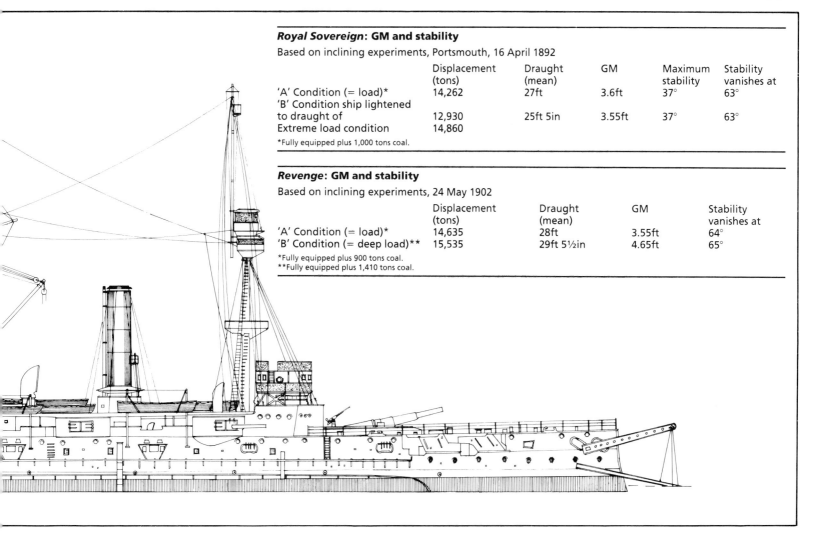

Royal Sovereign: GM and stability

Based on inclining experiments, Portsmouth, 16 April 1892

	Displacement (tons)	Draught (mean)	GM	Maximum stability	Stability vanishes at
'A' Condition (= load)*	14,262	27ft	3.6ft	37°	63°
'B' Condition ship lightened to draught of	12,930	25ft 5in	3.55ft	37°	63°
Extreme load condition	14,860				

*Fully equipped plus 1,000 tons coal.

Revenge: GM and stability

Based on inclining experiments, 24 May 1902

	Displacement (tons)	Draught (mean)	GM	Stability vanishes at
'A' Condition (= load)*	14,635	28ft	3.55ft	64°
'B' Condition (= deep load)**	15,535	29ft 5½in	4.65ft	65°

*Fully equipped plus 900 tons coal.
**Fully equipped plus 1,410 tons coal.

posal was not seriously considered by their Lordships who were certainly not prepared to sanction any considerable reduction in thickness of waterline armour.

As completed, the *Royal Sovereign* class were fitted with a main belt of 18, 16 and 14 inches, which ran for 250ft by 8½ft amidships. The upper edge was 3ft above the waterline, the lower edge 5½ft below. A thickness of 18in and 16in amidships between barbettes, with 14in abeam these. The belt bulkheads closed the forward and after extremities of the belt armour and were 16in thick forward and 14in aft. The upper side armour was 4in thick (¾in skin on top) and was 150ft by 6½ft in size, placed amidships above the main armoured belt, and running between the inner faces of the barbettes with the top edge 9½ft above water. The screen bulkheads were 3in thick and extended obliquely inwards from the forward and after extremities of the side armour to barbettes. The main deck was 3in and was placed flatly across the top of the belt. The lower deck at 2½in sloped at the ends from the forward and after ends of the belt to bow and stern respectively. The forward extremity was carried down to give some reinforcement to the ram bow.

Barbettes were 17in–16in–11in on the sides. The crowns were slightly above the upper deck level, with the bases on the middle deck at the top of the belt. They were 17in to 16in outside the screen bulkheads, and 11in uniform within these. There was a thin 1in steel roof plate partially covering the crown. The secondary casemates had 6in faces and sides, with 2in ammunition hoists for the main deck guns and 4in to the upper deck guns. The forward conning tower was 14in and 12in on the sides, with an 8in tube; the after conning tower was 3in with a 3in tube. Teak backing of 4in and 8in was placed behind the armour, and upper coal bunkers 10ft deep inboard behind the main belt also afforded extra protection. The lower coal bunkers were abreast the boiler rooms, extending upwards to the middle deck level.

Six-inch armoured casemates were provided for the main deck 6in guns. White wanted these for the upper deck 6in battery as well and wrote to the DNO in August 1900 about the possibility. A mock-up in *Revenge* at Chatham proved the idea impracticable. Topweight would be increased considerably, and the mountings were not easily adaptable; existing sights would have to be lowered or large holes cut in the casemate faces. The resultant 300-ton increase in displacement and reduction of GM from 3.6ft to 3.3ft was unacceptable to White. The Admiralty believed that the upper deck guns should be as unencumbered as possible so splinter shields only were provided—one of the major faults within the design. Provision was made, however, to enclose the end 6in guns (forward and aft) in casemates.

In October 1901 a proposal was submitted to rearm the class, substituting the 13.5in for the 12in; improved all-round loading was also considered. Moreover the First Sea Lord intimated that the changes might include some protection for the guns in the way of turrets. The matter seems to have received little attention, however, and was quickly dropped after the Controller saw the change as impracticable, and the new DNC, Philip Watts wrote to the First Sea Lord in July 1903 stating that it would mean too much cost, alteration and excessive topweight in ships that were almost ten years old. The matter was dropped.

MACHINERY

In the original design, provision was made to enable the ship to reach 15 knots with natural draught and 16.5 knots with forced draught as in *Trafalgar*, but it was subsequently found possible to raise this to 16 and 17.5 knots respectively without substantial increase in size and cost. When the design was under discussion, investigations were made as to the displacement and cost required to raise the speed to 17 knots natural draught, with a 30 per cent increase in coal supply, but as this was thought to be too extreme at that date, the idea was quickly abandoned.

The main machinery consisted of two sets of vertical, triple expansion engines driving twin screws. The cylinder sizes consisted of 40in (diameter) high pressure cylinders, 59in intermediate and 88in low pressure cylinders, with a stroke of 4½ft. There were eight single-ended, cylindrical return tube boilers located in four compartments, two each side of the centreline with ammunition passages between them. Each of the boilers had a working pressure of 155psi, a total heating surface of 19,560 sq ft, and a grate area of 700sq ft.

The machinery installation layout was similar to that of the *Trafalgar* class, but incorporated various improvements in detail. Reserve feedwater was introduced in this class while under construction,

Royal Sovereign class: Turning trials

	Ramillies (without bilge keels)	Royal Oak (with bilge keels)	Revenge (without bilge keels)	Revenge (with bilge keels)
Date	22 Aug 1893	12 March 1895		
Draught	24ft (mean)	27ft 11½in		
Tactical diameter:				
ahead at 14 knots	660 yards port	525 yards port		
	675 yards starboard	550 yards starboard		
ahead at 10 knots				456 yards port
				497 yards starboard
ahead at 8 knots	655 yards port	645 yards port	665 yards port	
	665 yards starboard	650 yards starboard	655 yards starboard	

and was made possible by utilizing some of the spaces within the double bottom of the hull.

Royal Sovereign was the first ship of the class to be completed, and as such was put through a lengthy series of steam trials which were studied very closely. Unfortunately the official records of these were not preserved apart from a few details. Only *Royal Sovereign* had her boilers forced to the design limit and consequently she achieved one of the highest recorded speeds. During full power trials at natural draught, which were run on the Stokes Mile stretch, she achieved 16.43 knots with 9,661ihp at 99rpm (mean) during the 8-hour trials, and 16.77 knots (mean) during the 4-hour trial. On the full-power forced-draught trials in the Channel, which were run in deep water when possible, she

Left: *Revenge.* Stern view, at Portsmouth dockyard, 1894. Note twin gaffs. *Inflexible* is moored ahead.

Below: Every year there were exhaustive sea manoeuvres when the combined Fleets exercised together – and what a wonderful sight it must have been. These photographs were taken during December 1900. The lower photograph shows *Royal Sovereign* and *Anson.* The upper photograph, *Royal Sovereign, Camperdown* and *Anson.*

produced mean figures of 18 knots with 13,360ihp at 106.3rpm on a displacement of 14,200 tons over a 3-hour period. During this trial, however, it was observed that sections of the boiler tubes were cracking under the pressure and were leaking as a result. It was subsequently decided that neither *Royal Sovereign* nor her sisters should be forced beyond 11,000ihp which would provide the boilers with a safety margin against similar breakdown.

While *Royal Sovereign* was on passage from Plymouth to Gibraltar the opportunity was taken to test her machinery and boilers over an extended period. The trial was run in fine weather over 72 hours, during which time she produced figures (mean) of 15 knots with 8,180ihp—an excellent result. When she left Plymouth her displacement was 14,650 tons at a draught of 28ft 6in and it was calculated that 484 tons of coal were consumed during the 72-hour run giving a consumption return of 1.84 pounds per hour/per hp—a record low for battleships which had never been equalled before. The ship also proved economical at cruising speeds, using only about 1 ton of coal per hour at 7.6 knots; the ihp for 10 knots was 2,500.

The class were the first British battleships to exceed 17 knots and at the time of completion were rated as the fastest such vessels in the world,

Below: *Ramillies* in 1903, prior to reconstruction when her upper deck 6in guns were placed in armoured casemates. All grey paintwork, W/T gaff to main, but retaining the old net shelf at this date, and shields fitted to upper quick-firing guns.

Right: *Revenge*, May 1903–May 1904. Note upper deck 6in guns now in casemates, small RF on bridge, no shields to upper QFs, masthead semaphore but she too still has the old upper deck net shelf in place at this late date.

although some foreign vessels showed paper speeds which equalled this figure.

Other units of the class achieved similar results to *Royal Sovereign*. *Empress of India* made 15.25 knots (natural draught); *Ramillies* 17.25 knots with 11,57ihp; *Repulse* 17.8 knots and *Royal Oak* a remarkable 18.27 knots with 11,608ihp. The majority of these trials were run in the load condition (14,050 tons).

APPEARANCE CHANGES

Without doubt they were the best-looking battleships to take the water since *Devastation* (1873) which had represented an initial attempt at pro-

ducing a seagoing battleship unobstructed by masts, rigging or superstructure. They were well proportioned and quite handsome with their high freeboard over the whole length, ram bow, cruiser stern and two tall, round, athwartships funnels.

As completed they were all very much alike, and difficult to tell apart. There were, however, minor differences in funnel detail, height of cowls and position of hawsepipes, etc.

Royal Sovereign: Low hawsepipes, no stay rim on funnels, bow scroll.
Revenge: One stay rim high and low.
Resolution: As *Revenge*.
Ramillies: Heavy set, high funnel caps (light caps

on other ships of class).
Repulse: High hawsepipes.
Empress of India: Very large, prominent bow scroll, low hawsepipes.
Royal Oak: Only unit with steam pipes abaft funnels, all others had them before. For steam pipe differences, *see* drawings.
1894–5 Bilge keels fitted in *Empress of India*, *Revenge*, *Royal Oak*, *Ramillies*, *Royal Sovereign* and *Resolution*. *Repulse* was fitted with hers prior to completion.
1899–1902 3pdrs removed from upper tops in all except *Empress of India* (retained until 1903–4). Shields removed from 3pdrs in lower tops. SL

removed from main deck and remounted port and starboard on each bridge. There was considerable variation in SL distribution in the class throughout this period. Wireless telegraphy fitted, W/T gaff to mainmast (1900). Bow scroll if fitted removed (1900). *Revenge* was used to carry out experimental colour schemes while serving in the Mediterranean, and for a short period was painted in a khaki and light-grey scheme.

1902–5 Above water broadside torpedo tubes removed in all. 3pdr in upper foretops in *Emperor of India* replaced by single searchlight (1903–4). Armoured casemates fitted to upper deck 6in secondary guns in all (1902–4). Net shelf lowered to main deck level to clear main deck 6in guns. Fixed maintopmast replaced by striking topmast (1904–5). Painting replaced by medium-grey. Early funnel bands were painted up, but these were usually Fleet markings and not used as vessel identification. *Empress of India*—2 dark bands, *Royal Sovereign* 1 dark.

1905–9 New fire control and rangefinding equipment fitted (1905–8). In *Revenge*, a new, square control top was fitted in place of the original upper foretop. Additional large top added below this. In others of the class, the original upper foretop was modified as the control top. There were various alterations in the number of light guns throughout the class, especially in the tops and superstructure, but generally all had been removed from the main deck level and tops by the end of 1909. One 24in SL added on platform below the control top in *Revenge* (1906). Stockless anchors fitted in *Revenge* during 1908–9. Forebridge SL remounted over forward upper deck casemates in *Empress of India* (1907). Torpedo nets removed in *Revenge* (1906). W/T gaff triced in *Revenge* (1907), in others 1907–8. Masthead semaphore removed from *Revenge*, in 1906, but in others from 1907 to 1908.

1910 After bridge removed in all except *Revenge*, leaving SL in wing platforms. Standard funnel bands painted up: *Royal Sovereign* three red on each;

Royal Oak two red on each; *Revenge* none; *Ramillies* one white on each; *Repulse* two white on each; *Resolution* three white on each; *Empress of India* none.

1912 13.5in guns in *Revenge* only were replaced by 10in for trial purposes while she was serving as gunnery firing ship. 13.5in were remounted in October 1912.

1914 *Revenge* was restored from disposal list in the autumn of 1914 for special bombardment of the Belgian coast. Her 13.5in guns were relined and reduced to 12in. Large bulges were added in 1915, which increased the guns' range by flooding one of the bulges and inclining ship farther than usual. Large rangefinder added over fore control top. 6in retained, plus some light QF. SL removed from mainmast, torpedo nets replaced. Yards removed from foremast, but retained on main. Strange camouflage painted over the whole of the ship (light-grey, dark-grey and white).

1915 Refit at Chatham, April to May. Became the first operational ship to be fitted with anti-torpedo bulges. Nets removed. Displacement increased to 16,011 tons (load), 16,720 (deep), with corresponding GM of 3.31ft and 3.19ft respectively. Special minesweeping gear fitted over bows. Camouflage painted out and bow wave added.

HISTORY: *ROYAL SOVEREIGN*

Built at Portsmouth Royal Dockyard under the financial provisions of the Naval Defence Act Programme of 7 Mar 1889, though originally included in the regular programme of the normal naval estimates for 1889–90. Laid down 30 Sept 1889; floated out of dock 26 Feb 1891. Queen Victoria performed the christening ceremony attended by her three sons, the Prince of Wales, the Duke of Edinburgh, and the Duke of Connaught. Her construction was accelerated as much as possible so as to gain experience of the design which might help the others of the class before they were completed.

Completed trials in May 1892 and commissioned at Portsmouth on 31st of that month to relieve *Camperdown* as Flagship, Channel Squadron.

May—13 Aug 1892 Flagship 'Red Fleet' taking part in annual manoeuvres off coast of Ireland.

27 July—6 Aug 1893 Again employed as Flagship, 'Red Fleet' in Irish Sea and Western Approaches.

June 1895 With British Naval Squadron attended opening of Kaiser Wilhelm Canal.

Below: *Ramillies* in 1913. Now quite obsolete and leaving Portsmouth after being sold by auction for £42,300 to an Italian firm by whom she was towed to Italy and scrapped.

With 'Fleet A' for annual manoeuvres in Irish Sea and off south-west coast of England during third week of July 1896.

7 June 1897 Paid off at Portsmouth, transferred crew to *Mars* which relieved her in Channel Squadron.

8 June Recommissioned to relieve *Trafalgar* in Mediterranean, but prior to departure took part in one of the largest Fleet reviews ever seen, for Diamond Jubilee of Queen Victoria at Spithead 26 June 1897.

7—11 July 1897 Took part in annual manoeuvres off coast of Ireland.

Sept 1897 Left England to join Mediterranean Fleet.

With Mediterranean Fleet until Aug 1902; recommissioned for further service on that station 13 May 1899.

9 Nov 1901 While in Greek waters, one of her 6in guns burst as a result of the breech not being properly closed; one officer, five marines killed; one officer, nineteen seamen injured.

On 9 July 1902 relieved by *London*, left Gibraltar bound for England, reaching Portsmouth 14 July.

30 Aug 1902 Commissioned as Port Guard Ship at Portsmouth for service in Home Squadron.

5—9 Aug 1903 Present during combined manoeuvres off coast of Portugal.

1903–4 Extensively refitted at Portsmouth.

1 Jan 1905 (officially) Home Fleet became Channel Fleet under new fleet reorganization scheme.

9 Feb 1907 Commissioned as Special Service Vessel in Reserve.

April 1909 Special Service Vessels of Reserve incorporated in 4th Division of Home Fleet.

Sept 1909 Paid off at Devonport into Material Reserve.

7 Oct 1913 Sold at auction to G. Clarkson & Co, London for £40,000. Later resold to GB Berterello, Genoa.

HISTORY: *RAMILLIES*

Built at Glasgow by J. G. Thompson and launched 1 March 1892. At so slight a tilt had she been constructed that it was only with the greatest of difficulty that she was made to take the water. She took one hour and twenty-six minutes to go down the slips, and her progress was so slow, that for some time it could not be measured by the naked eye. When she finally entered the water, pushed by rams and towed by tugs, most of the spectators had despaired of seeing her launched and long departed.

17 Oct 1893 Commissioned at Portsmouth as Flagship, Mediterranean Fleet.

28 Oct Left Spithead, arrived Malta 8 Nov to relieve *Sans Pareil*, which had been acting as Flagship since loss of *Victoria*.

9 Dec 1896 Recommissioned at Malta for further service on that station.

July 1899 Became private ship in Mediterranean Fleet, her place as Flagship taken by *Renown*.

12 Jan 1900 Hoisted Flag of Rear-Admiral Lord Charles Beresford as 2 i/c Mediterranean Fleet.

29 Sept—6 Oct 1902 Detained at Malta owing to illness of Rear-Admiral Watson; missed combined manoeuvres off Greece.

16 Oct 1902 Relieved as Flagship by *Venerable*, became private ship.

Aug 1903 Combined manoeuvres off coast of Portugal. Paid off from Mediterranean service into Portsmouth Reserve for refit at Chatham.

3 Jan 1905 Commissioned into Reserve at Chatham.

25 April 1905 Transferred crew to *London*; recommissioned next day with fresh nucleus crew for further service in Sheerness–Chatham Reserve Division.

30 Jan 1906 Transferred crew to *Albemarle*; recommissioned with fresh crew for further service with Chatham Reserve.

June 1906 Took part in naval manoeuvres of combined Atlantic, Channel and Reserve Fleets.

16 June During these operations collided with *Resolution*; stern damaged, propellers disabled.

6 Nov 1906 Transferred crew to *Africa*.

9 Mar 1907 Recommissioned in Special Service Division of Home Fleet at Devonport with reduced complement.

Oct 1910 Became Parent Ship in 4th Division, Home Fleet.

Aug 1911 Reduced to Material Reserve at Devonport.

July 1913 Stripped and laid up on Motherbank awaiting disposal.

7 Oct 1913 Sold at auction to George Cohen, of Swansea for £42,300. Later resold to an Italian firm and towed to Italy to be broken up in Nov 1913.

HISTORY: *ROYAL OAK*

Built at Birkenhead by Cammell Laird under the Naval Defence Act Programme of 7 March 1889.

29 Oct 1893 Arrived Portsmouth to be fitted out for sea trials. Completed trials June 1894.

14 Jan 1896 Commissioned for service in the Particular Service Squadron (soon renamed Flying Squadron) on its formation.

25 Nov 1896 Paid off from Flying Squadron on its disbandment, reduced to Fleet Reserve at Portsmouth.

9 March 1897 Commissioned at Portsmouth to relieve *Collingwood* in Mediterranean Fleet.

24 March Left Portsmouth, arrived Malta 5 April.

31 Mar 1899 Recommissioned at Malta for further service in Mediterranean Fleet.

7 June 1902 Paid off and relieved by *Bulwark*. Returned to England, arrived Portsmouth 6 June, proceeded soon afterwards to Chatham for a refit.

16 Feb 1903 Commissioned at Portsmouth for

service in Home Fleet, with nucleus crew of *Nile* which she relieved.

Summer 1903, Took part in annual manoeuvres in Atlantic by combined Channel, Mediterranean and Home Fleets, and Cruiser Squadron.

April 1904 With Home Fleet off Scilly Isles, she and *Revenge* struck sunken wreck, some bottom plates in both vessels dented.

9 May 1904 Hoisted Flag of 2 i/c Home Fleet, relieving *Empress of India*.

July and Aug 1904 Took part in manoeuvres for that year.

7 Mar 1905 Paid off at Portsmouth into Chatham Reserve, crew transferred to *Caesar*.

Following day, recommissioned with nucleus crew for service in Sheerness–Chatham Division of newly formed Fleet in Commission in Reserve at Home. On 11 May 1905 while under refit at Chatham, one workman killed, three injured in explosion caused by a naked light in gas and foul air in one of her compartments.

July 1905 Took part in Reserve Fleet manoeuvres.

On 17 Aug 1905 transferred crew to *Ocean*, recommissioned in Reserve at Chatham with fresh nucleus crew to serve as emergency ship.

12 June—2 July 1906 As unit of First Division, Blue Fleet took part in annual manoeuvres off coast of Portugal and eastern Atlantic (only member of her class present).

1 Jan 1907 Recommissioned in Reserve at Devonport with nucleus crew.

April 1909 Ships in Reserve at Devonport with reduced nucleus crews were formed into 4th Division, Home Fleet, on further reorganization.

June 1911 Relieved *Ramillies* as Parent Ship in 4th Division at Devonport; in Nov 1911 herself relieved by *Empress of India*.

Dec 1911 Paid off into Material Reserve.

August 1912 Towed to Motherbank by *Bellerophon*.

14 Jan 1914 Sold to T. W. Ward for £36,450 and broken up.

HISTORY: *REPULSE*

Commissioned at Portsmouth on 25 April 1894 for service in Channel Squadron, relieving *Rodney*; attached to Chatham.

Aug 1894 With 'Blue Fleet' took part in annual manoeuvres in Irish Sea and Atlantic.

July and Aug 1895 Took part in same manoeuvres.

19–24 June 1895 With British Squadron

attended opening of Kaiser Wilhelm Canal.

July Took part in annual manoeuvres as unit of 'Fleet A' in SW Approaches.

26 June 1897 Present at Spithead Review for Diamond Jubilee of Queen Victoria.

July 1897 Again took part in annual manoeuvres off southern coast of Ireland.

July and Aug 1899 Annual manoeuvres as unit of 'Fleet A' in Atlantic.

Aug 1900 The same, but with 'Fleet A1'.

4 Feb 1900 While leaving Sheerness driven by strong tide into barge anchored in fairway.

27 Oct 1901 While being towed to her moorings she was carried into the mud but refloated undamaged after two hours.

5 April 1902 Left England for Mediterranean Fleet.

Sept—Oct 1902 Annual manoeuvres with combined Channel and Mediterranean Fleets and Cruiser Squadron off coasts of Cephalonia and Morea.

29 Nov 1903 Left Malta for England, arrived Plymouth 10 Dec.

12 Feb 1904 Paid off at Chatham for extensive refit.

3 Jan 1905 Recommissioned in Reserve at Chatham.

6 June 1905 Recommissioned in Reserve at Chatham with fresh nucleus crew.

July 1905 Reserve Fleet manoeuvres.

24 March 1906 Again recommissioned in Reserve at Chatham.

27 Nov 1906 Transferred crew to *Irresistible*, recommissioned with fresh nucleus crew.

25 Feb 1907 Left Chatham for Devonport as special service vessel.

2 Aug 1910 Relieved of this duty by *Majestic*; Dec of that year to Portsmouth where she was paid off in Feb 1911.

11 July 1911 Sold to T. W. Ward for £33,500, subsequently broken up at Morecambe where she arrived 27 July 1911.

HISTORY: *REVENGE*

Laid down by Palmers on 12 Feb 1891, floated out 3 Nov 1892. Completed her sea trials March 1894, commissioned into Reserve at Portsmouth until Jan 1896.

14 Jan 1896 Commissioned at Portsmouth as Flagship of Special Flying Squadron organized as a result of the German Emperor's telegram to President Kruger and general European unrest following Jameson Raid in South Africa.

Flagship of this squadron from Jan 1896 until Nov of the same year. The squadron was held for ten months in readiness for any emergency and attached to the Mediterranean Fleet for a short period during mid-1896.

5 Nov 1896 Flying Squadron disbanded, *Revenge* paid off at Portsmouth. Recommissioned same day as 2nd Flagship Mediterranean Fleet, relieving *Trafalgar*.

Feb 1897—Dec 1898 Was unit of International Squadron sent to Crete to preserve order during the Greco-Turkish uprising.

April 1897 Major Bor landed with force of marines from *Revenge* to take over Fort Tzeddin.

Sept 1898 Sent to Candia to support British garrison following attack by Cretan insurgents and massacre of Christian inhabitants. Exacted reparations from Turkish authorities and saw last of Turkish troops expelled from Crete.

15 Dec 1899 Recommissioned at Malta for further

Top, left and right: *Redoubtable* painted in a one-off camouflage scheme. Note the AA gun on the forward barbette.

Bottom, left and right: *Redoubtable*; camouflage painted out (after April 1915) and sporting a false bow wave. Seen listing to increase the range of the 12in guns. Note the enlarged foretop, lower main top, tall topmast to main, and mine-sweeping equipment on bows (*see* drawing).

service with Mediterranean Fleet.

April 1900 Returned home having been relieved by *Victorious*; paid off into Fleet Reserve at Chatham.

18 April 1901 Commissioned at Chatham to relieve *Alexandra* as Coast Guard Ship at Portland, and as Flagship of Admiral Superintendent Commanding Reserves.

Early 1902 Under refit. Commissioned for service as Flagship, Home Squadron on its formation under the Fleet reorganization scheme of that year.

1 Jan 1905, Home Fleet became Channel Fleet.

July 1905 With Reserve Fleet for manoeuvres.

31 Aug 1905 Paid off at Portsmouth.

1 Sept 1905 Recommissioned in Portsmouth Reserve Division.

June 1906 Replaced *Colossus* as gunnery training ship at Portsmouth and as tender to *Excellent*.

13 June 1908 In collision with SS *Bengore Head* at Portsmouth.

7 Jan 1912 Broke from her moorings in Portsmouth Harbour during a gale and collided with new dreadnought *Orion*. *Revenge* damaged hull in several places.

October 1908 Carried out firing and explosives tests on *Edinburgh* with a new model 13.5in gun.

15 May 1913 Paid off as gunnery training ship, relieved by *Albemarle*, placed in Material Reserve. Laid up at Motherbank for disposal.

Sept—Oct 1914 Brought back into service and specially fitted out at Portsmouth for bombardment duties off coast of Flanders.

31 Oct 1914 Ordered to stand by at Portsmouth to relieve *Venerable* as Flagship.

4 Nov 1914 Ready for service with five 'Duncans' and formed new 6th BS of Channel Fleet (Special Service Squadron for projected attack on U-boat bases).

14 Nov 1914 Attack on U-boat bases abandoned owing to bad weather; with *Majestic* left Dover for Dunkirk.

22 Nov 1914 With *Bustard*, six British and four French destroyers and a French torpedo-boat, bombarded German troops off Nieuport.

22 Nov Recalled to Dover.

15 Dec 1914 With *Majestic* tried to locate German heavy guns which were giving trouble to British forces. Hit twice by 8in shells during this operation; second hit below waterline causing serious leak.

16 Dec Bombarded Flanders Coast again.

April to May 1915, Refit at Chatham, bulges fitted.

2–10 Aug 1915 Renamed *Redoubtable* to give name to new *Royal Sovereign* class dreadnought.

7 Sept 1915 During afternoon employed with a squadron bombarding Ostend and barracks at Westende from a position in the West Deep Channel. She then kept down German gunfire at Westende, in which she was assisted by the old gunboats *Bustard* and *Excellent*, all of which inflicted considerable damage to the enemy.

Oct to Dec 1915, Refit. Not recommissioned after refit; employed as accommodation ship at Portsmouth until Feb 1919.

Dec 1919 Placed on sale list; sold to T. W. Ward, Briton Ferry, for £42,750; later broken-up at Swansea.

HISTORY: *RESOLUTION*

Completed trials in Dec 1893, commissioned at Portsmouth for service with the Channel Squadron on 5th.

2–5 Aug 1894 with 'Fleet Red', in the annual manoeuvres in South-West Approaches.

9 April 1895 Recommissioned at Devonport for further service with Channel Fleet.

24–30 July 1896 With 'Fleet A', annual manoeuvres off SW coasts of England and Ireland.

18 July 1896 In collision with *Repulse*, sustaining slight damage to plating and keel.

26 June 1897 Present at Diamond Jubilee Fleet Review at Spithead.

29 July to 4 Aug 1899 With 'Fleet A', annual manoeuvres in Atlantic.

24 July to 3 Aug 1900, As unit of 'Fleet A2' in manoeuvres in SW Approaches.

Oct 1901 Paid off at Portsmouth and placed in Reserve.

17 Nov 1901 Recommissioned for service as coastguard ship at Holyhead.

8 April 1903 Paid off to dockyard reserve for refit.

5 Jan 1904 Commissioned for service as Port Guard Ship at Sheerness, relieving *Sans Pareil*.

20 June 1904 Transferred to Fleet Reserve at Chatham.

15 July 1906 Collided with *Ramillies* near Tongue Lightship during manoeuvres; slight damage.

1906 Refit at Chatham.

12 Feb 1907 Transferred to Special Service Division, Home Fleet, Devonport.

Feb 1907–Aug 1911 In this service.

8 August 1911 Paid off to disposal list, laid up at Motherbank.

2 April 1914 Sold to F. Rijsdijk for £35,650 and broken-up in Holland.

HISTORY: *EMPRESS OF INDIA*

Launched by Duchess of Connaught 7 May 1891, her name changed from 'Renown' prior to launch. Transferred from Pembroke to Chatham for completion and concluded her sea trials in September 1893.

11 Sept 1893 Commissioned at Chatham for service in Channel Fleet, relieving *Anson* as 2 i/c.

2–5 Aug 1894 Annual manoeuvres in Irish Sea and English Channel as unit of 'Blue Fleet'.

24 July to 30 Aug 1895 Annual manoeuvres.

June 1895 Represented British Navy at opening of Kiel Canal.

7 June 1897 Paid off at Chatham; recommissioned next day for service with Mediterranean Fleet. Present at Diamond Jubilee Fleet Review at Spithead before departing for Mediterranean Station.

Aug 1897 Arrived Malta.

Aug to Sept 1898, Unit of International Force preserving order during Greco-Turkish troubles.

24 Dec 1900 Recommissioned at Malta for further service on that station.

14 Sept 1901 Relieved in Mediterranean by *Implacable*.

12 Oct 1901 Paid off at Devonport; recommissioned following day for service as Port Guard Ship, Queenstown and Flagship, SNO Coast of Ireland, relieving *Howe*.

Early 1902 Extensive refit.

7 May 1902 Attached to Home Squadron as Flagship and as Flagship 2 i/c Home Fleet when cruising.

Sept 1905 Relieved of her duties by *Aeolus*.

Aug 1902 Present at Coronation Fleet Review (King Edward VII).

5 to 9 Aug 1903 Flagship, 'B Fleet' during combined manoeuvres of Home, Mediterranean and Channel Fleets off coast of Portugal, during which her port engine room broke down for 14 hours and she had to be left behind.

1 June 1904 Relieved by *Royal Oak* as 2nd Flagship, Home Fleet; became private ship.

22 Feb 1905 Relieved from Home Fleet by *Hannibal*; following day paid off and recommissioned in Reserve at Devonport, relieving *Barfleur* as Flagship, Rear-Admiral of newly formed Fleet in Commission in Reserve at Home.

1905–6 Refit at Devonport.

July 1905 Reserve Fleet manoeuvres.

31 Oct 1905 Recommissioned with fresh nucleus crew for same service.

30 April 1906 Collided with HM submarine *A10* submerged in Plymouth Sound.

Feb 1907 Reserve Fleet abolished and became Home Fleet, *Empress of India* continued as Flagship, Rear-Admiral, Devonport Division in new organization.

25 May 1907 Relieved as Flagship by *Niobe*.

28 May 1907 Recommissioned at Devonport as one of the Special Service vessels.

2 March 1912 Left Portsmouth in tow of *Warrior* to be laid up at Motherbank; collided with German barque *Winderhudder* and had to return to Portsmouth for repairs.

May 1912 Laid up awaiting disposal.

4 Nov 1913 Sunk as target off Portland by heavy shellfire at 7,000 yards' range.

HOOD

1889 ESTIMATES

DESIGN

When considering alternative designs for the *Royal Sovereign* class in November 1888, the low freeboard turret type, favoured by the First Sea Lord, Admiral Sir Arthur Hood, had been overwhelmingly rejected by the Design Committee in favour of the high freeboard, barbette plan greatly preferred by the DNC, William White. The advantages of the latter in respect of fighting efficiency in a sea-way were considered to outweigh the more complete protection to main armament that turrets would afford. It appears that with the single exception of Sir Arthur Hood, the Committee was unanimous in this respect, but pending practical experience of the new high freeboard type, and in concession to Hood's views, it was agreed that one of the first three ships to be laid down should carry the main armament in turrets, necessitating low freeboard forward and aft, to offset the additional topweight. The vessel was named after the Admiral.

As completed, her first sea trials showed that the reduced freeboard at the extremities and lower gun command made her a very qualified success compared to the *Royal Sovereign*, and distinctly inferior as a seagoing battleship type; all comparisons serving to vindicate the Design Committee's decision regarding the design of the high freeboard introduced in the *Royal Sovereign* group.

Hood was the last low freeboard battleship built for the Royal Navy, and the last British battleship to have the main guns mounted in circular turrets. The completely enclosed, armoured shield over the barbette (introduced in *Renown* and *Majestic*) was known as a 'barbette' for some years after its introduction, but gradually it became known as a 'turret', with the term 'barbette' referring only to the fixed armoured base.

Eventually, all enclosed shields or gunhouses, large or small, armoured or not, were known as turrets, the barbettes below these (where fitted) being referred to as turret bases.

In *Hood* the gun command was approximately six feet lower than in *Royal Sovereign*, which reduced fighting efficiency in a sea-way, but it was reported that she could fight her fore turret in a considerably stiff sea-way with moderate success. Furthermore, her 6in secondary guns amidships on the upper deck were found to be of little use owing to the reduced freeboard and were removed in 1904.

The number of 6-pounders was reduced from sixteen to eight as compared to *Royal Sovereign*, only four guns being mounted below decks. These four were carried in ports on the main deck forward and aft, but they were virtually uselesss because of the low command.

In service the ship had difficulty in reaching her norminal speed; she was actually about ½ knot slower than *Royal Sovereign* in smooth water. In moderate and rough weather this fell off rapidly

and placed her alongside the *Admirals*, *Sans Pareil*, *Victoria* and the *Trafalgar* class as regards seagoing performance.

Armour, machinery and armament were practically identical with that fitted in *Royal Sovereign*.

APPEARANCE CHANGES

Hood's appearance was generally similar to that of the *Trafalgar* pair, and owing to the rather large turrets forward and aft, gave a more formidable profile than *Royal Sovereign*.

Her funnels were slightly wider apart than in *Royal Sovereign* because of the central ammunition passage between the port and starboard boiler rooms.

A bow scroll was fitted as completed, striking topmasts stepped well clear ahead, with fixed topmast to main. Gaff on each mast and early-pattern mechanical semaphore halfway up mainmast as completed.

She was easily distinguishable from *Trafalgar* and *Royal Sovereign* groups by funnels equidistant from masts (closer to foremast in *Trafalgar*) and turrets as against barbettes in *Royal Sovereign*s.

1896 New type of masthead semaphore fitted to foremast, original on mainmast removed.
1897 One 3pdr mounted on each 13.5in turret top.
1899 Torpedo net shelf lowered to upper deck level to clear 6in gun blast.
1900 3pdrs in upper fighting top remounted in forward superstructure. Above water torpedo tubes removed. Main deck SL remounted on bridges. One additional SL on foretop. Bow scroll removed.
1902–3 6pdrs removed from main deck level, two remounted on superstructure, other two removed from ship. W/T gaff fitted on mainmast. Fixed topmast on mainmast replaced by striking topmast, stepped before.
1903–4 Victorian colours replaced by all-grey scheme.
1904 Upper deck 6in removed.
1905 3pdrs removed from forward superstructure.
1907–9 3pdrs removed from lower tops. W/T gaff triced (1908).

Left: *Hood*; fitting out at Chatham, 1893. The last low freeboard battleship built for the Royal Navy, built as a concession to the views of Sir Arthur Hood who favoured the type.

Left: *Hood*; port quarter as completed, 1893–4. She was every bit as powerful as the rest of the group, but was inferior in seakeeping qualities.

Bottom left: *Hood*; Often nicknamed the "'ood 'ave thought it?' In the autumn of 1896 she was stationed, for about six weeks, at Canea in Crete, and rendered splendid service in the cause of peace during the turmoil in the island (Greco-Turkish conflict).

Below: *Hood*, seen bow-on during Mediterranean service, 1901.

Hood: Particulars, as completed

Construction
Chatham DY; laid down 12 Aug 1889; launched 30 July 1891; completed 1 June 1893.

Displacement (tons)
14,780 (load), 15,588 (deep).

Dimensions
Length: 380ft pp, 410ft 6in oa
Beam: 75ft
Draught: 27ft 6in (mean), 28ft 6in max.
Freeboard: 11ft 3in forward, 17ft 3in amidships, 11ft 3in aft.

Armament
Four 13.5in 67ton BL
Ten 6in QF
Ten 6pdr
Twelve 3pdr
Seven 18in torpedo tubes (two submerged forward, one astern, four broadside above water).

Armour (Compound and nickel steel)
Main belt: 18in–16in–14in
Upper belt: 4⅜in
Bulkheads: 16in forward, 14in aft
Screen bulkheads: 3in
Decks: 3in–2in
Redoubts: 17in–16in–11in
Turrets: 17in–16in–11in–5in
6in Casemates: 6in
6in Ammunition hoists: 4in–2in
Conning tower: 14in–12in
Tube: 8in
After conning tower: 3in
Tube: 3in.

Machinery
Virtually identical with *Royal Sovereign*.

Ship's boats
Wooden torpedo-boats: one 56ft
Vedettes: one 56ft
Pinnaces (steam): one 40ft
Pinnaces (sail): one 36ft
Launches (steam): one 42ft
Cutters: two 30ft, one 26ft
Whalers: one 25ft
Gigs: one 30ft, one 28ft, one 24ft
Balsa rafts: one 14ft
Mail boats: one 18ft
Calculated life-saving capacity: 682 for crew of 690.

Searchlights
Five 24in: four in ports inside superstructure, two (P+S) forward and aft, one pair close before foremast, one close abaft mainmast.

Anchors
Three Martins, 115cwt
Two Martins, 55cwt
One 16cwt; 525 fathoms 2⁹⁄₁₆in cable.

Complement
690.

Costs
Estimated: £820,000
Actual: £849,252
Guns: £77,144
Hull (estimated): £749,000
Machinery, fittings and equipment: stores and first fittings: £11,000
Total: £926,396.

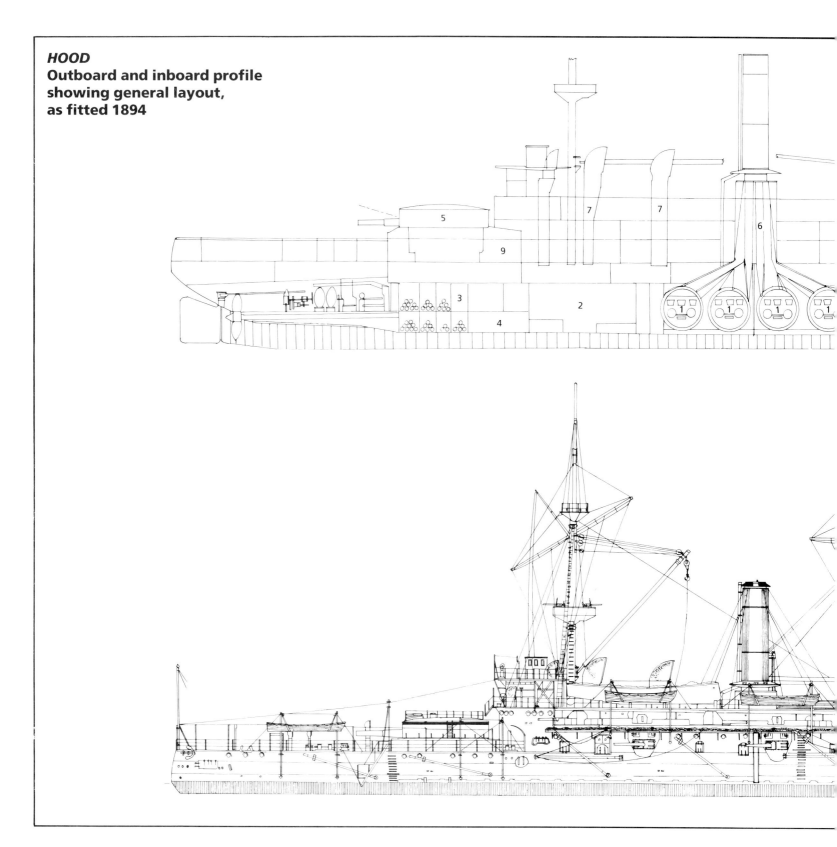

HOOD
Outboard and inboard profile showing general layout, as fitted 1894

5

9

3

2

4

7

7

6

1

1

1

1

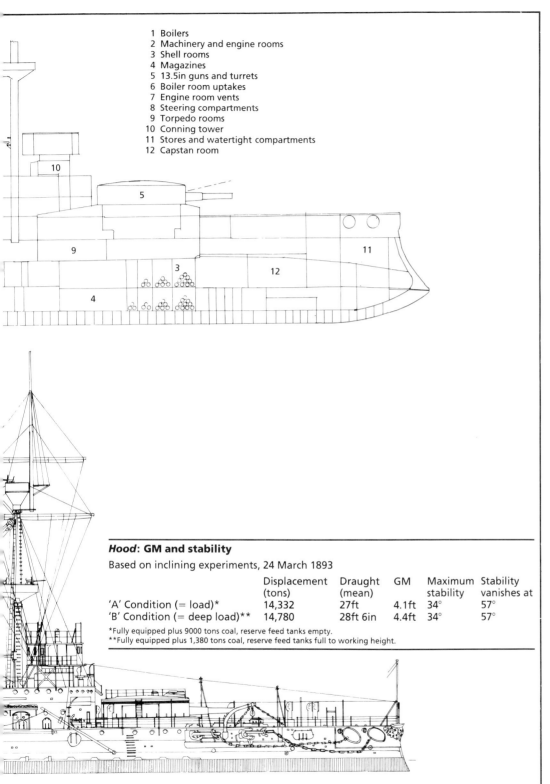

1 Boilers
2 Machinery and engine rooms
3 Shell rooms
4 Magazines
5 13.5in guns and turrets
6 Boiler room uptakes
7 Engine room vents
8 Steering compartments
9 Torpedo rooms
10 Conning tower
11 Stores and watertight compartments
12 Capstan room

Hood: GM and stability

Based on inclining experiments, 24 March 1893

	Displacement (tons)	Draught (mean)	GM	Maximum stability	Stability vanishes at
'A' Condition (= load)*	14,332	27ft	4.1ft	34°	57°
'B' Condition (= deep load)**	14,780	28ft 6in	4.4ft	34°	57°

*Fully equipped plus 9000 tons coal, reserve feed tanks empty.
**Fully equipped plus 1,380 tons coal, reserve feed tanks full to working height.

HISTORY: *HOOD*

Laid down at Chatham 12 Aug 1889, floated out 30 July 1891, the christening ceremony being performed by Viscountess Hood. Completed trials in May 1893 and commissioned at Chatham on 1 June 1893 for service with Mediterranean Fleet.

7 June 1893, while fitting out, a leak in her forward compartments was found. She was immediately docked for examination and the leak was found in the seams of two keel plates near the stem, the result of faulty riveting and a slight unevenness in the blocks at a previous docking which exerted excessive strain at this point. Damage was made good within two days and she was undocked on 9 June and left Chatham Dockyard on 12 June after being inspected by HRH the Duke of Edinburgh.

17 June 1893 Officially inspected by Vice-Admiral Sir Algernon C. F. Heneage, CinC at the Nore.

18 June Left Sheerness for Mediterranean, arriving Gibraltar 26 June. Left Gibraltar after coaling on 29th.

3 July Arrived Malta to relieve *Colossus*, having, owing to slight delay, just missed being present at the *Camperdown–Victoria* disaster.

Served with Mediterranean Fleet until April 1900; was a unit of international squadron preserving order during Greco-Turkish uprising in 1897–8.

29 April Paid off into Chatham Dockyard without relief; placed in Reserve until December 1900.

12 Dec 1900 Commissioned to relieve *Thunderer* as Port Guard Ship at Pembroke Dock.

End of 1901 Transferred to Mediterranean Fleet.

29 Sept—6 Oct 1902 Combined exercises of Mediterranean and Channel Fleets and Cruiser Squadron off coasts of Cephalonia and Morea.

4 Oct 1902 while on manoeuvres, fractured rudder on seabed while leaving Angostili Harbour. To Malta for repairs, then to England using her twin screws all the way.

5 Dec 1902 Paid off into Chatham for refit and repair. Transferred to Devonport for refit.

25 June 1903 Commissioned at Devonport for service in Home Fleet, relieving *Collingwood*.

5–9 Aug 1903 With combined Mediterranean, Home and Channel Fleets in annual manoeuvres off coast of Portugal as unit of 'Fleet B1'.

28 Sept 1904 Relieved from Home Fleet by *Russell*.

3 Jan 1905 Commissioned into Reserve at Devonport.

In Reserve until Feb 1907.

April 1909 Refitted and partially stripped at Devonport for service as Receiving Ship at Queenstown.

Sept 1910 Recommissioned for further service as Receiving Ship and Flag, SNO, Coast of Ireland.

Mar 1911 Towed to Portsmouth and placed on the disposal list.

1913–14 Used during first British experiments with anti-torpedo bulges. The tests were carried out in great secrecy and led to the fitting of bulges in later battleships and battlecruisers in the Royal Navy.

Nov 1914 Scuttled as blockship in south entrance of Portland Harbour, the wreck becoming known as 'Old hole in the wall'. Strangely, the Navy List for both Oct 1916 and Jan 1917 included her as being on the Sale List.

Hood: Legend weights (tons)

Water for 10 days	60
Provisions for 4 weeks	40
Officers' stores	25
Officers, men and effects	80
Masts and rig	70
Cables	98
Anchors	25
Boats	50
WO stores	50
Armament	1,720
Main machinery	1,050
Auxiliary machinery	55
Coal	900
Vertical armour on main belt	1,350
Horizontal armour	1,100
Protection to casemates	450
Teak backing	80
Turrets	1,490
Conning tower	90
Hull	4,750
Torpedo nets and booms	40
4% Board margin	530
Legend displacement	14,150

Top: *Hood* leaving Malta, 1898–9.

Bottom: *Hood* at Devonport, 1904. She had an inglorious end, being sunk as a blockship in Portland Harbour. On sinking, she turned turtle and broke her back before resting on the bottom with her keel awash.

CENTURION AND *BARFLEUR*

1890 ESTIMATES

DESIGN

The initiative to design the two second class battleships provided under the Naval Defence Act of 1889 had been under consideration at various times since that act was passed, but had been postponed until the building drawings and full specification had been completed for the first class battleships under the same programme (*Royal Sovereign*s). Moreover, the delay in proposals for these two was unavoidable owing to the very limited number of staff and extreme pressure of work imposed by the huge building programme then under way.

A meeting was held on 6 March 1889, attended by the DNC (White), the Controller and the DNO, to propose a provisional outline for the two second class battleships, and agree on approximate dimensions and particulars. Of primary importance was the requirement that the ships be designed with special regard to their employment as flagships on the China and Pacific Stations, able to match the most powerful foreign ships likely to be encountered (especially the large, Russian 8in-gunned armoured cruisers then appearing on the China Station). In order to navigate Chinese rivers a light draught was essential; a repeat of the cruiser *Imperieuse* (then serving on that station), which usually featured a draught of 27ft 3in, was to be avoided at all costs. Sir Vesey Hamilton subsequently stated that in his opinion a 26ft draught would be just permissable to navigate these waters safely and without difficulty.

Further discussions on that day paved the way for a design having a radius of operation not greater than that of *Imperieuse* (which carried 900 tons coal) and a speed superior to all first class battleships. The 10in guns were to be loaded and worked manually, with steam power for training. Because of the great number of men required for this, shield protection should be provided for the barbettes and guns.

Admiralty requirements, to which the outline design was initially drawn up, were:
1. Draught restricted to 26ft for navigation in Suez Canal and Chinese rivers.
2. Speed to be 16½ knots natural and 18 knots forced.
3. Radius of action to be the same as *Imperieuse*.
4. Cost to be 30 per cent less than that of *Royal Sovereign*.

On 9 March 1889 White wrote to R. E. Froude at the Admiralty Experimental Works, Haslar Gunboat Yard, Gosport, saying:

'With reference to our conversation two days ago, the full dimensions have been fixed upon providing for the new design (340ft x 63/4ft x 24ft 9in) and 9,200 tons. The form must be as such to reach our requirements with a centre of buoyancy which shall lie between 7 and 8½ feet abaft the middle of the length, and the height of the transverse metacentre (GM) above the centre of buoyancy (CB) should be between 14½ and 15ft. Will you be good enough to let me know, as early as convenient, your ideas as to the best form we can adopt under these conditions, together with a body plan, and an outside estimate of the HP for speed from 10 to 19 knots. If a model is necessary, please put in hand at once.'

Froude found it difficult to satisfy the demands of the Board, and told White that it was almost impossible to obtain the form he wanted on such

Centurion: Final legend, 17 February 1890

Displacement: 10,500 tons.
Length: 360ft
Beam: 70ft
Draught: 25ft 6in
Freeboard: 22ft forward, 17ft amidships, 19ft aft.

Armament
Four 10in
Ten 4.7in
Eight 6pdr
Nine 3pdr.

Armour
Belt: 12in–9in
Bulkheads: 8in
Casements: 6in–2in
Barbettes: 9in–8in–5in
Ammunition tubes: 1½in
Conning tower: 12in
Tube: 8in
Decks: 2½in–2in.

Weights (tons)
General equipment: 550
Machinery: 1,190
Armament: 895
Armour: 4,280
Coal: 750
BM: 370

9,000 IHP = 17 knots
13,000 IHP (forced) = 18½ knots.

dimensions. White increased the beam to 67.5ft and the corresponding draught to 24.75ft, and again, the following week, altered the dimensions to 345ft in length, 65ft beam and 23.5ft draught to achieve the body mould that was required. Finally, on 20 March, after much debate, Froude replied: 'Dear Mr White,
Very well, the 340ft x 67.5ft x 9,200-ton model was cast today, and I think that we had best defer any more alterations until we see what lines the model produces.'

On 30 August 1889 the early legend was agreed apart from the nature and arrangement of hull armouring (*see* notes) and other protective qualities, although the limitation on cost necessitated a reduction of 4,000 tons displacement from that of the *Royal Sovereign*, and the armament in the proposed design was correspondingly reduced from four 13.5in and ten 6in to four 10in and eight 4.7in, with belt armour reduced from 18in to 12in, and barbettes from 17in to 10in.

On 30 September 1889 protective deck layout was finalized and on 17 January 1890 casemates, barbettes and most of the armouring layout was agreed. On 24 February 1890 1/8in scale drawings were produced, submitted and approved, and on 28 April 1890 the sheer draught and midship section were sent to Portsmouth for construction to begin after further building drawings had been submitted for that purpose.

Initially the two vessels were well suited for their duties as cruiser squadron supports, and quite capable of dealing with the Russian cruisers they were intended to counter, but rising standards of cruiser speeds soon rendered them obsolete for this task, and they were otherwise only suitable for subsidiary employment. Their all-round qualitites were highly commended by Admiral E. R. Freemantle, while Admiral Sir John Hopkins expressed his opinion that: '*Barfleur* is indeed a model ship, except for her 4.7in guns.'

ARMAMENT

The 10in barbette mounting for *Centurion* and *Barfleur* was a new pattern, developed and produced by Whitworth while the design was still under discussion. It was exceptional in that a massive 35° elevation could be achieved (above 15° half charges had to be used, and a small piece of armour had to be unshipped from the upper part of the turret port to prevent the gun striking it on recoil).

The turntable was worked by a steam-driven engine, but arrangements for turning by hand were also provided. The engine had enough power to turn the guns and tables at one revolution per minute, which might seem slow by later standards but was adequate for the day. The steam and hand gear, however, proved unsatisfactory in service; the former could not arrest turning movement satisfactorily (liable to creep) while the latter was found to be completely inadequate.

No electric gear was fitted to the turntables. but some Siemens electric motors were provided in *Barfleur* as an experiment to elevate the guns. The later *Renown* was fitted with electric motors for elevation, working upper hoists from shell chamber to guns, and working shell hoists from magazine platform to shell chamber, which proved successful; so when these two came up for their big refit in 1901 they were both fitted with similar equipment. The electric elevating gear was capable of ranging from −7° to +35° in fourteen seconds.

All-round loading at any elevation was obtained by aligning the loading chamber below the gun platform and revolving with it. Ammunition was passed up a central tube and then taken up an incline to the gun breeches.

Four 10in Mk III 29-ton guns were provided. Their construction consisted of an A tube, over which were shrunk a 1B and a 2B tube, extending from the front of the chamber to the muzzle. At the

rear, the breech piece was shrunk into place, partly overlapping the 1B tube. In front of the breech piece, and over the 1B and 2B tubes the C tube and 2C hoop were shrunk. Around the breech piece, and a portion of the C tube, were shrunk the 1C hoop and trunnion hoop, interlocking longitudinally with the breech piece and tube. There was a 1D hoop shrunk over a 1C hoop at the breech, and the 2D hoop shrunk over the C tube, immediately in front of the trunnions. These guns were the first high-trajectory weapons of heavy calibre carried in the Royal Navy, and were seen as a big step forward in gun construction. They proved to be poor shooting pieces, however, with little value for the existing low battle ranges, and were generally disliked in service.

They were the largest hand-loaded guns in the British Navy at that date, and incorporated a very difficult breech mechanism. On the whole, they were much inferior to larger calibres and mountings.

The light secondary armament (4.7in) was the weak point in the design. The guns were ineffectual against armoured ships, and about 40 per cent of the main deck guns suffered from extremely low command and were difficult to fight in a sea-way.

These were the last British battleships completed with above-water beam torpedo tubes.

ARMOUR

When the design was first discussed on 6 June 1889, the arrangement of protection was to be similar to the *Royal Sovereign* class. No firm decision could be reached, however, owing to a lengthy debate with the DNC. He proposed three alternative arrangements:

1. A 12in thick waterline belt, with a flat deck across the top, and a light 4in upper side above this to the main deck.

2. Alternative arrangement providing the same displacement but with uniform armour (5in) from 5ft below the waterline to main deck level (about 10ft above) with a sloping uniform armoured deck (2½in) behind this.

3. Based on Admiralty proposals which combined a thick armoured belt, and light side armour with a sloping deck (as in 1 and 2) and involving a substantial increase of 300 tons in displacement.

White's proposal for a wide belt of uniform thickness with a sloping deck, instead of a thick belt with a flat deck with light side armour above

this, had been previously put forward by him for the *Royal Sovereign* class, and strongly pursued ever since. He stated his case:

'Regarding hull armour, attention to a suggestion made in my statement respecting the 1st class battleships. I would submit for consideration whether in the *Centurion* a more efficient protection might be secured by abolishing the thick waterline belt, substituting a stronger deck (curved as in *Blake*) for belt deck, and throwing the balance of weight into side armour of uniform thickness extending from the edge of curved deck up to the main deck over the same length as it is proposed to carry the thick armour. Assuming that the same total weight is appropriated to deck and side protection in each case, it is possible to have the arrangement as described.'

Unfortunately, the Board would have none of it; they did not approve of such a radical move and were not prepared, at that date, to sanction any reduction in armour thickness along the waterline.

For the first time in a British battleship lightly armoured shields were provided for the barbettes. This move had been initiated by the adoption of the alternative hand-training gear which necessitated the gun crews working above the top of the turntable, together with the fact that open barbettes had long been recognized as a weak point in the design of the *Admirals* and *Royal Sovereigns*. The shields did not afford complete protection for the crews

because the rears were left open to facilitate the working of the guns, but this was a respectable step towards the design of a better-protected and more efficient fighting ship.

Under the original (March 1889) proposals, all the 4.7in guns were to be carried on the upper deck with shield protection only, but in August the Board stipulated that four of them should be mounted in armoured casemates on the main deck, as in *Royal Sovereign*, although some naval authorities held that guns on an open deck, behind proper shields, stood a better chance against high-explosives than those between decks, even with armoured protection. Subsequent experience during the Sino-Japanese War of 1894–5 indicated, however, that thin shields had no real protective value at all, and frequently served to detonate projectiles which otherwise might have passed right across the deck without exploding (AP shells need to penetrate at least one inch before detonating).

As fitted, the main belt of *Centurion* was 12in–10in–9in–8in. The original length (225ft) was reduced to 200ft, by 7½ft amidships with the upper edge at middle deck level about 2½ft above the waterline. The lower edge was 5ft below waterline. The thickness of 12in–10in was between the inner faces of the barbettes and the 9in thickness was abeam these; the lower edge was 8in uniform thickness (all compound). Belt bulkheads were 8in and closed the forward and after extremities of the main belts. Upper side armour consisted of 4in plates (Harvey) 7ft 6in wide, run between the inner faces of the barbettes on top of the main strake about 10ft above the waterline.

Screen bulkheads of 3in (Harvey) extended obliquely inwards from the forward and after extremities of the side armour to barbettes. There was a 2in (mild) middle deck laid flat across the top of the belt and a lower deck of 2½in sloping from the forward and after citadel bases to bow and stern

respectively, below water at the ends. The barbettes extended down to the middle deck on top of the belt, and were 9in uniform thickness above the main deck before reducing to 8in below the outside screen bulkheads, and 5in inside these.

The new shields (nickel steel) had 6in sides and faces. As completed the secondary casemates had 4in faceplates and 2in sides to the main deck 4.7in guns only. The forward conning tower was 12in with an 8in tube; the after conning tower being 3in

Barfleur: GM and stability

Based on inclining experiments, 30 March 1894

	Draught (mean)	GM
'A' Condition (= load)*	25ft 7½in	4.35ft
'B' Condition (= deep load)**	26ft 8¾in	4.1ft

*Fully equipped plus 500 tons coal in upper bunkers, 250 tons in lower bunkers.
**Fully equipped plus 1,172 tons coal.

Centurion and Barfleur: Particulars, as completed

Construction
Centurion: Portsmouth DY; laid down 30 March 1890; floated out 3 Aug 1892; completed for trials Sept 1893; end of trials Feb 1894
Barfleur: Chatham DY; laid down 12 Oct 1890; launched 10 Aug 1892; completed trials June 1894.

Displacement (tons)
10,634 (load), 11,120 (deep), 12,213 (extreme deep).

Dimensions
Length: 360ft pp, 390ft 9in oa
Beam: 70ft
Draught: 25ft 7½in (mean) normal, 26ft 8¾in (mean) deep.

Armament
Four 10in 32cal
Ten 4.7in
Eight 6pdr
Twelve 3pdr
Two 9pdr boat and field guns
Seven MG
Seven 18in torpedo tubes, five above water, four beam one stern; two submerged (P+S) abeam fore barbette.

Armour
Main belt: 12in–10in–9in–8in
Side: 4in
Screen bulkheads: 3in
Barbettes: 9in–8in–5in
Turrets: 6in faces and sides (open backs)
Casemates: 4in faces, 2in sides
Forward conning tower: 12in
Tube: 8in
After conning tower: 3in
Tube: 2in
Decks: 2in middle, 2½in lower.

Machinery
Two sets 3-cylinder vertical triple expansion

engines, twin propellers
Boilers: eight cylindrical single-ended return tube arranged in four compartments, two each side of centre bulkhead. Arrangement similar to Royal Sovereign but no central ammunition passage.
Designed SHP: 9,000 = 17 knots natural draught, 13,000 = 18.5 knots forced draught
Fuel: 750 tons coal normal, 1,440 tons max. (Centurion 1,420 tons)
Coal consumption: approx. 10.5 tons per hour at 9,000shp (full normal power)
Radius of action: 5,230nm at 10 knots.

Ship's boats
Torpedo-boats: one 56ft
Pinnaces (steam): two 40ft
Pinnaces (sail): one 36ft
Launches (steam): one 42ft
Admiral's galley: one 32ft
Cutters: two 30ft, one 26ft
Whalers: one 25ft
Gigs: one 30ft, one 24ft, one 18ft
Mail boats: two 16ft
Balsa rafts: one 14ft.

Searchlights
One 24in high on main mast. Searchlight equipment, as completed, was considerably smaller than in contemporary first class battleships.

Anchors
Three improved Martins type 105cwt, two 30cwt, 525 fathoms of 2⅜in cable.

Complement (estimated)
606 January 1891
620 1895
600 1903.

Costs
Centurion £540,090
Barfleur £533,666.

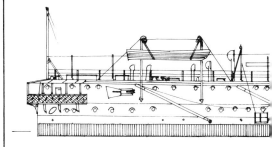

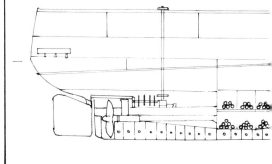

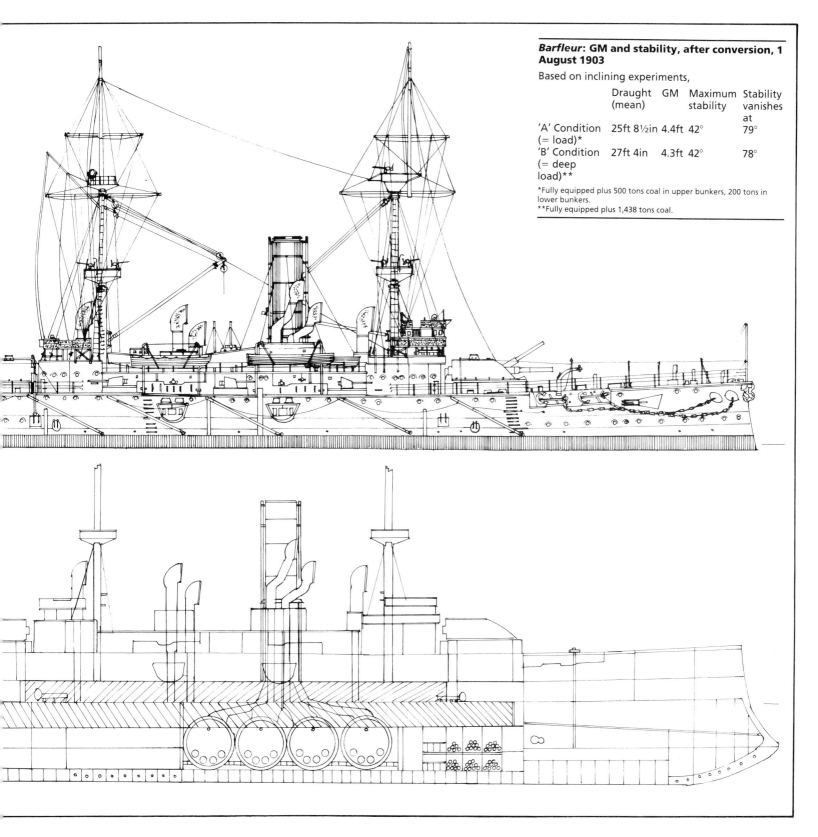

Barfleur: GM and stability, after conversion, 1 August 1903

Based on inclining experiments,

	Draught (mean)	GM	Maximum stability	Stability vanishes at
'A' Condition (= load)*	25ft 8½in	4.4ft	42°	79°
'B' Condition (= deep load)**	27ft 4in	4.3ft	42°	78°

*Fully equipped plus 500 tons coal in upper bunkers, 200 tons in lower bunkers.
**Fully equipped plus 1,438 tons coal.

with a 3in tube. The armour was backed up with 9in–6in of teak behind the main belts, with coal bunkers on each side affording some extra protection abreast the boiler and engine rooms.

MACHINERY

The basic installation was identical with that of the *Royal Sovereign* class; a designed 9,000shp for 17 knots with natural draught, and 18.5 knots with 13,000shp at forced draught.

The boilers were eight single-ended, cylindrical return tube boilers arranged in four compartments, two each side of the centre-line bulkhead. The arrangement was similar to that in *Royal Sovereign* except that there was no central ammunition passage between port and starboard boiler rooms; the absence of this enabled the funnels to be more closely paired.

They were nominally 1 knot faster than *Royal Sovereign*, and with the exception of the Italian *Sardegna* and *Lepanto* classes, were the fastest battleships in the world on completion.

In service both proved excellent steamers, capable of maintaining a steady sea speed of 17 knots, and often making more. This made them very popular when on foreign service, but the overshadowing fact that they were generally regarded as second class battleships always seemed to ignore this feature.

On preliminary sea trials, they were not pushed as hard as *Royal Sovereign* had been during her first

---

Barfleur and *Centurion*: Steam trials

No figures have survived in 'Covers' but 'Engineering' gives the following:

Barfleur: 9,934shp 17.1 knots (8 hours' natural)
Centurion: 9,703shp 17.05 knots (8 hours' natural)

Barfleur: 13,163shp 18.54 knots (4 hours' forced)
Centurion: 13,214shp 18.51 knots (4 hours' forced)

Continuous sea speed: 15.1 knots.

---

trials. It was not thought necessary given the ample power provided for the boiler/machinery installation, and their ability to reach their designed speed without too much effort.

APPEARANCE CHANGES

As completed, the two *Centurion*s presented quite a different appearance from the *Royal Sovereign* class. Their much lighter and smaller proportions, together with more closely spaced funnels, shields over main guns, bow scroll, and no stern walk, gave them a unique profile. They were easily distinguishable from *Renown* by their upper deck 6in guns in shields instead of casemates, open upper deck amidships, smaller upper top on the foremast and noticeable cowl differences.

It was also quite easy to distinguish one from the other by the bow scrolls (lion emblem in *Barfleur*, Roman soldier in *Centurion*). They were the last British battleships, apart from the Chilean *Triumph* and *Swiftsure*, to have bow crests. *Barfleur* had one

---

pair of cowls abeam the funnels and these were of the regular shape. *Centurion*, however, had irregular-shaped cowls (*see* drawings) abeam the funnels, and they were slightly smaller in size.

1896–99 Bilge keels added to hull in *Centurion* at Hong Kong (1896–7). Shields removed from guns in tops (1897–9). Masthead semaphore fitted to foremast in *Barfleur* only (early 1897).

1899–1901 Some 3pdrs removed from tops in *Centurion*.

1901–4 Both vessels were extensively reconstructed. These modifications followed a report submitted by Captain J. R. Jellicoe (C/O of *Centurion*) to the effect that the fighting value of both ships would be materially increased by the substitution of 6in guns for the 4.7in and the removal of the above water torpedo tubes. Moreover, the poor boat-handling times afforded by the main derricks had been recorded in Sept 1898 and on many other occasions. In one particular incident when raising a ship's boat at sea just off Wei-hai-wei at time of 13 to 14 minutes was logged. This was not only too slow, but in a seaway, downright risky. Jellicoe suggested that this feature needed rectification.

The refit took from 1901 until 1904 and resulted in the following:

1. 4.7in guns replaced by ten 6in 45cal in 5in KC casemates; four (two port, two starboard) on upper deck, six (three port, three starboard) on the main deck amidships.

2. The 3pdrs ex upper and lower foretops remounted in superstructure and on barbette shields.

3. Above water torpedo tubes removed.

4. Four 24in SL added (two on bridge, two close abreast on after superstructure).

5. Net shelf deck lowered to main deck level to clear upper 6in guns.

6. After bridge removed and majority of ventilator cowls replaced by windsails.

7. W/T fitted (gaff on mainmast).

8. Wooden military foremast replaced by new steel mast shorter than original fitting and without any tops.

9. Fixed topmast on mainmast replaced by striking topmast, stepped before.

10. New engines fitted for driving derrick winching gear.

11. Masthead semaphore fitted on mainmast in both ships.

Below: *Centurion*, paying off at Portsmouth from the China Station in August 1901, after which she was placed in Fleet Reserve.

Bottom: *Centurion* 10 November 1903, leaving for another commission on the China Station after being refitted 1902–3. her 4.7in were replaced by 6in fitted in casemates.

12. Bow scrolls removed, ships painted all-grey. New material added in reconstruction, 430 tons; material taken out, 352 tons. Net gain 78 tons.
1905 Topmast fitted to signal mast (tall in *Barfleur*, short in *Centurion*).
1906 Military top on mainmast modified as fire control position and 3pdrs removed. W/T gaff triced.
1908 Masthead semaphore removed.
No visible changes after 1909.

HISTORY: *CENTURION*

Ran trials from 19 Sept 1893 until Feb 1984.
14 Feb 1894 commissioned at Portsmouth to relieve *Imperieuse* as Flagship, China Station.
2 March 1894 Sailed for eastern waters; arrived Port Said 15 March, Singapore on the 11th. Here she met *Imperieuse* and flag was transferred after which she sailed to Hong Kong, arriving 21 April 1894.
June 1896 Grounded on sandbank while visiting Simonoseki, but refloated without damage.
1 April 1897 Recommissioned at Hong Kong for further service as Flagship, China Station.
1897–1900 Engaged in Allied operations in North China during Boxer Rebellion.
From 31 May 1900 her landing parties with Naval Brigades stormed Taku forts and relieved Tientsin legations.
10 April 1901 At Shanghai, lying in Woosung Roads during a gale, parted cables and drifted across bows of *Glory*. Holed below waterline, but not seriously damaged and repaired at Hong Kong.
10 June 1901 Relieved as Flagship by *Glory*.
3 July Left Hong Kong; arrived Portsmouth 19 Aug 1901.
19 Sept Paid off into Reserve.
Sept 1901 – Nov 1903 Reconstructed and partially rearmed at Portsmouth.
3 Nov 1903 Commissioned at Portsmouth for service on China Station.
10 Nov Left Portsmouth; reached Malta on 17th, Port Said on 25th, Aden 6 Dec, Colombo on 15th, Singapore on 27th and Hong Kong on last day of the year. On ratification of Anglo-Japanese Alliance in 1905, the China Squadron was reduced and all battleships were withdrawn.
7 June 1905 In company with *Ocean* left Hong Kong for home. At Singapore joined by *Albion* and *Vengeance*. The four ships left Singapore on 20 June and arrived at Plymouth on 2 Aug 1905.
25 Aug 1905 Paid off at Portsmouth but

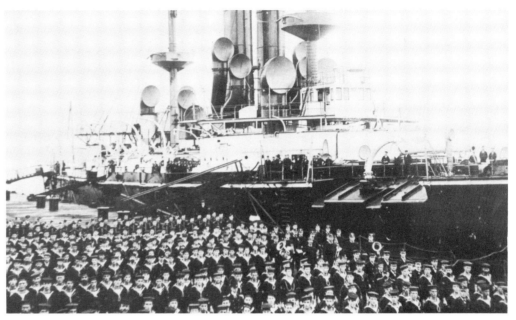

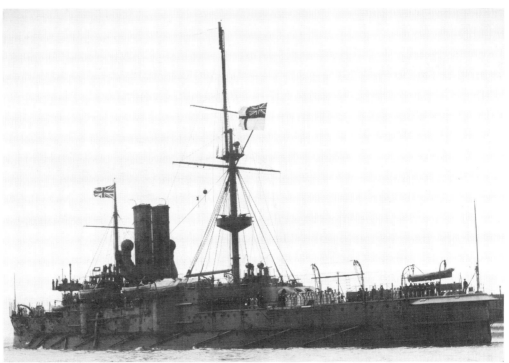

Below: *Centurion* in Chatham dockyard in the summer of 1903. Bow view showing new rig.

Opposite page, top: *Barfleur*, after refit at Devonport. Gone is the foremast and fighting tops, replaced by a light single pole with one yard. Note that all but two cowls have been removed.

Opposite page, bottom: *Barfleur* entering Portsmouth Harbour while serving with Portsmouth Division, Home Fleet during the summer of 1905.

recommissioned the following day with nucleus crew for service in Portsmouth Division of Reserve Fleet.

June 1906 Took part in combined manoeuvres with Atlantic, Channel and Reserve Fleets.

24 May 1907 Transferred crew to *Exmouth*; following day recommissioned with fresh crew for service as Special Service Vessel in Portsmouth Division of Home Fleet.

1 April 1909 Paid off at Portsmouth and placed on the sale list. At the end of June she was taken to Motherbank and moored to await disposal.

12 July 1910 Sold to T. W. Ward for £26,200.

4 Sept 1910 Arrived at Morecambe where she was broken up.

HISTORY: *BARFLEUR*

Completed for trials in June 1894, and commissioned at Chatham on 22 June for service in the Fleet Reserve. In July she was temporarily commissioned at Chatham to take part in the annual manoeuvres during July and August.

1 Sept 1894 Paid off into Reserve.

26 Feb 1895 Commissioned at Chatham for service with Mediterranean Fleet.

19 Mar Left UK; arrived Gibraltar 23 Mar to relieve *Sans Pareil*.

27 July 1895 Arrived Malta after being stationed at Gibraltar and working-up there.

15 Feb 1897 Assisted at Allied occupation of Candia (Crete); took part in operations during blockade of Turks in that island.

6 Feb 1898 Left Malta for China, to which station she was first lent, and afterwards transferred because of trouble in Far East.

4 Mar 1898 Arrived Singapore where she took *Fame* and *Whiting*, en route for China, under escort and with them sailed for Hong Kong.

1 Oct 1898 Recommissioned at Hong Kong and relieved *Grafton* as Flagship, 2 i/c on China Station.

1899–1900 Took part in Allied operations in North China during Boxer Rebellion.

31 May 1900–Sept 1900 Present at storming of Peking forts and Tientsin legations.

Sept 1900 Relieved as 2 i/c China Station by *Albion*.

11 Nov 1901 Left Hong Kong for England; arrived Plymouth 31 Dec 1901.

22 Jan 1902 Paid off at Devonport for extensive refit (new guns, etc.).

May 1904 Placed in Reserve.

18 July 1904 Temporarily commissioned to take

Below: *Barfleur* at Portsmouth, 1905–6. Note new air vents behind mast, and tall topmast to main.

Bottom: *Barfleur*, early 1907. She became Flagship of Rear-Admiral, Portsmouth Division in 1905, but was paid off on 4 March 1907 when she turned over the duties to *Prince George*.

Opposite page, top: *Renown* as completed July 1897. The last second class battleship built for the Royal Navy, she was an enlarged and improved *Centurion*.

Opposite page, botom: *Renown*, from the quarterdeck, showing 10in turret, guns and after bridge. The motto: 'England expects that every man will do his duty' (Lord Nelson's famous signal) appears on scrolls above the turret.

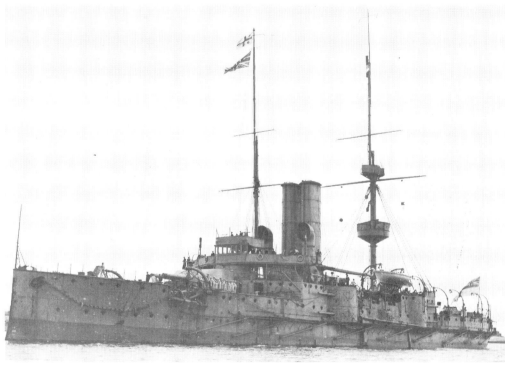

part in annual manoeuvres.

5 Aug Collided with *Canopus* in Mount's Bay, slightly damaged.

8 Sept Paid off at Devonport on conclusion of manoeuvres.

Feb 1905 Refit completed.

21 Feb 1905 Completed with full crew and sailed to recommission *Vengeance* on China Station.

30 Mar Met *Vengeance* at Colombo and exchanged crews.

7 May 1905 Arrived back at Portsmouth and paid off on the 9th.

10 May 1905 Recommissioned with nucleus crew for service as Flagship, Rear-Admiral Portsmouth Division of Reserve Fleet.

At about this time, the RNVR began sending parties of men for periods of sea training in ships of the Reserve Fleet, and during a cruise in June 1905 *Barfleur* carried six officers and 105 men of the London Division.

28 Nov 1905 Recommissioned with nucleus crew for same service, her old crew being drafted to *Duncan*.

June 1906 Took part in annual manoeuvres.

20 Sept 1906 Recommissioned with fresh nucleus crew. At the end of 1906 the Reserve Fleet was abolished and a new Home Fleet with an improved system of nucleus crews was organized. *Barfleur* became Flagship, Rear-Admiral Portsmouth Division of the new formation.

4 Mar 1907 Paid off after being replaced as Flagship by *Prince George*.

5 Mar Recommissioned with nucleus crew as Parent Ship of Special Service Vessels in Portsmouth Division, Home Fleet.

Reorganization of Home Fleet in March 1909 saw the Special Service Vessels becoming part of 4th Division, Home Fleet. A few weeks later (April) *Barfleur* ceased to act as Parent Ship.

June 1909 Paid off at Portsmouth and soon afterwards removed from active list. Towed to Motherbank to await disposal.

July 1910 Sold to C. Ewen of Glasgow (£26,550). Resold to Hughes Bolcklow, on the Tyne.

5 Aug 1910, while being towed up Tyne to scrappers, became jammed between piers of swing bridge at Newcastle, making it impossible to close bridge and holding up all road traffic. When some of her deck fittings had been cut away, she was released and was able to continue her journey to Blyth to be broken up.

RENOWN

1892 ESTIMATES

DESIGN

The basic design of *Renown* represented an enlarged and improved *Centurion* type; 1,850 tons heavier, with the same main armament, a more powerful and better protected secondary battery, modified arrangement of hull armouring with stronger all-round protection, about the same nominal speed and a considerably larger radius of action.

The original 1892 construction programme provided for three battleships (*Majestic* class) to carry a new model 12in (50ton) gun then in hand. In the spring of that year, however, it became apparent that this gun would not be ready for some time; commencement of two of these ships was temporarily postponed and it was decided (because of the urgent need to maintain continuity of employment at Pembroke Dockyard) to replace the third by a smaller, 10in gunned ship. It would seem that the vessel's construction stemmed from force of circumstances rather than from a deliberate policy.

The decision to build the smaller type was in fact strongly influenced by the views of the Controller (Rear-Admiral J. Fisher) and Captain Cyprian Bridge (Director of National Intelligence). At that time Fisher favoured the 'lightest practicable big gun and the heaviest secondary gun' as the ideal battleship armament, while Bridge was a strong advocate of moderate dimensions. During the early months of 1892, a proposal to substitute similar ships for the other two *Majestics* of the original programme was suggested and seriously considered (Fisher favoured a class of six), but it was rejected on the grounds that, although comparing satisfactorily in secondary armament, protection and speed with any of the battleships then building for foreign powers, the main armament was too weak for battlefleet work, and there was no pressing demand for more second class battleships to reinforce cruiser squadrons; for which purpose they constituted, in any event, a somewhat expensive luxury.

The Controller asked the DNC (White) to prepare a suitable design for an improved *Centurion* armed with four 10in, ten 6in and eight 12pdrs. In April 1892 White submitted to their Lordships three basic sketch designs for approval:
1. 13,050 tons, 29ft 11in draught and 1,500 tons coal capacity.
2. 12,750 tons, 27ft 5in draught and 1,200 tons coal.
3. 12,350 tons, 26ft 9in draught and 800 tons coal.

Within a few short weeks, the Board had decided, almost unanimously, to adopt plan 3 and on 11 April asked the DNC to prepare full plans for the vessel. White quickly appointed his trustworthy assistants, Narbeth, Beaton and Dunn, to be responsible for the design, and work began immediately.

During the early months of 1892, however, there were setbacks to the design, owing to non-agreement over the ship's armouring; a suitable compromise was reached, (*see* armour section) but construction progressed at a very slow pace indeed, and it took almost four years to complete against an average of about thirty months for the larger *Majestic* class ships.

Innovations within the design as completed comprised:

1. General use of Harvey armour in place of compound nickel or plain steel.
2. Adoption of sloping armoured deck behind main belt, instead of flat deck across the top of this.
3. Provision of closed armoured shields over the barbettes and armoured casemates for all secondary guns.

On completion, the ship turned out very well, being the same length (pp) as *Royal Sovereign*, with 3ft less beam and hull lines correspondingly finer. She was 1,850 tons heavier than *Centurion*, with an increase of 20ft (pp) in length, 2ft more beam and 9in draught. Her freeboard was 2½ft lower forward, and 1ft aft at normal load, and her bottom was sheathed and coppered for foreign service.

She handled well and was a good sea-boat, although somewhat lively in a sea-way.

During her first cruise, Captain Moore wrote (18 July 1897) to the Controller (Fisher) saying:

'Gun and torpedo practice went well, and most satisfactory but I feel doubtful as to the power of command with the casemates, and controlling the fire in action. We had a knot in hand of *Majestic* at full speed but I doubt for averaging more than 14 knots on our passage over. She certainly is a grand ship, and a pleasure to handle, the only difficulty being the lack of ventilation to the citadel deck.'

A glossier account (15 June 1898) came from Commander Moggridge to Captain Moore on *Renown*'s performance:

'The *Renown* has justified and improved on the promise she made on manoeuvres; her lines must be perfect. For seaworthiness and handling qualities I have never seen anything like her. She is the first man-o-war I have seen going astern with the wind before the beam. We left Burmuda last time, drawing 28ft 3in aft, and she was not a bit sluggish.'

As was the case with *Centurion*, *Renown*'s ability to operate effectively with cruiser squadrons declined somewhat rapidly with the rising standard of cruiser speeds and, being too lightly armed for battlefleet work, she was relegated to subsidiary service after an active career of less than ten years, this being shorter than any previous British battleship's with the exception of *Lord Clyde* (1866).

ARMAMENT

The main armament (four 10in) was disposed as in *Centurion*, but the gun command was slightly

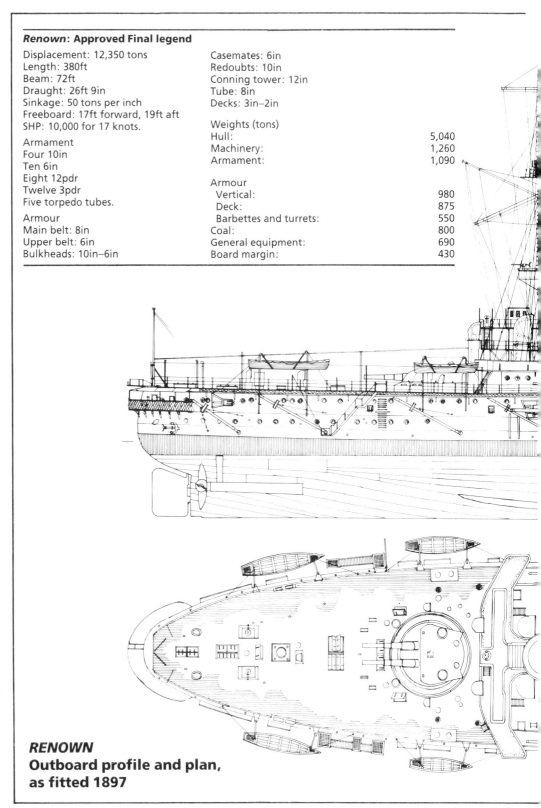

RENOWN
Outboard profile and plan,
as fitted 1897

Renown: Approved Final legend

Displacement: 12,350 tons	Casemates: 6in
Length: 380ft	Redoubts: 10in
Beam: 72ft	Conning tower: 12in
Draught: 26ft 9in	Tube: 8in
Sinkage: 50 tons per inch	Decks: 3in–2in
Freeboard: 17ft forward, 19ft aft	
SHP: 10,000 for 17 knots.	

Armament
Four 10in
Ten 6in
Eight 12pdr
Twelve 3pdr
Five torpedo tubes.

Armour
Main belt: 8in
Upper belt: 6in
Bulkheads: 10in–6in

Weights (tons)	
Hull:	5,040
Machinery:	1,260
Armament:	1,090
Armour	
Vertical:	980
Deck:	875
Barbettes and turrets:	550
Coal:	800
General equipment:	690
Board margin:	430

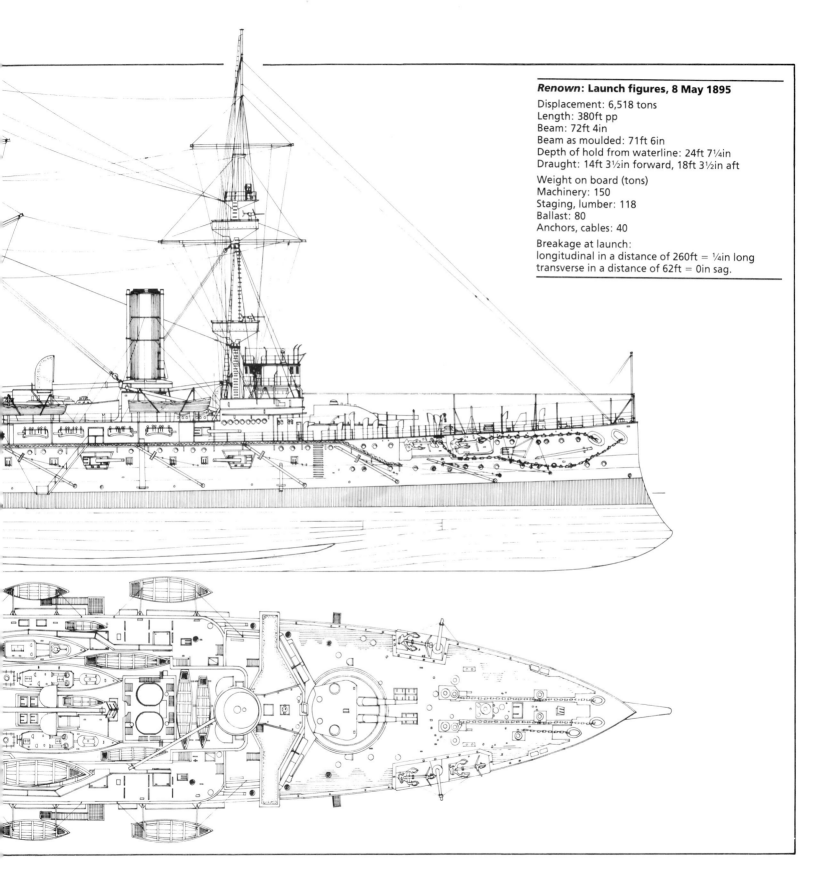

Renown: Launch figures, 8 May 1895

Displacement: 6,518 tons
Length: 380ft pp
Beam: 72ft 4in
Beam as moulded: 71ft 6in
Depth of hold from waterline: 24ft 7¼in
Draught: 14ft 3½in forward, 18ft 3½in aft

Weight on board (tons)
Machinery: 150
Staging, lumber: 118
Ballast: 80
Anchors, cables: 40

Breakage at launch:
longitudinal in a distance of 260ft = ¼in long
transverse in a distance of 62ft = 0in sag.

from that in *Royal Sovereign* and *Centurion* (as completed) in that 60 per cent of the guns were placed on the main deck, with the remainder on the upper deck. This meant that more than half of the battery had been cursed with a considerably low command (about 14ft above waterline) and consequently suffered from sea spray in anything other than calm weather.

Anti-torpedo armament was improved over all preceding classed by the adoption of the 12pdr QF in place of the 6pdr. An enclosed anti-torpedo battery was provided on the upper deck amidships by carrying the bulwarks up to the level of the 6in casemates at each end, with a narrow strip of deck overhead. Eight 12pdrs were mounted on this, firing through ports cut in the bulwarks. The 12pdr was subsequently retained as the principal anti-torpedo weapon in all later classes, up to and including *Dreadnought* (1905). They upper deck battery for these remained a feature in all ships prior to the *Lord Nelson* class, although in the *Duncan*, *Queen* and *King Edward VII* classes, the bulwarks were omitted.

Torpedo armament was slightly reduced from seven to five tubes, as compared with the two previous classes, the above water beam tubes being suppressed and submerged beam tubes increased from two to four. This reduction in the number of above water tubes was due, largely, to the difficulty of providing adequate protection against a torpedo being hit and exploding while still in the tube.

In 1903 consideration was given to a proposal to rearm *Renown* in a number of alternatives:

A. Four 10in to be replaced by a new, more powerful 10in as in *Triumph*.
B. Two 12in single guns (1 forward, 1 aft).
C. Renew all 6in guns.
D. Replace six 6in with six 7.5in on main deck.
E. Replace ten 6in with ten 7.5in.

When these alternatives had been carefully considered, all were rejected:
A, accepted in principle, but not worth the effort; B, not worth cost of alteration; C, no objection, but not done; D, not worth alteration; E, far too cramped, and not worth the effort.

ARMOUR

The armouring of *Renown* had been planned largely with a view to providing increased protection against the developing threat of attack

lower, arcs of fire approximately 30° wider, and loading end-on only instead of all-round.

Because of the difficulties experienced in *Centurion*'s turrets, hydraulic training and electric motor and elevating equipment was fitted instead of steam power, but the loading was still manual in an end-on position; she was the last British battleship to have this feature.

As in *Centurion*, closed armoured shields were fitted. Unlike *Centurion*, it had been planned to fit protection to the whole of the turret, but problems of weight distribution caused *Renown* to complete

with open-backed turrets; backs were fitted *c.* 1903–4.

Because of the large unarmoured areas in contemporary foreign battleships, which were open to attack by medium-calibre, high-explosive shells, the ship was given a powerful secondary armament, as in the *Royal Sovereigns*, this being the same as in those ships despite the considerably smaller displacement. It was a great deal more powerful than the 4.7in guns of *Centurion*, viewed by many as a retrograde step in modern battleship design. The arrangement of the secondary battery was different

Right: *Renown* painted white overall. In November 1902 she was detached from the Mediterranean Station, having been selected to take the Duke and Duchess of Connaught on a visit to India. The cruise lasted until 1903 when she returned to Portsmouth on 27 March as seen in photograph. Note the Royal Standard.

by medium-calibre, high-explosive projectiles. Armoured thickness was reduced along the waterline in order to provide extra thickness to the middle side above the belt, where the greatest number of hits was likely to occur. Greatly improved armouring methods (Harvey) allowed reduction of the really thick belts of the previous classes (18in and 12in, etc.). The principal innovations in protection were:

1. General use of Harvey steel in place of compound, nickel or plain steel.
2. Reduction in relative thickness of belt armour, with increase of protection to upper strakes, associated with sloping armoured deck behind belt, instead of flat deck on top of this.
3. Provision of armoured shields on main guns, and armoured casemates for all secondary guns.

Harvey armour had been used previously in *Royal Sovereign* and *Centurion*, but to a limited degree, and only for thicknesses below six inches. *Renown* was the first British battleship in which it was extensively adopted, and in which its superior resistance materially influenced the general scheme of protection. Reduction in thickness of belt as compared with *Centurion*, was easily offset by the improved quality of the armour and, backed by the 3in sloping deck, was estimated to present a deflecting resistance equal to 6in of vertical armour.

The length of unarmoured ends outside the

citadel was 10ft greater than in *Centurion*, but it was estimated that with either or both extremities flooded, the ship would still have adequate freeboard with only slight loss of manoeuvrability. The estimated sinkage with both ends completely flooded was 17 inches which still left 8 feet of armoured freeboard. Speed in this condition, however, would depend entirely on the nature of the damage inflicted.

The sloping deck, as fitted, adhered to in the British Navy for many years and widely copied abroad, had originated in a desire to provide a deck

protected cruiser with some degree of vertical armour, and had appeared for the first time in the *Leander* class cruisers (1880). In conjunction with a wide belt of medium thickness, it had been previously put forward by White for both *Royal Sovereign* and *Centurion*, but not approved, the Admiralty, at that date, being unwilling to sanction any reduction in the massive thick vertical armoured belts then being applied to HM warships. The edges of the flat section of the armoured deck were extended across to the sides by shell plating, with the triangular spaces below this

---

Renown: Particulars, as completed

Construction
Renown: Pembroke DY; laid down 1 Feb 1893; launched 8 May 1895; completed Jan 1897.

Displacement
11,690 (load), 12,865 (deep).

Dimensions
Length: 380ft pp, 412¼ft oa
Beam: 72ft 4in
Draught: 25ft 4¼in (load), 27ft 3½in (deep).

Armament
Four 10in 40cal Mk IV BL; 105 rpg
Ten 6in Mk II QF; 200rpg
Twelve 12pdr (12cwt); 200rpg
Two 12pdr (8cwt)
Eight 3pdr; 500rpg
Seven 0.45in MG
Five 18in torpedo tubes, one above water at stern, four submerged on beam (P+S).

Armour
Main belt: 8in–6in

Belt bulkheads: 10in–6in
Screen bulkheads: 6in
Casemates: 4in upper, 6in lower
Barbettes: 10in
Turrets: 6in faces
Conning tower: 9in, 1½in tube
After conning tower: 3in
Decks: 3in–2in.

Machinery
Two sets 3-cylinder vertical triple expansion engines, twin propellers
Boilers: eight cylindrical single-ended return tube, four furnaces to each boiler
Boiler house length: (four in all) forward 40ft, aft 40ft
Engine room length: 44ft
Designed SHP: 10,000 = 17 knots natural draught, 12,000 = 18 knots forced draught
Fuel: 800 tons coal normal, 1,890 tons max.
Radius of action: 6,400nm at 10 knots.

Ship's boats
Pinnaces (steam): two 56ft, one 40ft
Pinnaces (sail): one 36ft
Launches (steam): one 40ft
Cutters: three 30ft
Whalers: one 27ft
Gigs: one 30ft, one 28ft, one 24ft
Skiff dinghies: one 16ft
Balsa raft: one 13ft 6in.

Searchlights
Two 24in: one high on each mast.

Anchors
Three 110cwt, two 35cwt Martins approved type, two 13cwt Admiralty; 575 fathoms 2⅜in cable.

Complement
651–674 (1903)
638 (1905)
604 (1907).

Costs
£751,206.

providing a watertight flat on each side which could be filled with coal or water.

Overall protection to the main armament was improved over all preceding classes except *Centurion*, and these shields became known as turrets. After *Majestic* had been completed, it was mentioned that it would be possible at a later date to fit backs to the turrets of *Renown*. The proposal was put before the DNC and Controller who saw little objection if it was thought desirable, but it was not carried out until 1903–4.

In general protection was subordinated to speed, on the grounds that the ship (like *Centurion*) was not normally intended to engage anything more powerful than heavy cruisers. The percentage of armour displacement was actually slightly below acceptable battleship standards, and was even a little less than in *Centurion*. However, the extensive use of Harvey armour, together with improved arrangement of hull armouring, gave all-round protection that was thought to compare favourably with any battleships then building for European powers, and stronger than in *Centurion* despite reduced armoured thickness on belt and barbettes.

As completed her main belt was 8in to 6in, 210ft by 7½ft in size. The upper edge was at middle deck level, the lower edge 5 feet below the waterline at normal load. The 8in thickness was over machinery and boiler spaces amidships, with 6in elsewhere. The 10in and 6in belt bulkheads extended obliquely inwards from the extremities of the belt armour to the barbette faces. The upper 6in strake ran 180ft x 6¾ft between the inner faces of the barbettes from the top of the belt to the main deck (9ft 3in above waterline). The 6in screen bulkheads extended obliquely inwards from the side armour to the barbettes.

The middle deck (protective) was 2in on the flat, and 3in on inclines, and ran from barbette to barbette. The crown level was at the top of the main vertical strake (2½ft above waterline) with the lower edge at the ship's side along the lower edge of the belt, about 5 feet below waterline. Angle of incline was approximately 45° from slope to side.

The 3in lower deck curved down towards the forward and after bases of the ship's ends and was located below the waterline.

Barbettes were 10in uniform, and turrets were given 6in faces, 3in sides and 1in roof. Casemates on the upper deck were 4in on faces and sides, with 6in face and sides for those located on the main

RENOWN
Inboard profile and upper deck plan, 1897

***Renown*: Fuel consumption trials**

18 April 1896, 30 hours
Steam pressure (mean): 137psi
Revs (mean): 88.6rpm port; 85rpm starboard
SHP (mean): 3,044 port; 3,143 starboard
Max. speed: 15.3 knots
Coal consumption: 1.88lb per ihp.

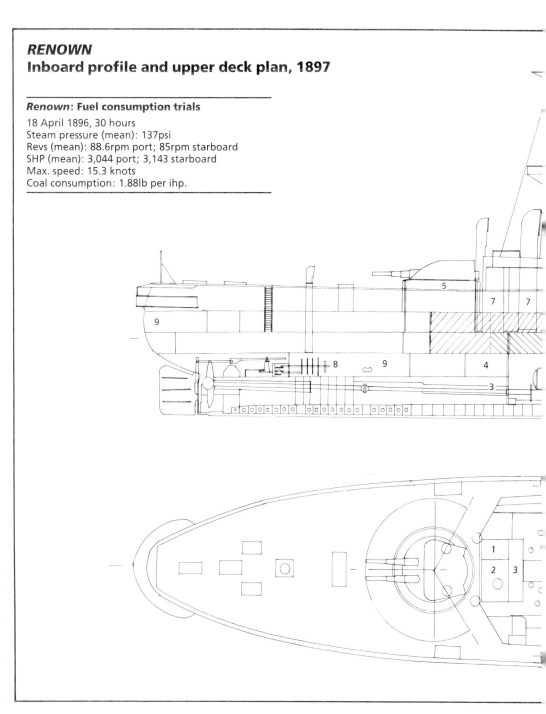

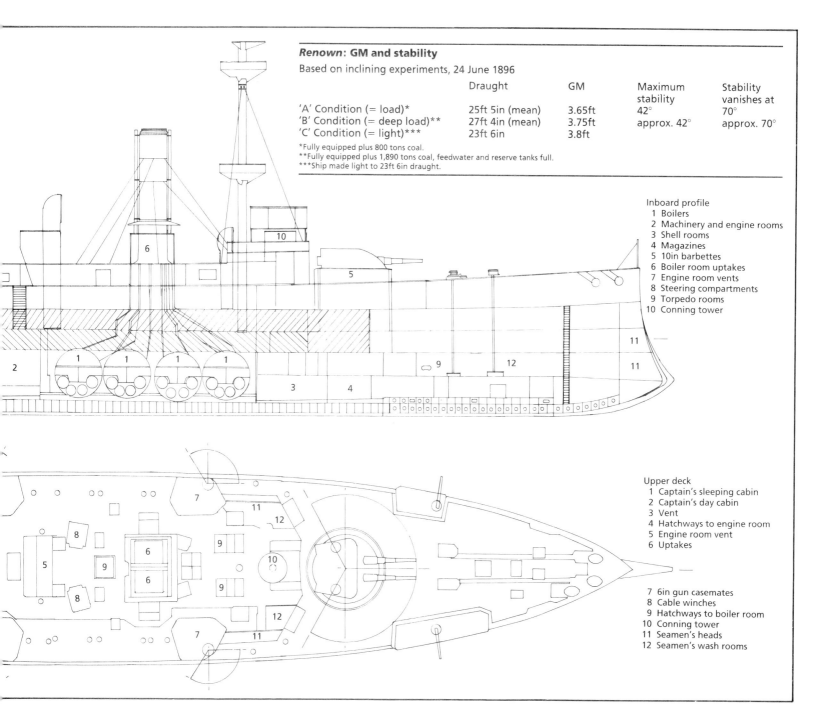

Renown: GM and stability

Based on inclining experiments, 24 June 1896

	Draught	GM	Maximum stability	Stability vanishes at
'A' Condition (= load)*	25ft 5in (mean)	3.65ft	42°	70°
'B' Condition (= deep load)**	27ft 4in (mean)	3.75ft	approx. 42°	approx. 70°
'C' Condition (= light)***	23ft 6in	3.8ft		

*Fully equipped plus 800 tons coal.
**Fully equipped plus 1,890 tons coal, feedwater and reserve tanks full.
***Ship made light to 23ft 6in draught.

Inboard profile
1 Boilers
2 Machinery and engine rooms
3 Shell rooms
4 Magazines
5 10in barbettes
6 Boiler room uptakes
7 Engine room vents
8 Steering compartments
9 Torpedo rooms
10 Conning tower

Upper deck
1 Captain's sleeping cabin
2 Captain's day cabin
3 Vent
4 Hatchways to engine room
5 Engine room vent
6 Uptakes

7 6in gun casemates
8 Cable winches
9 Hatchways to boiler room
10 Conning tower
11 Seamen's heads
12 Seamen's wash rooms

deck level. The mantlet to stern torpedo tube was 6in–3in. The forward conning tower was 9in with 1½in tube; the after conning tower had 3in plates and 1½in tube.

Renown: Steam trials

25 March 1896
8-hour natural power
Displacement: 12,471 tons
Oil pressure: 146psi
Revs (mean): 97.85rpm
IHP: 10,780
Speed: 17.91 knots

11 June 1897
Revs (mean): 97.7rpm
IHP: 10,028
Speed: 17 knots

4-hour full power
Displacement: 12,901 tons
Oil pressure: 150psi
Revs (mean): 104rpm
IHP: not recorded
Speed: 18.75 knots.

MACHINERY

Two sets of three-cylinder, vertical triple expansion engines driving twin screws. Eight cylindrical, single-ended boilers, arranged back to back in four compartments, two each side of centre-line bulkhead. Four furnaces to each boiler, and the boilers had a working pressure of 155psi.

The boiler room arrangement was practically identical with that of *Royal Sovereign*, necessitating the same twin funnel plan, but because of the absence of a central ammunition trunk (passages) between port and starboard boiler rooms, the funnels could be closer together—a feature which was fitted in the following *Majestic* class.

With a designed shaft horse power of 10,000 (normal) the ship easily reached her designed speed (17 knots). Her engine room registers showed that the machinery always performed most satisfactorily, and without any special attention other than boiler tube renewal.

Renown was always an excellent steamer in service, but she had some troubles early on when experiments with her propeller blades were being conducted, as shown by a letter from the Engineer A. D. Watson, who wrote to Admiral J. A. Fisher on 26 July 1897:

'Dear Sir John,
I should have written to you before this on the performance of the machinery during manoeuvres, had I not been aware of your absence abroad. There appears to be a distinct loss of speed for the same power and revolutions when compared with the original trials, which I put down to at least ½ knot. The only altered conditions are that of the new blades (thicker), but they do have the same pitch and diameter as the old ones, and we have a clean bottom.'

APPEARANCE CHANGES

An exceptionally good-looking vessel, with marked flare to the bows which rose up from the forward turret, made possible because of the longer forecastle which had not been practicable in *Royal Sovereign* or *Centurion*. *Renown*'s hull lines were extremely fine; the funnels were closely spaced, no bow scroll, enclosed upper deck amidships and two large military tops on the foremast with one low on the mainmast, made her one of the most graceful-looking warships of her period. Fitted with striking topmasts (stepped before), ensign gaff to fore and mainmast (removed from foremast in Aug 1897) and masthead semaphore at the mainmast head. Easily distinguished from *Centurion* and *Barfleur* by: enclosed upper deck amidships; no secondary guns in shields on upper deck amidships; larger upper top on foremast with SL platform above this.

From a distance *Renown* offered a similar appearance to that of *Majestic*, but the small differences to look for were: slightly different funnels (slimmer); smaller and different-shaped turrets (and guns); only three 6in casemates on each side of main deck amidships; only one military top low on mainmast.

As a whole, the ship was noticeably smaller and gave a lighter appearance.

1898–9 Shields removed from 3pdrs in fighting tops.

1900 Refitted at Malta Feb—May 1900, largely to conform with Vice-Admiral Fisher's requirements as his Flagship in Mediterranean. Main deck 12pdrs remounted in superstructure forward and aft. One 3pdr ex lower top remounted on each turret. Signal bridge aft relocated abaft foremast. Most ventilation cowls replaced by windsails. Various alterations to internal compartments. Top flagpole fitted to each mast (to accommodate outsized Admiral's flag).

1902 Specially refitted October 1902 as 'yacht' for Duke and Duchess of Connaught's tour to India. The main deck 6in guns were subsequently removed and not remounted again. Torpedo nets removed. Remaining ventilation cowls replaced by windsails. W/T fitted. Former flagpoles removed, and shorter pole fitted to mainmast only. Hull painted white, with yellow-ochre funnels and masts.

1903 Refitted for normal service Mar—April on return from Royal Tour. 3pdrs (ex upper foretop) remounted in lower tops (one in each). Two 24in SL added (P+S) on bridge. Torpedo nets replaced. Some cowls replaced, and ship painted all-grey.

1905 Refitted from April to Oct as 'yacht' for HM the Prince of Wales's Indian Tour. Upper deck 6in guns removed, torpedo nets removed, charthouse added on after superstructure, officers' cabins converted to royal suites, upper casemates to officers' cabins, tall flagpole replaced on each mast, large crest mounted on face of bridge; ship painted white again, but with green waterline, dark (possibly red) line to sheer on bows and yellow-ochre on funnels and masts.

1906–9 3pdr guns removed from over top of forward casemates (1906–7), W/T yards fitted to flagpoles and masthead semaphore removed (1906–8).

1910 Refitted Sept—Nov for service as stokers' Training Ship and was painted all-grey. Flagpoles removed.

HISTORY: *RENOWN*

Transferred to Devonport Dockyard on completion, and began her sea trials in January 1897. The trials were very extensive and she had her propeller blades changed which prolonged the issue. As a result of this and other circumstances, she took a total of four and a half years to complete.

8 June 1897 Commissioned for 'unappropriated service' during which she made a short cruise.

26 June 1897 Served as Flagship, CinC (Vice-Admiral J. A. Fisher) at Spithead Review by Prince of Wales honouring Diamond Jubilee of Queen Victoria.

7—12 July 1897 Temporarily attached to 1st Division, Channel Fleet as part of reinforcement added to that Fleet during farcical manoeuvres off south coast of Ireland.

24 Aug 1897 Hoisted Flag of Vice-Admiral J. A. Fisher and commissioned as Flagship on North

waterline. Accompanied by HMS *Terrible* (protected cruiser) they left Portsmouth on 8 October 1905. (Both views show her fitting out.) *Renown* leaving Portsmouth, 8 October 1905.

Below: *Renown*, on return from the Royal tour, 8 May 1906. Note the rig, empty 6in gun casemates, and crest on bridge face.

American and West Indies stations, relieving *Crescent*.

May—July 1899 Refit.

July 1899 Transferred to Mediterranean and became Fisher's Flagship again. As Controller of the Navy at that time, Fisher enjoyed his association with the ship's design, which he strongly endorsed, and this fact, together with *Renown*'s pleasing suitability for the social side of Flagship duty, probably influenced him in retaining her as his flagship on two consecutive occasions. It is reported that the Admiral even went as far as to have the flash plates of the 10in guns removed, as these interfered with ladies shoes during dance nights (probably correct, because photographs

show that they were removed during this period). Mediterranean Fleet until October 1902. (Flag until May 1902).

Feb—May 1900 Specially refitted at Malta; various modifications externally and internally to suit Fisher's requirements.

19 Nov 1900 Recommissioned for further service as Flagship, Mediterranean Fleet.

20 May 1902 On Fisher's relinquishing apppointment as CinC, became private ship in that formation.

29 Sept—6 Oct 1902 Unit of 'X Fleet' during combined manoeuvres off coasts of Cephalonia and Morea. Detached from Mediterranean to take Duke and Duchess of Connaught to India; specially fitted out at Portsmouth for this service (became known as the 'battleship yacht').

Nov 1902—Mar 1903 Royal Indian Tour.

April 1903 Rejoined Mediterranean Fleet.

Aug 1903 Temporary Flagship relieving *Venerable* for refit. Aug 1903 Manoeuvres with 'X Fleet' off the coast of Portugal.

15 May 1904 Paid off into Reserve at Devonport; withdrawn from Mediterranean, apparently without relief.

June 1904 Manoeuvres.

May 1904—April 1905 In Reserve (C Division).

21 Feb 1905 Specially refitted at Portsmouth for service as 'Royal Yacht' to carry Prince and Princess of Wales on Indian Tour (almost all secondary armament removed to provided extra accommodation). Refit completed early in October 1905.

8 Oct 1905 Left Portsmouth for Genoa where royal party joined ship. Escort provided by protected cruiser *Terrible*.

23 March 1906 Left Karachi for UK at conclusion of tour.

7 May 1906 Arrived Portsmouth; commissioned into Reserve 31 May 1906.

May 1907 Attached to Home Fleet organization as 'subsidiary yacht' for special service.

Oct—Dec 1907 Conveyed King and Queen of Spain to and from UK on official visit.

1 April 1909 Transferred to 4th Division, Home Fleet at Portsmouth.

25 Sept 1909 Paid off for refit as stokers' Training Ship. Refitted from Sept to Nov and commissioned at Portsmouth 1909 as STS. Stokers' Training Ship until January 1913.

24 June 1911 During Coronation Review (KGV) at

Spithead used as accommodation ship for visitors while at moorings in Portsmouth Harbour.

26 Nov 1911 Rammed by water tanker at Portsmouth, slightly damaged.

31 Jan 1913 Transferred to sale list and dismantled. In April 1913 it was rumoured that she might be used as depot ship at Cromarty, but this apparently dropped.

December 1913 Moored at Motherbank.

2 April 1914 Sold to Hughes Bolcklow, Middlesborough for £39,000 and later broken up at Blyth.

MAJESTIC CLASS

1893 ESTIMATES

DESIGN

In 1891 the Controller (Vice-Admiral J. A. Fisher) had asked the DNC (White) to prepare a sketch design for a 1st class battleship based on *Royal Sovereign*, but which would naturally incorporate the new 12in guns then under construction and make full use of the latest Harvey armour developments. On 27 January 1892 the DNC supplied the Board with provisional figures showing a displacement of 12,500 tons (excluding BM), four 12in guns, and a 9in uniform main armoured belt.

Approval was given to prepare suitable specifications for such a ship, but the DNC was asked to postpone progress a little because the new 12in gun was taking longer than expected to complete. Initially, three ships were laid down under the 1892 programme. The first two were of the new design (1st class), to be named the *Majestic* class, and these were finally allowed to proceed, under the normal 1893 programme, when the final layout had been approved. The third ship, however, was redesigned to smaller dimensions in an endeavour to provide an economical but strong ship for eastern waters (see *Renown*).

In August 1893, however, following considerable public agitation over the declining strength of the Royal Navy compared to the fleets of France and Russia, further building was called for which resulted in an emergency five-year programme. Initiated by the First Lord (Earl Spencer), it became known as the Spencer Programme. The original amendment called for an additional seven vessels all of which were grudgingly accepted by Parliament and finally approved in 1894.

Although general public satisfaction was guaranteed, the huge building programme caused much discontent in Government; some of the more eminent members speaking of resignation because of the enormous cost of such a mammoth, and in their opinion unjustified, programme.

It was agreed, however, that construction could be spread over a five-year period in order to minimize the cost in any one particular year, but in fact all were laid down in 1894 and 1895, and building times were varied to achieve a spread of time of completion.

All nine ships were completed by 1898 and represented the largest class of battleships ever built. Moreover, in all-round qualities, they were among the most efficient warships for their time ever built, the design being greatly admired and widely copied abroad and accepted as the standard battleship type in the Royal Navy for many years. (The design's main features were retained in the next twenty ships of the *Canopus, Formidable, London, Duncan* and *Queen* classes laid down from 1896 to 1901). The design and production of the *Majestic* class was truly Sir William White's *magnum opus* in a long and distinguished career.

The principal innovations of the *Majestic* design, over that of the *Royal Sovereign*, were:
1. The introduction of the new 12in wire-wound gun, very superior to the previous 13.5in in almost everything except weight of projectile.
2. General use of Harvey steel in place of compound armour.
3. Fitting of a deeper side armour belt of uniform

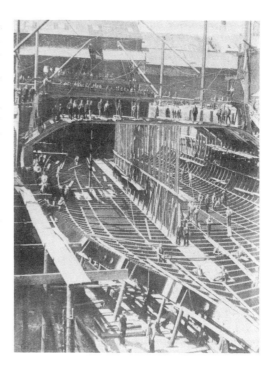

Right: *Mars.* On completion the Mighty *Majestic*s were the largest, and probably the most efficient battleships extant, generally admired, and greatly copied abroad. The frame work of *Mars* takes shape, 28 June 1894.

Below: *Prince George.* Launched by the Duchess of York (later Queen Mary) on 22 August 1896, *Prince George* takes the water.

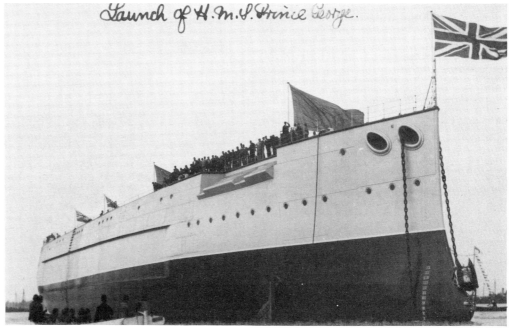

Launch of H.M.S. Prince George.

thickness, backed by a sloping armoured deck.

4. Provision of revolving armoured shields to protect the barbette-mounted guns.

The weight economies afforded by the lighter 12in gun and the Harvey armour, together with an improved arrangement of hull protection, made it possible to secure a substantial superiority in offensive and defensive qualities over the *Royal Sovereign* class with a relatively modest increase in displacement. In addition, the secondary armament was increased from ten to twelve guns, all of which were given the protection of casemates; the anti-torpedo boat defences were also greatly improved. Maximum designed speed remained the same as in *Royal Sovereign* but the steaming radius was increased.

The weaker points of the design, which were accepted in part to gain some of the above advantages, were:

1. Location of 6in secondary armament on the main deck with the attendant disadvantages of low command.

2. Reduced stability associated with longitudinal bulkheads without adequate counter-flooding arrangements (150 watertight compartments).

The original design leaned heavily, of course, on that of the *Royal Sovereign*, but the original displacement asked for (12,500 tons) was exceeded by a large increase (15,500 tons). White had wanted the entire 6in secondary battery to be mounted on the upper deck, and this arrangement is shown in a sketch design dated 3 January 1893 and bearing his signature. This sketch also shows one large top, low on each mast, with a small upper top as in *Royal Sovereign*, but this was later modified to provide two tops each capable of carrying a 6pdr gun.

The design load displacement was only approximately 750 tons more than in the *Royal Sovereign* class, while the length increased by 10ft(pp) and the freeboard by 5ft 10in forward and 6in aft (although reduced amidships by 9in), but the beam and nominal draughts were retained.

The all-round freeboard of the new vessels was never equalled in a pre-dreadnought of any succeeding class. The marked tumble-home was rather greater than in the previous class, with a marked sheer forward; this was criticized because it detracted from buoyancy on an already low metacentric height, but it was considered that the loss of initial stability through action damage was less likely owing to the deep armoured belt.

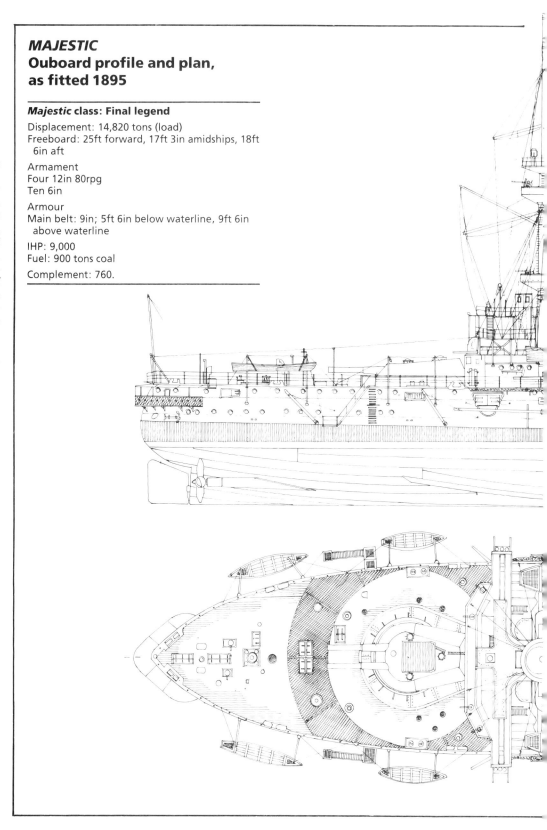

MAJESTIC
Ouboard profile and plan, as fitted 1895

Majestic class: Final legend

Displacement: 14,820 tons (load)
Freeboard: 25ft forward, 17ft 3in amidships, 18ft 6in aft

Armament
Four 12in 80rpg
Ten 6in

Armour
Main belt: 9in; 5ft 6in below waterline, 9ft 6in above waterline

IHP: 9,000
Fuel: 900 tons coal

Complement: 760.

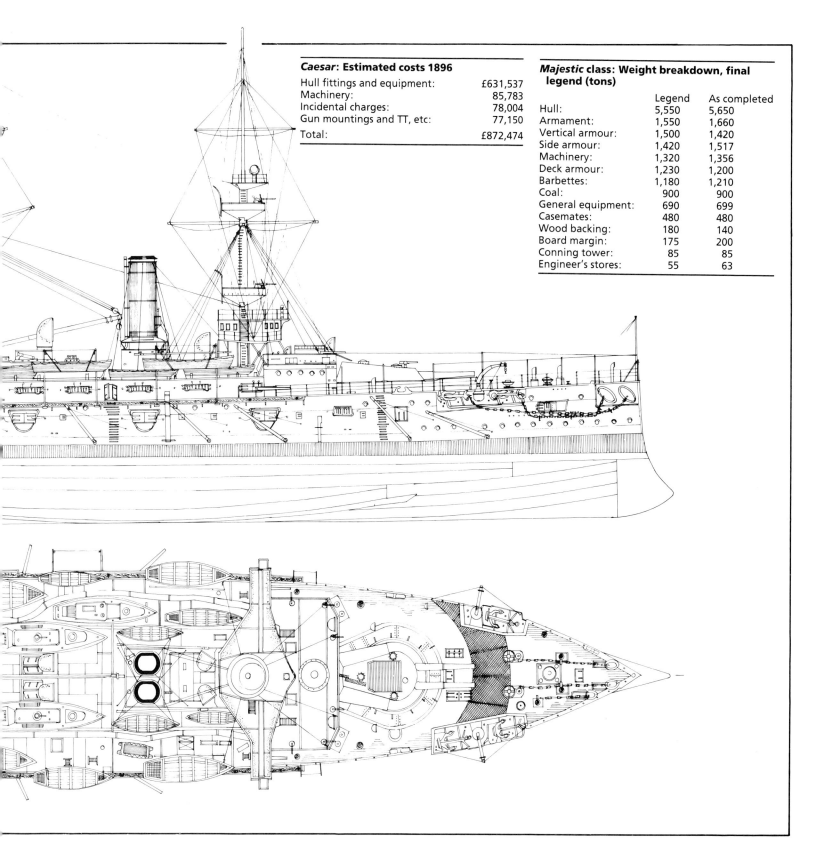

Caesar: Estimated costs 1896

Hull fittings and equipment:	£631,537
Machinery:	85,783
Incidental charges:	78,004
Gun mountings and TT, etc:	77,150
Total:	£872,474

Majestic class: Weight breakdown, final legend (tons)

	Legend	As completed
Hull:	5,550	5,650
Armament:	1,550	1,660
Vertical armour:	1,500	1,420
Side armour:	1,420	1,517
Machinery:	1,320	1,356
Deck armour:	1,230	1,200
Barbettes:	1,180	1,210
Coal:	900	900
General equipment:	690	699
Casemates:	480	480
Wood backing:	180	140
Board margin:	175	200
Conning tower:	85	85
Engineer's stores:	55	63

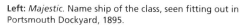

ARMAMENT

The *Majestic* class marked a reversion to the 12in calibre gun, which had not been fitted in a British battleship since that mounted in *Collingwood* in 1880. The new gun was the first large wire-wound gun in service with the Royal Navy and was such an advance on earlier designs that older guns could not hope to match its qualities.

The gun was designed by Vickers specifically for the *Majestic* class and on trials proved its ballistic superiority to the 13.5in gun of *Royal Sovereign*. It was also of superior strength, so much so that both Vickers and Armstrongs (also gun makers) thought that the Admiralty were over worried regarding this feature of the gun, and that it was 'over

---

Majestic class: Particulars, as completed

Construction
Majestic: Portsmouth DY; laid down 5 Feb 1894; launched 31 Jan 1895; completed Dec 1895
Mars: Cammell Laird; laid down 2 June 1894; launched 3 March 1896; completed June 1897
Prince George: Portsmouth DY; laid down 10 Sept 1894; launched 22 Aug 1895; completed Nov 1896
Magnificent: Chatham DY; laid down 18 Dec 1893; launched 19 Dec 1894; completed Dec 1895
Jupiter: John Brown; laid down 26 April 1894; launched 18 Nov 1895; completed May 1897
Caesar: Portsmouth DY; laid down 25 March 1895; launched 2 Sept 1896; completed Jan 1898
Illustrious: Chatham DY; laid down 11 March 1895; launched 17 Sept 1896; completed April 1898
Hannibal: Pembroke DY; laid down May 1894; launched 28 April 1896; completed April 1898
Victorious: Chatham DY; laid down 28 May 1894; launched 19 Oct 1895; Completed Nov 1896.

Displacement (tons) (*see* GM table)
14,980 (load), 15,630 (deep), 17,600 (extra deep).

Dimensions
Length: 390ft pp, 399ft wl, 421ft oa
Beam: 75ft
Draught: 27ft (load), 28ft 6in (deep), 31ft 4in (extra deep).

Armament
Four 12in 46ton Mk VIII; 80rpg
Twelve 6in 40cal Mk II; 200rpg
Sixteen 12pdr (12cwt); 300rpg
Twelve 3pdr
Eight MG

Five 18in torpedo tubes, two port and starboard (submerged), one aft.

Armour
Main belt: 9in Harvey, 220ft × 15ft
Bulkheads: 14in forward, 12in aft
Barbettes: 14in above armoured deck, reducing to 7in below
Turrets: 10½in faces, 5½in sides
Casemates: 6in faces
Decks: 3in on flat, 4in on inclines
Lower deck outside citadel: 2½in
Conning tower: 14in; 8in tube
After conning tower: 3in.

Machinery
Two sets 3-cylinder vertical triple expansion engines, two improved Griffiths propellers
Cylinder diameter: 40in, 59in, 88in
Stroke: 4ft 3in
Propellers: 4-bladed
Boilers: eight cylindrical single-ended, four furnaces each, working pressure 155psi
Weight of water in tubes to full working height: 120 tons
Heating surface: 24,400sq ft
Weight of machinery (tons): *Majestic* 1,356; *Mars* 1,328; *Jupiter* 1,315
Designed SHP: 10,000 for 16½ knots, 12,000 for 17½ knots (forced)
Fuel: 900 tons coal normal, 1,900 tons max. (400–500 tons oil added later, *see* Machinery)
Coal consumption: 250 tons per 24 hours full power; 140 tons ⅗th power; 50 tons per hour at economical power = 8 knots
Radius of action: 7,000nm at 10 knots (oil added), 4,420nm at 14.6 knots.

Ship's boats (average)
Pinnaces (steam): one 56ft, one 40ft, one 36ft
Launches (steam): one 42ft
Cutters: two 34ft
Whalers: two 27ft
Gigs: one 32ft, one 30ft, one 24ft
Skiff dinghies: one 16ft
Balsa rafts: one 13ft 6in.

Searchlights
Six 24in, two port and starboard on each bridge, one high on each mast (not always shown in photographs, and considerable variation in class).

Wireless
W/T Type I fitted to all during 1909–10.

Anchors
Two Inglefield 118cwt, one 117cwt, two Martins 55cwt.

Complement
794 *Mars* and *Jupiter* (1897)
672 *Majestic* (1895)
735 *Caesar* (as flagship 1905)
720 *Hannibal* (1905).

Costs
Majestic: £916,382 plus guns £70,100
Magnificent: £909,789 plus guns £70,100
Jupiter: £902,011 plus guns £65,640
Mars: £902,402 plus guns £61,950
Caesar: £872,474 plus guns £64,420
Victorious: £885,212 plus guns £70,100
Hannibal: £906,799 plus guns £57,360
Illustrious: £894,585 plus guns £57,610
Prince George: £895,504 plus guns £70,100.

designed'. There were also considerable improvements to the twin mountings for the 12in gun compared to those of the 13.5in, these being summarized below:

1. The turntables were balanced at their centre of rotation, making it possible to employ lighter training engines and allowing the fitting of hand-training gear.

2. The mountings were evenly balanced even with guns run out, allowing for lighter elevating gear and again, the use of alternative hand gear.

3. At the fixed loading positions the rammer was alongside instead of through the hoists, so the cages could be removed while the rammers were in motion (the main advantage here was that much time was gained in the loading cycle).

4. The loading trays worked with the rammers and the entry of the guides of their supply bogies locked the turntables, doing away with the need for separate outside locking bolts.

5. All-round loading was provided from a ready-use supply of eight shells stowed on the turntable.

6. The turrets, or shields as first called, had 10½in faces, 5½in sides, 4in back and a 2in floor and roof.

The guns were designed for either right- or left-hand breech, depending on which position in the mounting they occupied; the barrels, however, were interchangeable although some of the breech mechanism was different. The firing mechanism was designed for electric or percussion firing with vent sealed tubes and, following the usual practice of the day, the guns could not be fired until the breech screw was sealed fully home.

Gun trials in the completed ships passed without much trouble, although in November 1904 there was an accident in *Majestic* while she was engaged in prize firing. One of the guns blew off its muzzle while another had lining complications.

The latter complaint was due to the inner 'A' tube being out of line with the outer 'A' tube, at the first shoulder near the muzzle, and can be seen as an error in manufacture. The other gun, which had about 13in of the liner blown off, was found upon inspection to have a series of cracks in the inner tube. Both guns were fired with $^3/_4$-charges, made up of one ½-charge of $83^3/_4$lb and one $^1/_4$-charge of $41^7/_8$lb of Cordite 50 while the shells in use were solid shot. The accident was noticed after the seventh round was fired and observed to fall 500 yards short of the desired range. A crew member noticed a piece of alien metal flying through the air at the

MAJESTIC
Inboard profile, plan of upper deck and sections, 1895

Section 166
1 Admiral's dining room
2 Wardroom
3 Reading room
4 Steerage compartment

Section 152
1 Admiral's secretary
2 Cabins
3 Cabins
4 Feedwater tank
5 Towing lockers
6 Submerged torpedo room
7 Torpedo head magazine

Section 134
1 12in turret
2 12in barbette
3 Fleet flag equipment
4 Coal
5 Spares compartment
6 Auxiliary machinery
7 Working space
8 12pdr shell room
9 12in handing room
10 Store room
11 Spare equipment
12 12in shell room

Section 112
1 6in gun casemate
2 No. 5 sleeping cabin
3 Engine hatch
4 Coal
5 Passage
6 Engine room

Section 82
1 12pdr gun opening
2 6in gun casemate
3 Working area
4 Passage
5 Coal
6 Boiler
7 Uptake

Section 64
1 Bridge
2 Ventilator
3 6in gun casemate
4 Working area
5 Coal
6 Forced-draught fan
7 Boiler room
8 Wing

Section 36
1 12in turret
2 Middle turret level
3 Lower turret level
4 Working area
5 Wood locker
6 Spares for armament
   equipment
7 Passage
8 12in magazine
9 Boatswains' stores
10 Passage

11 Electrical spares
12 12in magazines
13 12in shell room
14 Electrical room

Section 26
1 Working area
2 Anchor bed
3 Mess space
4 Fresh water tank
5 Submerged torpedo room
6 Torpedo warheads
7 Spares for torpedo
   equipment

Section 18
1 Mess space
2 Cable room
3 Cable room
4 Capstan room
5 Canvas room

Inboard profile
1 Boilers
2 Machinery and engine rooms
3 Shell rooms
4 Magazines
5 12in barbettes
6 Boiler room uptakes
7 Engine room vents
8 Steering compartment
9 Torpedo rooms
10 Conning tower
11 Watertight compartments
12 Capstan room

Upper deck plan
1 Officers' WCs
2 Captain's cabin
3 Buffet
4 Captain's sleeping cabin
5 Admiral's deck cabin
6 Engine room hatch
7 Supply shaft to engine and
   boiler room
8 6in gun casemates
9 Dynamo room
10 Uptakes
11 Coaling winch
12 Beef screen
13 Vent supply to boiler room
14 Conning tower base
15 Seamen's heads

Section 166
looking aft

Section 152
looking aft

Section 134
looking aft

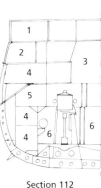

Section 112
looking aft

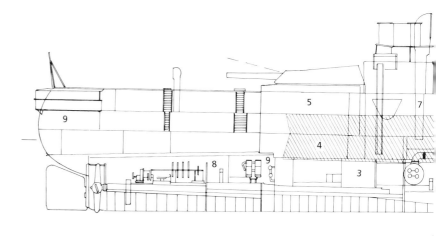

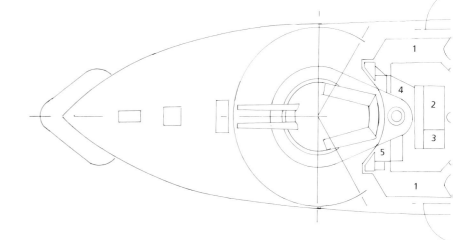

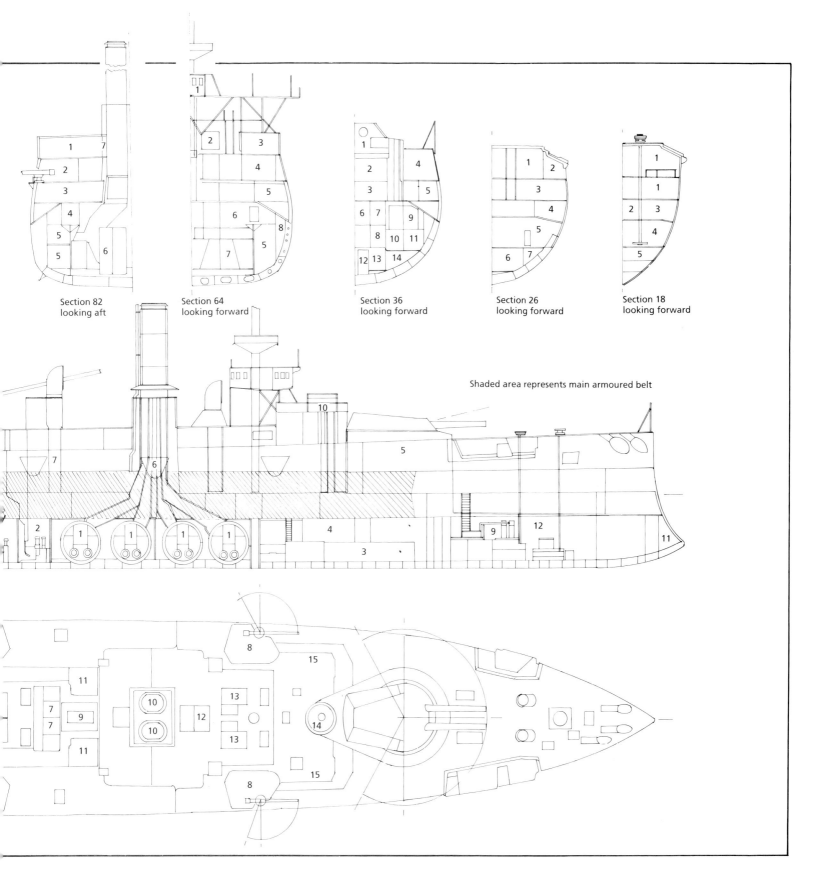

Section 82
looking aft

Section 64
looking forward

Section 36
looking forward

Section 26
looking forward

Section 18
looking forward

Shaded area represents main armoured belt

same time, but he thought it might have been a deck fitting—a common occurrence.

These incidents led to all the 46-ton 12in guns in use with the Fleet being subjected to close examination; it was concluded that, in their existing state, they were only good for 33 full charge firings before the risk of a similar occurrence became likely. The problem was 'muzzle choke', caused by the inner tube being contracted and bulging inwards around the muzzle opening, resulting in restriction and ultimately failure of the bore. Fortunately, because of the great strength of the gun, no one was hurt.

The faults in this otherwise excellent gun were rectified and it was later found, following tests with the damaged guns, that they could still fire to a distance of 10,605 yards with a 200lb cordite charge, at an elevation of 9°. The guns were mounted in pear-shaped turrets except in *Caesar* and *Illustrious* (last two completed) which had redesigned round mounts (Mk BIII). Those in *Majestic* were Mk BII.

Loading in the last two ships was slightly faster than in the others, with a better method of protection than before owing to the shell path being interrupted in the shell chamber, and not having a clear run from the magazines as in the first seven vessels of the class. This lessened the risk of an explosion in the turret reaching down to the magazines.

ARMOUR

When the time came to consider how the new battleships would be protected, the DNC insisted that they have the latest and best armour available. To this end he wrote on 27 January 1892 to the Controller and Board of Admiralty (Admiral Bedford, Sir Anthony Hoskins, Civil Lord, Mr Forwood, and Lord George Hamilton):

'It is submitted that in the new battleships if a modified plan of hull armour is adopted, the broadside protection should not be less than 9in thick. The thickness would, under service conditions make broadside over 60% of the length of the new ship practically impenetrable to even the best armour piercing projectiles from the largest of quick-firing guns.

For our 6in gun, the perforation at 1,000yds has been estimated at under 10in. I am disposed to think that with quality steel and steel faced armour now available this figure would be much less than this.

It would appear probable, therefore, that a thickness of 9in of the present quality would make the new ship practically proof against the best AP shells.'

The DNC also sent along two sketch plans showing how best the method should be applied, and also the following:

'Plan A: Everything disposed as in *Royal Sovereign*. (18in main belt and flat deck, etc.).

Plan B: The abolition of the thick waterline belt. The adoption of plating uniformly thick over the whole of the surface of broadside which is armoured in *Royal Sovereign*.

Construction of sloping steel deck which at its central part is at the height above water of belt deck in *Royal Sovereign*, but which is curved down at the sides to meet the lower edge of broadside armour. Minute subdivision of angular spaces near side and above protective deck, and the use of coal protection as packing for these spaces.

9in armour—250ft in length.

6in teak backing.

3in deck on flat, 4in on slopes.'

The DNC also made it clear that Plans A and B were practically equal as regards exposure of unarmoured bottom, but general thickness was seen as equal judging from gunnery experience.

The Controller (Fisher) and the Board—even the sceptics—were practically unanimous in agreeing that Plan B should be approved for any new battleship. The Controller wrote: 'I record the opinion I have previously expressed that Plan B is the best form of defence that could be applied in the new battleship.'

Magnificent: Displacements on inclining experiments at Chatham, 14 Dec 1895

Displacement (tons)	Draught
15,632	28ft 5½in
14,982	27ft 6in
13,900	26ft 0⅞in
13,400	25ft 2in

Majestic: GM and stability

Based on inclining experiments, 16 December 1895

	Displacement (tons)	Draught	GM	Maximum stability	Stability vanishes at
'A' Condition (= load)*	15,600	27ft (mean)	3.4ft	38°	62°
'B' Condition (= deep load)**		28ft 8in (mean)	3.7ft	39°	65°
'C' Condition (= light)		25ft 3in	3.3ft		

*Fully equipped plus 900 tons coal.
**Fully equipped plus 1,900 tons coal.

Top: *Majestic* leaves Portsmouth in 1896, passing Lord Nelson's Flagship, HMS *Victory.*

Bottom: *Majestic* in 1900, as Flagship, Channel Fleet. Note the black air cowls (unusual), no shields to quick-firing guns in tops, W/T gaff to main, and painted black line running through top of boat deck.

The suggested Plan (B) went ahead and the armour layout for *Majestic* was designed to give maximum protection against the ever growing threat of attack from medium-calibre guns and high-explosive shells. The main belt was reduced in thickness (from that of *Royal Sovereign*) to increase its area, and give improved protection to the middle side, above which the majority of hits were expected in any action.

To recap the situation as approved, the principal improvements in armour layout over that of *Royal Sovereign* were:

1. General use of Harvey armour for the vertical main belts, in place of nickel or compound steels.

2. Adoption of a much wider belt, made possible by the reduction of thickness over previous classes, backed by a sloping deck.

3. Provision of completely closed armoured shields (turrets) to protect the barbettes and gun crews.

At last White's proposal to apply a medium thickness belt together with a sloping armoured deck had become reality. As far back as 1888 he had conceived such a scheme for 1st class battleships, but the Admiralty Board would not approve any reduction in protective qualities until the coming of Harvey armour which proved to be much more resistant than any compound plates.

The Harvey process consisted of covering an all-steel plate with animal charcoal; another plate (given the same treatment) was placed on top of this to form a sandwich. The plates were then surrounded with bricks, the whole assembly placed in a large furnace for two or three weeks. The plates were then removed and left to cool for six or seven days. This treatment increased the carbon content of the surface of the plates; a high-carbon steel face was thus combined with a standard steel alloy back. The change from one to the other was gradual and without a joint (as in compound armour). Both plates were reheated in the furnace again and on withdrawal were plunged into cold water. The rapid cooling causing the high-carbon steel to become extremely hard, thus producing the ideal armour requirement of a super-hard face and a soft (resilient) back in one piece. Any forming of the armour plates was done prior to the hardening process.

As fitted, the main armoured strake was 220ft long by 15ft wide (all previously published material states that it was 16ft, but official records and 'as fitted' drawings show 15ft, so we must take that as

Right: *Resolution* and *Hannibal* anchored at Devonport, 1898.

Below: *Hood, Magnificent, Royal Sovereign* and *Majestic* class vessels on manoeuvres off Malta, 1899–1900.

fact) and extended to abeam the main barbettes. The upper edge was at main deck level, approximately 9ft 6in above the waterline at load draught, and the lower edge 5ft 6in below. The main bulkheads of 14in and 12in ran obliquely inwards from the extremities of the belt armour to the barbette faces. Total length of the armoured citadel was 250ft. Main armoured deck: 3in thickness on the flat section, and 4in on the inclines. The thickness consisted of two plates of 1½in for the flat section, and two plates of 1½in plus another of 1in for that on the inclines which was angled at 40° to the ship's side, and was estimated to represent a deflecting resistance equal to about 8in of vertical armour. Any armour-piercing shells hitting the ship would have to penetrate the 9in side armour and the 4in sloped deck before reaching the vitals of the ship. The method of application was seen as a great improvement over that used in *Royal Sovereign*.

The edges of the flat section of the deck were extended right across to the ship's side by shell plating (as in *Renown*). The triangular spaces thus formed between the flat and sides provided watertight flats on each side which could be filled with water or coal.

The main belt was backed with 4in of teak, and there were 78 watertight compartments outside the armoured citadel and 72 inside. A double bottom was provided from 8ft 9in past the citadel at both ends. Coal bunkers were approximately 11ft and 8ft inboard of the hull and behind the armoured belt above the middle deck and abreast engine and boiler rooms below this.

The ends were unarmoured and this was a point of criticism given the loss of *Victoria* in June 1893 (sunk by *Camperdown*). The construction of *Majestic* and *Magnificent* were delayed pending a special investigation into this accident, but it had been firmly established by the Board of Inquiry that the absence of armoured belt at the ends was not the cause of her loss.

The lower deck was 2½in thick, and ran from the bases of the citadel down to the extremities of the bow and stern.

The barbettes were 14in uniform thickness above the main deck, reducing to 7in inside the belt bulkheads. They were, however, 14in on the outer face of the citadel, even below the main deck.

Turrets had 10½in faces, 5½in sides, 4in rears and 2in floors and roofs.

Secondary casemates were given 6in on the faceplates, and 2in on the sides and rears; the ammunition hoists for these were also 2in. The mantlet to the stern torpedo tube was 6in and 3in. The forward conning tower was 14in on the face and sides, and 12in at the rear; the tube was 8in. The after tower was 3in uniform with a 3in tube.

MACHINERY

The *Majestic*s were given the same basic machinery as the *Royal Sovereign* class, but an extra 1,000shp was made available. This gave the same speeds, but the ships were able to achieve them more easily. The new class had improved radius of action, coal stowage having been increased to 1,900 tons maximum and 1,100 in the normal load, the latter raised from 900 tons because the Board margin was not entirely used up.

There were two sets of 3-cylinder inverted triple expansion engines driving two shafts with 4-bladed propellers. Boiler installation consisted of eight single-ended, cylindrical return tubed boilers arranged back to back in four watertight compartments, two each side of the centre-line bulkhead. There were four furnaces to each boiler.

With natural draught the nominal speed of the *Majestic* class was approximately 1 knot faster than that of the *Royal Sovereign*s and about the same with forced draught, although the latter was reached with 1,000shp less. *Illustrious* was fitted with induced instead of forced draught, although the results obtained were slightly less than the rest of the class, but the system was accepted as giving greater reliability and a wider margin of safety.

During *Royal Sovereign*'s preliminary sea trials the high level of forced draught caused her boilers to leak badly; steam pressure fell off so rapidly that she was in danger of complete failure. With this in mind the *Majestic* group were not forced to the same extent, but achieved the same speed having been given finer hull lines as in *Renown*.

On completion, the class had little trouble with

their machinery, but there were, as in any installation, minor technical mishaps such as the thrust blocks becoming overheated in *Prince George* while running at high power; which was caused by a perforated condenser. Similar troubles were experienced in *Illustrious* with leaking glands and valves, and some ships suffered from vibration. In general, however, they performed exceptionally well.

In 1903 two of the boilers in *Hannibal* and four in *Magnificent*, *Majestic* and *Mars* were converted to burn oil and coal simultaneously. Each boiler was fitted with eight oil sprayers giving a total output of 880lb of oil per boiler per hour at a pressure of 150psi. The radius of action using oil supplement was increased from 6,260 to approximately 7,000 nautical miles at 10 knots, and from 3,490 top 4,420 nautical miles at 14.6 knots.

Majestic, being first to complete, was put through a lengthy series of steam trials, but on her preliminary runs (19–20 October 1895) did not come up to expectations. On a displacement of 13,131 tons and a corresponding draught of 25ft 4in she made only 14.67 knots. Knowing that her bottom was clean, the sea smooth and the wind only Force 1, their Lordships were not pleased, but the cause was a blockage in the condensers which was soon rectified and *Majestic* made a better show during her next set of steam trials (*see* tables).

During these trials Vice-Admiral commanding Channel Squadron, Lord Walter T. Kerr, having watched the ship perform and taken careful notes, made the following statement (31 January 1896): 'I am thoroughly satisfied with the ship, and I think the result is most credible to the designers and fitters out.

We went through manoeuvres and target practice as though we had been in commission for a year already, and although everything was new, it went without hitch.

The new ship steers well, and is quicker off her helm than *Royal Sovereign*.'

Majestic: Steam trials, 19–20 October 1895

30-hour
Clean bottom
Wind Force 1, sea smooth
Displacement: 13,181 tons
Propeller: 4-bladed, Griffiths improved
Propeller diameter: 17ft 0¾in
Propeller pitch: 19ft 8⅝in
Revs: 85.5rpm (mean)
IHP: 6,075 (mean)
Speed: 14.67 knots (logged)
Coal consumption: 1.84lb per hp per hour
8-hour
Displacement: 13,360 tons
Revs: 100.6rpm (mean)
IHP: 10,453 (mean)
Speed: 16.9 knots
4-hour
Displacement: 13,225 tons
Revs: 107.2 (mean)
IHP: 12,554 (mean)
Speed: 17.8 knots.

Majestic class: Collective steam trials (over period of years)

	IHP	Speed (knots)			IHP	Speed (knots)	
Illustrious:	10,241	15.96	Contractors' 8-hour	*Victorious*:	10,300	16.92	Contractors' 8-hour
	10,323	15.7	3-hour commission trial		10,515	16.7	4-hour repair trial
	10,071	15.52	8-hour, 1903	*Caesar*:	10,692	16.7	Contractors' 8-hour
	10,316	15.9	trial at sea, 1899		12,695	18.7	Contractors' 4-hour
Majestic:	10,418	16.9	Contractors' 8-hour	*Prince George*:	10,466	16.52	Contractors' 8-hour
	10,365	15.81	8-hour, 1903		12,280	18.3	Contractors' 4-hour
Mars:	10,209	15.96	Contractors' 8-hour		10,243	16.05	4-hour, 1903
	12,483	17.7	Contractors' 4-hour				

Trial in Hannibal, 25 October 1906, Rame Head
Draught: 27ft 7in forward, 27ft 6in aft
Revs (mean): 94 port, 93.1 starboard
Steam in boilers: 155psi
Steam at engines: 145psi
IHP: 5,014 starboard, 5,224 port: Total 10,238
Speed: 15.2 knots on log, 14.8 knots on bearings.

	IHP	Speed (knots)	
Hannibal:	10,361	16.3	Contractors' 8-hour
	10,640	16	8-hour, 4 June 1904
	10,463	16.23	24-hours, 1902
Jupiter:	10,248	15.8	Contractors' 8-hour
	10,233	16	4-hour, 1902

Majestic class: Steam trials

Collective while in Channel Fleet (*Prince George* not present) 29–30 September 1904

8-hour trial					⅗ths power				
	Draught (mean)	IHP	Revs.	Speed (knots)		Draught (mean)	IHP	Revs.	Speed (knots)
Illustrious:	26ft 11½in	10,074	92.7	15.2	*Illustrious*:	26ft 11½in	6,521	84.1	13.6
Magnificent:	27ft 4½in	10,365	92.9	15.4	*Magnificent*:	27ft 4½in	6,519	80.1	13.1
Majestic:	27ft	9,315	95.9	15.2	*Majestic*:	27ft	6,765	87.5	14.4
Mars:	28ft	10,025	90.3	15	*Mars*:	28ft	6,976	84.2	13.97
Hannibal:	27ft 5½in	10,209	95.4	16	*Hannibal*:	27ft 5½in	6,291	84.1	14.03
Jupiter:	27ft 7in	10,539		16.2	*Jupiter*:	27ft 7in	7,047		14.45
Victorious:	27ft 6in	10,189	100	16.6	*Victorious*:	27ft 6in	6,416	88	14.50
Caesar:	27ft 6in	10,740	93.7	16.1	*Caesar*:	27ft 6in	6,608	83	14.17

Below: *Prince George* with the Channel Fleet, 1905–6. Note the quick-firing guns have been removed from tops and the bridge searchlights have been remounted in lower foretop.

Right: *Illustrious* bow-on, c.1898–9.

Far right: *Mars* at the Coronation Fleet Review, 16 August 1902. In the previous April whilst at firing practice, one of the 12in guns in the fore barbette was fired before the breech was properly closed, and the turret was completely wrecked. Two officers and nine men were killed, and seven were injured.

Below right: *Magnificent*; view over boat deck, c.1896. (A *Royal Sovereign* class ship is in the background.)

Above: *Caesar* at Portsmouth, c.1903, having just returned from a long Mediterranean commission.

Below: Aloft in *Prince George*, 1896. Keeping the rig in trim meant constant hard work, but men who could not stand heights were not forced to go aloft as had been the case some fifty years before.

Right: *Illustrious* in 1905, dressed overall. Note the smaller 12in turrets compared with those of her sisters (except *Caesar*).

APPEARANCE CHANGES

Well-proportioned and handsome ships, they were considered by many to be better-looking than the *Royal Sovereign*s, chiefly because of the closer spacing of the funnels and the pronounced sheer at the bows.

The masts, each with two large military tops, gave a rather impressive profile, while the modified arrangement of forebridge and conning tower introduced in the first six ships gave them a unique appearance.

In this latter arrangement the bridge was built up around the pole foremast, leaving the conning tower clear of obstruction, a departure from previous practice in which the bridge was built above the conning tower. The advantages of this layout were the increased all-round view from the conning tower, and the elimination of the risk of its being obstructed by the collapse of the bridge or parts of it in the event of action damage. Also, it increased the distance between bridge personnel and the blast of the forward 12in guns when being fired abeam or abaft that position.

In the last three ships (*Caesar*, *Hannibal* and *Illustrious*), however, the earlier system of fitting the bridge over the conning tower was reverted to, and this remained a feature of British battleships until the later Dreadnought-type *Orion* class in 1909. William White's early sketch plan shows the bridge over the conning tower, indicating that this had been the original idea, but later it was altered to suit the body of opinion who thought a stronger structure would evolve from placing it around the foremast base. A flying bridge was fitted in all the ships on completion except *Magnificent* which received hers shortly after commissioning. Accommodation was slightly inferior to that of the *Royal Sovereign*s, the cabin arrangements on the whole being more cramped. As completed the ships were extremely difficult to tell apart although there were many differences.

Caesar: Short steam pipes before and abaft the funnels and the upper stay rim on the funnels well below the top.

Hannibal: Steam pipes abaft the funnels only, and to the same height as the funnels. Solid points to the starfish below the searchlight platform.

Illustrious: Steam pipes abaft the funnels only, shorter than the funnels, and larger perforated points to her starfish.

Far left: *Illustrious*, showing standard funnel bands, 1909–10. Note the rangefinder drum on top and rangefinder on lower top.

Left: *Prince George* in 1903–4 (before 15 July 1904), showing fleet markings on funnels. Note lack of net booms.

Below left: *Jupiter* in 1907–8, while serving with the Channel Fleet. Note the searchlight above the 6in casemate.

Jupiter: Striking topmasts. A large starfish below the SL platforms. An upper yard high on the foremast. Tall steam pipes abaft the funnels. Heavy close-fitting caps to funnels and small brackets on the inner side of the funnels.

Magnificent: Fixed topmasts. Charthouse on after flying bridge by 1896. Starfishes and upper yard as in *Jupiter*.

Majestic: Light starfish below the SL platform. An upper yard low on the foremast. Tall steam pipes abaft the funnels and light funnels caps clear of the casings. Topmasts and charthouse as in *Magnificent*.

Mars: Topmasts and starfishes as in *Majestic*. Two widely spaced steam pipes before each funnel, and one abaft on the inner side of each funnel (all short).

Victorious: Topmasts and starfishes as in *Prince George*. Steam pipes as in *Prince George* except two before each funnel and heavy close-fitting caps.

Prince George: Striking topmasts, large starfishes. Short steam pipes abaft and before (one only) each funnel. Small light caps clear of casing.

1896 Flying bridge with charthouse fitted over bridge in *Magnificent*, and charthouse added on flying bridge in *Majestic*.

1898 Fixed topmasts in *Mars* replaced by striking topmasts (stepped before).

1899 Removal of 3pdr shields from tops; number of guns in tops reduced from this date onwards. In some vessels, the 3pdrs were remounted on the superstructure or in bridges (all shields removed by 1902).

1901–2 W/T fitted; gaff on main topmast.

1903 Electric hoists fitted to 6in guns in addition to original hand equipment. Experimental oil sprayers fitted to boilers in *Mars* and *Hannibal* late 1902 (completed late February). These two ships were the first British battleships to have oil-burning equipment. Experimental painting throughout the class to see what colour should be used to replace the Victorian livery buff (*see* notes).

1903–4 Net shelf in some ships lowered to main deck level to clear 6in gun blast. Fixed topmasts in *Jupiter*, *Magnificent* and *Majestic* replaced by striking topmasts. Victorian paintwork replaced by all-grey. Two boilers in *Hannibal* and *Mars*, four in *Magnificent*, *Majestic* and *Prince George* converted to burn oil. Spaces in double bottom used to carry oil. *Magnificent*: 560 tons (*Victorious* 552 tons, *Caesar* 563 tons, converted with others at later date).

1903–4 *Mars* refit:

Armament overhaul; reboring of 12in recoil cylinders; main deck 12pdrs shifted to shelter deck level; new positions for 3pdrs; general overhaul for all gun mountings; oil burners fitted to two boilers. Cost £70,037.

Funnel bands painted up in some ships. These early markings were used in the Atlantic and Channel Fleets from 1903 to 1908 while on manoeuvres to identify component ships of different squadrons, and were not meant for individual ship identification.

1905–9 Fire control and rangefinding equipment fitted in place of SL platform on foremast with small platform below this in place of original upper fighting top. In *Magnificent*, a new oval-shaped top was fitted. In others, original upper fighting top was roofed in and adapted as fire control position with extension for rangefinding at the forward end (not *Victorious*). Lower fighting top on mainmast was similarly adapted in all, with RF extension on back end (except *Magnificent* and *Victorious*). These modifications were effected 1905–6 in all except *Majestic* and *Victorious* (1907–8) and *Magnificent* (1908). Siemens-Martin fire control equipment was fitted experimentally in *Jupiter* for about six months in 1905. 12pdrs removed from main deck (1905–6), remounted on superstructure forward and aft. Forward ports plated-up. All 3pdrs removed from tops (1905–9); some suppressed, others remounted in various locations. SL removed (1905–9) from masts in all except *Majestic*, remounted over forward 6in casemates.

Net shelf lowered to main deck level (1905–6) in vessels not previously modified. Two-extra SL (24in) added on boat deck amidships in some ships. Oil-burning equipment extended to four boilers in *Mars* (1906) and four in *Caesar* (1907–8). *Victorious* last unit to be modified (1909). Masthead semaphore removed (1906–7). W/T gaff triced in 1907.

1906 *Magnificent* refit:

Broken joints at bottom of centre-line bulkheads repaired. Refitted 24 watertight doors in bunkers, and four quick-closing doors in machinery spaces. All defects on gun sights corrected. Boiler room overhaul. All 6in and 12pdr guns removed, checked and replaced. Electrical installation checked (found to be in poor condition). Torpedo equipment thoroughly overhauled. 12in guns

checked and mountings overhauled.

1909–14 A small rangefinder was mounted in the lower foretop in some ships (1909–10). Range indicators fitted in all. SL removed from masts in *Majestic* and remounted over forward 6in casemates (1910–11). Two 24in SL mounted on after flying bridge in *Caesar* and *Prince George*, and amidships on the boat deck in others. Flying deck SL relocated to boat deck in *Caesar* and boat deck SL to flying deck in *Mars*. Torpedo nets removed in *Illustrious*, *Magnificent* and others over a period of time (1912–13) (*Hannibal* and *Victorious* still show

PRINCE GEORGE
Outboard profile, as seen at Dardanelles 1915

Note anti-rangefinder baffles on topmasts, howitzer on forward 12in turret top, reduced bridgework and mine-catching equipment fitted to bow.

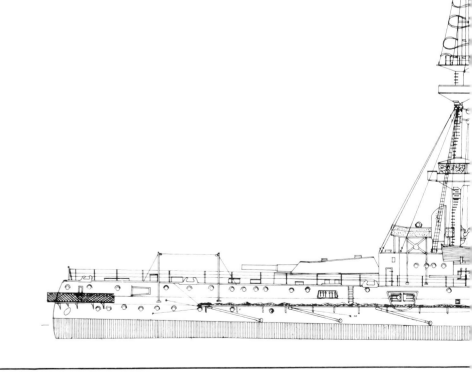

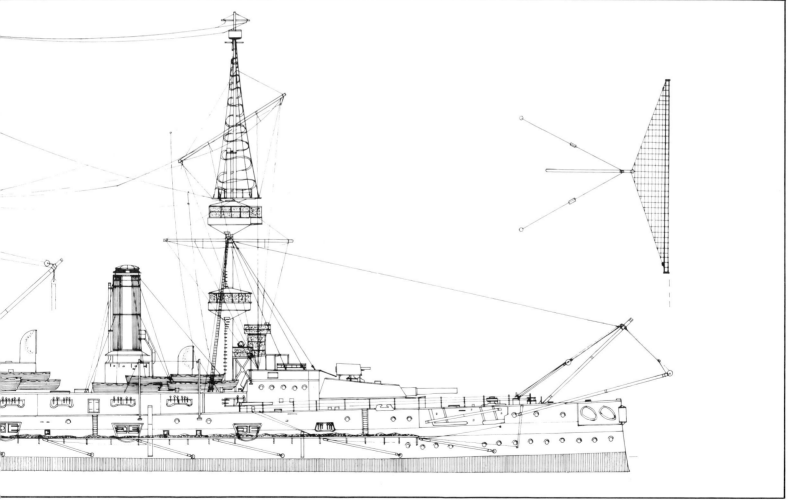

theirs in 1913.) W/T gaff replaced by tall topgallant in all except *Majestic* (1909–10) *Majestic* still had triced gaff in 1913. W/T topgallant fitted to foremast in *Illustrious, Jupiter, Magnificent* and *Prince George* (1909–11).

Heavy yards removed from mainmast in some ships (1910–14).

Standard funnel bands painted up (1909–10): *Caesar*, none; *Hannibal*, one white on each; *Jupiter*, three white on each; *Mars*, three red on each; *Magnificent*, one red on each; *Majestic*, two red on each; *Prince George*, one black on each; *Victorious*, two black on each; *Illustrious*, two white on each. Deleted on outbreak of war (August 1914).

Some vessels were modified for the Dardanelles campaign:

Prince George, Majestic

Small howitzer mounted on roof of each turret, although only apparent on 'A' turret. These were found of little use and were removed in April 1915. Casemates and boat deck SL removed. Torpedo nets fitted. Minesweeping gear fitted in bows. After flying bridge and charthouse removed in *Prince George*. Stockless anchors fitted in *Prince George*. Topgallant to each mast in *Majestic*. Small spotting 'crow's nest' fitted to top of fore topmast, and anti-rangefinder spirals fitted to topmasts in *Prince George* (soon removed as they proved of little use).

Jupiter as modified for Suez Canal Patrol (1915):

A 12pdr field gun on high-angle mounting added to fore turret in September 1915. SL reduced to four: two on lower foretop, two on forebridge. Torpedo nets fitted. After flying bridge removed. Topgallant to foremast only. Main topmast reduced to stump.

Hannibal, Mars and *Magnificent*:

Disarmed except for four 6in (upper deck) and some light guns. This was done with a view to provide 12in guns and mountings for the *Earl of Peterborough* monitors. Employed as troopships for Dardanelles. Two SL remounted on platform below foretop in *Magnificent*. Torpedo nets fitted. Topmasts reduced to stumps. From March 1916, remaining armament removed from all three.

Victorious: Disarmed and converted for harbour subsidiary duties from November 1915 to March 1916.

1917 *Jupiter* paid off and remaining guns removed.

1918 *Prince George*: Refitted at Malta for service with British light forces in Adriatic. Main deck 6in removed and two small AA guns fitted on after turret. Casemate and boat deck SL removed, two remounted on after flying bridge. Torpedo nets fitted, but were later removed. Topgallant to main only. Full topmast to each. Camouflage painted up. Used as ice breaker on one occasion during this service.

HISTORY: *MAJESTIC*

Laid down at Portsmouth Dockyard 5 February 1894 and floated out 31 January 1895. She began her preliminary sea trials in September 1895 but was unfortunate in striking the sea bottom on 19 September. There was no serious damage and she was able to proceed with trials after being freed.

12 December 1895 Joined Channel Fleet as Flagship. Channel Fleet until January 1905.

26 June 1897 Present at Jubilee Fleet Review.

16 Aug 1902 Coronation Review.

Feb—July 1904 Refit at Portsmouth.

Jan 1905 Under fleet reorganization Channel Fleet became Atlantic Fleet, Home Fleet became Channel Fleet. Served with Atlantic Fleet until Oct 1906.

1 Oct 1906 Paid off into Reserve at Portsmouth, until Feb 1907.

26 Feb 1907 Commissioned at Portsmouth as Flagship, Nore Division, new Home Fleet, which had been organized in January 1907. Served with Home Fleet until Aug 1914; Flagship, Nore Division until Jan 1908.

Jan—June 1908 Private ship, Nore Division.

June 1908–Mar 1909 Devonport Division.

Mar 1909–Aug 1910 3rd Division, Devonport.

Aug 1910–May 1912 4th Division, Devonport.

May 1912 7th BS, 3rd Fleet, Devonport. Two refits during this period: at Chatham 1907–9; at Devonport 1911.

14 July 1912 On manoeuvres, collided with *Victorious*, no serious damage.

Aug 1914 Assigned to Channel Fleet at outbreak of war. 7th BS, Channel Fleet until Oct 1914.

Aug–Sept 1914 Refit.

Sept 1914 Covered passage of BEF to France.

3–14 Oct Detached as unit of escort for first Canadian troop convoy.

Transferred to Nore as Guardship at end of Oct. Guardship at Nore until Nov, transferred to Humber after Gorleston raid of 3 Nov. Guardship at Humber until Dec.

Dec 1914 Unit of Dover Patrol.

15 Dec Bombarded Belgian coastal batteries in Nieuport area.

Jan 1915 Based at Portland; in Feb earmarked as unit of Dardanelles Force. Sailed for Malta early Feb; on arrival fitted with 'mine-catching' gear. Joined force 24 Feb. On 26th left Tenedos to bombard Dardanelles.

With *Albion* and *Triumph* carried out initial attack on the inner forts, opening fire at 09.14 and continuing until 17.40. These three battleships were the first Allied heavy vessels to enter the Straits during the campaign. *Majestic* was hit below the waterline, sustained a minor leak, but was able to patrol area on following day. Supported early landings, opening fire on forts 1 March from 11.25 until 16.45.

3 Mar On patrol; bombarded forts throughout day.

8 Mar Arrived Mudros Departed on patrol on 9th and circumnavigated entrance to Dardanelles, firing from 10.07 until 12.15. Returned to Tenedos on 10th; on patrol on 15th; back to Tenedos on 16th.

On the 18th took part in the main bombardment of the Narrows forts. Observed the sinking of the French battleship *Bouvet* which capsized at 14.05. *Majestic* took up position and engaged Fort 9 at 14.20, and also opened fire on field guns hidden in woods. Hit by two medium-calibre shells, one on lower top, one near forward lower top. Two more shells hit the port side forecastle abreast the fore turret, but no real damage sustained.

Fire was directed on Fort 9 for a lengthy period as

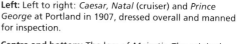

27 May While at anchor with nets out, she was torpedoed (hit twice) by *U21* just off West Beach at Gallipoli. Her log shows that she was carrying 1,728 tons coal which meant that she was in the deep condition, and her armour belt would have been low in the water. The torpedoes probably struck under the belt or at the edge on the unarmoured position. Listing heavily to port, she hung at about 40° for nearly six minutes before capsizing and sinking in 9 fathoms (40 lost). Her masts hit the mud and for a few months her keel could be seen out of water. At the end of 1915 the foremast gave way in a gale and the hulk disappeared.

HISTORY: *MAGNIFICENT*

that Fort was engaging the stricken battleship *Ocean*. Cease-fire was called at 18.35. Arrived back at Tenedos at 22.00 where wounded and one dead were brought off.

22 Mar Back on patrol. Opened fire on coastal positions on 28 Mar from 09.50 to 10.15; and again from 12.50 to 13.40. On patrol until 14 April when she fired on shore batteries at 14.58.

18 April Opened fire on the British submarine *E15* which had grounded near Fort Dardanos and was in danger of falling into enemy hands after being abandoned. *E15* was torpedoed and destroyed by one of *Majestic*'s picket boats together with one from *Triumph*. *Majestic*'s boat was sunk by gunfire while retiring.

21 April Returned to Tenedos.

25 April Signalled London 'Away all boats!' as troops were disembarked, under heavy rifle and machine-gun fire. Supported landing by bombarding coast; ceased fire at 19.10. Took 99 wounded troops aboard at 21.10 and all boats returned from landings. Anchored off Gallipoli.

26 April Opened fire at 06.17.

27 April Several shots fired at ship; very near misses; 11.30 firing on both sides ceased.

29 April Anchored off Gallipoli.

25 May Relieved *Triumph* as flagship of supporting squadrons off Cape Helles.

Laid down at Chatham 18 December 1893, and floated out 19 December 1894.

12 Dec 1895 Commissioned at Chatham to relieve *Empress of India* as 2nd Flagship, Channel Fleet. Special efforts had been made to construct *Magnificent* (and *Majestic*) in record time; the pace of building had been unprecedentedly rapid, *Magnificent* being commissioned within two years of laying down.

Dec 1895—Jan 1905 Channel Fleet.

26 June 1897 Present at Jubilee Fleet Review.

Feb—July 1904 Refit at Devonport.

Under Fleet reorganization in Jan 1905, Channel Fleet became Atlantic Fleet. With Atlantic Fleet until November 1906.

14 June 1905 Gun explosion on board, eighteen casualties.

15 Nov 1906 Paid off at Devonport and recommissioned on 16th into Reserve. In Reserve at Chatham until March 1907. Attached to Gunnery School, Sheerness, as gunnery training ship from Dec 1906. Transferred to Nore Division Mar 1907.

Mar 1907—Aug 1914 Home Fleet.

1908 Refit at Chatham.

Became Flagship of Vice-Admiral, 3rd and 4th Divisions 24 Mar 1909; Flag transferred to *Bulwark* 1 Mar 1910.

27 Sept 1910 Recommissioned for service as turret drill and Stokers' training ship Devonport and, 14 May 1912 as gunnery training ship.

16 June 1913 Grounded near Cawsand Bay in fog; slightly damaged.

1 July 1913 Recommissioned for 3rd Fleet.

27 July 1914, during the precautionary mobilization *Hannibal*, *Magnificent*, *Mars* and *Victorious*

Top: *Prince George*, 1911. 'Jack' takes a break for a smoke and some light refreshments during preparations for cleaning ship. Note the old-style hats. It was a hard life, but there was never any shortage of recruits for the Senior Service.

were selected to form 9th BS, outside main fleet organization, stationed in Humber under Admiral of Patrols pending completion of defences.

July–Aug 1914 Guardship Humber; 9th BS.

7 August Transferred to Scapa Flow with *Hannibal* to reinforce defences of Grand Fleet anchorage; 9th BS being broken up.

Aug 1914—Feb 1915 Guardship Scapa.

16 Feb 1915 Relieved by *Crescent* and paid off until September.

March—April 1915 Disarmed (except four 6in guns to provide 12in guns for *Earl of Peterborough* class monitors. Laid up at Loch Goil April—Sept 1915.

9 Sept 1915 Commissioned at Dalmuir for service as troopship for Dardanelles campaign.

Sept 1915—Mar 1916 Troopship service.

22 Sept Left (with *Hannibal* and *Mars*) on first leg of voyage; arrived Mudros 7 Oct.

18–19 Dec 1915 Took part in evacuation of troops at Suvla Bay.

Feb 1916 Returned home and paid off at Devonport 3 Mar 1916.

Mar 1916—Aug 1917 Devonport (overflow ship).

Aug 1917—Oct 1918 Refitted by Harland & Wolff, Belfast as ammunition storeship.

Oct 1918 Transferred to Rosyth.

Oct 1918—April 1921 Rosyth; Ammunition ship.

4 Feb 1920 Placed on disposal list but continued to serve as ammunition ship until April 1921.

9 May 1921 Sold to T. W. Ward. Broken up at Inverkeithing from 1922.

HISTORY: *CAESAR*

Built at Portsmouth Dockyard, and floated out on 2 September 1896. Commissioned at Portsmouth 13 Jan 1898 for service with the Mediterranean Fleet, but she was temporarily attached to the Channel Fleet until May 1898.

May 1898—Oct 1903 Mediterranean Fleet.

1900–1 Refit at Malta.

6 Oct 1903 Paid off at Portsmouth for refit until Feb 1904.

2 Feb 1904 Commissioned at Portsmouth to relieve *Majestic* as Flagship, Channel Fleet until Mar 1905. Channel Fleet became Atlantic Fleet, Home Fleet became Channel Fleet under reorganization of 1 Jan 1905.

Mar 1905—Feb 1907 Channel Fleet (2nd Flag).

3 June 1905 Collided with and sank barque *Afghanistan* off Dungeness bridge wings carried

Centre: *Prince George* in early 1915, coaling at Malta before proceeding to the Dardanelles. The *Majestic*s were the oldest class of British battleships to see action during the Great War. They proved invaluable in the Dardanelles where their guns gave continuous support to the troops.

Bottom: *Mars* in 1915–16; 12in guns now removed.

away, boats, davits and net booms on port side extensively damaged. Refitted at Devonport.
Feb—May 1907 Atlantic Fleet.
27 May 1907 Recommissioned for Devonport Division of new Home Fleet (formed Jan 1907) until Aug 1914.
1907–8 Refit at Devonport.
16 Jan 1911 Rammed by barque *Excelsior* in fog at Sheerness; no serious damage.
Aug 1914 Assigned to Channel Fleet (7th BS), formed at outbreak of war for defence of Channel, until Dec 1914.
25 Aug Took part in transporting Plymouth Marine Battalion for occupation of Ostend.
Sept 1914 Covered passage of BEF to France.
Dec 1914 Detached to Gibraltar as Guardship and Gunnery Training School until July 1915.
July 1915 Transferred to Bermuda for similar duties until Sept 1918.
Sept 1918 Transferred to Mediterranean to replace *Latona* as SNO, British Adriatic Squadron based at Corfu.
Sept—Oct 1918 Refitted at Malta for this service; equipped with repair shops, recreation rooms, reading rooms and leisure facilities.
Oct 1918 Attached to British Aegean Squadron as depot ship at Mudros.
Jan 1919 Transferred to Port Said.
Jan—June 1919 Egypt.
June 1919 Transferred to Black Sea as depot ship for British naval forces operating against Bolsheviks.
Mar 1920 Returned home and paid off to Disposal List at Devonport 23 April 1920.
8 Nov 1921 Sold to Slough Trading Co. Resold to German firm in July 1922 and towed from Devonport for scrapping. She was the last British predreadnought to serve as a Flagship, and the last to have served operationally overseas.

HISTORY: *PRINCE GEORGE*

Laid down at Portsmouth 10 Sept 1894 and began trials in Oct 1896. Commissioned at Portsmouth 26 Nov 1896 for service with Channel Fleet until July 1904.
Present at the Jubilee Fleet Review at Spithead 26 June 1897 and at Coronation Fleet Review 16 Aug 1902.
17 Oct 1903 Badly damaged in collision with *Hannibal* during night manoeuvres off Ferrol.
Hannibal rammed *Prince George* in heavy seas at 9

knots, making a large hole on starboard quarter below the waterline, and staving-in the side for about 1½ feet. *Prince George* was in danger for some hours, but eventually managed to reach Ferrol, steering with her engines and drawing 34ft 6in aft, with her sternwalk awash. Temporarily repaired at Ferrol, then left for Portsmouth 24 Oct under own steam. Completed repairs at Portsmouth.
July1904—Jan 1905 Refit at Portsmouth.
3 Jan until Feb 1905 Commissioned into Reserve at Portsmouth.
14 Feb 1905 Commissioned at Portsmouth for service with Atlantic Fleet (ex-Channel Fleet), until July 1905.
3 March 1905 In collision with German armoured cruiser *Friedrich Karl* at Gibraltar, no serious damage.
17 July 1905 Transferred to new Channel Fleet until Mar 1907.
4 Mar 1907 Paid off at Portsmouth and recommissioned on the 5th as Flagship, CinC, Portsmouth Division of new Home Fleet, organized in Jan 1907.
In Home Fleet until Aug 1914.
5 Dec 1907 Collided with armoured cruiser *Shannon* at Portsmouth sustaining considerable damage to plating below armoured shelf and to boat davits.
Mar–Dec 1909 Refit at Portsmouth.
Assigned to Channel Fleet (7th BS) on outbreak of war, until Feb 1915. Flagship of 7th BS until relieved by *Vengeance* on 15 Aug.
25 Aug Covered passage of Plymouth Marine Battalion to Ostend and BEF to France in Sept.
Feb 1915 Transferred to Dardanelles; arrived at Tenedos on 1 Mar, remained there until Feb 1916.
5 and 18 Mar Took part in the attacks on Narrows forts.
3 May Holed abaft armour strake by 6in shell while engaging Turkish batteries; returned to Malta for docking and repair.
12–13 July Supported French off Krithia and Achi Baba.
18–19 Dec Covered evacuation of troops from Suvla Bay and from West Beach 8–9 Jan 1916.
9 Jan Hit by torpedo during latter operation; torpedo failed to explode, no damage.
Jan—Feb 1916 Stationed at Salonika.
End of Feb 1916 Left for home; paid off at Chatham Mar 1916 to provide crews for A/S vessels.

Mar 1916—Oct 1918 At Chatham.
Care and maintenance until Feb 1918, then employed as accommodation ship Mar—May 1918.
May—Sept 1918 Refitted at Chatham for service as destroyer depot ship.
Aug 1918 Renamed *Victorious* II.
Oct 1918—Feb 1920 Destroyer depot ship.
Attached to *Victorious* (repair ship) at Scapa Flow until March 1919 as depot ship for Grand Fleet destroyers.
Mar 1919 Transferred to Sheerness as depot ship for Medway destroyers.
21 Feb 1920 Placed on disposal list at Sheerness.
22 Sept 1921 Sold to J. Cohen & Sons.
Dec 1921 Resold to Neugbaur, Germany.
30 Dec 1921 Stranded and wrecked on passage to scrapping yard off Camperduin, Holland and subsequently dismantled where she lay.

HISTORY: *MARS*

Laid down in dock by Lairds, Birkenhead 2 June 1894. Labour troubles delayed delivery of machinery and she was not completed and commissioned until 8 June 1897 for service with Channel Fleet until Jan 1905.
26 June 1897; Present at Jubilee Fleet Review; Coronation Review Aug 1902.
16 Aug—Mar 1905 Refit at Portsmouth.
Jan—Aug 1905 Atlantic Fleet (ex-Channel Fleet).
31 Mar 1906 Commissioned into Reserve at Portsmouth until Oct 1906.
31 Oct 1906 Commissioned at Portsmouth for new Channel Fleet until Mar 1907.
4 Mar 1907 Paid off at Portsmouth and recommissioned on 5th for Devonport Division, new Home Fleet, organized Jan1907; until August 1914.
1908–9, 1911, 1912 Refits.
27 July 1914 during precautionary mobilization, *Hannibal*, *Magnificent*, *Mars* and *Victorious* were selected to form 9th BS, outside main fleet organization, and stationed in Humber under Admiral of Patrols pending completion of new defences.
July—Dec 1914 Guardship, Humber.
7 Aug 9th BS broken up.
9 Dec Transferred to Dover (with *Majestic*) to reinforce Dover Patrol, but sent on to Portland on the 11th (*Majestic* remained in Dover).
Dec 1914—Feb 1915 at Portland.
Feb 1915 Transferred to Belfast and paid off on 15th.
Feb—Sept 1915 Paid off (Belfast and Loch Goil).

Top left: *Prince George* and *Jupiter*, 1910–11. Taking the train down to Portsmouth to see the King's ships was a popular excursion during this period. The vessels would often anchor at the end of the pier for all to see and photograph.

Top right: *Jupiter*, 1912–13. Three white bands, tall topmasts, enlarged tops and rangefinder drums.

Centre right: *Victorious*, early 1913 after repairs. In the summer of 1912 she had taken part in the annual manoeuvres after being inspected by members of Parliament. During the manoeuvres she collided with *Majestic* and damaged her propeller shaft.

Centre left: *Jupiter* during manoeuvres, c.1909. The high freeboard kept the ships of the class relatively dry forward; in fact they were dryer in a sea-way than later battleships.

Bottom left: *Jupiter* in 1915. Note the tall topmast on the fore and extension to fore of upper fighting top.

Bottom right: *Hannibal* in 1900–1, during her period with the Channel Fleet. She was a unit of the vast armada in the Solent while Queen Victoria's body was carried from Cowes to Portsmouth on 2 February 1901.

Mar—April 1915 Disarmed, except for four 6in and some lighter guns, by Harland and Wolff, Belfast, to provide 12in guns for *Earl of Peterborough* monitors.

April—Sept 1915 Laid up in Loch Goil.

Sept 1915 Commissioned for service as troopship in Dardanelles until Mar 1916.

5 Oct Arrived Mudros with *Hannibal* and *Magnificent*. Took part in evacuation of troops from Anzac Beach 18–19 Dec 1915, and from West Beach 8–9 Jan 1916.

On latter occasion, *Mars* was covered by two of her own 12in guns remounted in the monitor *Sir Thomas Picton*.

Feb 1916 Returned Devonport and paid off at Chatham. Remained at Chatham until Sept 1916. Refit for service as harbour depot ship and recommissioned for this on 1 Sept 1916.

Sept 1916—July 1920 Invergordon (depot ship).

7 July 1920 Placed on sale list at Invergordon.

9 May 1921 Sold to T. W. Ward & Co. Ltd.

Nov 1921 Left Invergordon for scrapping at Briton Ferry.

HISTORY: *JUPITER*

Laid down at Clydebank in April 1894 and transferred to Chatham Dockyard for completion in February 1897.

8 June 1897 Commissioned at Chatham for service with Channel Fleet until Jan 1905. Present at Jubilee Fleet Review 26 June 1897 and Coronation Review 1902.

Jan—Aug 1905 Atlantic Fleet.

27 Feb 1905 Paid off at Chatham for refit until Aug 1905.

15 Aug 1905 Commissioned at Chatham for Portsmouth Reserve.

20 Sept 1905 Commissioned at Portsmouth for service with Channel Fleet until Feb 1908.

3 Feb 1908 Paid off and recommissioned on 4th for Portsmouth Division, new Home Fleet until August 1914.

Refit at Portsmouth 1909–10 and 1911–12.

June 1912—Jan 1913 Employed as gunnery training ship, Nore. Assigned to Channel Fleet (7th BS) at outbreak of war until Oct 1914.

Sept 1914 Covered passage of BEF to France. Detached, with *Majestic*, at end Oct, for guardship duty at Nore.

3 Nov 1914 Transferred with *Majestic* from Nore to Humber after Gorleston raid, replacing *Hannibal*

and *Magnificent* which had been sent to Scapa.

Dec 1914 Transferred from Humber to Tyne.

5 Feb 1915 Detached to Archangel for special service as an icebreaker, and temporarily replaced the regular icebreaker for refit. *Jupiter* established a record as being the first ship to get into icebound Archangel in winter.

May 1915 Returned home for refit, and paid off at Birkenhead 19 May. Refit by Cammell Laird May until Aug 1915.

12 Aug 1915 Commissioned at Birkenhead for service in Suez Canal Patrol until Oct 1915.

21 Oct 1915 Transferred to Red Sea.

Guardship Aden and SNO, Red Sea Patrol until Dec 1915.

9 Dec Relieved by R.I.M. *Northbrook* and returned to Suez.

Dec 1915—Nov 1916 Suez Canal Patrol; stationed Port Said April—Nov 1916.

22 Nov 1916 Returned home and paid off at Devonport to provide crews for A/S vessels; at Devonport 1916—April 1919.

Feb 1918 Paid off. Subsequently auxiliary patrol ship and later accommodation ship.

April 1919 Placed on disposal list the first of the class to be disposed of.

15 Jan 1920 Sold to Hughes Bolcklow & Co.

11 Mar 1920 Towed from Chatham to Blyth for scrapping.

HISTORY: *ILLUSTRIOUS*

Laid down at Chatham, and floated out 17 September 1896. Began trials October 1897.

15 April 1898 Commissioned at Chatham for Fleet Reserve.

April—May 1898 Fleet Reserve.

10 May 1898 Commissioned at Chatham for Mediterranean Fleet until July 1904.

Sept—Dec 1898 Took part in Cretan insurrection operations.

1901 Refit at Malta.

July 1904 Transferred to Channel Fleet until Jan 1905.

Jan—Sept 1905 Atlantic Fleet (ex-Channel Fleet).

14 Sept 1905—Mar 1906 Refit at Chatham.

14 Mar 1906 Commissioned in Reserve, Chatham.

3 April 1906 Commissioned at Chatham for new Channel Fleet.

April 1906—June 1908 Channel Fleet (flag RA) (ex-Home Fleet).

13 June 1906 Collided with schooner *Christa* in fog

in the Channel.

1 June 1908 Paid off at Chatham and recommissioned on 2nd for Portsmouth Division, new Home Fleet, organized January 1907. With Home Fleet until August 1914.

22 Mar 1909 Collided with *Amethyst* in Portsmouth Harbour, no damage.

21 Aug 1909 Struck reef in Babbacombe Bay, sustaining damage to bottom.

Refit 1912.

1912 Manoeuvres as Flagship (VA) 7th BS.

Not included in initial mobilization of Third Fleet ships in July 1914, and intended to be paid off to provide crew for new battleship *Erin*. Subsequently selected, however, as Guardship for Grand Fleet base at Loch Ewe on 23 Aug 1914. Guardship, Loch Ewe, Loch Na-Keal, Tyne, Humber (Grimsby) Aug 1914—Nov 1915. Transferred from Loch Ewe to Loch Na-Keal 17 Oct; from Loch Na-Keal to Tyne in November, and from Tyne to Humber in Dec 1914.

26 Nov 1915 Paid off at Grimsby, for disarmed conversion to Harbour Subsidiary Service until March 1916.

Aug 1916 Transferred to Chatham as Overflow Ship.

20 Nov 1916 Commissioned at Chatham for service as Munition Storeship and transferred to Tyne on 24th, until April 1919 (Tyne to Nov 1917, Portsmouth later).

21 April 1919 Paid off.

24 Mar 1920 Placed on sale list at Portsmouth.

18 June 1920 Sold to T. W. Ward & Co Ltd and broken up at Barrow.

HISTORY: *HANNIBAL*

Laid down at Pembroke Dockyard 1 May 1894, launched in April 1896 and then transferred to Portsmouth for completion. Delayed by labour problems, she finally completed in April 1898, and was placed in Fleet Reserve at Portsmouth until May 1898.

10 May 1898 Commissioned at Portsmouth for service with Channel Fleet until Jan 1905.

Aug 1902 Present at Coronation Fleet Review.

17 Oct 1903 Collided with *Prince George* off Ferrol, latter badly damaged.

On Channel Fleet becoming Atlantic Fleet, and Home Fleet becoming Channel Fleet on 1 Jan 1905, *Hannibal* placed in Atlantic Fleet until Feb 1905.

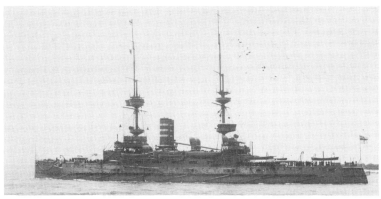

28 Feb 1905 Transferred to new Channel Fleet (old Home Fleet) until August 1905.

3 Aug 1905 Paid off into Reserve, Devonport until Jan 1907.

Jan 1907 Temporarily attached to Channel Fleet replacing *Ocean* for refit. Remained in Channel Fleet after return of *Ocean*, pending arrival of *Dominion* from refit in May. Transferred in May to Devonport Division of new Home Fleet, formed in January 1907, into which the Reserve Divisions were incorporated.

May 1907—Aug 1914 Home Fleet (Devonport).

19 Aug 1909 Struck reef in Babbacombe Bay, severely damaged bottom for about 60 feet.

29 Oct 1909 Collided with *TB 105* badly damaging forward part of the TB. No damage to *Hannibal*.

Nov 1911—Mar 1912 Refit at Devonport.

27 July 1914 With *Mars*, *Magnificent*, and *Victorious*, formed 9th BS to defend coast; stationed in Humber.

July—Aug 1914 Guardship (9th BS).

7 Aug Transferred to Scapa, with *Magnificent*, to reinforce defences of Grand Fleet anchorage, 9th BS being broken up.

Aug 1914—Feb 1915 Guardship Scapa.

20 Feb 1915 Relieved by *Royal Arthur* (cruiser) and paid off at Dalmuir until Sept 1915. Disarmed, except for four 6in and some lighter guns in Mar–April 1915 to provide 12in guns for *Earl of Peterborough* monitors.

April—Sept 1915 Laid up at Scapa and Loch Goil.

9 Sept 1915 Commissioned at Greenock for service as troopship to Dardanelles.

7 Oct Arrived at Mudros. Became depot ship for auxiliary patrol craft at Alexandria in Nov 1915, until June 1919. Served as depot ship for Egypt and Red Sea Forces.

Jan 1920 Placed on disposal list at Alexandria.

28 Jan 1920 Sold to Montague Yates. Broken up in Italy.

HISTORY: *VICTORIOUS*

Built at Chatham Dockyard and began sea trials in October–November 1896.

4 Nov 1896 Commissioned into Fleet Reserve at Chatham.

8 June 1897 Commissioned at Chatham to relieve *Anson* in Mediterranean Fleet. With Mediterranean Fleet until Feb 1898.

26 June 1897 Present at Jubilee Fleet Review at Spithead before proceeding to station.

Feb 1898 Detached to China Station until 1900.

1900–01 Refit at Malta.

8 Aug 1903 Paid off at Chatham for refit.

Aug 1903— Feb 1904 Refit at Chatham.

2 Feb 1904 Commissioned at Devonport as 2nd Flagship, Channel Fleet until Jan 1905.

14 July 1904 Rammed by *TB 113* in Hamoaze but sustained only slight plating damage. Joined Atlantic Fleet on Fleet reorganization.

Jan 1905—Dec 1906 Atlantic Fleet.

31 Dec 1906 Paid off at Devonport and recommissioned 1 Jan 1907 for Nore Division of new Home Fleet.

Jan 1907—Aug 1914 Home Fleet.

1908 Refit at Chatham.

14 July 1912 Collided with *Majestic* during manoeuvres in fog, damaging sternwalk.

1913 Refit at Chatham. From July 1914, stationed in Humber with 9th BS to defend east coast.

Dec 1914 Transferred to Tyne.

Dec 1914—Feb 1915 Guardship (Tyne).

4 Jan 1915 Paid off at Elswick.

Feb—Sept 1915 Tyne (paid off).

Sept 1915—Feb 1916 Converted by Palmer, Jarrow for service as Grand Fleet Repair Ship at Scapa Flow, to replace ex-merchantman *Caribbean*, lost Sept 1915.

22 Feb 1916 Commissioned at Jarrow for this service, and arrived Scapa 6 Mar 1916.

Mar 1916—Mar 1920 Fleet Repair Ship (Scapa).

Mar 1920 Transferred to Devonport to refit for service with Indus Establishment, and was renamed *Indus II*.

28 Mar Arrived Devonport and paid off into Care and Maintenance 14 April 1920 pending refit. This was abandoned and it was then proposed to fit her as a harbour depot ship at a cost of £6,000, but this was also cancelled in April 1922 after work had commenced.

April 1922 Placed on disposal list at Devonport.

19 Dec 1922 Sold to A. J. Purves (Channel Shipbreaking Co). Sale cancelled 1 Mar 1923. Sold to Stanlee Shipbreaking Co 9 April 1923 and towed to Dover for scrapping.

CANOPUS CLASS

1896/7 ESTIMATES

DESIGN

In March 1895 the DNC (William White) submitted to their Lordships a paper showing details of the new Japanese battleships *Fuji* and *Yashima*, then under construction in England, and suggested that the existence of such powerful ships, together with the recent general increase in Japanese naval strength, demanded the inclusion of more powerful battleship types in the British Far Eastern Squadron. White also suggested that some of the first class battleships to be laid down in the near future should be able to pass through the Suez Canal. White's ideas subsequently materialized in the *Canopus* class of the 1896–8 estimates.

On 13 May 1895 the Sea Lords met in the Controller's room to discuss and reach provisional agreement on the formulation of the new ships.

On the 15th White returned to his department and informed his staff (Mr Dunn, Mr W. E. Smith and Mr Cardwell) that a suitable design be prepared as quickly as possible around these suggestions:

1. Freeboard forward and aft to be the same as in *Centurion*.
2. Main armament the same as in *Caesar* and *Illustrious*.
3. Secondary armament to be ten 6in quick-firing guns.
4. Speed and fuel capacity to be the same as that of *Renown*.
5. Protection on the main belt to be 6in with barbette and deck as in *Renown*.

A sketch design fulfilling these conditions was submitted by the DNC to the Controller on 23 May 1895, together with a description of the principal features; the ships to be armed with four 12in, ten 6in and eight 12-pounders.

On the basis of this preliminary sketch, design work went ahead during the next few months.

In the first week of October 1895, the Assistant Constructor Mr J. Dunn sent a letter on behalf of the DNC to the Controller (J. Fisher) stating:

'As directed by you, I submit three sketches relating to the proposed new battleships.

Each plan provides four 12in and at least eight 6in. Sketch A shows gun arrangement as in sketch now before their Lordships, and it will be seen that a 6in gun is carried in a 6in armoured casemate on the main deck between two double stowed casemates; four 12-pounders are carried on the deck above.

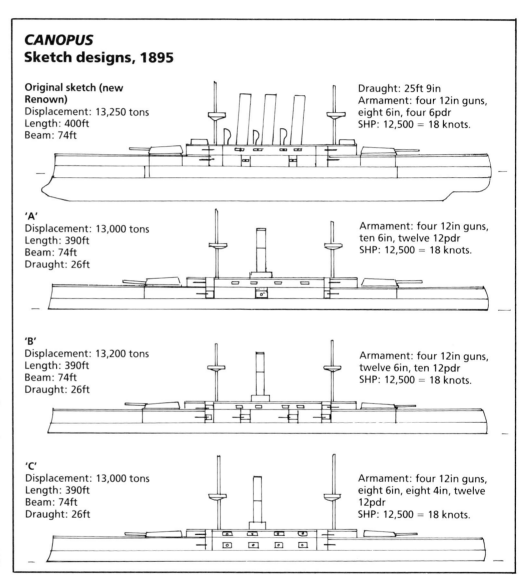

CANOPUS
Sketch designs, 1895

Original sketch (new Renown)
Displacement: 13,250 tons
Length: 400ft
Beam: 74ft

Draught: 25ft 9in
Armament: four 12in guns, eight 6in, four 6pdr
SHP: 12,500 = 18 knots.

'A'
Displacement: 13,000 tons
Length: 390ft
Beam: 74ft
Draught: 26ft

Armament: four 12in guns, ten 6in, twelve 12pdr
SHP: 12,500 = 18 knots.

'B'
Displacement: 13,200 tons
Length: 390ft
Beam: 74ft
Draught: 26ft

Armament: four 12in guns, twelve 6in, ten 12pdr
SHP: 12,500 = 18 knots.

'C'
Displacement: 13,000 tons
Length: 390ft
Beam: 74ft
Draught: 26ft

Armament: four 12in guns, eight 6in, eight 4in, twelve 12pdr
SHP: 12,500 = 18 knots.

The side of the ship, apart from the casemates, consists of only ordinary thin skin plating above the main deck.

B differs from A in having the side of the ship between the double stowed casemates, between the upper and main deck protected by 4in Harvey steel plates, whilst behind these plates two instead of one 6in gun is shown.

C shows 4in plates as in B, but instead of two 6in there are now four 4in.

Each plan represents equal stability and weight breakdown.'

The Controller quickly called a meeting to discuss the latest designs before sending an official reply to the DNC on 9 October.

'In view of the fact represented by you that there

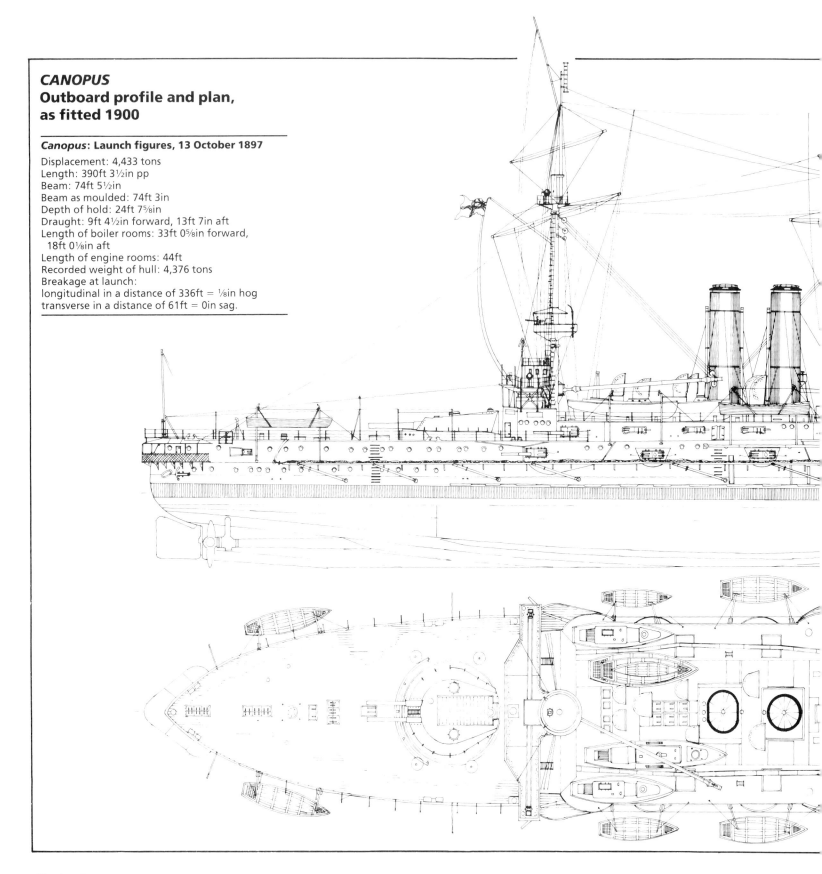

CANOPUS
Outboard profile and plan,
as fitted 1900

Canopus: **Launch figures, 13 October 1897**

Displacement: 4,433 tons
Length: 390ft 3½in pp
Beam: 74ft 5½in
Beam as moulded: 74ft 3in
Depth of hold: 24ft 7⅝in
Draught: 9ft 4½in forward, 13ft 7in aft
Length of boiler rooms: 33ft 0⅝in forward,
 18ft 0⅛in aft
Length of engine rooms: 44ft
Recorded weight of hull: 4,376 tons
Breakage at launch:
longitudinal in a distance of 336ft = ⅛in hog
transverse in a distance of 61ft = 0in sag.

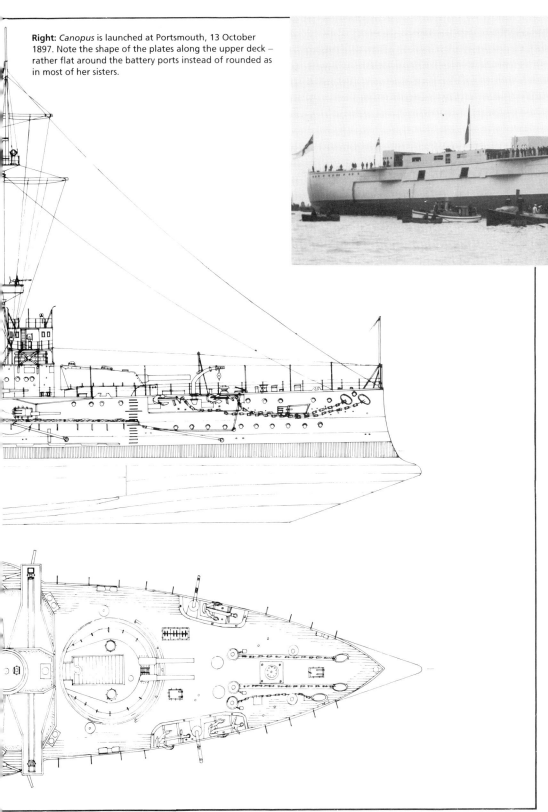

Right: *Canopus* is launched at Portsmouth, 13 October 1897. Note the shape of the plates along the upper deck – rather flat around the battery ports instead of rounded as in most of her sisters.

would be no alteration as regards stability, weight and draught of water, etc., and that from the construction point of view no objection exists, it was decided to adopt the suggested alternative in armament for the reason so fully discussed, and add a 6in quick-firing gun on each side of the main deck of the *Renown*s, doing away with the single 6in casemate on the main and substituting 4in Harvey steel on the side between the upper and main decks as shown in sketch B with an armoured traverse between the 6in guns instead of the arrangement suggested in sketch A.

If practicable, the four 12-pounders would be retained as originally proposed.

Present and agreeing in this discussion in the Controller's Room were: Sir Frederick Richards, Sir F. Bedford, Captain Noel, the Director of Ordnance, and the DNC.'

During the next few months the final design showed an amalgamation of the original sketch design submitted (3 funnels) and A+B, but before the final legend was approved on 2 September 1896, some alterations and additions were proposed and executed within the layout:

1. Two 6in guns were added to the first proposal bringing the total number to twelve as in *Majestic*.
2. It was arranged to have one fighting top on each mast instead of two.
3. The decision was taken to adopt water tube boilers after successful trials had been carried out in 'Sharpshooter'.
4. Four of the 6in battery guns were placed in armoured casemates.
5. The 4in side armour above the main belt, that had featured in the original design, was discarded, together with the 2in traverses and the armoured side was applied much the same as in *Majestic*.
6. The aft armoured strake was dropped, and the forward nickel steel strip was increased to a thickness of 2in.

7. The main deck plating inside the citadel was increased to 1in, outside to ³/₈in; and outside the citadel on the main deck level to ³/₈in.
8. Wood planking on main and middle decks was eliminated.
9. Bridgework extended over the conning tower as in previous designs.
10. Protective deck reduced inside citadel to two thicknesses of 2in plate (40lb).
11. Secondary casemate faces reduced from 6in to 5in.
12. Reduction in thickness of turret shields from 10in to 8in.
13. Reduction in thickness of forward armoured bulkhead.

Finally, in conclusion of the debate as to whether the ships would have two or three funnels, White wrote to the Engineer-in-Chief stating:

'We are to adopt the amended plan with two funnels; these are to be upright and not raking as in early designs. It is understood that the use of three funnels was in accordance with the Controller's wishes (Fisher), but as service opinion has shown, it makes the working of the boats difficult and in some cases possibly dangerous. The Controller, therefore, had concurred in the use of two funnels which has resulted in a saving of weight of 5 ton.'

The problem of making three funnels into two was cleverly overcome by White who ensured that the forward funnel served eight boilers, from the forward boiler house; the four boilers in the central and aft boiler houses had their flues trunked as they came up near the after funnel which was ingeniously trunked athwartships, thus giving an oval appearance, which, in fact, could not be seen unless viewing the uptake from the fore and aft position.

Compared to *Majestic*, the group of six ships were 1,950 tons lighter in the load condition, but with the same main and secondary armament; an increase of ¹/₄ knot on the maximum designed speed, and about two knots higher continuous sea speed and reduced radius of action.

The principal features of the design were:
1. Adoption of stronger Krupps Cemented armour with thin extension of belt to the bows, and a modified arrangement of deck protection.
2. Adoption of water tube boilers in place of cylindrical.
3. Slightly altered water plane, coefficient and hull lines, in the interest of manoeuvring ability.

4. Abandonment of upper fighting tops.
5. Improved bridge and navigation arrangements.
6. Improved and simplified ventilating arrangements.

Armament and speed were approximately the same as in the Japanese *Fuji*, with about 600 tons less displacement. Protection was equal except along the waterline where the armour was only one-third as thick, but this was partially offset by the use of improved KC quality, backed by the sloping deck (*see* armour) which was not fitted in *Fuji*. Furthermore, the fuel capacity and radius of action was substantially larger than in the Japanese vessels. With the application of the newly developed KC armour, White was able to secure maximum standards in offensive power on a moderate displacement and within the required draught limits.

At the same time, however, the securing of this quality on the restricted draught and displacement which their intended employment demanded, meant that certain sacrifices in protection had to be accepted and, although useful ships for the China Station, the class were never regarded as an entirely satisfactory type, fighting value being discounted to some extent by the thin armour which was considered inadequate against heavy-calibre shellfire.

Although conceived by White as 1st class battleships, and rated as such, the First Lord when introducing the 1896 estimates, referred to the group as 'improved *Renowns*' and in the Constructor's Department they were generally regarded as 2nd class battleships on account of their armouring (*see* White's remarks, armour section).

As completed, the ships turned out well in service and formed the backbone of the China Squadron for many years until the Anglo-Japanese Alliance of 1905 allowed them to be withdrawn.

At White's instigation, they were not copper sheathed owing to the additional draught that would have been involved (over 1ft) and because fouling was not considered a serious problem in view of the docking facilities at Hong Kong. In support of this the DNC pointed out that the new Japanese battleships then under construction were themselves unsheathed.

Compared with *Majestic*, the freeboard was 3¹/₄ft lower at the bows, but 6in higher aft. This reduction of freeboard forward did not have any adverse effect and the *Canopus* class were always good sea-

boats and steady gun platforms. The manoeuvring qualities were practically identical with *Majestic*, but the shallow draught on the same hull length tended to give a wider turning circle, and the ships were difficult to handle when steaming slowly into strong winds or going astern.

***Canopus*: Approved final legend, 2 September 1896**

Displacement: 12,950 tons
Length: 421ft 6in oa
Beam: 76ft 3in
Draught: 26ft (mean)
Sinkage: 53ft tons per inch.

Armament
Four 12in
Twelve 6in
Ten 12pdr
Six 3pdr
Four torpedo tubes.

Armour
Side: 6in
Bulkheads: 10in–8in–6in forward; 12in–10in–6in aft
Conning tower: 12in–3in
Casemates: 5in
Turrets: 8in
Barbettes: 12in–6in
Decks: 1in main, 2in middle, 2in lower.

Weights (tons)
Hull:	5,310
Armament:	1,485
Machinery:	1,290
Armour	
Vertical:	1,065
Deck:	950
Barbettes and turrets:	745
Casemates:	330
Conning tower:	80
Coal:	800
General equipment:	670

SHP: 13,500 for 18¹/₄ knots
Fuel: 800 tons coal normal, 1,600 tons max.

ARMAMENT

Originally it had been intended to fit the same turrets and loading arrangements as fitted in the last two vessels of the *Majestic* class (*Illustrious* and *Caesar*, BIII mountings), but a great deal of experimentation went on within the class which resulted in only *Canopus* herself actually being fitted with BIII mountings; the following four (*Glory*, *Albion*,

Ocean and *Goliath*) were fitted with improved BIV mountings. With *Vengeance*, the last of the class, came the BV arrangement. This variation had been proposed after it had been pointed out that in *Majestic*'s mounting, the shell hoist at the rear of the turret and barbette ran straight down to the shell rooms and magazines without interception. This was viewed by many as being highly dangerous. A shell exploding in the turret could cause a flashback which could easily reach down to the shell and magazine rooms.

Illustrious and *Caesar*, with their BIII mounting, countered the problem with an additional platform at main deck level which interrupted the path of the shell hoist (*see* drawings). *Glory*, *Albion*, *Goliath* and *Ocean*, however, took a retrograde step when fitted with the BIV which actually omitted the interception level because of the slower time taken to bring shells from below, than in previous

Canopus class: Particulars, as completed

Construction
Canopus: Portsmouth DY; laid down 4 Jan 1897; launched 12 Oct 1897; completed 5 Dec 1899
Glory: Cammell Laird; laid down 1 Dec 1896; launched 11 March 1899; completed Oct 1900
Albion: Thames Iron Works; laid down 3 Dec 1896; launched 21 June 1898; completed June 1901
Ocean: Devonport DY; laid down 15 Dec 1897; launched 5 July 1898; completed Feb 1900
Goliath: Chatham DY; laid down 4 Jan 1897; launched 23 March 1898; completed March 1900
Vengeance: Vickers; laid down 23 Aug 1898; launched 25 July 1899; completed April 1902.

Displacement (tons)
13,182 (load), 14,350 (deep) (*Albion*)
13,141 (load), 14,322 (deep) (*Canopus*).

Dimensions
Length: 390ft 3½in pp, 400ft wl, 421½ft oa
Beam: 74ft 5½in
Draught: 26ft 2in load, 30ft deep (mean).

Armament
Four 12in 35cal Mk VIII; 80rpg
Twelve 6in 40cal
Ten 12pdr (12cwt)
Two 12pdr (8cwt)
Six 3pdr
Two MG
Four 18in torpedo tubes, submerged on the beam, one pair abreast each barbette.

Armour
Main belt (KC): 6in amidships (196ft long)
Forward belt (nickel steel): 2in
Forward bulkheads (KC): 10in–8in–6in
After bulkheads (KC): 12in–10in–6in
Decks (mild steel): 1in main; 2in middle (slope, flat); 2in lower
Barbettes (KC): 12in–10in–6in
Turrets (KC): 8in faces, 2in roofs
Casemates (Harvey): 5in–2in
Forward conning tower (Harvey): 12in face, 8in tube
After conning tower (mild steel): 3in face, 3in tube.

Machinery
Two sets 3-cylinder triple expansion engines, twin in-turning propellers
Boilers: twenty Belleville water tube with economizers, working pressure 300psi (250psi at cylinders)
Heating surface: 33,780sq ft
Grate area: 1,055sq ft
Designed SHP: 13,500 = 18.25 knots
Fuel: 900 tons coal normal, 1,800 tons max.
Coal consumption: 336 tons per 24 hours at full speed, 52 tons per 24 hours at 8 knots
Radius of action: 5,320nm at 10 knots, 2,590nm at 16½ knots (sea-going speed).

Ship's boats
Pinnaces (steam): one 56ft, one 40ft
Pinnaces (sail): one 36ft
Launches (steam): one 40ft
Cutters: two 34ft, one 30ft
Galleys: one 32ft
Whalers: one 27ft
Gigs: one 30ft, one 28ft, one 24ft
Skiff dinghies: two 16ft
Balsa rafts: one 14ft.

Searchlights
Six 24in, two on each bridge, one high on each mast.

Anchors
Two 118cwt bower, one 117cwt sheet, two 55cwt Martins.

Wireless
Type I, later replaced by Type 2.

Complement
682 average as completed
737 *Goliath*, 1904
752 *Albion*, 1904 (as flagship)
739 *Goliath*, 1908
400 *Vengeance*, as seagoing gunnery ship 1912
371 *Albion*, 1916 as portguardship.

Costs
Canopus: £866,516 plus guns £54,800
Goliath: £866,006 plus guns £54,800
Ocean: £883,778 plus guns £54,800
Albion: £858,745 plus guns £54,800
Glory: £841,014 plus guns £54,800
Vengeance: £836,417 plus guns £55,000.

mountings. The reversion in *Vengeance*, shows that the dangers of the early straight-through system had at last been recognized, and sacrifices were made in favour of a greater safety margin for the hoisting of shells and charges to the turrets. The slowness of the loading arrangements in *Vengeance* were partially offset by an improved Vickers turret which provided all-round loading at all elevations which considerably improved the rate of fire.

The original proposal of ten 6in (May 1895) as in *Renown* was altered when the design was reviewed a few months later; it having been found possible to mount twelve 6in as in the *Majestic* group. The upper deck 6in were about 19 feet above the waterline, and the main deck guns 12½ feet above. As in *Majestic*, the siting of two-thirds of the secondary armament on the main deck was a particularly weak point in the design owing to their low command. The above-water torpedo tube, provided originally, was suppressed while under construction, and this marked the abandonment, for many years, of above-water torpedo tubes in British capital ships; probably because of the difficulty in providing adequate protection for them, and the risk of serious damage if a torpedo exploded in the tube.

The anti-torpedo armament originally consisted of six 12pdrs in the upper deck battery, and twelve 3pdrs in the tops of both masts, but when the design was finally reviewed in the summer of 1896, it was modified and strengthened by adding four 12pdrs in ports on the main deck level forward and aft; this enabled the upper top to be eliminated from each mast by reducing the number of 3pdrs from twelve to six.

ARMOUR

These were the first British battleships to have Krupps cemented armour with a 30 per cent greater resistance than the Harvey type it replaced; it was fitted on all main strakes except casemates, decks, ammunition hoists and the forward conning tower. They were also the first battle ships designed since *Dreadnought* (1870) to have vertical armour carried through to the extremities of the hull. The extension of the belt to the bow was originally proposed by White in 1888 for the *Royal Sovereign* class, but was rejected by the Board on the grounds that it was preferable to have the increased thickness amidships and rely on internal subdivision only, at the ends.

CANOPUS
Inboard profile and sections,
as fitted 1901

Section 162
1 Admiral's dining room
2 Wardroom
3 Wardroom stores
4 Steering compartment
5 Watertight compartment

Section 147
1 Admiral's secretary
2 Working space
3 Cabin
4 Electric light store
5 Torpedo room
6 Provision room

Section 134
1 Fleet surgeon
2 Coal
3 12in turret
4 Shell chamber
5 Passage
6 Hydraulic machinery
7 12pdr magazine
8 Hydraulic tank
9 Oil tank
10 Shaft passage
11 12in shell room

Section 104
1 Vent to engine room
2 Sergeants' mess
3 Coal
4 Ammunition passage
5 Engine room

Section 92
1 Casemate
2 Locker
3 Bag racks
4 Coal
5 Ammunition passage
6 Boiler room

Section 84
1 Electric winch
2 Uptake
3 Mess
4 Coal
5 Boiler room

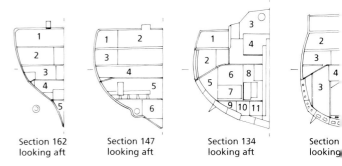

Section 162
looking aft

Section 147
looking aft

Section 134
looking aft

Section
looking

Section
1 Boilers
2 Machinery and engine rooms
3 Shell rooms
4 Magazines
5 12in barbettes
6 Boiler room uptakes
7 Engine room vent
8 Steering compartment
9 Torpedo rooms
10 Conning tower
11 Watertight compartments
12 Capstan room

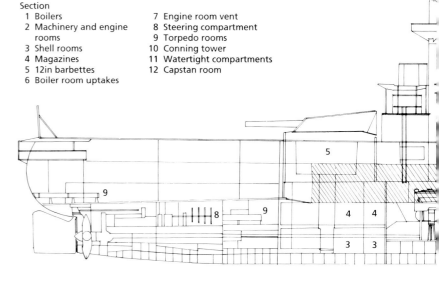

Section 56
1 Chart house
2 Shelter deck
3 Vent
4 Seamen's heads
5 Bag racks
6 Casemate
7 Conning tower base
8 Coal
9 Ammunition passage
10 6in magazine
11 12pdr magazine
12 6in shell room
13 3pdr magazine

Section 40
1 12in turret
2 Shell chamber
3 Passage
4 Lamp room
5 Coal
6 Working space
7 Engineers' workshop
8 12in magazine
9 Electric store
10 12in shell room
11 Provision room

Section 22
1 Mess
2 Chain lockers
3 Lime store
4 Capstan room
5 Mine store

Section 14
1 Mess
2 Boatswain's store
3 Boatswain's store
4 Locker
5 Cordage store

Goliath: Launch figures, 23 March 1898

Displacement: 5,735 tons
Length: 390ft 2in pp
Beam: 74ft 2⅝in
Beam as moulded: 74ft 1⅜in
Depth of hold: 23ft 11½in
Recorded weight of hull: 5,580 tons
Breakage at launch:
longitudinal in a distance of 320ft = ³/₃₂in hog
transverse in a distance of 64ft = ¹/₁₆in sag.

Weights on board (tons)
Men, launch gear, ballast, etc.: 100
Internal shoring: 80
Buoyancy of cradle: 60
Machinery: 25
Angle-iron, plates, etc.: 10

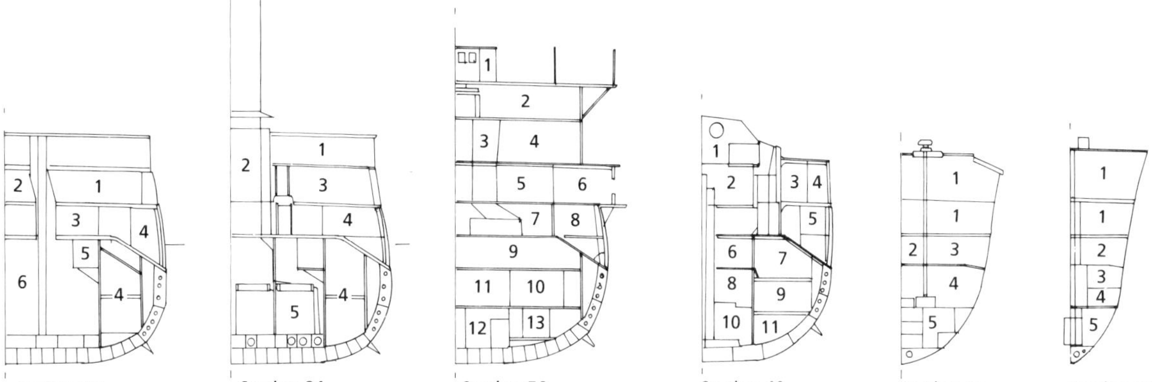

Section 92
looking forward

Section 84
looking forward

Section 56
looking forward

Section 40
looking forward

Section 22
looking forward

Section 14
looking forward

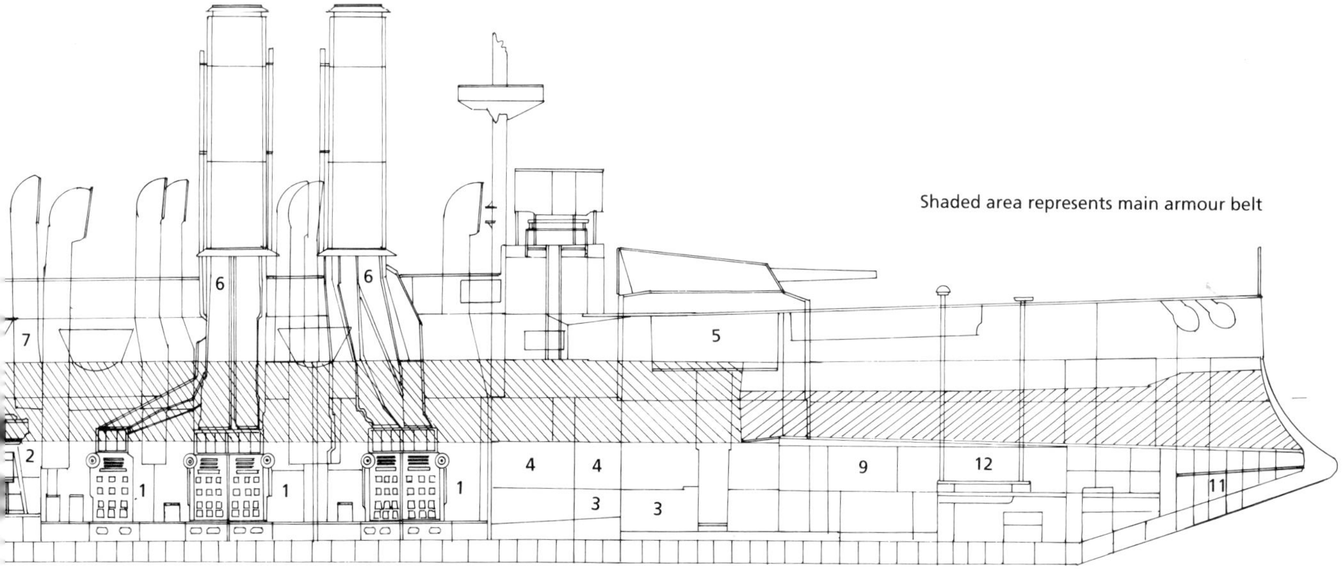

Shaded area represents main armour belt

Left: *Canopus.* Commissioned on 5 December 1899, she is seen here at Portsmouth on 19 December, shortly before leaving for the Mediterranean to relieve *Anson.*

Below left: *Goliath* at Chatham, 27 March 1900. Commissioned to relieve *Victorious* on the China Station, she did not leave England until 30 May.

They were the first British battleships to have two internal, above-water armoured decks, the extra deck resulting from a proposal to fit the latest French battleships with special howitzers for delivering plunging fire. This plan had become known while the *Canopus* group were being designed and, at White's instigation the ships were fitted to resist a threat of this kind. 1in armour was fitted to the main deck, over the citadel, with a view to bringing all high-explosive shells to detonate at that level. The flat section of the middle deck below, reduced from 3in to 2in as compared to the *Majestic*s, so that the total horizontal deck armour was the same in both classes. In the event, the proposed French ships were not given the howitzers (except one small coastal vessel for experiment), but the practice of fitting two or more complete or partial decks instead of one heavy one, was adhered to in all subsequent British battleships prior to the *Nelson* class (1925).

Below: *Glory* leaving Portsmouth for the China Station in December 1900.

Below right: *Canopus* leaving for the Mediterranean, 5 December 1899.

Canopus class: Steam trials, October 1899

Course: Rame Head to Dodman Point

	Revs (mean)	IHP	Speed (knots)
Goliath; 30-hour; 10 October			
Wind ESE, Force 1–2; sea smooth			
First run:	102	10,677	17.03
Second run:	101.4	10,638	17.67
Third run:	104.6	10,887	17.16
Fourth run:	102.1	10,939	17.42
Goliath; full power; 11 October			
First run:	109.8	13,878	18.14
Second run:	109.7	14,390	18.45
Third run:	109.3	13,980	18.68
Fourth run:	106.4	13,423	17.65
Glory; full power			
First run:	108.6	14,266	17.233
Second run:	110.6	14,420	19.266
Third run:	106.7	13,980	16.896
Fourth run:	107.4	13,696	19.291
Ocean; 20 October			
Wind E by S, Force 3; sea moderate			
First run:	113.7	13,994	18.81
Second run:	113	13,819	17.43
Third run:	114.2	14,332	19.18
Fourth run:	113.1	13,868	17.37
Fifth run:	112.4	13,429	18.61
Canopus (full power)	108.5	13,763shp	18.5
Albion	108	13,885shp	17.8
Vengeance	110.65	13,853shp	18.5

Average steam pressure in boilers: 265psi
Average coal consumption 1.58lb per hp per hour.

Protection was subordinated, to some extent, to offensive power and speed, with maximum armour thickness on belt, turrets and barbettes being reduced from that of *Majestic*, to help secure equal armament and higher speeds on a similar displacement, although reduction in thickness was partially offset by improved quality plates. The protection to the secondary armament and total thickness of horizontal armour was the same as in *Majestic*, but the sloping section (inclines) of the middle deck, behind the belt, were 1in thinner. Innovations to protection for the class were:

1. Adoption of Krupps armour in place of Harvey.
2. Thin extension to bows.
3. Provision of flat armoured section amidships over citadel, in addition to sloping deck behind belt within this.

The 2in bow belt fitted to the class was quickly seen by many to have been provided mainly as a sop to current public agitation against 'soft enders',

Below: *Goliath* in July 1903, homeward bound after ending her commission on the China Station.

Centre: *Vengeance* in the spring of 1905, on the China Station. *Furst Bismarck* and USS *Helena* in background.

Bottom: *Ocean* during 1906 fleet manoeuvres with Channel Fleet. Seen here at Portland and carrying her fleet markings.

Right: *Canopus*, all grey, showing fleet markings on funnels 1906–7. The class were built primarily for foreign service and when completed filled this role admirably, being able to out-steam most foreign contemporaries. Note the early range clock below the fore top.

which were inadequate against medium-calibre projectiles except at very long range. In fact, it had been fitted against the possibility of a completely unarmoured forecastle being riddled by light, quick-firing shells or splinters, and then flooded by the bow wave, although this was only part of White's theory of bow protection as envisaged for the *Royal Sovereign*s wherein he had planned at least medium thickness of armour plating.

At the time of construction, the class's protection came under severe criticism, and it was remarked in *The Times* that they were little more than 'second class battleships'.

Confronted by constant hostility towards his design White commented:

'Attention is specially directed to the armour thickness of 6in, and discussions in the Press and Parliament show a tendency to adverse criticism in general. I have no doubt, that at this early stage in the vessels' construction rumours about the class are widespread, and probably when they are completed, there will be more.

It is important, therefore, to recall the circumstances that when I first suggested the adoption of uniformly thick armour of the citadel in association with a strong protective lower deck, I also proposed that the lower limit of defence suitable for first class battleships intended for close action was such, that a thickness of armour as would be capable of resisting perforation by 6in AP projectiles under service conditions, and at fighting ranges.

All experience in actual warfare, and at the Battle of Yalu show that under the conditions of practice, the actual protection afforded by armour is much greater than that indicated by firing tests of targets with nominal impact, close range, and many blows delivered on a limited area. For example, the citadel armour of Chinese battleships was only dented 3 or 4in by the fire of the 12in guns mounted in some of the Japanese ships. The estimated penetrative power of these guns with normal impact at 2,500 yds was equal to 23in of iron armour, or 18 to 19in of wrought iron, whereas 8 to 14in of compound armour, by no means first class quality these days, was not penetrated or seriously damaged on the Chinese ships. The 6in citadel of *Canopus* will more than stand the attack of such ships.'

When comparing the *Canopus* class with foreign vessels, White said of the armour:

'The policy of the Admiralty has been to adopt the distribution of the armour which gives the best defence available with a given weight of material, and to consider the protected area, as well as the maximum thickness of armour. This was the reason which led to the abandonment of the thick armour belt, with thin side armour above it, after the construction of the *Royal Sovereign*s.

Royal Sovereign shows 18in against 9in in the *Majestic*, but it can scarcely be doubted that on the whole, the *Majestic* is the better protected ship, especially against modern quick-firing guns and explosives.

Of all the ships compared with *Canopus*, the *Majestic* was the best, but fortunately, the *Canopus* will not have to meet her in battle.'

The main belt was 6in thick; 196ft x 14$\frac{1}{4}$ft amidships extending to abeam the barbettes. The upper edge was at main deck level,

approximately 9ft above the waterline, with the lower edge 5$\frac{1}{4}$ft below.

The 2in strake forward ran straight through to the bows, with the forward extremity carrying down to support the ram. The upper edge was approximately 4ft above the waterline, rising to 9ft at the forward section. Lower edge was level with lower edge of midship 6in section.

All armour was laid over a double thickness of $\frac{1}{2}$in plating. The belt bulkheads were 10in–8in–6in forward, and ran obliquely inwards from the forward extremities of the 6in armour to the face of the forward barbette. Aft, the bulkhead ran at the same angle into the after barbette but at a thickness of 12in–10in–6in.

Turrets were given 8in faces and 2in roofs (*see* drawings for any variation in class). Barbettes had 10in on the fronts, 12in rears and then reduced to 6in once below the belt armour. Secondary

casemates (Harvey) were 5in on the face with 2in sides and rears.

The forward conning tower was 12in (Harvey) with an 8in communication tube; the after conning tower was 3in with a 3in tube (Harvey).

The main deck was 1in thick (mild steel) across the top of the citadel. The middle deck was 2in across the slope and flat, and extended over the length of the citadel between the outer facing of the barbettes, with the crown about 2ft above the waterline and the lower edge with the lower edge of the main belt, 5$\frac{1}{4}$ft below the waterline at normal load condition.

MACHINERY

Two sets of 3-cylinder triple expansion engines driving two screws. Twenty Belleville water tube boilers, with economizers and arranged in three compartments, all on the centre-line. Eight boilers

Right: *Vengeance* at Weymouth, c1906, during summer manoeuvres.

Far right: *Ocean* dressed overall, in August 1907 after a short refit. Note the rangefinder on bridge, SL positions, no quick-firing guns in tops, yards on topmast and W/T gaff.

in the forward and midships compartment, four in the after compartment; all having a working pressure of 300psi.

Engineering developments introduced in this class, especially the adoption of water tube boilers in place of cylindrical, materially influenced the design as a whole, and was largely responsible for the advance in speed over the *Majestic* group, an increase of 1,500ihp being obtained on a reduced total weight of machinery and boiler equipment.

The machinery was of the same general type as that fitted in the preceding classes, but of a lighter and more efficient design. In-turning screws were fitted which provided a greater drive and produced slightly higher revolutions but reduced fuel economy compared to the normal out-turning type. They also made the ships difficult to handle at low speeds or when going astern and the method was generally disliked in service. Nevertheless, they were retained until *Dreadnought* was again fitted with out-turning screws (1906).

The *Canopus* group were the first British battleships to have water tube boilers, which provided increased power on a greatly reduced weight. Their adoption in place of cylindrical boilers had been proposed when the design was first discussed in May 1895, but a decision was deferred pending a thorough and lengthy series of trials together with an investigation into the effect on stability which would result from the loss of weight low down in the ship's hull (*see* Boiler Committee results).

Compared to the eight cylindrical boilers in the *Majestic* class, working pressure was increased by approximately 145psi, heating surface by 9,300sq ft and horse power raised from 12,000 with forced draught to 13,500 with natural draught.

Forced draught was abandoned in this class, and a modified arrangement of the boilers meant that a reversion of the centre-line arrangement of funnels could be reverted to. The original design provided for 18 knots as in *Renown* but it was subsequently found possible to increase this to 18.25 knots. They were the fastest battleships in the Royal Navy until the *Duncan* class were completed.

Being the first large ships to have water tube boilers they did suffer from teething troubles—not just at first, but for most of their active careers. *Ocean* suffered badly from leaking tubes in the condensers shortly after completion, a condition which was cured in her refit of 1902–3. Later (1908), however, her machinery and boilers were in

such a bad state that a Court of Inquiry was held to investigate her poor condition, which resulted in her Engineer Commander being held responsible. The inquiry did show that her machinery was prone to deteriorate rapidly if not checked constantly. *Vengeance* also suffered from leaks and strains in her machinery, and was not an economical steamer as a result. Study of the machinery registers suggests that of all the ships in the class, *Canopus* herself seems to have been the best all-round steamer.

APPEARANCE CHANGES

Appearance was greatly changed from preceding classes because of their centre-line funnels instead of abreast as in *Majestic*, *Renown* and *Centurion*, etc. The *Canopus* group were noticeably smaller than *Majestic*, and sat lower in the water. The fore funnel was round, but the second was oval-shaped, the greatest diameter being athwartships and appearing much larger than the fore funnel when viewed from dead ahead or abaft (*see* drawings).

No flying bridge aft, and noticeably fewer cowls than *Majestic*. A single large fighting top on each mast was fitted low, with a searchlight placed high on each mast. W/T gaff fitted in *Albion*, *Glory*, *Vengeance* and *Canopus* as completed. Distinguishable from *Formidable*, *London*, *Duncan* and *Queen* classes by:
1. Funnels closer together and more amidships.
2. Masts shorter and closer together.
3. Enclosed upper deck battery (*Duncan* and *Queen* only).
4. Generally lower in the water, and looked smaller.

Glory: GM and stability

Based on inclining experiments, 27 October 1900

	Draught	GM	Maximum stability	Stability vanishes at
'A' Condition (= load)*	26ft 1in (mean)	3.7ft	38½°	64½°
'B' Condition (= deep load)**	28ft 0½in (mean)	3.8ft	36°	65½°
'C' Condition (= light)	24ft 5in	3.4ft		

*Fully equipped plus 300 tons coal in upper bunkers, 480 tons in lower bunkers.
**Fully equipped plus 1,880 tons coal, feed tanks full.

Individual differences:
Ocean and *Albion* Steam pipe before and abaft second funnel.
Ocean Steam pipe abaft fore funnel.
Albion No steam pipe abaft fore funnel.
Canopus, *Glory* and *Goliath* No steam pipes before fore funnel.
Canopus Steam pipes up to stay rib. Funnel caps well clear of casing.
Glory Large heavy funnel caps.
Goliath Lighter caps with centre rim well raised.
Vengeance No steam pipe abaft fore funnel. Heavy funnel caps. Angled instead of curved turrets (only unit).

There were individual differences in the number of scuttles around the anchors, and on the forward superstructure (*see* drawings).
1899–1900 Shields removed from 3pdrs in tops (1899–1902). Wireless telegraphy fitted in *Goliath*

and *Ocean* from 1901–2. W/T gaff on mainmast (high).

1903–4 Victorian paint scheme replaced by all-grey.
1905–9 Fire control and RF equipment fitted. Control top fitted to foretop instead of SL(1906–7). Large oval control top in *Albion* and *Glory*, but small square top in others. *Vengeance* retained her small square top throughout. Siemens-Martin fire control gear fitted temporarily in Vengeance in

***Glory*: GM and stability**

Based on inclining experiments, 14 August 1916

	Draught (mean)	GM	Maximum stability	Stability vanishes at
'A' Condition (= load)*	26ft	3.84ft	39°	65½°
'B' Condition (= deep load)**	28ft 7⅛in	4.56ft	36½°	71°

*Fully equipped plus 800 tons coal.
**Fully equipped plus 1,831 tons coal.

Below: *Goliath* bow-on during the summer of 1907. Note the lack of tumblehome as compared with the *Majestics*.

Right: *Goliath*, c.1908. She was the only unit of the class to be lost during the war, being torpedoed by a Turkish torpedo-boat in the Dardanelles on 13 May 1915.

Far right: *Canopus* at anchor in Weymouth Bay in 1907, while serving with the Portsmouth Division.

Bottom right: *Canopus* in 1907, anchored in Weymouth Bay while on manoeuvres with the Channel and Atlantic Fleets.

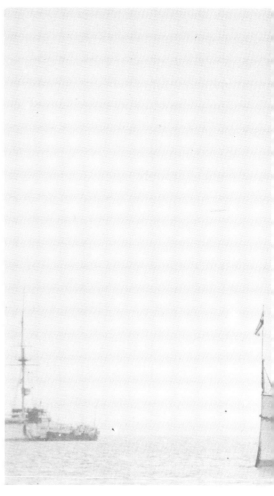

Left: *Albion*, at 15 knots. Note standard funnel bands.

Below left: *Albion* in 1909–10. From 17–24 July 1909 she was with the fleet that visited London to be entertained by the citizens (17–24 July 1909), and was present at the review of the Home and Atlantic Fleets by the King and Queen at Cowes on 31 July.

Below: *Canopus* at anchor in the Dardanelles. Note the modifications: SL on lower top, no wings to bridge, vents instead of cowls, mine-sweeping gear at bows, short top masts, crow's nest on foremast, no torpedo nets.

1906 for experiment only. Small range indicators fitted in some of class for short period. Removal of 3pdrs from tops from 1905–6. Maintop guns all out by the end of 1907, foretop by 1909. Two remounted on forebridge in *Vengeance*, and in superstructure forward or aft in the others. 12pdrs removed from main deck in all (1906–7) and remounted in forward superstructure in all except *Vengeance*. Forward ports plated up. SL removed from masts and remounted over 6in casemates (1905–7). In all except *Albion*, forward SL removed

first being temporarily suppressed in *Canopus*, remounted on new platform well below control in *Goliath*, *Ocean* and *Vengeance*, and in foretop in *Glory*. Both SL relocated over casemates in all by 1907. Two 24in SL added on boat deck amidships in all (1907–9). Masthead semaphore removed and W/T gaff triced (1907–8). W/T gaff replaced by W/T topgallant in *Canopus* in 1908. Funnel bands painted up in some ships in 1905 (*see* drawings).
1909–10 Standard system of funnel bands painted up (*see* drawings).

1910–11 Modified and larger type of range indicators fitted in some ships, being carried on forward military top, after control top, or on platform below fore control top. These, together with the 1905 pattern, were for experimental purposes and were finally discarded in 1914. W/T gaff in *Ocean*, *Vengeance*, *Glory*, *Albion* and *Goliath* replaced by W/T topgallant as in *Canopus*. W/T topgallant fitted to foremast in *Vengeance* only. Heavy yards began to be removed from masts during this period, and were all out by 1914.
1912 Casemate and boat-deck SL in *Vengeance* remounted on forebridge, ship then carrying six on this.
1912–13 Torpedo nets removed in *Vengeance*. Others later, but at different dates.
1914 Funnel bands painted out in August 1914. A dummy third funnel is stated to have been rigged up in *Canopus* during the operations against Von Spee in October. Extra control position added over fore control top, topmasts struck, and painted up in strange camouflage (*see* drawings), while stationed at Port Stanley.
1915 Small howitzer temporarily mounted on fore turret in *Canopus* Feb 1915 for engaging Turkish batteries in Dardanelles at close range. Proving of little use, this was removed early spring. Small AA gun (probably 3pdr) added to quarter-deck in *Albion* and on each turret in *Vengeance* by late 1915.
SL ex forward 6in casemate remounted on forward fighting top in *Canopus* and *Vengeance*. *Glory* and *Ocean* also received similar alterations while on this particular service. Torpedo nets not fitted. Special mine-sweeping gear fitted over bows of *Canopus* in Feb 1915. Wings removed from both bridges in *Canopus*, *Goliath*, *Ocean* and *Vengeance*. Stockless anchors fitted in all, but old anchor beds retained. Rigs of class very variable at this stage. Topgallant masts fitted in *Ocean* during Suez Canal Patrol early 1915, removed later at Dardanelles. Topmasts in others, but usually housed well down. No heavy yards on mainmast. Various forms of camouflage painted up at Dardanelles (*Canopus* grey patches to resemble cloud formations). False bow wave painted up in *Ocean* and *Vengeance*. Range baffles in rigging in *Canopus*.
1916 *Canopus* Main deck 6in guns removed, four remounted in shields on upper deck. 12pdrs reduced from ten to eight, all fitted in forward and aft superstructure. *Glory* refitted for service in

North Russia–6in and 12pdr modifications as in *Canopus*. Torpedo nets fitted, *Glory* being the last British battleship to carry these. Full-height topmasts, and topgallant to main.

1918 *Vengeance* disarmed for service as depot ship.

HISTORY: *CANOPUS*

Commissioned at Portsmouth 5 December 1899 for Mediterranean Fleet until April 1903.

Dec 1900—June 1901 Refit at Malta.

25 April 1903 Paid off into Reserve at Portsmouth.

May 1905 Reserve at Portsmouth.

May 1903—June 1904 Extensive refit by Cammell Laird, Birkenhead.

5 Aug 1904 Rammed by the battleship *Barfleur* in Mounts Bay during manoeuvres, slightly damaged.

9 May 1905 Commissioned at Portsmouth to replace *Centurion* on China Station, but recalled from Colombo June 1905 while en route as a result of the reduction of forces in that area by the new Anglo-Japanese agreement. Joined Atlantic Fleet (ex-Channel Fleet) 22 July 1905 on her return. Atlantic Fleet until Jan 1906.

Jan 1906 Transferred to Channel Fleet (ex-Home Fleet) until Mar 1907.

10 Mar 1907 Transferred to Portsmouth Division of new Home Fleet (organized Jan 1907) until April 1908.

Nov 1907—April 1908 Refit at Portsmouth.

28 April 1908 Commissioned at Portsmouth for service with Mediterranean Fleet until Dec 1909.

Dec 1909 Reduced to 4th Division, Home Fleet, Nore until Aug 1914.

July 1911—April 1912 Refit at Chatham.

Assigned to Channel Fleet (8th BS) at outbreak of war in August.

Channel Fleet (8th and 7th BS). Detached to Cape Verde–Canary Islands 21 Aug to support cruiser squadron in that area. Cape-Verde–Canary Islands (Guardship, St. Vincent) until Sept. Relieved by *Albion* and transferred to South America Station 1 Sept as Guardship, Albrolhos Rocks, and support for Rear-Admiral Craddock's cruiser squadron. Arrived at Abrolhos Rocks 22 Sept. South America Station until Jan 1915. Operations against Von Spee's squadron until December 1914. Transferred to Falklands Islands 7 Oct to join Craddock's squadron in search for Von Spee. Arrived at Falklands 18 Oct, but owing to low speed was only employed as escort ship and was not present at the Coronel action in which Craddock was lost with his ship. Returned to Falklands after Coronel (arrived 12 Nov) and stationed at Port Stanley as Guard-ship, being moored head and stern to cover entrance to harbour and command fire landwards to the south-east. Observation post established ashore with telephone communication to ship, enabling indirect fire to be carried out against approaching vessels. Topmasts were struck, and she was camouflaged to blend with surroundings. Some 12pdrs were landed for harbour defence with a Marine detachment of 70 men.

She opened fire on the German squadron on their approach on the morning of 8 Dec but enemy turned away before coming into effective range of her 12in guns. One hit, however, was scored on *Gneisenau*'s after funnel by a ranging shell which ricocheted off the water.

Canopus left Falklands on 18 Dec for Abrolhos Rocks, on reorganization of South America forces after the Falklands action.

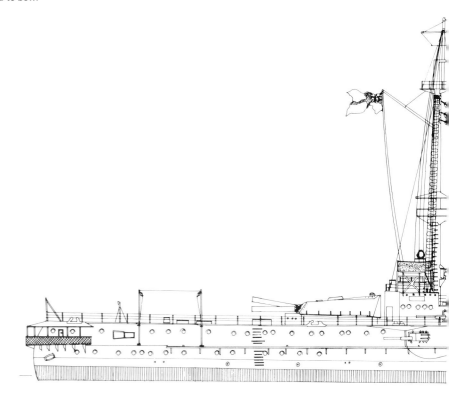

CANOPUS
Outboard profile, as seen at Dardanelles 1915

Note short topmasts, reduced bridgework, searchlights on forward lower fighting top, windsails and mine-catching equipment fitted to bow.

Feb 1915 Transferred to Dardanelles until Jan 1916.

2 Mar 1915 Took part in second attack on entrance forts. Hit several times, main topmast carried away, after funnel riddled, and wardroom damaged. Demonstrated off Aegean Coast 4 March during third landings.

Covered indirect bombardment of forts by *Queen Elizabeth* 8 Mar and supported sweepers in Kephes minefield 10–12 Mar. Took part in attack on

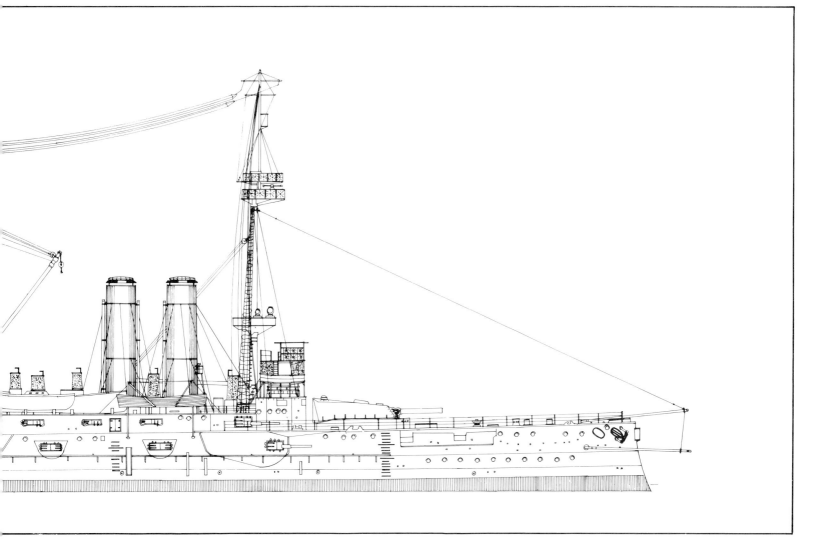

Right: *Ocean* at Suez in 1915. She anchored at the mouth of the Suez Canal on 29 December 1914 and stayed in the area until the middle of January 1915. She then went up the canal to lend support against a half-hearted Turkish attack. She rejoined the fleet in mid-February to ready herself for the Dardanelles campaign.

Far right, top: *Vengeance* in dry dock for hull inspection and small refit, 1915.

Far right, centre: *Vengeance*. She was nicknamed 'the Lord's Own'. Note the extremely small bridge fitted during the early months of the war.

Far right, bottom: *Vengeance* seen from the air at Dar es Salaam in 1916.

Narrows forts 18 Mar and with *Talbot* escorted the damaged *Inflexible* from Mudros to Malta after the attack. Towed *Inflexible* stern first during latter part of passage when the battlecruiser became unable to steam ahead because of damage. Escorted troop transports from Egypt early 1915. Covered diversionary attack on Bulair 25 April during main landings. 23 May Towed *Albion* off-shore at Gaba Tepe under heavy fire after latter had grounded within range of enemy batteries.

May—June 1915 Refit at Malta.

Jan 1916 Attached to Eastern Mediterranean Squadron after evacuation of Gallipoli. Eastern Mediterranean until April 1916.

28 April 1916 arrived at Plymouth, and paid off at Chatham to provide crews for anti-submarine vessels. At Chatham until April 1919. Refit 1916. Deployed as accommodation ship from Feb 1918.

April 1919 Placed on Disposal List at Chatham.

18 Feb 1920 Sold to Stanlee Shipbreaking Co, Dover for £35,500.

26 Feb 1920 Arrived Dover for scrapping.

HISTORY: *OCEAN*

Laid down at Devonport Dockyard, the first large armoured ship to be built there.

20 Feb 1900 Commissioned at Devonport for service with Mediterranean Fleet, until Jan 1901, when transferred to China because of Boxer Rebellion. In China until June 1905.

Sept 1902 Damaged in typhoon; section of net shelf carried away and cutter lost. Refit 1902–3.

June 1905 Recalled owing to reduction of China Squadron following Anglo-Japanese agreement. Reserve at Chatham until Jan 1906.

2 Jan 1906 Recommissioned for Channel (ex-Home) Fleet, until April 1908. Refit at Chatham Jan—Mar 1907, and April—June 1908.

2 June 1908 Recommissioned for service with Mediterranean Fleet until Feb 1910. Refit at Malta 1908–9.

16 Feb 1910 Transferred to 4th Division of new Home Fleet (organized Jan 1907) until August 1914. Refit at Chatham 1910 and 1911–12. Assigned to Channel Fleet (8th BS) on outbreak of war. With Channel Fleet. Detached to Queenstown 21 Aug as Guardship and support for cruiser squadron in that area. Queenstown Guardship until Sept 1914. Transferred to East Indies Station (with *Goliath*) to support cruisers on convoy duty against possibility of attack by Von Spee's squadron.

Ordered to relieve *Albion* on Cape Verde–Canary Islands Station but diverted to East Indies en route; arrived Aden mid-October. Oct 1914 Escorted Indian troop convoy to Bahrein. Subsequently in Persian Gulf and Suez Canal. Oct—Dec 1914 Senior Officer's ship of squadron covering military operations against Basra. This squadron consisted of *Ocean*, *Espiègle*, *Odin* and RIM *Dalhousie*.

Dec 1914 Stationed at Suez to assist in defence of the Canal, and supported troops in action during Turkish attack 3—4 Feb. Transferred to Dardanelles late Feb 1915, until March 1915.

1 Mar Took part in the bombardment of the entrance forts and hit by gunfire from mobile batteries, but no serious damage. Supported landings at Sedd el Bahr 4 Mar. Took part in attack on Narrows forts 18 Mar. Hit drifting mine while retiring from this engagement under heavy fire. Her coal bunkers and forward and after passages on the starboard side were flooded. The helm had jammed hard to port and the ship took a list of 15° to starboard. She came under shellfire and her starboard engine room became flooded which prevented her steering gear from being temporarily repaired. *Ocean* was finally abandoned at 19.30, and later drifted into Morto Bay and sank there at about 22.30. Most of her crew were taken off by destroyers and loss of life was small.

HISTORY: *GLORY*

Floated out 11 March 1899 with most of her armour in place and nearly all machinery installed; masts were stepped but funnels were not in.

1 Nov 1900 Commissioned at Portsmouth for service on China Station. Left for China 24 Nov.

17 April 1901 Collided with *Centurion* in Woosung Roads, no damage. Refit at Hong Kong 1901–2. Withdrawn from station July 1905. Left Hong Kong for home 22 July.

2 Oct 1905 Paid off at Portsmouth and completed to full crew 24 Oct for Channel Fleet (ex-Home). With Channel Fleet until Oct 1906.

31 Oct 1906 Transferred to Portsmouth Reserve. Reserve until Jan 1907 when Portsmouth Reserve Division became Portsmouth Division of new Home Fleet. Home Fleet (Portsmouth Division) until Sept 1907. Refit at Portsmouth Mar—Sept 1907.

18 Sept 1907 Commissioned at Portsmouth for service with Mediterranean Fleet, until April 1909.

20 April 1909 Paid off at Portsmouth and

recommissioned for 4th Division, Home Fleet, Nore, until August 1914.

Assigned to Channel Fleet at outbreak of war. Detached to Halifax 5 Aug as Guardship and support for North America and West Indies cruiser squadron in Oct 1914. Unit of escort for Canadian troop convoy in Oct 1914. Transferred to Dardanelles May 1915, and joined Dardanelles Squadron in June of that year. Dardanelles until Dec 1915. At end of Dec detached with *Cornwallis* to Suez Canal Patrol and joined this 4 Jan 1916, until April 1916, then returned home.

April–July 1916 Refit at Portsmouth.

1 Aug 1916 Commissioned at Portsmouth as Flag (RA) of the British North Russia Squadron. This squadron was based at Archangel to protect supplies landed there for Russian armies. Early in 1917 the squadron consisted of *Glory* (Flag), *Vindictive* and six minesweeping trawlers. Aug 1916—Sept 1919 North Russia Squadron, Murmansk.

Sept 1919 Returned home at close of North Russia campaign and paid off at Sheerness to Care and Maintenance 1 Nov 1919.

With Caesar she was the last British predreadnought to remain in operational service overseas. Sheerness until May 1920.

1 May 1920 Transferred to Rosyth as harbour depot ship, Rosyth until Sept 1921.

17 Sept 1921 Paid off on to disposal list.

19 Dec 1922 Sold to Granton Shipbreaking Co.

HISTORY: *VENGEANCE*

She was the first British battleship to be completely built, armed and engined by a single firm. After her launch on 25 July 1899 completion was delayed by damage incurred to the fitting-out dock.

8 April 1902 Commissioned at Portsmouth for service with Mediterranean Fleet.

Mediterranean Fleet until July 1903.

July 1903 Transferred to China to relieve *Goliath*. In China until June 1905. Refit at Hong Kong 1903–4.

1 June 1905 Recalled.

23 August 1905 Paid off into Devonport Reserve, until May 1906. Refit 1905–6.

15 May 1906 Commissioned at Devonport for service with Channel Squadron. Channel Fleet until May 1908.

6 May 1908 Transferred to Home Fleet, until Aug 1914.

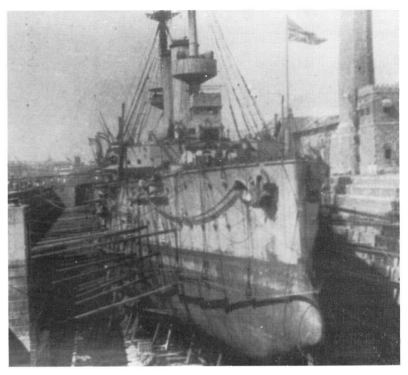

13 June 1908 Collided with SS *Begore Head* at Portsmouth; damaged side plating, net shelf and booms.

28 Feb 1909 Grounded in Thames estuary, no damage.

April 1909 Tender to Chatham gunnery school.

29 Nov 1910 Collided with SS *Biter* in fog, damage to net shelf and booms.

Jan 1913 Gunnery Training Ship at the Nore.

Aug—Nov 1914 Channel Fleet.

15 Aug Transferred to 7th BS relieving *Prince George* as Flagship. Took part in transporting Plymouth Marine Battalion for occupation of Ostend 25 Aug.

Detached to Egypt early Nov 1914 as Guardship at Alexandria, relieving *Black Prince* and *Warrior*.

Below: *Vengeance* in 1916. Note the AA guns on the 12in turret.

Right: *Albion* at Gaba Tepe. With *Triumph* and *Majestic* she carried out the initial attacks on the inner forts in February 1915. She was hit badly on 28 April and again on 2 May. She ran aground off Gaba Tepe on the night of 22/23 May and came under extremely heavy fire, being hit about 200 times by shrapnel shells.

Egypt until late Nov 1914. 1914 Transferred to Cape Verde–Canary Islands to replace *Albion* as support for cruiser squadron operating in that area. Cape Verde–Canary Islands Station (Guardship, St. Vincent) until Jan 1915. Transferred to Dardanelles 22 Jan 1915 as 2nd Flag of that squadron. Arrived Feb 1915. Dardanelles until July 1915.

18–19 Feb Took part in opening bombardment of entrance forts, sustained damage to spars and rigging from returning gunfire. Subsequent bombardments of entrance and Narrows forts and initial landings during Feb and early Mar. Main attack on Narrows forts 18 Mar. Supported main landings at Helles (Morto Bay area) 25 April. Supported army during Turkish attack on positions at Anzac 19 May. Attacked by submarine 25 May.

July 1915 Returned home to pay off owing to boiler defects.

July—Dec 1915 Refitted at Devonport.

Dec 1915 Transferred to East Africa to support operations against Dar es Salaam, left Devonport for Cape 30 Dec. Took part in operations against and capture of Dar es Salaam 1916. East Africa and Cape until Feb 1917.

Feb 1917 Returned home. Paid off until Feb 1918 for experimental service.

Feb—April 1918. Used for experiments with anti-flash equipment. Disarmed in 1918 and employed as ammunition storeship from May 1918.

9 July 1920 Placed on sale list at Devonport.

1 Dec 1921 Sold to Stanlee Shipbreaking Co. Towed to Dover 27 Dec 1921, but tow-rope parted in Channel on 29th. Relocated by French tugs and taken to Cherbourg. Finally reached Dover from Cherbourg on 9 Jan 1922.

HISTORY: *GOLIATH*

Commissioned at Sheerness 27 March 1900 for service on the China Station, until July 1903.

Sept 1901—April 1902 Refit at Hong Kong.

9 Oct 1903 Paid off into Reserve at Chatham, until May 1905. Refit at Palmers, Tyne Jan—July 1904. Took part in manoeuvres 1904.

9 May 1905 Commissioned at Chatham to relieve *Ocean* on China Station but recalled from Colombo in June, while *en route*, and attached to Mediterranean Fleet, until Jan 1906. Transferred to Channel Fleet (ex-Home) Jan 1906—Mar 1907.

15 Mar 1907 Transferred to Portsmouth Division of new Home Fleet. Refit at Portsmouth Aug 1907—Feb 1908.

4 Feb 1908 Commissioned at Portsmouth for service in Mediterranean Fleet, until April 1909.

20 April 1909 Paid off at Portsmouth and recommissioned on 22nd for 4th Division, Home Fleet, Nore, until August 1914. Refit at Chatham 1910–11. Assigned to Channel Fleet at outbreak of war, until Sept 1914. Took part in transporting Plymouth Marine Battalion for occupation of Ostend 25 August. Transferred to East Indies Station 20 Sept to support cruisers on convoy. Escorted Indian convoy to Persian Gulf and German East Africa until Oct 1914. Took part in blockade of *Königsberg* in River Rufiji Oct—Nov 1914. Bombarded Dar es Salaam 28 and 30 Nov, and sent in boats to destroy shipping and installations.

Dec 1914—Feb 1915 Refit at Simonstown.

25 Feb Hoisted Flag of Vice-Admiral King Hall on completion of refit, and employed in further operations against *Königsberg* during March.

25 Mar Ordered to Dardanelles and transferred flag to *Hyacinth*.

1 April Left for Dardanelles, there until May 1915. Supported landings at 'Y' Beach 25 April and covered evacuation on 26th. Sustained some damage from gunfire on 25th. Supported army during first battle of Krithia 25 April; Damaged in action with batteries 2 May.

13 May 1915 Torpedoed and sunk by a German-manned Turkish torpedo-boat *Muvenet-i-Milet* with the loss of 570 men. The atack was carried out at night under foggy conditions when the ship was anchored off Morto Bay, supporting French troops at Kereves Dere. Two torpedoes hit almost simultaneously, one abreast fore turret and the other abeam the fore funnel. The ship listed rapidly to port, and was almost on her beam ends when a

third torpedo hit near the after turret. She capsized and started to sink by the bows before the majority of her crew could reach the upper deck. The *Muvenet-i-Milit* was sighted and fired on shortly after the first torpedo hit, but escaped into the darkness.

HISTORY: *ALBION*

Built by Thames Ironworks at Blackwall and launched on 21 June 1898. After the launching ceremony had been performed by the Duchess of York, a wave caused by her displacement ran up a side creek and brought about the collapse of a staging on which 200 people were standing; 34 of them were drowned, mostly women and children. Her completion was delayed by the late delivery of some of the main machinery, partly caused by the contractor's financial difficulties. She began her trials late in 1900, and was finally commissioned (after more delays because of defects in machinery and guns, etc.) 25 June 1901 at Chatham, to relieve Barfleur on the China Station.

9 Sept 1901 2nd Flag transferred from *Barfleur* at Hong Kong; with China Fleet until June 1905. Refits at Hong Kong 1902 and 1905.

June 1905 Returned home and joined Channel Fleet, until April 1906. Collided with *Duncan* at Lerwick 26 Sept 1905, but received no damage.

3 April 1906 Transferred to the Reserve at Chatham, until Feb 1907. Refit at Chatham 1906.

25 Feb 1907 Paid off at Portsmouth and recommissioned 26th for temporary service with Portsmouth Division, new Home Fleet; Feb—Mar 1907.

26 Mar 1907 Commissioned at Portsmouth for Atlantic Fleets. Refitted at Gibraltar and Malta 1908–9.

25 Aug 1909 Paid off to 4th Division, Home Fleet, Nore until Aug 1914. Refit at Chatham 1912. Assigned to Channel Fleet at outbreak of war.

15 Aug 1914 The 7th and 8th BS Channel Fleet merged into one following the transfer of four *Majestics* from the original 7th BS for Guardship duties. *Albion* became 2nd Flagship of new 7th BS. As a result of a decision to provide battleship escort for Atlantic cruiser squadrons against possible breakthrough of German heavy ships, *Albion*, *Canopus*, *Glory* and *Ocean* were detached from the 7th BS from 5 to 21 Aug and were sent to Cape St. Vincent–Finisterre, Cape Verde Islands, Halifax and Queenstown respectively. *Goliath* and

Below: *Albion* c.1917–18, showing deck layout. Note the forward barbette is painted black, and net booms are out.

Bottom: *Albion* at the scrapyard (T. W. Ward) in January 1920. Note the huge ram and the fact that her nets are still fitted.

Opposite page: *Formidable* at Portsmouth in October 1901, shortly before leaving for the Mediterranean. Whereas the *Canopus* group had been designed specifically as light battleships capable of passing through the Panama Canal for foreign service, the *Formidable*s were modified versions of *Majestic* and were of exceptionally strong construction. *Formidable* was commissioned on 10 October 1901 with the crew of *Resolution* for service in the Mediterranean.

Vengeance (Flag) remained with 7th BS until Sept and Nov respectively.

21 Aug *Albion* was detached to Gibraltar as Guardship and support for the St. Vincent–Finisterre Squadron.

3 Sept *Albion* transferred to Cape Verde–Canary Islands to relieve *Canopus*, and became a private ship.

Oct 1914–Jan 1915 Cape Station. Guardship Walfiach Bay to Nov.

Dec 1914—Jan 1915 Took part in operations against German West Africa.

Jan 1915 Transferred to Dardanelles and was there until Oct 1915.

Took part in bombarding entrance forts 18/19 Feb. With *Majestic* and *Triumph* carried out initial attack on inner forts 26 Feb. These three ships were the first battleships to enter the straits during the campaign. Supported the first landings in Feb and early Mar. *Albion* was repeatedly hit in action with forts 1 Mar, but sustained no serious damage.

Took part in main attack on forts 18 Mar.

Supported main landings at Helles ('V' Beach) 25 April.

28 April Heavily hit during attack on Krithia and forced to retire and seek repairs in Mudros. Returned to the fight, only to receive more punishment on 2 May, resulting in a further period for repair at Mudros.

22/23 May Went aground at night at Gaba Tepe and came under heavy fire. She received about 200 hits from shrapnel shells but sustained no serious damage. Towed clear by *Canopus*. Refit at Malta May—June 1915.

4 Oct 1915 Returned to Salonika as unit of 3rd Detached Squadron, formed to assist the French in blockading Greece and the Bulgarian coast, and to reinforce the Suez Canal Patrol. Embarked first British contingent of 1,500 troops for Salonika, and escorted transports for French second contingent.

Oct 1915—April 1916 Salonika Station.

April 1916 Returned home and stationed at Queenstown as Guardship, April—May 1916. May—Aug 1916 Refit at Devonport. Transferred to Humber as Guardship on completion of refit, Aug 1916—Oct 1918. Reduced to accommodation ship in October.

Aug 1919 Placed on disposal list at Devonport.

11 Dec 1919 Sold to T. W. Ward for £32,755.

3 Jan 1920 Left Devonport under own steam for scrapping at Morecambe arriving 6 Jan.

FORMIDABLE CLASS

1897 ESTIMATES

DESIGN

Designs for the battleships of the 1897 programme were first discussed by the Board at a meeting on 3 May 1897 when it was agreed that a repeat of the *Canopus* class would be inadvisable in view of:

1. The advance to 15,000 tons displacement in Japanese battleships (*Shikishima* and *Hatsuse*) already laid down or projected.

2. Displacement of the *Canopus* was insufficient to carry the new 12in 40cal gun produced since *Majestic* and *Canopus* because of the increase in weight for the new mountings, turntables and barbettes, etc., amounting to about 150 tons of topweight.

It was decided therefore to include one further unit of the *Canopus* class (*Vengeance*) in this programme, in order to complete a tactical group of six ships, and to adopt a larger and more powerful design for the other three which were allowed for to make up the total for the year of 1897.

By utilizing the advantages of the newly developed Krupps armour plating, improved machinery and water tube boilers, introduced in the *Canopus* group, and affording increased efficiency on reduced weight, it was found possible to incorporate the new guns, together with generally stronger protection and higher seagoing speed than the *Majestic*s without any substantial increase in displacement.

The DNC (White) accordingly proposed a modified *Majestic* which embodied these developments and, on 18 June 1897, submitted two alternative sketch designs, each having a main armament of four 12in guns, with an 8in armoured belt and a nominal speed of 18 knots. The first plan showed a secondary armament of twelve 6in on a displacement of 14,700 tons, this number being the same as in *Majestic* on 200 tons less displacement. The second layout had fourteen 6in (as in the Japanese ships) with a displacement of 14,900 tons.

White recorded his opinion favouring the fourteen 6in layout, but the majority of the Board did not consider the additional guns necessary. They approved the twelve gun plan, but with an extra 1in of armour bringing it up to 9in, even though the extra cost showed a figure of £17,000 and the displacement rose to 15,000 tons. On 19 June 1897 the Board agreed that for the three later battleships provided for under the 1897–8 naval estimates, an improved *Majestic* with the above

features would be most desirable and asked the DNC to prepare full sets of drawings.

After the preliminary features had been decided, White placed J. H. Narbeth in charge of the basic design with J. H. Cardwell to assist him. On 17 August 1897 a model was put in hand by R. E. Froude at Haslar to work out the details of her hull and coefficient.

Compared to *Majestic*, the new design was 100 tons heavier, with a more powerful 12in gun, stronger protection due to the Krupp process, increased maximum designed speed and a 2-knot

Formidable class: Particulars, as completed

Construction
Formidable: Portsmouth DY; laid down 21 March 1898; launched 17 Nov 1898; completed Sept 1901

Implacable: Devonport DY; laid down 13 July 1898; launched 11 March 1899; completed July 1901

Irresistible: Chatham DY; laid down 11 April 1898; launched 15 Dec 1898; completed Oct 1901.

Displacement (tons)
Formidable: 14,658 (load), 15,805 (deep)
Implacable: 14,480 (load), 15,805 (deep)
Irresistible: 14,720 (load), 15,930 (deep)

Dimensions
Length: 400ft pp, 411ft.wl, 431ft 9in oa
Beam: 75ft
Draught (mean): 26ft 9in (load), 28ft 8in (deep)
Freeboard: 23ft forward, 16ft 9in amidships, 18ft aft.

Armament
Four 12in 40cal Mk IX; 80rpg
Twelve 6in 45cal Mk VII; 200rpg
Sixteen 12pdr (12cwt); 300rpg
Two 12pdr; (8cwt)
Six 3pdr 500rpg
Two MG
Four 18in torpedo tubes (submerged).

Armour
Main belt: 9in
Bulkheads: 12in–10in–9in
Side plating: 3in forward, 1½in aft
Barbettes: 12in–6in
Turrets: 10in–8in
Casemates: 6in
Conning tower: 14in–3in

Communication tube: 8in–3in
Decks: main 1in, middle 3in–2in, lower 2½in–2in
Total weight: 4,335 tons.

Machinery
Two sets 3-cylinder vertical triple expansion engines, two propellers
Cylinder diameter: two at 31½in, two at 51⅛in, two at 84in
Stroke: 4ft 3in
Boilers: twenty Belleville, working pressure 300psi
Total heating surface: 37,000sq ft
Designed SHP = 15,000 for 18 knots
Fuel: 900 tons coal normal, 1,920–2,000 tons max.
Consumption: 350 tons per day at full power, 209 tons at ⅗ths power, 50 tons at 7 knots
Radius of action: 5,100nm at 10 knots.

Ship's boats (average complement)
Pinnaces (steam): two 56ft, one 36ft
Pinnaces (sail): one 36ft
Launches (sail): one 40ft
Cutters: two 34ft, one 30ft
Galleys: one 32ft
Whalers: three 27ft
Gigs: one 28ft
Skiff dinghies: one 16ft
Balsa rafts: one 13ft 6in.

Searchlights
Six 24in, two on each bridge, one high on masts.

Anchors
Two 115cwt Halls close-stowing, one 115cwt Byers stockless (*Formidable*); others three Halls 115cwt.

Complement
711 *Formidable*, 1910
361 *Implacable*, 1918 (nucleus crew).
788 *Irresistible*, 1901

increase in continuous seagoing speed. On the same displacement as the Japanese *Hatsuse*, they carried the same main armament, but two fewer 6in guns and a stronger all-round protection owing to the superior quality of armour (KC against HN), the same speed and an 18 per cent larger fuel capacity.

At Haslar R. E. Froude had managed to secure an improved hull shape by cutting away the deadwood forward and aft, which in return gave increased handiness. This had featured in the *Canopus* class but to a much lesser degree. The class proved good sea-boats, but not quite up to the standards of *Majestic* owing to reduced freeboard.

ARMAMENT

The Mk IX 12in 40cal gun produced by Vickers was introduced in this class. The weapon differed in many ways from the older MK VIII which had been fitted in the *Majestic* and *Canopus* classes. The principal differences were:

1. Abolition of the 'C' hoop, the jacket being connected directly to 'B' tube, which it overlapped a good deal by means of shoulders, and the thrust collar was formed on the jacket. The effect of this alteration was greatly to increase the girder strength.

2. The gun was four tons heavier.

3. The heavier charge of cordite gave a greater muzzle velocity, and necessitated a larger chamber.

4. The new gun had Vickers rifling.

5. The new gun had the 'Welin' breech.

The gun was constructed of steel, and consisted of a number of tubes within a layer of steel wire with a jacket. It was of exceptionally strong construction and was well received in service, but as a matter of interest, the gun received a certain amount of criticism from Captain Percy Scott in 1903–4 in a general paper about gunnery:

'The Mark VIII 12in gun was designed some eleven years ago, and was the first wire gun above 9.2in made. It was an immense improvement as regards power over its predecessors. It is of course now getting slowly obsolete, and is not in the first rank, neither are the ships which have these guns mounted. It has one great defect, and that is the inner 'A' tube. The original idea was that owing to the high velocity required of the gun, and the erosion due to cordite, that the inner 'A' tube should be practically a thin cylinder which was driven into the outer 'A' tube, having a taper of 1in in 200, so that when it is required to be renewed,

Below: *Implacable* approaching Malta in 1902.

Bottom: *Implacable*, *c.*1903, painting out Victorian colours. Note the ship is cleared for action.

owing to wear, erosion and splitting, it could be easily driven out, and a new one put in at small cost. This was false economy, for the following reasons:

1. It is nearly impossible to obtain the very neat mechanical fit of the inner and outer 'A' tube, so consequently they would be rarely bearing against each other throughout their whole length.

2. After proof rounds, and a certain amount of service rounds, some parts of the inner 'A' tube would be expanded more than others, and would be breaking up against the outer 'A' tube leaving other portions unsupported with a consequent tendency to split.

3. The thin inner 'A' tube being able to expand and contract as the projectile passes along the bore results in the projectile being badly centered with its consequent erratic flight making for bad shooting.

Curiously enough, I was lecturing at Gibraltar to the ex-Channel Fleet in long-range firing, and laid stress on the weakness of these 12in guns.

Three weeks afterwards I went out in the *Majestic* to umpire for her prize firing (*see Majestic* class) and was sitting on top of her fore turret when a portion of her inner 'A' tube was blown overboard. At the time we did not notice it, and fired two more rounds. The piece blown out was seen gyrating in the air by the Chaplain who was on the quarter-deck, and it fell close to the ship. Two cracks in other guns were not discovered until firing was completed.

I am not an alarmist, I hope, but up to date not a breath of suspicion has been cast against the 12in Mk IX. The manufacture is nearly identical, except the inner 'A' tube is a little thicker, but it is put to a much greater strain. One or two have failed already, and as the guns get older, I am much afraid they will develop similar defects to those in the Mark VIII gun.'

A great deal of experimentation in gun mountings was taking place during the period of construction of the *Formidable* and *Bulwark* classes, and as a result *Formidable* and *Implacable* were fitted with BVI mountings, while *Irresistible* was given an improved Vickers arrangement (BVII), tested in the ship when she was still under construction (*London*, *Bulwark* Type BVI, *Venerable* Type BVII). Both types had interruption chambers within the barbette trunk, but there were considerable differences in the hoists and internal fittings.

Two alternative plans were submitted by White for the secondary armament; one providing twelve 6in as in *Majestic*, the other for fourteen 6in, with six guns on the upper deck and eight on the main (as in the new Japanese *Hatsuse* and *Shikishima*). In preference, the Board approved the former layout, on the grounds that while the extra upper deck guns would increase offensive power, especially in a seaway, a secondary armament of twelve 6in guns could be regarded as sufficiently heavy in relation to that carried in foreign contemporary battleships. Moreover, the additional guns would overcrowd the upper deck and certainly require an increase in complement.

A body of opinion was of the mind that rather than increase offensive power, it might be better to increase the thickness of armour belt, especially when gun calibres and high muzzle velocities were increasing on an alarming scale.

The original design showed twelve 3pdrs carried in four fighting tops (two on each mast) as in *Majestic*, but as the upper tops were abandoned in the layout, the complement of guns was reduced to six only.

ARMOUR

White's original proposals provided for an 8in armoured belt of the latest quality armour (Krupp) against the 9in Harvey in the *Majestic* class. Taking advantage of the latest developments in armour, a saving of at least 300 tons was envisaged. In view of further possible ordnance developments abroad, however, the Board decided that it would be preferable to retain the same thickness as in *Majestic* and build ships having an armoured belt that would be virtually invulnerable at the normal battle ranges of the day.

The armouring arrangement of the *Formidable* group embodied the modifications to the *Majestic*s which had been introduced in the intervening, and somewhat smaller, *Canopus* class. Improvements were:

1. Krupp cemented instead of Harvey armour for most of the vertical strakes.

2. Thin extensions of belt to the bow and stern (after extension not provided in *Canopus*).

3. Provision of flat armoured deck over citadel in addition to the sloping deck behind belt within this.

The forward extension of the belt was carried about 3½ft higher above the waterline than in the

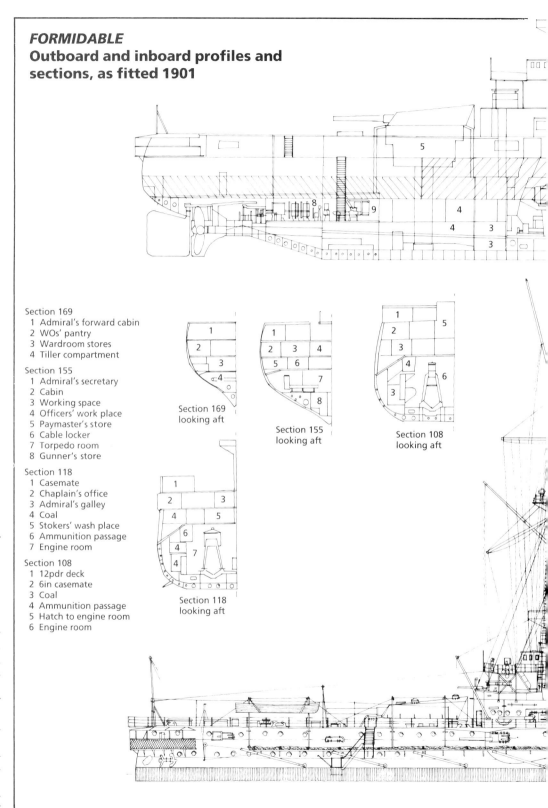

FORMIDABLE
Outboard and inboard profiles and sections, as fitted 1901

Section 169
1 Admiral's forward cabin
2 WOs' pantry
3 Wardroom stores
4 Tiller compartment

Section 155
1 Admiral's secretary
2 Cabin
3 Working space
4 Officers' work place
5 Paymaster's store
6 Cable locker
7 Torpedo room
8 Gunner's store

Section 118
1 Casemate
2 Chaplain's office
3 Admiral's galley
4 Coal
5 Stokers' wash place
6 Ammunition passage
7 Engine room

Section 108
1 12pdr deck
2 6in casemate
3 Coal
4 Ammunition passage
5 Hatch to engine room
6 Engine room

Section 169
looking aft

Section 155
looking aft

Section 108
looking aft

Section 118
looking aft

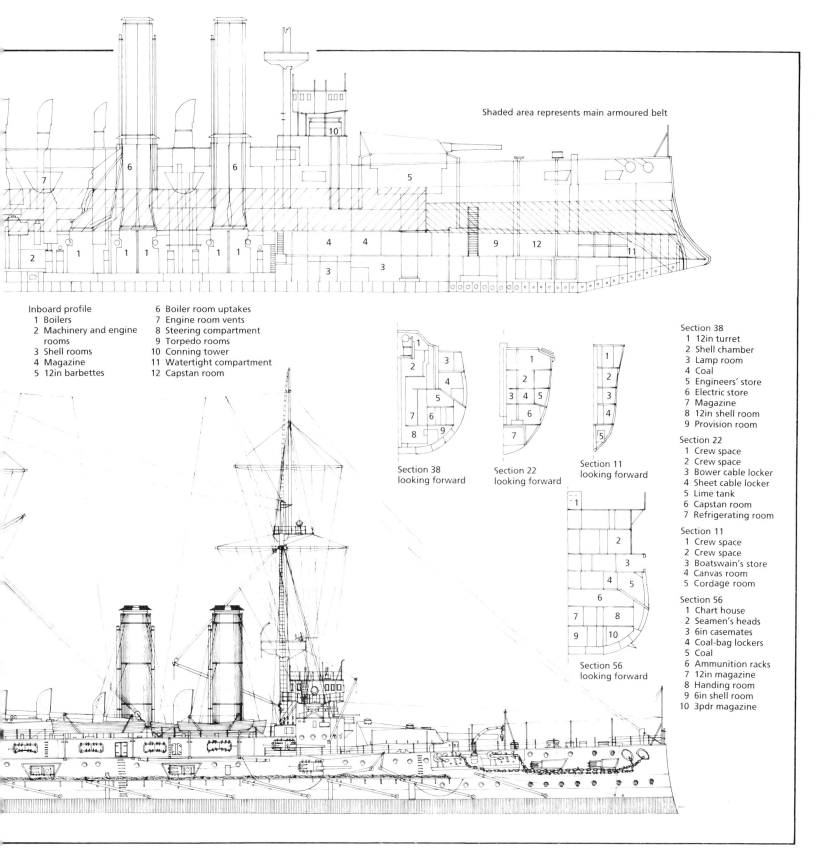

Inboard profile
1 Boilers
2 Machinery and engine rooms
3 Shell rooms
4 Magazine
5 12in barbettes
6 Boiler room uptakes
7 Engine room vents
8 Steering compartment
9 Torpedo rooms
10 Conning tower
11 Watertight compartment
12 Capstan room

Shaded area represents main armoured belt

Section 38
looking forward

Section 22
looking forward

Section 11
looking forward

Section 56
looking forward

Section 38
1 12in turret
2 Shell chamber
3 Lamp room
4 Coal
5 Engineers' store
6 Electric store
7 Magazine
8 12in shell room
9 Provision room

Section 22
1 Crew space
2 Crew space
3 Bower cable locker
4 Sheet cable locker
5 Lime tank
6 Capstan room
7 Refrigerating room

Section 11
1 Crew space
2 Crew space
3 Boatswain's store
4 Canvas room
5 Cordage room

Section 56
1 Chart house
2 Seamen's heads
3 6in casemates
4 Coal-bag lockers
5 Coal
6 Ammunition racks
7 12in magazine
8 Handing room
9 6in shell room
10 3pdr magazine

Canopus class, associated with a reduction of ½in thickness of the lower deck forward. Maximum thickness of turrets was reduced from that of *Majestic* in order to offset the extra weight of the belt armour at the extremities. No centre-line bulkhead in boiler spaces provided, but internal sub-division was more complete than in *Majestic*.

The 9in Krupp belt amidships was 218ft long by 15ft wide which brought it abeam the barbettes. The upper edge was at main deck level (9ft 6in above waterline); the lower edge was 5ft 6in below waterline. From this belt, a 2in strake ran forward at a height of 7ft 6in above waterline, the lower edge level with the lower edge of the midships main strake, except that the forward extremity carried down to meet the ram at the bows. The armour on the forward run, sometimes interpreted as being 3in, was in fact 2in laid over two sheets of ½in plating. 1in armour was provided for the after belt, which extended completely to the stern of the vessel. The upper edge was approximately 4ft above the waterline; the lower edge was at the same level as that of the amidships section.

The belt bulkheads were 9in (forward) and ran obliquely inwards from the forward extremities of the 9in main armour to the outer face of the fore barbette. The bulkhead aft was 10in-9in thick and ran obliquely inwards from the after extremity of the 9in main belt to the outer face of the barbette. Its thickness was 9in above the main deck, and 10in below. The total length of the armoured citadel at the centre-line was 250ft.

There were some differences in barbette and turret thicknesses within the class (*see* drawings). Formidable had 12in thick uniform barbettes, while her turrets were 8in on the faces and sides,

---

Formidable: Original legend, 29 December 1897

(modified *Majestic*)

Displacement: 15,000 tons
Length: 400ft
Beam: 75ft
Draught: 26ft 9in mean
Freeboard: 23ft forward, 16ft 9in amidships, 18ft aft.

Armament
Four 12in
Twelve 6in
Sixteen 12pdr
Six 3pdr.

Armour
Main belt: 9in
Barbettes: 12in–6in
Forward conning tower: 12in
Turrets: 10in max.
Casemates: 6in
Decks: 3in–2½in.

Complement: 758.

Weight breakdown (tons)	
Hull:	9,150
Guns:	1,730
Machinery:	1,415
Coal:	900
General equipment:	710
Board margin:	200
Armour weight breakdown (tons)	
Vertical:	1,265
Decks:	1,240
Barbettes:	1,035
CT:	110
Casemates:	425

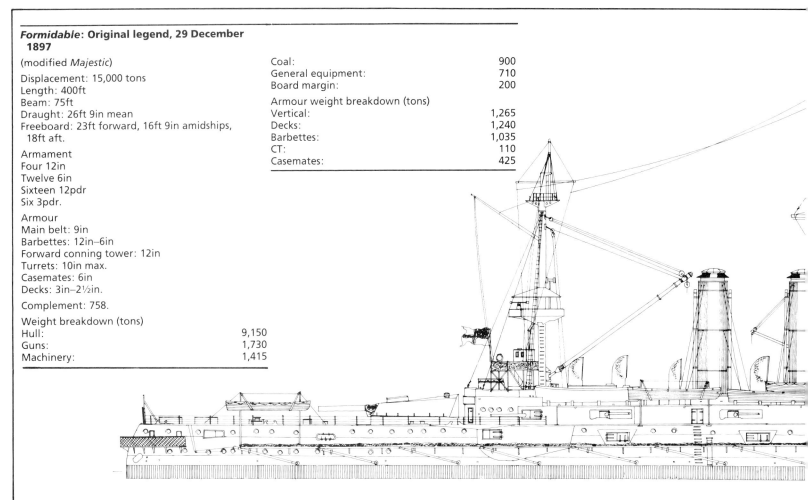

10in rear and 2in–3in roofs. *Irresistible*, however, was given 12in barbettes above the belt armour, but reduced to 10in on the forward part below this, and 6in on the rears. Turret thickness was practically identical except for a shorter 3in run on the roofs. Secondary casemates were given 6in faceplates and 2in rears and roofs made of Harvey steel; the ammunition hoists for these were 2in mild steel.

The main deck, which ran flat across the top of the citadel, was 1in thick (mild steel); the middle deck 2in on the flat and 3in on the inclines and extended over the whole length of the citadel

between the outer faces of the barbettes. The crown was about 2ft 6in above the waterline, the lower edge being level with the lower edge of the main belt. The lower deck forward was 2in thick, curved, and ran underwater from the base of the citadel to the bow. Aft this was 2½in thick and fitted in the same way.

The forward conning tower had 14in–10in plates (Harvey) with an 8in tube (mild steel); the after tower had 3in plates with a 3in tube.

The usual provision of coal bunkers behind the belt armour was fitted, and ran between main and

middle decks abreast boiler rooms, and a cellular layer of watertight compartments was fitted at the extremities outside the citadel.

Armour thicknesses were about the same as in *Majestic*, any reduction being compensated by the improved quality of the Krupp armour process which was considered to have about 30 per cent greater resisting power than the Harvey type.

MACHINERY

The machinery of the *Formidable* group, although of the same general type as that of *Majestic*, benefited from basic improvements in the design, and gave increased efficiency on a slightly reduced weight. The installation of the improved machinery and water tube boilers in the *Canopus* group had provided substantially greater horsepower than in *Majestic*, for an approximate increase of only 95 tons. It was realized that if the same machinery were put in *Formidable* the shaft horse power could be raised from 12,000 (*Majestic*) to 15,000 using natural draught, and full advantage should be taken of this in the design.

Twenty Belleville boilers were fitted, with economizers, arranged in three compartments, eight in the forward and midships section, and four in the after section. Two sets of 3-cylinder vertical triple expansion engines driving twin in-turning screws were fitted.

On sea trials, except for a few minor problems, the boilers and machinery worked satisfactorily, but as the installations grew older, there were various incidents in the class (and others of this group) concerning machinery/boilers from 1909 to 1914.

Formidable appears to have been the worst case. During the autumn of 1912 a Court of Inquiry was held to investigate the causes of the defective condition of her boilers which had deteriorated since a refit at Gibraltar in 1911. After a lengthy hearing, the Board concluded that as the vessel had received no special attention since that refit, and in fact had been subjected from August to October 1911 to hard and continuous steaming with a nucleus crew, no single individual or individuals were to blame.

On 12 July 1905 a boiler explosion occurred in *Implacable* through admission of steam into the main steam pipe while there was water in the pipe. Two men were killed and several injured. The Court of Inquiry found blame attributable to the

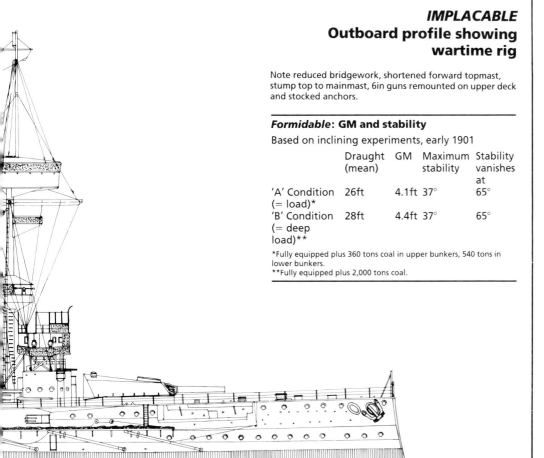

IMPLACABLE
Outboard profile showing wartime rig

Note reduced bridgework, shortened forward topmast, stump top to mainmast, 6in guns remounted on upper deck and stocked anchors.

Formidable: GM and stability

Based on inclining experiments, early 1901

	Draught (mean)	GM	Maximum stability	Stability vanishes at
'A' Condition (= load)*	26ft	4.1ft	37°	65°
'B' Condition (= deep load)**	28ft	4.4ft	37°	65°

*Fully equipped plus 360 tons coal in upper bunkers, 540 tons in lower bunkers.
**Fully equipped plus 2,000 tons coal.

Formidable class: Steam trials, 1901

	Displacement (tons)	Draught (mean)	Revs.	IHP	Speed (knots)
Formidable					
30-hour ⅕th power:	15,084	26ft 3in	65.2	3,281	11.5
30-hour at 11,500 shp:	15,372	26ft 6in	100.95	11,618	17.65 (measured mile)
8-hour full power:	14,797	26ft 4in	109.3	15,511	18.13 (measured mile)
Implacable					
30-hour ⅕th power:	15,117	26ft 8in	66.1	3,179	11 (logged)
30-hour at 11,500shp:	15,046	26ft 7in	100.05	11,858	16.75 (measured mile)
8-hour full power:	15,017	26ft 10in	108.55	15,262	18.22
Irresistible					
30-hour ⅕th power:	15,162	26ft 10in	69.25	3,243	11.76
30-hour at 11,500shp:	15,262	27ft	101.9	11,726	17.5 (logged)
8-hour full power:	15,205	27ft 1in	110.2	15,603	18.2 (logged)

Engineer Commander and two Engineer Lieutenants. Another boiler exploded in *Implacable* the following year, on 16 August, which was later traced to overheating from loss of feedwater.

Although each Court of Inquiry found good reason for these, and other mishaps, time was to prove that although the machinery of the vessels was more or less reliable, the boilers were subject to frequent breakdown. Average life of a boiler was about three years depending on how hard it was used, but the economizer and general tubes were in need of constant renewal.

APPEARANCE CHANGES

This trio were rather pleasant-looking vessels; their wider funnel and mast spacing gave them a somewhat heavier appearance that the *Canopus* group. They could be distinguished from the *Canopus* class by the following:

Fore funnel closer to the foremast; masts wider apart and slightly taller; extra pair of 12pdrs in ports on main deck level forward and aft; slightly higher freeboard and general heavier appearance.

Distinguishable from the *Bulwark* group by: curved turret faces and lower-deck scuttles forward (there were considerable differences in scuttle formation around the bows). They were quite different from the *Duncan*s whose funnels were equal sized. *Formidable*'s funnels were of unequal size and the second funnel was athwartship.

The numerous individual differences were sometimes difficult to spot. *Formidable* had no caging to her funnels, and had heavy raised funnel caps. *Implacable* had caging to funnels and caps almost

identical with *Formidable*. *Irresistible* had caging to funnels, but much lighter type of caps fitted closer to funnels. *Irresistible* had no steam pipe abaft the fore funnel.

1902 Shields removed from 3pdrs in *Formidable* and *Implacable* (*Irresistible* completed without these). *Implacable* was temporarily painted light-grey while in the Mediterranean Fleet. The repaint-

ing is reported to have been carried out as a special exercise to determine the length of time required to change from peacetime to wartime colours.

The grey was under consideration as 'war colour' at that time, although the livery buff was still in general use for peacetime (*see* camouflage and paintwork). During the same exercise, *Implacable* was cleared for action with topmasts housed down, yards and ensign gaff removed, windsails fitted in place of cowls and lashings passed around the boats as splinter protection.

1903–4 Foremast SL in *Implacable* replaced by small rangefinder.

1904–6 Fire control and RF equipment fitted. Control top in place of SL platform fitted to foremast. Military top on main roofed in and adapted as control position with extension fitted to the rear for the rangefinder.

These modifications were effected in *Formidable* during 1904–5 refit; *Implacable* 1904–6, and *Irresistible* 1905–6. 3pdrs removed from tops (main only). Foremast SL temporarily remounted on new small platforms below control top.

1906–7 3pdrs removed from foretop. Some 3pdrs were remounted on bridges or superstructure; the

Below: Forecastle of *Irresistible*, c.1905.

Bottom: *Irresistible*'s quarterdeck, seen shortly before beginning coaling at Malta in 1905. Note the gun and turret have been completely covered as have the quick-firing guns on the turret top and after bridge. This was to protect gun muzzles and mechanisms from coal dust which might ignite when guns were fired later.

rest were suppressed. Considerable variation in the location of these guns within the group. SL removed from mainmast and temporarily re-mounted over forward casemates.

1907–8 Main deck 12pdrs remounted on super-structures, four forward, and four aft. Forward ports plated-up in *Formidable* and *Implacable*.
SL ex-foremast and after charthouse were remounted over forward casemates.
W/T gaff triced and masthead semaphore removed.

1908–9 W/T gaff removed and W/T topgallant mast fitted to fore and mainmast in *Implacable*. Heavy yards to mainmast removed in all three ships. Funnel bands painted-up in *Implacable* and *Irresistible* in 1908 (2 red, close together on each in *Implacable*; 2 red, widely spaced *Irresistible*). These were temporary bands used only as identification features during Fleet manoeuvres and were not intended to identify individual ships. They were also frequently changed while at sea.

1909–10 Range indicators fitted to one or both tops and over after charthouse (varied in each ship). W/T topgallant fitted to fore in *Formidable*. Standard funnel bands painted-up: *Formidable* one white on second funnel; *Irresistible* one white on each funnel; *Implacable* one white on fore funnel.

1910–11 W/T gaff in *Formidable* replaced by topgallant. W/T topgallant mast fitted to each mast in *Irresistible* and W/T gaff removed.

1913–14 After casemate SL in *Irresistible* re-mounted on after charthouse. Anti-torpedo nets removed in all.

1914 Funnel bands painted out.

1915 (*Formidable* lost Jan 1915) Other two: Fore-bridge SL in *Irresistible* remounted on lower foretop. Torpedo nets replaced; special mine sweeping gear fitted to bows. Forebridge wings taken out in *Implacable*. Stockless anchors fitted but billboards retained. Both topgallant and main topmasts removed; small spotting top fitted at the head of foremast.
'One-off' camouflage painted-up in *Irresistible*.
Sandbag protection fitted around bridges in *Implacable* and painted-up in strange camouflage of grey-blue hull and sand-coloured upperworks while in Suez Canal late 1915. Barbed wire was also fitted to her net booms to stop any attempted boarding of the ship at night while at anchor.

1916 *Implacable* only: Main deck 6in guns removed. 4 remounted in shields in 12pdr battery amidships.

Below: *Irresistible* coaling at Malta in 1905. During this unpleasant job the Captain usually took a break, leaving his officers in charge. Captain Tufnall is seen here relaxing in his rather luxurious day cabin.

Below: Up spirits! A tot of pure nectar was most welcome after arduous tasks such as coaling, stoking or cleaning. The lads dish it out on *Irresistible* after coaling. Malta 1905.

Upper deck battery amidships suppressed.
Two 3pdr AA guns provided.
1918 Refitted for service as Depot Ship.
Main armament and four upper deck 6in retained. Remaining 6in removed. Anti-torpedo nets removed. Rig remained unaltered from 1916.
Service History: *Formidable*.
Laid down at Portsmouth Dockyard 21 March 1898 and launched 17 November 1898 in a very incomplete state to clear the slip for laying down *London*.

HISTORY: *FORMIDABLE*

Formidable's completion was greatly delayed by financial difficulties of her machinery contractor (Earle).
10 Oct 1904 Commissioned at Portsmouth for service with Mediterranean Fleet, until Aug 1908.
1904—April 1905 Refit at Malta.
17 Aug 1908 Paid off at Chatham for refit.
Aug 1908—April 1909 Refit at Chatham.
20 April 1909 Commissioned at Chatham for 1st Division, Home Fleet, Nore, until May.
29 May 1909 Transferred to Atlantic Fleet, until May 1912.
May 1912—Aug 1914 Home Fleet (5th BS Second Fleet, Nore).Assigned to Channel Fleet (5th BS) as part of a force to defend Channel and cover passage of BEF to France.

Dec 1914 Channel Fleet. 5th BS based at Portland but transferred to Sheerness 14 Nov in anticipation of possible invasion attempt. Replaced at Sheerness by 6th BS (*Duncan* class) and she returned to Portland on 30 Dec 1914. *Formidable* took part in transferring a Portsmouth Marine battalion to Ostend and supporting the occupation on 25 Aug.
Loss of *Formidable*:
On 1 Jan 1915, while on exercises and patrol duties in the Channel, *Formidable* was torpedoed by *U24* at approximately 02.20. The torpedo hit near the forward funnel on the starboard side. Immediately after the explosion the order was given to shut down steam and bring the ship into the wind to get her head to the rising sea.
The weather was deteriorating, but it was thought that she might be saved if she could reach the coast. After about twenty minutes, however, she had taken a list of about 20° to starboard, and Captain Loxley ordered 'Abandon ship!' and some of the lifeboats were lowered. The darkness and worsening weather severely hampered the procedure and some of the small boats were thrown into the water upside down.
Counter-flooding of the port side put *Formidable* back on an even keel more or less, although dangerously low in the water; the final flooding of the port side compartments was taking place when, at approximately 03.05 another torpedo hit her on

the starboard side near the bows. By 04.45, after the small cruisers *Topaze* and *Diamond* had stood by taking off some of the crew, *Formidable* showed signs of going over. A few minutes later she gave a sudden lurch and dipped her bows. The call, 'Every man for himself!' was heard, but almost immediately the stricken battleship turned turtle, crashing down on those men already in the water.
She lay in the water, down by the bows, very still for a short while, before taking the final plunge.
When last seen Captain Loxley was on the bridge with his terrier dog, as cool as ever, going down with his ship. Official records give a loss of 35 officers and 512 men.
Commander K. G. B. Dewar, an eye-witness aboard *Prince of Wales*, wrote a letter to a fellow officer:
'During the whole of 31st December 1914 ships of the Fleet carried out manoeuvres in the vicinity of Portland. After sunset, we steamed to the eastward at 10kts, five ships in single line ahead. There was a full moon, and it was extraordinarily clear and bright until about 3am on 1st January.
Visibility of a battleship probably about 2 to 3 miles. At 7pm the Fleet turned 16 points and returned back over the same ground still proceeding at 10kts. At about 11.30pm Portland Bill was abeam 15 miles. Shortly after *Formidable* had been torpedoed at 2.15am (approximately) the

Below: *Irresistible* in 1908. The class were easy to distinguish from the *Canopus* group by their heavier appearance, and wider spaced funnels and masts.

Formidable class: Cost breakdown

Armour	Formidable	Implacable	Irresistible
Citadel sides:	£125,163	£124,745	£124,868
Upper barbettes:	65,983	66,529	66,802
Citadel ends:	41,805	41,370	41,370
Main turret shields:	37,660	37,606	37,632
Casemates:	26,552	26,552	26,667
Lower barbettes:	13,329	12,786	12,835
Bow plating:	8,372	8,302	8,592
Forward conning tower:	5,410	5,410	5,547
Barbette tops:	1,925	1,925	1,925
Communication tubes:	1,415	1,412	1,410
After conning tower:	685	685	685
Propelling and auxiliary machinery:	£140,481	£148,803	£144,845
Gun mountings (excluding turntables): £80,245 (average)			

Labour: £220,000 (average)
Materials: £134,000 (average)
Steam boats: £6,530

Total cost, as estimated:	£911,256	£918,883	£917,535
Total cost, as completed:	£1,022,745	£989,116	£1,048,136
plus guns:	74,500	74,500	74,500

Fleet turned 16 points and steamed back over the same ground passing within a mile of the same position occupied at 7pm. At 3am the Fleet moved and increased speed to the North East. No one minds taking risks when there is an adequate object in view, but our only object was Fleet exercises and gunnery. Surely we should have carried this out to the westward and out of sight of land. Portland is the Channel port where we have kept battleships throughout the war, and surely it is the place where hostile submarines might be expected to operate. The submarine probably followed us to the eastward, and *Formidable* was the last ship in line. I do not think it would have been possible to take greater risks than were taken on that night.

After *Formidable* had been hit, the rest of the ships stayed on the same course until altering course 180 back to the *Formidable*'s position. Still in single line at slow speed (10kts) was exceedingly difficult to understand. There is no doubt that the *Formidable* was sacrificed to the gross stupidity of a

Left: *Implacable* at Weymouth in 1911. Note that she has a darker grey paintwork scheme, which appeared in ships at about this period.
Centre left: *Irresistible* in July 1914. Seen from the port quarter as she moves off after the Fleet Review at Spithead. This view shows her general pre-war appearance.
Bottom left: *Formidable* in July 1914. A nice view of the ship just before the outbreak of war. Note that the nets have been removed.

very ignorant man—and long before the incident occurred, both Officers and men criticised the folly of taking such risks for no object whatever. One does not blame the Admiral (Sir L Bayley)—he is God—the Navy made him—a thoroughly obstinate and stupid man. One blames only the system which makes it possible for such a man to command a Fleet. In peacetime, he has continually shown himself as ignorant of the personnel, as he is of the material. Every Fleet he has been in has been unhappy and thoroughly discontented. No one thought he would be employed again until Winston Churchill gave him command of the 3rd BS.'

HISTORY: *IMPLACABLE*

Laid down at Devonport 13 July 1898, and launched on 11 March 1899 in a very incomplete state in order to clear the slipway for laying down *Bulwark*.
10 Sept 1901 Commissioned at Devonport for service with Mediterranean Fleet, until Feb 1909. Refit at Malta 1902, 1903–4, 1904–5.
1908–9 Refit at Chatham.
Feb—May 1909 Channel Fleet.
15 May 1909 Transferred to Atlantic Fleet, until May 1912.
13 May 1912 Transferred to Second Home Fleet, Nore under Fleet reorganization of 1 May 1912. Home Fleet: (Second Fleet, 5th BS, Nore) Assigned to Channel Fleet (5th BS) on outbreak of war in August 1914.
Aug 1914—Mar 1915 Channel Fleet (5th BS Portland and Sheerness). Temporarily attached to Dover Patrol in late Oct for bombardment of Belgian coast in support of Allied left flank.
Mar 1915 Transferred to Dardanelles.
Left England 13th, arrived Lemnos on 23rd. Dardanelles until May 1915. Supported main landings at Helles ('X' Beach) on 25 April and subsequent support operations from April to May. Detached to Adriatic 22 May with *London*, *Prince of Wales* and *Queen*, as units of 2nd Detached Squadron, organized to reinforce Italian Navy in containing the Austrian Fleet in accordance with agreement of 26 April 1915 by which Italy undertook to declare war on Austria. Squadron based at Taranto, supporting Italian Army's drive to head of Adriatic.
27 May Arrived Taranto, there until Nov 1915.
Nov 1915 Transferred to 3rd Detached Squadron based at Salonika, to reinforce Suez Canal Patrol

Below: *Irresistible* in March 1915, shortly before her loss. Note the one-off camouflage scheme, mine sweeping gear at bows, nets replaced, additions to fore and aft bridge work and searchlights on lower foretop.

Bottom: A rare view of *Implacable* entering Taranto Harbour during hostilities, clearly showing her mine-sweeping gear in the bows; reduced bridge work (wings, etc.); one yard on the foremast, none on mainmast. The squadron was based at Taranto to support the advance of the Italian Army to the head of the Adriatic.

and assist French in blockading Greece and Bulgarian coast.

Nov 1915—July 1917 Suez Canal Patrol and Aegean.

Nov 1915—March 1916 Stationed at Port Said.

22 Mar 1916 Left for UK, arrived Plymouth 9 April 1916 for refit.

June 1917 At Athens during abdication of King Constantine; only three British battleships remaining in the Mediterranean at that date, the other two being *Agamemnon* and *Lord Nelson*.

July 1917 Returned home and paid off at Portsmouth to provide crews for anti-submarine vessels, until March 1918.

Mar 1918 Selected for service as depot ship for Northern Patrol, Lerwick, Kirkwall and Buncrana.

Portland Nov 1918 Placed on disposal list.

4 Feb 1920 Placed on sale list.

8 Nov 1921 Sold to Slough Trading Co. Resold to German firm and towed to Germany for scrapping in April 1922.

HISTORY: *IRRESISTIBLE*

Laid down at Chatham Dockyard 11 April 1898 and launched on 15 December 1898 in a very incomplete state to clear the slip for *Venerable*. Began trials in October 1901, and finally commissioned at Chatham 4 Feb 1902 for service in Mediterranean Fleet, relieving *Devastation* as Port Guardship at Gibraltar. With Mediterranean Fleet, until April 1908.

3 Mar 1902 Collided with Norwegian SS *Clive* in fog, sustained considerable damage to side plating.

9 Oct 1905. Grounded at Malta. Refit at Malta and again Oct 1907—Jan 1908.

April 1908 Transferred to Channel Fleet, until June 1910.

4 May 1908 Collided with schooner in fog, no damage.

1 June 1910 Paid off at Chatham for refit until Feb 1911.

28 Feb 1911 Commissioned at Chatham for service in 3rd Division, Home Fleet, Nore, until Aug 1914. Assigned to Channel Fleet (5th BS) from outbreak of war 1914 until Feb 1915. Took part in transferring Portsmouth Marine Battalion to Ostend and generally supporting occupation.

Oct—Nov 1914 Temporarily attached to Dover Patrol for bombardment of Belgian coast in support of Allied left flank. Detached to support East Coast

H.M.S. IMPLACABLE

Patrols during Gorleston Raid 3 Nov.
1 Feb 1915 Transferred to Dardanelles, temporary Flag of British Squadron until March. Took part in opening bombardment of entrance forts 18–19 Feb and subsequent bombardments of entrance and Narrows forts and initial landings Feb and early Mar (she knocked out two 9.4in guns in Fort Orkanieh on 25 Feb).
28 Feb—6 Mar Relieved *Vengeance* as 2nd Flag.
18 Mar Took part in main bombardment of Narrows forts; badly damaged and later sank at about 19.30, with 150 casualties, her exact movements have not been recorded. During the bombardment of the Narrows forts, it is almost certain that she hit a mine which exploded below the starboard engine room, very near the centre-line. At approximately 16.15 the engine room flooded so rapidly that only three of the crew were able to escape. The midship bulkhead collapsed, flooding the port engine room and leaving her with no motive power. She took a list of 6° or 7° to starboard and appeared down by the stern. She drifted slightly out of control into range of the enemy's heavy guns which saturated her with shells. Her main turrets were by now partially inoperative, and she was almost hidden by dense black smoke and spray.

It was decided to send in *Ocean* to tow her out of the action area, but this was found to be impossible because of her heavy list, dense fire from the shore, and the fact that *Ocean* herself had grounded and was trying to extricate herself.

When darkness had fallen destroyers and sweepers could find no trace of *Irresistible*, and it was rightly assumed that she had sunk. Subsequent Turkish reports stated that she had been caught in a cross-current and drifted nearer to the shore batteries which severely pounded her.

BULWARK CLASS

1898 ESTIMATES

DESIGN

The first meeeting of their Lordships to discuss the battleship programme for 1898 was held in the First Lord's room on 7 January.

Although no firm commitments were made on that day, it was agreed that the new Russian threat (the proposed laying down of 18-knot battleships) should be adequately met with similar strength of numbers. There was, however, at that time a great deal of argument as to whether British yards could supply sufficient quantities of armour plate for new battleship construction. Addressing the problem, White told the Board:

'I state my opinion that the production of armour could be made sufficient in 1899/1900 and later years to permit of an extended programme of construction for battleships and armoured cruisers to be begun in this financial year if that becomes neccessary on grounds of public enquiry.

The pinch of armour supply comes in this year, and arises from the concurrent influence of recent labour difficulties, and of change of quality of armour, which needs reconstruction of plant and large additions to machinery.

This reconstruction is now fairly in hand, and several firms are now using every means to perfect and extend their appliances, as well as increase their output.'

On 14 June 1898 a second meeting to debate new construction was held. More information had become available regarding the Russian programme. White pointed out that in fact only one vessel, a first class battleship, had been laid down to date (at Cramps) and had a provisional completion date of 30 months. There was, however, a strong suggestion that the full Russian programme allowed for four such vessels. With this in mind, it was agreed that in order to gain time to prepare a new British design, the decision to defer commencement of these ships, and substitute a slightly modified edition of *Formidable* as suggested by White, was a sound move. They would of course embody certain modifications in protection and elsewhere which White already had in mind for the vessels that would follow these.

It was agreed that a total of three additional battleships be commenced towards the end of the year, or the beginning of the next year, which seemed sufficient until more definite knowledge about the projected Russian ships was available.

Launch of HMS London, 1899.

***Bulwark* class: Final legend, July 1898**

Displacement: 15,000 tons
Length: 400ft pp
Beam: 75ft
Draught: 26ft 3in forward, 27ft 3in aft
Freeboard: 23ft forward, 16ft 9in amidships, 18ft aft
Sinkage: 56.5 tons per inch
Height of upper deck from keel: 43ft 9in
Height of guns at above draught: 25ft forward, 23ft aft
Coal: 900 tons, 2,000 tons max.

Armament
Four 12in Mk IX
Twelve 6in
Sixteen 12pdr (12cwt)
Six 3pdr
Four 18in torpedo tubes.

Armour
Main belt: 9in Krupp
Backing (wood): 7in–6in–4in
Barbettes: 12in–8in–6in
Decks: 2½in–1in

Conning tower: 14in–3in
Bulkheads: 12in–10in–9in.

Machinery:
IHP: 15,000 for 18 knots.

Estimated GM: 3.14ft
Estimated CG: 7.7ft.

Complement: 758.

Weight breakdown (tons)	
Hull:	5,625
Armament:	1,730
Vertical armour and backing:	1,565
Machinery:	1,415
Bow and stern plating:	1,255
Barbettes:	900
Coal:	900
Casemates:	425
Board margin:	200
Conning tower:	110
Barbette backing:	105

Below, left and right: *London* seen at Chatham Dockyard on completion. Commissioned on 7 July 1902 to relieve *Royal Sovereign* on the Mediterranean station. Prior to her departure, however, it was planned to use her as Flagship at the Coronation Review, but the sudden illness of the King caused the event to be postponed and *London* sailed for Malta on 3 July, reaching her destination on the 14 of that month.

Below: *Bulwark*, nameship of the class that was usually referred to as the *London* group. Seen here from the starboard quarter, as completed. The difference in funnel size is particularly highlighted from this angle.

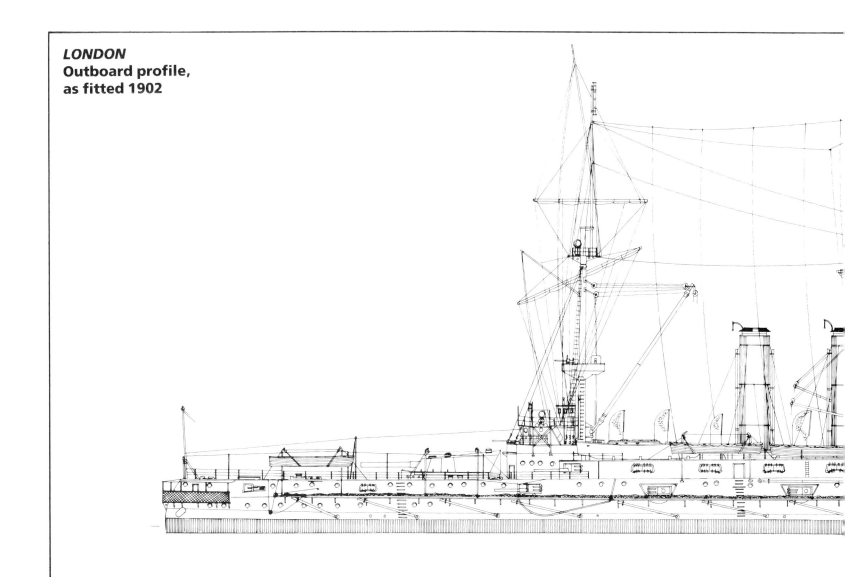

LONDON
Outboard profile,
as fitted 1902

The new designs for a further six ships (as agreed on that date) must completely outclass the Russian vessels, and would be commenced in December 1898 (*Duncan*s). A further meeting was held on 27 June 1898 when the following Minutes were recorded:

'Three new *Formidable* class are to be built in HM Dockyards. The design is to be further considered and got on with.

Subject to the Naval Lords' agreement, it would be advisable to adopt for the *Formidable* arrangement of armour, but to allow extra protection to the bows as suggested by the DNC (White) who pointed out the following: "Instead of having the citadel terminated at the fore end by an armoured bulkhead across the ship, it is proposed to carry on the side armour at its full thickness for some distance before the fore barbette, and then gradually diminish its thickness toward the bow, bringing it to a minimum of 2in right forward as in *Formidable*." '

On 9 July 1898, the Controller (A. K. Wilson) wrote to the Admiralty Superintendent at Portsmouth saying:

'The new battleships provided for in the current programme are to be repeat *Formidable*s, with the exception of the bow armour which is modified in accordance with the attached tracing. The armoured bulkhead at the fore end as in *Formidable* will be omitted. In all other respects, details remain the same—please put drawings and details in hand.'

The sheer, draught and midship section were ready and approved on 18 October 1898.

Bulwark class: Particulars, as completed

Construction
Bulwark: Devonport DY; laid down 20 March 1899; launched 18 Oct 1899; completed March 1902
London: Portsmouth DY; laid down 8 Dec 1898; launched 21 Sept 1899; completed June 1902
Venerable: Chatham DY; laid down 2 Jan 1899; launched 2 Nov 1899; completed Nov 1902.

Displacement
Bulwark: 15,366 (load), 15,955 (deep)
London: 15,316 (load), 15,962 (deep)
Venerable: 15,290 (load), 15,853 (deep).

Dimensions
Length: 400ft pp, 411ft wl, 431ft 9in oa
Beam: 75ft

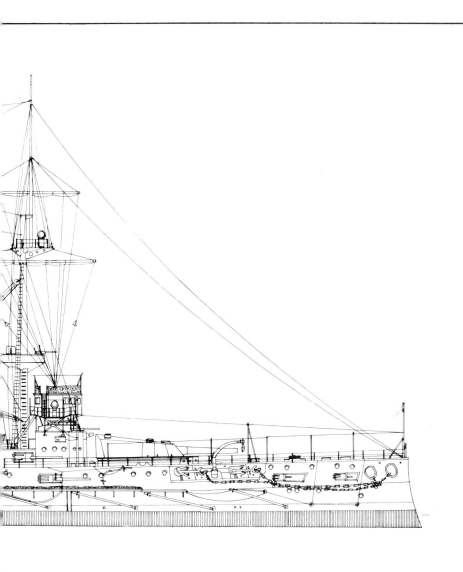

Machinery
Two sets 3-cylinder vertical triple expansion
  engines, two in-turning propellers
Cylinder diameter: two 31½in, two 51½in, two 84ir
Stroke: 4ft 3in
Propeller diameter: 17ft 6in
Propeller pitch: 19ft 3in; developed area 83ft
Boilers: twenty Belleville water tube with
  economizers, working pressure 300psi
Heating surface: 37,000sq ft
Designed SHP: 15,000 for 18 knots
Fuel: 900 tons coal normal, 2,000 tons max.
Coal consumption: 50 tons per day at 7 knots, 350
  tons per day at full power
Radius of action: 5,550nm at 10 knots.

Ship's boats (*Venerable*, 1905)
Pinnaces (steam): two 56ft, one 40ft
Barges (steam): one 40ft
Pinnaces (sail): one 36ft
Launches (sail): one 42ft
Cutters: two 34ft, one 30ft
Galleys: one 32ft, one 28ft
Whalers: one 27ft
Gigs: one 32ft, two 24ft
Skiff dinghies: two 16ft
Balsa rafts: one 13ft 6in.

Searchlights
Six 24in, two on each bridge, one high on each
  mast.

Anchors
Three 115cwt Halls close-stowing, one 54cwt, one
  42cwt; 525 fathoms 2⁹⁄₁₆in cable (83 tons).

Wireless
Type 1, replaced by Type 2, 1909–10.

Complement
760 *Venerable*, 1902
766 *Bulwark* as flagship, 1904
768 *London* in Channel Fleet, 1908
724 *London*, 1910
361 *Venerable*, 1918.

Costs
Hull: £367,550 (average)
Armour: 330,000
Machinery: 145,565 (average)
Gun mountings: 84,350 (*London, Bulwark*), 87,541
  (*Venerable*).

Total cost
Bulwark: £997,846 plus guns £67,970
London: £1,036,353 plus guns £67,100
Venerable: £1,092,753 plus guns £67,100.

Draught
Bulwark: 27ft 3⅛in (load), 28ft 2in (deep)
London: 27ft 5in (load), 28ft 1in (deep)
Venerable: 27ft 1in (load), 27ft 10¼in (deep).

Armament
Four 12in Mk IX, BVI mountings (*Venerable* BVII);
  80rpg
Twelve 6in Mk VII, PIV mountings; 200rpg
Sixteen 12pdr (12cwt) PIII mountings; 300rpg
Two 12pdr (8cwt) boat and field; 300rpg
Six 3pdr, recoil mountings; 500rpg
Two MG (mountings)
Four 18in torpedo tubes submerged (one pair
  abreast each barbette); fourteen 18in torpedoes,
  five 14in for boats.

Armour (KC, non-cemented, Harvey, nickel steel,
  mild steel)
Main belt: 9in KC
Bulkheads: 10in–9in
Forward extension to belt: 7in–5in–3in–2in
Aft extension: 1in
Barbettes: 12in uniform (*London* and *Bulwark*),
  12in–10in–6in (*Venerable*)
Turrets: 10in–8in
Main deck: 2in–1½in
Middle deck: 2in–1in
Lower deck: 2½in–2in–1in
Conning tower: 14in–10in
Casemates: 6in–2in
After conning tower: 3in.

Above: *Venerable* as completed, 1902 taking on supplies at Chatham. She was commissioned at Chatham on 17 November 1902 wearing all-grey paintwork, the first British battleship to enter service in this colour.

Right: *London* leaving Portsmouth on 8 May 1905, having been recommissioned with the crew of *Ramillies* for further service in the Mediterranean.

VENERABLE
Outboard profile, 1912

Note tall topgallant masts and improved W/T rig. Funnel
bands were red.

ARMAMENT

The armament of these three vessels was identical with that of *Formidable* and *Implacable* (not *Irresistible*). In some cases shields were fitted to 3pdrs as fitted, but only during trials period as photographs show. They were removed, and these were the last British battleships to have shields on the upper 3pdr guns. Angled armour plates on the main turrets, instead of round curved fittings as in *Formidable* and *Implacable*.

ARMOUR

The armouring of the *Bulwark*s embodied simple modifications of the *Formidable* layout which had been designed and approved for the temporarily postponed *Duncan* class, but with thicker armour than provided in those ships, and which was intended still further to reduce risk of damage along the waterline forward. A reduction of speed was accepted (due to increased weight), but increased horizontal protection against plunging fire at main deck level would be achieved. These modifications, which represented a development of the arrangement introduced into the *Canopus* class and repeated in the *Formidable*s consisted of:

1. Maxium thickness of belt armour carried to just beyond the fore barbette instead of terminating abeam this.

2. Forward extension of belt to bows raised 2ft higher and thickness increased from 2in uniform to 7in–5in–3in. and 2in respectively, and afforded substantially greater overall protection.

3. Forward citadel bulkhead was abandoned to offset the increased weight involved in supplying the bow armour.

4. Main deck armour increased from 1in to 2in between outer faces of barbettes with a 2in-1½in extension to the bows—not fitted in the *Formidable* group.

The middle deck was fitted with 2in slopes and 1in flat which was a reduction from the 3in and 2in of *Formidable*. The lower deck was also reduced from 2in to 1in (forward) except for a short section immediately before the fore barbette where it increased to 2in and sloped steeply upwards to meet the middle deck, forming a low, inclined bulkhead, partially replacing the normal citadel bulkhead.

The maximum armour thickness on belt and gun positions remained the same as in *Formidable*; the total thickness of flat armour deck, although

remaining the same, had positions altered by having the main and middle deck reversed, the former becoming the heavier.

Angled instead of curved turret faces were fitted in this class, the special advantage of this being that Krupp cemented armour was more easily applicable to flat surfaces than Harvey. A change in turret shape was first seen in *Vengeance* (last unit of *Canopus* class), but *Formidable* and *Implacable* had reverted to curved types.

The main 9in Krupp cemented belt amidships as fitted was 238ft long by 15ft wide and extended from just ahead of the forward barbette to abeam the after barbette. The upper edge was at main deck level, approximately 9ft 6in above water; the lower edge was 5ft 6in below water when the ship was in the normal load condition.

The 7in-5in-3in-2in forward was complete to the stem over the same width as the midships section, except that the forward extremity was carried down to support the ram. The 2in thickness right forward, quickly increased to 3in, 5in and 7in. The 5in thickness reached about 30ft abaft, the stem and the 2in plating was laid over two ½in layers of shell plating.

Aft the 1in armour ran complete to stern, with the upper edge about 4ft above the waterline, the lower edge level with the midships 9in section. Again, as with the forward 2in armour, this 1in thickness aft, was laid over two layers of ½in shell plating.

The belt bulkhead (aft only) ran obliquely inwards from the after extremities of the 9in belt to the outer face of the after barbette. Thickness was 9in above the armoured deck and 10in below.

Barbettes varied in the class: *London* and *Bulwark* had 12in uniform barbettes, but *Venerable* had 12in above the main armoured deck only, then reduced to 10in at the front and sides, and 6in at the rear below this. Turrets had 8in faces, 10in rears and 2in–3in roof. Casemates had 6in faces and 2in sides and rear. Ammunition hoists for the secondary armament were 2in uniform thickness.

The main deck ran flat across the top of the armoured belt from stem to after bulkhead; 2in from the after bulkhead to the end of the 5in

Bulwark: Full-power steam trials, 1909
(to ascertain whether ship could still achieve original speed)

	25 March	25 May	22 August
Date:	25 March	25 May	22 August
Place:	North Sea	North Sea	Atlantic
Duration:	8 hours	8 hours	2 hours
Draught:	28ft 3in forward	27ft 3in	27ft 9in forward
	28ft 9in aft		27ft 6in aft
Steam in boilers:	280psi	280psi	285psi
Steam at engines:	257psi	260psi	260psi
Revs port/starboard:	109.2/109.2	108.2/108.1	108.3/108.5
Total IHP:	15,152	15,263	15,377
Distance run (nm):	146.2	140.3	34.6
Average speed (knots):	18.27	17.5	17.3
Total coal consumption (tons):	109.1	131.6	29.3
Average IHP for 1lb coal per hour:	2.01lb	2.41lb	2.13lb
Vacuum in condenser:	26.5	25.5	25.5

Below: *London*, leaving Portsmouth during Fleet manoeuvres, 1910–11. Note SL over 6in casemates; funnel bands; four yards on foremast; rig; no 3pdrs in tops; and badge on bridge face.

armour, and 1½in forward of this. The middle deck extended from the after bulkhead to the forward extremity of the 9in belt armour; the crown was about 2ft above waterline, with the lower edge level with the main belt armour. It was 2in on the inclines, and 1in on the flat. The lower deck was curved, underwater, and ran from the outer base of each barbette to the stem and stern respectively. The inner extremity of the forward section was 2in thick and sloped steeply upwards to meet the middle deck before the fore barbette; 1in elsewhere. Thicknesses were 1in–2in forward but 2½in aft.

Forward conning tower was 14in-10in thick with an 8in tube; the after conning tower had 3in armour (nickel) and a 3in tube (mild steel).

Bulwark class: Steam trials, 1902
One month out of dock; clean bottom; sea fair

Full power	SHP	Speed (knots)
Bulwark:	15,355	18.09
London:	15,293	18.13
Venerable:	15,355	18.4

30-hour ⅘sths power		
Bulwark:	11,755	16.83
London:	11,720	16.4
Venerable:	11,366	16.8

Summary of London, 1904–09 (full power)

Time out of dock	Bottom	SHP	Speed (knots)
8 months	fair	15,300	17.8
12¾ months	foul	15,192	17.8
1 month	clean	15,435	18.06
12 months	foul	15,440	17.9
15 months	dirty	15,423	17.6

Venerable: Machinery weights (tons)
Based on inclining experiments, 18 December 1902

Boilers:	643.96
Engines and gear, etc.:	512.06
Propellers:	123.77
Auxiliary machinery and gear:	86.40
Extras including workshop machinery, etc.:	63.45
Water for boilers:	37
Feedwater and tanks:	27
Water in condensers:	17.66
Water in distillers:	5.10
Water in auxiliary condenser:	3.60
Water in refrigeration plant:	.30
Total:	1,520.30

Bulwark: GM and stability
Based on inclining experiments, 8 February 1902

	Draught (mean)	GM	Maximum stability	Stability vanishes at
'A' Condition (= load)*	26ft 3in	4.1ft	36°	63°
'B' Condition (= deep load)**	28ft 2in	4.1ft	35°	64°

*Fully equipped plus 360 tons coal upper bunkers, 540 tons lower bunkers.
**Fully equipped plus 2,000 tons coal, all tanks full.

MACHINERY

Machinery and boiler installation was identical with that of *Formidable*: two sets of 3-cylinder vertical triple expansion engines driving twin in-turning screws. Twenty Belleville water tube boilers, with economizers, arranged in three compartments, eight in the forward and midships section, four in the after section. Working pressure was 300psi which reduced at the cylinders to 250psi. With a designed shaft horse power of 15,000 the estimated speed was easily reached, and

VENERABLE
Outboard profile, 1915/16

Note reduced bridgework, searchlights on lower foremast fighting top and after chart house top, false bow wave, anti-rangefinder rigging to forward topmast and back of top to mainmast.

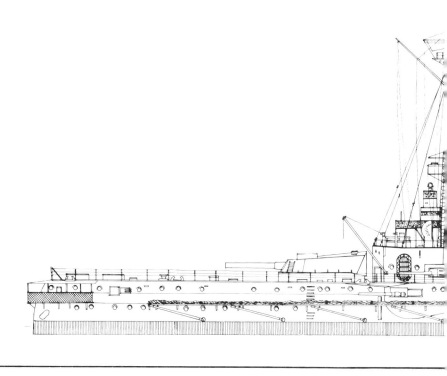

they were capable of a continuous seagoing speed of just over 16 knots in the normal load.

On completion of *London*, the Chief Constructor at Portsmouth (Deadman) went out with the vessel on her preliminary sea trials. He reported:

'In accordance with your instructions (DNC's) I attended the 8-hour full-power trials of *London* which was carried out at Portsmouth on Saturday 8th February 1902. The sea was smooth, and wind westerly with force varying from 3 to 5. The ship was run to Portland and back, and then made 5 runs on a measured mile course between St Catherine's Point and Ventnor. The mean of means of the first 4 runs was 18.35kts on a draught of 26ft 2in forward, 27ft 2in aft and 15,264shp with 107.8 revolutions.

On that early trial, reports show that there was considerable difficulty experienced with overheating of the main bearings generally, and with leaking condensers, but other than this, no serious problems arose.

After that trial it was also reported that she sailed very well, rolled easily and steered well; except when going slow, and then she steered very badly (partially due to inward-turning propellers).

APPEARANCE CHANGES

Practically identical, and very difficult to distinguish from the *Formidable* group. *Bulwark* and *London* were the last British battleships to enter service in the Victorian colours, although the scheme was painted up in *Duncan*, *Russell* and possibly *Exmouth* and *Montague* while the vessels were fitting out. They were, however, repainted all-grey before entering service. *Venerable* commissioned in November 1902 with her new all-grey

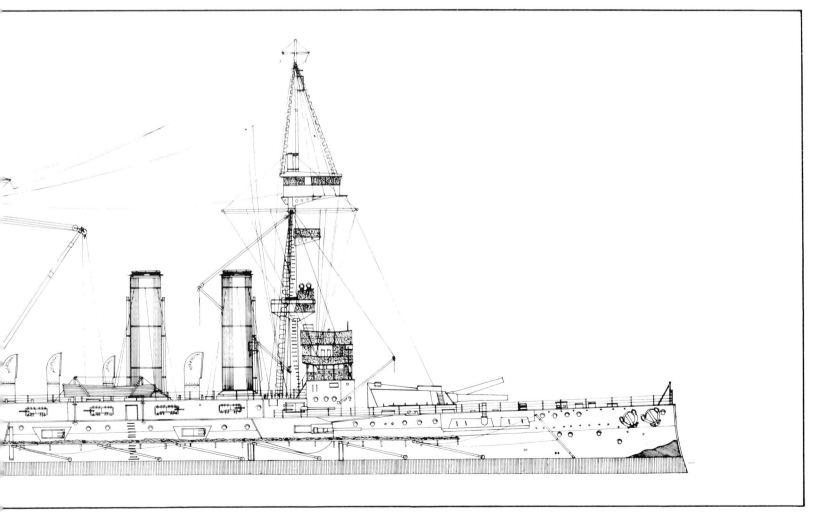

paintwork—the first British battleship to enter
service with the new colours.

The ships were easily distinguishable from the
Canopus group by their general appearance of being
heavier than that class. The fore funnel was closer
to the foremast; the masts were wider apart and
taller, and an extra pair of 12pdrs was shipped in
ports on the main deck forward and aft. Distinguishable from the *Formidable*s by different-
shaped main gun turrets (curved in *Formidable*)
and no lower deck scuttles forward. Easily
distinguishable from the *Duncan* group because of
that class's equal funnels and no cowls for ventilation.

Individual differences were very small in the
Bulwark class, and from some angles in
photographs it is very difficult to identify the ship
in question. They differed only in minor funnel and
rig details which were:
Bulwark Steam pipe before and abaft fore funnel
(double abaft).
London No steam pipes before fore funnel; no
caging to funnels, and heavy raised caps.
Venerable No steam pipe abaft fore funnel; no
caging to funnels; light funnel caps; upper yards at
lower mastheads (higher up in other two); gaff
when fitted carried low (high in other two)
1903–4 Experimental fire control equipment fitted
in *Venerable* for trial purposes.
1904–5 SL removed from foremast in *London* and
Venerable, *Bulwark* later (date uncertain).
1905–7 Fire control and RF equipment fitted.
Control top fitted in place of SL platform on
foremast. Military top on mainmast roofed in and
used as control position with extension at the rear
for rangefinder in *Bulwark* and *London*. 3pdrs
began to be removed from 1905. All out in *Bulwark*
by end of 1906, two being remounted on forebridge, others suppressed. All removed from
maintop in *London* in 1906 and *Venerable* 1906–7.
Main deck 12pdrs remounted on superstructure
forward and aft 1906–7. Forward ports plated up in
Venerable (1909) and *Bulwark* (1914) but never
plated over in *London*. Both mast SLs were remounted over forward casemates 1905–7. One 24in
SL mounted over each after casemate in all three
ships. After flying bridge added in *Bulwark* in
1906. W/T gaff triced and masthead semaphore
removed in *Bulwark* (1906) and *Venerable* (1907).
Bulwark was one of the first vessels to get this
modification.

Right: Boat deck of *Venerable* looking forward over starboard side. Here she is preparing for the Fleet Review at Spithead in July 1914. She still has dark-red funnel bands. Note the SL distribution on bridge wings and boat deck.

Below: *Venerable* at Portsmouth Dockyard, 1914 showing final pre-war appearance.

1908 Remaining 3pdr removed from foretop in *London* and *Venerable*. Two 3pdrs (ex-tops) remounted on after bridge in *London*. All suppressed in *Venerable*. Two SLs (ex-forward casemates) restored to after bridge in *London*. After flying bridge added to *London*. W/T topgallant fitted to each mast in *Venerable*. W/T Mk 1 fitted. W/T gaff and semaphore removed. Fleet marking type funnel bands painted in *Bulwark* and *Venerable*; two red low on each funnel in both ships.

1908–9 RF added in lower foretop in *Bulwark* and *Venerable*. Heavy yards removed from mainmast in all.

1909–10 Range indicators fitted on platform below fore control top and over after charthouse in *Bulwark* (early type, all discarded by 1914). 24in SL on forebridge in *Bulwark* replaced by 36in, and after bridge SL temporarily restored. This 36in

Below: *Bulwark* in 'C' line at the Spithead Review, July 1914.

Bottom: *Venerable* at war, Malta 1915. Note crow's nest on foremast; SL arrangement on lower foretop and after bridge.

lamp was experimental and was later removed, there being insufficient space for such a large lamp. After flying bridge in *London* and *Bulwark* removed. Standard funnel bands painted up: *Bulwark* two white on second funnel; *London* nil; *Venerable* one red on each.

1910–11 Remaining 3pdrs removed from *London* and *Bulwark*. W/T topgallants fitted to each mast in *London*, but only foremast in *Bulwark*. Type II W/T fitted.

1911–12 Two 24in SL added on after bridge. W/T topgallant fitted to mainmast in *Bulwark* and W/T gaff and semaphore removed.

1912–13 *London* May 1912 experimental flying-off platform. Fitted over forecastle from forward superstructure; removed 1913.

1913–14 Torpedo nets removed in all. Extra pair 24in SL added on forebridge in *Venerable*.

1914 Funnel bands painted out.

1915 *London* and *Venerable* fitted out for Dardanelles operations: two 3pdr AA added on quarterdeck. After casemate SL in *London* transferred to lower foretop. Forebridge and after casemates SLs transferred to lower foretop in *Venerable*. After bridge SL remounted on after charthouse in both ships. Nets temporarily replaced. Forebridge wings shortened, after bridge wings removed. After charthouse enlarged in *Venerable*. Stockless anchors fitted. Both topgallants and topmast removed; small spotting top fitted at head of foremast. False bow wave painted-up in *London*.

1916 *London* and *Venerable*: Main deck 6in guns removed. Four remounted in shields in 12pdr battery on upper deck amidships (2P+S) firing through large ports in bulwarks. Upper deck 12pdr taken out.

1918 *London*: Converted to minelayer early 1918 (completed by April). Main armament removed; fore turret and barbette retained, but after turret and mounting completely removed. Secondary armament reduced to three 6in, one in each forward upper deck casemate, and one in shield in place of after turret. One 4in AA added later on quarterdeck and 3pdr AA removed. Mines stowed on rails on quarterdeck behind canvas screen. SL reduced to four, all on forebridge. After charthouse removed. Foretopmast always housed in down position. Painted-up in experimental dazzle-type camouflage similar to Norman Wilkinson's schemes, but of a different type from that used in

Below: *Bulwark* sails past after one of the largest fleet reviews ever held at Spithead in July 1914. Ship fully manned for inspection by King George V. The photograph was taken from the Royal yacht by the official photographer, Stephen Cribb.

Below: *Bulwark* blows up, 26 November 1914 (see report).

other battleships (very different scheme for each side of vessel). Painted grey again after the war.

HISTORY: *BULWARK*

Laid down at Devonport 20 March 1899 and launched 18 October 1899. Began her trials in May 1901.

11 Mar 1902 Commissioned for service with Mediterranean Fleet, until Feb 1907.

1 May 1902 Relieved *Renown* as Flag.

1905–6 Refit at Malta.

11 Feb 1907 Paid off at Devonport and recommissioned on 12th as Flag (RA) Nore Division, the new Home Fleet; with Home Fleet until Oct 1908.

26 Oct 1907 Grounded near Lemon Light, North Sea while trying to avoid fishing vessels; slightly damaged. Refit at Chatham 1907–8.

3 Oct 1908 Transferred to Channel Fleet until Mar 1909.

Under reorganization of 24 Mar 1909, Channel Fleet became 2nd Division, Home Fleet; with Home Fleet until Aug 1914. Refit at Devonport 1909.

1 Mar 1910 Commissioned at Devonport as Flag (VA) 3rd and 4th Divisions, Home Fleet, Nore.

Sept 1911—June 1912 Refit at Chatham. Grounded twice on Barrow Deep off the Nore during refit trials May 1912 (some damage to bottom).

Assigned to Channel Fleet (5th BS) at outbreak of war, until Nov 1914. 5th BS normally based at Portland, but temporarily transferred to Sheerness 14 Nov 1914 in anticipation of enemy raid.

LOSS OF *BULWARK*

On 26 November 1914, while lying at anchor, *Bulwark* suddenly blew up at approximately 07.53—07.55. After the smoke had cleared there was no sign of the ship, only some wreckage. She had been lying at buoy number 17 in about 58 feet of water and all was normal so far as has been ascertained. No submarines had been sighted.

A Court of Inquiry was quickly convened, but as all the officers in *Bulwark* had been killed, it was a question of piecing together reports of the twelve survivors who had been thrown clear of the blast. Those questioned, however, although hearing a rumbling noise, remembered nothing until entering the water. Eye-witnesses from the battleship *Agamemnon*, anchored nearby, stated that first thick smoke came out of the ship, the first explosion taking place in the after magazine and lifting the stern before another explosion covered her stern in a sheet of flame. This was confirmed by an eye-witness in *Prince of Wales* who, again, stated

that smoke had definitely come from the rear of *Bulwark* before the explosion occurred.

Divers found wreckage over a very large area; no guns were found, only bits of masts and fragments. The chief find was the gunnery log, and a sunprint of the 12in guns' electrical circuit (latter item found by children on a far shore the next day). The gunnery log recorded that on the day of the explosion and throughout the year, temperatures of magazines and passages had been normal.

On the day before the explosion, however, a working party had been engaged in separating great quantities of 6in shells and charges in the two cross-passages, and this work was resumed early in the morning of the 26th. Some 15 minutes before 08.00 the company had been sent to breakfast, and at least thirty bare 6in charges had been left in the passages. Sentries had been posted, and correct procedure was observed at all times, but it was recorded that magazine doors had been left open.

Since the outbreak of war, quantities of 6in cordite charges were kept in casemates, and those in the upper deck casemates, were occasionally sent up to the ammunition passages except when circumstances render it inadvisable (coaling or when recorded temperatures were too high).

At the forward and after ends of the ammunition

BULWARK CLASS   191

passages in *Bulwark* (and others of the group) were hooks for twenty charges of 6in cordite, and along the passages were hooks for twenty lyddite fuzed shells, and 24 common. There were also three 6in armour-piercing shells and 47 rounds for the 12-pounder guns available.

It was recorded that on the day of disaster, as on any day during the early months of the war, there would have been 275 6in shells plus 178 12-pounder shells actually touching one another while stacked along these passages. The unanimous conclusion was that some of the charges had been placed too close to one of the boiler room bulkheads, which at that time would have been increasing in temperature as the ship got up steam for the day. One or more of the charges ignited and set off 6in shells in the area (causing smoke seen by other ships at the time) which reached the main 12in magazines in the stern of the ship causing a tremendous explosion and resulting in the complete loss of the vessel. When records were checked it was noted that some of the cordite charges in *Bulwark* were more than thirteen years old, but no significance was attached to this; *Bulwark* was not the only ship to have old cordite on board. The Court of Inquiry finally blamed the dead officers for not checking that all safety measures had been carried out (such as charges left against bulkheads).

On 27 November 1914, the day after her loss, three photographs appeared in the *Daily Mirror* showing explosions at different heights; it was stated that this was '*Bulwark* blowing up'. The headlines caused quite a stir, and a stream of correspondence poured into the Admiralty saying that this could not be possible, and how did the newspaper get such photographs in wartime. The stories (and the photographs) were soon discredited and the *Mirror* was made to retract its statement, and saying: These photographs show how *Bulwark* would have looked after the explosion, and are not of the actual ship herself.'

The photograph reproduced in this book, however, is reported to be of *Bulwark* exploding; it was taken by one of the crew in *Agamemnon* or *Prince of Wales*, and not brought forward until after the war.

HISTORY: *LONDON*

Laid down at Portsmouth Dockyard 8 December 1898 and launched 21 September 1899.

7 June 1902 Commissioned at Portsmouth for service in the Mediterranean Fleet (Flag at Coronation Review 16 Aug 1902).
With Mediterranean Fleet until Mar 1907.
1902–3 and 1906 Refit at Malta.
Mar 1907 Transferred to Nore Division, Home Fleet, until June 1908.
2 June 1908 Transferred to Channel Fleet, until April 1909.
1908 Refit at Chatham.
19 April 1909 Paid off at Chatham for extensive refit until Feb 1910.
8 Feb 1910 Commissioned at Chatham as 2nd Flag (RA), Atlantic Fleet, until May 1912.
1 May 1912 Transferred to Second Home Fleet, Nore, on Fleet reorganization, until August 1914.
11 May 1912 Collided with SS *Don Benite* off Hythe. Used in experiments in flying-off aircraft May 1912 until 1913. Assigned to Channel Fleet on outbreak of war.
Aug 1914—Mar 1915 Channel Fleet.
19 Mar 1915 Ordered to Dardanelles and joined the Squadron at Lemnos on 23 Mar. In Dardanelles until May 1915.
25 April 1915 Supported main landings at Gaba Tepe and Anzac.
22 May Detached to Adriatic as unit of 2nd Detached Squadron. Based at Taranto. In Adriatic until Oct 1916.
Oct 1915 Refit at Gibraltar.
Oct 1916 Returned home and paid off at Devonport to provide crews for anti-submarine vessels. At Devonport until Jan 1918.
1916–17 Refit.

LONDON
Outboard profile, after conversion to minesweeper, 1918

Note reduced bridgework, removal of 12in guns and after 12in turret, canvas screen over whole length of quarterdeck to hide minelaying equipment, and removal of nets.

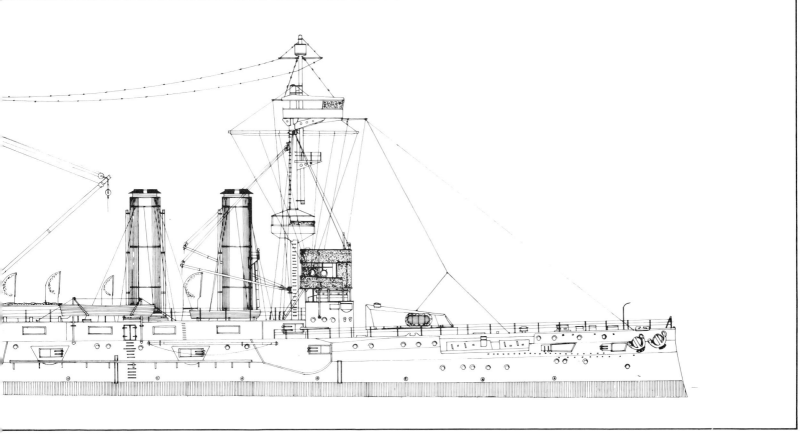

Below: *Venerable* taking on supplies at Mudros in 1915 during the Dardanelles campaign. Note that nets are out in the defensive position.

Bottom: *Venerable* showing final rig, 1917. She was laid up from December 1916 to February 1918 before becoming depot ship for Northern Patrol minesweeping trawlers.

Opposite page: *Russell* running her preliminary sea trials in the summer of 1902. Having more speed and less armour than most contemporary battleships, the *Duncans* could claim, with *Canopus*, to be the embodiment of early battlecruiser principles. Unusually, for this late date, she is wearing Victorian colours.

Feb—April 1918 Converted to minelayer at Rosyth.

18 May 1918 Commissioned at Rosyth for 1st Minelaying Squadron (*Angora*, *Princess Margaret*, *Amphitrite* and *London*). Joined Grand Fleet until Jan 1919.

Laid 2,640 mines in Northern Mine Barrage.

Jan 1919 Reduced to Reserve at Devonport, until Jan 1920. Became unit of Devonport 3rd Fleet on post-war reorganization.

Jan 1920 Placed on disposal list at Devonport.

31 Mar 1920 On sale list.

4 June 1920 Sold to Stanlee Shipbreaking Co, Dover for £30,500. Subsequently resold to Slough Trading Co, and again resold to German scrappers.

April 1922 Towed to Germany for scrapping.

HISTORY: *VENERABLE*

Laid down at Chatham Dockyard 2 January 1899 and launched 2 November 1899.

12 Nov 1902 Commissioned at Chatham after many delays to her completion because of difficulties with her machinery contractors. Commissioned for service with Mediterranean Fleet as 2nd Flag (RA), until Jan 1908.

26 June 1905 Grounded outside Algiers harbour, slight damage to hull plating.

1906–7 Refit at Malta.

12 Aug 1907 Flag transferred to *Prince of Wales*.

6 Jan 1908 Paid off at Chatham and recommissioned on 7th for service with Channel Fleet, until Feb 1909.

Feb 1909 Paid off at Chatham for extensive refit.

19 Oct 1909 Commissioned at Chatham for Atlantic Fleet, until May 1912.

13 May 1912 Transferred to Second Home Fleet, Nore until Aug 1914. Assigned to Channel Fleet (5th BS) on outbreak of war, until May 1915. Took part in transporting Portsmouth Marine Battalion to Ostend. Attached to Dover Patrol for bombardment duties. Bombarded enemy positions between Westende and Lombartzyde 27–30 Oct 1914.

Flagship of Admiral Hood, CinC, Dover Patrol 27–29 Oct.

3 Nov 1914 Detached to support East Coast Patrols during Gorleston Raid. Bombarded batteries near Westende 11 Mar and 10 May 1915.

12 May 1915 Ordered to Dardanelles to replace new battleship *Queen Elizabeth*. In Dardanelles until Oct 1915.

21 Aug Supported attacks on Turkish positions at Suvla Bay.

Oct—Dec 1915 Refit at Gibraltar.

Dec 1915 Transferred to Adriatic, until Dec 1916.

19 Dec Returned to Portsmouth, until Feb 1918.

Feb—Mar 1918 Refitted at Portsmouth as depot ship and moved to Portland on 27th for service as depot ship for Northern Minelaying trawlers; depot ship until Dec 1918. Attached to Northern

Patrol Mar—Aug and Southern Patrol Sept—Dec. Paid off into Care and Maintenance at Portland at end Dec 1918. Used in experiments.

May 1919 Placed on disposal list at Portland.

4 Feb 1920 On sale list.

4 June 1920 Sold to Stanlee Shipbreaking Co, Dover; Resold to Slough Trading Co in 1922; Resold to German scrappers mid-1922 and towed to Germany to be scrapped.

DUNCAN CLASS

1898/9 ESTIMATES

DESIGN

Designed as a fast battleship type, this class was specifically intended as a reply to the Russian battleships of the *Peresviet* class, the first two of which were launched in 1898, erroneously reported to have a nominal speed of 19 knots. These Russian ships were at first (late 1896) thought to be large armoured cruiser types, but a report by Captain Paget on 30 December 1897 showed them to be fast, second class battleships, although their designed speed was only 18 knots.

Proposals for the *Duncan* class were submitted as early as February 1898, but in order to allow more time for working out the design it was decided to defer their commencement, and a modified' *Formidable* design, embodying certain changes in armouring, provisionally accepted for the *Duncans*, was adopted, at White's suggestion, for three battleships of the 1898 programme and these were built as units of the *Bulwark* class. So it was not until 14 June 1898 that the DNC (White) submitted his sketch designs for 19-knot battleships—vessels in which the greatest possible economies in weight had been made in order to achieve the required speeds on the dimensions laid down.

On 2 June White instructed Haslar to prepare models (L1 and LE2) on his preliminary dimensions and after a beam increase of 6in (to 75ft 6in) to secure a greater metacentric height, the sheer had been prepared by 15 July 1898 and sent back to the Construction Department. A final legend was approved in September 1898 and tenders were sent out on 25 October 1898.

After publication of the British 1898 programme, proposed large increases to the French and Russian Fleets were made known and in view of this and the fact that the British programme included only three battleships (all supposedly inferior in speed to the Russian *Peresviets*), a Special Supplementary Programme for 1898 was introduced and approved during the latter part of 1898. This provided for the commencement of at least four of the *Duncans* as early as possible, and these were put in hand from March to July 1899, the remaining two being laid down in November 1899 and January 1900 under the 1899 programme.

Influenced by a powerful lobby favouring moderate dimensions and cost, displacement at the design stage was kept to about 1,000 tons less than in the *Formidable* group; in order to provide equal

armament with an increase of 1 knot designed speed, undesirably heavy sacrifices in protection had to be accepted which adversely affected their all-round value as first class battleships. The design did not, therefore, constitute a direct development of the *Formidable* type, but represented an enlarged and improved version of the earlier *Canopus* class, bearing much the same relation to those ships as *Formidable* did to the *Majestics*.

Having less protection, but higher speeds than contemporary British battleship types, the *Duncans* have some claim to being regarded, with the *Canopus* class, as embodying early battlecruiser ideas, although in contrast to the later bona fide battlecruisers, offensive power was not reduced, and the increase in speed was relatively much less.

Innovations in the design were:

1. Provision of increased protection to hull side forward with some rearrangement of deck armour against plunging fire (also adopted in *Bulwark* group).

2. Open deck 12pdr battery.

3. Abandonment of ventilator cowls.

4. Adoption of stockless anchors (in last two ships).

On an increase of 1,050 tons displacement over the *Canopus* class, the *Duncans* carried more powerful guns (Mk IX), stronger protection, except over a 4ft-wide strip along the waterline amidships, an increase of 1—2 knots seagoing speed, but a slightly smaller fuel-carrying capacity.

Designed for the then unusually high speed of 19 knots and handicapped by a displacement limit inadequate to provide this speed without considerable sacrifices to protection, the *Duncans* could not fail to displease, and were always regarded as an altogether unsatisfactory type, although certainly superior to the Russian *Peresviet* type in every aspect except fuel stowage. They enjoyed the distinction of being, for some years, among the fastest battleships afloat.

They all turned out be fair sea-boats owing to the fine lines incorporated in the hull to assist in securing the high speed without undue increase in shp installation, but as a result suffered from being wet ships because of the lowered freeboard from that of the *Canopus*, *Formidable* and *Bulwark* groups (approx. 6in forward and 15in less aft).

ARMAMENT

Except for smaller barbettes and a lower gun command, the main armament was identical with that of the *Bulwark* groups.

The need to conform to strict weight saving, however, led to the reduction of barbette size. The barbettes of *Formidable* and *Bulwark* were 37ft 6in outside diameter, and it was proposed to reduce the clearance from the turntables to the inside framing of the barbette. This was made possible because there were no shells kept in this space or any traffic passing through. The proposal was immediately accepted and the *Duncans*' barbettes were con-

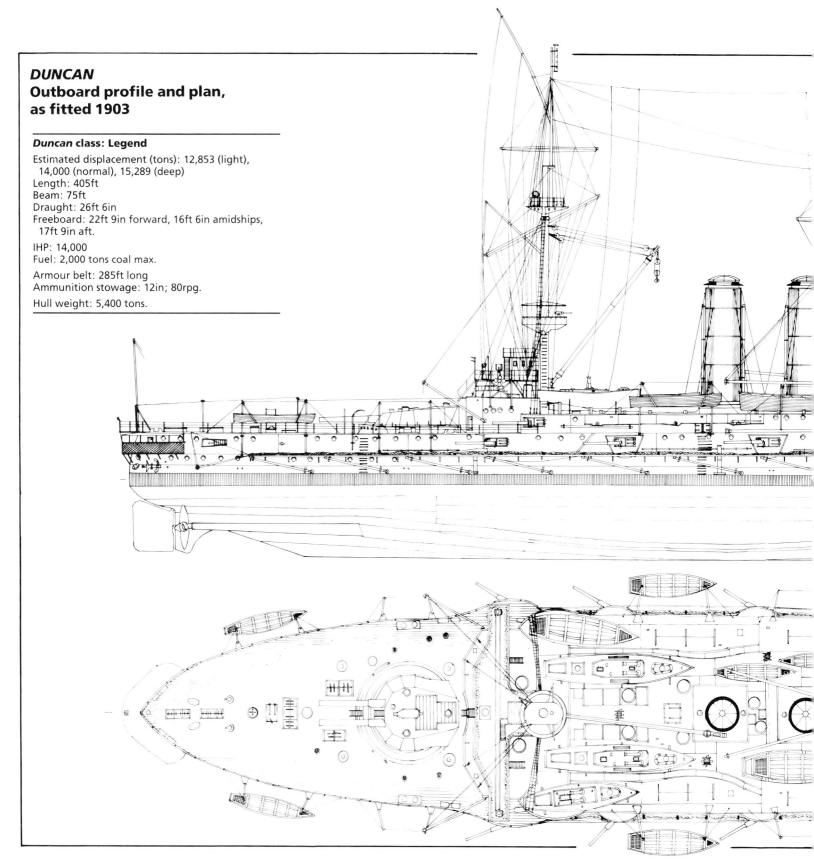

DUNCAN
Outboard profile and plan,
as fitted 1903

Duncan class: Legend

Estimated displacement (tons): 12,853 (light),
  14,000 (normal), 15,289 (deep)
Length: 405ft
Beam: 75ft
Draught: 26ft 6in
Freeboard: 22ft 9in forward, 16ft 6in amidships,
  17ft 9in aft.

IHP: 14,000
Fuel: 2,000 tons coal max.

Armour belt: 285ft long
Ammunition stowage: 12in; 80rpg.

Hull weight: 5,400 tons.

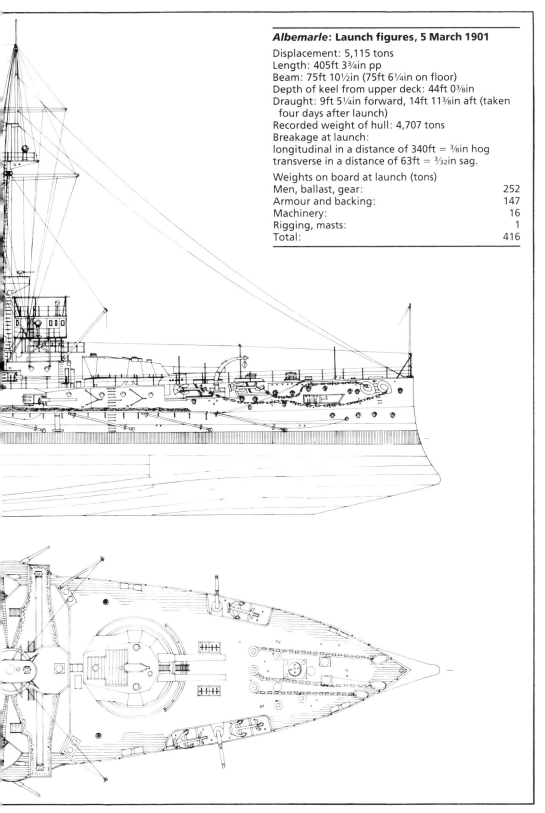

Albemarle: Launch figures, 5 March 1901

Displacement: 5,115 tons
Length: 405ft 3¾in pp
Beam: 75ft 10½in (75ft 6¼in on floor)
Depth of keel from upper deck: 44ft 0⅜in
Draught: 9ft 5¼in forward, 14ft 11⅜in aft (taken four days after launch)
Recorded weight of hull: 4,707 tons
Breakage at launch:
longitudinal in a distance of 340ft = ⅜in hog
transverse in a distance of 63ft = ³⁄₃₂in sag.

Weights on board at launch (tons)
Men, ballast, gear:	252
Armour and backing:	147
Machinery:	16
Rigging, masts:	1
Total:	416

structed at 36ft 6in. Accordingly, the turrets were altered slightly in shape to conform with the barbettes, and given angled faces rather than round faces as in *Formidable*; other than this they were identical with those in that ship (BVI).

Secondary armament was identical with that of *Formidable* although the main deck forward and after casemates were well sponsoned to increase blast-free end-on arcs. When the design layout was first reviewed by the Captain of *Excellent* he remarked:

'I would prefer to have the inner pair of main deck casemates on the upper deck with the 12pdrs between them, as the guns would be in a better fighting position especially when there is any seaway; if the extra weight for protecting the ammunition supply and bases of pedestal could be allowed, it would be to a great advantage, and this protection should also be given to the foremost and after upper deck casemates, unless the foremost and after main deck casemates are brought underneath the former.'

After a review of this situation, the conclusion reached did not agree with the above remarks, and it was generally thought that fitting 6in guns amidships on the upper deck level would bring problems in hampering the clearways for ammunition supply.

The number of 12pdrs was reduced from sixteen to ten by suppression of the inner pair on the main deck forward and aft, and reduction of the upper deck battery from eight to six guns.

The upper deck battery was entirely open along the sides, with the guns firing over a low breastwork instead of through ports in high bulwarks, as in *Majestic* and *Bulwark*.

ARMOUR

Protection was subordinated to armament and speed, with considerable sacrifices in armour thickness being accepted to provide the same armament as in *Formidable*, and with a knot more speed on 1,000 tons lighter displacement. The blame for accepting these sacrifices to protection lay with the strong body of opinion that was opposed to any increase in size or cost at that date.

The arrangement of hull armouring was modified from that of *Formidable* with a view to securing better protection to hull side forward, with thicker horizontal armour at main deck level to meet the threat of plunging shellfire. These

Opposite page, top: *Duncan* in November 1905. Unofficially known as the '*Admirals*' they appeared much lower in the water than the *Formidable* and *Bulwark* groups and had two round funnels rather than the unequal-sized funnels of the latter.

Opposite page, bottom: *Cornwallis* completing at Chatham, early 1904. She was commissioned on 9 February 1904 to relieve *Renown* in the Mediterranean.

Duncan class: Particulars, as completed

Construction

Duncan: Thames Ironworks; laid down 10 July 1899; launched 21 March 1901, completed Oct 1903

Cornwallis: Thames Ironworks; laid down 19 July 1899; launched 13 July 1901; completed Feb 1904

Exmouth: Cammell Laird; laid down 10 Aug 1899; launched 31 Aug 1901; completed May 1903

Russell: Palmer; laid down 11 March 1899; launched 19 Feb 1902; completed Feb 1903

Albemarle: Chatham DY; laid down 8 Jan 1901; launched 5 March 1901; completed Nov 1903

Montague: Devonport DY; laid down 23 Nov 1899; launched 5 March 1901; completed Nov 1903.

Displacement (tons)

13,305 tons normal condition. 14,845 tons deep condition. (*Montague*)

13,272 tons normal condition. 14,048 tons deep condition. (*Cornwallis*)

14,870 tons deep condition. (*Russell*).

Dimensions

Length: 405ft 3¾in pp, 418ft wl, 432ft oa (*Albemarle*)

Beam: 75ft 10in (*Albemarle*)

Draught: 25ft 3in – 27ft 7½in (mean).

Armament

Four 12in Mk IX

Twelve 6in Mk VII (PIII mountings)

Ten 12pdr (12cwt) (PIII mountings)

Two 12pdr (8cwt) boats (field mountings)

Six 3pdr (recoil mountings)

Two Maxims

Four 18in torpedo tubes submerged; eighteen 18in Mk V, six 14in torpedoes.

Shell stowage

12in (80rpg): 64 AP shells, 216 common steel, 28 practice, 40 AP shot

6in (200rpg): 480 AP shells, 1,272 common steel, 240 Lyddite common, 288 shrapnel, 168 practice, 120 AP shot.

Armour

Main belt: 7in KC

Forward belts: 5in–4in–3in

Stern belt: 1½in

After bulkhead: 11in–7in

Barbettes: 11in–4in

Turrets: 8in faces and sides

Conning tower: 12in–3in

Casemates: 6in faces, 2in backs

Decks: main 2in–1in, middle 1in, lower 2in.

Machinery

Two sets 4-cylinder vertical inverted triple expansion engines, twin in-turning propellers

Propeller diameter: 17ft

Propeller pitch: 18ft 6in, developed area 82ft

Cylinder diameter: 33½in HP, 54½in IP, 63in LP

Stroke: 4ft

Boilers: twenty-four Belleville water tube, working pressure 300psi, 250psi at engines

Heating surface: 43,260sq ft

Grate area: 1,375sq ft

Revs: 120rpm

Designed SHP: 18,000 for 18 knots

Fuel: 900 tons coal normal, 2,182–2,240 tons max.

Coal consumption: 100 tons per day at 10 knots, 420 tons per day at full power, 50 tons per day at 7 knots

Radius of action: 6,070nm at 10 knots

Length of boiler room: 94ft 1in

Length of engine room: 54ft 0½in

Weight of auxiliary machinery: 115.769 tons (*Duncan*).

Ship's boats (*Russell*, as completed)

Pinnaces (steam): one 56ft, one 40ft

Pinnaces (sail): one 36ft

Launches (steam): one 56ft, one 42ft

Cutters: two 34ft

Whalers: one 27ft

Gigs: one 30ft, one 28ft

Jolly boats: one 24ft

Skiff dinghies: one 16ft

Balsa rafts: one 13ft 8in.

Searchlights

Six 24in, two on each bridge, one high on each mast (as completed) *Albemarle*, 1913: two 24in on after bridge, two 36in on boat deck, two 24in on fore bridge, two 24in on shelter deck. (Varied a great deal within class – see Appearance notes).

Anchors

Three 115cwt Halls close-stowing; *Albemarle* and *Montague* fitted with stockless.

Wireless

Duncan: Type 1, replaced by Types 2 and 3

Cornwallis: Type 1, replaced by Types 2 and 3

Exmouth: Type 2, replaced by Types 1 and 3

Russell: Type 1, replaced by Types 2 and 3

Albemarle: Type 1, replaced by Type 2

Montague: Type 1.

Complement

762 as designed

762 (*Exmouth*, as Flagship 1904)

736 (*Russell*, 1904)

761 (*Exmouth*, 1905)

781 (*Russell*, 1915).

Costs

Duncan: £1,023,147 plus guns £65,750

Cornwallis: £1,030,302 plus guns £65,750

Exmouth: £1,032,409 plus guns £65,750

Russell: £1,038,301 plus guns £65,750

Albemarle: £1,009,835 plus guns £68,560

Montague: —.

---

changes represented ideas originally introduced in the earlier *Canopus* class and repeated in *Formidable*. This difference in layout was adopted in the *Bulwark* group, although proposed, in the first instance for the *Duncan* class.

Provision of a thicker armour belt forward was intended to reduce the risk of damage from flooding at the bows with consequent loss of speed and manoeuvring ability; maintenance of speed being especially important in the *Duncan* class in view of their role as fast battleships. Additional armour on the main deck was designed to afford more effective protection against plunging fire, but

the corresponding reduction to 1in maximum thickness of the middle deck in *Duncan* was severely criticized on the grounds that this provided inadequate reinforcement to the 7in belt which could be pierced by the French 9.4in gun at close ranges of 3,000 yards and under.

Compared with *Formidable* the armouring was:

1. Maximum thickness of armoured belt reduced from 9in to 7in although carried slightly before the forward barbette instead of terminating abeam it.

2. Forward extension to belt at bows raised 2ft 6in (to main deck level) and thickness increased from 2in uniform to 5in-4in-3in and 2in.

3. Usual belt bulkhead forward was abandoned to offset additional weight of bow armour, and maximum thickness of the after bulkhead was reduced from 10in to 7in.

4. Main deck between barbettes increased from 1in to 2in with a 2in-1in extension forward to the stem (not fitted in the *Formidable*s).

5. Middle deck reduced from 3in slopes and a 2in flat to 1in uniform.

6. Lower deck forward reduced from 2in uniform to 2in and 1in, and aft from 2½in to 2in.

7. Maximum thickness of barbettes reduced from 12in to 11in.

Referring to the *Peresviet* class the DNC explained:

'Comparing with the *Osliabia* it will be seen that the new ships are much superior in protection. The *Osliabia* it is true has 9in armour at the waterline for 224ft but maximum thickness only extends about 3ft above the waterline and not more than 1ft below.

Citadel armour in *Osliabia* rising to the main deck from the top of the thick belt is 7ft 6in wide and extends only over extreme length of about 188ft. It is 4in thick and even if the same quality as the 7in in the new ships it would only be $^1/_3$rd as strong in its resistance to perforation – but it is exceedingly doubtful if such 4in armour could be treated by the Krupps process.

For about 60ft at each end there is no armour whatsoever in *Osliabia*.'

As fitted, the main armoured belt in *Duncan* was 238ft long by 14ft 3in wide and extended from just before the fore barbette to abeam the after barbette.

The upper edge was at main deck level, approximately 10ft above the waterline; the lower edge approximately 4ft 3in below at normal condition.

The 5in-4in-3in and 2in forward was carried right through to the stem over the same width as the midships section except that the forward extremity was carried down to support the ram. The 2in thickness, right forward, quickly increased to 3in-4in and 5in with the 5in section reaching about 25ft abaft the stem. The 2in section was laid over a double thickness of ½in shell plating.

The 1in after strake was complete to the stern, the lower edge being level with the lower edge of the midships section, the upper edge being about 4ft above the waterline.

Again this armour was laid over two thicknesses of ½in shell plating.

The belt bulkhead aft was 7in thick and ran obliquely inwards from the after extremities of the 7in belt armour to the outer face of the after barbette.

The forward gun barbette was 11in on the outer face above the side armour, and 7in below. The inner face was 10in above the side armour and 4in below. The after gun barbette was 11in on the outer face above the middle deck and 10in below. The inner face was 10in above the side armour and 4in below this. Turrets were given 8in faces, 8in sides, 10in rears and 2in-3in roofs. Casemates had 6in faces and sides and a 2in rear. Ammunition hoists for the 6in guns were 2in.

The main deck ran flat across the top of the belt from stem to after bulkhead at 1in-2in thick, 2in to outer end of 4in armour, 1in forward of this to stem. The middle deck was 1in on the slope and flat and extended from the after bulkhead to the forward extremity of the 7in armour belt. The lower deck was curved, underwater, and ran from the outer base of each barbette to stem and stern respectively, 2in-1in forward, 1in aft. The inner extremity of the forward section (2in) sloped steeply upwards to meet the middle deck before the fore barbette.

The forward conning tower was 12in-10in and had an 8in tube; the after conning tower was 3in with a 3in tube.

Coal bunkers were placed behind the main belt between the middle and main decks, and abreast the boiler rooms below the middle deck.

A cellular layer of watertight compartments was fitted at the extremities between the middle and lower deck levels. The internal sub-division was more complete than in the *Formidable*s and included provision of a centre-line bulkhead between the engine rooms, not fitted in those ships.

Russell: GM and stability

Based on inclining experiments, 31 January 1903

	Draught	GM	Maximum stability	Stability vanishes at
'A' Condition (= load)*	25ft 3¼in (mean)	4.1ft	38°	65°
'B' Condition (= deep load)**	27ft 8⅝in (mean)	4.2ft	36°	66°
'C' Condition (= light)***	23ft 5¾in	4ft		

*Fully equipped plus 360 tons coal in upper bunkers, 540 tons in lower bunkers, reserve feed tanks empty, boilers to full working height.
**Fully equipped plus 2,287 tons coal, all tanks full.
***Lightened to draught shown, but boilers to working height.

DUNCAN
Inboard profile and sections, as fitted 1903

Section 174
1 Admiral's after cabin
2 Warrant Officers' mess
3 Admiral's store
4 Tiller compartment

Section 158
1 Admiral's secretary
2 Warrant Oficers' cabin
3 Paymaster's store
4 Submerged torpedo room
5 Gunners' store

Section 145
1 12in barbette
2 Paymaster's cabin
3 Coal
4 Shell chamber
5 Auxiliary machinery compartment
6 Compressor compartment
7 Training engine compartment
8 6in gun magazine
9 Light box
10 12in handing room
11 Engineers' stores
12 Shaft passage
13 12in shell room

Section 120
1 After fighting top
2 Signal house
3 6in casemate
4 Vent to engine room
5 Captain's day cabin
6 Engineer Commander's cabin
7 Coal
8 Stokers' washplace
9 Ammunition passage
10 Engine room

Section 87
1 Seamen's heads
2 Boiler uptake
3 6in casemate and crew mess
4 Coal
5 Ammunition passage
6 Wing
7 Boiler room

Section 51
1 Boatswain's ready-use store
2 Vent from auxiliary machinery
3 CPOs' heads
4 Bakery
5 Canteen
6 Forward transmitting station
7 Leading stokers' washplace
8 Coal
9 Hydraulic machinery compartment
10 12pdr magazine
11 6in maghazine
12 6in shell room
13 Small-arms magazine

Section 39
1 12in barbette
2 Canvas room
3 Shell chamber
4 Electric light store
5 Turning engine compartment
6 Hydraulic tank
7 Engineers' store
8 12in handing room
9 Electrical store
10 12in shell room
11 Provisions room

Section 18
1 Crew space
2 Crew space
3 Cable locker
4 Capstan engine room
5 Bread room

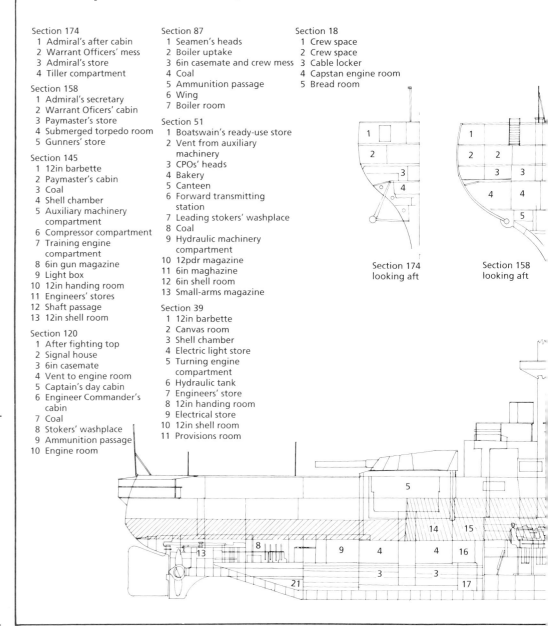

Section 174
looking aft

Section 158
looking aft

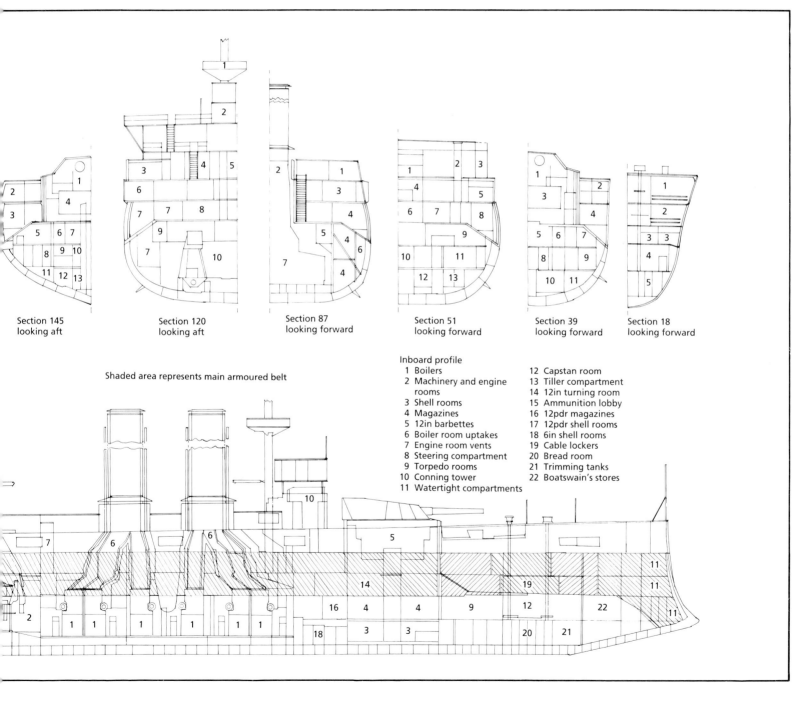

Section 145
looking aft

Section 120
looking aft

Section 87
looking forward

Section 51
looking forward

Section 39
looking forward

Section 18
looking forward

Shaded area represents main armoured belt

Inboard profile
 1 Boilers
 2 Machinery and engine
   rooms
 3 Shell rooms
 4 Magazines
 5 12in barbettes
 6 Boiler room uptakes
 7 Engine room vents
 8 Steering compartment
 9 Torpedo rooms
10 Conning tower
11 Watertight compartments

12 Capstan room
13 Tiller compartment
14 12in turning room
15 Ammunition lobby
16 12pdr magazines
17 12pdr shell rooms
18 6in shell rooms
19 Cable lockers
20 Bread room
21 Trimming tanks
22 Boatswain's stores

Left: *Montague*, dressed overall and showing her early fleet markings (funnel bands).

Bottom left: *Exmouth* in Weymouth Bay, c.1906. Note that she has the old-style anchor beds – only *Montague* and *Albemarle* of the class were fitted without Trotman anchor beds.

At the same time, the usual low reserve of stability (designed to secure a relatively steady gun platform) associated with longitudinal bulkheads, without adequate counter-flooding arrangements was a very weak point in the system of underwater protection, and there is no doubt that this fact contributed greatly to the loss of both *Cornwallis* and *Russell*, each of which assumed a heavy list before turning over and going down.

MACHINERY

As they were specially built to counter the Russian ships which were reported to be 19-knot ships, it is natural that special attention was given to the machinery of the new class. Designed with 18,000shp for speeds up to 19 knots, they were the fastest battleships in the Royal Navy on completion, and the fastest predreadnoughts ever built with the exception of *Swiftsure* and *Triumph*. The designed speed was $^3/_4$ knot higher than in the *Canopus* class, which hitherto had been the fastest battleships in the Royal Navy.

The propelling machinery consisted of two sets of 4-cylinder, vertical inverted triple expansion engines driving two in-turning screws at approximately 120rpm at full speed. Twenty-four Belleville boilers with economizers arranged in two groups of eight, and two of four (24) and all had a working pressure of 300psi which reduced to 250psi at the engines. The 4-bladed propellers were manganese bronze.

As completed, all the ships except *Albemarle*, carried out their steam trials successfully. *Albemarle*, however, had difficulties with leaking glands during her runs, but apart from that all was satisfactory. Reports from sea trials indicate that there was less trouble with the machinery installation in this group, than in earlier classes fitted with basically the same equipment.

The *Duncan*s were always regarded as good steamers, steering very well at most speeds, and rolling easily.

APPEARANCE CHANGES

Generally similar to the last three groups in appearance but sat lower in the water than *Formidable*, and looked much lighter. Distinguishable from *Canopus*, *Formidable* and *Bulwark* groups by:
1. Only one 12pdr port and starboard forward and aft (from *Formidable* and *Bulwark* only).
2. Open upper deck battery amidships.

3. Equal-sized, round larger funnels.
4. No ventilation cowls.

Distinguishable from the *Queens* by: Circular fighting tops (kidney-shaped in *Queen*). Stocked anchors with billboards, cat davits, etc. (except *Albemarle* and *Montague*).

As completed, all ships of the class were painted in the new grey colours, but *Russell* was given the Victorian buff scheme during her trials period, and *Duncan* also received this during the summer of 1903.

Individual differences:
Sometimes difficult to tell apart as completed, except for *Albemarle* and *Montague* with their stockless anchors.

Albemarle also had steam pipes up to the stay rib, while *Montague* had quite short steam pipes. The hawseholes were oval-shaped in *Albemarle* and circular in *Montague*.

Exmouth was fitted with heavy, close-fitting funnel caps; *Cornwallis* light, close-fitting caps, *Russell* heavy caps. *Duncan* had light, close-fitting caps and, as completed, she was almost identical with *Cornwallis* and extremely difficult to pick out. The only reliable identification feature was a slight variation in three scuttles abaft the cat davit on the port side of the forecastle.

1905 Range indicators fitted to SL platform on foremast in *Cornwallis*, *Duncan* and *Exmouth*, and to after fighting tops in *Duncan*. Very small rangefinder fitted to SL platform on foremast in *Montague*. Foremast SL in *Ablemarle* remounted in forward military top. Both mast SL in *Montague* transferred to roof of fore turret. Tall, light W/T pole temporarily fitted to fore topmast in *Duncan*, and W/T gaff triced (pole removed and gaff lowered to original position in 1905–6). Atlantic and Channel Fleet funnel bands painted-up for use as Fleet identification (*see* sketches): *Albemarle* one narrow band on each funnel; *Russell* one wide on each; *Cornwallis* two narrow on each; *Montague* one wide over one narrow on each; *Duncan* one narrow over one wide on each.

1905–6 Fire control and RF equipment added in all. Control top fitted in place of SL platform on foremast. Fighting top on mainmast roofed in and adopted as control position with extension at rear for RF in *Albemarle*, *Exmouth* and *Montague*. Small, square control top in *Albemarle*, *Cornwallis* and *Duncan*. Range indicators fitted to fore control top in *Cornwallis* and *Duncan* (removed from after control top in *Duncan*). Main deck 12pdrs removed and remounted in forward superstructure in all except *Montague*. In *Russell* only two remounted, others suppressed. 3pdrs removed from fighting tops.

Foremast SL remounted on new small platform below control top in all except *Montague*. Platform

fitted in *Montague* but lamp not actually carried prior to loss (1906). *Duncan* had temporary (1906) arrangement with both mast SL on fore turret, and forebridge SL remounted over forward casemates.

1907–8 Original square control top in *Albemarle* and *Duncan* replaced by large, oval type as in *Exmouth* and *Russell*. *Cornwallis* retained her small, square top throughout. Range indicators removed in *Duncan* and *Cornwallis*. Two 24in SL added (P+S) on boat deck amidships in all. W/T topgallant fitted to both masts in *Exmouth* and W/T gaff removed. W/T gaff triced in others. Masthead semaphore removed in all.

Albemarle Refit Mar 1907
Fitted with speed sights; covers fitted to fire control switch boards for protection to delicate instruments; Bowden cable deflective gear fitted to turret sights; fire gongs fitted to both 12in turrets; Captain's cease-fire bell fitted to CT linked directly to 12in turrets; equipment for dynamo firing fitted; W/T office fitted on after bridge; wire stays and rigging insulated for W/T; additional ventilation to engine rooms; new director tops; enlargement of sighting ports of 12in turrets; modification to mountings of 12pdrs; two 36in SL lamps fitted on forebridge.

1909–10 Modified range indicator fitted to control top in *Albemarle*. Boat deck SL remounted on forebridge in *Duncan* and *Cornwallis*. W/T topgallant fitted to each mast in *Albemarle*, *Duncan* and *Russell*; to mainmast only in *Cornwallis*. W/T gaff removed in all. Standard funnel bands painted-up:

Albemarle one white on each funnel; *Cornwallis* one white on second funnel; *Russell* two wide white on fore funnel; *Duncan* one white on fore funnel; *Exmouth* one wide white on each (*Albemarle* had hers painted out later, and *Russell*'s was changed to two white on second funnel in 1911).

Russell Gun refit 1909. New central sighting gear for 12in guns; creep training control gear for 12in fitted; single-wheel elevating gear for 12in fitted; enlargement of sight ports in the 6in PIII mountings; train and creep gear fitted in 12in; deflection teachers fitted on 12in modification to sights of 12in; transmitting station for fire control fitted; dynamo firing gear fitted; hinged doors in ammunition passage riveted-up; barbette heating system connected to live steam instead of the exhaust system.

1911–12 Modified range indicator fitted to platform

below fore control top in *Duncan* and *Russell*; also in after charthouse in *Duncan* and to rear of after control top in *Russell*. Range indicator removed from fore control top in *Albemarle*. These indicators, together with the 1905–6 pattern were an early, experimental type, discarded by 1914 but retained in *Duncan* as late as 1915 which was very unusual (removed later). Boat deck SL remounted on forebridge in *Exmouth* and *Russell* (1911) and on after charthouse in *Albemarle* (1912). Bridge and casemate SL in *Albemarle* (1912) transposed, the 36in being carried on casemates and 30in on bridge. Casemate SL in *Exmouth* remounted on roof of forward fighting top in 1912. Forebridge in *Albemarle* rebuilt in 1912 (after being damaged at sea). Heavy yards removed from mainmast in *Albemarle*.

1913–14 Small RF mounted on fore turret in *Exmouth* (1914). 36in SL in *Exmouth* transferred from forebridge to forward casemates. Torpedo nets removed in *Albemarle*, *Exmouth* and *Russell*. Forebridge in *Exmouth* rebuilt as in *Albemarle*.

W/T topgallant fitted to foremast of *Cornwallis*. Heavy yards removed from mainmast in *Cornwallis*, *Duncan*, *Exmouth* and Russell.

1914 Funnel bands deleted.

1915 Two 3in AA added: *Albemarle* on after superstructure; *Cornwallis* over forward 6in casemates; *Duncan* on after bridge (others probably similar); *Russell* on quarterdeck. 36in SL in *Albemarle* removed and boat deck SL remounted on lower foretop (3) and on after charthouse (1). Torpedo nets replaced in *Cornwallis*, *Duncan* and *Exmouth* for Dardanelles. Stockless anchors fitted, but original billboards retained. Topgallants removed in all, and main topmast in all except *Exmouth*. Short W/T pole fitted in place of main topmast in *Albemarle* and *Cornwallis*. Spotting top added on foretop mast in *Albemarle* and *Cornwallis*. Identification letters painted up on turret sides in *Duncan* (DU) and *Exmouth* (EX) in Mediterranean during 1915. *Exmouth* showed single dark red funnel bands on fore funnel at Dardanelles, in 1915.

1916–17 Main deck 6in guns removed in *Albemarle* (1916): four remounted in shields (2P+S) in 12pdr battery space on upper deck amidships. 12pdrs reduced to eight, all in superstructures forward and aft. SL removed from casemates in *Duncan*, two ex forebridge remounted on platform below fore control top and two 36in lamps added on roof of lower foretop. Torpedo nets temporarily replaced in *Albemarle* at Murmansk Jan—Sept 1916. Removed on return home. Nets removed in *Duncan* and *Exmouth* 1916–17 (still fitted in *Cornwallis* at time of loss). After bridge wings in *Albemarle* curtailed.

1917–18 12pdrs removed in *Albemarle*. Other vessels of class sometimes stripped of various small fittings.

HISTORY: *DUNCAN*

Laid down under the 1898 Supplementary Programme at Thames Iron Works, Blackwall on 10 July 1899.

8 Oct 1903 Commissioned at Chatham for service in

Duncan class: Collective steam trials

	IHP	Revs.	Speed (knots)		IHP	Revs.	Speed (knots)
Duncan				**Russell**			
30-hour				30-hour			
⅕th power (3,600ihp):	3,755	72.5	11.9	⅕th power:	3,768	74.65	12.1
¾ power (13,500ihp):	13,541	111.9	17.9	¾ power:	13,690	114	17.95
8-hour full power:	18,262	121.25	19.11	8-hour full power:	18,199	123.4	19.4
Cornwallis				**Albemarle**			
30-hour				30-hour			
⅕th power:	3,724	71.45	10.9	⅕th power:	3,606	70.85	12.05
¾ power:	13,765	113.45	17.94	¾ power:	13,837	–	17.75
8-hour full power:	18,056	121.65	18.98	8-hour full power:	18,213	121	18.65
Exmouth				**Montague**			
30-hour				30-hour			
⅕th power:	3,667	73.45	12.4	⅕th power:	3,767	71.1	12
¾ power:	13,839	113.25	17.928	¾ power:	13,611	111.5	17.63
8-hour full power:	18,604	122.5	19.015	8-hour full power:	18,206	118	18.6

Cornwallis: Steam trials, 4 March 1903
Rame Head and Dodman Point. Wind NW, Force 4

Runs	Port	Starboard	Total	Speed (knots)
	IHP			
30-hour, ¾ power				
First:	7,203	6,811	14,014	18.3
Second:	6,861	6,653	13,514	17.72
Third:	6,829	6,519	13,348	17,87
Fourth:	7,297	6,888	14,185	18.60

Runs	Port	Starboard	Total	Speed (knots)
	IHP			
8-hour, full power				
First:	9,763	9,262	18,998	19.62
Second:	9,228	8,731	17,959	18.42
Third:	8,993	8,390	17,353	19.43
Fourth:	9,150	8,765	17,915	18.65

On second full-power trials, weather had turned squally, and on two runs the ship was hampered by sailing vessels crossing her path.

Mediterranean Fleet, until Feb 1905.

Feb 1905 Transferred to Channel Fleet (ex-Home Fleet), until Feb 1907.

26 Sept 1905 Collided with *Albion* at Lerwick; sternwalk carried away, side holed below waterline, plating, frames and rudder damaged. Later, after repair, she grounded off Lundy Island during salvage operations of *Montague*, 23 July 1906.

Feb 1907 Transferred to Atlantic Fleet, until Dec 1908.

Nov 1907—Feb 1908 Refit at Gibraltar.

1 Dec 1908 Transferred to Mediterranean Fleet as 2nd Flagship, with Mediterranean Fleet until May 1912.

1909 Refit at Malta. Under Fleet reorganization of 1 May 1912, Mediterranean Fleet became 4th BS, Home Fleet, being based at Gibraltar instead of at Malta.

May 1912—Aug 1914 With Home Fleet.

Reduced to Second Fleet (6th BS) and for service as gunnery training ship, Portsmouth May 1913. Recommissioned at Chatham for this service 27 May 1913.

May—Sept 1914 Refit at Chatham.

Transferred to Grand Fleet (3rd BS) on outbreak of war in Aug 1914. Joined Grand Fleet at Scapa Flow Sept 1914 on completion of refit. With Grand Fleet until Nov 1914; with cruisers on patrol duties in Northern Patrol area.

2 Nov 1914 Squadron temporarily attached to Channel Fleet.

Feb 1915 Reduced to Reserve for extended refit at Chatham, until July.

19 July 1915 Recommissioned at Chatham and attached to 9th CS, Finisterre-Azores-Madeira Station, until August 1915.

Aug 1915 Transferred to 2nd Detached Squadron, Adriatic. This force was organized in May 1915 to reinforce the Italian Navy in containing the Austrian Fleet in accordance with the agreement of 26 April 1915, under which Italy undertook to declare war on Austria. Squadron was based at Taranto to support the advance of the Italian Army at the head of the Adriatic.

Aug 1915—June 1916 In Adriatic.

June 1916 Transferred to 3rd Detached Squadron based at Salonika; in Aegean until Jan 1917. Took part in operations against Greek royalists from Oct to Dec 1916, including landings of Marines at Athens 1 Dec.

Jan 1917 Rejoined Adriatic Squadron, until Feb 1917. Returned home in Feb and paid off at Sheerness to provide crews for anti-submarine vessels.

Feb 1917—Mar 1919 In Reserve (Sheerness until April, then Chatham).

April 1917—Jan 1918 Refit at Chatham; employed as accommodation ship from Jan 1918.

Mar 1919 Placed on disposal list.

18 Feb 1920 Sold to Stanlee Shipbreaking Co Ltd, Dover.

June 1920 Towed to Dover for scrapping.

HISTORY: *MONTAGUE*

Laid down at Devonport 23 November 1899 and began trials in February 1903.

28 July 1903 Commissioned at Devonport for service in Mediterranean Fleet, until Feb 1905.

Feb 1905 Transferred to the Channel Fleet (ex-Home Fleet, until May 1906.

30 May 1906 Wrecked on Lundy Island in thick fog (*see* report). Her foremast raked forward by the force of impact, and later the ship finally settled in such a way that water rose and fell through the holes in the hull, and at times little more than the upper deck was above water (longest hole reported to be nearly 91 feet). Strenuous efforts made to salvage her, but finally abandoned. £85,000 spent on salvage operations. Wreck later sold for £4,250.

THE GROUNDING OF *MONTAGUE*

Montague ran aground near Shutter Rock, at the south-west tip of Lundy Island in the Bristol Channel at about 02.00 on 30 May 1906. The ship sustained a long gash on the starboard side and was held fast. Twenty-four hours after striking the bottom, many of her compartments were full of water including all the boiler rooms, steering compartment, starboard engine room and capstan engine room forward. The port engine room was flooded as a counter-measure to stop the vessel from listing any farther and steps were taken to secure all movable objects on board. At daybreak divers surveyed the extent of the damage. A large sharp rock had pushed in the hull to at least 10ft inboard of the ship, and the damage done was far more serious than had at first been envisaged.

The port propeller and part of the bracket and shaft had been completely ripped off, and the screw had received severe damage. Help arrived for the stricken vessel on the afternoon of the 30th. On inspection, it was seen that getting her off the rock was going to take a long time and there was no quick solution. During June, July and August the 12in guns, all heavy fittings, parts of the boilers and heavy machinery were unshipped with great

difficulty. Water pumps were fitted throughout the damaged areas and pumping commenced, but with little effect. Huge air-compressing machinery was fitted on her upper decks in an attempt to force the water out of her boiler and machinery spaces, but again, to no avail. Some of the armour plating on the bows was removed to lighten her, small hatches and scuttles in the vicinity were sealed and her 6in guns were removed.

Every conceivable method was used to free *Montague*, but with little success; it was decided to leave her until the following year. Further inspections were carried out on 1 and 10 October 1906 when it was found that rough sea had driven her bows another 15 feet deeper onshore, and her stern was swinging out of the water considerably with the heavy swell. The hull between the barbettes was hogging very badly and damage almost beyond

repair was found. The deck planking was all coming away, frames were bending internally (above armour) and many of the joints in the hull were opening to about $\frac{1}{4}$in. Some of the internal bulkheads were buckled, boat davits had crashed down on the deck and the upper deck was in a terrible mess from the previous salvage attempts.

A guard was put aboard, and when taken off later, it was necessary to guard the wreck from shore or small boats because of reports about looters waiting to get aboard and strip her. The Court Martial blamed the thick fog and inefficient navigation.

The following year *Montague* was beyond all help, and the go ahead for her scrapping was given by the Admiralty—a sorry end, and an expensive one, to such a fine ship.

Left: Montague on the rocks of Lundy Island.

Below: *Albemarle* cleared for battle practice in the Mediterranean in early 1905, when she was Flagship of Rear-Admiral, Mediterranean Fleet.

Below: *Duncan* in 1907, showing new control top.

Bottom: *Duncan* in June 1908, while serving as a unit of the Atlantic Fleet. She paid off before recommissioning for further service in that fleet in August. Note unofficial white bands.

HISTORY: *CORNWALLIS*

Laid down and built by Thames Ironworks, Blackwall. Her completion was delayed by labour troubles in the engineering trade and she was not commissioned until 9 February 1904 at Chatham, for service with the Mediterranean Fleet, until Feb 1905.

17 Sept 1904 Collided with Greek brigantine *Angelica* in Mediterranean; no serious damage.

Feb 1905 Transferred to Channel Fleet (ex-Home Fleet), until Jan 1907.

14 Jan 1907 Transferred to Atlantic Fleet, until Aug 1909.

Jan—May 1908 Refit at Gibraltar; Became 2nd Flagship (RA) 25 Aug 1908.

Aug 1909 Transferred to Mediterranean Fleet, until May 1912.

Under Fleet reorganization of 1 May 1912, Mediterranean Battle Squadron became 4th BS, Home Fleet, being based at Gibraltar instead of Malta. Reduced to 2nd Fleet (6th BS) Mar 1914. With Home Fleet until Aug 1914. Transferred to Grand Fleet (3rd BS) with rest of class on outbreak of war.

Dec 1914 Withdrawn with rest of class to form new 6th BS.

Channel Fleet (6th BS Dover and Sheerness).

Dec 1914—Jan 1915 Detached to West Ireland area (Clew and Killarney Bays) during latter part of Dec.

Jan 1915 Transferred to Dardanelles; left Portland 24 Jan, arrived Tenedos 13 Feb.

Feb—Dec 1915 In Dardanelles.

Took part in opening bombardment of entrance forts 18-19 Feb, firing first shell of bombardment on 18th. Subsequent bombardments of entrance and Narrows forts and initial landings during Feb and early Mar. With *Vengeance*, *Albion* and *Triumph* silenced forts Sedd el Bahr and Kum Kale with secondary armament at close range 25 Feb. Main bombardment of Narrows forts 18 Mar. Supported landings at Morto Bay 25 April. 18-20 Dec 1915 Covered evacuation of Suvla Bay, being last big ship to leave the area.

Dec 1915 Detached to Suez Canal Patrol after evacuation and joined 4 Jan 1916. Suez Canal Patrol and East Indies Command until Mar 1916. Employed on Indian Ocean convoy duty during part of this period.

Mar 1916 Returned to eastern Mediterranean, until Jan 1917.

Below: *Exmouth* at Weymouth, 1911.

Bottom: *Duncan* entering Portsmouth, 1912–13. Note standard funnel bands and range indicators below top on the foremast and on the roof of the after charthouse; very unusual at this date.

May—June 1916 Refit at Malta.

7 Jan 1917 Hit by torpedo from *U32*. First explosion occurred in after boiler room on starboard side near bulkhead 88. The middle and after stokeholds were flooded, and the ship took a list of about 9°-10°. To counteract this the port wings, port engine room and after 6in magazines were flooded, which brought the ship back on a more or less even keel. She was visibly sinking, but information as to the actual damage was not recorded because of the confusion on board. All watertight hatches were tightened down and all measures to save the ship were under way. Approximately 75 minutes after the first explosion a second torpedo hit the starboard side. She started to roll over very quickly, but remained afloat long enough for most of the crew to be taken off (fifteen men killed in the explosions). *Cornwallis* sank about 30 minutes after the second torpedo exploded.

HISTORY: *RUSSELL*

Laid down at Palmer and commissioned at Chatham 19 Feb 1903 for service with Mediterranean Fleet, until April 1904.

7 April 1904 Recommissioned at Devonport for Home Fleet, until Jan 1905.

Jan 1905—Feb 1907 Channel Fleet.

Feb 1907 Transferred to Atlantic Fleet, until July 1909.

16 July 1908 Collided with cruiser *Venus* off Quebec, but sustained only light plating damage.

30 July 1909 Transferred to Mediterranean Fleet, until May 1912.

May 1912—Aug 1914 Home Fleet (First Fleet 4th BS to Sept 1913; 6th BS, Second Fleet later. Flag 6th BS and Flag RA Home Fleets at the Nore from Dec 1913.)

Transferred to 3rd BS, Grand Fleet on outbreak of war, joined at Scapa 8 Aug. With Grand Fleet (3rd BS) until Nov 1914. Squadron temporarily detached to Channel Fleet 2 Nov 1914, until April 1915. Became Flagship, 6th BS Channel Fleet on its formation in Nov 1914. Took part in bombardment of Zeebrugge 23 Nov.

April 1915 Rejoined Grand Fleet (3rd BS Rosyth), until Nov 1915.

Oct—Nov 1915 Refit at Belfast.

6 Nov Detached to eastern Mediterranean with a division of 3rd BS, comprising *Hibernia* (Flag),

Above: After exhaustive fleet manoeuvres from January to May 1911, *Exmouth* is seen leaving Portsmouth bound for the Mediterranean to serve as Flagship of that fleet.

Left: *Russell* taking on supplies in Weymouth Bay, 1912–13.

Top right: *Exmouth* taking on supplies in the Dardanelles, 1915.

Centre and bottom right: *Exmouth* during the Dardanelles campaign, 1915. Forecastle and quarterdeck seen during a lull in the bombardments.

Zealandia and *Albemarle* to reinforce Dardanelles Squadron.

Dec 1915—April 1916 Eastern Mediterranean. Took part in evacuation of Helles 7—9 Jan 1916, being last battleship of British Dardanelles Squadron to leave. Relieved *Hibernia* of divisional flag (RA) Jan 1916.

Steaming off Malta early in the morning of 27 April 1916, *Russell* ran into two mines in quick succession and was mortally stricken. The after part of the ship caught fire after the explosions, and the order to abandon ship was given; shortly afterwards there was an explosion in the vicinity of the after 12in turret and the ship rapidly inclined to a dangerous degree. After this, however, she took her time in sinking, and many of her crew were saved.

The Court of Inquiry found that there had been problems below decks in the area of the explosion caused mainly by burning cordite which, in fact, was responsible for the deaths of fourteen men who died later. A total of 98 ratings and 27 officers were lost. (The minefield was laid by *U73*.)

HISTORY: *ALBEMARLE*

Built at Chatham and commissioned there on 12 November 1903 for service with the Mediterranean Fleet as Flag extra, Rear-Admiral.

Nov 1903—Feb 1905 Mediterranean Fleet (Flag extra RA).

Feb 1905 Transferred to Channel Fleet (ex-Home Fleet) as 2nd Flag. With Channel Fleet until Jan 1907.

31 Jan 1907 Transferred to Atlantic Fleet (ex-Channel Fleet) as 2nd Flag, until Feb 1910.

11 Feb 1907 Collided with *Commonwealth* near Lagos, sustaining light damage to bows.

May—Aug 1909 Refit at Malta.

25 Feb 1910 Recommissioned for 3rd Division, Home Fleet, Portsmouth, until Aug 1914.

30 Oct 1911 Paid off at Portsmouth for refit.

Jan—Dec 1912 Refit at Portsmouth.

17 Dec 1912 Recommissioned at Portsmouth for First Fleet (4th BS).

15 May 1913 Reduced to Second Fleet (6th BS) for service as gunnery training ship, Portsmouth. Under the original war organization, the *Duncan* class were to form, with *Agamemnon* and *Vengeance*, the 6th BS in the Channel Fleet, constituted for the defence of the Channel and to cover passage of the BEF to France. It was

Opposite page, left: Exmouth, 1915 during the Dardanelles campaign.

Opposite page, right: *Cornwallis* opens fire on the forts, 18/19 February 1915. In fact she fired the first shell of the bombardments.

intended, however, that under certain conditions, they should join the Grand Fleet, and immediately after the outbreak of war in Aug 1914, they were assigned to the 3rd BS, Grand Fleet at Jellicoe's request to offset his shortage of cruisers for patrol duties. The 6th BS was temporarily abolished, with *Agamemnon* being transferred to the 5th and *Vengeance* to the 8th BS, Channel Fleet.

8 Aug *Albemarle* joined Grand Fleet at Scapa.

Aug—Nov 1914 3rd BS, Grand Fleet. Employed with cruisers on Northern Patrol. Squadron temporarily attached to Channel Fleet 2 Nov as reinforcement against enemy activity in this area of North Sea.

Nov 1914—April 1915 Channel Fleet. The *King Edward*s returned to the Grand Fleet (Rosyth) on 13 Nov, but the *Duncan*s remained in the Channel as a reformed 6th BS from 14 Nov, this squadron being specifically intended for bombarding operations against German submarine bases on the Belgian coast. The squadron was transferred from Portland to Dover 14 Nov, but reverted to Portland on the 19th because of inadequate submarine defences at Dover.

Dec 1914 Returned to Dover; transferred to Sheerness at the end of Dec to relieve 5th BS which had been stationed there since mid-November against the threat of an enemy invasion.

Jan—May 1915 6th BS finally dispersed when *Albemarle* and *Russell* rejoined 3rd BS, Grand Fleet; *Cornwallis* and *Exmouth* were sent to the Dardanelles. *Duncan* was withdrawn in Jan for extended refit and went to Finisterre-Azores-Madeira Station on completion of this in July. *Albemarle* returned to 3rd BS in April 1915, until Jan 1916.

Oct 1915 Refit at Chatham.

Nov 1915 Ordered to Mediterranean with a division of 3rd BS, comprising *Hibernia* (Flag), *Zealandia*, *Albemarle* and *Russell* to reinforce the Dardanelles Squadron.

6 Nov The Division left Rosyth and ran into very bad weather in the Pentland Firth during the night of 6/7 Nov. *Albemarle* was badly damaged, her forebridge being washed away with all bridge personnel; the conning tower was displaced and superstructure considerably damaged. Repaired during Dec and rejoined Grand Fleet instead of proceeding to Mediterranean.

Jan 1916 Detached to Murmansk as guardship and icebreaker.

Jan—Sept 1916 North Russia; guardship and SNO, Murmansk. Employed as icebreaker in approaches to port.

Sept 1916 Returned home and paid off at Portsmouth to provide crews for A/S vessels.

Oct 1916—Mar 1917 Refit at Liverpool. Placed in Reserve at Devonport on completion, until April 1919. Employed as accommodation ship and attached to Gunnery School in 1919.

April 1919 Placed on disposal list.

From Aug 1919 On sale list.

19 Nov 1919 Sold to Cohen Shipbreaking Co.

April 1920 Arrived at Swansea for scrapping.

HISTORY: *EXMOUTH*

Laid down by Laird, Birkenhead on 10 August 1899, she was completed in May 1903, after some delay due to troubles in the engineering trade.

2 June 1903 Commissioned at Chatham for service with Mediterranean Fleet, until May 1904.

18 May 1904 Commissioned at Chatham as flagship (VA, Home Fleet), until Jan 1905.

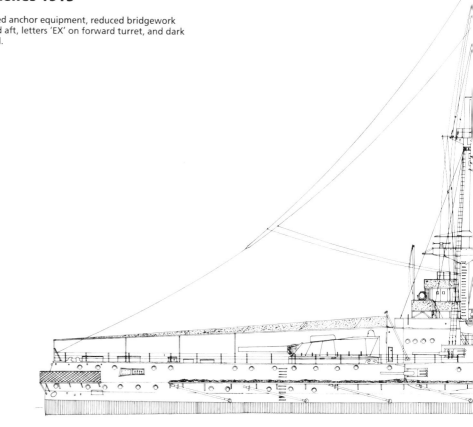

EXMOUTH
Outboard profile, as seen at Dardanelles 1915

Note reduced anchor equipment, reduced bridgework forward and aft, letters 'EX' on forward turret, and dark funnel band.

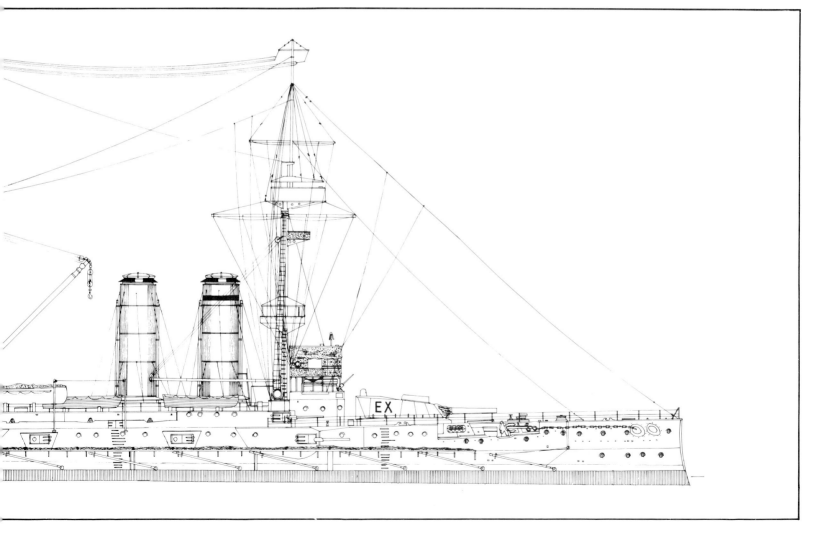

Top: *Exmouth, c.*1916, taking on supplies at Imbros during her period as Flagship of the 3rd Detached Squadron in the Aegean from November 1915 to March 1917.

Centre: *Cornwallis* turns over after being fatally struck by torpedoes from *U32*, 60 miles off Malta on 9 January 1917.

Bottom: *Duncan* arrives at Dover in June 1920, to await the scrapper's torch. Note that she has been stripped of guns and small fittings.

Opposite page: *Prince of Wales*, at Chatham on completion, May 1904. *Queen* and *Prince of Wales* represented the final development of the basic *Majestic* design by the DNC, William White, and were the last British battleships for which he was entirely responsible.

Jan 1905—May 1907 Channel fleet (flag until April 1907.
April—May 1907 Refit at Portsmouth.
25 May 1907 Recommissioned at Portsmouth as Flagship, (VA) Atlantic Fleet, until Nov 1908.
20 Nov 1908 Transferred to Mediterranean Fleet as Flagship, until May 1912.
1908-9 Refit at Malta.
May 1912—Aug 1914 Home Fleet.
Dec 1912 Replaced in 4th BS (First Fleet) by *Dreadnought*.
Dec 1912—July 1913 Refit at Malta.
1 July 1913 Recommissioned at Devonport for 6th BS, Second Fleet and gunnery training ship, Devonport. Transferred to Grand Fleet (3rd BS) at outbreak of war. Joined at Scapa 8 Aug, until Nov 1914. With cruiser squadrons on Northern Patrol.
2 Nov detached to Channel Fleet until May 1915.
23 Nov Took part in bombardment of Zeebrugge.
12 May 1915 Transferred to Dardanelles (flag RA, supporting squadron) until Nov 1915. Supported attack on Achi Baba 4 June, and attacks in Helles area during Aug.
Nov 1915 Became 3rd Flag, Detached Squadron; this force, based at Salonika, organized to assist French in blockading Greece and the Bulgarian coast and to provide reinforcement for Suez Canal Patrol.
Nov 1915—Mar 1917 Aegean (flag, 3rd Detached Squadron). Embarked personnel of British Belgrade Naval Force at Salonika 28 Nov 1915 following Serbian retreat from Belgrade.
Sept—Dec 1916 Unit of combined British and French naval force supporting Allied demands on Greek Government, including seizure of Greek Fleet at Salamis 1 Sept, and landing marines at Athens 1 Dec.
Mar 1917 Transferred to East Indies Command for Indian Ocean convoy duty owing to activities of German raider *Wolf*. Mar—June 1917 East Indies. Employed on convoy duty on Colombo and Bombay route.
June 1917 Left for home, via Cape and Sierra Leone.
Aug 1917 Arrived Devonport and paid off to provide crews for anti-submarine vessels.
Aug 1917—April 1919 Reserve (Devonport).
From Jan 1918 Employed as accomodation ship.
April 1919 Placed on sale list.
15 Jan 1920 Sold (£39,600) to Forth Shipbreaking Co (hull broken up in Holland).

QUEEN CLASS

1900 ESTIMATES

DESIGN

To complete a tactical group of eight ships, White proposed a further pair of battleships, identical with the *Formidable* group, for the 1900 estimates. Although this was accepted, however, the proposal for these two ships came at a time when a design for larger and more powerful *King Edwards* was under consideration and being subjected to severe criticism as being grossly undergunned for their size.

Modern additions to the battlefleet were gratefully accepted in service, and a letter from Rear-Admiral Charles Beresford to the *Morning Post* on 26 April 1900 made the position quite clear:

'Any Government that sent out men to fight on blue water, or relied for harbour protection on the vessels in the British Navy armed with muzzle-loading guns would certainly get a short shrift. No other nation in the whole World has ships on the effective list armed with muzzle-loading guns.'

Naming them, he quoted the following: *Ajax* (1876), *Agamemnon* (1876), *Temeraire* (1873), *Inflexible* (1873), *Superb* (1873), *Dreadnought* (1872), *Neptune* (1874), *Triumph* (1868), *Swiftsure* (1868), *Sultan* (1868), *Iron Duke* (1868), *Invincible* (1867), *Audacious* (1867), *Monarch* (1866), *Hercules* (1866).

Reaction to this letter from Government was more than acrid and not for the first time, Beresford found himself in hot water. Nevertheless, he pushed home his ideas about the declining state of the British Navy, and in a letter to Sir John Fisher from *Ramillies* in the Mediterranean on 15 June 1900, he stated with a degree of euphemism:

'I send you an official letter on the strength of the present fleet under your commission in the Mediterranean. Strictly speaking, such a letter might be regarded as improper for a second in command (who has no respect whatsoever) to write to his Commander-in-Chief. Please except my two excuses. The first, my anxiety to the future having regard to what appears to me probable, viz: difficulties with France and Russia.

Secondly, the fact of me being a public man outside my naval profession. If we did meet with any disaster through want of preparation, on a station where I might be serving, questions would naturally be asked, did I perceive danger, and did I represent my views? It would not be according to my views of patriotism to take refuge behind a plea

that I was not responsible, true though it would be. I do not know what you may decide right with my letter, that is naturally no business of mine, but it is right to tell you that I shall be sending a copy privately to Lord Salisbury and Mr Balfour, as I believe that our position is more serious with regard to numbers of ships which we need to enable

the British Commander-in-Chief to prevent a reverse if hostilities were suddenly forced upon us by France or Russia.'

A copy of this letter was sent to *The Times* and was published on 25 June 1900 provoking lively correspondence from all quarters; it practically ensured construction of the two *Queen*s and the

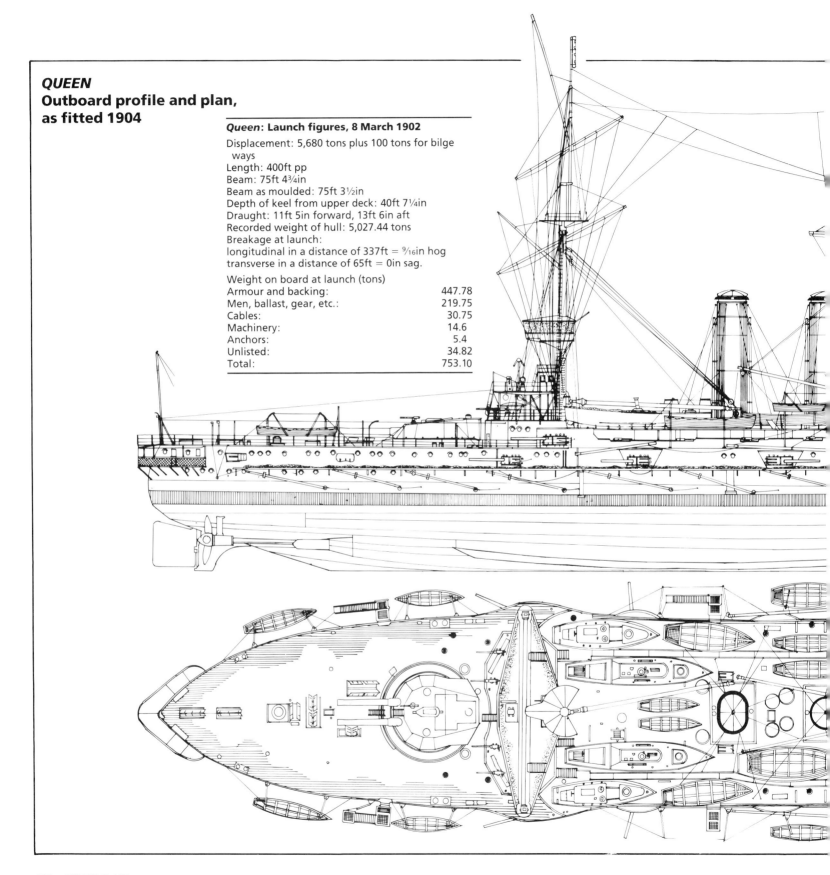

QUEEN
**Outboard profile and plan,
as fitted 1904**

Queen: Launch figures, 8 March 1902

Displacement: 5,680 tons plus 100 tons for bilge
  ways
Length: 400ft pp
Beam: 75ft 4¾in
Beam as moulded: 75ft 3½in
Depth of keel from upper deck: 40ft 7¼in
Draught: 11ft 5in forward, 13ft 6in aft
Recorded weight of hull: 5,027.44 tons
Breakage at launch:
longitudinal in a distance of 337ft = ⁹⁄₁₆in hog
transverse in a distance of 65ft = 0in sag.

Weight on board at launch (tons)	
Armour and backing:	447.78
Men, ballast, gear, etc.:	219.75
Cables:	30.75
Machinery:	14.6
Anchors:	5.4
Unlisted:	34.82
Total:	753.10

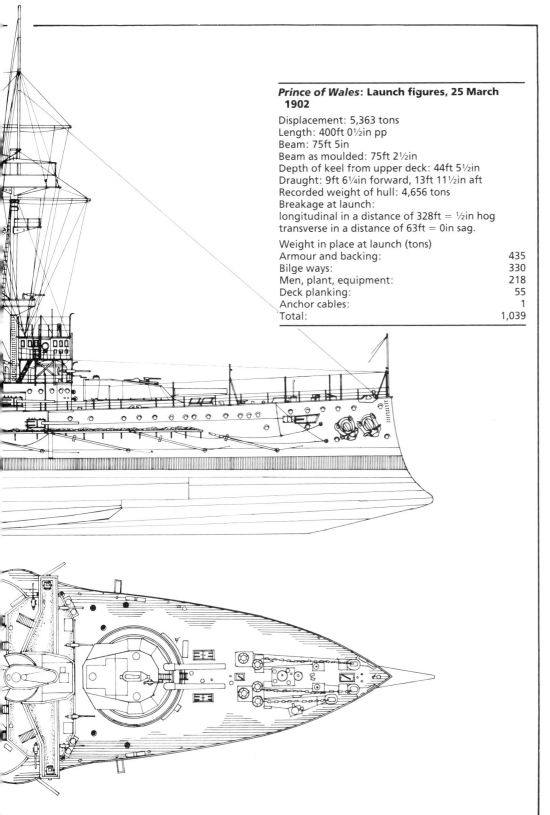

Prince of Wales: Launch figures, 25 March 1902

Displacement: 5,363 tons
Length: 400ft 0½in pp
Beam: 75ft 5in
Beam as moulded: 75ft 2½in
Depth of keel from upper deck: 44ft 5½in
Draught: 9ft 6¼in forward, 13ft 11½in aft
Recorded weight of hull: 4,656 tons
Breakage at launch:
longitudinal in a distance of 328ft = ½in hog
transverse in a distance of 63ft = 0in sag.

Weight in place at launch (tons)
Armour and backing:	435
Bilge ways:	330
Men, plant, equipment:	218
Deck planking:	55
Anchor cables:	1
Total:	1,039

following six *Duncan*s without any intimation of a cutback.

This pair were the last British battleships for which Sir William White (DNC) was entirely responsible, and being practically identical with the *Bulwark* group, represented the final development of the basic *Majestic* design, comprising 29 ships, all of a single standard type but with successive improvements in the later classes, mainly due to developments in ordance, armour and machinery. They differed from the *Bulwark*s only in minor detail: open instead of enclosed upper deck 12pdr battery; only one pair of 12pdrs carried on main deck forward and aft with one pair in forward superstructure. Kidney-shaped instead of circular fighting tops. Stockless anchors, and no ventilating cowls.

ARMAMENT

The main and secondary armaments were practically identical with the *Formidable* and *Bulwark* groups although some modification was effected in the torpedo armament. The main deck 12-pounders were reduced from eight to four by the removal of the inner pair forward and aft, two of the guns being relocated in the forward superstructure before the bridge, where they had a higher command and could be fought in a sea-way. The other pair were supressed, reducing the total number from sixteen to fourteen. The upper deck battery was open instead of closed by bulwarks; the enclosed battery, which had been introduced in the *Renown* and *Majestic* classes, had been continued throughout until this pair were designed. It was finally abandoned in this class, and the *Duncan*s on the grounds that the thin bulwarks merely served to detonate, directly over the guns, high-explosive projectiles which might otherwise pass right through without exploding.

The kidney-shaped fighting tops provided more room for the gun crews than had been afforded by the older circular tops. They were the only British battleships to have fighting tops of this shape and, with the ex-Chilean *Swiftsure* and *Triumph*, purchased in 1903 while completing, were the last British battleships to have fighting tops for light, quick-firing guns, or with any of these guns carried in ports on the main deck where they had been found of limited value owing to the very low command.

During their construction it was frequently

Queen and *Prince of Wales*: Particulars, as completed

Construction
Queen: Devonport DY; laid down 12 March 1901; launched 8 March 1902; completed March 1904
Prince of Wales: Chatham DY; laid down 20 March 1901; launched 25 March 1902; completed March 1904.

Displacement (tons)
Queen: 14,160 (load), 15,415 (full load), 16,105 (deep)
Prince of Wales: 14,140 (load), 15,380 (full load).

Dimensions
Length: 400ft pp, 411ft wl, 431ft 9in oa
Beam: 75ft
Draught: 25ft 4in – 27ft 3in (mean).

Armament
Four 12in Mk IX; 80rpg
Twelve 6in Mk VII
Fourteen 12pdr
Six 3pdr
Two MG
Four 18in torpedo tubes, submerged, beam, one pair abreast each barbette.

Armour
Main belt: 9in KC
Forward belt: 7in–5in–3in–2in KNC

Belt bulkhead: 10in–9in KC
Barbettes: 12in–10in–6in KC
Turrets: 10in–8in–3in–2in KC
Decks: main 2in–1½in mild steel, middle 2in–1in, lower 2½in–2in–1in
Conning tower: 10in–4in Harvey
After conning tower: 3in nickel steel
Tubes: forward 8in, aft 3in mild steel.

Machinery
Two sets 3-cylinder vertical triple expansion engines, two in-turning propellers
Boilers: thirteen Babcock in *Queen* (270psi), twenty Belleville in *Prince of Wales* (300psi)
Heating surface: 38,400sq ft in *Queen*, 37,000sq ft in *Prince of Wales*
Length of boiler rooms: 33ft 11¾in forward, 34ft 0½in middle, 17ft 11½in aft *Queen*; 86ft overall *Prince of Wales*
Length of engine rooms: 45ft 10½in *Queen*, 46ft *Prince of Wales*
Fuel: 900 tons coal normal, 2,000 tons max. *Queen*, 1,950 tons max. *Prince of Wales*
Coal consumption: 310–350 tons per day at full power
Radius of action: 5,550nm at 10 knots *Queen*, 5,400nm at 10 knots *Prince of Wales*; 2,510nm at 16½ knots.

Ship's boats (*Prince of Wales*)
Pinnaces (steam): two 56ft, one 40ft
Pinnaces (sail): one 36ft
Launches (steam): one 42ft
Cutters: two 34ft, one 32ft
Whalers: two 27ft
Gigs: one 30ft, one 28ft, two 24ft
Skiff dinghies: one 16ft
Balsa rafts: one 13ft 6in.

Anchors
Three 115cwt, one 54cwt, one 42cwt, one 16cwt, one 8cwt; 525 fathoms 2⁹⁄₁₆in cable (136 tons).

Wireless
Mk I, Mk II later.

Searchlights
Six 24in, two on each bridge, one high on each mast.

Complement
747 *Queen*, Feb 1904
803 *Queen*, 1908 Flagship, Mediterranean
747 *Prince of Wales*, 1904.

Cost
Queen: £1,074,999 plus guns £71,670
Prince of Wales: £1,114,074 plus guns £71,670.

reported that they might be given a secondary armament of eight 7.5in and eight or ten 6in. Official documents show this to have been erroneous; the idea probably stemming from the outcome of tests then being carried out in connection with new 7.5in mountings for eventual use in armoured cruisers. The main 12in gun mountings were the same as those in *Irresistible* and *Venerable* (BVII).

ARMOUR

The armour protection was identical with that of the *Bulwark* class, with a 9in Krupp cemented main belt, 238ft by 15ft, extending from close behind the forward barbette to abeam the after barbette. The upper edge was at main deck level, 9ft 6in above the waterline at normal condition. The lower edge was approximately 5ft 6in below the waterline.

Thicknesses of 7in-5in-3in and 2in ran forward from the main 9in strake, over the same width as the belt. The 2in thickness being right forward only, the 5in section reached about 30ft abaft the

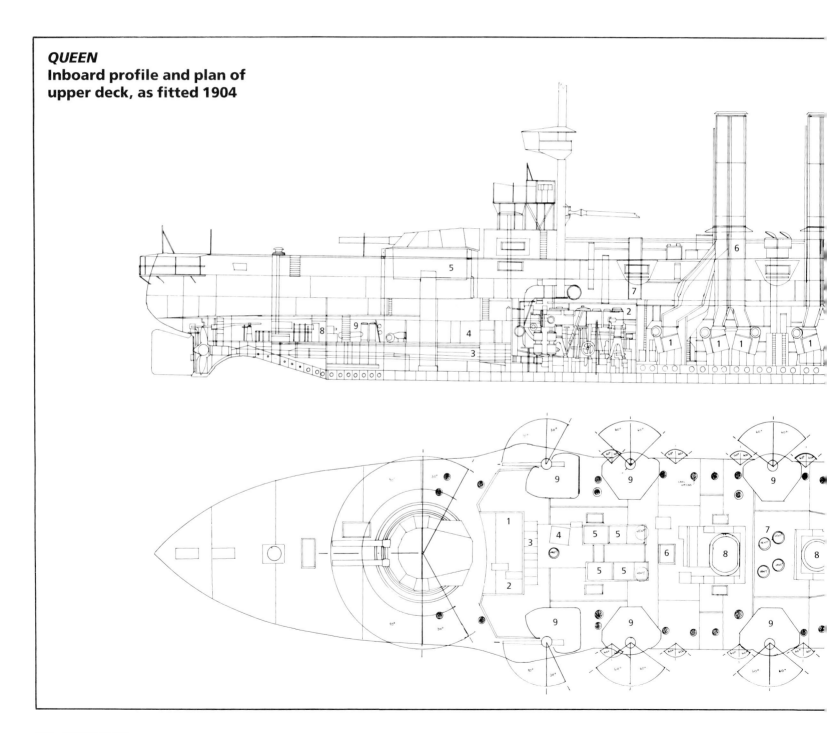

QUEEN
Inboard profile and plan of upper deck, as fitted 1904

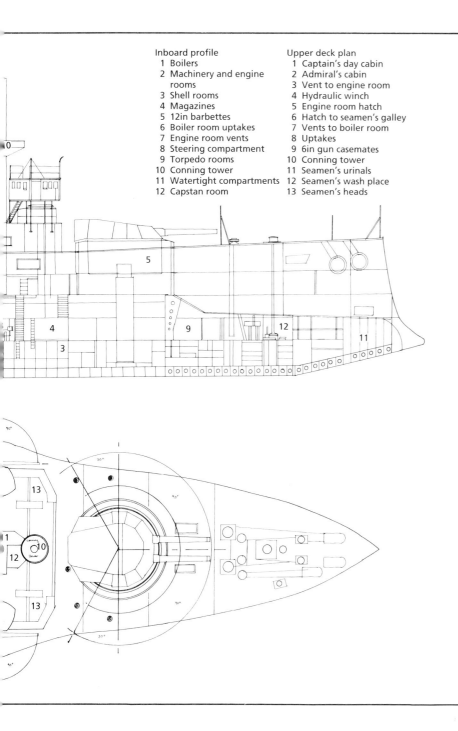

Inboard profile
1 Boilers
2 Machinery and engine rooms
3 Shell rooms
4 Magazines
5 12in barbettes
6 Boiler room uptakes
7 Engine room vents
8 Steering compartment
9 Torpedo rooms
10 Conning tower
11 Watertight compartments
12 Capstan room

Upper deck plan
1 Captain's day cabin
2 Admiral's cabin
3 Vent to engine room
4 Hydraulic winch
5 Engine room hatch
6 Hatch to seamen's galley
7 Vents to boiler room
8 Uptakes
9 6in gun casemates
10 Conning tower
11 Seamen's urinals
12 Seamen's wash place
13 Seamen's heads

stem, with the 7in meeting the 9in belt. Aft there was a 1in belt running from the 9in belt which reached the stern of the vessel. The upper edge was 4ft above the waterline, and the lower edge level with the midships main belt.

Belt bulkheads (aft only) ran obliquely inwards from the after extremities of the 9in belt to the outer face of the after barbette, 9in thick above the middle deck, and 10in below.

The forward and after barbettes were 12in-10in and 6in as in *Irresistible* and *Venerable* (see those ships). Turret thicknesses were also identical with those two ships (BVII mountings, *see* drawings).

Decks, conning towers, ammunition hoists, tubes and general layout were identical with those of *Bulwark*. Internal sub-division was the same as that in the last two classes, which in fact, left a great deal to desire. Although fitted with longitudinal bulkheads, the means to counter-flood opposite compartments was limited, which greatly reduced adequate ability quickly to right the ship—one of the main reasons for the rapid loss of *Majestic*, *Goliath*, *Formidable*, *Cornwallis* and *Russell*.

MACHINERY

Both ships were originally intended to have twenty Belleville water tube boilers as in the four preceding classes (*Canopus*, *Formidable*, *Bulwark* and *Duncan*) but the constant defects appearing in those installations indicated that a change was needed. During the immediate months after the pair had been laid down their Lordships wondered whether it might be possible to install new cylindrical boilers in *Queen* rather than the Belleville types which had already been ordered.

Queen and *Prince of Wales*: Comparative machinery weights

Admiralty estimate

	Queen (Babcock)	Prince of Wales (Belleville)	
	tons	tons	cwt
Boilers, funnels, casings:	734	614	6
Engine shafting:	507	579	
Shafting, screws, fittings:	119	112	17
Freshwater to working height in boilers:	78	40	10
Auxiliary machinery:	68	65	2
Main and auxiliary water:	24	18	
Totals:	1,530	1,429	15

H.M.S. Prince of [Wales]

Below: *Prince of Wales*, pre-war appearance, 1912–13. Hardly noticeable in this photograph, three crew members are working on the funnel cap – while the ship is under way – no mean feat!

Right: *Bulwark*, *Venerable* and *Queen* (nearest) form part of the 5th BS and put to sea after the Fleet Review at Spithead in July 1914.

Below: *Prince of Wales* in 1915, entering Malta Harbour
during the Dardanelles campaign. Note reduced
bridgework, SL on lower top, and no nets.

Right: *Queen* enters Taranto Harbour, 1915.

Her machinery and boiler contractors (Harland & Wolff) were asked by the Admiralty whether such an installation were feasible. Harland & Wolff replied on 4 April 1901 that although it was possible to fit the new Babcock & Wilcox boilers, some internal modifications would have to be made to the boiler rooms, the increase in cost being from £87,150 to £89,450, and the weight increase approximately 100 tons.

In reply to this, and other correspondence received, the DNC (White) accepted the weight increase, which would be absorbed by the Board margin, and dispersed any fears of the Board regarding installation of a new type of boiler for one of the Royal Navy's battleships:

'We have the advantage of following the *Formidable* class, the leading vessels of which are approaching completion. On the basis of information obtained from *Formidable*, the 100 ton increase in weight can easily be accepted—in fact, the Engineer-in-Chief estimates that if new boilers of this type, and machinery to suit is adopted, an increase of 370 tons has been calculated which will increase the vessels' draught by only 7in.'

Accordingly, Babcock & Wilcox cylindrical boilers were fitted in *Queen*, but apparently it was found impracticable to make any change in *Prince of Wales* because her internal state was too advanced; she became the last British battleship to enter service with Belleville boilers.

Prince of Wales was fitted with twenty Belleville water tube boilers with economizers; *Queen* received thirteen Babcock & Wilcox. Working pressure was 300psi in *Prince of Wales* compared to the lower 270psi in *Queen*. Consumption in *Queen* was much better than in her sister, and showed figures of 310 tons coal at full power, 180 tons at ³/₅-power (per day) and 40 tons at 7 knots. *Prince of Wales*: 350 tons at full power, 209 tons at ³/₅-power and 50 tons at 7 knots.

Queen and *Prince of Wales*: Steam trials, 1903–4

Queen
Dodman Point, 8 December 1903
Mean SHP: 15,660
Mean revs: 116.7
Mean speed: 18.04 knots

Prince of Wales
Left Portsmouth, wind westerly Force 3–5, sea smooth
Mean draught: 26ft 2in forward, 27ft 2in aft
IHP: 15,264
Mean revs: 107.8
Mean speed: 18.35 knots (3 runs)

Prince of Wales left Portsmouth on Saturday, 8 February 1904 for her full-power sea trials in calm water and against a wind of Force 3–5. Her mean speed on the first three runs was 18.57 knots and 18.1 knots on the last two runs. *Queen* held her first trials on Saturday, 8 December 1903 on the Rame Head and Dodman Point run, and made 18.04 knots with 15,660shp and 116.7 revolutions. Of *Queen* it was said:

'No special difficulties have been experienced with the machinery, and the ship has proved singularly economical and a successful steamer.'

Summary of trials during first eighteen months of service

Queen			
Out of dock	Bottom	IHP	Speed (knots)
1 month	clean	15,564	18.04
5 months	fair/foul	15,800	17.4
2 weeks	clean	15,173	18.3
14 months	foul	15,738	18

Prince of Wales			
Out of dock	Bottom	IHP	Speed (knots)
1 month	clean	15,364	17.84
1 month	clean	15,441	17.87
5 months		14,975	18.57
3 months	clean	15,275	18.5
11 months	dirty	15,495	17.3

APPEARANCE CHANGES

Very similar to the *Bulwark* group, but with variation in details. Distinguished from the *Formidable*s and *Bulwark*s by: kidney-shaped fighting tops; open deck battery amidships; stockless anchors; no scuttles along lower deck side forward; no cowls; slightly different turret shapes within group. Easily distinguished from the *Duncan* class by: Unequal-sized funnels; kidney-shaped fighting tops; stockless anchors (except *Albemarle* and *Montague*).

Both *Queen* and *Prince of Wales* were very similar as completed, and differed only in minor detail:
Queen Slightly shorter funnels; double steam pipe abaft second funnel.
Prince of Wales Slightly taller funnels; single steam pipe abaft second funnel; W/T gaff on topmast lower set.
1904–5 SL removed from foremast in *Prince of Wales*.
1905–6 Primary system of fire control and range-

finding equipment fitted, and dynamo firing installation fitted. Fighting top on mainmast roofed in and adopted as control position. Control top fitted in place of SL platform on foremast. 12pdrs removed from main deck in *Prince of Wales*: two remounted on after superstructure, others temporarily suppressed. 3pdrs removed from after fighting tops in both ships. Foremast SL temporarily mounted on platform below fire control top in *Prince of Wales*. SL ex-mainmast temporarily remounted over after charthouse in both.

Bridge SL (four) remounted over forward and after casemates.

1906–7 12pdrs removed from main deck in *Queen* (May 1906): all four remounted on superstructures.

Masthead semaphore removed in both. W/T gaff triced in *Prince of Wales* (May–Sept 1906 refit). W/T topgallant mast fitted to both masts in *Queen*. New refrigerating machinery fitted in after dynamo room.

1908–9 *Prince of Wales* Refit at Malta (*Queen* at Gibraltar). Items that received attention: Extra ventilation to engine rooms. Main condenser parts renewed. Smoke deflectors in rear of boiler rooms improved. Ammonia machine fitted. Oil glands

---

Prince of Wales: GM and stability

Based on inclining experiments, 12 March 1904

	Draught (mean)	GM	Maximum stability	Stability vanishes at
'A' Condition (= load)*	25ft 4⅛in	4.21ft	37°	64°
'B' Condition (= deep load)**	27ft 1⅞in	4.27ft	36°	64°

*Fully equipped plus 900 tons coal.
**Fully equipped plus 1,957 tons coal, 107 tons reserve feedwater, 130 tons fresh water.

altered to increase efficiency. 12in guns fitted with
hydraulic breech working gear. 6in guns given
cross connection sights. Additional fire control
fitted, and also night fire control. 12pdr guns fitted
with automatic elevating brakes. All guns fitted
with telescopic sights. W/T room built on after
bridge. Type 1 W/T and a short-range set fitted in
Prince of Wales. 36in SL lamps replaced the 24in on
fore bridge (found to be too large for that position).
Two cabins built on forebridge (POW). Old W/T
room converted to Midshipmen's study. Reduction
of net shelving to 14in wide.

1909–10 3pdrs removed from forward fighting
tops. Heavy yards removed from mainmast.
Standard system of funnel bands painted up: *Prince
of Wales* two white on fore funnel; *Queen* two white
on each funnel.

1911 After charthouse in *Queen* considerably
enlarged.

1913–14 Torpedo nets removed.

1914 (Aug) Funnel bands painted out.

1915 Two 3pdr AA guns added. 36in SL
remounted on forward fighting top. One 24in
mounted on platform below fore control top in

QUEEN
Outboard profile, 1916

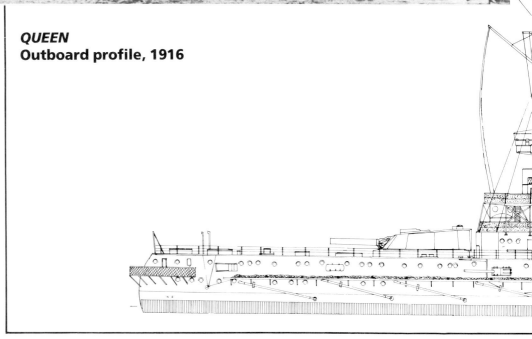

Prince of Wales (platform removed in *Queen*). Torpedo nets temporarily replaced in both. Forebridge wings curtailed and after bridge wings removed in *Prince of Wales*.
Both topgallant masts and main topmast removed. Small spotting top added on fore mast.
1916–17 *Queen*: Main and secondary armaments removed (turrets retained). In April 1917 she still had four 6in secondary guns. 12in guns taken out in Oct 1917 for use as land artillery on Italian front. 6in used for arming patrol vessels. SL reduced to one 24in in forward fighting top, two 24in on forebridge. Extra deckhouses added abeam fore

funnel, on after superstructure and on after bridge (replacing charthouse). Main topmast and both topgallants replaced.

HISTORY: *QUEEN*

Laid down at Devonport Dockyard on 12 March 1901 and launched by Queen Alexandra on 8 March 1902.
7 April 1904 Commissioned for service with Mediterranean Fleet, until Dec 1908.
1906–7 Refitted at Malta for flag duty.
20 Mar 1907 Became Fleet flag (VA).
14 Dec 1908 Paid off at Devonport and recom-

missioned on the 15th for service in Atlantic Fleet, until May 1912.
1 Feb 1909 Collided with Greek SS *Dafni* at Dover; no serious damage.
1910–11 Refit at Devonport.
15 May 1912 Transferred to 2nd Home Fleet, until Aug 1914.
April 1914 Became 2nd Flag (RA) 5th BS, 2nd Fleet, employed as gunnery training ship at Portsmouth. Assigned to Channel Fleet (2nd Flag, 5th BS) on outbreak of war in Aug 1914, until Mar 1915.
17 Oct Joined Dover Patrol for bombardment

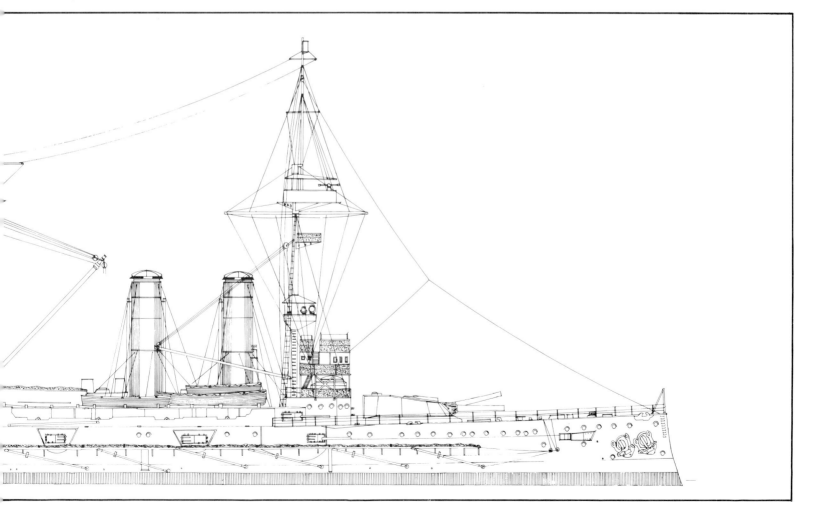

Below: *Prince of Wales* awaits the scrapper's torch.

Opposite page: Launch of *New Zealand*. A new breed of warship takes to the water after being christened by Lady Onslow on 4 February 1904.

operations and escort duties.

3 Nov 1914 Detached to support east coast patrols during Gorleston Raid.

March 1915 Transferred to Dardanelles leaving England on 13th, arrived Lemnos on 23rd.

Mar—May 1915 Dardanelles: (Flag RA, 2nd Squadron). Supported Anzac landings at Gaba Tepe 25 April.

22 May 1915 Detached to Adriatic as Flag, 2nd Detached Squadron. Arrived Taranto 27 May. In Adriatic until April 1919.

Dec 1916—Feb 1917 Refitted for service as depot ship for personnel of Adriatic anti-submarine net barrage patrol. As such, was last British battleship remaining in Adriatic at that date; most of her crew had returned home by that date, leaving only a care and maintenance party on board. Majority of 6in guns were removed by April 1917. Her main armament was removed (guns only) in Oct 1917, the guns having been requested by the Italian military command to assist in repelling heavy Austrian attacks. *Queen* was Flag, British Naval Forces, Taranto until Feb 1918.

April 1919 Returned home and placed on disposal list at Chatham in May.

June 1919 Restored and attached to Pembroke Establishment, as overflow ship, replacing *Hindustan*, until Nov 1919.

Mar 1920 Placed on sale list.

4 Sept 1920 Sold to T. W. Ward and Co for £30,100; arriving Birkenhead 25 Nov 1920 to be lightened sufficiently to allow her to reach the scrapping berth at Preston.

5 Aug 1921 Arrived Preston.

HISTORY: *PRINCE OF WALES*

Laid down at Chatham 20 March 1901 and launched by the Princess of Wales. Completed in March 1904 and placed in Fleet Reserve at Chatham.

18 May 1904 Commissioned at Chatham for service in Mediterranean Fleet, until May 1906. Collided with SS *Enidiven* in Mediterranean 29 July 1905; no serious damage.

28 May 1906 Paid off at Portsmouth for refit.

May—Sept 1906 In Reserve at Portsmouth.

8 Sept 1906 Commissioned at Portsmouth for further service with Mediterranean Fleet, until Feb 1909.

Aug 1907 Became 2nd Flag (VA).

1908 Refit at Malta.

Feb 1909 Transferred to Atlantic Fleet as Flag (VA) until May 1912.

1911 Refit at Gibraltar.

13 May 1912 Transferred to Home Fleet until Aug 1914.

2 June 1913 Rammed by submarine *C 32* during exercises; no damage. Assigned to Channel Fleet (Flag, 5th BS) on outbreak of war, August 1914, until Mar 1915. Based at Portland, but moved to Sheerness. Replaced at Sheerness by *Duncan* class and returned to Portland 30 Dec 1914. Took part in transporting Portsmouth Marine Battalion to Ostend and covering occupation 25 August.

19 Mar 1915 Ordered to Dardanelles and left Portland on 20th. Joined Dardanelles Squadron 29 Mar 1915, until May 1915. Supported Anzac landings at Gaba Tepe 25 April. Detached to Adriatic 22 May, with *Implacable*, *London* and *Queen* as 2nd Detached Squadron, based at Taranto, arrived 27 May.

In Adriatic May 1915—Feb 1917 (Flag, Mar—June 1916).

Summer 1916 Refit at Gibraltar.

Feb 1917 Ordered home; arrived Gibraltar 28th. Left for Devonport 10 Mar. Placed in Reserve on arrival, until Nov 1919. Employed as accommodation ship.

10 Nov 1919 Placed on disposal list.

12 April 1920 Sold to T. W. Ward and Co for £36,500.

June 1920 Arrived at Milford Haven for scrapping.

KING EDWARD VII CLASS

1901/2/3 ESTIMATES

DESIGN

When these battleships were originally considered in the spring of 1901, a provisional displacement and length of 16,000 tons and 420ft respectively was specified. Many official documents for this class, however, which include the Ships Books' (destroyed) and Ships' Covers (missing) are not available to show how the conception of the type was fully developed.

What is known, however, is that the basic principle of the design was initiated by the Controller (Wilson), and Chief Constructor (Deadman), and then finally drawn up by J. H. Narbeth, the Assistant Constructor to the DNC (White).

News of foreign construction, giving details of the Italian *Benedetto Brin* class, carrying four 12in, four 8in and twelve 6in guns on a displacement of 13,427 tons, and the American *New Jersey* class with four 12in, eight 8in and twelve 6in on 14,948 tons, became known to the Controller during 1900, and as the British *Queen* pair only mounted four 12in and twelve 6in on 15,000 tons, a series of alternative designs embodying stronger secondary armaments was called for before any new construction of battleships would be considered.

In White's absence, because of illness, proposals were put forward by Deadman for a very powerful and extravagant type representing such a marked advance on anything previously attempted as to rule out the likelihood of foreign competition. Details of these proposals were not worked out in great detail, however, and nothing of this nature has been uncovered, but it is almost certain that their Lordships, at that time, would have rejected it as being impracticable.

During this period, J. H. Narbeth prepared a series of sketch designs based on the later *Formidables* (*Queen* group) which showed an intermediate armament of 9.2in or 7.5in guns, and dimensions varying according to length, stability and speed. These were submitted without comment and one particular layout, which showed a secondary armament of eight 7.5in guns in twin turrets on the upper deck at the corners of the superstructure with ten 6in in a main deck battery amidships, was provisionally accepted, without the usual Board Conference.

Work was put in hand on the design, which marked the first radical departure from the basic *Majestic* type, and was mainly influenced by the following:
1. The adoption by foreign navies of intermediate-calibre guns in addition to the standard 12in and 6in armament.
2. Severe criticism of existing British battleships as being under-gunned for their displacement.
3. Improvements in armour had reduced the 6in gun's effectiveness as a battleship weapon.

While the work was in hand, the DNC (White) returned to office. After studying the plans with great care, he congratulated Narbeth and told him that he had probably paved the way for the construction of a very powerful battleship that would be included in the next naval estimates. White worked with Narbeth, and on the former's advice they agreed to replace the twin 7.5in by single 9.2in guns, which would still be on the same basic dimensions and cost. It was then submitted again to their Lordships, and in April 1901 accepted by all concerned.

Work on the new design was completed before White left office on 31 January 1902, but orders for the first ships were deferred pending an examination of the plans by his successor, Philip Watts. The new DNC had no hesitation, however, in completely approving the plans and accepting full responsibility which showed his faith, not only in White, but in the Assistant Constructor, Narbeth, who he now hoped would work with him, as closely as he had done with White. Although officially, the *King Edwards* fall into the Watts era, they are rightfully regarded (and historically recorded) as the last British battleships produced under Sir William White as DNC.

Compared with *Queen* the design was nominally 1,350 tons heavier, with the same main armament, but had a substantially heavier and differently arranged secondary armament. Armour thickness was generally similar, but with certain modifications in arrangement of side and deck armour, mainly to conform to provision of a continuous battery instead of separate casemates for the 6in guns.

The principal innovations of the design, as compared with preceding classes, were the introduction of the 9.2in gun, with a three- instead of two-calibre armament, and the provision of the continuous battery cleverly arranged along the main deck. Other novel features were: abandonment of fighting tops for light QF guns, and suppression of the after bridge.

The first three ships were laid down under the 1901 programme and a following two were planned for the 1902 estimates. This meagre proposal for the latter, however, brought about severe agitation in Parliament and in public.

A few days before Lord Charles Beresford was to make his feelings felt to Government and their Lordships, he received a letter from J. H. Fisher (27

KING EDWARD VII
Outboard profile and upper deck plan, as fitted 1905

King Edward VII class: Final legend, weights (tons)

Hull:	5,900
Armour:	4,175*
Armament:	2,525
Machinery:	1,800*
Coal:	950
General equipment:	690
Engineer's stores:	60
Displacement:	16,350

*Average.

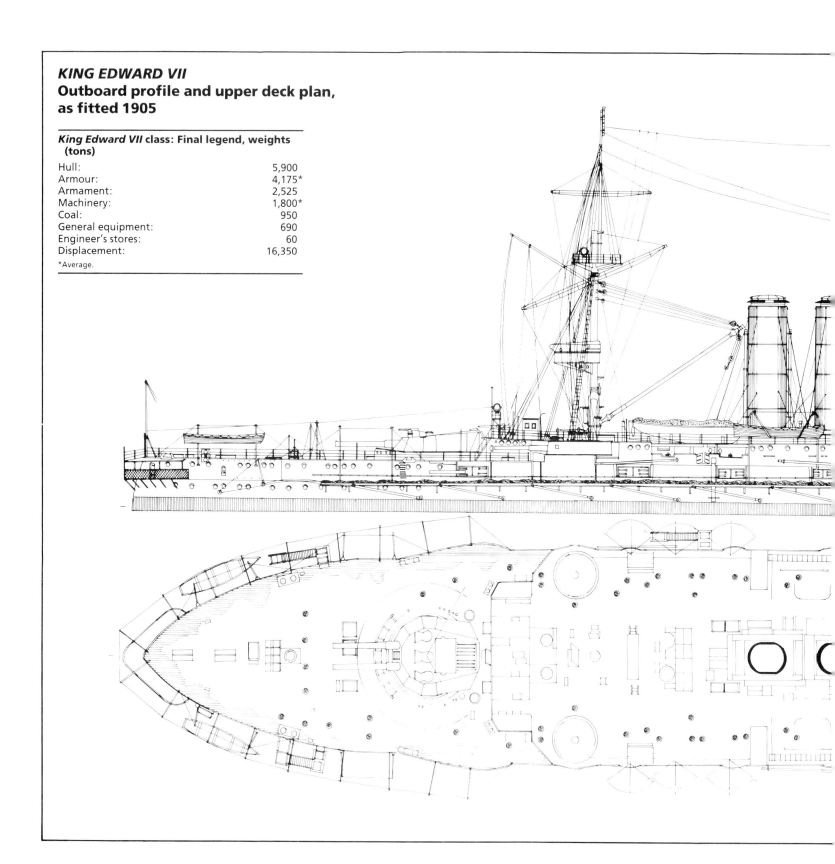

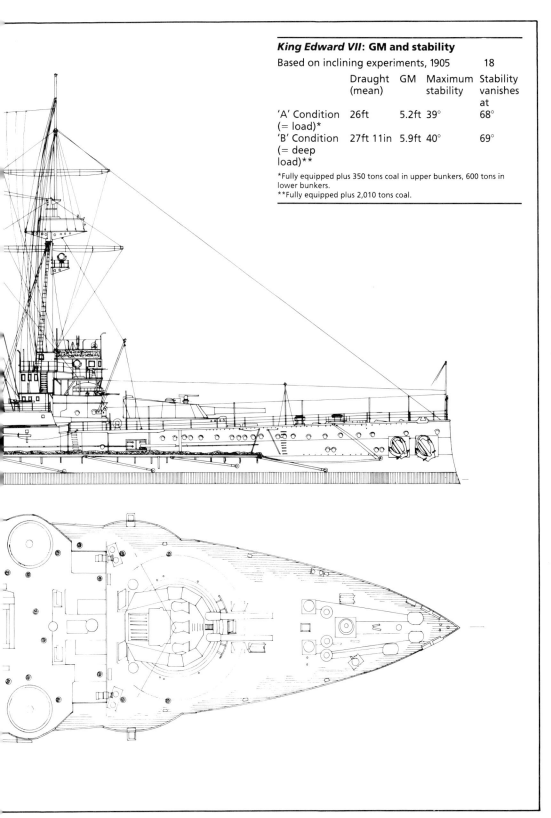

King Edward VII: GM and stability

Based on inclining experiments, 1905   18

	Draught (mean)	GM	Maximum stability	Stability vanishes at
'A' Condition (= load)*	26ft	5.2ft	39°	68°
'B' Condition (= deep load)**	27ft 11in	5.9ft	40°	69°

*Fully equipped plus 350 tons coal in upper bunkers, 600 tons in lower bunkers.
**Fully equipped plus 2,010 tons coal.

Feb 1902) who had no hesitation in telling everyone what he thought of the programme:

'My dear Beresford, when I wrote to you yesterday, I had not read the speeches on the Navy estimates of which I see you were present. I think Sir Charles Dilke was correct and admirable in all he said. May I suggest you reiterate the following words in his speech:

"Mr Goschen's view was that the paramount safety of the country required that we should maintain a fleet which would *cause three powers to pause* before they attacked England."

Mr Goschen also said that as a Cabinet member, and responsible for the safety of the country, he was also responsible for the Navy, and Mr Asquith as an ex Cabinet Minister states the precise truth when he says "the Navy is our only efficient protection." Can anyone say that two battleships and two heavy cruisers is a sufficient new building programme? It is absurd to say because our figures affording new construction show 9 millions we cannot spend more – that is not true. You may depend on it that Dilke was right. Hicks Beach put on the screws, and you should repeat Dilke's unanswerable arguments. "We must go into a naval war with ships ordered 4 or 5 years before that war was declared." You cannot build them in a hurry with a supplementary estimate, it is madness to underbuild.
Walter Kerr will fight tooth and nail against this idea.

Patriotism and commonsense confirm this—it is vital to our existence, they are the points to rule out to the British public, and I say it is shocking only to lay down two battleships and two cruisers. Goschen's dictum "3 power pause" you must hang onto that in your speech like a bulldog—reiteration is the secret of conviction. I say more can be done, and I know how to do it, and in the last resort they can build ships for us in Italy to any extent—but ask Noble how many battleships and cruisers he could build. Consult Thursfield before you make your speech—indeed I should ask him to revise your speech were I in your place, He knows how to put things to the British public.'

A further attack on naval matters appeared in the Malta *Daily Chronicle* in February saying:

'The needs of the Navy, and the means at the disposal of My Lords constitute a long worn policy. The needs of the Navy are nine in number, viz;- the creation of 2½ power standard of strength; the fighting fleets being ready to fight; better gunnery;

younger Admirals; the sale or destruction of ships useless in war, and costly in peace; the redistribution of nine squadrons, and the concentration of strength where it is needed; the elimination of the political element in the Board of Admiralty; the absorption of the Engineering Department in the executive branch and ninthly the addition of twelve battleships, sixty cruisers and fifty destroyers in the Royal Navy. Parliamentary criticism is almost unknown outside the naval element of the House of Commons.

If Germany is assured that England thoroughly understands her ambitions, peace not war, will be the result.'

Lord Charles Beresford delivered his broadside speech against just two battleships being proposed for the 1902 estimates, as did other eminent members of naval staff. Their words, however, fell on stony ground and 1902 passed into history recording the parsimonious attitude of the Government toward naval construction.

During 1902, however, following Watts' appointment as DNC, the whole question of battleship design came under complete reconsideration, and with a view to competing strongly with foreign contemporaries a new, more powerful design, providing a secondary armament of twelve 9.2in guns was produced.

King Edward VII class: Particulars, as completed

Construction
King Edward VII: Devonport DY; laid down 8 March 1902; launched 23 July 1903; completed Feb 1905

Britannia: Portsmouth DY; laid down 4 Feb 1902; launched 10 Dec 1904; completed Sept 1906

Dominion: Vickers; laid down 23 May 1902; launched 25 Aug 1903; completed July 1905

Commonwealth: Fairfield; laid down 17 June 1902; launched 13 May 1903; completed March 1905

Hindustan: Clydebank; laid down 25 Oct 1902; launched 19 Dec 1903; completed March 1905

New Zealand: Portsmouth DY; laid down 9 Feb 1903; launched 4 Feb 1904; completed June 1905

Hibernia: Devonport DY; laid down 6 Jan 1904; launched 17 June 1905; completed Jan 1907

Africa: Chatham DY; laid down 27 Jan 1904; launched 20 May 1905; completed Nov 1906.

Displacement (tons)
14,313 (light), 15,630–15,826 (load), 16,434–17,075 (deep).

Dimensions
Length: 425ft pp, 443ft wl, 457 oa

Beam: 78ft (hull 77ft 10¼in), 80ft oa (as moulded)

Draught: 26ft 3in – 26ft 9in (load), 28ft 3in (deep)

Freeboard: 22ft forward, 16ft 6½in amidships, 18ft aft

Height of 12in guns above wl: 25ft forward, 22ft 9in aft at normal load

Depth of keel from upper deck: 43ft 4in

Sinkage: 62.001 tons per inch.

Armament
Four 12in Mk IX; 80rpg

Four 9.2in Mk X; 150rpg

Ten 6in Mk VII; 200rpg

Twelve 12pdr (12cwt) PIII mountings; 250rpg

Two 12pdr (8cwt) field mountings; 250rpg

Fourteen 3pdr recoil mountings; 400rpg

Five 18in torpedo tubes (four beam, one stern underwater)

'A' turret centre 107ft 9in from bows

'X' turret centre 109ft 9in from stern.

Armour
Main belt: 9in KC

Upper belt: 8in KC

Top of belt: 7in KC

Main bulkheads: 12in–10in–8in

Decks: main 1½in, upper 1in, lower 2½in–1in

Barbettes: 12in–8in–6in

Turrets: 12in–10in–6in

9.2in turrets: 4in

Conning tower: 12in–10in.

Machinery
Two sets 4-cylinder inverted triple expansion surface condensing engines, two in-turning propellers

Cylinder diameter: 33½in HP, 54½in IP, 63in LP

Stoke: 4ft

Boilers:

King Edward VII ten Babcock, three cylindrical

Britannia eighteen Babcock, three cylindrical

Dominion sixteen Babcock

Commonwealth sixteen Babcock

Hindustan eighteen Babcock, three cylindrical

Below: *King Edward VII* during trials period, January 1905. The actual breakaway from the basic *Majestic* type was seen in these ships, and although often criticised for their mixed calibres they were, nevertheless, extremely powerful ships.

The design in general was quickly approved by all, but to enable it to be given ample consideration, it was deferred until the following year, and for 1903 it was decided to built three additional *King Edward*s. This decision was taken on the following grounds:

1. The situation in dockyard employment necessitated commencement of the 1903 programme ships at an early date and the new design was not sufficiently far advanced for this to be done.

2. For tactical reasons, it was considered desirable to complete a homogeneous squadron of eight ships of the *King Edward* class.

These three later ships, laid down during 1904, had the benefit of the latest technology, which had not been fitted in the sister ships: a newer model of 12in gun (Mk X); the latest 18cwt 12pdr; certain machinery improvements, a modified type of control top and improved searchlight equipment.

The new design (1903) subsequently materialized in the *Lord Nelson* class of the 1904 programme, but with its 9.2in reduced from twelve to ten. Although distinctly more powerful than the preceding classes, the fighting value of the *King Edward*s, on completion, was rather less than had appeared on paper when designed, the inherent disadvantages of the three-calibre armament being accentuated by developments in long-range firing

New Zealand eighteen Niclausse, three cylindrical
Hibernia eighteen Babcock, three cylindrical
Africa eighteen Babcock, three cylindrical
Working pressure: 210–220psi (*Dominion*, *Commonwealth*) 270psi
Grate area: 1,400sq ft
Length of boiler rooms: 107ft overall (*King Edward VII*)
Length of engine rooms: 75ft 3in overall (*King Edward VII*)
Designed SHP: 18,000 for 18.5 knots forced draught (*Dominion*, *Commonwealth* 18,000 for 18.5 knots natural draught)
Fuel: 2,164–2,238 tons coal max. plus 380 tons oil
Coal consumption: 380 tons per day at full power, 55 tons per day at 8 knots
Radius of action: 5,270nm at 10 knots.

Ship's boats
Pinnaces (steam): two 56ft
Pinnaces (sail): one 36ft
Launches (steam): one 42ft
Cutters: two 34ft

Whalers: three 27ft
Gigs: one 34ft, one 28ft
Skiff dinghies: one 16ft
Balsa rafts: one 13ft 6in.

Searchlights
Six 24in, two on after superstructure, one high on each mast (*Britannia*, *Hibernia*, *Africa* two 36in on bridge, six 24in: two on bridge, two on W/T office abaft mainmast, two in wing platforms on after superstructure).

Anchors
Three 125cwt stockless Admiralty, one 42cwt close-stowing, one 16cwt Admiralty, one 8cwt Admiralty; 525 fathoms 2¹¹⁄₁₆in cable.

Wireless
Type 1 in some, Type 2 in others. Type 3 (short-range) fitted 1912–13.

Complement
755 as private ship
800–815 wartime.
Breakdown of complement in *Dominion* as completed:

Executive and navigating branch	390
Engineers' branch	193
Artificers	30
Medical	6
Accountants	8
Miscellaneous	9
Domestic	18
Chaplain's branch	2
Royal Marines	101
Butchers	2
Lamptrimmers	2
Bandsmen	15
Servant to Commander	1
Total:	777

Costs
King Edward VII: £1,382,675 plus guns £89,400
Britannia: £1,316,983 plus guns £91,070
Dominion: £1,364,318 plus guns £89,400
Commonwealth: £1,382,127 plus guns £89,400
Hindustan: £1,361,762 plus guns £88,890
New Zealand: £1,335,753 plus guns £88,890
Hibernia: £1,347,620 plus guns £91,070
Africa: £1,328,970 plus guns £91,070.

KING EDWARD VII
Plan of boat deck and forward bridgework, as fitted 1905

1 Signal house
2 9.2in gun turrets
3 56ft steam pinnace
4 30ft cutter
5 27ft whaler, 34ft pinnace, 42ft launch
6 34ft cutter
7 27ft whaler
8 32ft galley
9 30ft gig
10 28ft gig, 16ft skiff dinghy
11 Boiler house vents
12 Conning tower
13 Admiral's sea cabin
14 Admiral's bridge
15 Admiral's bridge house
16 Chart house
17 Compass platform
18 Admiral's signal house
19 Forward fire-control platform
20 After fire-control platform
21 30ft cutter

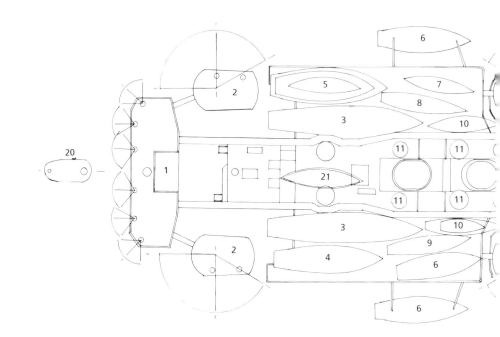

KING EDWARD VII
Inboard profile showing general layout and main armoured belt, as fitted 1905

1 Boilers
2 Machinery and engine rooms
3 Shell rooms
4 Magazines
5 12in barbettes
6 Boiler room uptakes
7 Engine room vents
8 Steering compartment
9 Torpedo rooms
10 Conning tower
11 Watertight compartments
12 Capstan room
13 Tiller compartment
14 9.2in barbettes

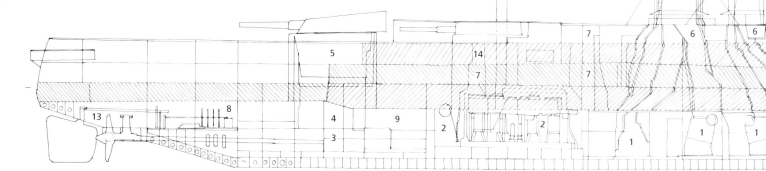

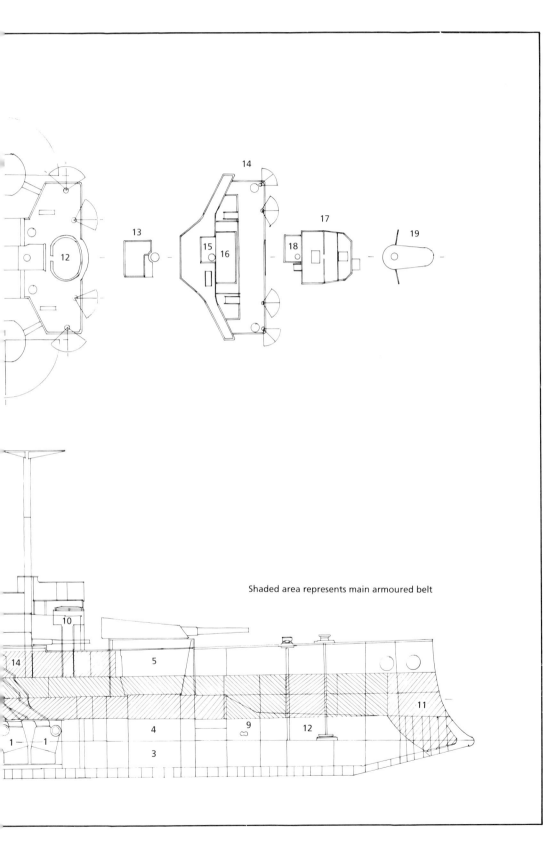

Shaded area represents main armoured belt

which had taken place during their building period; the longer battle ranges increased the difficulties of mixed calibre fire control, and further reduced the effectiveness of the 6in gun as a battleship weapon. Service opinion was especially critical of the multiplicity of calibres and regarded the ships as still being undergunned for the displacement in comparison with contemporary foreign types.

Nevertheless, as a bridge between the *Majestic*, *Formidable*, *Bulwark* and *Duncan* types and the *Lord Nelson* pair, they were of excellent design, and compared favourably with any of the foreign mixed-calibre types built during the same period.

All ships of the class turned out well as completed. Constructional savings in weight of hull and equipment averaged about 400 tons, apart from the Board margin which was not called upon (200 ton) and was responsible for the substantial reduction in nominal draught and displacement as completed. Reductions in weight, compared with preceding classes were effected by: suppression of fighting tops, after bridge, one 40ft steam pinnace, stream cable and stern anchor. Also, a reduction in storing the ship was applied; the usual four-month supply was reduced to three.

As completed, they were satisfactory sea-boats, although owing to the reduced freeboard and the additional topweight of the 9.2in turrets they proved very wet ships and were less steady than the *Bulwarks*; also they were prone to roll easily because of their higher metacentric height, stated to be 14 seconds for the period of a double roll.

They were exceptionally handy ships, but when the class formed the 3rd Battle Squadron, Grand Fleet during 1914–16 they became known as the 'Wobbly eight' because of their crablike movements in a sea-way; they were exceptionally tender under helm and liable to sheer considerably if not carefully handled.

Early in the war, it was customary, during Grand Fleet sweeps in the North Sea, to station one ship of the class at the head of each division to give warning and protect the more valuable 'Dreadnoughts' in the event of the Fleet's running into an enemy minefield—such was their value by 1914.

ARMAMENT

When the final legend was approved, and the general layout published, the ships were received with mixed feelings. The public were pleased because they were seeing vessels that were considerably larger, better-armed than, and a breakaway from, the traditional British type of battleship. In the service there was an immediate dislike for the arrangement of the mixed calibres.

The main armament, which remained the same (four 12in), was now greatly supplemented by four single 9.2in turrets while retaining a powerful secondary battery of ten 6in all mounted in a central

Dominion: Net weights (tons), as built
Plates, bars and rivet heads: 4,108.761
Middle and lower deck protection: 582.006
Main deck forward: 142.200
Upper deck within citadel: 246.784
Remainder of protective material: 57.539
Armour bars: 88.169
Communications tube: 20.578
Conning tower: 52.538
Armour and nickel steel: 2,722.322
Armour fixings: 97.250
Smithwork: 177.366
Steel castings: 83.124
Other castings: 41.168
Carpenters' timber: 251.548
Armour backing and fastening: 145.315
Joiners' timber and fittings: 91.441
Pumping, ventilation and sheet ironwork: 179.266
Fitters' work and brasswork: 300.533
Oakum, paint, cement, etc.: 225.843
Auxiliary machinery: 162.347
Rigging, etc.: 29.661
Anchors, chains and warps: 129.500
Boats and gear: 59.400
Armament including air compressors: 1,708.043
Ammunition including torpedo gear: 555.889
Machinery gear for working ammunition: 94.441
Torpedo net defence: 45.950
Ammunition tubes: 9.650
Electrical fittings: 78.876
Remainder of fittings: 95.542
Hull: 12,581.020
Machinery feedwater: 1,731.980
Equipped weight: 14,313.000
Engineers' stores: 35.200
Men and effects: 95.000
Fresh water and sanitary water: 159.840
Warrant officers' stores: 34.700
Officers' stores: 55.000
Provisions and spirits: 45.000
Coal: 950.000
Reserve feedwater: 109.280
Remainder of feedwater: 20.000
Gunners' stores: 9.100
Displacement: 15,826.120.

battery amidships. When preparing the general layout the Assistant Constructor, J. H. Narbeth, had considerable difficulty in siting a powerful intermediate battery without greatly hindering the main 12in turrets, or placing them too high as to cause excessive topweight.

Narbeth knew that any designer worth his salt, and in line with current trends, would need to secure the highest maximum of gun power consistent with other claims in the design—armour protection, machinery/speed, etc. Moreover, it was necessary to dispose the guns in such a manner as to ensure the greatest attack on any adversary—irrespective of the position of the ship. Looking abroad, the US Navy had recently constructed battleships (*Kearsarge* class) which attempted to answer problems of gun layout in limited lengths by placing a pair of secondary guns in turrets which were actually seated on top of the main turrets. (directly superimposed).

The Admiralty Constructor's Department, however, viewed this system with a great deal of scepticism, because although the arrangement permitted easy training of all four guns on each broadside, the disadvantages outweighed their relative value:

1. Severe blast problems when firing the uppermost guns directly over those of the lower turret.

2. Cramped conditions (turret and barbettes) and problems regarding adequate shell supplies to upper guns.

3. Both turrets could be knocked out simultaneously from a single heavy hit—resulting in a loss of 50 per cent of the principal armament.

Narbeth believed that his arrangement of placing intermediate turrets on the upper deck, at the corners of the superstructure, was preferable and considerably superior to any foreign disposition. Various alternatives were submitted by Narbeth, all in the temporary absence of the DNC (White) from office, but a suggested arrangement of eight 7.5in guns in four twin turrets mounted on the upper deck, with ten 6in in an armoured main deck amidships was generally favoured by their Lordships, and initially approved.

Later, however, on White's return to office, and at his suggestion, the 7.5in twins were replaced by single 9.2in guns. In support of his proposal, White pointed out that the 7.5in was not fully effective against heavily armoured ships, whereas the 9.2in

combined good hitting power and rate of fire to a very satisfactory degree and, furthermore, had a good reputation with the Fleet's gunnery officers.

The adoption of the 9.2in gun in the secondary armament constituted the outstanding innovation in the design, as compared with preceding classes.

The class were the only battleships designed for the Royal Navy during the White era to carry the 6in secondary guns in a continuous battery instead of in the separate casemates introduced by White in the *Royal Sovereigns* and retained in all intervening classes. Adoption of this battery arrangement resulted from the considerably increased space taken up by the 9.2in turrets which necessitated closer spacing of the 6in guns and precluded use of the separate casemate system. In the *King Edwards*, the three centre guns on each side were required to be accommodated within a space of approximately 90ft between the 9.2in turrets against some 160ft allowed for four casemate guns in *Formidable*. The main deck box battery had been adopted in the Japanese battleship *Mikasa* (built by Vickers) and also in contemporary Austrian, German and American ships, whereas France, Russia and later Italy favoured secondary turrets on the upper deck.

The battery was regarded as being more economical in weight and cost of armour, but on the other hand it offered the maximum target compared with casemates and turrets, and the thin internal screens supplied between the individual guns did not in any way afford the same degree of isolation as casemates.

Owing to a slightly reduced freeboard in the design, the battery guns were placed some eight-inches lower than the main deck casemates in *Formidable*, and after the ships were completed it was found that the gun muzzles touched water at about 14° of roll, and they were practically unfightable in any sort of sea-way. Official records give anti-torpedo armament as eight 12pdrs and twelve 3pdrs, but photographs show twelve 12pdrs in all with twelve 3pdrs in the first five ships as completed, but only eight in the last three (*Africa*, *Britannia* and *Hibernia*). A new 18cwt 12pdr was introduced in the last three ships in place of the 12cwt pattern previously used. Also, the 3pdr was updated in *Africa*, *Britannia* and *Hibernia* by using a semi-automatic gun introduced by Vickers and first tested in the torpedo-boat destroyer *Daring*. Main deck and fighting top locations for any anti-torpedo guns was finally abandoned in this class

Right and below: *Hindustan* as completed, seen during her trials period, March to May 1905, putting to sea to undergo strenuous tests imposed by the Royal Navy.

and the 12pdrs were carried in a short open deck battery amidships and in superstructures forward and aft. 3pdrs were mounted on 9.2in turrets in all ships, with four on the bridge.

The turret roof location for anti-torpedo guns was retained in all later classes prior to the dreadnought *Neptune* (1911) and was adopted with a view to securing an armoured base below the guns.

By 1903, the 3pdr was generally considered to be too light to deal with contemporary torpedo-boat destroyers and although the new Vickers gun was held by many to be the ideal anti-torpedo gun, and was retained in the succeeding *Lord Nelson* class, it was finally abandoned in *Dreadnought*.

In the completed ships, the percentage of armament weight increased to 15.7 per cent against

11.5 per cent in the *Formidable* group, but the three-calibre armament was severely criticized in the service on the grounds that the ships were still undergunned, and that if the 9.2in gun was desirable (naval opinion unanimous in support of this), the 6in gun was superfluous and the whole secondary armament could have been 9.2in.

It has often been suggested that if any of the gunnery officers had been consulted over the design, the unsatisfactory step in armament layouts (*King Edwards*) between the basic *Majestic* and *Lord Nelson* would have been omitted. At the time of considering the design, however, there was no question of consulting anyone but the Constructor's Department on the subject of Her Majesty's warship designs; service opinion tended to be biased and individual, and likely to change with the breeze; and it was not Admiralty policy to consult the fleets' leading officers. It has to be remembered that with standard Admiralty designs, flaws in the layout only came to light after the ships had been built and tested.

Although often quoted as having a difficult armament layout the group were, nevertheless, very powerful warships indeed and could, if necessary, put up a terrific volume of fire, far superior to preceding classes and certainly on a par with any foreign design. On the whole the Construction Department had accomplished what it set out to do, and in practice had some measure of success. They were the first British battleships completed with fire control tops and long-range fire control equipment (not in the original design, but added during construction).

ARMOUR

The arrangement of armour protection was generally based on that of the *Bulwark* group, but with modifications to conform to the continuous main deck battery instead of separate casemates for the 6in guns. The principle modifications were:

1. 9in section of belt carried slightly further forward beyond fore barbette, and the extremity increased from 7in-5in-3in to 7in-5in-4in and 3in. After extension of belt was increased from 1½in to 2in with two ½in plates over this (3in).

2. Side armour on citadel from about 1ft 6in above waterline to main deck reduced from 9in to 8in.

3. 7in battery armour added between main and upper deck amidships (this being unarmoured in *Formidable* types).

4. 1in armour fitted to upper deck amidships over battery instead of 2in on main deck below this; main deck within citadel being unarmoured in the *King Edwards*. Protection to the battery was considered essential, and its provision together with the side armour between main and upper decks over nearly the whole length of the citadel was considered to obviate the necessity for any main deck armour within this.

For reasons of stability (avoiding excessive topweight) 1in armour was accepted for the upper deck over the battery, the saving in weight as compared with the 2in main deck in *Formidable*, largely offsetting the weight required for the battery side armour.

5. Maximum thickness of turrets increased from 10in to 12in.

6. After conning tower suppressed, being replaced by torpedo control tower, accommodating the directors for the after pair of tubes, and protected by ½in plates.

With the exception of the ex-Chilean *Swiftsure* and *Triumph* (completed 1904), the *King Edwards* were the first British battleships since the *Trafalgar* class (1890) to have side armour above the main deck, or any armour on the upper deck.

The 9.2in turrets were substantially armoured, but advantage was taken of the protection afforded by the battery armour to save weight on the depth and thickness of the barbettes, these being carried only about 3ft 6in below the upper deck, with 4in sides, thin 1in floor and 3in ammunition tubes. These shallow barbettes were subjected to severe criticism on the grounds that a shell exploding below them would probably blow the entire barbette over the side, although against this it was contended that the chance of a shell explosion exactly in this position was relatively slight. This was certainly an optimistic view on the part of the Construction Department, and a major weakness in an otherwise carefully thought-out design.

Because of the risk of disablement of several of the guns by a single shell hit or explosion, the 6in battery was distinctly inferior from the standpoint of protection to the two-deck, separate casemates of the preceding classes, but this was necessitated by space considerations resulting from the 9.2in turrets on the upper deck at the corners of the superstructure.

Internally the battery was divided into two by an athwartships armoured bulkhead and short traverses between the guns; this reduced the risk to some extent, but the absence of a centre-line bulkhead or rear screens to the guns was another of the ships' weak points.

Admiral Sir Arthur Wilson (Controller) would have preferred a rearrangement of the hull armouring, with the belt carried three to four feet lower down, and the slope of the middle deck shifted about six feet further inboard, with a thick longitudinal bulkhead extending downwards from that point over the full length of the citadel, the space between bulkhead and ship's side forming a coal bunker. This plan, which was intended to provide additional protection against heavy shells bursting in the water close alongside the ship, was subsequently withdrawn by him, with great reluctance, owing to the difficulty in transporting

Below: *Britannia* taking on stores at Portsmouth shortly after completion in October 1906, having been commissioned into the Reserve with the nucleus crew from *Revenge*. Note square top compared with *King Edward VII* and *Commonwealth*.

coal from this outer bunker. Doors in the bulkhead would have reduced its protective value, while hoists to the armoured deck with trunks running down to the stockholds from this, where required, would involve considerable wastage of space and also constitute too slow an operation for high-speed steaming. Had oil fuel instead of coal been in use at the date when the design was under consideration, the idea could probably have been accepted, anticipating the 1½in to 3in anti-torpedo bulkhead introduced in the *Bellerophon*s (1906–7), but would have increased displacement in the *King Edward VII* class to over 17,000 tons in the normal load. As completed the armour protection in the *King Edward*s was as follows.

The main belt and side armour (above 2in), main bulkhead, barbettes, turrets, battery plus forward conning tower were all made from Krupp cemented plates; the belt and side (2in section) battery screens were Krupp non-cemented.

The decks, secondary barbette floors, ammunition hoists and conning tower tubes, etc., were all mild steel. The main 9in belt amidships, was 259ft 4in long, and extended from about 25ft ahead of the fore barbette to abeam the after barbette. The upper edge was approximately 2ft 2in above the waterline; the lower edge being about 5ft 6in below (normal condition). Forward of this belt the thickness reduced to 7in for a length of 15ft 8in, then to 5in for 21ft 11in, 4in for 18ft 10in and then 2in right through to the stem (2in armour section backed by two thicknesses of ½in mild steel plating = 3in).

Aft of the 9in main belt amidships was 2in nickel steel which ran over the same width as the midships section (9in) and extended for a length of 120ft toward the stern before terminating. This was backed by two ½in mild steel plates which ran from the after barbette right through to the stern of the ship.

The middle side belt was 8in thick, 259ft 4in long by 7ft 6in wide, and extended over the same length as the 9in between main and middle deck levels. The extensions to the 8in belt were of the same thicknesses and lengths as that for the 9in belt (total width of armour protection amidships including 7in battery armour was 20ft from bottom to top).

The main bulkhead (aft only) ran obliquely inwards from the after extremities of belt and side armour to the outer face of the after barbette. It was 10in thick below and 8in above the middle deck,

but was 12in uniform as it ran around the barbette. The forward barbette was 12in uniform above the main deck, 8in below, and had a 6in inner face.

MACHINERY

Originally all the ships were to have had Belleville water tube boilers only, but they were modified following the lengthy report (*see* boiler and machinery installations) of the Special Boiler Committee appointed by the Admiralty to investigate differences experienced with marine boilers then in use in Her Majesty's Ships.

This report recommended that Belleville boilers be discarded and that four other large tube types be fitted in the new ships for trial purposes with a proportion of cylindrical boilers in each case.

The four types selected were the British Babcock and Yarrow, the French Niclausse, and the German Durr (a variant of the Niclausse). As a result of this, the *King Edward*s were given a mixture of water tube (Babcock or Niclausse) and cylindrical boilers although two (*Dominion* and *Commonwealth*) received all Babcock water tube, and no other.

The ships were carefully monitored while on trials and many reports were made about their behaviour. Unfortunately the official material (Covers) for this class is missing but owing to the fact that there was no general embargo on detailed information about the class, other secondary sources show that experience during trials proved that the Niclausse boilers were generally inferior to the Belleville type, while the Babcock and Yarrow were entirely satisfactory. They were the last British battleships to have any cylindrical boiler fitted, and *New Zealand* was the last to have any foreign type installed. Machinery and boiler installations varied from ship to ship:

They all had two sets of 4-cylinder vertical inverted triple expansion engines driving twin, 4-bladed 17ft 6in diameter inward-turning propellers. The cylinders, which in each set consisted of one high pressure, one intermediate and two low pressure, were 33½in (HP), 54½in (IP) and 63in (LP) in size respectively, with a piston stroke of 48in. The engine room machinery occupied two separate watertight compartments.

Boiler installations were a little more complex within the group. *King Edward VII* had ten Babcock water tube and six Scotch cylindrical single return tube boilers; *Africa*, *Britannia*,

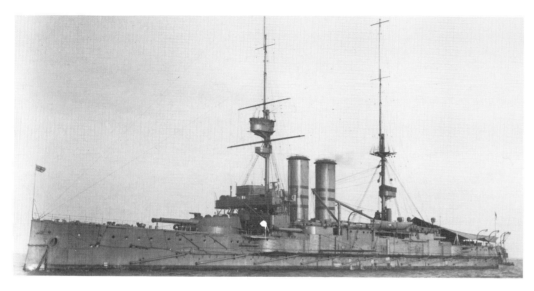

Hibernia and *Hindustan* had eighteen Babcock water tube and three cylindrical return tube boilers. *New Zealand* was given eighteen Niclausse and three cylindrical return tube. Only *Dominion* and *Commonwealth* received any homogeneity in the installation of boilers, being fitted with sixteen Babcock water tube type.

Each Babcock boiler in *Hindustan* was fitted with two oil fuel sprayers, and each cylindrical with six. Total output of oil sprayed per boiler, per hour, at 150psi was 600lb in the Babcock, and 1,080lb in the cylindrical. *Dominion* and *Commonwealth* had all sixteen Babcock fitted with eight oil fuel sprayers with a total output of 880lb oil per boiler, per hour, at 150psi. *King Edward VII* was different yet again, with eight sprayers on the Babcock boilers, and six on the cylindrical. *New Zealand* was not fitted with any.

All proved reliable steamers in service, although speeds in some did not come up to expectations.

King Edward VII class: Steam trials

Commonwealth 25 June 1904 8-hour full power

Run	IHP	Revs	Speed (knots)
First:	18,478	120.35	19.1082
Second:	17,931	119.1	19.1285
Third:	18,213	119.5	18.6721
Fourth:	17,747	120.15	19.3029
Fifth:	17,987	119.3	18.8382
Sixth:	18,205	119.4	19.5546

Dominion 1 November 1904 8-hour full power (severely hampered by fog)

First:	12,967	112.75	17.630
Second:	13,904	117.60	18.310
Third:	12,652	114.60	18.000
Fourth:	12,420	111.70	17.647
Fifth:	12,435	109.45	17.110
Sixth:	12,414	114.70	18.018

Hindustan December 1904

	Draught forward	aft	Boiler pressure (psi)	Mean IHP	Revs	Speed (knots)
30-hour at 3,600shp:	26ft 3in	27ft 2in	149	3,718	71/2	11.8 logged
8-hour full power:	26ft 4½in	27ft 2½in	191	18,521	120.4	19.01 measured mile

Africa 1 June 1906

30-hour at 12,600shp:	26ft 4in	27ft 1½in	194	12,847	115.8	17.547 mean of six runs
3 June 8-hour full power:	26ft 4in	27ft 1½in	199	18,671	129.1	18.953 measured mile

Britannia December 1906

8-hour full power:			198	18,725		18.24

Dominion: Contractor's Preliminary steam trial results

Engines: 8 cylinders. HP: 33½in; Intermediate: 54½in; Low: 63in
Length of stroke: 48in
Diameter of propellers: 17ft 6in
Number of blades: 4
Pitch of propeller: 18ft 6in
Developed surface: 86sq ft
Surface of condensers: 9,500sq ft
Total weight of machinery: 1,763.50 tons plus 27.4 tons for oil fittings
8-hour full power trial:
Draught forward: 26ft 3in
Draught aft: 26ft 9in
Displacement: 16,434 tons
Maximum HP: 19,054
Maximum revolutions: 126.7
Mean speed attained: 19½ knots
Pressure of steam at boilers 248.1psi
Pressure of steam at engines 228.7psi
Vacuum: 25.55
Speed results:

SHP	Revs	Speed (knots)
3,330	73.2	12
4,230	80.2	13
5,410	87.2	14
6,880	94.2	15
8,700	101	16
10,880	108	17
13,480	115	18
16,600	122	19

Admiral Sir Arthur Wilson (Controller) had stated that he favoured a still higher speed (19.5—20 knots was being recorded by some foreign battleships), but at the time of design, the Board were not prepared to recommend the increased displacement and cost involved.

With the exception of *New Zealand* they were the first British battleships completed with any oil fuel, and with mixed firing arrangements. All were originally laid down as coal-burning only, but during 1903–4 and 1905 while under construction all boilers were provided with capacity to burn oil and were fitted with oil sprayers. These alterations were not practicable in *New Zealand* because her Niclausse boilers could not be satisfactorily adapted for oil. This modification, which was approved late in 1904, resulted from successful mixed-firing trials, using oil sprayers, carried out in 1902–3 in the *Majestic* class battleships *Hannibal* and *Mars*, and the destroyer *Surly*.

Oil fuel was carried in double bottom compartments. Success was achieved during the 1906 Fleet manoeuvres when units of the class were easily able to draw away from a superior force by using the oil sprayers to increase steam pressure quickly; the performance giving considerable impetus to the general adoption of oil fuel.

Fuel capacity and radius, as originally designed with coal only, was approximately the same as in *Formidable*; the failure to provide any increase in the new ships was subjected to adverse criticism when details of the design were first released. With the addition of oil, however, the average nominal radius was about 1,600 miles greater than in the *Formidable* groups.

The practice of fitting combinations of boilers ended with this group, and was always strongly opposed by the Engineer-in-Chief. The justification for this, was seen in the actual performance of the completed ships—those with combinations being inferior in general, to those with a uniform outfit. In general, the combination had the effect of complicating the arrangements of machinery, and subsequently reducing the working process and speed at full power without any compensating gain.

FLIGHT EXPERIMENTS IN *AFRICA*

For some years before the First World War it had been thought possible that aircraft could be launched from ships at sea. Experiments had been carried out in early aircraft to see if it were feasible for them to carry extra weights for use on runways and, of course, floats so that they could come down on the water.

In January 1912, *Africa* was fitted with a long runway which ran like a ski slope from her lower forebridge down to the bows.

On the occasion of the first take-off from a British warship, the rails were first tested by the crew who jumped up and down on it. The aircraft was a Short biplane with a Gnome engine, and was held in place by members of the crew before the pilot, Lieutenant Samson, boarded her. The engine was started and the aircraft shot down the runway. She dipped her nose slightly when she left the runway, but soon pulled clear of the bows and rose to a fair height and circled *Africa* with ease. The runway, approximately 100 feet long, had proved adequate for the purpose. Cheer after cheer rose from the crew of the ship. Samson circled the vessel many times (coming too close for comfort on one occasion) before rising to a height of about 800ft and guiding his aircraft back to base. History had been made in those few short minutes.

The equipment was removed from *Africa* and was fitted in *Hibernia*, and was then shipped to *London* for further tests.

After these tests, however, it was concluded that although it was desirable to have aircraft on board for many purposes (spotting, general fleet duties, etc.), it was not considered worth the expense of hampering the forward (or perhaps the after) 12in guns and turret. Moreover, the fact that the aircraft had to come down on the sea in order to be lifted back on board, a task which would be practically impossible in rough weather, assured the dismissal of the fixed runway on any warship.

These, and other tests carried out, were the start of aircraft being used at sea. Indeed, the system was expertly developed, and by 1917/18 it was contemplated that an aircraft attack at sea might be feasible upon the German High Seas Fleet—should they ever show themselves again.

APPEARANCE CHANGES

The height of masts and funnels and their relative positions (rear of second funnel midway between masts) together with the thickness of the funnels, all combined to produce an ensemble of balance and symmetry unequalled in any contemporary battleship. They were generally conceded to have been the best proportioned and finest-looking battleships of their day.

Easily distinguishable by their single 9.2in turrets at the corners of the superstructure; unusually large funnels, and pole masts with control top high on the foremast, and low on the main, and no fighting tops. As completed however, they were, very difficult to tell apart. No topgallant masts as completed; W/T gaff on maintop in all; mechanical semaphore at head of main topmast in all except *Hibernia* and *Hindustan*; no yards on mainmast (carried in *KEVII* during trials only); derrick stump (P+S) amidships.

Individual differences were: *Dominion*, *Commonwealth*, *King Edward VII*, *New Zealand* and *Hindustan* all had large, oval control tops on foremast with single small top below. *Africa*, *Britannia* and *Hibernia* had small, square control tops on foremast with two smaller tops below this. Funnel cap differences: *King Edward VII* heavy caps clear of casing with flat caging; *Dominion* heavy caps close to casing with flat caging; *Hindustan* medium caps rather close to casing with low flat caging; *Commonwealth* medium to heavy caps slightly raised from casing with low flat caging; *New Zealand* medium to light caps slightly raised from casing with prominent caging; *Africa* medium caps close to casing; *Britannia* very light caps close to casing; *Hibernia* heavy caps raised slightly above casing.

Other differences were: *Dominion* short steampipes; *King Edward VII* as *Dominion*, but W/T gaff carried higher, and very tall topmasts to derrick stump amidships. *Commonwealth* W/T gaff halfway up topmast. *Hindustan* upper yard on foremast close above lower mast cap. *Africa* lower yard on foremast on or below second top. *Brittania* lower yard on foremast touching top. *Hibernia* lower yard clear of tops. *New Zealand* upper yard well clear of cap.

1907 12pdr ex-superstructure forward and aft in *King Edward VII* temporarily remounted on 12in turrets; four guns abreast on each turret. This arrangement is reported to have been instigated by Admiral Lord Charles Beresford when *King Edward VII* served as his flagship. The guns reverted to the superstructures later in 1907. W/T gaff triced and masthead semaphore (where fitted) removed. Tall light topmasts fitted to derrick stumps amidships in *Africa* and *King Edward VII*.

1907–8 Special fire control equipment fitted following trials carried out against the old battleship *Hero* in Nov 1907. Bridge 3pdrs in *Commonwealth*, *Dominion*, *Hindustan* and *King Edward VII* suppressed (*NZ* later).

Two 36in SL added in bridge wings in *Commonwealth*, *Dominion*, *Hindustan*, *New Zealand* and on forward 9.2in turrets in *King Edward VII*. Mast SL in first five ships remounted on W/T office abaft mainmast.

Two 24in SL added on platform high on starboard side of upper deck amidships in *Hindustan* (1908). W/T topgallant fitted to each mast in all; Type 1 W/T fitted and W/T gaff removed. Topmasts removed from derrick stump in *Africa* and *King Edward VII*. Early funnel bands painted up in 1907–8 (fleet markings only): *Africa* two white close together, halfway up funnels; *Dominion* one white high up, but also two red wide apart and low down later into 1908; *Hibernia* one red halfway up; *King Edward VII* none; *New Zealand* two white, close together and low; *Britannia* one white halfway up

(1907); three white close together and low (1907–8); one white halfway up (1908).

1909–10 Range indicators fitted in all except *Britannia*. Location varied—face or roof of forward or after control top; below control top; SL platform on foremast. One 3pdr removed from each after 9.2in turret in *Commonwealth* to accommodate SL, and remounted P+S on after superstructure. SL (two ex-W/T office) in *Commonwealth* temporarily remounted on after 9.2in turrets. One SL removed from W/T office in *Hindustan*. Compass platform

over bridge in *Africa* removed. Standard funnel bands painted up: *Africa* nil; *Britannia* one white on second funnel; *King Edward VII* two white on each funnel; *Dominion* one white on each funnel; *Hindustan* two white on fore funnel; *Hibernia* two white on second funnel; *Commonwealth* white on fore funnel; *New Zealand* one red on each funnel.

1911–12 RF added on after superstructure in *Hibernia* and *Hindustan* (*removed from Hindustan* 1913–14). AS modifications varied a great deal: *Africa*, *Dominion* wing SL on after superstructure removed; *Commonwealth* SL on after 9.2in turret restored to W/T office; *Hibernia* SL removed from W/T office; *Hindustan* SL platform amidships removed and SL remounted on after 9.2in turrets; *New Zealand* single 24in SL on W/T office and after superstructure replaced by two twin 24in mounted on W/T office.

1912 *Africa* and *Hibernia* used in 1912 for experimental flying-off of aircraft from turret tops. *Africa* was first British battleship to fly off aircraft in January 1912 (*see* aircraft).

1913–14 Further SL modifications: *Britannia*, *Commonwealth* SL ex-W/T remounted in bridge wings; *Hindustan* SL ex-9.2in turrets remounted in bridge wings; *KEVII* 36in ex-forward 9.2in turrets remounted in bridge wings. SL removed from W/T office. Torpedo nets removed from all.

1914 Funnel bands deleted.

1914–15 One 12pdr ex-*Zealandia* transferred to Q-ship in July 1915; two 3pdrs added. Almost all were mounted on quarterdeck, or after superstructure. Bridge in *Dominion* enlarged and extended abaft mast. Both topgallants and main topmast removed. Short light pole fitted in place of topmast in some. Identification letters painted-up on sides of 12in turrets in some (or all) ships: *Africa* AF; *King Edward* KE; *Dominion* DOM; *Zealandia* Z.

1916 6in guns removed from main deck level in all. Four remounted in shields on 12pdr battery deck amidships. This modification was effected by April 1917 in all except *Dominion* and *Hindustan*. Upper deck 12pdr suppressed *Dominion* only: one 24in SL mounted on new platform low on foremast; after control top replaced by SL platform with two 36in ex-bridge lamps; high platform with two 24in SL added on after superstructure.

1918 *Commonwealth* and *Zealandia* Specially refitted for service as gunnery training ships. Director control fitted with latest control and RF equipment; fore control top enlarged and tripod

legs fitted to foremast to stiffen it for control purposes; 12in director located over control top and 6in tower platform close below this; 6in armament unchanged; remaining 12pdrs removed; two 3in AA added right aft; after control top replaced by SL platforms with two 36in ex-bridge; high platform with four 24in SL added on after superstructure. Anti-torpedo bulges added in *Commonwealth* only; bridge extended around foremast; rig unchanged from 1917. Norman Wilkinson dazzle camouflage painted-up, consisting of two shades of blue, grey and black. It was reported that *Zealandia* was painted in the same manner, but lack of official and photographic evidence rules this out.

HISTORY: *KING EDWARD VII*

Laid down at Devonport 8 March 1902 and launched by HM King Edward VII 23 July 1903. In giving consent for the ship to bear his name, King Edward is reported to have stipulated that she should always serve as Flagship. This was carried out, although at the date of her loss, when *en route* from Rosyth to Devonport for refit, the flag had been temporarily transferred.

7 Feb 1905 Commissioned at Devonport as Flagship CinC, Atlantic Fleet, until Mar 1907.
1906–7 Refit.
4 Mar 1907 Paid off at Portsmouth and recommissioned on 5th for service as Flagship of Admiral

Lord Charles Beresford, CinC, Channel Fleet, until Mar 1909.
1907–8 Refit at Portsmouth. Channel Fleet became 2nd Division, Home Fleet on reorganization in Mar 1909, and *King Edward VII* was commissioned at Portsmouth 27 Mar as Flagship (VA), Home Fleet, Mar 1909—Aug 1914.
Dec 1909—Feb 1910 Refit at Portsmouth.
1 Aug 1911 Commissioned at Portsmouth as Flagship (VA), 3rd and 4th Divisons, Home Fleet.
14 May 1912 Completed to full crew at Sheerness as Flagship (VA), 3rd BS, First Fleet.
Nov 1912 3rd BS detached to Mediterranean because of troubles in the Balkans. Took part in blockade of Montenegro by International Force,

Left: *King Edward VII, c.*1910. Flagship of Vice-Admiral 2nd Division, Home Fleet. Note searchlight arrangement of after bridge.

Below: *Hindustan* entering Portsmouth Harbour *c.*1910 during naval manoeuvres which continued throughout June of that year and involved all of the 3rd BS.

and subsequent occupation of Scutari.

27 June 1913 Rejoined Home Fleet.

Aug—Nov 1914 Grand Fleet (Flagship, 3rd BS). Squadron employed with Grand Fleet cruisers on Northern Patrol area, augmented by five *Duncan*s for this purpose.

2 Nov 1914 Detached to reinforce Channel Fleet, (Flagship, 3rd BS) until end of month. Returned to Grand Fleet on last day of November 1914. With Grand Fleet until Jan 1916.

6 Jan 1916 Mined and sunk off Cape Wrath in field laid by German raider *Moewe*. Explosion occurred under starboard engine room, and ship immediately listed slightly to starboard. Attempts to tow her by the collier *Princess Melita* and the leader *Kempenfelt* in a strong wind and rising sea

proved unsuccessful, the ship becoming very low in the water and quite unmanageable. About five hours after being hit, the list had become so heavy that it was decided to abandon ship, and the crew were taken off by the destroyers *Fortune, Marne Musketeer* and *Nessus* without loss of life. In fact *King Edward VII* took a very long time to capsize and sink; approximately nine hours after being hit. The best official description of the incident is that from her Captain which was given to the Court of Inquiry which followed the ship's loss. This and other reports were sent in, but at that time it was difficult to ascertain whether she had been mined or had been the victim of a submarine attack.

After the war, as fresh evidence came to light, it was concluded that she had struck a mine.

The report from Captain MacLachlan, RN, 12 January 1916 at the Court of Inquiry ran as follows.

'On Thursday, 6th January 1916, in accordance with orders the *King Edward VII* left Scapa Flow for Belfast, passing through Hoxa Gate at 7.12 am. After rounding Gantlick Head course was shaped west, speed 15 knots, for the swept line and on reaching it course was altered to N.71° W. Wind SSW Force 4, sea slight. At 9 am commenced zigzagging two points at a time. Visibility 3 miles, rain.

At 10.47 am when in a position latitude 58° 43' N. longitude 4° 12' W. and three minutes before the helm would have been put over for the next turn, a violent explosion took place under the starboard engine room. I had just gone into the

Below: *Zealandia* at Portland, 1911. *New Zealand* was re-named on 1 December 1911 to release the name for a new battlecruiser then under construction. Originally it was proposed to re-name her *Caledonia*, but this met with disapproval on the part of people in New Zealand.

Below: Stern view of *Africa* preparing for the Coronation Review in July 1911.

charthouse when the explosion occurred, and I ran out to give orders to close watertight doors, but found that the officer-of-the-watch had already done so.

The helm was put hard a'starboard with the intention of closing the land and beaching the ship if necessary. The helm was reported jammed hard a'starboard when trying to steady the ship on south. The Engineer Commander sent me a message a few minutes after the explosion that both engine rooms were flooded and in another few minutes reported personally that both engines were

stopped. The door between two engine rooms being open admitted water to the port engine room. An attempt was made to close it, but the rush of water was too great to allow this. It was then reported to me that all watertight doors were shored up and holding well and that all watertight doors were closed, with the exception of the one mentioned between the two engine rooms. The engines being stopped and both engine rooms flooded, and the ship having a list of 8° to starboard I considered it advisable to get all the boats into the water while we had pressure on the main derrick. It

was now blowing from the westward, Force 6 with a rising sea. At the same time in order to reduce the list, orders were given to flood the port wings, this righted her 3 degrees. A few minutes after the explosion, guns and rocket signals were made to attract the attention of a steamer bearing SSE and about 5 miles off which started to close after about a quarter of an hour and proved to be the *Princess Melita*. A 5in wire was sent to her, and while she was preparing to tow, the *Kempenfelt* arrived and 1 6½in wire was sent to her. They started towing at 2.15 pm but owing to strong wind and sea the ship

Below: *Britannia* in Weymouth Bay, 1911. The 9.2in barbettes made a bulge in the ship's side, and a low, curved dwarf wall prevented seas from entering the upper deck 12pdr battery. No after bridge or fighting tops in these ships, fire control tops having taken their place.

was unmanageable, and in spite of working the helm with the hand wheel, it was found impossible to keep her from getting beam onto the wind and sea. At first the ship was heading to the southward, but after the tow was started, she swung to the northward and it was found impossible to straighten her up again. The ship was now low in the water and having a list of 15°.

At about 2.40 pm the *Kempenfelt*'s tow parted, and seeing that any further attempt at towing was useless I gave orders to the SS *Princess Melita* to slip her tow. The ship was now getting deeper in the water, with the starboard side of the quarterdeck awash and water washing onto the upper deck abreast of A 9.2in. Although the bulkheads showed no signs of giving, it was reported to me by the Engineer Commander that 'C' strokehold was gradually filling, so an attempt was made to keep it under with the Downtons but this was found to be of little use. The starboard ammunition passage was flooded and water was getting into the after cross passage. I also knew that the bulkheads between the engine rooms and 9.2in magazines were not water-tight, though every attempt had been made in the ship to render them so; both these magazines were cleared at Rosyth in order that this defect could be put right during the ship's refit at Belfast. Taking into consideration the amount of water in the ship, the increasing heavy weather, the towing having failed and the approaching darkness, I decided to abandon ship for the night.

The destroyer *Musketeer* came alongside at 2.45 pm and then *Marne* and *Fortune*, and took all officers and men off the ship and I embarked in *Nessus* at 4.10 pm. I ordered the tugs and *Nessus* to stand by the ship, and the other destroyers were

Above: *Hindustan* in 1911. Increasing the armament with four 9.2in seemed the natural way towards the all big gunned battleship, but the usual mistake of mounting the 6in guns on the main deck in sponsons prevailed, and the low freeboard, meant that the guns were often washed out in a seaway.

Left: *Zealandia* leaving Portsmouth in 1912.

Right and below: *Britannia*, c.October 1914. Two photographs taken aboard *Britannia*, showing her forecastle, forward 12in turret and bridgework; also quarterdeck looking back at *Hindustan* which is rolling well.

sent back to harbour. It was now blowing strong from the westward, force 6 to 7 with a moderate heavy sea. At 5.20 pm the *Nessus* stood to the westward till 7.45 pm when course was altered back toward the ship but nothing more was seen of her. At 0.45 am the course was shaped for Scrabster in compliance with orders from Commander-in-Chief, and at daylight *Nessus* returned to Scapa Flow. On reporting myself on board *Iron Duke* I was informed that the tugs standing by the ship had reported that *King Edward VII* had turned over at 8.10 pm.'

The centre of the explosion was apparently at about the fourth longitudinal between 116 and 124 stations, in the neighbourhood of the main sea inlet, and just before the 9.2in magazine. The coal bunkers there flooded very quickly, and water made its way from there into the ammunition passages, and probably into the bunkers above the protective deck. Information gained from this experience as to watertight thoroughness was applied to all warships constructed after the war, the incident showing that principal bulkheads must not be pierced even for pipe fittings, etc.

HISTORY: *BRITANNIA*

Built at Portsmouth Dockyard, and commissioned into the Reserve at Portsmouth on 8 Sept 1906, until Oct 1906.
2 Oct 1906 Completed with full crew for service with Atlantic Fleet, until Mar 1907.
4 Mar 1907 Transferred to Channel Fleet, until Mar 1909 when Channel Fleet became 2nd Division, Home Fleet. With Home Fleet until Aug 1914.
1909–10 Refit at Portsmouth.
14 July 1910 Collided with barque *Loch Trool*, slight damage. On Fleet reorganization in May 1912, all eight *King Edward*s were assigned to form 3rd BS, First Home Fleet
Nov 1912 3rd BS detached to Mediterranean because of trouble in Balkans (arrived 27th). Took part in blockade of Montenegro by International Force and subsequent occupation of Scutari.
27 June 1913 Rejoined Home Fleet.
Aug—Nov 1914 3rd BS, Grand Fleet Rosyth.
26 Jan 1915 Grounded in the Forth, but refloated after 36 hours, although bottom was considerably damaged. Refitted at Devonport.
29 April 1916 Squadron transferred to Sheerness, and separated from the Grand Fleet organization.

HIBERNIA
Outboard profile, as fitted for
aircraft take-off experiments 1912

Note runway over forecastle and aircraft handling derrick
to foremast.

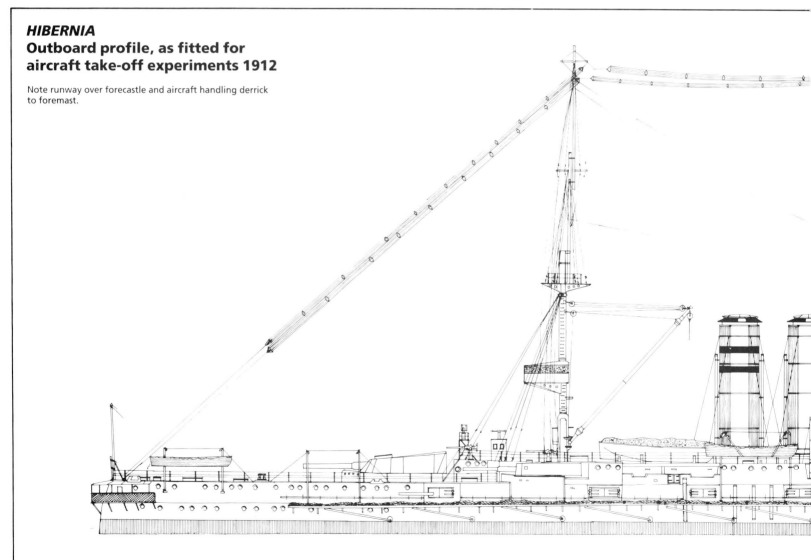

Left: *Hibernia* at Sheerness, January 1912 (see report). General view of ship showing her flying-off runway. The close-up was taken shortly before Commander Sampson made his historical flight. Note the large derrick for retrieving the aircraft from the water.

Right: Loss of *King Edward VII*. Fatally stricken off Pentland Firth on 6 January 1916, she inclines slowly to starboard which allowed her crew time to abandon ship. Note 'KE' on turret sides; netting around tops, no anti-torpedo nets and no topmast to main.

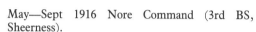

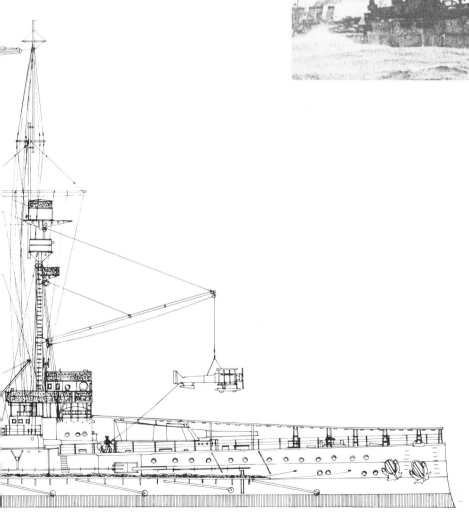

May—Sept 1916 Nore Command (3rd BS, Sheerness).
Aug—Sept 1916 Refit at Portsmouth and transferred to Adriatic on completion.
Sept 1916—Feb 1917 Adriatic (2nd detached squadron).
Feb—Mar 1917 Refit at Gibraltar.
Mar 1917 Attached to 9th CS for Atlantic Patrol and convoy duties until Nov 1918, based mainly at Sierra Leone.
Mar 1917 relieved *King Alfred* (cruiser) as Flagship of the Squadron.
May 1917 Refit at Bermuda.
9 Nov 1918 Torpedoed by U50 *en route* to Gibraltar. Minutes after the first explosion, there was a second, which started a fire in one of the 9.2in magazines, exploding a quantity of cordite. Before the second explosion, however, the ship took a list of 10° but this did not increase after the second and she remained in this position for more than 2½ hours before sinking. Fifty men were lost and eighty were injured.

The Court of Inquiry highlighted some interesting points: It was found practically impossible to locate all flooding valves for the magazines because of darkness below decks, and when some were found it proved extremely difficult to turn them because of their location; had they been sited on the upper deck, it might have been possible to flood the magazine and the ship might have been saved. Most of the fatal casualties were caught in the passages near the magazine and were overcome by poisonous fumes from the burning cordite. *Britannia* was the last British warship to be sunk by enemy action in the First World War.

COMMONWEALTH
Outboard profile, as refitted 1918

Note removal of nets, shortened topmasts, increased
elevation to 12in guns, 6in guns fitted on upper deck,
improved fire control, tripod to foremast and anti-torpedo
bulges.

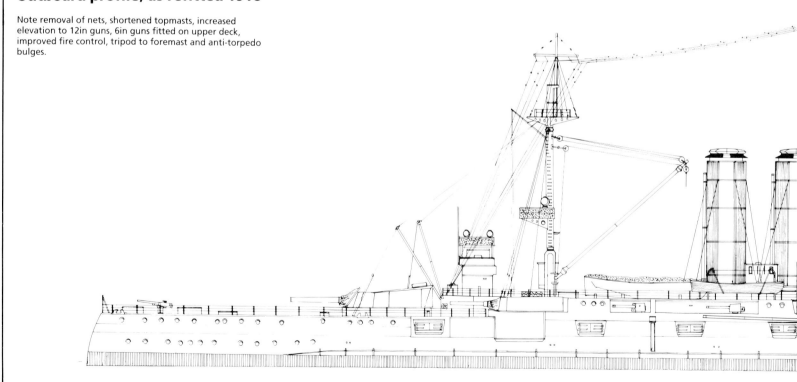

HISTORY: *COMMONWEALTH*

Laid down and built by Fairfield, Govan.
14 Mar 1905 Delivered to Portsmouth and placed in reserve until May 1905.
9 May 1905 Completed to full crew at Devonport for service in Atlantic Fleet, until Mar 1907.
11 Feb 1907 Collided with *Albemarle* near Lagos, sustaining damage to bulkheads, plates and frames.
Feb—May 1907 Repaired at Devonport. Transferred to Channel Fleet Mar 1907 while still in dockyard hands and did not actually commission until 28 May 1907. With Channel Fleet until Mar 1909. Channel Fleet became 2nd Division, Home Fleet in Mar 1909. With Home Fleet until Aug 1914.

Oct 1910—June 1911 Refit at Devonport.
On Fleet reorganization May 1912, all eight *King Edwards* assigned to form the 3rd BS, First Home Fleet.
Nov 1912 Detached to Mediterranean because of troubles in the Balkans (arrived Malta 27 Nov). Took part in subsequent blockade of Montenegro.
27 June 1913 Rejoined Home Fleet.
Aug—Nov 1914 with Grand Fleet. Squadron employed with Grand Fleet cruisers in Northern Patrol areas.
2 Nov Detached to reinforce Channel Fleet.
Nov 1914 Channel Fleet (3rd BS, Portland).
13 Nov The *King Edwards* returned to Grand Fleet (Rosyth).
Nov 1914—April 1916 With Grand Fleet.

29 April 1916 Squadron transferred to Sheerness and separated from Grand Fleet organization 3 May.
May 1916—Aug 1917 Nore Command (3rd BS, Sheerness).
Aug 1917 Paid off at Portsmouth for extensive refit for service as gunnery training ship.
Aug 1917—April 1918 Refit at Portsmouth.
16 April 1918 Commissioned for Northern Patrol work, until Aug 1918.
21 Aug 1918 Transferred to Grand Fleet command as seagoing gunnery training ship, Invergordon, until Feb 1921.
Feb 1921 Paid off and placed on disposal list at Portsmouth in April 1921.
18 Nov 1921 Sold to Slough Trading Co. Subsequently resold to German scrappers and towed to Germany to be broken up.

HISTORY: *DOMINION*

Laid down by Vickers, Barrow on 23 May 1902 and began her trials in May 1905.
15 Aug 1905 Completed to full crew at Portsmouth for service in Atlantic Fleet, until Mar 1907.
16 Aug 1906 Grounded in Gulf of St Lawrence and sustained severe pitted plating, and some double bottom compartments flooded.
Sept 1906—Jan 1907 Temporarily repaired at Bermuda and then repairs completed at Chatham Feb—June 1907. Mar 1907 Transferred to Channel Fleet while still in dockyard hands, and did not actually commission for this until completion of refit in May 1907.
Mar 1907—Mar 1909 Channel Fleet.
On Fleet reorganization 24 Mar 1909 Channel Fleet became 2nd Division, Home Fleet.
Mar 1909—Aug 1914 Home Fleet. All *King Edwards* assigned to 3rd BS, First Home Fleet.
Dominion remained temporarily in 2nd BS, but transferred to 3rd BS in June. 3rd BS detached to Mediterranean (Balkans trouble), arrived at Malta 27 Nov. Took part in blockade of Montenegro.
27 June 1913 Rejoined Home Fleet.
Aug—Nov 1914 Grand Fleet 3rd BS. Temporarily working with cruisers Northern Patrol.
29 April 1916 Squadron transferred to Sheerness. Nore Command (separated from Grand Fleet organization).
May 1916—Mar 1918 3rd BS Sheerness.
Unsuccessfully attacked by German U-boat in May 1916.

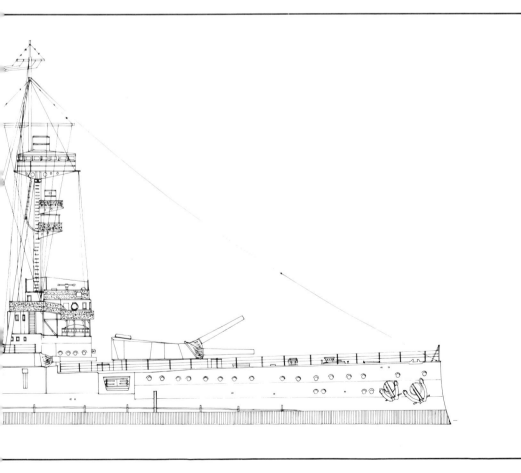

Left: *Commonwealth* in 1918. Reconstructed and painted-up in one of Norman Wilkinson's dazzle efforts before being used as Training Ship for gun layers and director experiments. Colours were light-blue, dark-blue and shades of grey.

Centre and bottom: Loss of *Britannia*, 9 November 1918. The last British battleship lost during the war. Most of her crew were safely taken off by destroyers because she remained upright for about three hours before capsizing and sinking.

June 1917 Refit at Portsmouth.
Mar 1918 Paid off on breaking up of 3rd BS. By 1 Mar 1918, *Dreadnought* (Flagship) and *Dominion* were the only remaining units of 3rd BS.
Mar 1918 Selected as additional parent ship for preparation of Zeebrugge and Ostend Expeditions and stationed in the Swin, until May 1918.
2 May 1918 Paid off to Nore Reserve, until May 1919. Employed as accommodation ship.
29 May 1919 Placed on disposal list at Chatham.
9 May 1921 Sold to T. W. Ward & Co Ltd.
30 Sept 1923 Towed to Belfast to be stripped.
28 Oct 1924 Arrived at Preston for scrapping.

HISTORY: *HINDUSTAN*

Built at Clydebank and began trials in January 1905.
22 Aug 1905 Completed to full crew at Portsmouth for service with Atlantic Fleet, until Mar 1907.
Mar 1907 Transferred to Channel Fleet, until Mar 1909.
Mar 1909—Aug 1914 Home Fleet.
1909 and 1910 Refit at Portsmouth.
Nov 1912 With 3rd BS detached to Mediterranean during Balkans trouble. Took part in blockade of Montenegro and subsequent occupation of Scutari. *Africa* and *Hindustan* returned home in Feb 1913 and temporarily attached to 4th BS pending return of squadron 27 June 1913.
Aug—Nov 1914 Grand Fleet (3rd BS). Working with cruiser squadron on Northern Patrol.
2 Nov 1914 Detached to reinforce Channel Fleet.
13 Nov 1914 Returned to Grand Fleet, until April 1916. Based at Sheerness and separated from Grand Fleet organization 29 April 1916.
May 1916—Feb 1918 Nore Command (3rd BS Sheerness).
Feb 1918 Selected for service as parent ship for preparation of Zeebrugge and Ostend Expeditions and stationed in the Swin, until May 1918. Collided with destroyer *Wrestler* May 1918, *Wrestler* badly damaged.
15 May 1918 Paid off into Reserve, Nore.
May 1918—June 1919 Reserve (Nore). Employed as accommodation ship for RN Barracks, Chatham.
June 1919 Placed on disposal list at Chatham.
Aug 1919 On sale list.
9 May 1921. Sold to T. W. Ward & Co Ltd.
1923 Towed to Belfast to be stripped.
14 Oct 1923 Arrived at Preston for scrapping.

HISTORY: *HIBERNIA*

Laid down at Devonport on 6 January 1904 and completed in December 1906.

2 Jan 1907 Commissioned at Devonport as 2nd Flag, Atlantic Fleet, until Feb 1907.

27 Feb 1907 Transferred to Channel Fleet as 2nd Flag, until Mar 1909.

Mar—Aug 1914 Home Fleet.

14 July 1910 Rammed by barque *Loch Trool* just after latter had been in collision with *Britannia*.

Jan 1912 Relieved in 2nd Division by *Orion* and reduced to 3rd Division, Nore.

Equipment for experiments in flying-off aircraft fitted and first flight ever made from British warship **underway** was carried out during tests.

Gear tranferred from *Africa* to *Hibernia*, in May 1912, and flights were witnessed by HM the King during a four-day visit to the Fleet at Portland. Equipment later transferred to *London*.

14 May *Hibernia* completed to full crew at Sheerness as 2nd Flag (RA) 3rd BS.

Nov 1912 3rd BS detached to Mediterranean during Balkans trouble.

27 June 1913 Rejoined Home Fleet.

Aug—Nov 1914 Grand Fleet (2nd Flag, 3rd BS). Detached to reinforce Channel Fleet. All *King Edwards* returned to Grand Fleet (Rosyth) 13 Nov.

Nov 1914—Nov 1915 Grand Fleet.

One division of 3rd BS detached to Mediterranean, arrived 14 Dec.

Dec 1915—Jan 1916 Eastern Mediterranean.

Covered evacuation of Helles ('V' and 'W' Beaches) 8–9 Jan 1916. Stationed at Milo later in Jan in case pressure on Greece became necessary to save French force at Salonika. Relieved as Divisional Flag by *Russell* and left for home late in Jan. Arrived at Devonport 5 Feb.

Feb—Mar 1916 Refit at Devonport and joined Grand Fleet.

Mar—April 1916 Grand Fleet (2nd Flag, 3rd BS, Rosyth). Squadron transferred to Sheerness 29 April 1916 and separated from Grand Fleet organization.

May 1916—Oct 1917 Nore Command.

Oct 1917 Paid off to Nore Reserve at Chatham, until July 1919. Overflow ship at Chatham.

July 1919 Placed on disposal list at Chatham.

8 Nov 1921 Sold to Stanlee Shipbreaking Co, Dover. Resold to Slough Trading Co, 1922, and towed to Germany for scrapping in Nov 1922.

HISTORY: *AFRICA*

Laid down at Chatham Dockyard 27 Jan 1904 and completed in November 1906.

6 Nov 1906 Commissioned at Chatham for service in Atlantic Fleet, until Mar 1907.

4 Mar 1907 Transferred to Channel Fleet, until June 1908. Collided with SS *Ormuz* off Portland 23 Mar 1907, slight damage.

June 1908 Transferred to Nore Division, Home Fleet, until Aug 1914.

25 April 1911 Commissioned at Chatham as Flagship (VA), 3rd and 4th Divisions, Home Fleet.

24 July 1911 Relieved by *King Edward*.

Jan 1912 Specially fitted for flying-off aircraft; first flight ever made from large British warship while at Sheerness. Equipment transferred to *Hibernia* May 1912.

1912 Refit at Chatham. All *King Edwards* formed 3rd BS, Home Fleet on reorganization.

Nov 1912 Detached to Mediterranean for Balkans trouble. Took part in blockade of Montenegro, and occupation of Scutari. *Africa* and *Hindustan* returned home Feb 1913.

Aug—Nov 1914 Grand Fleet (3rd BS). Working with cruisers on Northern Patrol.

2 Nov 1914 Whole squadron eight *King Edwards*, five *Duncans*) detached to reinforce Channel Fleet against threat of enemy attack. *King Edwards* returned to Grand Fleet, *Duncans* remained in Channel to form new 6th BS.

Nov 1914—April 1916 Grand Fleet (3rd BS).

Dec 1915—Jan 1916 Refit at Belfast.

29 April 1916 3rd BS transferred to Sheerness, arrived 2 May.

May—Sept 1916 Nore Command (3rd BS, Sheerness).

Aug—Sept 1916 Refit at Portsmouth and transferred to Adriatic on completion.

Sept 1916—Jan 1917 In Adriatic.

Jan—Mar 1917 Refit at Gibraltar.

Mar 1917 Attached to 9th CS for Atlantic Patrol and convoy duty, until Oct 1918.

9th CS originally in Finisterre—Madeira area, but from Aug 1916 the ships were held available for service anywhere in the Atlantic. *Africa* was based mainly at Sierra Leone and was employed on the Sierra Leone–Capetown convoys.

Dec 1917—Jan 1918 Refit at Rio de Janerio.

Oct 1918 Returned home and reduced to Reserve at Portsmouth in Nov, until Mar 1920. Employed as accommodation ship. Selected in Dec 1919 to replace *Diadem* (cruiser) as Stokers' TS, Portsmouth, but this was later cancelled.

Below: *Commonwealth* as training ship, paying off at Portsmouth in February 1921. Note the tripod to foremast; directors in tops; searchlight distribution; tops cut out of 12in turrets for increased elevation to guns; and large anti-torpedo bulge on waterline.

Bottom: *Commonwealth* on the sale list at Portsmouth, 1921. Note sternwalk has been removed.

Opposite page: *Triumph* as completed, leaving Vickers' yard in January 1904 (note colours of ship). Originally described as armoured cruisers of a powerful type, they were built for the Republic of Chile, and consequently were not easy to incorporate into the Royal Navy. Their 10in guns had to have ammunition specially made for these two ships.

Mar 1920 Placed on sale list.
30 June 1920 Sold to Ellis & Co, Newcastle for £32,825. Broken up at Newcastle.

HISTORY: *NEW ZEALAND*

Built at Portsmouth from 1903, completed in 1905.
11 July 1905 Commissioned with full crew at Devonport for service with Atlantic Fleet, until Mar 1907.
Oct—Dec 1906 Refit at Gibraltar.
4 Mar 1907 Transferred to Channel Fleet, until Mar 1909.
Mar 1909—Aug 1914 Home Fleet.
1 Dec 1911 Renamed *Zealandia* to release name for new battlecruiser presented to British Navy by New Zealand Government. It was originally proposed to rename the ship *Caledonia*, but this did not meet with the approval of New Zealand people. With 3rd BS when detached to Mediterranean for Balkans trouble. Took part in blockade of Montenegro and occupation of Scutari.
27 June 1913 Rejoined Home Fleet.
Aug—Nov 1914 Grand Fleet (3rd BS). Working with cruisers on Northern Patrol.
10 Sept 1914 Rammed German U-boat in North Sea.
Nov 1914 Channel Fleet (3rd BS Portland).
6 Nov 1915 Detached to Dardanelles, arrived 14 Dec.
Dec 1915—Jan 1916 Eastern Mediterranean.
Late Jan 1916 Left for home with *Hibernia*, arrived Portsmouth 6 Feb.
Feb—Mar 1916 Refit at Portsmouth.
26 Mar Rejoined Grand Fleet (Rosyth), until April 1916.
29 April 1916 Transferred to Sheerness.
May 1916—Sept 1917 Nore Command (3rd BS Sheerness).
Dec 1916—June 1917 Refit at Chatham.
20 Sept 1917 Paid off into Reserve at Portsmouth, until June 1919.
Jan—Sept 1918 Refitted at Portsmouth as gunnery training ship. Many experiments carried out including director control equipment of different varieties. Never actually employed as gunnery training ship and remained paid off at Portsmouth.
2 June 1919 Placed on disposal list.
8 Nov 1921 Sold to Stanlee Shipbreaking Co.
Resold to Slough Trading Co Ltd 1922 and left Portsmouth for Germany and scrapping 23 Nov 1923.

SWIFTSURE AND *TRIUMPH*

PURCHASE FROM CHILE

DESIGN

Projected late in 1901 as a reply to the Argentinian armoured cruisers *Moreno* and *Rivadavia*, during a period of acute political tension between the South American countries of Chile and Argentina. Examination of official documents (Covers, etc.) of this pair of ships reveals many gaps in the recording of their conception and history. The Admiralty has tended to lean on Sir Edward Reed's personal account which was read before the Institution of Naval Architects at the spring meeting on 23 March 1904.

'Their origin is to be found in the fact that towards the end of 1901 the relations between Chile and Argentina, over their mutual-boundary question, were so severely strained as to bring the two countries to the brink of war. Happening to visit Chile at the time for the benefit of my health, just before reaching Valparaiso I met a powerful Chilean Squadron proceeding south in battle array. All the ships composing it had been built by Sir W. G. Armstrong, Whitworth & Co., at Elswick under my own superintendence and responsibility, in more or less association with some Admiral of the Chilean Navy, but so as to embody all that was forthcoming from the ability and experience of that great company, and especially from their extremely able naval architect Mr Philip Watts, then the Shipbuilding Director at Elswick, and now the Director of Naval Construction at the Admiralty. The leading ship, flying the flag of my friend Rear-Admiral Goni, was that *O'Higgins* which by her remarkable combination of gun power, speed, and coal carrying power with very moderate dimensions excited so much comment four or five years ago.

I had scarcely arrived at Valparaiso when the question of reinforcing the Chilean Navy by purchase or construction of two powerful battleships came under urgent consideration. The purchase of such ships being found impracticable, the steps for building them had to be taken, and to this end I was put into close communication with one of the most capable and influential men in Chile, Vice-Admiral Montt, the Director General of the Chilean Navy, a man of singularly quiet and reserved manner, but one who nevertheless had conducted war successfully, and had subsequently presided over the destinies of Chile, as President of the Republic, with marked distinction. No existing design of any kind, or emanating from any source whatever, was seen or mentioned during my conference with ex-President Admiral Montt, but it was his desire (in order to limit the cost) to keep the tonnage, if possible, down to 11,000 tons; but, with a speed of 19 knots, to carry an armament of four 10in guns, as bow and stern chaser, and at least ten, and if possible twelve, 7½in guns, of which four were to be upon the upper deck.

This left either six or eight of the 7½in guns to be disposed of, according as I might decide upon providing ten or twelve of these guns; and it was

TRIUMPH
Outboard profile and plan, as fitted 1904

Constitucion (Swiftsure): Launch figures

Displacement: 5,725 tons
Length: 435ft 11in pp
Beam: 71ft 1¼in
Beam as moulded: 71ft
Depth of keel from upper deck: 42ft 0¾in
Draught (shortly after launch): 11ft 5in forward,
17ft 6in aft
Recorded weight of hull: 4,244 tons
Breakage at launch:
longitudinal in a distance of 259ft 0¼in = ¼in hog
transverse in a distance of 84ft 1¼in = 0in sag.

Weights on board (tons)
Armour: 1,220
Men, ballast, gear: 191
Machinery: 70
Total: 1,481.

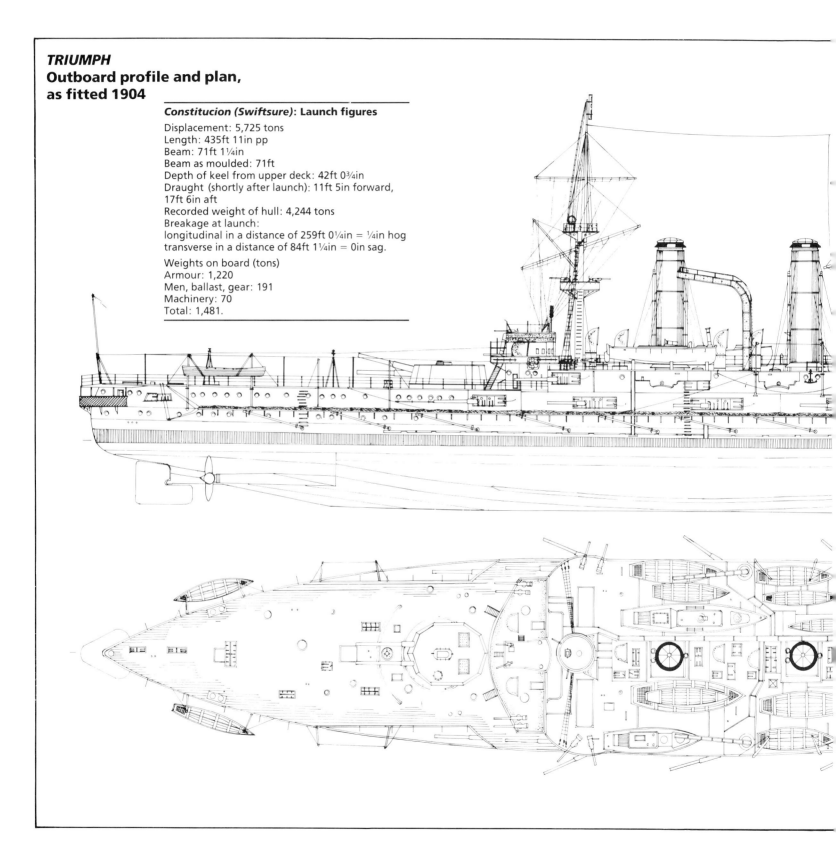

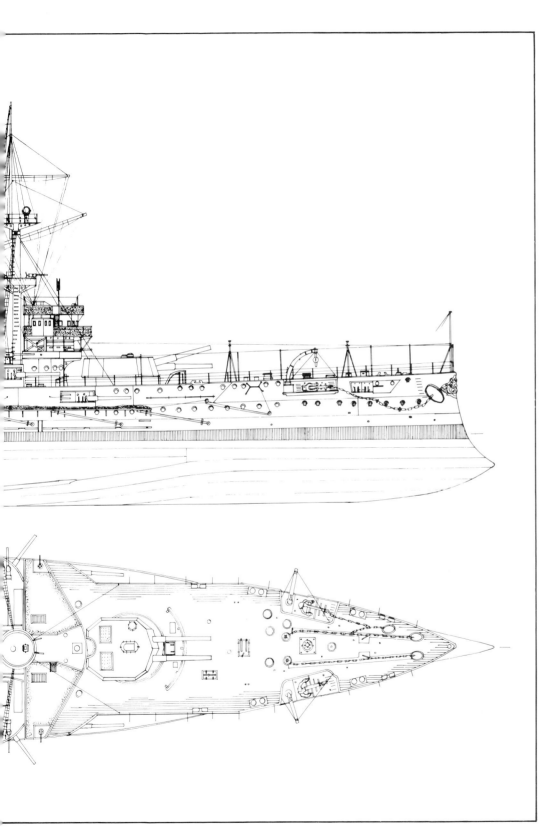

further arranged—as was, in fact, almost a matter of necessity—that if I could not succeed on the voyage home in placing six remaining 7½in guns in turrets or barbettes, so as to give them a greater height above the sea, and a greater range than the main deck guns—a matter which I desired to attempt, but without success—then the main deck battery was to be resorted to, and was to contain eight of these 7½in guns.

Many other matters were settled between Admiral Montt and myself. Owing to the pressing necessity of rapid building I was authorized to proceed to England as quickly as possible, and to obtain tenders for ships of the design thus settled upon from the Armstrong Company, and from another firm which could quickly produce hull, machinery, and armament complete, on which account, among others, we selected the eminent firm of Vickers, Sons & Maxim.'

Orders were placed with Armstrongs and Vickers on 26 February 1902 and it is probable that

---

Libertad and Constitucion: Final legend

Displacement (tons): 11,728 normal
Length: 436ft pp
Beam: 71ft
Draught: 24ft 7½in (mean)
Freeboard: 22ft forward, 17ft amidships, 19ft aft
Sinkage: 53.79 tons per inch.

Armament
Four 10in
Fourteen 7.5in
Fourteen 14pdr
Four 6pdr
Four MG
Three 18in submerged torpedo tubes.

Armour
Main belt: 7in–3in
Bulkheads: 10in–6in
Casemates: 7in
Conning tower: 11in
Decks: 1½in–1in, 3in inclines
Weight: 3,074 tons.

SHP: 12,500 for 19 knots
Fuel: 800 tons coal normal, 2,000 tons max.
Machinery weight: 1,020 tons
Hull: 4,630 tons

Hull was to be divided into 170 watertight compartments, to be fitted with double bottom under magazines and machinery spaces, with framing at 4ft intervals.

Top right: *Triumph* 1904. Although taken over by the Admiralty during the Russo-Japanese war of 1904, when British relations with Russia were somewhat strained, they were never popular in the service because of their extensively foreign design.

Bottom right: *Swiftsure* as completed. The two ships were quite easy to tell apart; note the smaller bow crest in this ship; no houses at end of bridge; 10in turrets differently shaped; and light funnel caps compared with *Triumph*.

the final design was one from either Vickers' or Armstrongs' archives modified by Reed to suit the requirements of the Chilean Navy. The design called for:

1. Displacement of about 11,000 tons with ability to use docking facilities at Talcahuano, which limited beam and draught.

2. Armament to be four 10in and ten or twelve 7.5in (four on upper deck).

3. Speed of 19 knots.

The demand for heavy armament and high speed, on restricted dimensions and displacement, necessitated a long, narrow-hulled, lightly built and only moderately protected design, the direct antithesis of Reed's earlier ships, all of which had been characterized by a short, handy hull, very strongly constructed, with armament subordinated to protection. Owing to a change of heart, and

financial problems, both ships were put up for sale early in 1903, shortly after they had been launched, and were subsequently purchased by the Royal Navy for £2,432,000 in December 1903, just prior to the outbreak of the Russo-Japanese War, possibly to prevent their sale to Russia.

Although powerfully armed for the displacement and, on completion, among the fastest battleships extant, they were not generally regarded as an altogether satisfactory type for the British Navy on the grounds that the calibre of the main armament was below exisiting standards for first class battleships, and speed was too slow for any type of cruiser work. They were renamed *Swiftsure* and *Triumph* (*Constitucion* and *Libertad*) respectively, on 7 December 1903.

The DNC asked what would be required to bring them into line with existing British capital ships. A

report was returned from the respective builders' yards which had been visited by leading British naval staff:

1. Conning tower communications need regrouping for the 7.5in guns; present arrangement is only fitted with voice pipes.

2. None of the small guns such as rifles, machine-guns, etc., are of the same pattern as RN—suggest that all these should be removed.

3. The casemates of the secondary guns seem to be satisfactory with 20rpg in the racks, plus electrical hoists for such.

4. Magazines and shell rooms are somewhat different to our ships, with the shell rooms leading into each other. Ammunition supply is quite good with 40rpg stowed in the passage.

5. The 7.5in are of a different design from our cruisers, and it would seem that the 7.5in guns

---

Swiftsure and *Triumph*: Particulars, as completed

Construction
Swiftsure (ex-*Constitution*): Elswick; laid down 26 Feb 1902; launched 12 Jan 1903; completed June 1904
Triumph (ex-*Libertad*): Vickers; laid down 26 Feb 1902; launched 15 Jan 1903; completed June 1904.

Displacement (tons)
Swiftsure: 11,740 (load), 13,432 (deep)
Triumph: 11,985 (load), 13,640 (deep).

Dimensions
Length: 436ft pp, 462ft 6in wl, 475ft 3in oa (*Swiftsure*)
Beam: 71ft 1¼in
Draught: 24ft 7½in (load) (mean), 27ft 3in (deep).

Armament
Four 10in 45cal Mk VI (*Swiftsure*)
Four 10in 45cal Mk VIII (*Triumph*) *see* Gunnery notes
Fourteen 7.5in 50cal
Two 12pdr (8cwt)
Four 6pdr
Four 3pdr (saluting)
Four MG
Two 18in torpedo tubes submerged; nine 18in torpedoes.

Shell stowage
10in; 90rpg
90 AP shot capped
126 AP shells
144 common steel

216 fighting charges
144 reduced charges
450 electric primers
7.5in; 150rpg
525 AP shot capped
735 AP shells
840 common steel
14pdr; 400 rpg.

Armour
Main belt: 7in–6in–3in
Lower deck sides: 7in with 2in bulkhead
Battery: 7in
Casemates: 7in–3in
Barbettes: 10in–3in–2in
Turrets: 9in–8in–3in
Conning tower: 11in
Decks: 3in–1in
Total weight: approximately 3,122 tons.

Machinery
Two sets 4-cylinder vertical inverted direct-acting triple expansion surface condensing engines, twin propellers
Cylinder diameter: 29in HP, 47in IP, 54in LP
Stroke: 3ft 3in
Boilers: twelve large tube Yarrow separated in four compartments, working pressure 280psi
Total heating surface: 37,524sq ft
Grate area: 664sq ft
Weight of each boiler with water: 34½ tons, 1,008 tubes in each boiler (average length 6ft 9in)
Length of boiler rooms: 84ft 1¼in

Length of engine rooms: 42ft 0⅛in
Designed SHP: 12,500 for 19 knots.
Fuel: 800 tons coal normal, 2,048 tons max.
Coal consumption: 350 tons per day at full power, 179 tons per day at ⅗ths power, 50 tons per day at 8 knots
Radius of action: 6,210nm at 10 knots.

Ship's boats
Pinnaces (steam): one 56ft
Pinnaces (sail): one 36ft
Launches (steam): two 36ft
Cutters: three 30ft
Whalers: one 27ft
Gigs: three 30ft
Dinghies: two 18ft
Skiff dinghies: one 16ft.

Searchlights
Five 30in: two on forebridge P+S, one starboard side of signal house; three 24in: two on platform abreast mainmast, one port side of after signal house.

Complement
729 *Swiftsure*, 1906
741 *Triumph*, 1906; 732, 1908; 803, 1914.

Costs
Triumph: £847,520 plus guns £110,000
Swiftsure: £846,596 plus guns £110,000.

Wireless
Type 1 then type 2.

would need their chambers enlarged to take our shells.

6. 14pdrs would not at present take service ammunition, and the 12pdrs also require attention.

7. Modification of the boats and their arrangement are required.

Obviously, little was needed to bring the ships into line with Royal Navy requirements, but the question was, where to place the two odd vessels within the Fleet?

The Chilean requirements had called for a displacement of about 11,000 tons with beam and draught restricted to permit use of the double graving dock at Talcahuano and increased length required to offset this, the ships being considerably longer, narrower and nominally of lighter draught than contemporary designs.

They were nominally 2,000 tons lighter than the *Duncan* class, with an increase of 47ft 9in in overall length, but on a reduction of 4ft 6in beam and 2ft designed mean draught. As, however, the *Duncan*s turned out well under and the *Swiftsure*s well over their normal draught and displacement figures, the actual differences in these figures was considerably

less, averaging about 3in and 1,343 tons in the normal load.

The scantlings were considerably lighter than in British practice and at one time *Swiftsure* developed some degree of structural weakness which had to be overcome by strengthening, at various times, certain parts of the hull. *Triumph*, however, always proved sound, and there is no record of her receiving similar treatment.

ARMAMENT

There is no doubt that, for their size and displacement, they were powerfully armed ships which could, if necessary, put up a terrific volume of semi-heavy gunfire. In principle, the armament embodied Admiral J. Fisher's views of the early 1890s (but reversed in 1904) that the ideal battleship armament consisted of the smallest effective big gun, and the largest practicable secondary gun relative to displacement.

In service, however, the 10in gun was generally regarded as too light for battle fleet units, and the 7.5in secondary gun as too long for carrying on the main deck. Nevertheless, Admiral J. O. Hopkins

recorded his view that: 'The new 10in mounted in these ships is an adequate battleship weapon.' It was, admittedly, effective against the $7^3/4$in and 9in belts of the latest Russian and German battleships, although it would not penetrate the thick 11in belt of the French *République* at normal battle ranges.

Moreover, an effective comparison, it was claimed, was that these two ships, because of their innovatory armament, could 'fight the whole five ships of the *Royal Sovereign* class, now serving in the Home Fleet, with every fair chance of success'—obviously the writer had turned a blind eye to the new ships' inadequate armour protection, especially around the barbettes, which might have to withstand eight to twelve 13.5in shells every few minutes.

Swiftsure and *Triumph* were armed by their respective builders, and accordingly featured slight variations in detail. The turrets carrying the 10in guns differed in many respects, and most notably to the eye (*see* drawings). The 10in BL guns in *Swiftsure* were Mk VI and special to that ship. They were of wire construction, but had no inner 'A' tube. The 'A' tube extended from the seat of the

Left: *Triumph* was one of the British ships present at a review alongside the French Fleet at Spithead, held to enhance relations between the two countries (1905). Both fleets were reviewed by the King and Queen, the Prince and Princess of Wales, and the Princes Edward and Albert, from the Royal Yacht *Victoria and Albert*.

Below: *Swiftsure* leaving Portsmouth to join the Mediterranean Fleet in April 1909.

Bottom: *Triumph* and *Commonwealth* on manoeuvres in 1908. Note water smothering bows, and unusual funnel bands in *Triumph*.

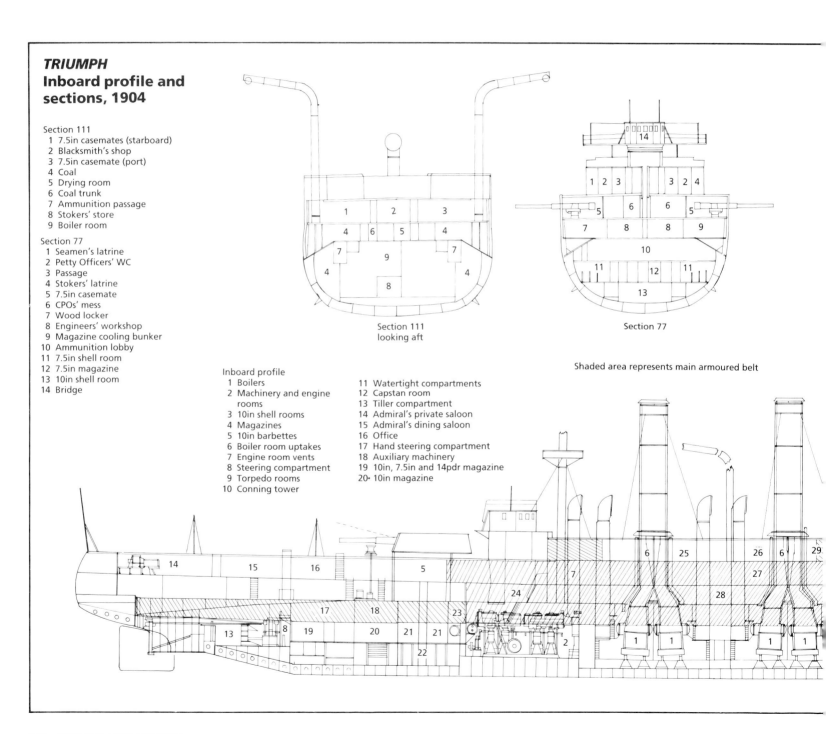

TRIUMPH
Inboard profile and sections, 1904

Section 111
1 7.5in casemates (starboard)
2 Blacksmith's shop
3 7.5in casemate (port)
4 Coal
5 Drying room
6 Coal trunk
7 Ammunition passage
8 Stokers' store
9 Boiler room

Section 77
1 Seamen's latrine
2 Petty Officers' WC
3 Passage
4 Stokers' latrine
5 7.5in casemate
6 CPOs' mess
7 Wood locker
8 Engineers' workshop
9 Magazine cooling bunker
10 Ammunition lobby
11 7.5in shell room
12 7.5in magazine
13 10in shell room
14 Bridge

Inboard profile
1 Boilers
2 Machinery and engine rooms
3 10in shell rooms
4 Magazines
5 10in barbettes
6 Boiler room uptakes
7 Engine room vents
8 Steering compartment
9 Torpedo rooms
10 Conning tower
11 Watertight compartments
12 Capstan room
13 Tiller compartment
14 Admiral's private saloon
15 Admiral's dining saloon
16 Office
17 Hand steering compartment
18 Auxiliary machinery
19 10in, 7.5in and 14pdr magazine
20 10in magazine

Section 111
looking aft

Section 77

Shaded area represents main armoured belt

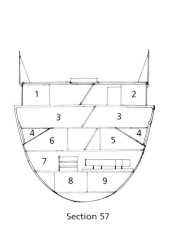
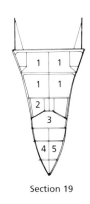

Section 57
1 Gunners' store
2 Dispensary
3 Crew space
4 Stores
5 Bread room
6 Issue room
7 Submerged torpedo room
8 Submerged mine room
9 Stowage for cable net

Section 19
1 Crew space
2 14pdr ammunition
3 Provision room
4 Canteen
5 Doctor's store

Section 57

Section 19

21 10in shell room	31 Engineers' workshop	41 Dry gun-cotton magazine
22 7.5in magazine	32 Ammunition lobby	42 Spirit room
23 Ammunition lobby	33 Auxiliary machinery	43 Provision room
24 Engineers' office	34 Provision room	44 Doctor's store
25 Engineers', gun room, galley	35 Feedwater tank	45 Wet gun-cotton magazine
26 Crew's galley	36 Cabin locker	46 Print store
27 Stokers' wash place	37 Paint room	47 Sand tank
28 Drying room	38 Cold store	48 Carpenters' stores
29 Bakery	39 Boatswains' stores	49 Carpenters' stores
30 Lamp room	40 Submarine mine store	50 14pdr auxiliary engine

obturator to the muzzle, and over it were shrunk breech pieces which were prolonged at the rear for the breech bush, and a 'B' tube extending to the muzzle. The wire was wound over the breech piece and a section of the 'B' tube. The 'C' tube and jacket were fitted over the 'B' tube and wire. The 10in gun in *Triumph* was Mark VII, and again, special to that ship. The gun was of wire construction, and consisted of an inner 'A' tube, and 'A' tube, a series of layers of wires and a 'B' tube and jacket. The wire only extended to a point about halfway along the bore. The 10in in both ships were 45cal; *Swiftsure*'s were 467.6 inches in length, and *Triumph*'s were 462.75in. The Armstrong Co made up extra 10in guns for *Swiftsure* which were Mk VI★ and these had an inner 'A' tube like those fitted in *Triumph*.

After trials in the ships, it was claimed that the rate of fire for the 10in in *Swiftsure* was nominally 50 per cent higher than that of the Vickers in *Triumph*, the latter being about the same as for contemporary 12in guns.

They were the only British battleships to carry 7.5in guns, although these had been considered for the *King Edward*s in 1901, and they were being adopted in British cruisers. The 7.5in shell was too heavy to be manhandled and needed mechanical handling equipment. The gunnery trials indicated that the envisaged nominal rate of fire could be

***Swiftsure*: GM**

Based on inclining experiments, February 1904

	Draught	GM
'A' Condition (= load)*	24ft 7½in (mean)	3.44ft
'B' Condition (= deep load)**	27ft 3in (mean)	4.01ft
'C' Condition (= light)***	23ft	2.75ft

*Fully equipped plus 800 tons coal, plus 60 tons fresh water.
**Fully equipped plus 2,048 tons coal, plus 110 tons fresh water.
***Lightened to 10,694 tons.

***Triumph*: GM**

Based on inclining experiments, March 1904

	Draught	GM
'A' Condition (= load)*	24ft 10in (mean)	3.45ft
'B' Condition (= deep load)**	27ft 4½in (mean)	4ft

*Fully equipped plus 800 tons coal, plus 80 tons fresh water.
**Fully equipped plus 2,000 tons coal, plus 110 tons fresh water.

maintained, but the arrangement was disliked owing to the rather large guns being placed on the main deck and taking up too much room amidships.

Main deck battery guns were about 13ft 2in above the waterline at normal load, but as both ships considerably exceeded the designed draught, they were actually only about 12ft 6in above in this condition, and even lower at 10ft in the deep load,

muzzles of the 7.5in dipping readily in any sea-way. During their careers, it was reported that these guns were practically unfightable at anything over 15 knots or even in a slight sea.

The hull side was recessed before and abaft the 7.5in battery to increase the end-on arcs of fire of the forward and aft guns, but those amidships, because of the severe blast to one another, were severely limited in their training. The secondary

armament was the heaviest extant (1904) in respect of weight of broadside delivered in one minute; the shell stowage was also on the generous side, in having 90 rounds per gun for the 10in and 150 rounds for the 7.5 (compared with 80rpg 12in and 200rpg 6in in ships designed for the Royal Navy).

Anti-torpedo armament was more powerful than in any contemporary British design, and except for the four main deck guns, was well placed. They

Below: *Swiftsure* at Devonport, 1908–9.

Bottom: *Swiftsure* in 1912–13, showing searchlight arrangement in lower top.

were the only British battleships to carry 14pdrs, but in fact, as altered, these were little more effective than the 12pdr 8cwt. Large shields were fitted to these guns in *Swiftsure*, but much smaller ones in *Triumph*. With the contemporary *Queen* class, they were the last battleships completed for the British Navy with fighting tops for QF guns, or with any of these guns carried in ports on the main deck where they had always been found of limited value owing to the extremely low command.

ARMOUR

The armour plates for these ships were constructed at their respective builders' yards. Little is known about *Swiftsure*, but the armour for *Triumph* was made at Vickers' River Don Works, and thoroughly tested at the Company's Eskmeale range in the presence of Captains Stuven, Nef, Schroder and other important officers in the Chilean Navy. The 7in plates, to be used for the main strakes, were 8ft by 6ft in size, and were attacked by 6in guns at 1,000 yards using AP shells. Penetration of the plate ranged from $1\frac{1}{4}$in to $1\frac{3}{4}$in, but other than this the armour facing suffered only mild abrasion. Against the British 12in gun, however, it would have been a different story, because it was capable of piercing the 7in plates from 3,000 yards.

All in all, the protection of *Swiftsure* and *Triumph* compared favourably with the *Duncan* group (to which they were always compared), having the same percentage of armour weight to displacement, but with some rearrangement of the armouring mainly so as to conform with the continuous battery adopted in place of separate casemates for the main deck secondary guns.

The citadel bulkheads were not carried below the middle deck and the main deck was unarmoured, nor was an armoured deck (lower) fitted at each extremity as in contemporary British practice. The horizontal protection above the middle deck, within the citadel, was located at upper deck level to provide an armoured roof for the battery; underwater protection was afforded by extensions to the middle deck.

Side armour (including battery) was carried up to upper deck level amidships, instead of terminating at main deck level, as in *Duncan*, and the belt abaft the citadel was increased from 1in to 3in.

The middle deck, within the citadel, was ½in thicker, and underwater protection at the ends, outside this, was increased from 1in—3in to 3in.

Casemate armour was considerably improved at 7in and 3in against 6in and 2in in *Duncan*. On the other hand, the belt armour abreast the barbettes was 1in thinner than in *Duncan*, and forward extension to the bows was reduced one deck in height, with a uniform thickness of 3in against a graduated 5in—4in—3in and 2in in *Duncan*.

Deck protection above the middle deck, was 1in thinner amidships, and non-existent outside the citadel, as against 2in and 1in armour on the main deck forward in *Duncan*. Maximum thickness of the barbette armour was about 1in less, and the inner faces of the barbettes, below upper deck, were only 3in and 2in against 10in and 4in in *Duncan*. This thin armour of the barbettes once below certain levels was a distinct weak point in *Swiftsure* and *Triumph*, and made the magazines extremely vulnerable to oblique hits in this area where combined thickness of deck and barbette armour totalled only 3in to 4in.

The turret faces and sides were less sloped than in British designs, and consequently slightly less effective against armour-piercing shells. Net defence was not carried so far forward as in usual British practice, and terminated just short of the forward 10in turret.

As completed, the main belt extended to just outside the barbettes, with the upper edge at middle deck level, approximately 2ft 9in above water in the normal load. Width of the belt was

TRIUMPH
Outboard profile, as seen at
Dardanelles, 1915

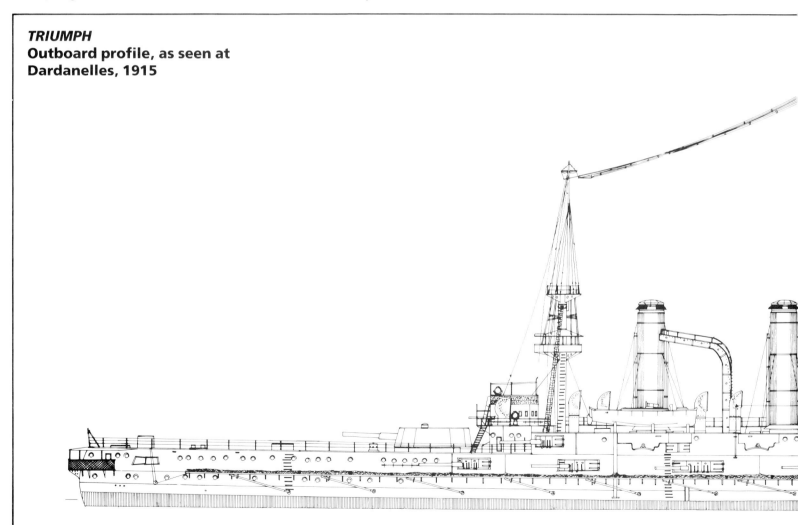

about 8ft, the lower edge being 5ft 3in below the waterline. Thickness was 7in to just inside the barbettes, then reduced to 6in beyond this, to just outside the barbettes.

The end belts ran right to the stem and almost to the stern over the same width as the midships section, except that the forward extremity was carried right down to support the ram. The thickness was 3in reducing to $2^3/4$in (including shell plating) over the ram. Belt bulkheads (aft only) were right aft and closed the extremities of the 3in belt armour.

The middle side armour was 7in thick, and ran between main and middle decks over the same length as the 7in main belt. Middle side bulkheads of 2in ran obliquely inwards from the forward and after extremities of the middle side armour to the barbette faces. Barbettes were 10in on the outer faces, 8in on inner faces above the upper deck, and then reduced to 3in and 2in below this. Turrets had 9in faces, 8in sides and rears, 2in roof, 3in floor, $1^1/2$in sighting hood.

The 7.5in battery was 7in amidships between upper and main deck level over the same length as the 7in main belt and side armour. The 6in bulkheads ran obliquely inwards from forward and after extremities of the battery side armour to the outer faces of the barbettes. Within the battery, 1in longitudinal screens were fitted along the centreline, with three transverse screens between the guns. Casemates were 7in on faces, 7in sides, and a 3in rear. The conning tower had an 11in face and 8in rear fitted to an 8in tube. Funnel uptakes were $1/2$in (shell plating).

The upper deck was 1in thick, flat over the whole length of the citadel. The middle deck was $1^1/2$in to 3in thick, sloping, and ran from the stem to the belt bulkhead right aft. Crown level was at the top of the belt, about 2ft 9in above waterline, and lower edge at ship's side at lower edge of belt, about 5ft 3in below waterline at normal load.

Coal bunkers were placed behind the belt and side armour between main and middle decks, and abreast the boiler rooms below the middle deck.

MACHINERY

The machinery consisted of two sets of inverted vertical direct-acting, 4-cylinder triple expansion engines, driving twin screws. The engine rooms were divided by a centre-line bulkhead. Cylinder sizes were 29in HP, 47in Int, and 54in LP in diameter, with a stroke of 3ft 3in. Each ship had twelve Yarrow water tube boilers housed in four compartments, and a designed SHP and speed of 12,500 and 19.5 knots.

On completion, they were the fastest battleships in the British Navy, and among the fastest in the world. In service, however, although being nominally a $1/2$-knot faster than the *Duncan* group, they proved unable to keep up with them over long runs, except to get ahead in short sprints. Being the first British battleships to attain a speed of 20 knots, it was suspected that their steam trials had been carried out under different, more favourable conditions than normally obtained for contemporary British battleships. *Triumph* left Vickers with members of the Press and public relations officers on board, to give a 'good show'. She reached speeds of 20.17 knots during her runs, but when the DNC inquired whether that was the mean speed or just a sprint on a run, the designer (Reed)

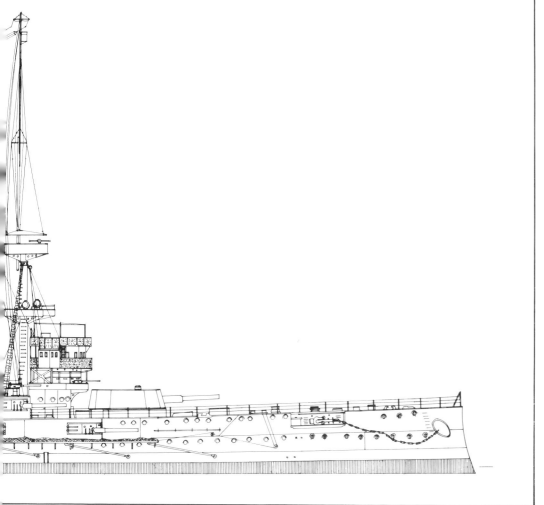

Below: After three years in the Mediterranean Fleet, *Triumph* returns to the UK in 1912 to join the Home Fleet.

Bottom: *Triumph* in 1909.

had to admit that it was one the six runs on the full-power measured mile.

Swiftsure left Armstrong's yard with many Royal Navy officers on board, and prepared herself for a completely different set of trials under standard Admiralty conditions. She reached a high of 20.870 knots on one of her six measured mile runs. Both *Swiftsure* and *Triumph* ran full-power trials for six hours which showed an average speed of 19 knots which was more or less the same as in the *Duncan* group which reached 18–19 knots over eight hours' full-power trials.

Great controversy arose because of the high speeds these two ships achieved on preliminary sea trials; the DNC going so far as to accuse Reed of pushing the machinery far beyond its normal capacity. The charge was quite unfounded. The ships proved every bit as good as most of the big ships in service at the time—they could not have failed to be; they were fitted with the latest British boilers, and built by the same firms that built British ships. Although designed to conform with Chilean standards, the machinery and boiler installations were not; the only requirement had been that they reach 19 knots.

Swiftsure: **Steam trials, March 1904**

Mean figures:
Steam in boilers: 253psi
Steam at engines: 229psi
Revolutions: 151.2 port; 151.1 starboard
Total IHP: 13,469
Speed: 20.046 knots

Runs	Revs (port)	Revs (starboard)	Speed (knots)
First:	131.1	130.9	18.136
Second:	132.3	132.1	17.341
Third:	129.9	130.2	17.476
Fourth:	131.1	131.7	17.561
Six runs at full power			
First:	148.1	147.8	20.339
Second:	153.1	153.4	19.459
Third:	157.1	152.4	20.690
Fourth:	152.9	152.6	19.407
Fifth:	152	151.6	20.870
Sixth:	151.8	151.2	19.099

APPEARANCE CHANGES

These two ships looked distinctly foreign, mainly because of the heavy cranes between the funnels, short masts, and tall, thin round, funnels. They

Below: *Triumph* on manoeuvres in 1912.

Below: On 9 November 1914 the destruction of the German raider *Emden* by HMS *Sydney* removed the threat against British shipping in the Indian Ocean, and *Swiftsure* (in the area for that reason) had just arrived in Aden and was ordered to proceed to the Suez area against a possible Turkish attack in December 1914.

Below: Arriving at Tsingtau on 22 September, *Triumph* gave full co-operation to the Japanese Fleet for the next six weeks. Seen here bombarding forts at Tsingtau in October 1914.

Right: *Triumph*; fixing the topmasts, and shipping the 12pdr gun after being hit during bombardment of the forts in the Dardanelles on 8 March 1915.

Opposite page, bottom: *Swiftsure* covers landings at Helles ('W' Beach) on 25 April 1915.

were the last British battleships to enter service with the Royal Navy sporting bow crests, and the last to have ventilation cowls.

The hull sides were prominently recessed before and abaft the main deck battery, and very deep embrasured ports were set in the main deck level right forward. They also carried a mix of stocked and stockless anchors; two anchors carried to port and one to starboard in contrast to British standard practice.

No after bridge, two tall, thin, round funnels, single fighting tops on each mast, very short lower-masts, short topmasts, which were housed below the starfish instead of above, as in British practice, gave them a completely unique appearance, unlike any other battleship serving with the Royal Navy at that time.

It was also quite easy to distinguish them from

each other. *Swiftsure* had steam pipes abaft the funnel, small funnel caps, and a bow scroll higher and more conspicuous than in *Triumph*. *Triumph* had steam pipes before the funnel, larger funnel caps, much smaller bow scroll, and very prominent box shelters, with MGs on top, at each wing of the bridge.

1905–6 Small rangefinder added on SL platform on foremast in *Swiftsure*. Foremast SL remounted in forward fighting top. One red band painted on each funnel in *Triumph*.

1906–8 Fire control and RF equipment fitted. Vickers deflection system fitted in *Swiftsure*. Control top fitted in place of SL platform on foremast.

In both ships, the SL platform was temporarily adopted as the control position (1906–7), but permanent control top was not fitted until 1907–8. Range indicators fitted to fore control top in *Swiftsure*, and small RF added in forward fighting top in *Triumph*. 6pdrs removed from tops and 14pdrs from main deck. Main deck 14pdrs remounted in superstructures, two forward, two aft. Forward ports plated up.

Shields removed from 14pdrs in both ships (1907–8).

SL, ex-mainmast remounted over after charthouse (1906–7).

W/T added (Type 2). W/T gaff to main topmast.

W/T gaff triced and masthead semaphore removed (1907–8).

Heavy yards removed from mainmast.

New squadron bands painted-up on funnels: one white, low on each in *Triumph*.

1908–9 SL equipment increased in *Triumph*. SL ex-upper deck amidships (two) remounted on fore-bridge shelters, replacing MGs. Four extra 24in SL added. W/T topgallant fitted to each mast in *Swiftsure*, and W/T gaff removed.

1909–10 W/T topgallants fitted in *Triumph*, and W/T gaff removed. Starboard system of funnel bands painted-up; none in *Swiftsure*; one white, high on second funnel, in *Triumph*.

1910–11 Range indicators removed from *Swiftsure*. SL equipment increased in *Swiftsure*. SL ex-upper deck amidships remounted on wing platforms abeam after charthouse. Four 24in added: three in forward fighting top, one over after charthouse.

1912 Range indicator fitted to each control top in *Triumph* (removed 1913–14).

These together with the indicators fitted in

Swiftsure 1907–8 were an early experimental type, and all were discarded by 1914. SL removed from bridge shelters in *Triumph* and remounted in bridge wings below these.

1914 Torpedo nets may have been removed at some time during this period, as were those from other capital ships. *Triumph* at Tsingtau in Oct 1914 showed no apparent alterations, but it is reported that she was fitted with a modified 6pdr for AA while on the China Station. Torpedo nets still (or refitted) fitted.

Swiftsure Suez Canal Patrol, Dec 1914: two light guns (calibre unknown) mounted in after control top. SL ex-superstructure (two) remounted on original SL platform on mainmast. Shields replaced on 14pdrs. Sandbag protection fitted around bridge and superstructure. No torpedo nets. Full topgallant masts.

1915 *Swiftsure* in Dardanelles: Light guns removed from after control top (early). SL ex-mainmast remounted in original position on after super-structure. Nets fitted (later in 1915). Bridge wings cut away leaving short wings at each side (later in 1915). Bow waves painted-up. Topgallants removed.

1915 *Triumph* at Dardanelles: Nets fitted. Main topmast out.

1917 *Swiftsure* completely disarmed and stripped in autumn 1918, for proposed second attempt to block Ostend.

HISTORY: *SWIFTSURE*

Built by Armstrong-Whitworth & Co as *Constitucion* and laid down on 13 March 1902. Completed June 1904.

21 June 1904 Commissioned at Chatham for service with Home Fleet, until Jan 1905. Fleets re-organized, Home Fleet became Channel Fleet. Jan 1905—Oct 1908 Channel Fleet.

3 June 1905 Collided with *Triumph* sustaining damage to propellers, sternwalk and part of hull aft.

June—July 1906 Refitted at Chatham.

7 Oct 1908 Reduced to Reserve, Portsmouth, until April 1909.

6 April 1909 Transferred to Mediterranean Fleet, until May 1912.

8 May 1912—Mar 1913 Following Fleet reorgani-zation transferred to 3rd Home Fleet, Portsmouth. Sept 1912—Mar 1913 Refit.

26 Mar 1913 Commissioned at Portsmouth as

Flagship (RA), East Indies Station, until Feb 1915 (Suez Canal Patrol from Dec 1914). Escorted Indian troops from Bombay to Aden Sept—Nov 1914.

1 Dec 1914 Detached to Suez, but remained Flagship, East Indies Squadron.

27 Jan—4 Feb 1915 Took part in repelling Turkish attack in Kantara area. Relieved by *Euryalus* and transferred to Dardanelles.

28 Feb 1915 Joined Dardanelles Squadron until Feb 1916.

2 Mar 1915 Took part in attack on Fort Dardanos.

5—9 Mar Detached (with *Triumph*) for operations against Smyrna forts. Took part in main attack on Narrows forts 18 Mar Supported main landings at Helles (West Beach) and subsequent landings, including attack on Achi Baba 4 June. Attacked by

German U-boat (possibly *U21*) 18 Sept *en route* Mudros to Suvla.

18 Jan 1916 Took part in bombardment of Dedeagatch.

Feb 1916 Attached to 9th Cruiser Squadron for Atlantic Patrol and Convoy duty; left Kephale for Gibraltar 7 Feb 1916.

Feb 1916—Mar 1917 Atlantic Patrol. Withdrawn from 9th CS Mar 1917.

26 Mar Left Sierra Leone for home, arrived Plymouth 11 April and paid off at Chatham 26 April to provide crews for A/S vessels.

April 1917—autumn 1918 Reserve.

Mid-1917 Refit at Chatham. Employed as accommodation ship from Feb 1918.

Autumn 1918 Dismantled at Chatham for use as blockship in proposed second attempt to block

Ostend, but Armistice signed before this operation could be carried out. Used as target ship for short period.

Mar 1920 Placed on sale list at Portsmouth.

18 June 1920 Sold to Stanlee Shipbreaking Co, Dover, for scrapping.

HISTORY: *TRIUMPH*

Ordered by Chilean Government from Vickers in February 1902 as *Libertad*. Purchased from Vickers by British Navy 3 Dec 1903.

21 June 1904 Commissioned at Chatham for service with Home Fleet, until Jan 1905.

17 Sept 1904 Rammed by SS *Siren* at Pembroke, sustained slight damage to side plating.

Jan 1905—April 1909 Channel Fleet, ex-Home Fleet.

3 June 1905 Collided with *Swiftsure*, sustained damage to bows.

Oct 1908 Refit at Chatham.

6 April 1909 Transferred to Mediterranean Fleet, until May 1912. Transferred to 3rd Home Fleet on Fleet reorganization.

May 1912—Aug 1913 Home Fleet.

28 Aug 1913 Commissioned at Devonport for service on China Station, until Jan 1915. In Reserve at Hong Kong until Aug 1914. Recommissioned at outbreak of war with crews of demobilized river gunboats, together with 2 officers, 100 men and 6 signallers from the Duke of Cornwall's Light Infantry, and was ready for sea by 6 Aug. Took part in operations against Von Spee's squadron in early

Below: *Swiftsure* early in 1916, anchored alongside the French Fleet (*République* (left), *Gaulois* and *Henri IV*) during the Dardanelles campaign. Note bow wave still painted-up at this late date.

Bottom: Not needed any more. *Zealandia* (left), *Prince of Wales* and *Swiftsure* laid up and awaiting their fate, 1919.

August, and captured one of his colliers. Attached to Japanese Second Fleet for operations against Tsingtau 23 Aug, until Nov 1914, including capture of fortress on 7 Nov.

Nov 1914—Jan 1915 Refit at Hong Kong.

Jan 1915 Transferred to Dardanelles; left Hong Kong 12 Jan, arrived Suez 7 Feb. Left for Dardanelles 12 Feb.

Feb—May 1915 Dardanelles.

Took part in opening attack on entrance forts 18–19 Feb (together with *Albion, Cornwallis* silenced Fort Sedd el Bahr with secondary armament at close range 25 Feb). With *Majestic* and *Albion* carried out initial attacks on inner forts 26 Feb, these three battleships being the first to enter the Straits during the campaign. Took part in attack on Fort Dardanos 2 Mar. Took part in main attack on Narrows forts 18 Mar. Carried out experimental firing on enemy trenches at Achi Baba 15 April. On 18 April, one picket boat from *Triumph* and one boat from *Majestic*, torpedoed and destroyed British submarine *E15* which had been stranded near Fort Dardanos, and was in danger of falling into enemy hands. Supported main landings (Anzacs at Gaba Tepe) 25 April. Supported Anzac position at Gabe Tepe against heavy Turkish attacks 19 May.

LOSS OF *TRIUMPH*

On 25 May 1915 while under way engaging enemy positions off Gaba Tepe, *Triumph* was torpedoed by *U21*.

The ship's torpedo nets were out, guns manned and most watertight doors shut. 'Submarine alarm' was sounded and the crew went to action stations (all water-tight doors now shut). Steaming west, a periscope was seen at approximately 12.30 about 300 to 400 yards off the starboard beam. Firing commenced, but almost immediately *Triumph* was hit by a torpedo on the starboard side abreast No. 2 boiler room. As with *Majestic* the torpedo sliced through the nets as if they were paper and struck the ship with maximum force.

A tremendous explosion almost lifted the ship out of the water. A heavy shower of coal and debris fell back on to deck after the blast. Within minutes the ship heeled 10° to starboard and then stopped. Five minutes later she had listed almost 30° and it was obvious that she was going to turn over. She did not capsize for about ten minutes and, the order to abandon having been given, many of the crew were rescued. *Triumph* then turned turtle, but remained afloat for about half an hour. She then sank slowly by the bows, and there was another large explosion inside the ship (some reports say that this noise was caused by weights shifting within the ship, and was not an explosion). She went down in about 30 fathoms of water, with the loss of three officers and 75 ratings.

At the Court of Inquiry, the loss of the ship was attributed to two main causes:

1. The complete failure of the anti-torpedo nets, and no one was to blame for this.

2. There was inadequate destroyer protection at the time. (The destroyer *Chelmer* took off most of the survivors).

Operating off Gaba Tepe at this stage was known to be hazardous, but it was necessary, and, because of this, no blame was put on the Captain or *Triumph*'s officers.

LORD NELSON CLASS

1904/5 ESTIMATES

DESIGN

The *Lord Nelson* class were the last of the British predreadnoughts, often called intermediate dreadnoughts, and the first British battleships for which Philip Watts, as DNC, was entirely responsible.

They were designed to meet requirements of a new policy; the objective being to initiate battleship types having a definite superiority over their foreign contemporaries rather than merely matching them, as had been the tendency in recent years. It was now being seen that British designs had procrastinated so far as anything innovatory was concerned.

When Watts took office early in 1902, he undertook the task of completely reconsidering the entire scope of battleship design. At the same time, exhaustive investigations were being carried out by the Controller, Sir William May, into the relative efficiency of armament and protective qualities provided in British and foreign battleships. Results from these investigations showed that:

1. The destructive effect of secondary guns (especially the 6in) was very small in relation to that of larger calibres up to 12in.

2. Damage caused by heavy projectiles was very extensive and the lightly protected secondary armament always received considerable damage, and would probably be completely destroyed before getting into its effective range.

3. Heavier armouring was required over a much larger area than had previously been the case.

Designs were prepared on the basis of these findings, but it took a long time for their Lordships to agree as to what was the best alternative to what had been classed as the standard procedure in design, which had been adhered to for the last ten years, with only a slight breakaway in the *King Edwards*. New layouts were submitted for consideration as early as July 1902 (*see* tables), but although May was pleased with what he received, he asked that much more thought be given to various alternatives in general armament and armour application.

Work continued at the DNC's Department, and in December another set was forwarded for perusal (variations of Design B) from which B3[a] was favoured most by members of the Board. After this, the design proceeded at a very slow pace indeed until in August 1903 three further sketches were drawn up ('A', 'B', 'C'). Also submitted was a

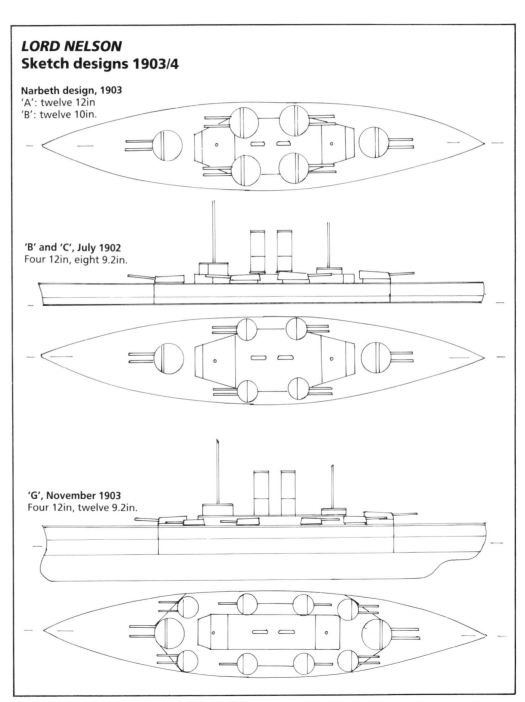

LORD NELSON
Sketch designs 1903/4

Narbeth design, 1903
'A': twelve 12in
'B': twelve 10in.

'B' and 'C', July 1902
Four 12in, eight 9.2in.

'G', November 1903
Four 12in, twelve 9.2in.

Lord Nelson: Early designs, 22 July 1902

	A	B*	B5	B6	B7	C	D	E
Displacement:	14,000 tons	14,000 tons	15,800 tons		16,350 tons	14,000 tons	14,000 tons	15,800 tons
Length:	405ft pp	410ft pp	400ft pp	same as B5	415ft pp	410ft pp	410ft pp	400ft pp
Beam:	79ft	to suit requirements	80ft	except armament	80ft	to suit requirements	to suit requirements	80ft
Draught:	26ft 6in		27ft mean		27ft mean			27ft mean
SHP:	15,000 = 19kts	15,000 = 18½kts	18kts			13,500 = 18kts	13,500 = 18kts	
Armament:	four 12in, four 9.2in, ten 6in	four 12in, eight 9.2in, twelve 6in	four 12in, ten 9.2in	twelve 10in	four 12in, twelve 9.2in	four 12in, eight 9.2in	four 12in, twelve 9.2in	twelve 10in
Main belt:	9in–4in	9in–4in	12in–4in			9in–4in	7in–4in	12in–4in

*There was also B2 which was the same as B except armament of four 12in, eight 9.2in and four 7.5in. B3 was the same except four 12in and ten 9.2in. B4 same as B, but displacement rise to 16,000 tons.

Lord Nelson class: designs submitted to Board

December 1902

	B3[a]	A*	B*	C*	**	***
Displacement:	15,400 tons	16,350 tons	16,350 tons	16,350 tons	16,500 tons	15,600 tons
Length:	400ft pp	405ft pp	400ft pp	425ft pp	405ft pp	400ft pp
Beam:	80ft	81ft	82ft	78ft	80ft	80ft
Draught:	27ft mean	27ft mean	26ft 9in	26ft	27ft mean	26ft 6in mean
SHP:	15,500 = 18kts	16,500 = 18kts	same as A	18,000 = 18½kts	16,500 = 18kts	15,500 = 18kts
Armament:	four 12in, eight 9.2in, fourteen 12pdr	four 12in, twelve 9.2in, fourteen 12pdr	sixteen 10in	four 12in, four 9.2in, ten 6in	four 12in, twelve 9.2in, fourteen 12pdr	four 12in, eight 9.2in, fourteen 12pdr
Main belt:	12in–4in	12in–4in	9in–4in	9in–4in	12in–4in	12in–4in

*Further designs submitted 6 August 1903
**Design dated 19 October 1903
***Design dated 24 October 1903.

Designs submitted 13 November 1903

	G	G1	G2	G3	G4	G5	G6
Displacement:	16,350 tons	16,500 tons	16,900 tons	16,550 tons	16,500 tons	16,500 tons	17,040 tons
Length:	405ft pp	405ft pp	415ft pp	405ft pp	405ft pp	405ft pp	425ft pp
Beam:	79ft 6in	80ft	80ft	80ft	80ft	79ft 6in	79ft 6in
Draught:	27ft	27ft	27ft	27ft	27ft	27ft	27ft
SHP:	16,500 = 18kts	16,500 = 18kts	same as G1	same as G1		16,500 = 18kts	16,500 = 18kts
Armament:	four 12in, twelve 9.2in, fourteen 12pdr	four 12in, twelve 9.2in, fourteen 12pdr	same as G1	same as G1	four 12in, ten 9.2in	four 12in, ten 9.2in	four 12in, twelve 9.2in
Main belt:	12in–4in	12in–4in			12in–4in	12in–4in	12in–4in

Further design submitted by DNC (Watts) December 1903.   Watts submitted another alternative 6 February 1904

	E1	
Displacement:	16,500 tons	18,400 tons
Length:	405ft pp	445ft pp
Beam:	79ft 6in	82ft
Draught:	27ft mean	27/28ft
SHP:	16,500 = 18kts	17,000 = 18kts
Armament:	twelve 10in	sixteen 10in
Main belt:	12in–4in	12in–4in

Below: *Lord Nelson* during trials period, 1908. Designed to carry the maximum possible number of armour-piercing guns on a limited displacement, the *Lord Nelson*s as completed were remarkable ships in many ways.

proposal by the Assistant Constructor, J. H. Narbeth, on 25 September, for an all big gun ship carrying twelve 12in or sixteen 10in (*see* sketch). Other designs dated 19 and 24 October 1903 (no letter prefix) were sent along for consideration.

On 21 October 1903, the Controller called for a legend of weights and a picture sketch of B3ª. The design was discussed in general terms by senior Naval Lords, but it was considered under-armed and too lightly protected at the ends, so it was dropped.

On 27 October 1903 the Controller received a communication from the DNC stating that ships to be built at Barrow should not exceed 79ft 6in in beam, because the entrance to the basin (and other

docks) was too narrow. From November to 4 December 1903, there was serious discussion about widening the entrances to the docks at Portsmouth and Chatham.

On 13 November 1903, in response to verbal instructions from the Controller, the DNC and his staff submitted a further six alternative sketches (G to G5), having a Board margin of 200 tons except for G and G1.

After the layouts had been studied by everyone concerned with the procedure, the Controller called a meeting on 4 December 1903 where a sheer, midship section and various alternative sketches were deliberated by their Lordships, in an endeavour to reach a definite decision.

Design G5 was unanimously preferred to G4, but a beam of 79ft 6in was not be be exceeded; this restriction, many felt, marred an otherwise balanced design. In view of the fact that the Renerable shell (a shell which carried its burster through thick armour) was being introduced into foreign navies, it was thought that the lower armoured deck should receive more armour than had been indicated in the provisional layout; at least 12in should be applied to the main strake to protect the new ships from the future possibility of a shell of even greater penetrative power. Another meeting was held on 21 December 1903 when general armour distribution and relative thicknesses were seriously discussed.

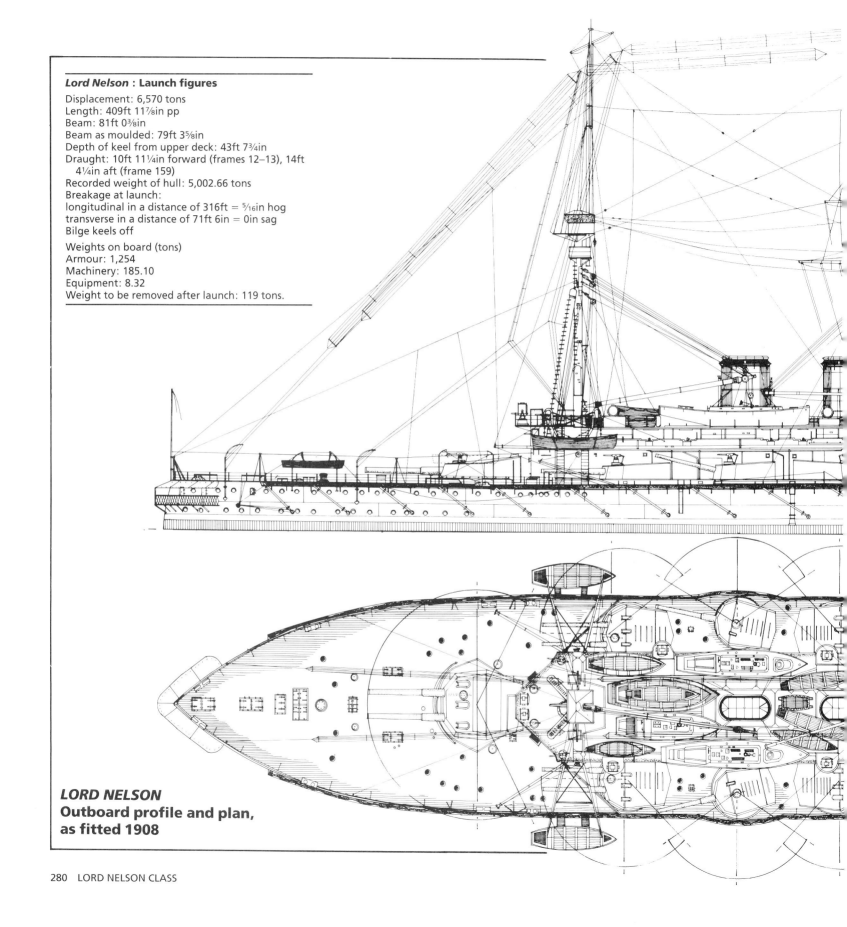

Lord Nelson : Launch figures

Displacement: 6,570 tons
Length: 409ft 11⁷⁄₈in pp
Beam: 81ft 0³⁄₈in
Beam as moulded: 79ft 3⁵⁄₈in
Depth of keel from upper deck: 43ft 7³⁄₄in
Draught: 10ft 11¼in forward (frames 12–13), 14ft
    4¼in aft (frame 159)
Recorded weight of hull: 5,002.66 tons
Breakage at launch:
longitudinal in a distance of 316ft = ⁵⁄₁₆in hog
transverse in a distance of 71ft 6in = 0in sag
Bilge keels off

Weights on board (tons)
Armour: 1,254
Machinery: 185.10
Equipment: 8.32
Weight to be removed after launch: 119 tons.

LORD NELSON
Outboard profile and plan,
as fitted 1908

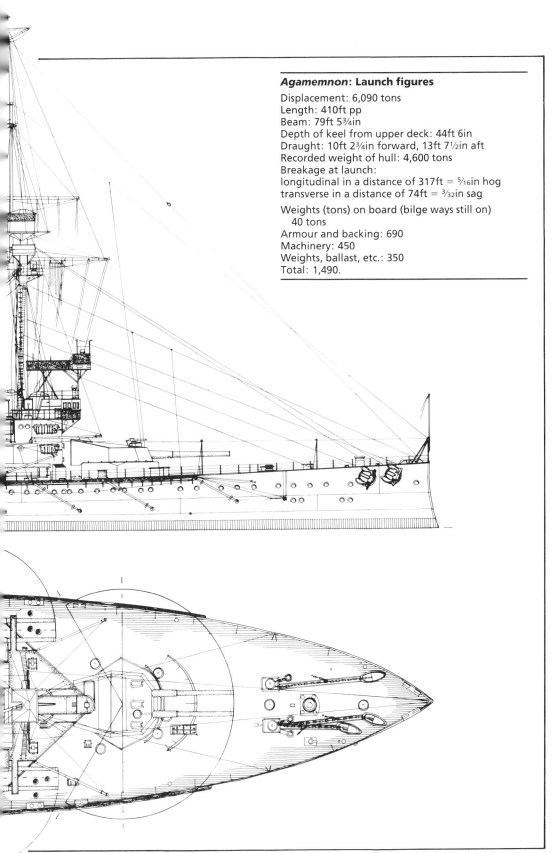

***Agamemnon*: Launch figures**

Displacement: 6,090 tons
Length: 410ft pp
Beam: 79ft 5¾in
Depth of keel from upper deck: 44ft 6in
Draught: 10ft 2¾in forward, 13ft 7½in aft
Recorded weight of hull: 4,600 tons
Breakage at launch:
longitudinal in a distance of 317ft = ⁵⁄₁₆in hog
transverse in a distance of 74ft = ³⁄₃₂in sag

Weights (tons) on board (bilge ways still on)
   40 tons
Armour and backing: 690
Machinery: 450
Weights, ballast, etc.: 350
Total: 1,490.

On 6 February 1904, the DNC showed the Controller another design which departed somewhat from the desired G5 layout in that it was considerably increased in size, and sported sixteen 10in guns which the DNC had always favoured. The dimensions (beam of 82ft) (*see* tables) made it impossible to dock the ship in Chatham and other private docks, however, and it was discarded. Mention was made of another possibility (G6); giving G2 an extra 20 feet in length and shipping a pair of 9.2in guns in the centre turret instead of the single as featured in the G2 layout.

With so many sketches and layout alternatives before them, it became increasingly difficult to decide which was the best, but when a further

***Lord Nelson* class: Final legend, 1 August 1904**

Displacement: 16,500 tons
Length: 410ft pp
Beam: 79ft 6in
Draught: 27ft mean
Freeboard: 24ft forward, 16ft 6in amidships, 18ft
   aft
Sinkage: 61 tons per inch
Main gun heights: 27ft forward, 22ft aft
9.2in gun heights: 23ft forward, 22ft amidships,
   22ft aft.

Armament
Four 12in
Ten 9.2in
Twelve 12pdr (18cwt)
Ten 3pdr.

Armour
Main belts: 12in–4in
Bulkheads: 8in
Barbettes: 12in–3in
Turrets: 12in max.
9.2in turrets: 8in–7in
Glacis for 9.2in guns: 6in
Conning tower: 12in
Main deck: 1½in, middle 4in–1in, lower 3in–1in.

SHP: 16,500 for 18 knots
Fuel: 900 tons coal, 2,000 tons max.

Complement: 750.

General equipment: 650 tons
Armament: 3,110 tons
Armour: 4,200 tons
Machinery: 1,720 tons
Hull: 5,720 tons
Total weight of ship 16,500 tons plus 200 tons
Board margin.

Right: *Agamemnon*, 1908–9. She and *Lord Nelson* were very successful in service and would have received greater recognition had they not been preceded by the revolutionary *Dreadnought* in 1906.

Below right: *Agamemnon* in 1910. She was easy to distinguish from *Lord Nelson* because of bridge and charthouse differences.

Lord Nelson class: Particulars, as completed

Construction
Lord Nelson: Palmer; laid down 18 May 1905; launched: 4 Sept 1906; completed Oct 1908
Agamemnon: Beardmore; laid down 15 May 1905; launched 23 June 1906; completed June 1908.

Displacement (tons)
15,358 (load), 17,820 (deep), 18,910 (extra deep).

Dimensions
Length: 410ft pp, 435ft wl, 443ft 6in oa
Beam: 79ft 6in
Draught: 25ft (light), 30ft (extra deep).

Armament
Four 12in 45cal Mk X, Mk VIII mountings
Ten 9.2in Mk XI, Mk VII mountings (singles on Mk VIII)
Twenty-four 12pdr
Two 3pdr
Five 18in torpedo tubes submerged; twenty-three torpedoes.

Shell stowage
12in; 80rpg
9.2in; 100rpg
12pdr; 230rpg.

Shell types carried
12in 160 AP, 160 common
9.2in 500 AP 500 common
12pdr 5,520 common.

Armour
Main belt, main bulkhead, conning tower, turrets KC
Ammunition hoists, glacis to 9.2in middle deck KNC
Communications tube 'Era' steel
Remainder mild steel.
Main belt: 12in

Upper tier: 8in
Bulkheads: 8in
Barbettes: 3in–12in
Turrets: 13½in–12in
9.2in turrets: 7in–3in
9.2in barbettes: 8in
9.2in glacis: 6in
Conning tower: 12in
Tube: 6in
Torpedo director: 3in
Decks: main 1½in; middle 4in slopes, 2in elsewhere; 3in–1in lower.

Machinery
Two sets 4-cylinder inverted vertical triple expansion, surface condensing, engines, twin in-turning propellers
Cylinder diameter: 32¾in HP, 52¾in IP, 60in LP
Stroke: 4ft.
Boilers: fifteen Babcock (*Agamemnon* Yarrow) water tube, working pressure 275psi, 250psi at engines
Heating surface: 50,265sq ft
Grate area: 848sq ft
Auxiliary machinery included for the first time two diesel-driven dynamos for emergency use
Length of boiler rooms: 52ft forward, 19ft 11in amidships, 38ft aft
Length of engine rooms: 52ft
Designed SHP: 16,750 for 18 knots
Fuel: 900 tons coal normal, 2,170 tons coal max. plus 1,090 tons oil *Lord Nelson*; 2,193 tons coal plus 1,048 tons oil max. *Agamemnon*
Coal consumption: 410 tons per day full power, 270 tons ⅗ths power, 55 tons at 7 knots (economical speed)

Radius of action: 5,390nm at 10 knots coal only (2,180 tons), 9,180nm at 10 knots oil added (1,090 tons) *Lord Nelson*.

Ship's boats
Pinnaces (motor): one 50ft
Pinnaces (steam): one 50ft
Barges (steam): one 40ft
Pinnaces (sail): one 36ft
Launches (sail): one 24ft
Cutters: two 32ft, one 30ft
Galleys: one 32ft
Whalers: three 27ft
Gigs: one 28ft
Skiff dinghies: two 16ft
Balsa rafts: two 13ft 6in.

Searchlights
Eight 36in: two on forward superstructure, four on raised platform on sides of flying deck, two close abreast after superstructure, one 24in on platform below forward control top.

Anchors
3 125cwt stockless (bower and sheet).

Wireless
Mk I W/T (short-range set fitted in 1910).

Complement
752 *Lord Nelson*, 1910
749 *Agamemnon*, 1908; 756, 1913
800 average in wartime.

Costs
Lord Nelson: £1,540,939 plus guns £110,400
Agamemnon: £1,541,947 plus guns £110,400.

Lord Nelson: GM and stability

Based on inclining experiments, November 1908

	Draught	GM	Maximum stability	Stability vanishes at
'A' Condition (= load)*	26ft 6¼in	3.42ft	32°	58°
'B' Condition (= deep load)**	30ft 3¾in	5.27ft	33°	57°

*Fully equipped plus 900 tons coal
**Fully equipped plus 2,171 tons coal, 1,090 tons oil, 204 tons reserve feed water.

meeting was called on 10 February 1904 nearly all the Board members were still in hearty agreement about the G5 design, and asked for this to be given further consideration and worked out to the full, so that it could be given approval quickly and the design could then be prepared for the naval estimates of the 1904 construction programme.

Consideration was seriously given to the very powerful, all big gun designs as proposed by the DNC and his assistant, in which the results of the 1902 investigation were carried to their ultimate conclusion; the intermediate calibres being discarded entirely in favour of an increased number of big guns, and only light quick-firing 12pdrs in

addition for anti-torpedo boat work. Unfortunately, at that date (1903–4), the majority of the Board were not in favour of an all big gunned ship. They even had great difficulty in choosing an ideal

big gun layout for the later *Dreadnought* in 1905 (*see* R. A. Burt. *Battleships of WW1*) and considered that such a radical advance, with corresponding increase in size and cost, was not worthy of consid-

eration without an intermediate step in construction so as to fully judge the merits or faults of the mixed-calibre battleship.

The final legend for the *Lord Nelson* pair was drawn up on 1 August 1904, but the ships were not laid down until May 1905 during the controversy raging about the innovatory *Dreadnought*, which would render this pair obsolete overnight, not to mention the older predreadnoughts which were equipped with as few as four 12in and little else.

Consideration was given to providing the *Lord Nelson*s with a single-calibre armament while the *Dreadnought* design was under way, but at that late date (January 1905), although they had not yet been laid down work was too far advanced to make any drastic alterations, and the pair passed into history as being the last British battleships with mixed-calibre guns, a feature which was short-lived in Royal Navy warships.

On an increase of approximately 250 tons displacement the *Lord Nelson* design compared with the *King Edward* group essentially as follows:
1. More powerful models of 12in and 9.2in guns.
2. A uniform, and considerably heavier secondary armament of ten 9.2in, all mounted on the upper deck, instead of a mixture of four 9.2in and ten 6in, the latter mounted on the main deck where they were more or less unfightable in a heavy sea.
3. A larger, and more effectively arranged anti-torpedo armament.
4. Stronger hull armouring, and improved internal protection.
5. Nominal speed of ½-knot less, although, in service, they turned out as fast as the *King Edward* group.
6. Steaming radius substantially increased.

Such a marked advance in general all-round fighting efficiency over the *King Edward VII* class, on a slightly increased displacement, was an especially noteworthy achievement for all concerned with the design and construction of the pair.

Although classed as less, they were only slightly less powerful than the following *Dreadnought*, which featured a broadside of eight 12in against four 12in and five 9.2in. At long range *Lord Nelson* was outclassed, but under 10,000 yards, she was indeed a powerful ship against any of the early dreadnoughts—especially given that her scale of armour protection was greater than that of *Dreadnought* whose principal modifications on the

Below: After the battleship *Irresistible* sank on 18/19 March, the survivors were distributed in various ships of the force. Some are seen here on *Agmemnon's* quarterdeck.

Bottom: *Agamemnon* opens up with her 9.2in battery against fortifications in Sedd el Bahr on 4 March 1915.

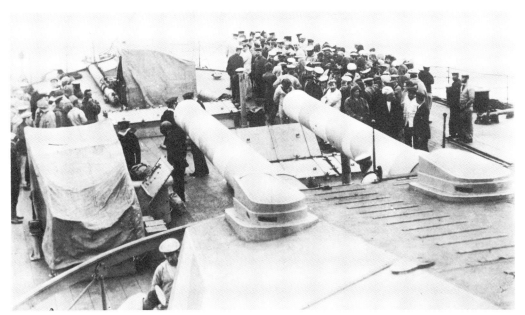

Lord Nelson comprised a maximum thickness of belt reduced from 12in to 11in, and the 8in upper side armour omitted.

Other novel features of *Lord Nelson* included:
1. Provision of a large flying deck to accommodate anti-torpedo guns and searchlights on a high command.
2. Absence of any normal bridge structure.
3. Tripod mainmast.

The principal weak points in an otherwise good design were: 1. Difficulty in controlling two different gun calibres, especially as longer battle ranges were coming into use. 2. A general cramping due to dimensions being restricted in design by the Admiralty requirement of being able to use existing docking arrangements.

In service, both ships proved successful within the limits of the design, and certainly fitted the bill for pre-1904 requirements in most respects, so much so, that a suggestion was made in 1908 to construct two more to make a tactical group of the type, but this idea was discarded owing to the success of the *Dreadnought* and the ever-changing demand for more and more bigger gun calibres.

During the design stage, the Admiralty had stipulated that the ships be able to use No. 5 dock at Devonport, and No. 9 at Chatham, the former limiting length to 13ft less than the *King Edwards*, and the latter restricting beam to 79ft 6in. Under these restrictions, which were actually unnecessary, as by the time the ships entered service, there was ample docking accommodation available in all the dockyards, considerable difficulty was experienced in combining the degree of fineness of the hull required for the designed speed, with displacement adequate for the load to be carried. With the benefit of a little foresight, the class could have been just that much better in design with the possibility of featuring all big guns instead of their mixed calibres.

To meet this problem of docking, the sides amidships were made vertical and parallel to conform with the entrance to Chatham dock; the bottom was constructed quite flat giving maximum midships section and displacement, while hull lines before and abaft this were made as easy as practicable. The results proved very satisfactory, with the hull being driven easily, despite the unusual full midships section, which incidentally, offered a greater resistance to rolling.

They were the last British battleships to have a

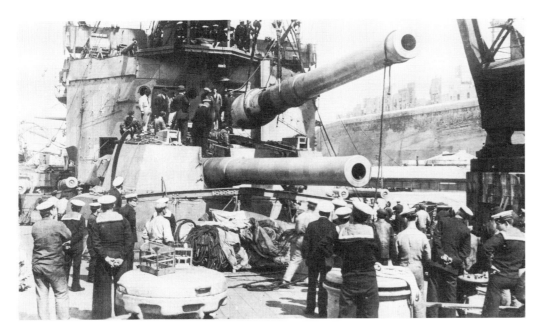

Below: After constant firing in the Dardanelles, the gun linings needed renewing. *Agamemnon* in Malta May–June 1915, for refit and replacement of her 12in guns. Note the entire turret roof has been removed.

full pointed ram with armoured support, although all ideas of ramming at the long battle ranges then in use, had long been abandoned.

Their reduced GM as compared with the *King Edwards*, coupled with the damping effect from the 9.2in gun turrets, made them comfortable sea-boats, and exceptionally good gun platforms with a much drier command.

ARMAMENT

As designed, the basic requirements had always been four 12in guns, but problems arose when it came to the secondary battery.

As can be seen in the tables, there were many alternatives before the Board, which had to be discussed, but for most of the time, the whole emphasis was on a strong 9.2in battery with no 6in guns included.

In general, the Board would have liked to have seen the maximum of twelve 9.2in guns in pairs as in many of the G designs, but the requirements restricting the beam necessitated reducing the centre 9.2in turret on each side from twin mountings to single. The size of the twin turrets was restricted for the same reason, and they were cramped internally and it proved awkward to maintain a high rate of fire.

The concentration of eight turrets on the upper deck (two 12in and six 9.2in) posed problems for the design, and special measures had to be taken to avoid blast interference. This was accomplished by fitting an electrical danger signal, which sounded a loud buzzer in any turret liable to cause damage to its neighbour. Although the 9.2in gun was a good semi-heavy calibre, combining hitting power and high rate of fire, and was popular in service, consideration was given to the two designs that featured all big guns. The DNC was most forceful in his pursuit of an all big gun ship, but he favoured a 10in gun as mounted in *Swiftsure* and *Triumph* and not all 12in as favoured by the Assistant Constructor, J. H. Narbeth. At that time, however, the Board was not looking at anything as innovatory as that, but had their sights set on a heavy mixed battery of 12in and 9.2in.

Both layouts of 10in and 12in, appear to be the first official British all big gun proposals, although the DNC had worked on such a ship, with J. Fisher as early as 1882 when they presented a combination of *Devastation* and *Inflexible* to mount all big guns, and little else. In January–February 1905, when *Dreadnought* was under discussion, it was suggested that the *Lord Nelson* pair might indeed have modifications and mount all 12in guns in place of

their 9.2in, but after it was pointed out that such a major alteration would hold up the completion of the ships drastically, and the fact that the new model of 12in gun (Mk X) and Vickers' new mountings to house them were not yet available in sufficient quantity, the suggestion was dropped.

Lord Nelson and *Agamemnon* were completed with guns and turrets (12in) exactly identical with those fitted in *Dreadnought* (Mk VIII). During the final layout stage, and when the *Lord Nelsons* were being laid down, it was suggested also, during a conference in the Controller's room, that it might be possible to fit the class with electrically worked turrets. After debate, however, the Officers were practically unanimous that the present hydraulic mountings left little to be desired and that it was unlikely that a turret worked electrically would be of any great advantage. It was acknowledged that an electrical turret would have certain advantages

Lord Nelson class: Armament, legend weights (tons)	
12in turret weights	
Four 12in:	232
Shields:	355
Turntables:	180
Turning gear:	31.1
Slides:	88
Pumps (3):	45
Hydraulic revolving pipes:	9
Shell machinery:	6.5
Transport gear:	40.5
Spare gear:	10
Water in tanks, etc.:	30
Pipes, etc.:	22.5
Shells in shield (8):	3
Shells in shell room (40):	15.5
Propellent (80rpg):	51.5
9.2in in pairs	
Eight guns:	226
Training gear:	24
Turntables:	180
Slides:	106
Revolving pipes:	8
Shell room machinery:	16.7
Transporting gear:	54.3
Pipes, etc:	6
Shields:	432
Shells in shield (12):	2
Shells in shell room:	134
Propellant:	57
Spare gear:	4
378.3 tons calculated for single 9.2in mountings.	

over the hydraulic turret, but one of the weaknesses of electrically-worked guns, and a very important one, was in the taking up of the recoil, and the rapid retraining of the gun.

At that time this was all done hydraulically, but in the electrical turret it was done by either springs or a pneumatic system. The Board agreed that although there were many such mountings fitted in our defensive forts on land, it was not satisfactory for fitting to heavy guns at sea.

With one disentient, the Board decided that trials should be carried out with these mountings under all conditions at sea. The Controller stated his opinion that he should like to see trials carried out in one of the new battleships to be laid down in 1905–6 as it was generally accepted that it was too late to fit such an experiment in the *Lord Nelsons* without the risk of considerable delay to their completion.

As late as 30 November 1904 it was again suggested to fit one of the electrical turrets in the after mounting of *Lord Nelson*, but this was dropped for the same reason. (It was later fitted in a turret of the battlecruiser *Invincible*.) As fitted the armament, was considerably stronger than in the *King Edwards* with more powerful models of both 12in and 9.2in, and an additional six 9.2in guns on the upper deck in place of the ten 6in a deck lower, which could not be fought properly in a sea-way.

The *Lord Nelson* pair were the last British battleships to carry intermediate-calibre guns, specifically intended for use against armoured ships, and the first to have no 6in guns since the old

Inflexible (1882). The intervening *Trafalgar* and *Centurion* classes (1890 and 1894 respectively) were completed with 4.7in, but were modified later to carry 6in. As reintroduced in the *Iron Duke* class (1912), the 6in gun was intended solely for anti-torpedo work.

Particularly attention was paid to the anti-torpedo armament, and its arrangement, which was considerably heavier than in any of the preceding classes. Compared to the *King Edwards*, the number of 12pdrs was practically doubled, with the same number of 3pdrs as in the last three ships of that class.

A large flying deck amidships was fitted to provide accommodation for about two-thirds of the 12pdrs and four of the eight 36in searchlights, which proved a great convenience and comfort at sea; the guns, although being greatly exposed to shellfire, had a very high command (about 30ft above the waterline at normal load), and were entirely free from interference from the main and secondary armaments. On the other hand, the deck involved considerable topweight, and offered a good target; it was also frowned upon in service because it was thought the structure might collapse after hits in action, and fall and hamper the 9.2in turrets. Moreover, the layout was criticized for mounting nothing larger than 12pdrs; many officers were of the opinion that the 12pdr was no longer efficient against the ever-growing sizes of torpedo-boats.

The retention of the 12pdr (at 18cwt it was better than previous 12pdrs) appears to have been influ-

enced by current official opinion that it was not absolutely essential to sink an attacking torpedo-boat —but merely to stop her before she got within torpedo range. This was seriously questioned by an extremely large body of opinion (including the former DNC, William White), but not enough evidence against the 12pdr was available at that date, and the gun was retained in this pair and the following *Dreadnought*.

ARMOUR

Lord Nelson was armoured as a result of the investigations carried out during 1902 which indicated the obvious necessity for heavier armour, and more extensive protection in general than had previously been provided. The principle modifications over *King Edward VII* were:

1. Belt increased from 9in to 12in amidships, and from 1½in to 4in aft.
2. Thickness of fore barbette was 6in uniform against a graded 7in-5in-4in and 2in.
3. Lower side forward of fore barbette was 6in and 4in against 8in-7in-5in-4in-2in.
4. Upper side (above main deck) over citadel increased from 7in to 8in.
5. Main bulkhead (aft) not carried below middle deck, being replaced by slope of middle deck to meet the lower outside of after barbette.
6. Upper deck over citadel, reduced from 1in to ³⁄₄in.
7. Maximum thickness of main deck reduced from 2in to 1½in.
8. Middle deck increased 1in of flat between end barbettes, 1in on slope and 2in on flat around these, and 2in on slope to lower deck outside.
9. Maximum thickness of lower deck aft, increased by ½in.
10. Barbette armour within citadel reduced from 6in to 3in.
11. Faces of turret unchanged, but sides increased to 12in and rears to 13in.
12. 9.2in turrets 1in thinner on faces, 1in thicker on sides.
13. 6in glacis fitted around these turrets, but no shallow barbettes as in *King Edward*.

Weak points of the armour protection were:
1. The 12in belt was usually submerged at deep load.
2. Thin (3in) armour on inner faces of main barbettes below the upper deck. These were protected against flat trajectory fire by the 8in

Top: Partially painted in an unofficial camouflage scheme, *Agamemnon* is seen here in the Dardanelles. Note bow wave and painted upperworks, 1915.

Centre: *Agamemnon* in May 1915. A rare photograph of the ship under way during the Dardanelles campaign, showing her full camouflage scheme. Note the bow wave has been painted out.

Bottom: *Lord Nelson* and *Agamemnon* on patrol in the Dardanelles; during the campaign their duties included watch and ward, blockade, support for army forces at Salonika, and search for the German battlecruiser *Goeben*, reputed to be in the area.

Lord Nelson: Armour weights (tons), as fitted

Taken from Record Book at Palmer

Upper and lower tier:	1,398.3
2in bow protection:	22.25
Bulkheads and barbettes:	468.4
Backing:	88.65
Splinter protection to 9.2in:	126.75
Glacis plates to 9.2in:	77
CT and tubes:	83.30
Decks	
Main:	188.6
Middle:	550.5
Slopes:	88.5
Lower:	198.5

citadel, but were vulnerable against plunging fire from long-range shooting, which only had the $^3/_4$in upper deck to penetrate in this vicinity.

General internal protection was improved over all earlier classes, by the provision, for the first time in a British battleship, of solid bulkheads (watertight) to all main compartments, these being unpierced even by doors or pipes, etc. Additional security was obtained by the installation of separate pumping and ventilating arrangements in each compartment in place of the single main drainage system previously used.

Absence of any doors, however, occasioned great inconvenience, especially in the machinery and boiler room spaces. Access throughout the ship was by lifts fitted in each compartment. Solid bulkheads had first appeared some years previously in the Russian battleships *Tsarevitch* and the cruisers *Pallada* and *Bayan*, the first two of which survived torpedo damage at Port Arthur in 1904, although in the British Navy, their inconvenience, especially regarding access, led to the subsequent abandonment of the system in the early dreadnoughts.

The anti-torpedo armament being completely exposed, and the flying deck being a particular large target, were considered weak points in the system, but they were armoured more heavily than in any of the preceding ships, and were unequalled in area or thickness in any of the later dreadnoughts prior to the *Orion* group in 1909.

The high standard of all-round protection in these ships was demonstrated during the Dardanelles operations when, on 7 March 1915, *Agamemnon* received eight, and *Lord Nelson* seven hits from heavy or semi-heavy calibre shells (14in or 9.4in) with no serious damage and only a few casualties.

There was a reversion to the high fitting (upper deck) anti-torpedo net shelf, which facilitated the handling of the nets. This was rendered possible by the absence of any main deck secondary armament. The upper deck net shelf had last been seen in the *Majestic*s (*Mars* excepted) as completed, but was abandoned in the intervening classes because of interference with the main deck 6in guns.

As fitted the main armoured belt was 12in-9in-6in thick, and ran for approximately 190ft amidships from the outer face of the forward barbette to abeam the after barbette. The upper edge was at middle deck level, about 2ft above the waterline. The lower edge was 5ft below the waterline. There was 12in from abeam the after barbette to the inner face of the fore barbette, the lower edge over the entire length being 6in thick. Forward there was 6in to 2in complete to the stem over the same width as the midships section except that the forward extremity was carried right down to support the ram. Thickness was 6in uniform except when reducing to 2in down to support ram (2in section supported by two ½in shell plates). Aft there were 4in armour plates complete to stern over the same width as the midships section. The lower side was 8in thick amidships from the outer face of the forward barbette to abeam the after barbette between middle and main deck levels.

There was 6in to 4in forward, and complete to the stem over the same width as the midships section; 6in for about one-third of the length, and then reducing to 4in outside this. The citadel amidships was 8in thick (sides) between the forward and after 9.2in turrets, from main to upper deck. The 8in bulkheads extended obliquely inwards from the forward and after extremities of the side armour of the citadel to the outer faces of the 12in barbettes.

The main bulkhead (aft only) was 8in, and ran obliquely inwards from the after extremity of the

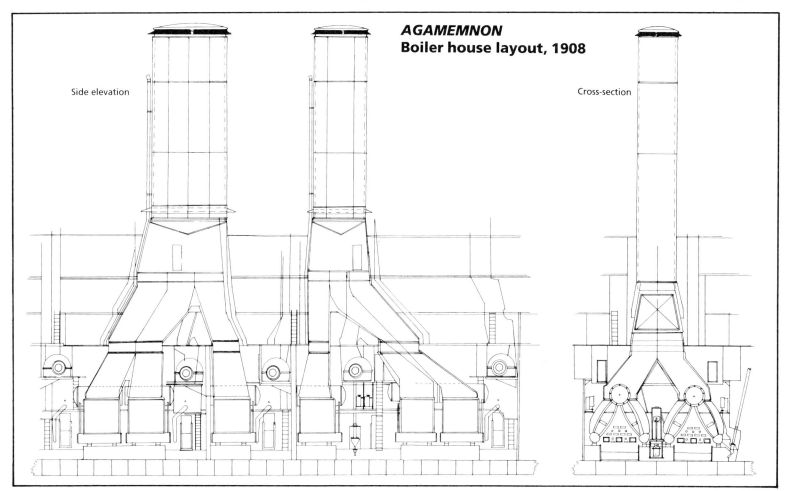

**AGAMEMNON
Boiler house layout, 1908**

Side elevation

Cross-section

lower side armour to the outer face of the after barbette.

The forward barbette had a 12in face, above the main deck, and then 8in to 4in from main to middle deck. The inner face, inside the citadel bulkhead was 12in above and 3in below upper deck level. The after barbette was 12in uniform on the outer face, but the inner face, inside the citadel bulkhead, was 12in above and 3in below upper deck level. The turrets had 12in sides and faces, 13in backs with 4in to 3in crowns. The 9.2in turrets had 8in faces, 7in sides and 2in roofs. The glacis to the 9.2in turrets were 6in thick. Ammunition hoists to the 9.2in turrets were 2in.

The upper deck was ³/₄in thick amidships and was laid over the citadel. The main deck was 1½in from the forward citadel bulkhead to the stem. The middle deck extended to just outside the 12in barbettes; extremities sloped sharply down to meet the lower deck, with the lower edge at the ship's side along the lower edge of the belt, 5ft below waterline; 2in on slope and 1in on flat amidships and 3in slope and flat outside this except on slopes to lower deck outside barbettes where it increased to 4in.

The lower deck was 1in on slopes and flat from the forward extremity of the middle deck to the stem, and 3in-2in on the slope and 2in on the flat on the after extremity of the middle deck to the stern.

The forward conning tower was 12in on the face and sides, with a 3in roof and 3in floor. The tube was 6in uniform. The after conning tower was 3in uniform with a 3in tube. Coal bunkers were located behind the belt and side armour between main and middle deck levels, and abreast boiler rooms below middle deck.

MACHINERY

From the very start it was generally agreed that *Lord Nelson* should have all large tube water boilers. Very early in the proceedings the DNC had pointed out that such a move to fit all Yarrow or Babcock boilers, rather than a mixture of cylindrical and Yarrow would mean a saving of about 70—75 tons which could be used to great advantage in other areas. Moreover, the Boiler Committee had concluded that it was more than desirable to fit boilers all of one type rather than a mixture (*see* boiler installations). As a result *Lord Nelson* received fifteen Babcock boilers, and *Agamemnon* fifteen Yarrow.

Agamemnon: Steam trials, 1907

Sea: moderate
Ship's bottom: clean
Propellers: two 4-bladed
Propeller diameter: 15ft 1in
Propeller pitch: 19ft
Developed area: 90ft
Coal consumption at full power: 2.141 pounds per hp per hour.

	Date	Draught forward	aft	Cylinder pressure psi	Boiler pressure psi	IHP	Revs	Average speed (knots)
⅕th power	20 Aug	26ft 6in	27ft 6in	222	222	3,515	77.37	11.794
⁷/₁₀th power	22 Aug	26ft 10in	27ft 2in	–	268	12,070	115.93	16.865
full power	26 Aug	26ft 6½in	27ft 6in	–	262.5	17,270	130.05	18.547
						17,526 (mean)	131.387 (mean)	18.735 (mean)

Maximum speed attained: 18.735 knots with 17,526ihp.

Agamemnon: Turning trials, 11 September 1907

Firth of Clyde
Wind: Northerly
Sea: calm
Ship's bottom: clean

	Full power		⅗ths power	
	Port	Starboard	Port	Starboard
Angle of rudder:	35°	35°	35°	35°
Time to reach angle (seconds):	5	5	7	7
Advancement (yards):	373	439	350	440
Revs:	116	116	76	76
Tactical diameter:	340	386	376	398
Speed:	17 knots		11.6 knots	
Comparison:	*Dreadnought*: 455 yards at 12 knots			
King Edward VII: 460 yards at 12 knots	*Lord Nelson*: 398 yards at 12 knots.			

Lord Nelson: Steam trials, 28 January 1908

Measured mile, full power
Estimated displacement: 15,000 tons
Draught: 25ft 7½in forward, 27ft 4½in aft

Run	Wind	SHP	Revs	Speed (knots)	SHP 4-hour trial	
First:	S.	Figures	125	18.072	15,911	
Second:	N.	not	124.2	18.614	16,616	gave mean speed
Third:	S.	taken	122.65	17.928	16,888	of 16.384 knots
Fourth:	N.		122.3	18.461	16,124	

1 February 1908
Wind: Force 6–7
Draught: 26ft 7in forced, 27ft 6¾in aft
Boiler pressure: 234psi
IHP: 17,445
Revs: 125.21
Speed: 18.53 knots (estimated by E. L. Attwood)
Trials abandoned because of weather; measured mile posts could not be seen.

They were the last British battleships to be fitted with reciprocating engines and twin screws; turbines and quadruple screws were used in all later types of battleship. They were also the last to have in-turning screws, which had been introduced in the *Canopus* class, and retained in all intervening classes. These screws afforded a greater drive, slightly higher speed and slightly reduced fuel consumption compared to the normal type; but they had an adverse effect on handiness at slow speeds or when going astern, and were generally disliked in service.

As fitted the installation consisted of two sets of 4-cylinder inverted vertical, triple expansion, surface condensing engines driving twin screws. Cylinder sizes were 32³/₄in (HP), 52³/₄in (IP), and 60in (LP) with a stroke of 48in.

The boilers were arranged in two compartments and had a working pressure of 275psi, heating surface of 50,265sq ft, and a total grate area of 848sq ft.

The Babcock boilers in *Lord Nelson* were fitted with six oil sprayers, with a total output of 940lb oil sprayed, per boiler, at 150psi. *Agamemnon* had only five oil sprayers, being sprayed at the same pressure of 150psi but delivered only 900lb.

They were the first British battleships designed

LORD NELSON
Outboard profile, as seen at
Dardanelles 1915

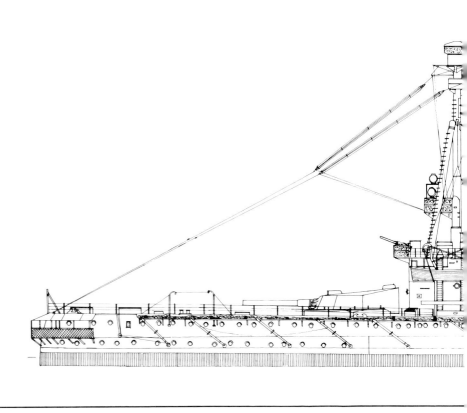

to carry oil; provision had been made in the *King Edward*s while under construction, but not in the original design. Oil was stowed in the bottom compartments which were considerably larger than usual in order to minimize the number of pipes and fittings.

This pair were fitted with a system of forced lubrication to the main engines (principal bearings), first tried out in *Africa*, which had proved very successful in destroyers during earlier experiments. The lubrication (oil) was pumped under pressure around the machinery, then after being used, discharged through the bearings and drains to an oil well fitted between the centre crank pits. This oil was drawn through a strainer box from the well by means of another pump, and discharged through filters back to reservoir tanks for further use. The great advantages of such a system are obvious. In general, the machinery/boiler installation in *Lord Nelson* and *Agamemnon* proved very satisfactory, and just as reliable as that in the later dreadnoughts.

APPEARANCE CHANGES

Having a distinct French appearance, this pair were quite unlike any other contemporary British battleship. They were by no means handsome

Lord Nelson class: Machinery, legend weights (tons)

Machinery and water in feed tanks:	1,545
Spare gear:	30
Boat hoists:	15
Coal hoists:	40
Dynamos and engines:	4
Ash hoists:	2
Engineers' workshop motors:	1
Ice machine:	5
Steam heating apparatus:	15
Total:	1,657

Deep condition as above except:
Water tanks full, plus feed tanks full to working height: 12 tons
Reserve feedwater: 120 tons

Coal capacity (tons):
Upper bunkers 700
Lower bunkers 500
Outer bunkers 800
Total 2,000 tons.

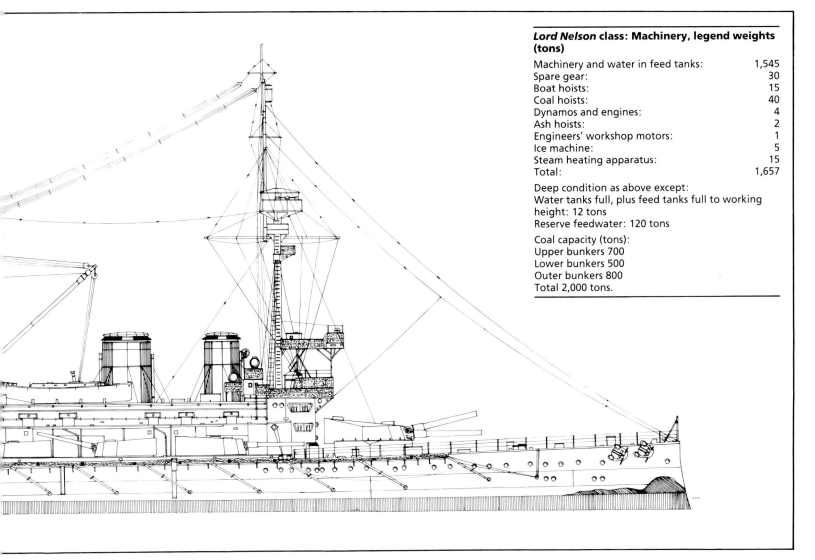

Below: Aboard *Lord Nelson*, late 1918.

Bottom: *Agamemnon*, 1918.

ships, in fact they were ugly; they did, however, present a picture of grim fighting efficiency seldom equalled. Features included:

1. A row of turrets on each beam amidships.
2. Piled up superstructure, and large flying deck.
3. Short, flat-sided, unequal-sized funnels; fore funnel noticeable smaller than second.

4. Light flying bridge over forward superstructure.
5. Prominent topping davits on superstructure abeam mainmast.

W/T topgallant on each mast as completed. Fore topmast and topgallant stepped abaft, main before. Not at all easy to tell apart, especially at a distance.

Lord Nelson No steam pipe abaft fore funnel; brackets high on fore funnel; small charthouse below flying bridge.

Agamemnon Steam pipe abaft fore funnel. Low brackets before second funnel.

1909 Range indicators fitted to the faces of each control top in *Agamemnon* and to second top on each mast in *Lord Nelson*. 3pdrs reduced to four in *Agamemnon*, and two in *Lord Nelson*. Standard system of funnel bands painted-up. *Agamemnon* none, *Lord Nelson* one white on each.

1910–11 Fore control top in *Agamemnon* enlarged to accommodate rangefinder. RF mounted on fore turret in both ships. SL removed from foremast in both ships. SL remounted over conning tower in *Agamemnon*, and on flying bridge in *Lord Nelson*.

1912 Fore control top in *Lord Nelson* modified as in *Agamemnon*. SL removed from flying bridge in *Lord Nelson*.

1913–14 Small RF added on bridge in *Lord Nelson*. Remaining 3pdrs removed from both ships. Various SL modifications in *Lord Nelson*. Flying deck SL (four) remounted on platform low on main tripod legs on two levels. After superstructure SL (two) remounted (P+S) abeam fore funnel. Forward superstructure SL (two) remounted on high platforms (P+S) before second funnel.

1914 Funnel bands painted out.

1914–15 RF removed from fore turret in both ships, and from bridge in *Lord Nelson*. Two 12pdrs removed from after superstructure in both ships. Two AA guns added. One at after extremity of quarterdeck in both ships, other on forward superstructure (port) in *Agamemnon*, and on forecastle, before fore turret in *Lord Nelson*. After pair, flying deck SL remounted close beside forward pair in *Agamemnon*. Main tripod SL platform in *Lord Nelson* enlarged. Extra flying bridge added in *Agamemnon* below original. Charthouse removed in *Lord Nelson*. Main topmast removed in both ships; fore topmast and topgallant retained. Small spotting top fitted at head of fore topmast in *Lord Nelson*.

Special camouflage painted-up in *Agamemnon* for Dardanelles operations. *Lord Nelson* painted on turrets, superstructure and funnels, in light-grey colour with false bow wave; *Agamemnon* blotched paintwork (*see* camouflage). The camouflage in *Agamemnon* was intended to blend with the landscape, so that when moored off Gallipoli she would be difficult for enemy submarines to see. In

practice, however, the scheme (and others of this nature) proved somewhat ineffective, because at a few thousand yards or so, the shades merged, and produced an overall grey appearance.

1916–17 Forward pair of flying deck 12pdrs removed from both ships, and lower pair in forward superstructure removed in *Agamemnon*. 24in SL restored in *Lord Nelson*, and mounted on original platform below fore control top. Various SL modifications in *Agamemnon*: After pair of flying deck SL restored to original position. Forward pair, together with SL (two) ex-after superstructure, remounted on platform low on tripod legs. Forward superstructure SL suppressed. 24in SL remounted on platform below control top (1917). Funnels raised to clear bridge. Main topmast and topgallant replaced in both.

1918 Remaining 12pdrs removed from after structure in *Lord Nelson*. Forward AA gun in *Agamemnon* transferred to starboard side of superstructure. 24in SL remounted on new platform, low on foremast. Torpedo nets removed. Charthouse replaced in Lord Nelson late in year. Topgallant masts removed in both.

AGAMEMNON AS TARGET SHIP

On 14 September 1918, CinC, David Beatty, wrote to their Lordships at the Admiralty, explaining his theory that practical gunnery experience was required for many of the ships in the battle fleet, because they had not seen action, or had the chance to fire their guns at a suitable target even in practice shoots.

'War experience has emphasized the importance of observation of fire as the principal factor in successful fire control. The newly introduced system of 'throw off' firing provides excellent practice for the control personnel in all respects except observation of fire which is not furnished in a realistic manner during target firings under modern conditions.

It is over two years since the Battle fleet have had any action experience, and a large number of control officers have joined. Important decisions governing fire control and concentration now have to be decided largely on conjecture, so far as observation of fire is concerned; this leaves an element of doubt, as to what is, or is not, practicable under action conditions. It is therefore considered a matter of urgency that some practice in spotting against a ship target under realistic

conditions should be afforded to control officers.

To meet the requirements, it is proposed that a bulk target be provided—either an obsolete warship or damaged merchant vessel—and that a full calibre firing with practice shot be carried out periodically and witnessed by control officers who can be accommodated in the firing ship or ships. It is requested that this important matter may receive their Lordships early consideration.'

Agreeing with all that was said in this letter, their Lordships at the Admiralty made moves to sanction use of one of the many obsolete warships available at that time, and asked the various departments involved to carry out tests to see which vessel would be the most suitable. Early in 1919 firing tests were carried out at Shoeburyness on plates of similar thickness to those fitted in the old predreadnoughts (decks), but it was soon realized that to fire on any warship with 15in shells would quickly sink her.

In the tests, plates were placed at a range corresponding to 25,500 yards. All the plates were completely destroyed, and it was therefore decided to use any target provided, but only against 6in shells or lesser sizes.

Test 1. Plates equivalent to upper deck of *Agamemnon* ($^3/_4$in) completely pierced with a hole of 15in x27in.

Test 2. Plates equivalent to main deck ($^3/_8$in plate plus 1in); same as before, but hole was 17in x 27in.

Test 3. Plates equivalent to middle deck (1in plus 1in sandbags behind). Target completely destroyed, with plates being pierced and scattered some 45 yards away—sandbags smashed to bits.

At first it was suggested that the old *Hibernia* of the *King Edward VII* class be used, but when *Agamemnon* was put forward on offer, she was eagerly accepted. Work proceeded from 6 December 1920 and was completed on 8 April 1921.

There were, however, problems concerning the removal of all of the big guns (12in and 9.2in) which, it was thought, would seriously affect the stability. To overcome this, to some extent, it was decided to place ballast in compartments below the main deck, and fill others with cork for extra buoyancy if the material could be acquired in such great quantities. She was completely rewired for extra communication, and many electrical controls were placed all over the ship; she would be wireless-controlled at times. When being prepared for use as a target, *Agamemnon* was completely stripped, with the following alterations:

1. Removal of all 12in guns and mountings, plus all hydraulic gear associated with them.
2. Removal of all 9.2in guns and mountings, plus turrets and hydraulic gear.
3. Removal of all 12pdrs and equipment.
4. Removal of all coamings, unneeded hatches, scuttles and lifts; open ports plated up after removal.
5. Removal of all mess gear, and spaces cleared.
6. All CO_2 machinery removed.
7. All ventilation trunks removed and plated-up.
8. Lower conning tower removed.
9. 1,000 tons ballast placed in various parts of the ship as seen neccessary.
10. All torpedo equipment removed.
11. All refrigeration equipment removed.
12. Flying deck removed.
13. Sea cabins removed.
14. Main derrick and boat booms removed. W/T office replaced by new control office.
15. All small fittings such as boat davits, anchor gear, coal winches and storage boxes, etc., removed.
16. All mast and yards removed.

Estimated cost: Labour £26,874; Material £7,182; Dockyard work £19, 692.

The first trials were carried out on 19 March 1921 to see how a modern battleship would stand up against gas attack, but unfortunately no record of this trial has been found. What is known, however, is that the Admiralty was well aware that in a future war, a ship might pass through a large cloud of noxious gas and staff in the upper parts of the ship could be at risk. Scuttles, hatches and small openings in the vessel would let such gases in, but as *Agamemnon* was not properly sealed because of her partial stripping, accurate results could not be obtained.

On 21 September 1921 trials were carried out to ascertain the effect of machine-gun fire from aircraft. It was appreciated that in such tests conditions were artifically favourable to the attacking craft, as any modern warship would not just sit there in the water and would certainly return any fire. Nevertheless, the test was to see if any of the personnel would be in danger in exposed areas. The trials showed that a modern, well-equipped squadron of aircraft, with efficient machine-guns, could do no better than harass the ship. The plating (vertical) protecting exposed parts was $^3/_{16}$in thick and at times had been pene-

trated. The horizontal plating ($^1/_{16}$in) had also been mutilated and in places penetrated, but at the expense of the bullets, which had been destroyed. Accordingly, it was agreed that future protection for bridge personnel should be confined to that area only and be at least $^1/_4$in thick which would give complete immunity.

Controlled by wireless, she underwent a series of tests in which she was fired upon by 6in, 5.5in and 4in shells. 6in shells: 400 rounds at 14,000 yards (down to 11,000 yards); 5.5in and 4in: 300 rounds at 14,000 yards. After the first tests, constructor E. L. Attwood went aboard and reported: 'Out of the 400 rounds of 6in fired, only 22 hits were scored. For the 300 rounds of 5.5in and 4in it was 20 hits.'

Most of the shells had hit broadside on and did not get past the upper deck, but were brought to a halt there. Three rounds did penetrate the thin side plating below the upper deck, but the shells were broken up and did not penetrate to the middle deck level. There seemed to be little damage in general.

Two outstanding shots were fired from *Renown* and *Repulse*, which struck *Agamemnon* stern on as

---

Agamemnon: As target ship, 13 April 1921

Condition of ship
Fuel: none on board
Reserve feedwater: none on board
Boilers: all without water
Condensers: empty
Anchors: only 19 shackles on board

Five Carley rafts on quarterdeck
Fresh water: none on board, but 44 tons to come
Provisions: 14½ tons on board, 4 tons to come
Warrant officers and Engineer's stores: none on
  board
Crew: 153
There were also about 5 tons of rubbish scattered on the upper and main deck levels.

Ship inclined to establish stability:
'A' Condition: Displacement: 13,320 tons
                Draught: 20ft 11in forward, 24ft aft
                GM: 7.6ft
'B' Condition: Displacement: 14,185 tons
                Draught: 23ft 2½in forward, 24ft
                3in aft
                GM: 8.56ft
'C' Condition: Displacement: 15,830 (some
                compartments filled with water)
                Draught: —
                GM: 9.55ft

AGAMEMNON
Outboard profile, as converted to gunnery target ship 1923

Note radio control equipment on tops of masts and turrets.

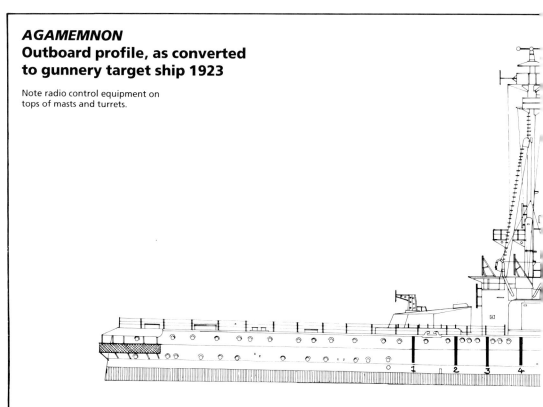

she was moving away. One of the rounds struck over a beam and ripped up the wood and scored the upper plating; some fragments of the beam and plating did perforate a thin bulkhead below this area. The other shell penetrated the upper deck over the washroom, and the middle deck transverse bulkhead below, before coming to a halt in the feedwater tank. These two shells were stated to have descended at 35°–36° and had a striking velocity of 840fps. If the shells had been fired from larger calibres—especially from any main armament, considerable damage would have been caused. Much attention was paid to this area in future.

Tests also showed that ships built like *Agamemnon* or stronger (some of the dreadnoughts, etc.) had little to fear from secondary batteries except wrecked upperworks and general havoc, but owing to long battle ranges—small calibres were generally ineffective. *Agamemnon* was used as a target until 1926 and then replaced by *Centurion*.

HISTORY: *LORD NELSON*

Laid down by Palmer at Jarrow on 18 May 1905 and commissioned at Chatham with a nucleus crew on 1 Dec 1908. The completion of these two was considerably delayed by labour troubles, and appropriation of some of the 12in guns to expedite delivery of the all big gunned *Dreadnought*.

5 Jan 1909 Completed with full crew to relieve *Magnificent* as Flagship Nore Division, Home Fleet, until Aug 1914.

Sept 1913 Temporarily attached to 4th BS.

April 1914 Relieved as Flag from *Queen* (VA), 2nd Home Fleet.

7 Aug 1914 Became Flagship (VA), Channel Fleet as constituted for Channel defence, and to cover passage of BEF to France.

Aug 1914—Feb 1915 With Channel Fleet. Normally based at Portland, but moved to Sheerness owing to possibility of German invasion. 30 Dec 1914 Squadron replaced at Sheerness by *Duncan*s (6th BS) and returned to Portland.

Feb 1915 Transferred to Dardanelles; *Lord Nelson* left Portland 18 Feb and joined British Squadron at Mudros on 26th. In Dardanelles until Jan 1916. Took part in bombardment of the inner forts and initial landings early in Mar 1915. Heavily engaged by forts 7 Mar, being hit several times, sustaining splinter damage, superstructure and rigging cut up, and one hit below waterline which flooded two bunkers. Other than this, no substantial damage. Refitted at Malta. Took part in main attack on Narrows forts 18 Mar. Engaged German battle-cruiser *Goeben* briefly off Gaba Tepe, and bombarded field batteries prior to second battle of Krithia on 6 May. Became Flagship VA, British

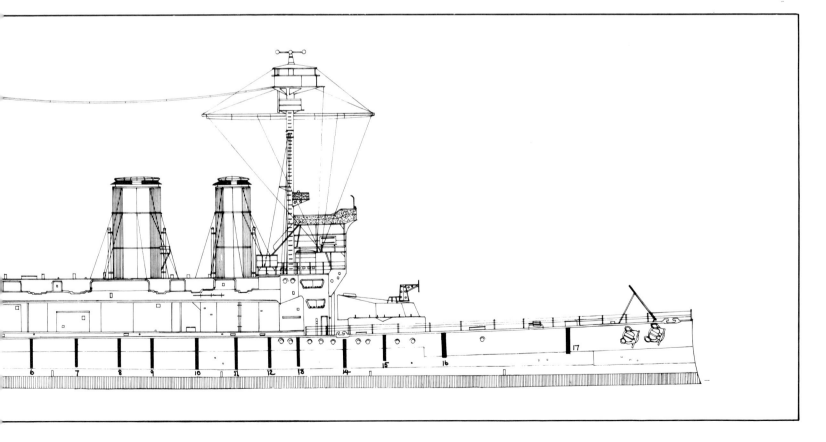

Below: *Agamemnon* as target ship 1924–25.

Dardanelles Squadron, after *Queen Elizabeth* was ordered home 12 May 1915.

Bombarded docks and shipping at Gallipoli on 20 June, with kite balloon spotting, inflicting considerable damge. Lord Kitchener set up headquarters aboard *Lord Nelson* at Mudros in Nov 1915. Became Flag (VA), British Eastern Mediterranean Squadron on reorganization following evacuation of Gallipoli Jan 1916, until Aug 1917.

Stationed at Salonika and Mudros (alternating with *Agamemnon*) against any sorties by *Goeben* from Dardanelles. *Lord Nelson* mainly at Salonika.

Aug 1917 Eastern Mediterranean Squadron redesignated British Aegean Squadron. With British Aegean Squadron, until May 1919.

20 Jan 1918 Attempted to intercept *Goeben* after latter had been mined *en route* to raid Mudros, but *Lord Nelson* was unable to make contact before *Goeben* reached shelter of Dardanelles.

Oct 1918 Refit at Malta. Unit of British Squadron sent to Constantinople Nov 1918 following Turkish Armistice. Conveyed Grand Duke Nicholas and Peter of Russia from Black Sea to Genoa April 1919. Returned home May 1919.

May—Aug 1919 Reserve.

August 1919 Placed on sale list.

4 June 1920 Sold to Stanlee Shipbreaking Co, Dover. Resold to Slough Trading Co, 8 November, and again to German scrappers.

Jan 1922 Towed to Germany for scrapping.

HISTORY: *AGAMEMNON*

Laid down by Beardmore at Dalmuir, and commissioned at Chatham on 25 June after considerable delay.

June 1908 Joined Home Fleet, Nore Division, until Aug 1914.

11 Feb 1911 She grazed an uncharted rock on entering Ferrol Harbour, sustaining damage to bottom and frame work.

Sept 1913 Temporarily attached to 4th BS.

7 Aug 1914 Transferred to Channel Fleet (5th BS) as constituted for defence of Channel.

Aug 1914—Feb 1915 Channel Fleet (5th BS Portland and Sheerness).

Feb 1915 Transferred to Dardanelles. Left Portland 9 Feb and joined Dardanelles Squadron on 19th, until Jan 1916. Took part in opening bombardment of entrance forts 19 Feb, and subsequent bombardments of entrance forts and initial landing during Feb and early Mar. She was hit seven times in ten minutes by 9.4in shells from Fort Helles 25 Feb, three fatal casualties. Holed above the waterline, but sustained no serious damage. *Agamemnon* came under heavy fire from field batteries and Fort Hamidieh 7 Mar: one hit, alleged to be a 14in shell penetrated the quarterdeck, blowing a large hole and wrecking wardroom and gunroom. She received seven more hits, plus several from lighter guns later than day. Her upper works were cut up but there was no serious hindrance to the working of the ship. Took part in the attack on the Narrows forts 18 Mar.

Hit twelve times in twenty-five minutes by a 6in howitzer battery, five times on the armour without injury, and seven times outside it. Considerable structural damage was sustained, and one of her 12in guns was temporarily out of action. She supported main landings 25 April and was employed in protecting the sweeping and net-laying vessels in the Straits. Hit twice in action against field batteries from 28 to 30 April. Supported troops during Turkish counterattack 1 May and bombarded batteries prior to second attack on Krithia on 6th. May—June 1915 Under refit at Malta. With the cruiser, *Endymion*, and monitor *M33*, destroyed central spans of Kavak bridge 2 Dec 1915, cutting enemy communications across Bulair Lines, to Gallipoli Peninsula. Became unit of Eastern Mediterranean Squadron on reorganization, following evacuation of Gallipoli Jan 1916: this force being broken up into several detached squadrons deployed at various bases in the Aegean. Jan 1916—Aug 1917 British Eastern Mediterranean Squadron. The duty of these squadrons was to 'watch the Dardanelles' and safeguard the Greek islands under British occupation, as well as support the army at Salonika. *Agamemnon* based mainly at Mudros. Shot down the Zeppelin L85 5 May. Redesignated British Aegean Squadron Aug 1917. Sent from Mudros to intercept *Goeben*, but missed her. Refit at Malta 1918. Terms of the Armistice were signed on board at Mudros 30 Oct 1918 and ship subsequently proceeded to Constantinople with British Squadron in Nov 1918. Returned home, and paid off at Chatham into Reserve 20 Mar 1919. Refit at Chatham September to April 1923 for service as wireless-controlled target ship (*see* notes). Replaced by *Centurion* Dec 1926. Sold 1927. Left Portsmouth for Newport and scrapping 1 Mar 1927.

APPEARANCE CHANGES

1 *Royal Sovereign* as completed, 1893.
2 *c.* 1896: no white line along hull.

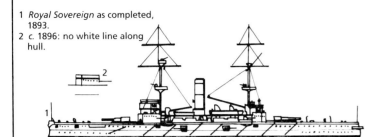

1 *Ramillies* as completed, 1893; no white line at waterline; buff paintwork.

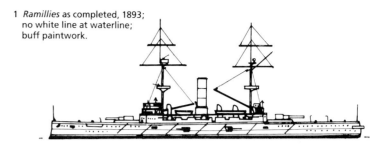

1 *Royal Sovereign*, 1903/4, showing casemates, lowered net shelf, W/T gaff and all-grey paintwork.
2 1910: red funnel bands.

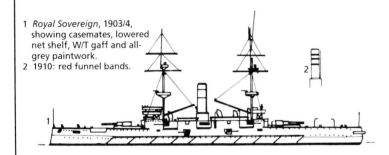

1 *Ramillies*, 1905/6, with casemates and low net position; gaff and searchlight removed later.
2 1910: white funnel bands.

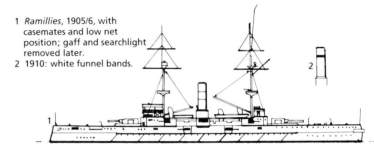

1 *Empress of India* as completed 1893.
2 1894: buff top to upper level and black line. (Also seen 1894/5 with brown masts and lower funnel coaming.)
3 Rig as modified 1902.

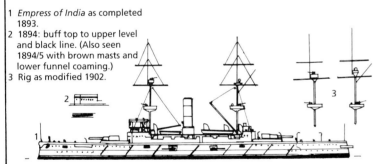

1 *Royal Oak*, 1904/5, with lowered net shelf, casemates; gaff still in position.
2 1910: red funnel bands. (Only unit of Class to have steam pipes *in front of* funnels.)

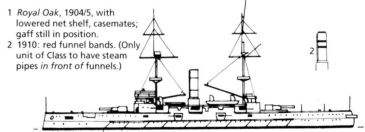

1 *Empress of India*, 1894, with red funnel bands and all-grey paintwork.
2 Rig as in 1906; no bands; foretopmast.

3 1905: W/T gaff to mainmast and yards closer together.

1 *Repulse*, 1910, with white funnel bands.
2 1904: 3pdrs removed from tops.

3 Mainmast 1904/5. (*Repulse* had white vents as completed, 1894.)

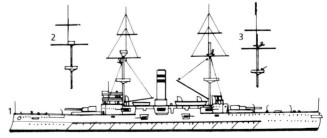

1 *Resolution* as completed, 1893, with buff bridge, masts and funnels, white vents, all-white bridge.
2 1894/5: buff top to superstructure and vents; later during same period, dark vents (probably brown) were evident; gaffs removed early.
3 Rig as in 1905.
4 1910: white funnel bands.

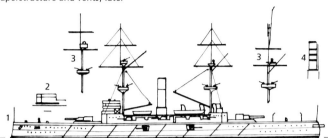

1 *Centurion* as completed, 1894, with buff paintwork, white line at upper deck level, white upper works; searchlight added to maintop 1901; painted all-white during China Station period.

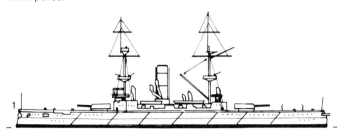

1 *Revenge*, 1905/6; nets removed 1906.
2 Rig in 1908; maintopmast and W/T removed 1911.
3 Foremast rig in 19
4 Rig in 1915.

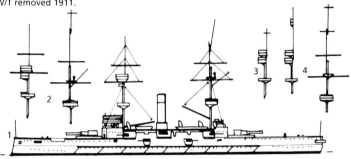

1 *Centurion* as reconstructed 1904; grey paintwork, vents removed amidships, new bridgework aft, vent removed behind foremast.
2 Foretopmast added 1905/6.
3 W/T gaff added on mainmast in 1904.

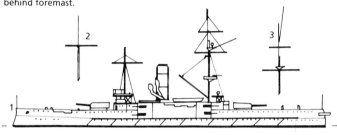

1 *Hood* as completed, 1894; two gaffs, buff paintwork.
2 1899: modified paintwork to turrets and superstructure.
3 1899/1900: upper yard to mainmast and semaphore.
4 1898: 3pdr in lower mainmast top.

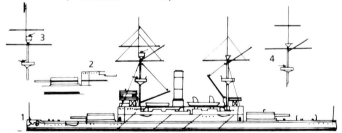

1 *Barfleur* as completed, 1894; buff paintwork.

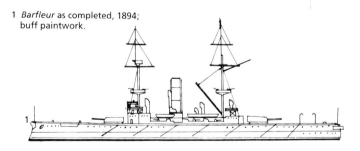

1 *Hood*, 1904/5; grey, W/T gaff, low net position.

1 *Barfleur* as reconstructed 1904; grey paintwork, W/T gaff added to mainmast during 1904; maintopmast added 1905; foretopmast added 1905/6 and maintopmast removed; topmasts to both in 1906/7.

1 *Renown* as completed, 1897; buff paintwork. 1903, first cruise: flagstaff to mainmast, large vents removed, white paintwork; reported to have had green waterline.

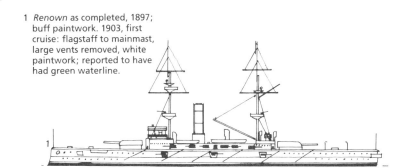

1 *Magnificent* as completed, 1896; buff paintwork; after chart house not seen in early period.

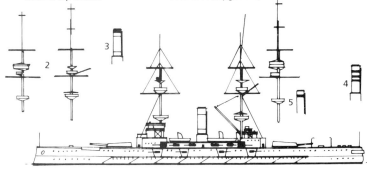

1 *Renown*, 1905; second Royal Cruise. White paintwork, red waterline, tall topmasts; repainted all-grey after cruise.

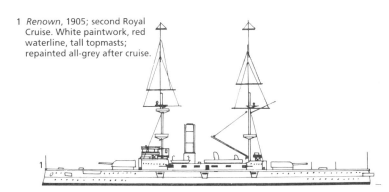

1 *Magnificent*, 1906; new net shelf, W/T gaff.
2 Rig in 1908; special fire-control top added.

3 1903: black tops painted on funnels.
4 1910: red funnel bands; rig to foremast (topgallant).

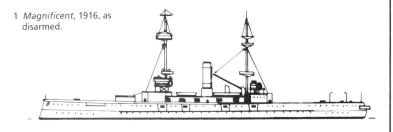

1 *Majestic* as completed, 1895; no vents, buff paintwork, black line.

2 1895/6: vents added, brown masts, no white line on upper deck level, no main yards.

1 *Magnificent*, 1916, as disarmed.

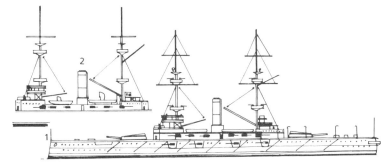

1 *Majestic*, 1906, with red funnel bands, tall gaff to main.

2 1911: new topmast to main.
3 1915: crow's nest on foremast.
4 1910: red funnel bands.

1 *Mars* as completed, 1897; buff paintwork.

2 No lower yards, no semaphore or gaff (early period); gaff to mainmast 1902.

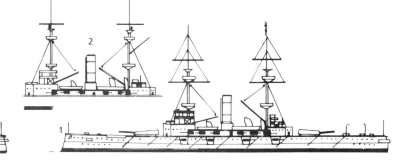

1 *Mars* 1903/4; early red funnel
  bands, W/T gaff to mainmast,
  new net level, new top to
  foremast.
2 1910 rig and red funnel
  bands; fire control added.

1 *Jupiter* as completed; buff
  paintwork.
2 Early period: no guns in tops,
  searchlights in tops, no yards
  on masts.

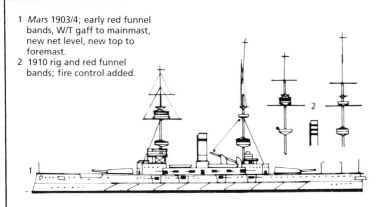

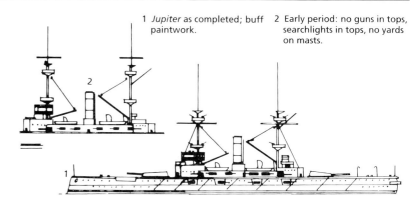

1 *Prince George* as completed,
  1896; buff paintwork.
2 W/T gaff added to mainmast.

3 Two black funnel bands.
4 1906: gaff added to mainmast
  and no funnel bands.

1 *Jupiter*, 1904; low net shelf,
  grey paintwork, new large
  foretop, single black funnel
  band, no guns in tops.
2 Guns seen in tops during that

  period and no funnel bands at
  times up to 1906.
3 Rig as 1906, showing fire-
  control on lower foretop and
  back of after bridgework.

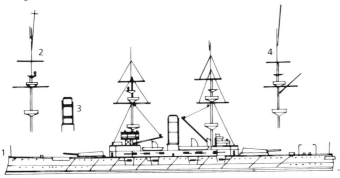

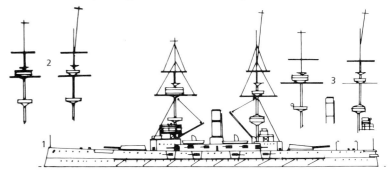

1 *Prince George*, 1905; black
  funnel bands; new torpedo
  shelf level.
2 Maintopmast added 1907.
3 1909: retained black funnel

  bands when standard
  markings were introduced.
4 Tops to both masts and no
  yards on mainmast, 1911–12.

1 *Jupiter*, 1908; top to
  mainmast, caging to funnel,
  no guns in tops.
2 Standard funnel bands,

  1907–10; three, white.
3 1912: tall tops to both masts,
  bands on funnels seem thicker
  and wider apart.

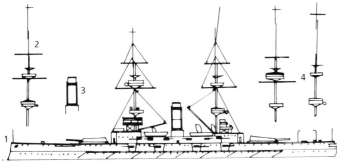

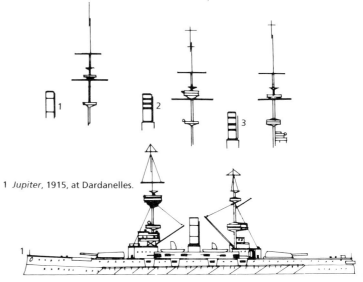

1 *Prince George*, 1918,
  completely disarmed and
  modified as Torpedo Boat
  Destroyer Depot Ship.

1 *Jupiter*, 1915, at Dardanelles.

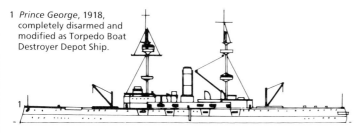

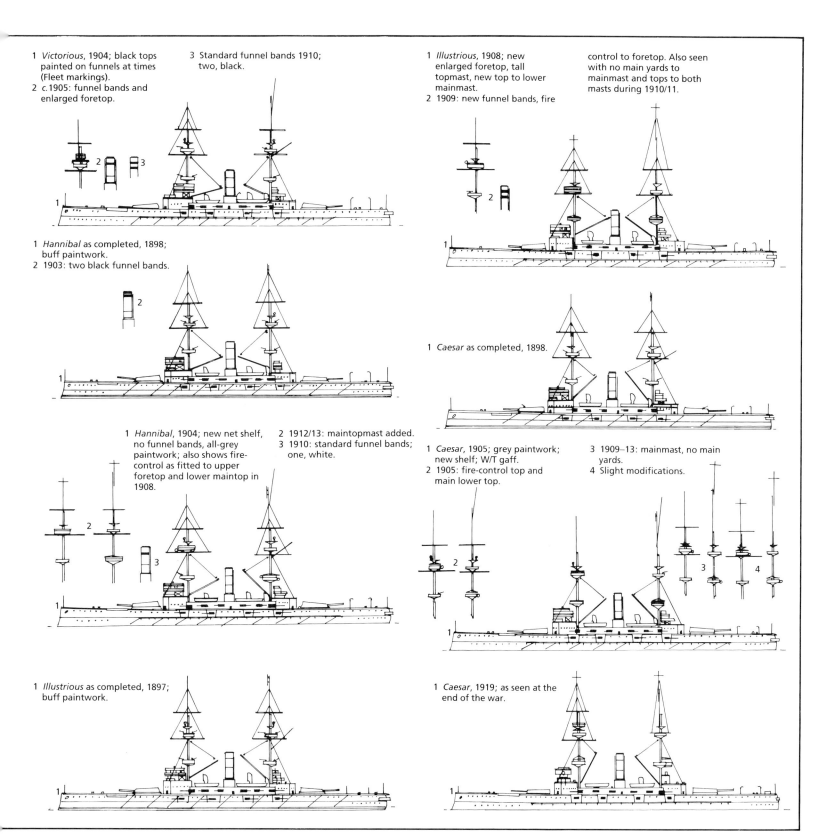

1 *Victorious*, 1904; black tops painted on funnels at times (Fleet markings).
2 *c.*1905: funnel bands and enlarged foretop.

3 Standard funnel bands 1910; two, black.

1 *Hannibal* as completed, 1898; buff paintwork.
2 1903: two black funnel bands.

1 *Hannibal*, 1904; new net shelf, no funnel bands, all-grey paintwork; also shows fire-control as fitted to upper foretop and lower maintop in 1908.

2 1912/13: maintopmast added.
3 1910: standard funnel bands; one, white.

1 *Illustrious* as completed, 1897; buff paintwork.

1 *Illustrious*, 1908; new enlarged foretop, tall topmast, new top to lower mainmast.
2 1909: new funnel bands, fire control to foretop. Also seen with no main yards to mainmast and tops to both masts during 1910/11.

1 *Caesar* as completed, 1898.

1 *Caesar*, 1905; grey paintwork; new shelf; W/T gaff.
2 1905: fire-control top and main lower top.

3 1909–13: mainmast, no main yards.
4 Slight modifications.

1 *Caesar*, 1919; as seen at the end of the war.

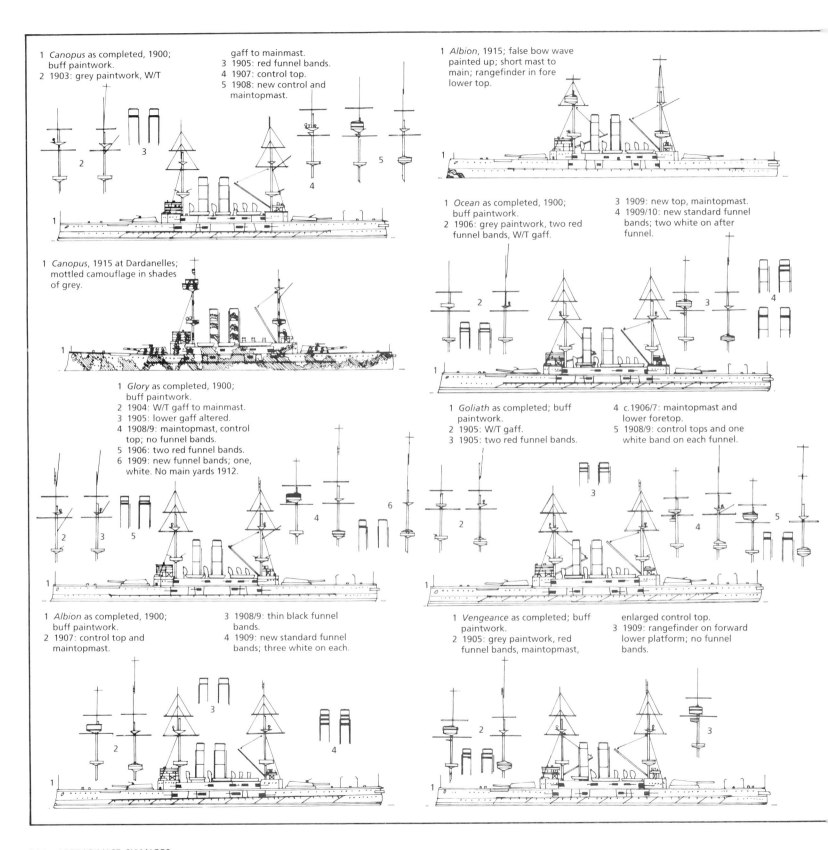

1 *Canopus* as completed, 1900;
  buff paintwork.
2 1903: grey paintwork, W/T

gaff to mainmast.
3 1905: red funnel bands.
4 1907: control top.
5 1908: new control and
  maintopmast.

1 *Canopus*, 1915 at Dardanelles;
  mottled camouflage in shades
  of grey.

1 *Glory* as completed, 1900;
  buff paintwork.
2 1904: W/T gaff to mainmast.
3 1905: lower gaff altered.
4 1908/9: maintopmast, control
  top; no funnel bands.
5 1906: two red funnel bands.
6 1909: new funnel bands; one,
  white. No main yards 1912.

1 *Albion* as completed, 1900;
  buff paintwork.
2 1907: control top and
  maintopmast.

3 1908/9: thin black funnel
  bands.
4 1909: new standard funnel
  bands; three white on each.

1 *Albion*, 1915; false bow wave
  painted up; short mast to
  main; rangefinder in fore
  lower top.

1 *Ocean* as completed, 1900;
  buff paintwork.
2 1906: grey paintwork, two red
  funnel bands, W/T gaff.

3 1909: new top, maintopmast.
4 1909/10: new standard funnel
  bands; two white on after
  funnel.

1 *Goliath* as completed; buff
  paintwork.
2 1905: W/T gaff.
3 1905: two red funnel bands.

4 c.1906/7: maintopmast and
  lower foretop.
5 1908/9: control tops and one
  white band on each funnel.

1 *Vengeance* as completed; buff
  paintwork.
2 1905: grey paintwork, red
  funnel bands, maintopmast,

enlarged control top.
3 1909: rangefinder on forward
  lower platform; no funnel
  bands.

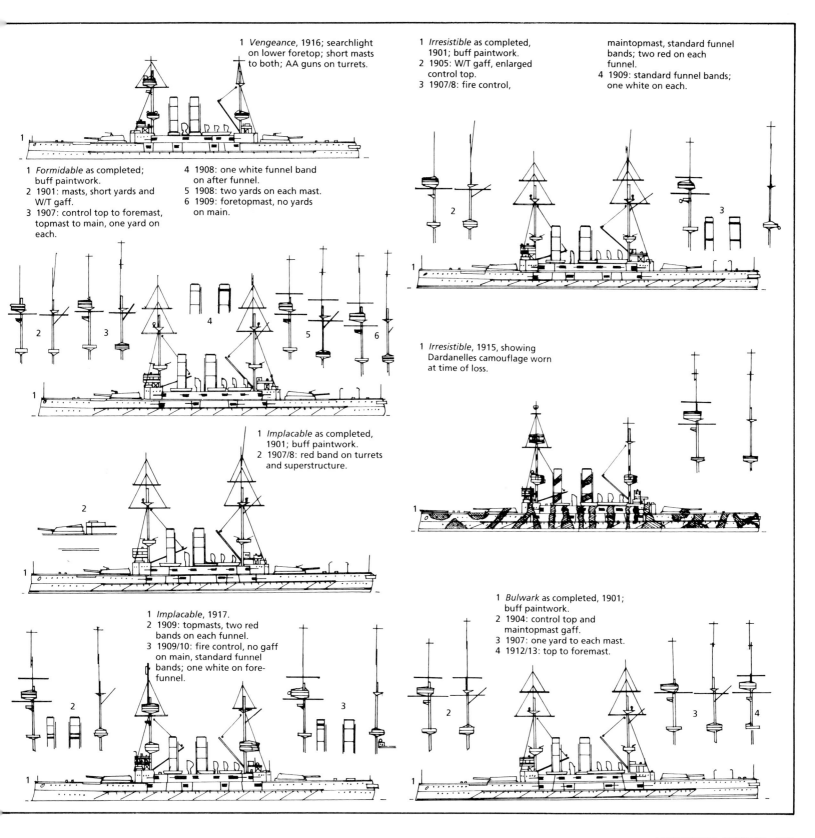

1 *Vengeance*, 1916; searchlight on lower foretop; short masts to both; AA guns on turrets.

1 *Formidable* as completed; buff paintwork.
2 1901: masts, short yards and W/T gaff.
3 1907: control top to foremast, topmast to main, one yard on each.

4 1908: one white funnel band on after funnel.
5 1908: two yards on each mast.
6 1909: foretopmast, no yards on main.

1 *Implacable* as completed, 1901; buff paintwork.
2 1907/8: red band on turrets and superstructure.

1 *Implacable*, 1917.
2 1909: topmasts, two red bands on each funnel.
3 1909/10: fire control, no gaff on main, standard funnel bands; one white on fore-funnel.

1 *Irresistible* as completed, 1901; buff paintwork.
2 1905: W/T gaff, enlarged control top.
3 1907/8: fire control,

maintopmast, standard funnel bands; two red on each funnel.
4 1909: standard funnel bands; one white on each.

1 *Irresistible*, 1915, showing Dardanelles camouflage worn at time of loss.

1 *Bulwark* as completed, 1901; buff paintwork.
2 1904: control top and maintopmast gaff.
3 1907: one yard to each mast.
4 1912/13: top to foremast.

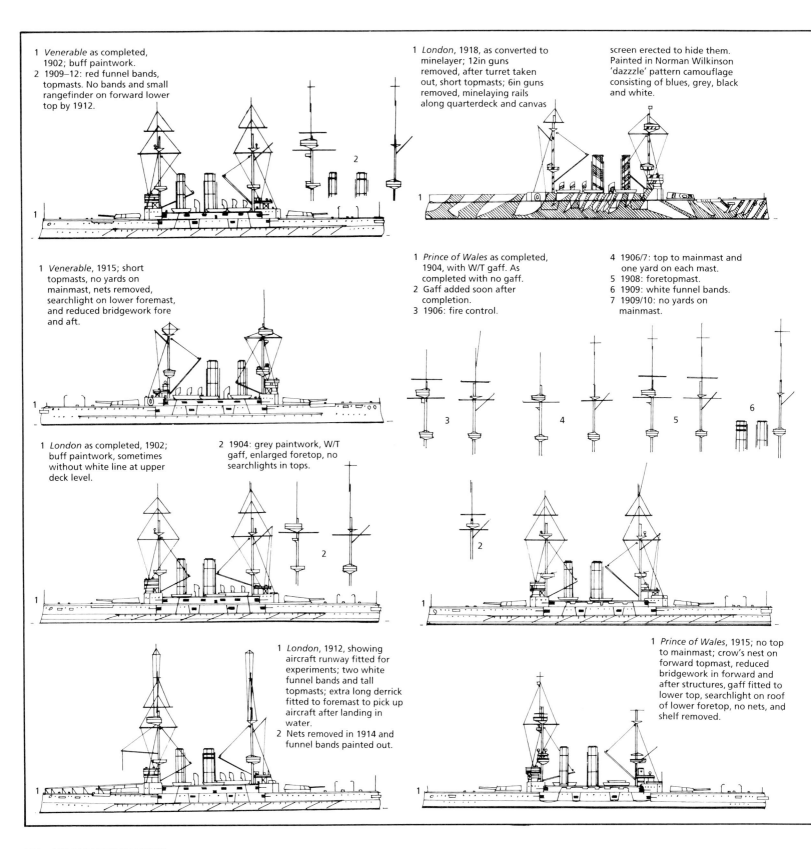

1 *Venerable* as completed, 1902; buff paintwork.
2 1909–12: red funnel bands, topmasts. No bands and small rangefinder on forward lower top by 1912.

1 *Venerable*, 1915; short topmasts, no yards on mainmast, nets removed, searchlight on lower foremast, and reduced bridgework fore and aft.

1 *London* as completed, 1902; buff paintwork, sometimes without white line at upper deck level.
2 1904: grey paintwork, W/T gaff, enlarged foretop, no searchlights in tops.

1 *London*, 1912, showing aircraft runway fitted for experiments; two white funnel bands and tall topmasts; extra long derrick fitted to foremast to pick up aircraft after landing in water.
2 Nets removed in 1914 and funnel bands painted out.

1 *London*, 1918, as converted to minelayer; 12in guns removed, after turret taken out, short topmasts; 6in guns removed, minelaying rails along quarterdeck and canvas screen erected to hide them. Painted in Norman Wilkinson 'dazzle' pattern camouflage consisting of blues, grey, black and white.

1 *Prince of Wales* as completed, 1904, with W/T gaff. As completed with no gaff.
2 Gaff added soon after completion.
3 1906: fire control.
4 1906/7: top to mainmast and one yard on each mast.
5 1908: foretopmast.
6 1909: white funnel bands.
7 1909/10: no yards on mainmast.

1 *Prince of Wales*, 1915; no top to mainmast; crow's nest on forward topmast, reduced bridgework in forward and after structures, gaff fitted to lower top, searchlight on roof of lower foretop, no nets, and shelf removed.

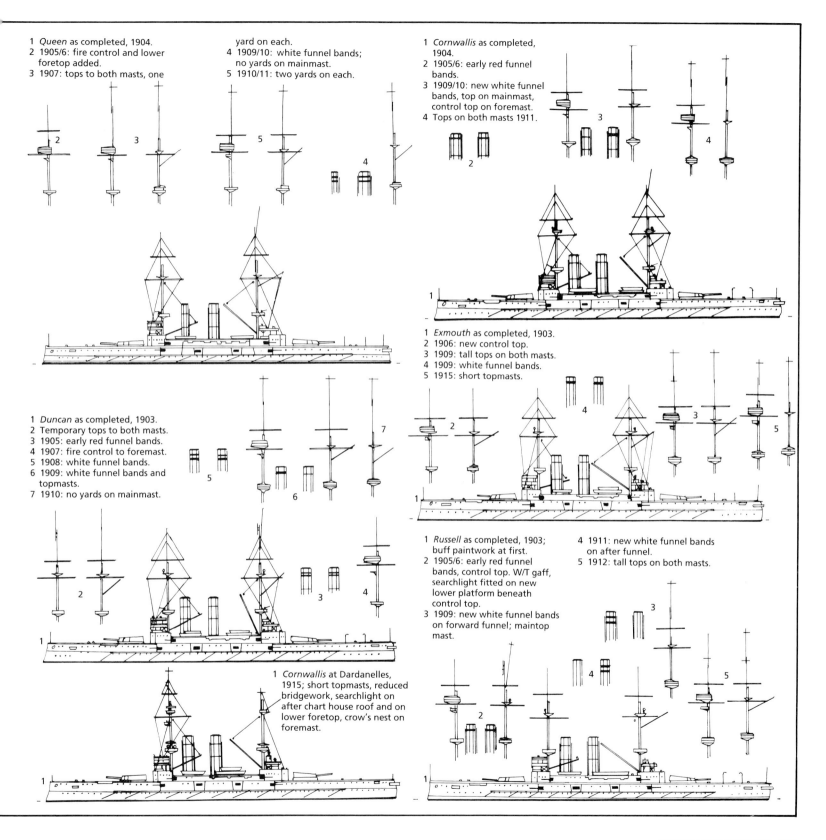

1 *Queen* as completed, 1904.
2 1905/6: fire control and lower foretop added.
3 1907: tops to both masts, one yard on each.
4 1909/10: white funnel bands; no yards on mainmast.
5 1910/11: two yards on each.

1 *Cornwallis* as completed, 1904.
2 1905/6: early red funnel bands.
3 1909/10: new white funnel bands, top on mainmast, control top on foremast.
4 Tops on both masts 1911.

1 *Duncan* as completed, 1903.
2 Temporary tops to both masts.
3 1905: early red funnel bands.
4 1907: fire control to foremast.
5 1908: white funnel bands.
6 1909: white funnel bands and topmasts.
7 1910: no yards on mainmast.

1 *Exmouth* as completed, 1903.
2 1906: new control top.
3 1909: tall tops on both masts.
4 1909: white funnel bands.
5 1915: short topmasts.

1 *Cornwallis* at Dardanelles, 1915; short topmasts, reduced bridgework, searchlight on after chart house roof and on lower foretop, crow's nest on foremast.

1 *Russell* as completed, 1903; buff paintwork at first.
2 1905/6: early red funnel bands, control top. W/T gaff, searchlight fitted on new lower platform beneath control top.
3 1909: new white funnel bands on forward funnel; maintop mast.
4 1911: new white funnel bands on after funnel.
5 1912: tall tops on both masts.

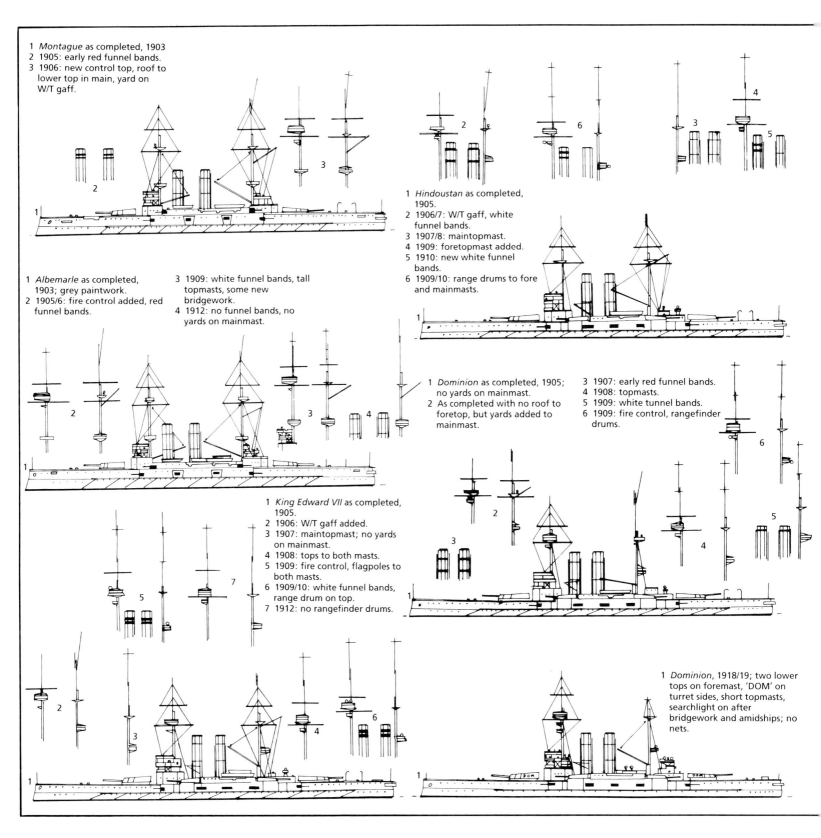

1 *Montague* as completed, 1903
2 1905: early red funnel bands.
3 1906: new control top, roof to lower top in main, yard on W/T gaff.

1 *Albemarle* as completed, 1903; grey paintwork.
2 1905/6: fire control added, red funnel bands.
3 1909: white funnel bands, tall topmasts, some new bridgework.
4 1912: no funnel bands, no yards on mainmast.

1 *King Edward VII* as completed, 1905.
2 1906: W/T gaff added.
3 1907: maintopmast; no yards on mainmast.
4 1908: tops to both masts.
5 1909: fire control, flagpoles to both masts.
6 1909/10: white funnel bands, range drum on top.
7 1912: no rangefinder drums.

1 *Hindoustan* as completed, 1905.
2 1906/7: W/T gaff, white funnel bands.
3 1907/8: maintopmast.
4 1909: foretopmast added.
5 1910: new white funnel bands.
6 1909/10: range drums to fore and mainmasts.

1 *Dominion* as completed, 1905; no yards on mainmast.
2 As completed with no roof to foretop, but yards added to mainmast.
3 1907: early red funnel bands.
4 1908: topmasts.
5 1909: white tunnel bands.
6 1909: fire control, rangefinder drums.

1 *Dominion*, 1918/19; two lower tops on foremast, 'DOM' on turret sides, short topmasts, searchlight on after bridgework and amidships; no nets.

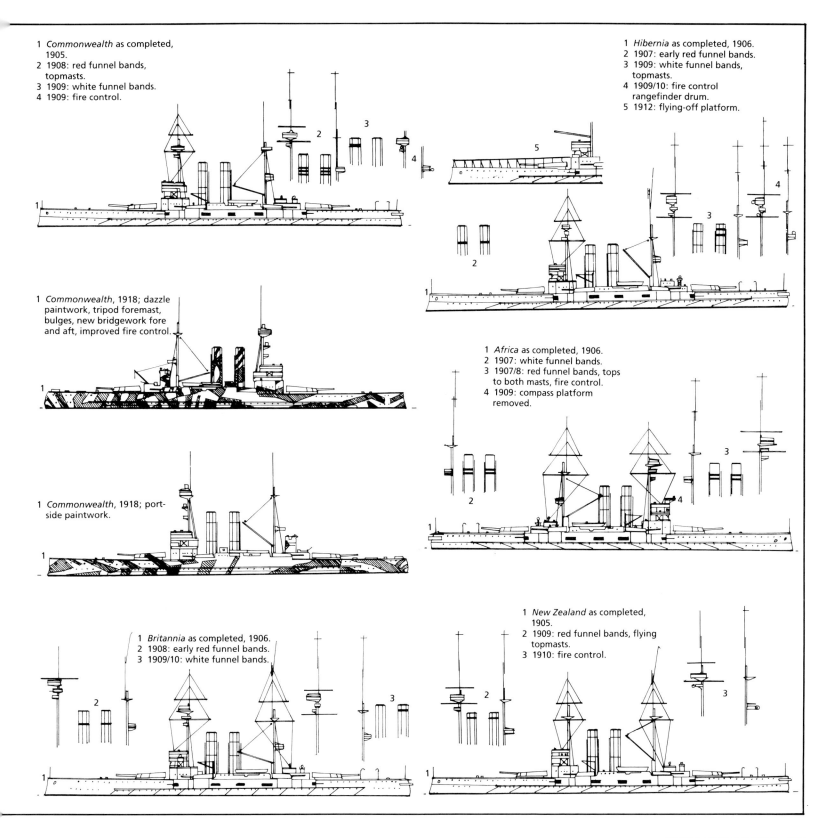

1 *Commonwealth* as completed,
  1905.
2 1908: red funnel bands,
  topmasts.
3 1909: white funnel bands.
4 1909: fire control.

1 *Commonwealth*, 1918; dazzle
  paintwork, tripod foremast,
  bulges, new bridgework fore
  and aft, improved fire control.

1 *Commonwealth*, 1918; port-
  side paintwork.

1 *Britannia* as completed, 1906.
2 1908: early red funnel bands.
3 1909/10: white funnel bands.

1 *Hibernia* as completed, 1906.
2 1907: early red funnel bands.
3 1909: white funnel bands,
  topmasts.
4 1909/10: fire control
  rangefinder drum.
5 1912: flying-off platform.

1 *Africa* as completed, 1906.
2 1907: white funnel bands.
3 1907/8: red funnel bands, tops
  to both masts, fire control.
4 1909: compass platform
  removed.

1 *New Zealand* as completed,
  1905.
2 1909: red funnel bands, flying
  topmasts.
3 1910: fire control.

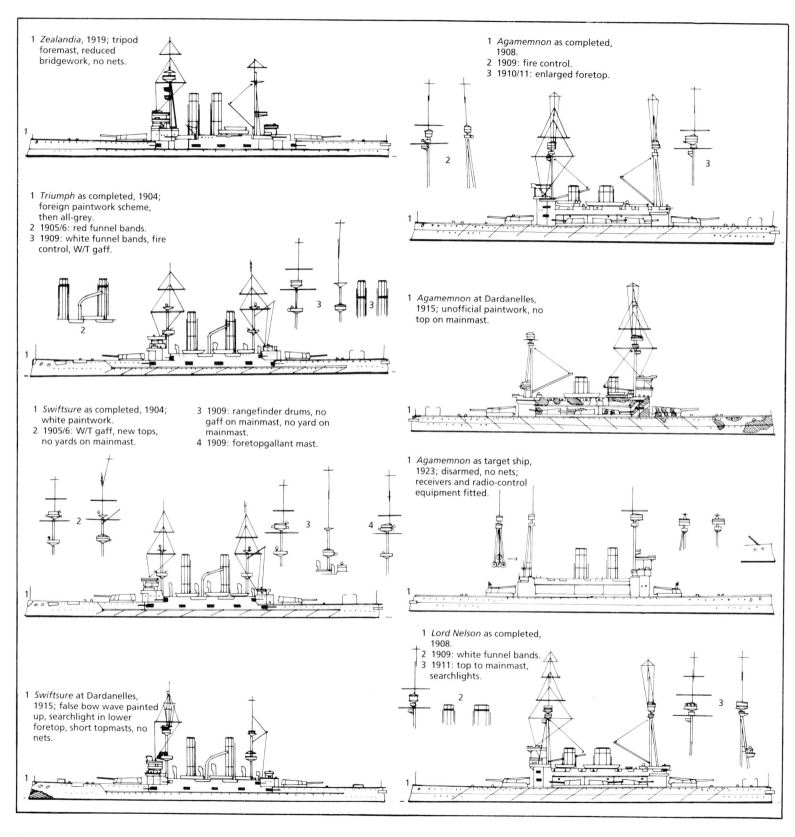

1 *Zealandia*, 1919; tripod foremast, reduced bridgework, no nets.

1 *Triumph* as completed, 1904; foreign paintwork scheme, then all-grey.
2 1905/6: red funnel bands.
3 1909: white funnel bands, fire control, W/T gaff.

1 *Swiftsure* as completed, 1904; white paintwork.
2 1905/6: W/T gaff, new tops, no yards on mainmast.
3 1909: rangefinder drums, no gaff on mainmast, no yard on mainmast.
4 1909: foretopgallant mast.

1 *Swiftsure* at Dardanelles, 1915; false bow wave painted up, searchlight in lower foretop, short topmasts, no nets.

1 *Agamemnon* as completed, 1908.
2 1909: fire control.
3 1910/11: enlarged foretop.

1 *Agamemnon* at Dardanelles, 1915; unofficial paintwork, no top on mainmast.

1 *Agamemnon* as target ship, 1923; disarmed, no nets; receivers and radio-control equipment fitted.

1 *Lord Nelson* as completed, 1908.
2 1909: white funnel bands.
3 1911: top to mainmast, searchlights.

CONCLUSION

How did these ships compare with their counterparts in other navies? To begin with, the *Royal Sovereign*s, a class of seven (plus one) on completion during 1892–4 certainly constituted the finest homogeneous group of battleships in the world. But let us take one of them and compare it with contemporaries completed at about the same time—the French *Brennus* or the Russian *Navarin*.

Both had thick compound armoured belts (18in and 16in respectively), were armed with four 13.4in and four 12in and were capable of 16 to 17 knots at full power; they seemed to be formidable opponents. Items that do not compare, however, were coal consumption, steaming and sea-keeping qualities, and general stability in all parts of the world. The big guns of the French ship were reported to be very slow in their rate of fire, and the Russian ship was, in fact, based on our own *Trafalgar* class, whose design was considered to be rapidly approaching obsolescence.

Majestic could be matched against the Japanese *Fuji*, the French *Bouvet*, and US *Alabama*. All were approximately equal in displacement, armament, armour and speed (*see* tables), but *Fuji* was completely based on the *Royal Sovereign*, and built in a British yard—she could hardly fail to compare well with British ships—she was one. The US *Alabama*, not completed until 1899–1900, was a direct reply to *Majestic*, but her armoured belt of 178ft x 7½ft x16in did not show well on paper, against 250ft x 15ft x 9in. *Alabama* was well armed and reached speeds of up to 17 knots, but was often reported as being a poor sea-boat.

The French *Bouvet* was not completed until a year after all nine *Majestic*s had put to sea. Giving a good impression on paper, in fact she was often

---

Navarin
Country: Russia

Date of launch: Sept 1891

Displacement: 9,476 tons (load)
Length: 338ft pp
Beam: 67ft
Draught: 25ft mean.

Armament
Four 12in 40cal
Eight 6in
Many smaller guns plus MG
Six torpedo tubes (submerged).

Armour (compound)
Main belt: 16in–14in–12in; 212ft long
Battery: 5in
Deck: 3in–2½in
Redoubt: 12in
Conning tower: 14in.

Machinery
Two sets triple expansion engines, two propellers
Boilers: twelve cylindrical
Designed SHP: 9,000 for 16 knots.

Brennus
Country: France

Date of launch: Oct 1891

Displacement: 11,190 tons (load)
Length: 361ft 10in pp
Beam: 66ft 11in
Draught: 26ft 3in.

Armament
Three 13.4in
Ten 6.4in
Four 9pdr
Two MG
Six torpedo tubes (above water).

Armour (Creusot steel)
Main belt: 18in amidships reducing to 12in at ends, and 11½in at lower edge
Turret bases: 8in
Turrets: 18in faces, 8in rears
Battery redoubt: 4½in
Small turrets: 4¾in
Decks: 3in
Lower deck side: 4½in.

Machinery
Two sets vertical triple expansion engines, two propellers
Thirty-two Belleville boilers without economizers
Designed SHP: 13,600 for 18 knots
Fuel: 550 tons coal normal, 800 tons max.
Coal consumption: approx. 13 tons per hour at full power.

Searchlights: five.

Complement: 673.

Fuji
Country: Japan

Date of launch: March 1896

Displacement: 12,450 tons (load)
Length: 374ft pp, 406ft 6in oa
Beam: 73ft
Draught: 27ft mean.

Armament
Four 12in 40cal BL Armstrong
Ten 6in
Twenty 47mm QF
Two 47mm (3pdr) Hotchkiss
Five 18in torpedo tubes, 4 submerged, 1 above water.

Armour (Harvey)
Main belt: 18in tapering to 14in, 226ft long, 8ft wide
Bulkheads: 14in and 12in

Citadel: 4in
Barbettes: 14in–9in–4in
Turrets: 6in–3in
Casemates: 6in–2in
Decks: 2½in
Conning tower: 14in, 1in roof
After tower: 3in.

Machinery
Two sets 3-cylinder triple expansion engines, two 4-bladed propellers
Ten cylindrical boilers, single-ended, in four compartments, working pressure: 155psi
Designed SHP: 10,200 normal, 14,100 forced draught, for 18.5 knots
Fuel: 700–1,200 tons coal.

Searchlights: five.

Complement: 600.

Bouvet
Country: France

Date of launch: April 1896

Displacement: 12,007 tons
Length: 386ft 6in pp, 401ft 3in oa
Beam: 70ft 2in
Draught: 27ft 6in mean.

Armament
Two 12in (1893 model); 52rpg
Two 10.8in (1893 model)
Eight 5.5in
Eight 4in
Twelve 47mm, four in each top
Five 37mm
Two 37mm Maxim
Two 17.7in torpedo tubes (submerged).

Armour (Harvey and nickel steel)
Main belt: 15¾in tapering to 12in at bow and stern, 8in at stem

quoted as being undergunned for her size. She was, however, very very cramped internally, partly due to her numerous turrets, also cramped together, which made for severe blast problems, and great danger of hits disabling more than one turret at a time. *Bouvet* was a good steamer, and a fair sea-boat, but suffered from a limited fuel carrying capacity which limited her radius of action.

The *Canopus* group never fared well on paper against most contemporaries, mainly owing to their being fitted with a mere 6in armoured belt instead of the 9in belt fitted to most possible antagonists.

Against the French *St Louis*, which had just been completed at the time, *Canopus* was faced with a 15in waterline belt, equal speed and four 12-in guns which could pierce her 6in belt with ease at almost all ranges. The French vessel was a good sea-boat (*Canopus* a little better) and in general was well thought of. Her thick armoured belt, however, was extremely shallow, and the huge, heavy super-structure and fat funnels made a superb target. Although not completed until about 1904, we can compare the Russian *Panteleimon* with *Canopus*. A good ship, although a little slower than *Canopus*,

she sported a 9in Krupp armoured belt. A particular weakness was her meagre 860 tons coal fuel against 1,800 tons in *Canopus*.

Even before the final legend for the *Formidables* was approved, a close eye had been kept on the Japanese *Asahi* and *Shikishima*. Both vessels, however, were built in Great Britain and it is doubtful if there were much between them. *Asahi*, *Shikishima* and the British *Formidable* class were extremely well-built vessels with great internal structual strength. British official documents do favour the *Formidables*, but in general efficiency

---

Lower edge: 10in
Upper side: 3.9in (4ft wide amidships, 8ft forward, 6ft aft)
Turrets: 15¾in
Armoured tubes: 8in
5.5in turrets: 4¾in with 2½in tubes
Conning tower: 12in
Tube: 8in.

Machinery
Vertical triple expansion, three 4-bladed propellers
Thirty-two Belleville boilers in four rooms, working pressure 250psi
Designed SHP: 15,000 for 18 knots
Fuel: 600–810 tons coal
Coal consumption: 251 tons per day at 17 knots; 63.5 tons per day at 10 knots
Trials: 18.18 knots at full power; sea-going speed was 17 knots; speed had dropped to just over 10 knots by 1900.

Searchlights: six.

Complement: 666.

St. Louis
Country: France

Date of launch: Sept 1896

Displacement: 11,090 tons (load)
Length: 374ft pp, 385ft 6in oa
Beam: 66ft 5in
Draught: 27ft 6in.

Armament
Four 12in (1893/6 model); 48rpg
Ten 5.5in (1893 model); 49rpg
Eight 4in (1891 model)
Two 65mm field guns
Twenty 3pdr Hotchkiss QF
Four 37mm MG
Four 17.7in torpedo tubes, two above water; Fiume torpedoes.

Armour (Harvey and nickel)
Main belt: 14.2in (1ft 6in above, 5ft below wl), 8in lower edge
Side: 3.9in
Battery: 3in
Turrets: 15in
Loading tube: 8in
Conning tower: 12.7in
Admiral's position: 1in
Decks: 3.3in over belt, 1.57in on lower level.

Machinery
Three sets 4-cylinder of vertical triple expansion engines, three propellers
Twenty Belleville boilers with economizers in four separate rooms, working pressure 250psi
Designed SHP: 15,000 for 18 knots
Fuel: 1,080 tons max.
Coal consumption: 266 tons per day at full power, 60.3 tons at 10 knots
Trials: 18.1 knots with 15,221shp, 17 knots with 11,250shp.

Searchlights: six 23.6in.

Complement: 694.

Alabama
Country: USA

Date of launch: May 1898

Displacement: 11,552 tons (load)
Length: 368ft pp, 374ft oa
Beam: 72ft 2½in
Draught: 23ft 6in.

Armament
Four 13in 35cal Mk II; 50rpg
Fourteen 6in 40cal Mk IV ; 200rpg
Sixteen 6pdr
Four MG
Two 3in field guns
Torpedo tubes: nil.

Armour: (Harvey)
Main belt: 16½in–13½in–9½in
Citadel and battery: 5½in
Casemates: 6in
Barbettes: 15in fronts, 10in rear
Turrets: 14in faces and sides, 2in roof
Deck: 3in–2¾in
Conning tower: 10in, 2in roof
Signal tower: 6in.

Machinery
Two sets vertical triple expansion engines, two 3-bladed propellers
Eight cylindrical single-ended boilers in four compartments, working pressure 180psi
Designed SHP: 10,000 for 17 knots
Fuel: 1,339 tons max.
Coal consumption: 132 tons at seagoing speed (14.4 knots)
Trials: 17.01 knots with 11,366shp.

Searchlights: four 30in.

Complement: 713.

Osliabia
Country: Russia

Date of launch: Nov 1898

Displacement: 12,674 tons
Length: 401ft 3in pp, 426ft 6in wl, 435ft oa
Beam: 71ft 6in
Draught: 27ft 3in

Armament
Four 10in 43cal Obuchov guns; 540 shells carried (normal stowage)
Eleven 6in
Twenty 3in
Twenty-six smaller including 75mm and MG
Five 15in torpedo tubes (three submerged).

Armour (Krupp, Harvey and nickel steel)

---

only. Both foreign vessels were present at the Battle of Tsushima in 1904, and proved themselves of excellent design when compared to those of the Russian Navy.

Comparisons of the later *Bulwark* groups against the German *Wittelsbach*, one of the latest battleships from that country, favoured the British vessel because of the smaller 9.4in guns mounted in the latter. The US *Maine* however, compared very well with *Bulwark*; she sported an 11in belt and identical speed. The secondary armaments of both ships suffered badly in a seaway. The French *Suffren* also compared well with *Bulwark* in all except speed and width of armoured belt (13^1/4ft against 15ft). She was considered a good ship by British designers and worthy of respect.

The *Duncan*s saw their concept in the Russian *Osliabia* class, and were built to match them. The British four 12in were more than a match for four 10in; secondary armaments compared favourably; armour protection compared well (although thinner in *Duncan*) and speeds were almost equal, although *Duncan* could keep her speeds high for much longer and steam much further. The Admir-alty thought that the *Duncan*s was more than a match for the Russian vessels—even individually.

The *King Edward*s had many rivals and were, in fact, by the time of completion faced with stiff opposition. The Japanese *Katori* featured a 9in Krupp belt, excellent armament, and adequate speeds. Built in a British yard, she inherited all the latest features, and was considered an extremely well-built and powerful vessel.

Until then (1904) the German Navy had never been considered a threat at sea, but were now building ships showing good qualities. The

---

Main belt: 9in amidships tapering to 5in at lower edge, 7in at ends
312ft in length, 3ft above waterline, 4ft 9in below
Upper belt: 5in; 188ft long
Bulkheads: 4in
Casemates: 5in–2in
Turrets: 9in–5in
Conning tower: 10in–6in–4in
Decks: 2½in on flat, 3in on slopes.

Machinery
Three sets vertical triple expansion engines, three 4-bladed propellers
Thirty Belleville boilers in three compartments
Designed SHP: 14,500 for 18.5 knots
Fuel: 1,500 tons/2,000 tons
Trials: 18.33 knots with 15,053shp.

Complement: 730.

Asahi
Country: Japan

Date of launch: March 1899

Displacement: 15,200 tons normal load
Length: 400ft pp, 425ft oa
Beam: 75ft
Draught: 27ft 2in.

Armament
Four 12in 40cal (not same gun as Mk IX mounted in *Formidable* groups)
Fourteen 6in Mk VII
Twenty 3in
Four 18in torpedo tubes, submerged.

Armour (Harvey and nickel steel)
Main belt: 9in (250ft long)
Barbettes: 14in–10in
Turrets: 10in faces, 6in sides
Casemates: 6in faces
Conning tower: 14in face, 3in roof
Decks: 3in amidships.

Machinery
Two sets of vertical triple expansion engines, two propellers
Twenty-five Belleville boilers
Designed SHP: 14,500 for 18 knots
Fuel: 700 tons coal normal, 1,400 tons max.
Coal consumption: 14 tons per hour at full power
Trials: 16,360shp for 18.3 knots.

Searchlights: five.

Complement: 743.

Suffren
Country: France

Date of launch: July 1899

Displacement: 12,527 tons (load)
Length: 411ft 9in wl
Beam: 70ft 2in
Draught: 27ft 6in mean.

Armament
Four 12in (1893/6 model); 106rpg
Ten 6.4in
Eight 4in
Twenty-two 3pdr
Two 37mm QF
Two 17.7in torpedo tubes submerged.

Armour: (Harvey)
Main belt: 11.8in tapering to 9in forward and aft on top, 4in at bottom; 3ft 7in above, 4ft 7in below waterline
Sides: 5.1in above main belt (6ft 7in wide)
Armoured bulkhead: 4.3in
Turrets: 12.6in–11in
Turret bases: 10in
6.4in turrets: 5in KNC
Ammunition chambers for 6.4in: 4in
Casemates: 5.1in
Conning tower: 11in–9in–8in
Communication tube: 5.9in

Decks: 2.7in upper, 1.6in lower.

Machinery
Three sets vertical triple expansion engines, three propellers
Twenty-four Niclausse boilers in 8 groups, working pressure 256psi
Designed SHP: 16,200 for 18 knots
Fuel: 1,120 tons coal
Coal consumption: 269 tons per day (24 hours) full power; 64.7 tons at 10 knots
Trials: 17.92 knots with 16,715shp.

Searchlights: six.

Complement: 714.

Panteleimon
Country: Russia

Date of launch: Oct 1900

Displacement: 12,582 tons (load)
Length: 371ft 3in wl, 378ft 6in oa
Beam: 73ft
Draught: 27ft.

Armament
Four 12in 40cal; 80rpg
Sixteen 6in 45cal; 126rpg
Fourteen 3in
Six 47mm
Two 37mm Hotchkiss
Four MG
Two Baranovski QF
Five torpedo tubes (submerged).

Armour (Krupps process, made in USA)
Main belt: 9in amidships, 8in at ends; 237ft in length, by 7ft 6in wide
Citadel: 6in at 156ft long and closed by 6in bulkheads
Battery: 5in at 156ft in length
Casemates: 6in outside, 2in inside
Turrets: 10in

Schlesien was a potential threat indeed, and matched *King Edward* in all respects. Armed with 11in guns, which were considered too small a calibre for such ships, they, nevertheless could easily pierce the 9in belt of *King Edward*, and, for a change, there were five ships in the class, whereas previously the German Navy, like the French, tended to build one or two at most. *King Edward* was a better seagoing ship than practically all foreign contemporaries within her period. Often compared with the Italian *Benedetto Brin* class, which were very fast ships and could practically outrun *King Edward*. The former, however, was in many essentials, a hybrid of the battlecruiser type, sporting only a 6in belt and having high sea speeds. *Lord Nelson* can be compared with the Japanese *Satsuma* which was the first large warship built in Japan, and mainly from Japanese materials. They compared very favourably in all areas except armour protection. The thick belts of *Lord Nelson* (12in) against 9in in *Satsuma*, as well as a much wider armoured freeboard in *Lord Nelson*, made the British ship easily comparable with soem of the earlier dreadnoughts.

During the Victorian era, British battleships were constructed for the primary purpose of engaging contemporary units of the world's battlefleets. In this respect, they had little to fear. There were no torpedo attacks, no flotillas of little ships to hinder them, no aircraft, and no potential enemy fleet big enough to force the issue. They were, as usual, designed and constructed with the greatest of care, but it was always paramount that they should be able to steam into any part of the globe without too much trouble, a feature that often cramped the design. On completion, the ships performed their

---

Ammunition tubes: 5in
Conning tower: 9in
Communication tube: 5in
Decks: 2in on flat, 2½in on slopes
Upper deck over 5in side armour: 1½in.

Machinery
Two sets vertical triple expansion engines, two
    4-bladed propellers
Twenty-two, Belleville boilers (made in Belgium)
Designed SHP: 10,600 for 16 knots
Coal consumption: 195 tons per day (24 hours) at
    full power
Fuel: 1,760 tons coal
Trials: seagoing speed: 15 knots.

Searchlights: six.

Complement: 750.

Wittelsbach
Country: Germany

Date of launch: Oct 1900

Displacement: 11,830 tons (load)
Length: 400ft wl, 416ft 6in oa
Beam: 67ft
Draught: 27/28ft mean.

Armament
Four 9.4in 40cal
Eighteen 5.9in
Twelve 3in
Eight MG
Five 17.7in torpedo tubes.

Armour (Krupp)
Main belt: 9in amidships
Ends: 4in
Barbettes: 10in
Turrets: 10in faces
Battery: 5in
Conning tower: 10in face
Decks: 3in on slopes.

Machinery
Three sets vertical triple expansion engines, three
    propellers
Six cylindrical and six Schulz-Thornycroft boilers
Designed SHP: 15,000 for 18 knots
Fuel: 653/1,400 tons coal, plus 200 tons oil
Trials: 18.1 knots with 14,488shp.

Searchlights: four:

Complement: 650.

Maine
Country: USA

Date of launch: July 1901

Displacement: 12,500 tons (load), 13,500 tons
    (deep)
Length: 388ft pp, 393ft 11in oa
Beam: 72ft 2½in
Draught: 23ft 6in, 26ft 8in mean.

Armament
Four 12in 40cal
Sixteen 6in 50cal
Six 3in
Eight 3pdr Hotchkiss
Four MG
Two 18in torpedo tubes, submerged.

Armour (Krupp belt)
Main belt: 11in tapering to 7in at lower edge; 8½
    and 5½in abreast barbette, 4in to bow
Casemates: 6in
Bulkheads: 9in
Barbettes: 12in–8in
Turrets: 12in–11in
Conning tower: 10in–7in
Decks: 4in–2¾in–2½in

Machinery
Two 3-cylinder vertical triple expansion engines,
    two propellers

Twenty-four Niclausse boilers
Designed SHP: 16,000 for 18 knots
Fuel: 1,000/1,800 tons coal
Trials: 18 knots with 15,841shp.

Searchlights: six.

Complement: 648.

Benedetto Brin (class of two ships, *Regina Margherita*)
Country: Italy

Date of launch: Nov 1901

Displacement: 13,207 tons (load)
Length: 426ft 6in pp
Beam: 78ft 2in
Draught: 27ft.

Armament (1,519 tons)
Four 12in (mounting and loading arrangements
    similar to *Formidable*); 100rpg
Four 8in in casemates on upper deck; 100rpg
Twelve 6in in main deck battery
Twenty 3in QF
Two 75mm
Two 37mm
Two 6.5in Maxim
Four 18in torpedo tubes (two submerged)

Armour (Harvey and nickel steel) (3,103 tons)
Main belt: 5.9in amidships reducing to 3.9in
    forward, 2in aft; 4ft 3in below waterline, 4ft 9in
    above
Citadel: 5.9in above belt for 262ft, closed by 7.8in
    bulkheads
Barbettes: 7.8in
Turrets: 5.9in
Casemates: 5.9in
Conning tower: 5.9in (two)
Communication tube: 3.14in
Decks: 2in over battery, 4in lower (slopes), 1in flat;
    3in outside citadel.

duties with ease and did everything that was asked of them; but when the First World War started in 1914 most of the battleships described in this book were practically obsolete. They were not built to face new types of armour-piercing shell, mines, extremely powerful torpedoes (with wire-cutters) or ships as large and powerful as the new dreadnoughts. Nevertheless, they did see considerable war service; without them, the resources of the Royal Navy would have been pushed beyond limit.

Judgements in hindsight that there was no real necessity to build such a large fleet so as to achieve a two-power standard need to be balanced by consideration of the naval scares of the 1880s, when quantity was low and numbers near parallel with France and Russia. For Britain, at the zenith of her imperial responsibilities, there could be no doubts. Indeed, the events of the First World War demonstrated the importance of numbers, for major units could not be replaced quickly. Nelson himself saw this: 'Only numbers can annihilate.'

Victorian battleships are remembered with much affection: long lines of brightly coloured battleships steaming out of harbour; long summers, lazing in the Mediterranean; frequent fleet reviews; constant reports about the fleet in the press. The British battle fleet had never before, and has never since, 'ruled the waves' as she did during the latter part of the 19th century. It was not an easy period, certainly not trouble-free, and hardly a romantic one (especially for those serving in the vessels), and it was one of considerable change within the system as well as in terms of ship design. Because the Royal Navy was able through practical experience to rectify many of the problems that arose, on the whole its ships had little to equal them.

Machinery (1,577 tons)
Two sets 4-cylinder vertical triple expansion engines, two 3-bladed in-turning propellers
Twenty-eight Belleville boilers in three compartments, working pressure 285psi
Designed SHP: 20,475
Fuel: 1,968 tons coal, plus 200 tons oil
Coal consumption: 335 tons per day, at full power, 66.5 tons at 10 knots
Trials: 18.25 knots on 6-hour trial with 15,700shp; 20.36 knots on 2-hour, forced draught with 20,400shp.

Searchlights: two 75cm, two 65cm.

Complement: 809.

Katori
Country: Japan

Date of launch: July 1905

Displacement: 16,400 tons (load)
Length: 425ft pp, 455ft oa
Beam: 78ft 6in
Draught: 27ft mean.

Armament
Four 12in
Four 10in
Twelve 6in
Twelve 3in
Six MG
Five 18in torpedo tubes, submerged.

Armour (Krupp belt, nickel steel and mild steel)
Main belt: 9in (7ft 6in wide, 5ft of it below water)
Ends: 6½in
Lower edge: 3½in
Barbettes: 9in–5in
Turrets: 9in faces
Decks: 3in–2in
Conning tower: 9in

Upper deck battery: 4in.

Machinery
Two sets 4-cylinder quadruple expansion engines, two propellers
Twenty Niclausse boilers with economizers
Designed SHP: 17,000 for 18.3 knots
Fuel: 800 tons coal normal, 2,100 tons max.
Trials: 18,500shp for 20.62 knots.

Searchlights: four.

Complement: 865.

Schlesien (class of four ships)
Country: Germany

Date of launch: May 1906

Displacement: 13,200 tons (load)
Length: 410ft wl
Beam: 72ft
Draught: 25ft 5in mean.

Armament
Four 11in 40cal
Fourteen 6in
Twenty 24pdr
Four MG
(17.7in) six torpedo tubes (submerged)

Armour (Krupp, nickel steel and mild steel)
Main belt: 9½in amidships reducing to 8in at ends
Ends: 4in
Barbettes: 11in
Turrets: 10in faces
Battery: 6½in
Casemates: 6½in
Decks: 3in on inclines
Conning tower: 12in face.

Machinery
Three sets 3-cylinder vertical triple expansion engines, three propellers
Twelve Schulz-Thornycroft boilers

Designed SHP: 16,000 for 18 knots
Fuel: 800 tons coal normal, 1,800 tons max., 200 tons oil
Trials: 18,465shp for 18.3 knots.

Searchlights: four.

Complement: 730.

Satsuma
Country: Japan

Date of launch: Nov 1906

Displacement: 19,372 tons (load)
Length: 479ft wl, 482ft oa
Beam: 83ft 6in
Draught: 27ft 6in load (mean).

Armament
Four 12in
Twelve 10in
Twelve 4.7in
Four 3in
Five 18in torpedo tubes (submerged).

Armour (Krupp)
Main belt: 9in reducing to 4in at ends; 6in portion at bow
Barbettes: 9in–7in
Turrets: 9in–7in–2in
Decks: 2in main
Conning tower: 6in.

Machinery
Two sets vertical triple expansion engines, two propellers
Twenty Miyabara boilers
Designed SHP: 17,300 for 18.3 knots
Fuel: 1,000 tons coal normal, 2,800 tons max.; 377 tons oil
Trials: 18.95 knots with 18,507shp.

Searchlights: five.

Complement: 800.

BATTLESHIP FORTS
and
BATTLESHIP EXTERMINATORS

It would seem that during the Victorian period there was never any shortage of ideas as to how to improve the military might of Great Britain. One of the most interesting schemes propounded is worthy of mention.

In June 1898 a suggestion was put forward by Major-General Crease, CB which called for the construction of mobile battle forts and fast battleship exterminators.

The General's thesis was as follows:

'The Channel and coast of the United Kingdom, as far as the Navy is concerned, are protected by the Channel and Reserve Fleets. The Channel Fleet in case of war is supposed to go to Gibraltar to keep touch with the Mediterranean Fleet, but the arrangement is contemplated really for the purpose, that it may be in a position to extricate that fleet, should it be overwhelmed in the Mediterranean, but as this presupposes a war with more than one great power, it is certain in such a case, that the English public would not permit the Channel Fleet to leave the Channel, running as we should, did it do so, the danger of invasion or other troubles. The generally expressed naval idea, is that we should defend our coasts by attacking those of the enemy, but if this were carried out, even then a very strong reserve at home in the English Channel would not the less be necessary; indeed the safety of our coasts is a vital necessity about which there must not be the shadow of doubt, or whatever it costs to obtain.

In the case of attack in our home naval fortresses and Harbours nothing is laid down as to by what authority, naval or military, their defence is to be carried out; it is a mixed and unsettled question, although one of paramount importance. The scheme now proposed is intended to meet this grave difficulty by establishing all round the coast, in selected positions, mobile floating battle forts in contra distinction to battleships, floating forts which shall be in reality very powerful heavily armed and armoured ships of the line, well manned, of large coal-carrying capacity, moderate speed and of such light draught as to be capable of fighting in shallow waters, and of entering small harbours inaccessible to ships of normal draught. These battle forts are designed to be torpedo proof, and of such great beam, reserve of flotation and interior divisibility as to be capable of undergoing the ramming of a battle ship under ordinary conditions, without being sunk thereby.

These battle forts are designed only, for preventing an enemy's descent upon our coasts, for protecting the entrance of the Channel, or for bombardment of towns around our coasts; not being intended for service abroad, I propose that they should be manned with a certain number of militia and volunteers trained especially for the purpose, and located at certain points around the coast, at or near where their battle forts should be stationed.'

The General went on to state that the construction of these battle forts was simple, and therefore comparatively inexpensive as compared with battleships. Moreover, the guns were to be of the heaviest and most modern construction, and the forts should carry at least 16in twin turrets as shown in the sketch. Not content with just the battle forts, and to complement them, it was suggested that smaller, partly protected vessels of 3,000/4,000 tons, of greater speed (35/40kts) and of enormous destructive power, should be constructed and used for dispatch and search purposes, and to build them with the primary purpose of destroying battleships, which could escape from the much slower battle forts. Ram and torpedoes were to be provided, and just enough small guns to repel possible torpedo-boat destroyers which might be so bold as to come close enough to attack.

When the document was privately circulated among their Lordships at the Admiralty, it was naturally received with a great deal of apprehension, but was studied very carefully. After considerable thought and debate it was seen that the whole question of the forts and exterminators was viewed as little more than folly, by officers in service, public sectors and construction staff alike. The idea was sound enough, but the practical side of it had not been given consideration. The following obejctions were sent to the General:

1. New private dockyards would have to be constructed for the forts, as no existing dockyard would be capable of building them, especially given the 100ft beam.

2. At 8 knots forts were much too slow, and enemy battleships would always avoid action with them, and probably concentrate on the coastline without battlefort protection and escape before the forts could come up.

3. Soldiers, as suggested, not suitable to man ships of this size. It was pointed out, that years before, in the French war, this had been done in their ships, and the Royal Navy took advantage of it with much success.

4. The cost of the eighteen contemplated battle forts at £600,000 each would be more usefully spent on eighteen contemporary battleships, especially when these vessels could travel world-wide, unlike the coastal battle forts and exterminators.

The General forwarded some arguments against these objections, but the paramount issued seemed to be the actual construction of the forts and exterminators on the dimensions provided by him. The General said:

'Had we not, in Sir William White, one of the most skilful and able naval architects I suppose England has ever produced, and excellent officers to man these forts – I should then seen a problem.'

On close inspection the General's proposal, in theory, was feasible if, as he suggested, the forts were just for coastal defence, leaving conventional battleships to carry out important work elesehwere and not worry about Channel and port defences. The very important question of construction, however, is the major factor in discarding the whole issue as tactical folly.

Let us consider the following:

1. Sixteen of the largest naval guns possible– probably 12in Mk 1X (as in *Formidable*, *Bulwark*, etc.).

2. 12in to 15in armoured belt, heavily armoured deck, heavily armoured turrets and barbettes for guns, all on a displacement of 11,500 tons with dimensions of 400ft x 100ft x only 11ft 6in draught!

3. 5,000shp to push this giant vessel at 8 knots.

4. Colossal topweight of the main and many light guns (as featured in the fighting tops), creating considerable problems in providing the vessel with a substantial metacentric height which was of the greatest importance if the guns were to have a steady platform.

Weights suggested for battle forts: 11,500 tons.
Actual weights needed:
Sixteen 12in guns, 800 tons.
Armour at thicknesses suggested, about 5,000 tons.
Machinery, about 850 tons.
Sixteen 12in barbettes and turrets, about 3,500 tons.
400ft x 100ft, 4-bottomed hull, about 6,500 tons.
Coal as suggested, 1,500 tons.
Total: 18,150 tons.

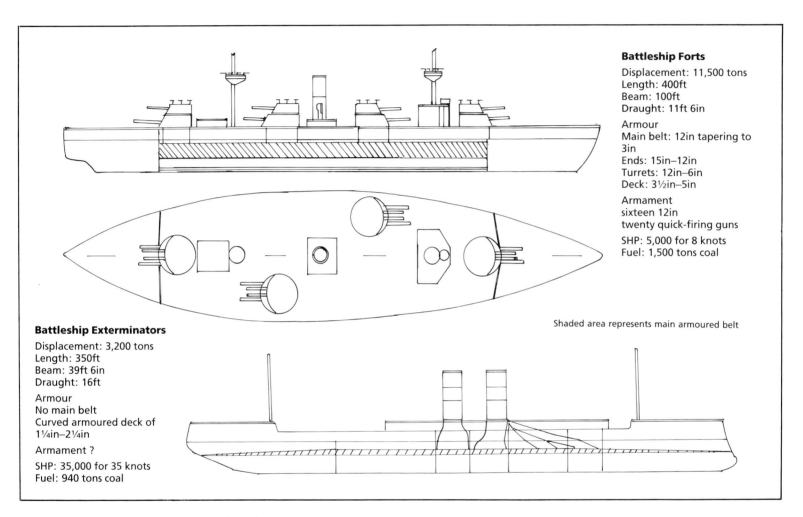

Battleship Forts

Displacement: 11,500 tons
Length: 400ft
Beam: 100ft
Draught: 11ft 6in

Armour
Main belt: 12in tapering to 3in
Ends: 15in–12in
Turrets: 12in–6in
Deck: 3½in–5in

Armament
sixteen 12in
twenty quick-firing guns

SHP: 5,000 for 8 knots
Fuel: 1,500 tons coal

Shaded area represents main armoured belt

Battleship Exterminators

Displacement: 3,200 tons
Length: 350ft
Beam: 39ft 6in
Draught: 16ft

Armour
No main belt
Curved armoured deck of 1¼in–2¼in

Armament ?

SHP: 35,000 for 35 knots
Fuel: 940 tons coal

These figures are approximate and do not include any of the smaller weights involved or, indeed, any Board margin.

The General's suggestion showed great enterprise and consideration towards the defence of his country, but sadly was not at all practical.

BIBLIOGRAPHY

Attwood, E. L. *Warship*. Longman, 1911

Barnaby, N. *Naval Developments of the Century*. W. & R. Chambers, 1904

Berlin, L. E., and Robertson, L. S. *Marine Boilers*. John Murray, 1906

Biles, J. H. *The Construction of Ships*, 2 vols. Charles Griffin & Co. Ltd., 1908

Brassey, Sir Thomas. *The British Navy*, 5 vols. Longman, 1882

Brown, J. *The Log of HMS* Repulse. Westminster Press Ltd., 1904

Corbett, J., and Newbolt, H. *Naval Operations*, 5 vols. Longman, Green & Co., 1920–31

Clowes, Sir William Laird. *The Royal Navy*, 7 vols. Sampson Low, Marston & Co. Ltd., 1897–1903

Eardley-Wilmot, Captain S. *Our Fleet Today*. Seeley & Co., 1900

— *The Development of Navies*. Seeley & Co., 1892

Fisher, Admiral Sir John. *Memories*. Hodder & Stoughton, 1919

— *Records*. Hodder & Stoughton, 1919

Frothingham, T. G. *The Naval History of the World War*. Harvard University Press, 1927

Hamilton-Williams, M. A. *Britain's Naval Power*. Macmillan & Co., 1902

Herival, P. G. *The Log of HMS* Ramillies. Westminster Press Ltd., 1903

Jane, F. T. *Jane's Fighting Ships*. Sampson Low, Marston & Co. Ltd., 1897–1921

— *The British Battle Fleet*, 2 vols. Library Press Ltd., 1915

Jellicoe, Admiral Sir J. *The Grand Fleet, 1914–16*. Cassell, 1919

Low, C. R. *Her Majesty's Navy*, 3 vols. J. S. Virtue, 1897

Marder, A. J. *British Naval Policy, 1880–1905*. Putnam, 1941

McDermaid, N. J. *Shipyard Practice*. Longman, 1911

Milton, J. T. *Water Tube Boilers for Marine Purposes*. 1903

Parkes, Dr. Oscar. *British Battleships*. Seeley Service, 1957

Pollen, Arthur. *The Navy in Battle*. Chatto & Windus, 1919

Price, W. H. *With the Fleet in the Dardanelles*. Andrew Melrose Ltd., 1915

Protheroe, Ernest. *The British Navy*. G. Routledge & Sons, 1916

Reed, E. J. *Our Ironclad Warships*. John Murray, 1870

Reid, J. S., and Pearce, T. H. *The Log of HMS* Victorious. Westminster Press Ltd., 1903

Seaton, A. E. *Manual of Marine Engineering*. Charles Griffin & Co. Ltd., 1907

Stenzel, A. *The British Navy*. T. Fisher Unwin, 1898

Stewart, A. T., and Peshall, Revd. C. J. E., *The Immortal Gamble*. A. C. Black, 1917

White, W. H. *Manual of Naval Architecture*. Clowes, 1882

Williams, H. *The Steam Navy of England*. W. H. Allen, 1894

Wilson, H. W. *Battleships in Action*. Sampson Low, Marston & Co. Ltd., 1896

Wood, Walter. *Battleship*. Kegan Paul, 1912

Barr & Stroud Rangefinders. HMSO, 1896

Brassey's Naval Annual. J. Griffin & Co. and Clowes, 1886–1919

HMS Glory *1901–2–3, a Cruise*. Charpentier & Co

The Navy League Annual. John Murray, 1907–14

Navy Lists. Sampson Low, 1888–1910

Transactions of the Institute of Naval Architects, 1870–1911

Journals: *Blue Jacket; Engineer; Engineering; Fleet; Navy and Army Illustrated; Navy and Military Record; Navy League Journal*

Newspapers: *Daily Graphic; Daily Mail; Daily Telegraph; Evening Standard; Hampshire Telegraph; Pall Mall Gazette; Portsmouth Evening News; St. James's Gazette; The Times*

INDEX